POKÉMON
Pocket Pokédex ®

Eric 'ECM' Mylonas

Prima Games
A Division of Random House, Inc.
3000 Lava Ridge Court
Roseville, CA 95661
1-800-733-3000
www.primagames.com

Product Manager: Mario De Govia
Project Editor: Alaina Yee
Design: Keating Design
Layout: Jamie Knight and Jose J. Ramirez

© 2006 Pokémon. © 1995-2006 Nintendo/Creatures Inc./GAME FREAK inc.

ISBN: 0-7615-5376-2
Library of Congress Catalog Card Number: 2006901932
Printed in the United States of America

07 08 09   10 9 8 7

Contents

The Bare Essentials

The Essentials

FIRE [AND ICE AND WATER AND...] IT UP!

Normal	Grass	Fighting	Flying	Rock	Dark
Fire	Electric	Poison	Psychic	Ghost	Steel
Water	Ice	Ground	Bug	Dragon	

There are seventeen different types of Pokémon, with many actually being dual-types: Bulbasaur, for example, is both Grass- and Poison-type. These different types determine the best matches. Check out the Damage Multiplier table to determine which types work best against one another.

The most effective way to play the game is with a well-balanced party made of six of the seventeen Pokémon types (many Pokémon actually belong to two types). This way, you are always equipped, in some fashion, to take advantage of Pokémon's Rock, Paper, Scissors-style gameplay.

Essentially, each type of Pokémon has strengths and weaknesses versus other types, with damage multipliers applied accordingly. For example, while a Fire-type Pokémon may be super effective against a Grass type, Water has the same damage multiplier effect against Fire. Thus, succeeding in battle really comes down to effectively matching Pokémon type for type.

A well-balanced party has enough Pokémon straddling each category so that you almost always have the right team to devastate your opponent.

The following tables show how the various matches shake out. Damage can go as high as 4x if a Pokémon is comprised of two classes that would each normally take 2x damage from a specific type. For example, a Pokémon that is both Steel- and Electric-type would be *very* vulnerable to Ground-type attacks and, if the attacking Pokémon's level is within 5 levels of the defending Pokémon's level, it means an instant KO.

Damage Multiplier Table

Condition	Multiplier
Move is the same type as Pokémon	1.5x
Move is effective against opponent's type	2–4x
Move scores a Critical Hit!	2x
Pokémon has an item that raises the move's Strength	1.1x
Rain Dance or Sunny Day effects (depending on move)	1.5x or .5x

Pokémon Move Compatibility

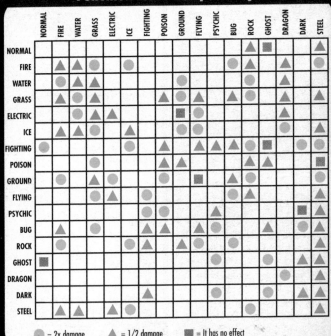

	NORMAL	FIRE	WATER	GRASS	ELECTRIC	ICE	FIGHTING	POISON	GROUND	FLYING	PSYCHIC	BUG	ROCK	GHOST	DRAGON	DARK	STEEL
NORMAL													▲	■			▲
FIRE		▲	▲	●		●						●	▲		▲		●
WATER		●	▲	▲					●				●		▲		
GRASS		▲	●	▲				▲	●	▲		▲	●		▲		▲
ELECTRIC			●	▲	▲				■	●					▲		
ICE		▲	▲	●		▲			●	●					●		▲
FIGHTING	●					●		▲		▲	▲	▲	●	■		●	●
POISON				●				▲	▲				▲	▲			■
GROUND		●		▲	●			●		■		▲	●				●
FLYING				●	▲		●					●	▲				▲
PSYCHIC							●	●			▲					■	▲
BUG		▲		●			▲	▲		▲	●			▲		●	▲
ROCK		●				●	▲		▲	●		●					▲
GHOST	■										●			●		▲	▲
DRAGON															●		▲
DARK							▲				●			●		▲	▲
STEEL		▲	▲		▲	●							●				▲

● = 2x damage ▲ = 1/2 damage ■ = It has no effect

Catch 'Em All!

If you want to fill your Pokédex, you're going to have to catch a lot of Pokémon. Bear in mind that each edition of *Pokémon* has its own unique roster and you have to trade with the other versions (either your own or a friend's) to fill out the National Pokédex.

The following sections detail exactly how to collect the vast majority of the Pokémon in the games.

TALL GRASS

If you've played the game(s) before, you know that the best source of Pokémon is tall grass. Simply wading into these vast fields of foliage, lilting in the breeze, sends Pokémon running—hopefully into you. Contact here is entirely random and, once you find a Pokémon, a battle begins. From there, your goal is to wear it down and use the various Poké Balls at your disposal to capture it and add it to the Pokédex.

FISHING

While running through the tall grass is a great way to catch lots of Pokémon, you may need to head to a pond, bay, or sea to obtain those elusive Water-type Pokémon. To do this, however, you need to locate the various fishing rods (Old, Good, and Super) scattered throughout the games. Once equipped, you simply need to move to a body of water and use the rod to fish. If you get a bite, a battle ensues with the Pokémon you hooked. Poké Balls determine whether you walk away empty-handed.

Tools of the Trade: Poké Balls

There's only one way to catch a wild Pokémon, and that's via the Trainer's tool of choice: the Ball! Poké Balls come in various types, each with specific traits.

The shops scattered about each of the continents sell three types of Balls: standard Poké Balls, Great Balls, and Ultra Balls. Each is slightly more expensive than the previous one and each is successively more efficient.

That being said, luck does play a very large part in how effective Poké Ball can be in a given situation. While you might guess that Ultra Balls are the best in every situation, it isn't always so.

Your best bet is to learn through experimentation which works best for you. After all, there's no need to lay down the big bucks for Ultra Balls if a regular Poké Ball does the trick.

Bear in mind that *Ruby* and *Sapphire* have a great many more Poké Balls than *FireRed* and *LeafGreen* including a whole host of specialty Balls. These are *not* transferable.

SURFING

First off, before even attempting to Surf, you need to track down HM03 Surf and teach it to a compatible Pokémon. From there, approach a body of water and hit Ⓐ to take to the sea astride your Pokémon. Simply swim about until a Pokémon throws itself at you. From there, you know the drill: Weaken the invader and then cap things off with a handy Poké Ball.

EVOLVING

After you've caught a Pokémon, there's every chance that, at some point, you'll want to evolve it into another form. This is a good idea for a number of reasons:

● Every time a Pokémon evolves, that new form is added to your Pokédex as another Pokémon, so that's one less Pokémon

you'll have to trade or catch. This is the easiest way to add Pokémon to your Pokédex—especially if you have access to a Day Care Center (more on those in the breeding section).

● An evolved Pokémon, generally, ends up more powerful than its forebear, giving you a decided edge in combat. For example, a Level 55 Venusaur is stronger than a Level 55 Bulbasaur (Venusaur's initial form).

Clearly there's value in seeing your Pokémon attain newer levels of development, but that naturally begs the question of how to do it….

Evolve Via Experience

The most straightforward way to evolve a Pokémon is simply by having your Pokémon fight, and defeat, other Pokémon throughout your adventure. This way they gain experience which, once you reach a certain level, automatically triggers the change into that particular Pokémon's next form. Of course, the Pokémon you want to evolve in this manner *must* battle and cannot simply sit on the sideline, as it won't gain any experience that way.

note Experience is shared if you use multiple Pokémon in the course of a single battle.

Evolution Canceling

You may occasionally not want a Pokémon to evolve. The transformation begins when the Pokémon reaches the minimum number of experience points required to trigger it. At that point, during the animation sequence, quickly press Ⓑ to cancel the Evolution, keeping the Pokémon in its current state.

Why would you want to prevent the Evolution? Sometimes a Pokémon learns better moves by staying in a less-evolved state until reaching a predetermined level.

Evolution Canceling (cont.)

For example, Sandshrew automatically evolves into Sandslash when it reaches Level 22. However, if you'd like to earn the move Swift a bit sooner, you would do well to cancel the Evolution. Normally Sandslash would get Swift at Level 33, but Sandshrew earns it at Level 30, thus you get that move three levels earlier.

caution Unless you have an Everstone, every time your Pokémon reaches another level (and you want it to stay in its current form), you'll need to hit Ⓑ to cancel the Evolution. Otherwise, let it go to automatically transition to its next state.

Trade 'Em All!

One of the most fun (and only) ways to collect a large quantity of Pokémon is via trading with other players. Whether it's trading via the Game Link Cable or the new wireless adapter, meet your friends in the Union Room located above each and every Pokémon Center in the games.

Evolve via Trade

Pokémon in this category include Kadabra and its next evolutionary state, Alakazam. You must trade it to a friend to induce this Evolution and no amount of leveling up will do Kadabra any good after it evolves from Abra.

Evolution via Trade with Item

Pokémon in this group include the evolved form of Onix, Steelix. It won't go on to its final Evolution without being traded with a Metal Coat attached. Needless to say, once your friend has hold of a Pokémon who's fairly tricky to acquire, you may have some trouble getting it back!

Via Evolution Stones

The final special Evolution category includes those Pokémon such as Vulpix and Pikachu who won't evolve into their final forms (Ninetales and Raichu) without the use of a specific stone. To trigger these transitions, simply select the Item in question from your bag and use it on the Pokémon you want to evolve. From there, nature will take its course.

note See the Pokédex section for exactly when a given Pokémon will evolve to its next stage and how.

Via Friendship

On rare occasions, a few Pokémon (basically all those that fall into the pre-evolutionary category) will only evolve when their Friendship level is maxed out. How do you know when you're on the right track? Well, in *Ruby* and *Sapphire* you need to visit the Friendship Rater in Verdanturf Town and in *FireRed* and *LeafGreen* you need to visit your Rival's sister in Pallet Town *after* you conquer the Elite Four.

note A Pokémon's Friendship level is determined by how well you treat it: Letting it faint too much, letting negative Status Effects linger, and feeding it bitter-tasting berries and potions all have a negative effect on your Pokémon's Friendship.

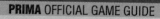

Pokémon Breeding 101

note **For starters, in order to even consider breeding, you need access to a Day Care Center in either *Ruby* and *Sapphire* or *FireRed* and *LeafGreen*.**

THE BASICS

When you drop off two of your Pokémon at Day Care, there's a chance that they'll end up producing an Egg. Of course, there is a whole host of rules involved for those two Pokémon to begin down the path of parenthood and we cover these rules in levels, starting here with the most basic.

First, you need a male and a female Pokémon, as two of the same gender cannot reproduce. You also cannot breed relatives, for example, mother with son or father with daughter. You can, however, check their compatibility with the Day Care attendant, though the tables that follow tell you all you need to know in that area.

Also, certain Pokémon are not capable of being bred at all. Typically this involves the very powerful or very rare Pokémon, so don't think you're going to have Groudon and Mewtwo produce any earth-shattering offspring.

note **The offspring of two Pokémon will be the base form of the mother; for example, breeding a female Fearow with a male Togepi will yield a Level 5 Spearow. Gender, however, is determined at random.**

So why breed Pokémon when you can simply catch them in the vast majority of cases? Simply put, you get much more powerful Pokémon by breeding than you could ever catch in the wild, as well as moves that are only obtainable via breeding (Egg Moves are listed in the Pokédex).

Inheriting Stats

The entire inheritance process, while semi-scientific, also features pitfalls because of the random nature of gender-assignment.

Because a female baby inherits her stats from her father and a male baby inherits his stats from his mother, it can take several tries to get the desired effect. Patience, in these cases, is a virtue.

Inheriting Moves

Your efforts at customizing a Pokémon show in the moves with which your new Pokémon is born. These moves come in three types: Learned Moves, Inherited Moves, and Hereditary Moves.

Learned Moves are the ones that your Pokémon would start with if caught in the wild at Level 5.

Inherited Moves cover any move or TM your Pokémon would normally learn, although not at Level 5. These Moves are inherited from the male Pokémon used in the breeding.

Hereditary Moves (also known as "Egg Moves") are also inherited from the father, but they are special. Egg Moves are ones the newly hatched Pokémon would not normally be able to learn. Of the Pokémon you can obtain through breeding, most of them can inherit up to eight moves through breeding that they would not normally learn.

Here's how it works: When a baby Pokémon hatches from its Egg, it starts with the moves that a wild Pokémon of the same level would know. So, for example, a newly hatched Bagon will know one move, Rage, while a newly hatched Pichu will know two, Thundershock and Charm. The remaining spaces, not filled with Learned Moves, can be filled with other types of Inherited Moves.

Don't worry if your bred Pokémon starts with too many naturally Learned Moves. Inherited and Egg moves take precedence over Learned Moves, so if your target Pokémon starts with three moves and stands the chance to inherit two more moves, the first move on the list of Learned Moves is erased and replaced by one of the two Inherited Moves.

Next, if both the male and female Pokémon used in breeding know a move that the baby Pokémon would learn later in life (after Level

5), then the baby Pokémon hatches with this move. For example, if you breed two Pokémon who currently know Defense Curl, then the baby Pokémon starts with that move too. This works well when you want your baby Pokémon to start with a high-powered move that it would otherwise learn later in life.

Similarly, if the male Pokémon knows an attack that the offspring can learn in the form of a Technical Machine, the baby Pokémon will inherit that move. This lets you "reuse" your TMs by breeding the attacks they contain into other Pokémon.

BREEDING FOR HEREDITARY MOVES

To breed for Egg Moves, find a compatible male Pokémon who can learn the desired Hereditary Move, then mate it with a female version of the target Pokémon.

Sometimes, the Pokémon who learn the desired Egg Move are not compatible with the target Pokémon. In this case, you need to find another compatible Pokémon to act as an inter-mediate. Breed the two Pokémon, and if the baby born is male (and you should continue breeding those two Pokémon until they produce a male Pokémon), then you can breed it with the target female Pokémon.

CRACK 'EM ALL!

Hatching the Eggs is a pretty straightforward process: After you collect the Egg (remember an Egg takes up one slot in your roster) you simply have to carry it around with you till it hatches. And, to make things more interesting, there isn't a universal number of steps required to hatch an Egg, so some take longer than others to yield a bouncing baby Pokémon.

To speed up the process a bit, you can do two things:

- Breed two of the same Pokémon, for example, two Doduo (unfortunately this isn't terribly practical or very useful).

- Transfer Pokémon from a different version of the game, as they have different ID

numbers, which speeds up the process—this is fairly easy if you have a Pokémon in *Ruby/Sapphire* and transfer it to *FireRed/LeafGreen* or vice versa.

Pokémon Compatibility

The following charts provide all the info you need to determine whether Pokémon are compatible with one another. This way, you know what to expect. And, as is usually the case, there are a couple of rules:

- Pokémon belonging to Group X cannot produce Eggs, period.

- In order to breed, the two Pokémon in question, in addition to the aforementioned rules, can only produce Eggs with members of the same group.

With that in mind, check out the following charts and see what kind of super-Pokémon you can come up with!

Group X: Cannot Breed

Articuno	Latias	Metagross	Staryu
Azurill	Latios	Nidoking	Tangela
Baltoy	Lunatone	Nidoqueen	Togepi
Beldum	Mew	Rayquaza	Tyrogue
Claydol	Mewtwo	Regice	Unown
Cleffa	Moltres	Regirock	Voltorb
Elekid	Pichu	Registeel	Wynaut
Electrode	Magby	Shedinja	Zapdos
Igglybuff	Magnemite	Smoochum	
Groudon	Magneton	Solrock	
Kyogre	Metang	Starmie	

Group 1: Plant-Group Pokémon

Bayleef	Exeggutor	Nuzleaf	Sunflora
Bellossom	Gloom	Oddish	Sunkern
Bellsprout	Hoppip	Paras	Tropius
Breloom	Ivysaur	Parasect	Venusaur
Bulbasaur	Jumpluff	Roselia	Victreebel
Cacnea	Lombre	Seedot	Vileplume
Cacturne	Lotad	Shiftry	Weepinbell
Chikorita	Ludicolo	Shroomish	
Exeggcute	Meganium	Skiploom	

Group 2:
Bug-Group Pokémon

Ariados	Heracross	Parasect	Venomoth
Beautifly	Illumise	Pineco	Venonat
Beedrill	Kakuna	Pinsir	Vibrava
Butterfree	Ledian	Scizor	Volbeat
Cascoon	Ledyba	Scyther	Weedle
Caterpie	Masquerain	Shuckle	Wurmple
Dustox	Metapod	Silcoon	Yanma
Flygon	Nincada	Spinarak	
Forretress	Ninjask	Surskit	
Gligar	Paras	Trapinch	

Group 3:
Flying-Group Pokémon

Aerodactyl	Golbat	Pidgeot	Togetic
Altaria	Hoothoot	Pidgeotto	Wingull
Crobat	Murkrow	Skarmory	Xatu
Dodrio	Natu	Spearow	Zubat
Doduo	Noctowl	Swablu	
Farfetch'd	Pelipper	Swellow	
Fearow	Pidgey	Taillow	

Group 4: Humanshape-
Group Pokémon

Abra	Hitmonchan	Machamp	Mr. Mime
Alakazam	Hitmonlee	Machoke	Sableye
Cacnea	Hitmontop	Machop	Spinda
Cacturne	Hypno	Magmar	Volbeat
Drowzee	Illumise	Makuhita	
Electabuzz	Jynx	Medicham	
Hariyama	Kadabra	Meditite	

Group 5:
Mineral-Group Pokémon

Geodude	Graveler	Porygon	Steelix
Glalie	Nosepass	Porygon2	Sudowoodo
Golem	Onix	Snorunt	

Group 6: Indeterminate-
Group Pokémon

Banette	Gastly	Koffing	Slugma
Castform	Gengar	Magcargo	Swalot
Chimecho	Grimer	Misdreavus	Weezing
Dusclops	Gulpin	Muk	Wobbuffet
Duskull	Haunter	Ralts	
Gardevoir	Kirlia	Shuppet	

Group 7:
Ground-Group Pokémon

Absol	Golduck	Phanpy	Slakoth
Aipom	Granbull	Pikachu	Smeargle
Ampharos	Growlithe	Piloswine	Sneasel
Arbok	Grumpig	Ponyta	Snubbull
Arcanine	Houndoom	Poochyena	Spheal
Blaziken	Houndour	Primeape	Spinda
Camerupt	Jolteon	Psyduck	Spoink
Combusken	Kecleon	Quagsire	Swinub
Cyndaquil	Linoone	Quilava	Tauros
Delcatty	Loudred	Raichu	Teddiursa
Delibird	Manectric	Rapidash	Torkoal
Dewgong	Mankey	Rattata	Torchic
Diglett	Mareep	Raticate	Typhlosion
Donphan	Mawile	Rhydon	Umbreon
Dugtrio	Meowth	Rhyhorn	Ursaring
Dunsparce	Mightyena	Sandshrew	Vaporeon
Ekans	Miltank	Sandslash	Vigoroth
Electrike	Nidoran ♀	Sealeo	Vulpix
Eevee	Nidoran ♂	Seedot	Wailmer
Espeon	Nidorina	Seel	Wailord
Exploud	Nidorino	Sentret	Walrein
Flaaffy	Ninetales	Seviper	Whismur
Flareon	Numel	Shiftry	Wooper
Furret	Nuzleaf	Skitty	Zangoose
Girafarig	Persian	Slaking	Zigzagoon

Group 8:
Water 1-Group Pokémon

Azumarill	Gorebyss	Milotic	Slowbro
Blastoise	Horsea	Mudkip	Slowking
Clamperl	Huntail	Omanyte	Slowpoke
Corphish	Kabuto	Omastar	Spheal
Corsola	Kabutops	Pelipper	Squirtle
Crawdaunt	Kingdra	Politoed	Surskit
Croconaw	Lapras	Poliwag	Swampert
Dewgong	Lombre	Poliwhirl	Totodile
Dragonair	Lotad	Poliwrath	Walrein
Dragonite	Ludicolo	Psyduck	Wartortle
Dratini	Mantine	Quagsire	Wingull
Feebas	Marill	Seaking	Wooper
Feraligatr	Marshtomp	Sealeo	
Golduck	Masquerain	Seel	

Group 9:
Water 2-Group Pokémon

Barboach	Lanturn	Seaking	Wailord
Carvanha	Luvdisc	Sharpedo	Whiscash
Chinchou	Magikarp	Quilfish	
Goldeen	Octillery	Remoraid	
Gyarados	Relicanth	Wailmer	

Group 10:
Water 3-Group Pokémon

Anorith	Cradily	Krabby	Staryu
Armaldo	Crawdaunt	Lileep	Tentacool
Cloyster	Kabuto	Omanyte	Tentacruel
Corphish	Kabutops	Omastar	
Corsola	Kingler	Shellder	

Group 11:
Monster-Group Pokémon

Aggron	Feraligatr	Marshtomp	Snorlax
Ampharos	Flaaffy	Mudkip	Squirtle
Aron	Grovyle	Nidoran ♀	Swampert
Bayleef	Ivysaur	Nidoran ♂	Totodile
Blastoise	Kangaskhan	Nidorina	Treecko
Bulbasaur	Lairon	Nidorino	Tropius
Charizard	Lapras	Pupitar	Tyranitar
Charmander	Larvitar	Rhydon	Venusaur
Charmeleon	Lickitung	Rhyhorn	Wartortle
Chikorita	Loudred	Sceptile	Whismur
Croconaw	Meganium	Slowbro	
Cubone	Mareep	Slowking	
Exploud	Marowak	Slowpoke	

Group 12:
Fairy-Group Pokémon

Azumarill	Delcatty	Mawile	Skiploom
Blissey	Glalie	Minun	Skitty
Breloom	Granbull	Pikachu	Snorunt
Castform	Hoppip	Plusle	Snubbull
Chansey	Jigglypuff	Raichu	Togetic
Clefable	Jumpluff	Roselia	Wigglytuff
Clefairy	Marill	Shroomish	

Group 13:
Dragon-Group Pokémon

Altaria	Dragonair	Gyarados	Sceptile
Arbok	Dragonite	Horsea	Seadra
Bagon	Dratini	Kingdra	Seviper
Charizard	Ekans	Magikarp	Shelgon
Charmander	Feebas	Milotic	Swablu
Charmeleon	Grovyle	Salamence	Treecko

Move Tutor Stats

You'll find lists of all the moves a Pokémon can perform at the end of their entries in the Pokédex. To find the stats for each of those moves refer back to this table.

MOVE TUTOR

Name	Type	Power	ACC	PP	Name	Type	Power	ACC	PP
Body Slam*†	Normal	85	100	15	Mimic*	Normal	—	100	10
Counter*†	Fighting	—	100	20	Mud-Slap**†	Ground	20	100	10
Defense Curl**†	Normal	—	—	40	Psych Up**†	Normal	—	—	10
Double-Edge*	Normal	120	100	15	Rock Slide*†	Rock	75	90	10
Dream Eater*†	Psychic	100	100	15	Rollout**	Rock	30	90	20
Dynamicpunch**	Fighting	100	50	5	Seismic Toss*†	Fighting	—	100	20
Endure**†	Normal	—	—	10	Sleep Talk**	Normal	—	—	10
Explosion*	Normal	250	100	5	Snore**†	Normal	40	100	15
Fire Punch**†	Fire	75	100	15	Softboiled**				
Fury Cutter**	Bug	10	95	20	Substitute*	Normal	—	—	10
Ice Punch**†	Ice	75	100	15	Swagger**	Normal	—	90	15
Icy Wind**†	Ice	55	95	15	Swift**†	Normal	60	—	20
Mega Kick*†	Normal	120	85	5	Swords Dance*†	Normal	—	—	30
Mega Punch*†	Normal	80	75	20	Thunderpunch**†	Electric	75	100	15
Metronome**	Normal	—	100	10	Thunder Wave*†	Electric	—	100	20

* FireRed/LeafGreen and Emerald Only   ** Emerald Only   † Battle Frontier tutor move (Emerald)

PRIMA OFFICIAL GAME GUIDE

Pokédex

Pokédex Alphabetical Listing

PRIMA OFFICIAL GAME GUIDE

001 Bulbasaur™

GRASS   POISON

GENERAL INFO
SPECIES: Seed Pokémon
HEIGHT: 2'04"
WEIGHT: 15 lbs.
ABILITY: Overgrow

Bulbasaur's Grass-type attack power multiplies by 1.5 when its HPs get low.

STATS

EVOLUTIONS

LV16   LV32

LOCATION(s):

RUBY	Rarity: **None**	Trade from *FireRed/LeafGreen*
SAPPHIRE	Rarity: **None**	Trade from *FireRed/LeafGreen*
FIRERED	Rarity: **Only One**	Starter Pokémon from Professor Oak in Pallet Town
LEAFGREEN	Rarity: **Only One**	Starter Pokémon from Professor Oak in Pallet Town
COLOSSEUM	Rarity: **None**	Trade from *FireRed/LeafGreen*
EMERALD	Rarity: **None**	Trade from *FireRed/LeafGreen*
XD	Rarity: **None**	Trade from *FireRed/LeafGreen*

MOVES

Level	Attack	Type	Power	ACC	PP	Level	Attack	Type	Power	ACC	PP
—	Tackle	Normal	35	95	35	20	Razor Leaf	Grass	55	95	25
4	Growl	Normal	—	100	40	25	Sweet Scent	Normal	—	100	20
7	Leech Seed	Grass	—	90	10	32	Growth	Normal	—	—	40
10	Vine Whip	Grass	35	100	10	39	Synthesis	Grass	—	—	5
15	Poisonpowder	Grass	—	75	15	46	Solarbeam	Grass	120	100	10
15	Sleep Powder	Grass	—	75	15						

TM/HM

TM/HM#	Name	Type	Power	ACC	PP	TM/HM#	Name	Type	Power	ACC	PP
TM06	Toxic	Poison	—	85	10	TM36	Sludge Bomb	Poison	90	100	10
TM09	Bullet Seed	Grass	10	100	30	TM42	Facade	Normal	70	100	20
TM10	Hidden Power	Normal	—	100	15	TM43	Secret Power	Normal	70	100	20
TM11	Sunny Day	Fire	—	—	5	TM44	Rest	Psychic	—	—	10
TM17	Protect	Normal	—	—	10	TM45	Attract	Normal	—	100	15
TM19	Giga Drain	Grass	60	100	5	HM01	Cut	Normal	50	95	30
TM21	Frustration	Normal	—	100	20	HM04	Strength	Normal	80	100	15
TM22	Solarbeam	Grass	120	100	10	HM05	Flash	Normal	—	70	20
TM27	Return	Normal	—	100	20	HM06	Rock Smash	Fighting	20	100	15
TM32	Double Team	Normal	—	—	15						

EGG MOVES*

Name	Type	Power	ACC	PP
Charm	Normal	—	100	20
Curse	—	—	—	10
Grasswhistle	Grass	—	55	15
Light Screen	Psychic	—	—	30
Magical Leaf	Grass	60	—	20
Petal Dance	Grass	70	100	20
Safeguard	Normal	—	—	25
Skull Bash	Normal	100	100	15

*Learned Via Breeding

MOVE TUTOR
FireRed/LeafGreen and Emerald Only

Body Slam*	Mimic	Swords Dance*
Double-Edge	Substitute	

*Battle Frontier tutor move (*Emerald*)

002 Ivysaur™

GRASS | POISON

GENERAL INFO

SPECIES: Seed Pokémon
HEIGHT: 3'03"
WEIGHT: 29 lbs.
ABILITY: Overgrow

Ivysaur's Grass-type attack power multiplies by 1.5 when its HPs get low.

STATS

EVOLUTIONS

  LV16 LV32

LOCATION(s):

RUBY	Rarity: **None**	Trade from *FireRed/LeafGreen*	
SAPPHIRE	Rarity: **None**	Trade from *FireRed/LeafGreen*	
FIRERED	Rarity: **Evolve**	Evolve Bulbasaur	
LEAFGREEN	Rarity: **Evolve**	Evolve Bulbasaur	
COLOSSEUM	Rarity: **None**	Trade from *FireRed/LeafGreen*	
EMERALD	Rarity: **None**	Trade from *FireRed/LeafGreen*	
XD	Rarity: **None**	Trade from *FireRed/LeafGreen*	

MOVES

Level	Attack	Type	Power	ACC	PP	Level	Attack	Type	Power	ACC	PP
—	Tackle	Normal	35	95	35	22	Razor Leaf	Grass	55	95	25
—	Growl	Normal	—	100	40	29	Sweet Scent	Normal	—	100	20
—	Leech Seed	Grass	—	90	10	38	Growth	Normal	—	—	40
10	Vine Whip	Grass	35	100	10	47	Synthesis	Grass	—	—	5
15	Sleep Powder	Grass	—	75	15	56	Solarbeam	Grass	120	100	10
15	Poisonpowder	Grass	—	75	15						

TM/HM

TM/HM#	Name	Type	Power	ACC	PP	TM/HM#	Name	Type	Power	ACC	PP
TM06	Toxic	Poison	—	85	10	TM36	Sludge Bomb	Poison	90	100	10
TM09	Bullet Seed	Grass	10	100	30	TM42	Facade	Normal	70	100	20
TM10	Hidden Power	Normal	—	100	15	TM43	Secret Power	Normal	70	100	20
TM11	Sunny Day	Fire	—	—	5	TM44	Rest	Psychic	—	—	10
TM17	Protect	Normal	—	—	10	TM45	Attract	Normal	—	100	15
TM19	Giga Drain	Grass	60	100	5	HM01	Cut	Normal	50	95	30
TM21	Frustration	Normal	—	100	20	HM04	Strength	Normal	80	100	20
TM22	Solarbeam	Grass	120	100	10	HM05	Flash	Normal	—	70	20
TM27	Return	Normal	—	100	20	HM06	Rock Smash	Fighting	20	100	15
TM32	Double Team	Normal	—	—	15						

MOVE TUTOR
FireRed/LeafGreen and Emerald Only

Body Slam*	Mimic	Swords Dance*
Double-Edge	Substitute	

*Battle Frontier tutor move (*Emerald*)

PRIMA OFFICIAL GAME GUIDE

003 Venusaur™

| GRASS | POISON |

GENERAL INFO

SPECIES: Seed Pokémon
HEIGHT: 6'07"
WEIGHT: 221 lbs.
ABILITY: Overgrow

*Venusaur's Grass-type attack power
multiplies by 1.5 when its HPs get low.*

STATS

(Stat chart: HP, ATK, DEF, SP ATK, SP DEF, SPEED)

EVOLUTIONS

LV16   LV32

LOCATION[s]:

RUBY	Rarity: **None**	Trade from *FireRed/LeafGreen*
SAPPHIRE	Rarity: **None**	Trade from *FireRed/LeafGreen*
FIRERED	Rarity: **Evolve**	Evolve Ivysaur
LEAFGREEN	Rarity: **Evolve**	Evolve Ivysaur
COLOSSEUM	Rarity: **None**	Trade from *FireRed/LeafGreen*
EMERALD	Rarity: **None**	Trade from *FireRed/LeafGreen*
XD	Rarity: **None**	Trade from *FireRed/LeafGreen*

MOVES

Level	Attack	Type	Power	ACC	PP		Level	Attack	Type	Power	ACC	PP
—	Tackle	Normal	35	95	35		22	Razor Leaf	Grass	55	95	25
—	Growl	Normal	—	100	40		29	Sweet Scent	Normal	—	100	20
—	Leech Seed	Grass	—	90	10		41	Growth	Normal	—	—	40
—	Vine Whip	Grass	35	100	10		53	Synthesis	Grass	—	—	5
15	Sleep Powder	Grass	—	75	15		65	Solarbeam	Grass	120	100	10
15	Poisonpowder	Grass	—	75	15							

TM/HM

TM/HM#	Name	Type	Power	ACC	PP		TM/HM#	Name	Type	Power	ACC	PP
TM05	Roar	Normal	—	100	20		TM27	Return	Normal	—	100	20
TM06	Toxic	Poison	—	85	10		TM32	Double Team	Normal	—	—	15
TM09	Bullet Seed	Grass	10	100	30		TM36	Sludge Bomb	Poison	90	100	10
TM10	Hidden Power	Normal	—	100	15		TM42	Facade	Normal	70	100	20
TM11	Sunny Day	Fire	—	—	5		TM43	Secret Power	Normal	70	100	20
TM15	Hyper Beam	Normal	150	90	5		TM44	Rest	Psychic	—	—	10
TM17	Protect	Normal	—	—	10		TM45	Attract	Normal	—	100	15
TM19	Giga Drain	Grass	60	100	5		HM01	Cut	Normal	50	95	30
TM21	Frustration	Normal	—	100	20		HM04	Strength	Normal	80	100	20
TM22	Solarbeam	Grass	120	100	10		HM05	Flash	Normal	—	70	20
TM26	Earthquake	Ground	100	100	10		HM06	Rock Smash	Fighting	20	100	15

MOVE TUTOR

FireRed/LeafGreen and Emerald Only

Body Slam*	Frenzy Plant	Substitute
Double-Edge	Mimic	Swords Dance*

*Battle Frontier tutor move (*Emerald*)

004 Charmander™

FIRE

GENERAL INFO

SPECIES: Lizard Pokémon
HEIGHT: 2'00"
WEIGHT: 19 lbs.
ABILITY: Blaze
Charmander's Fire-type attack power multiplies by 1.5 when its HPs get low.

STATS

EVOLUTIONS

LV16   LV36

LOCATION(s):

RUBY	Rarity: None	Trade from *FireRed/LeafGreen*
SAPPHIRE	Rarity: None	Trade from *FireRed/LeafGreen*
FIRERED	Rarity: Only One	Starter Pokémon from Professor Oak in Pallet Town
LEAFGREEN	Rarity: Only One	Starter Pokémon from Professor Oak in Pallet Town
COLOSSEUM	Rarity: None	Trade from *FireRed/LeafGreen*
EMERALD	Rarity: None	Trade from *FireRed/LeafGreen*
XD	Rarity: None	Trade from *FireRed/LeafGreen*

MOVES

Level	Attack	Type	Power	ACC	PP
—	Scratch	Normal	40	100	35
—	Growl	Normal	—	100	40
7	Ember	Fire	40	100	25
13	Metal Claw	Steel	50	95	35
19	Smokescreen	Normal	—	100	20

Level	Attack	Type	Power	ACC	PP
25	Scary Face	Normal	—	90	10
31	Flamethrower	Fire	95	100	15
37	Slash	Normal	70	100	20
43	Dragon Rage	Dragon	—	100	10
49	Fire Spin	Fire	15	70	15

TM/HM

TM/HM#	Name	Type	Power	ACC	PP
TM01	Focus Punch	Fighting	150	100	20
TM02	Dragon Claw	Dragon	80	100	15
TM06	Toxic	Poison	—	85	10
TM10	Hidden Power	Normal	—	100	15
TM11	Sunny Day	Fire	—	—	5
TM17	Protect	Normal	—	—	10
TM21	Frustration	Normal	—	100	20
TM23	Iron Tail	Steel	75	75	15
TM27	Return	Normal	—	100	20
TM28	Dig	Ground	60	100	10
TM31	Brick Break	Fighting	75	100	15
TM32	Double Team	Normal	—	—	15

TM/HM#	Name	Type	Power	ACC	PP
TM35	Flamethrower	Fire	95	100	15
TM38	Fire Blast	Fire	120	85	5
TM40	Aerial Ace	Flying	60	—	20
TM42	Facade	Normal	70	100	20
TM43	Secret Power	Normal	70	100	20
TM44	Rest	Psychic	—	—	10
TM45	Attract	Normal	—	100	15
TM50	Overheat	Fire	140	90	5
HM01	Cut	Normal	50	95	30
HM04	Strength	Normal	80	100	20
HM06	Rock Smash	Fighting	20	100	15

EGG MOVES*

Name	Type	Power	ACC	PP
Ancientpower	Rock	60	100	5
Beat Up	Dark	10	100	10
Belly Drum	Normal	—	—	10
Bite	Dark	60	100	25
Dragon Dance	Dragon	—	—	20
Outrage	Dragon	90	100	15
Rock Slide	Rock	75	90	10
Swords Dance	Normal	—	—	30

*Learned Via Breeding

MOVE TUTOR
FireRed/LeafGreen and Emerald Only

Body Slam*	Mega Kick*	Substitute
Counter*	Mimic	Swords Dance*
Double-Edge	Rock Slide*	
Mega Punch*	Seismic Toss*	

*Battle Frontier tutor move (*Emerald*)

005 Charmeleon™

FIRE

GENERAL INFO
SPECIES: Flame Pokémon
HEIGHT: 3'07"
WEIGHT: 42 lbs.
ABILITY: Blaze

Charmeleon's Fire-type attack power multiplies by 1.5 when its HPs get low.

STATS

EVOLUTIONS

LV16 · LV36

LOCATION[s]:

	Rarity	
RUBY	**None**	Trade from *FireRed/LeafGreen*
SAPPHIRE	**None**	Trade from *FireRed/LeafGreen*
FIRERED	**Evolve**	Evolve Charmander
LEAFGREEN	**Evolve**	Evolve Charmander
COLOSSEUM	**None**	Trade from *FireRed/LeafGreen*
EMERALD	**None**	Trade from *FireRed/LeafGreen*
XD	**None**	Trade from *FireRed/LeafGreen*

MOVES

Level	Attack	Type	Power	ACC	PP	Level	Attack	Type	Power	ACC	PP
—	Scratch	Normal	40	100	35	27	Scary Face	Normal	—	90	10
—	Growl	Normal	—	100	40	34	Flamethrower	Fire	95	100	15
—	Ember	Fire	40	100	25	41	Slash	Normal	70	100	20
13	Metal Claw	Steel	50	95	35	48	Dragon Rage	Dragon	—	100	10
20	Smokescreen	Normal	—	100	20	55	Fire Spin	Fire	15	70	15

TM/HM

TM/HM#	Name	Type	Power	ACC	PP	TM/HM#	Name	Type	Power	ACC	PP
TM01	Focus Punch	Fighting	150	100	20	TM35	Flamethrower	Fire	95	100	15
TM02	Dragon Claw	Dragon	80	100	15	TM38	Fire Blast	Fire	120	85	5
TM06	Toxic	Poison	—	85	10	TM40	Aerial Ace	Flying	60	—	20
TM10	Hidden Power	Normal	—	100	15	TM42	Facade	Normal	70	100	20
TM11	Sunny Day	Fire	—	—	5	TM43	Secret Power	Normal	70	100	20
TM17	Protect	Normal	—	—	10	TM44	Rest	Psychic	—	—	10
TM21	Frustration	Normal	—	100	20	TM45	Attract	Normal	—	100	15
TM23	Iron Tail	Steel	75	75	15	TM50	Overheat	Fire	140	90	5
TM27	Return	Normal	—	100	20	HM01	Cut	Normal	50	95	30
TM28	Dig	Ground	60	100	10	HM04	Strength	Normal	80	100	20
TM31	Brick Break	Fighting	75	100	15	HM06	Rock Smash	Fighting	20	100	15
TM32	Double Team	Normal	—	—	15						

MOVE TUTOR
FireRed/LeafGreen and Emerald Only

Body Slam*	Mega Kick*	Substitute
Counter*	Mimic	Swords Dance*
Double-Edge	Rock Slide*	
Mega Punch*	Seismic Toss*	

*Battle Frontier tutor move (*Emerald*)

006 Charizard™

FIRE | FLYING

GENERAL INFO
SPECIES: Flame Pokémon
HEIGHT: 5'07"
WEIGHT: 200 lbs.
ABILITY: Blaze

Charizard's Fire-type attack power multiplies by 1.5 when its HPs get low.

STATS

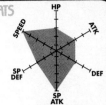

EVOLUTIONS

LV16 | LV36

LOCATION(S):

RUBY	Rarity:	None	Trade from *FireRed/LeafGreen*
SAPPHIRE	Rarity:	None	Trade from *FireRed/LeafGreen*
FIRERED	Rarity:	Evolve	Evolve Charmeleon
LEAFGREEN	Rarity:	Evolve	Evolve Charmeleon
COLOSSEUM	Rarity:	None	Trade from *FireRed/LeafGreen*
EMERALD	Rarity:	None	Trade from *FireRed/LeafGreen*
XD	Rarity:	None	Trade from *FireRed/LeafGreen*

MOVES

Level	Attack	Type	Power	ACC	PP	Level	Attack	Type	Power	ACC	PP
—	Heat Wave	Fire	100	90	10	27	Scary Face	Normal	—	90	10
—	Scratch	Normal	40	100	35	34	Flamethrower	Fire	95	100	15
—	Growl	Normal	—	100	40	36	Wing Attack	Flying	60	100	35
—	Ember	Fire	40	100	25	44	Slash	Normal	70	100	20
—	Metal Claw	Steel	50	95	35	54	Dragon Rage	Dragon	—	100	10
20	Smokescreen	Normal	—	100	20	64	Fire Spin	Fire	15	70	15

TM/HM

TM/HM#	Name	Type	Power	ACC	PP	TM/HM#	Name	Type	Power	ACC	PP
TM01	Focus Punch	Fighting	150	100	20	TM32	Double Team	Normal	—	—	15
TM02	Dragon Claw	Dragon	80	100	15	TM35	Flamethrower	Fire	95	100	15
TM05	Roar	Normal	—	100	20	TM38	Fire Blast	Fire	120	85	5
TM06	Toxic	Poison	—	85	10	TM40	Aerial Ace	Flying	60	—	20
TM10	Hidden Power	Normal	—	100	15	TM42	Facade	Normal	70	100	20
TM11	Sunny Day	Fire	—	—	5	TM43	Secret Power	Normal	70	100	20
TM15	Hyper Beam	Normal	150	90	5	TM44	Rest	Psychic	—	—	10
TM17	Protect	Normal	—	—	10	TM45	Attract	Normal	—	100	15
TM21	Frustration	Normal	—	100	20	TM47	Steel Wing	Steel	70	90	25
TM23	Iron Tail	Steel	75	75	15	TM50	Overheat	Fire	140	90	5
TM26	Earthquake	Ground	100	100	10	HM01	Cut	Normal	50	95	30
TM27	Return	Normal	—	100	20	HM02	Fly	Flying	70	95	15
TM28	Dig	Ground	60	100	10	HM04	Strength	Normal	80	100	15
TM31	Brick Break	Fighting	75	100	15	HM06	Rock Smash	Fighting	20	100	15

MOVE TUTOR
FireRed/LeafGreen and Emerald Only

Blast Burn	Mega Punch*	Seismic Toss*
Body Slam*	Mega Kick*	Substitute
Counter*	Mimic	Swords Dance*
Double-Edge	Rock Slide*	

*Battle Frontier tutor move (*Emerald*)

PRIMA OFFICIAL GAME GUIDE

007 Squirtle™

 WATER

GENERAL INFO

SPECIES: Tiny Turtle Pokémon
HEIGHT: 1'08"
WEIGHT: 20 lbs.
ABILITY: Torrent

Squirtle's Water-type attack power multiplies by 1.5 when its HPs get low.

STATS

EVOLUTIONS

LV16   LV36

LOCATION(s):

RUBY	Rarity: None	Trade from *FireRed/LeafGreen*
SAPPHIRE	Rarity: None	Trade from *FireRed/LeafGreen*
FIRERED	Rarity: Only One	Starter Pokémon from Professor Oak in Pallet Town
LEAFGREEN	Rarity: Only One	Starter Pokémon from Professor Oak in Pallet Town
COLOSSEUM	Rarity: None	Trade from *FireRed/LeafGreen*
EMERALD	Rarity: None	Trade from *FireRed/LeafGreen*
XD	Rarity: None	Trade from *FireRed/LeafGreen*

MOVES

Level	Attack	Type	Power	ACC	PP
—	Tackle	Normal	35	95	35
4	Tail Whip	Normal	—	100	30
7	Bubble	Water	20	100	30
10	Withdraw	Normal	—	—	40
13	Water Gun	Water	40	100	25

Level	Attack	Type	Power	ACC	PP
18	Bite	Dark	60	100	25
23	Rapid Spin	Normal	20	100	40
28	Protect	Normal	—	—	10
33	Rain Dance	Water	—	—	5
40	Skull Bash	Normal	100	100	15
47	Hydro Pump	Water	120	80	5

TM/HM

TM/HM#	Name	Type	Power	ACC	PP
TM01	Focus Punch	Fighting	150	100	20
TM03	Water Pulse	Water	60	95	20
TM06	Toxic	Poison	—	85	10
TM07	Hail	Ice	—	—	10
TM10	Hidden Power	Normal	—	100	10
TM13	Ice Beam	Ice	95	100	10
TM14	Blizzard	Ice	120	70	5
TM17	Protect	Normal	—	—	10
TM18	Rain Dance	Water	—	—	5
TM21	Frustration	Normal	—	100	20
TM23	Iron Tail	Steel	75	75	15
TM27	Return	Normal	—	100	20

TM/HM#	Name	Type	Power	ACC	PP
TM28	Dig	Ground	60	100	10
TM31	Brick Break	Fighting	75	100	15
TM32	Double Team	Normal	—	—	15
TM42	Facade	Normal	70	100	20
TM43	Secret Power	Normal	70	100	20
TM44	Rest	Psychic	—	—	10
TM45	Attract	Normal	—	100	15
HM03	Surf	Water	95	100	15
HM04	Strength	Normal	80	100	20
HM06	Rock Smash	Fighting	20	100	15
HM07	Waterfall	Water	80	100	15
HM08	Dive	Water	60	100	10

EGG MOVES*

Name	Type	Power	ACC	PP
Flail	Normal	—	100	15
Foresight	Normal	—	100	40
Haze	Ice	—	—	30
Mirror Coat	Psychic	—	100	20
Mist	Ice	—	—	30
Mud Sport	Ground	—	100	15
Refresh	Normal	—	100	20
Yawn	Normal	—	100	10

*Learned Via Breeding

MOVE TUTOR
FireRed/LeafGreen and Emerald Only

Body Slam*	Mega Punch*	Seismic Toss*
Counter*	Mega Kick*	Substitute
Double-Edge*	Mimic	

*Battle Frontier tutor move (*Emerald*)

008 Wartortle™

WATER

GENERAL INFO

SPECIES: Turtle Pokémon
HEIGHT: 3'03"
WEIGHT: 50 lbs.
ABILITY: Torrent

Wartortle's Water-type attack power multiplies by 1.5 when its HPs get low.

STATS

HP, SPEED, ATK, DEF, SP ATK, SP DEF

EVOLUTIONS

LV16   LV36

LOCATION(S):

RUBY	Rarity: **None**	Trade from *FireRed/LeafGreen*
SAPPHIRE	Rarity: **None**	Trade from *FireRed/LeafGreen*
FIRERED	Rarity: **Evolve**	Evolve Squirtle
LEAFGREEN	Rarity: **Evolve**	Evolve Squirtle
COLOSSEUM	Rarity: **None**	Trade from *FireRed/LeafGreen*
EMERALD	Rarity: **None**	Trade from *FireRed/LeafGreen*
XD	Rarity: **None**	Trade from *FireRed/LeafGreen*

MOVES

Level	Attack	Type	Power	ACC	PP
—	Tackle	Normal	35	95	35
—	Tail Whip	Normal	—	100	30
—	Bubble	Water	20	100	30
10	Withdraw	Normal	—	—	40
13	Water Gun	Water	40	100	25

Level	Attack	Type	Power	ACC	PP
19	Bite	Dark	60	100	25
25	Rapid Spin	Normal	20	100	40
31	Protect	Normal	—	—	10
37	Rain Dance	Water	—	—	5
45	Skull Bash	Normal	100	100	15
53	Hydro Pump	Water	120	80	5

TM/HM

TM/HM#	Name	Type	Power	ACC	PP
TM01	Focus Punch	Fighting	150	100	20
TM03	Water Pulse	Water	60	95	20
TM06	Toxic	Poison	—	85	10
TM07	Hail	Ice	—	—	10
TM10	Hidden Power	Normal	—	100	15
TM13	Ice Beam	Ice	95	100	10
TM14	Blizzard	Ice	120	70	5
TM17	Protect	Normal	—	—	10
TM18	Rain Dance	Water	—	—	5
TM21	Frustration	Normal	—	100	20
TM23	Iron Tail	Steel	75	75	15
TM27	Return	Normal	—	100	20

TM/HM#	Name	Type	Power	ACC	PP
TM28	Dig	Ground	60	100	10
TM31	Brick Break	Fighting	75	100	15
TM32	Double Team	Normal	—	—	15
TM42	Facade	Normal	70	100	20
TM43	Secret Power	Normal	70	100	20
TM44	Rest	Psychic	—	—	10
TM45	Attract	Normal	—	100	15
HM03	Surf	Water	95	100	15
HM04	Strength	Normal	80	100	15
HM06	Rock Smash	Fighting	20	100	15
HM07	Waterfall	Water	80	100	15
HM08	Dive	Water	60	100	10

MOVE TUTOR

FireRed/LeafGreen and Emerald Only

Body Slam*	Mega Punch*	Seismic Toss*
Counter*	Mega Kick*	Substitute
Double-Edge	Mimic	

*Battle Frontier tutor move (*Emerald*)

009 Blastoise™

WATER

GENERAL INFO

SPECIES: Shellfish Pokémon
HEIGHT: 5'03"
WEIGHT: 189 lbs.
ABILITY: Torrent

Blastoise's Water-type attack power multiplies by 1.5 when its HPs get low.

STATS

EVOLUTIONS

  LV16   LV36

LOCATION(s):

RUBY	Rarity: None	Trade from *FireRed/LeafGreen*
SAPPHIRE	Rarity: None	Trade from *FireRed/LeafGreen*
FIRERED	Rarity: Evolve	Evolve Wartortle
LEAFGREEN	Rarity: Evolve	Evolve Wartortle
COLOSSEUM	Rarity: None	Trade from *FireRed/LeafGreen*
EMERALD	Rarity: None	Trade from *FireRed/LeafGreen*
XD	Rarity: None	Trade from *FireRed/LeafGreen*

MOVES

Level	Attack	Type	Power	ACC	PP
—	Tackle	Normal	35	95	35
—	Tail Whip	Normal	—	100	30
—	Bubble	Water	20	100	30
—	Withdraw	Normal	—	—	40
13	Water Gun	Water	40	100	25

Level	Attack	Type	Power	ACC	PP
19	Bite	Dark	60	100	25
25	Rapid Spin	Normal	20	100	40
31	Protect	Normal	—	—	10
42	Rain Dance	Water	—	—	5
55	Skull Bash	Normal	100	100	15
68	Hydro Pump	Water	120	80	5

TM/HM

TM/HM#	Name	Type	Power	ACC	PP
TM01	Focus Punch	Fighting	150	100	20
TM03	Water Pulse	Water	60	95	20
TM05	Roar	Normal	—	100	20
TM06	Toxic	Poison	—	85	10
TM07	Hail	Ice	—	—	10
TM10	Hidden Power	Normal	—	100	15
TM13	Ice Beam	Ice	95	100	10
TM14	Blizzard	Ice	120	70	5
TM15	Hyper Beam	Normal	150	90	5
TM17	Protect	Normal	—	—	10
TM18	Rain Dance	Water	—	—	5
TM21	Frustration	Normal	—	100	20
TM23	Iron Tail	Steel	75	75	15
TM26	Earthquake	Ground	100	100	10

TM/HM#	Name	Type	Power	ACC	PP
TM27	Return	Normal	—	100	20
TM28	Dig	Ground	60	100	10
TM31	Brick Break	Fighting	75	100	15
TM32	Double Team	Normal	—	—	15
TM42	Facade	Normal	70	100	20
TM43	Secret Power	Normal	70	100	20
TM44	Rest	Psychic	—	—	10
TM45	Attract	Normal	—	100	15
HM03	Surf	Water	95	100	15
HM04	Strength	Normal	80	100	20
HM06	Rock Smash	Fighting	20	100	15
HM07	Waterfall	Water	80	100	15
HM08	Dive	Water	60	100	10

MOVE TUTOR

FireRed/LeafGreen and Emerald Only

Body Slam*	Hydro Cannon	Mimic
Counter*	Mega Punch*	Seismic Toss*
Double-Edge	Mega Kick*	Substitute

*Battle Frontier tutor move (*Emerald*)

010 Caterpie™

GENERAL INFO

SPECIES: Worm Pokémon
HEIGHT: 1'00"
WEIGHT: 6 lbs.
ABILITY: Shield Dust

Protects Caterpie from being hit by any additional move effects.

STATS

EVOLUTIONS

  LV7   LV10

LOCATION(s):

RUBY	Rarity: **None**	Trade from *FireRed/LeafGreen*	
SAPPHIRE	Rarity: **None**	Trade from *FireRed/LeafGreen*	
FIRERED	Rarity: **Common**	Viridian Forest, Six Island, Route 25	
LEAFGREEN	Rarity: **Common**	Viridian Forest, Six Island, Route 25	
COLOSSEUM	Rarity: **None**	Trade from *FireRed/LeafGreen*	
EMERALD	Rarity: **None**	Trade from *FireRed/LeafGreen*	
XD	Rarity: **None**	Trade from *FireRed/LeafGreen*	

MOVES

Level	Attack	Type	Power	ACC	PP
—	Tackle	Normal	35	95	35
—	String Shot	Bug	—	95	40

TM/HM

TM/HM#	Name	Type	Power	ACC	PP
None					

EGG MOVES*

Name	Type	Power	ACC	PP
None				

*Learned Via Breeding

MOVE TUTOR

FireRed/LeafGreen and Emerald Only

None

PRIMA OFFICIAL GAME GUIDE

011 Metapod™

BUG

GENERAL INFO
SPECIES: Cocoon Pokémon
HEIGHT: 2'04"
WEIGHT: 22 lbs.
ABILITY: Shed Skin

Enables Metapod to only have a status effect for one turn. Has a 30% chance of success.

STATS

EVOLUTIONS

LV7   LV10

LOCATION(s):

RUBY	Rarity: None	Trade from *FireRed/LeafGreen*
SAPPHIRE	Rarity: None	Trade from *FireRed/LeafGreen*
FIRERED	Rarity: Common	Evolve Caterpie, Viridian Forest, Six Island, Route 25
LEAFGREEN	Rarity: Common	Evolve Caterpie, Viridian Forest, Six Island, Route 25
COLOSSEUM	Rarity: None	Trade from *FireRed/LeafGreen*
EMERALD	Rarity: None	Trade from *FireRed/LeafGreen*
XD	Rarity: None	Trade from *FireRed/LeafGreen*

MOVES

Level	Attack	Type	Power	ACC	PP
—	Harden	Normal	—	—	30

TM/HM

TM/HM# Name	Type	Power	ACC	PP
None				

EGG MOVES*

Name	Type	Power	ACC	PP
None				

*Learned Via Breeding

MOVE TUTOR
FireRed/LeafGreen and Emerald Only

None

012 Butterfree™

BUG

GENERAL INFO

SPECIES: Butterfly Pokémon
HEIGHT: 3'07"
WEIGHT: 71 lbs.
ABILITY: Compoundeyes
Raises Butterfree's Accuracy by 30%.

STATS

HP
SPEED — ATK
SP DEF — DEF
SP ATK

EVOLUTIONS

LV7 LV10

LOCATION[s]:

RUBY	Rarity: **None**	Trade from *FireRed/LeafGreen*
SAPPHIRE	Rarity: **None**	Trade from *FireRed/LeafGreen*
FIRERED	Rarity: **Common**	Evolve Metapod
LEAFGREEN	Rarity: **Common**	Evolve Metapod
COLOSSEUM	Rarity: **None**	Trade from *FireRed/LeafGreen*
EMERALD	Rarity: **None**	Trade from *FireRed/LeafGreen*
XD	Rarity: **Only One**	Cipher Key Lair (Capture from Cipher Peon Targ)

MOVES

Level	Attack	Type	Power	ACC	PP	Level	Attack	Type	Power	ACC	PP
—	Confusion	Psychic	50	100	25	23	Whirlwind	Normal	—	100	20
13	Poisonpowder	Poison	—	75	35	28	Gust	Flying	40	100	35
14	Stun Spora	Grass	—	75	30	34	Psybeam	Psychic	65	100	20
15	Sleep Powder	Grass	—	75	15	40	Safeguard	Normal	—	—	25
18	Supersonic	Normal	—	55	20	47	Silver Wind	Bug	60	100	5

TM/HM

TM/HM#	Name	Type	Power	ACC	PP	TM/HM#	Name	Type	Power	ACC	PP
TM06	Toxic	Poison	—	85	10	TM29	Psychic	Psychic	90	100	10
TM10	Hidden Power	Normal	—	100	15	TM30	Shadow Ball	Ghost	80	100	15
TM11	Sunny Day	Fire	—	—	5	TM32	Double Team	Normal	—	—	15
TM15	Hyper Beam	Normal	150	90	5	TM40	Aerial Ace	Flying	60	—	20
TM17	Protect	Normal	—	—	10	TM42	Facade	Normal	70	100	20
TM18	Rain Dance	Water	—	—	5	TM43	Secret Power	Normal	70	100	20
TM19	Giga Drain	Grass	60	100	5	TM44	Rest	Psychic	—	—	10
TM20	Safeguard	Normal	—	—	25	TM45	Attract	Normal	—	100	15
TM21	Frustration	Normal	—	100	20	TM46	Thief	Dark	40	100	10
TM22	Solarbeam	Grass	120	100	10	TM48	Skill Swap	Psychic	—	100	10
TM27	Return	Normal	—	100	20	HM05	Flash	Normal	—	70	20

EGG MOVES*

Name	Type	Power	ACC	PP
None				

*Learned Via Breeding

MOVE TUTOR

FireRed/LeafGreen and Emerald Only

Double-Edge	Substitute	Dream Eater*
Mimic		

*Battle Frontier tutor move (*Emerald*)

013 Weedle™

BUG   POISON

GENERAL INFO

SPECIES: Hairy Bug Pokemon
HEIGHT: 1'00"
WEIGHT: 7 lbs.
ABILITY: Shield Dust
Protects Weedle from being hit by any additional move effects.

STATS

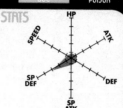

EVOLUTIONS

LV7   LV10

LOCATION[s]:

RUBY	Rarity: **None**	Trade from *FireRed/LeafGreen*
SAPPHIRE	Rarity: **None**	Trade from *FireRed/LeafGreen*
FIRERED	Rarity: **Common**	Viridian Forest, Six Island, Route 25
LEAFGREEN	Rarity: **Common**	Viridian Forest, Six Island, Route 25
COLOSSEUM	Rarity: **None**	Trade from *FireRed/LeafGreen*
EMERALD	Rarity: **None**	Trade from *FireRed/LeafGreen*
XD	Rarity: **None**	Trade from *FireRed/LeafGreen*

MOVES

Level	Attack	Type	Power	ACC	PP
—	Poison Sting	Poison	15	100	35
—	String Shot	Bug	—	95	40

TM/HM

TM/HM# Name	Type	Power	ACC	PP
None				

EGG MOVES*

Name	Type	Power	ACC	PP
None				

*Learned Via Breeding

MOVE TUTOR
FireRed/LeafGreen and Emerald Only

None

014 Kakuna™

GENERAL INFO

SPECIES: Cocoon Pokémon
HEIGHT: 2'00"
WEIGHT: 22 lbs.
ABILITY: Shed Skin

Enables Kakuna to only have a status effect for one turn. Has a 30% chance of success.

STATS

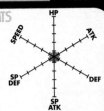

EVOLUTIONS

 ► ►

LV7   LV10

LOCATION(S):

RUBY	Rarity: **None**	Trade from *FireRed/LeafGreen*
SAPPHIRE	Rarity: **None**	Trade from *FireRed/LeafGreen*
FIRERED	Rarity: **Rare**	Evolve Weedle, Viridian Forest, Six Island, Route 25
LEAFGREEN	Rarity: **Rare**	Evolve Weedle, Viridian Forest, Six Island, Route 25
COLOSSEUM	Rarity: **None**	Trade from *FireRed/LeafGreen*
EMERALD	Rarity: **None**	Trade from *FireRed/LeafGreen*
XD	Rarity: **None**	Trade from *FireRed/LeafGreen*

MOVES

Level	Attack	Type	Power	ACC	PP
—	Harden	Normal	—	—	30

TM/HM

TM/HM# Name	Type	Power	ACC	PP
None				

EGG MOVES*

Name	Type	Power	ACC	PP
None				

*Learned Via Breeding

MOVE TUTOR

FireRed/LeafGreen and Emerald Only

None

PRIMA OFFICIAL GAME GUIDE

015 Beedrill™

	BUG	POISON

GENERAL INFO
SPECIES: Poison Bee Pokémon
HEIGHT: 3'03"
WEIGHT: 65 lbs.
ABILITY: Swarm

Beedrill's Bug-type attacks multiply by 1.5 when its HPs get low.

STATS

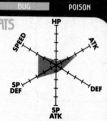

EVOLUTIONS

    LV7 LV10

LOCATION(s):

RUBY	Rarity: **None**	Trade from *FireRed/LeafGreen*
SAPPHIRE	Rarity: **None**	Trade from *FireRed/LeafGreen*
FIRERED	Rarity: **None**	Evolve Kakuna
LEAFGREEN	Rarity: **None**	Evolve Kakuna
COLOSSEUM	Rarity: **None**	Trade from *FireRed/LeafGreen*
EMERALD	Rarity: **None**	Trade from *FireRed/LeafGreen*
XD	Rarity: **Only One**	Cipher Key Lair (Capture from Cipher Peon Lok)

MOVES

Level	Attack	Type	Power	ACC	PP	Level	Attack	Type	Power	ACC	PP
10	Fury Attack	Normal	15	85	20	30	Pursuit	Dark	40	100	20
15	Focus Energy	Normal	—	—	30	35	Pin Missile	Bug	14	85	20
20	Twineedle	Bug	25	100	20	40	Agility	Psychic	—	—	30
25	Rage	Normal	20	100	20	45	Endeavor	Normal	—	100	5

TM/HM

TM/HM#	Name	Type	Power	ACC	PP	TM/HM#	Name	Type	Power	ACC	PP
TM06	Toxic	Poison	—	85	10	TM32	Double Team	Normal	—	—	15
TM10	Hidden Power	Normal	—	100	15	TM36	Sludge Bomb	Poison	90	100	10
TM11	Sunny Day	Fire	—	—	5	TM40	Aerial Ace	Flying	60	—	20
TM15	Hyper Beam	Normal	150	90	5	TM42	Facade	Normal	70	100	20
TM17	Protect	Normal	—	—	10	TM43	Secret Power	Normal	70	100	20
TM19	Giga Drain	Grass	60	100	5	TM44	Rest	Psychic	—	—	10
TM21	Frustration	Normal	—	100	20	TM45	Attract	Normal	—	100	15
TM22	Solarbeam	Grass	120	100	10	TM46	Thief	Dark	40	100	10
TM27	Return	Normal	—	100	20	HM01	Cut	Normal	50	95	30
TM31	Brick Break	Fighting	75	100	15	HM06	Rock Smash	Fighting	20	100	15

EGG MOVES*

Name	Type	Power	ACC	PP
None				

*Learned Via Breeding

MOVE TUTOR
FireRed/LeafGreen and Emerald Only

Double-Edge	Substitute	Swords Dance*
Mimic		

*Battle Frontier tutor move (*Emerald*)

016 Pidgey™

GENERAL INFO

SPECIES: Tiny Bird Pokémon
HEIGHT: 1'00"
WEIGHT: 4 lbs.
ABILITY: Keen Eye
Protects Pidgey from having its Accuracy lowered.

STATS

HP, SPEED, ATK, SP DEF, DEF, SP ATK

EVOLUTIONS

LV18   LV36

LOCATION[s]:

RUBY	Rarity: **None**	Trade from *FireRed/LeafGreen*
SAPPHIRE	Rarity: **None**	Trade from *FireRed/LeafGreen*
FIRERED	Rarity: **Common**	Routes 1, 2, 3, 5, 6, 7, 8, 12, 13, 14, 15, 25
LEAFGREEN	Rarity: **Common**	Routes 1, 2, 3, 5, 6, 7, 8, 12, 13, 14, 15, 25
COLOSSEUM	Rarity: **None**	Trade from *FireRed/LeafGreen*
EMERALD	Rarity: **None**	Trade from *FireRed/LeafGreen*
XD	Rarity: **None**	Trade from *FireRed/LeafGreen*

MOVES

Level	Attack	Type	Power	ACC	PP
—	Tackle	Normal	35	95	35
5	Sand-Attack	Ground	—	100	15
9	Gust	Flying	40	100	35
13	Quick Attack	Normal	40	100	30

Level	Attack	Type	Power	ACC	PP
19	Whirlwind	Normal	—	100	20
25	Wing Attack	Flying	60	100	35
31	Featherdance	Flying	—	100	15
39	Agility	Psychic	—	—	30
47	Mirror Move	Flying	—	—	20

TM/HM

TM/HM#	Name	Type	Power	ACC	PP
TM06	Toxic	Poison	—	85	10
TM10	Hidden Power	Normal	—	100	15
TM11	Sunny Day	Fire	—	—	5
TM17	Protect	Normal	—	—	10
TM18	Rain Dance	Water	—	—	5
TM21	Frustration	Normal	—	100	20
TM27	Return	Normal	—	100	20
TM32	Double Team	Normal	—	—	15

TM/HM#	Name	Type	Power	ACC	PP
TM40	Aerial Ace	Flying	60	—	20
TM42	Facade	Normal	70	100	20
TM43	Secret Power	Normal	70	100	20
TM44	Rest	Psychic	—	—	10
TM45	Attract	Normal	—	100	15
TM46	Thief	Dark	40	100	10
TM47	Steel Wing	Steel	70	90	25
HM02	Fly	Flying	70	95	15

EGG MOVES*

Name	Type	Power	ACC	PP
Air Cutter	Flying	55	95	25
Faint Attack	Dark	60	—	20
Foresight	Normal	—	100	40
Pursuit	Dark	40	100	20
Steel Wing	Steel	70	90	25

*Learned Via Breeding

MOVE TUTOR
FireRed/LeafGreen and Emerald Only

Double-Edge	Mimic	Substitute

017 Pidgeotto™

NORMAL | FLYING

GENERAL INFO
SPECIES: Bird Pokémon
HEIGHT: 3'07"
WEIGHT: 66 lbs.
ABILITY: Keen Eye

Protects Pidgeotto from having its Accuracy lowered.

STATS

HP · ATK · DEF · SP ATK · SP DEF · SPEED

EVOLUTIONS

   LV18   LV36

LOCATION[s]:

RUBY	Rarity: **None**	Trade from *FireRed/LeafGreen*
SAPPHIRE	Rarity: **None**	Trade from *FireRed/LeafGreen*
FIRERED	Rarity: **Rare**	Evolve Pidgey, Route 13, Route 14, Route 15, Three Island, Five Island
LEAFGREEN	Rarity: **Rare**	Evolve Pidgey, Route 13, Route 14, Route 15, Three Island, Five Island
COLOSSEUM	Rarity: **None**	Trade from *FireRed/LeafGreen*
EMERALD	Rarity: **None**	Trade from *FireRed/LeafGreen*
XD	Rarity: **Only One**	Cipher Key Lair (Capture from Cipher Peon Lok)

MOVES

Level	Attack	Type	Power	ACC	PP	Level	Attack	Type	Power	ACC	PP
—	Tackle	Normal	35	95	35	20	Whirlwind	Normal	—	100	20
—	Sand-Attack	Ground	—	100	15	27	Wing Attack	Flying	60	100	35
—	Gust	Flying	40	100	35	34	Featherdance	Flying	—	100	15
13	Quick Attack	Normal	40	100	30	43	Agility	Psychic	—	—	30
						52	Mirror Move	Flying	—	—	20

TM/HM

TM/HM#	Name	Type	Power	ACC	PP	TM/HM#	Name	Type	Power	ACC	PP
TM06	Toxic	Poison	—	85	10	TM40	Aerial Ace	Flying	60	—	20
TM10	Hidden Power	Normal	—	100	15	TM42	Facade	Normal	70	100	20
TM11	Sunny Day	Fire	—	—	5	TM43	Secret Power	Normal	70	100	20
TM17	Protect	Normal	—	—	10	TM44	Rest	Psychic	—	—	10
TM18	Rain Dance	Water	—	—	5	TM45	Attract	Normal	—	100	15
TM21	Frustration	Normal	—	100	20	TM46	Thief	Dark	40	100	10
TM27	Return	Normal	—	100	20	TM47	Steel Wing	Steel	70	90	25
TM32	Double Team	Normal	—	—	15	HM02	Fly	Flying	70	95	15

MOVE TUTOR
FireRed/LeafGreen and Emerald Only

Double-Edge	Mimic	Substitute

018 Pidgeot™

NORMAL | FLYING

GENERAL INFO

SPECIES: Bird Pokémon
HEIGHT: 4'11"
WEIGHT: 87 lbs.
ABILITY: Keen Eye

Protects Pidgeotto from having its Accuracy lowered.

STATS

HP · ATK · DEF · SP ATK · SP DEF · SPEED

EVOLUTIONS

LV18 · LV36

LOCATION[s]:

RUBY	Rarity: **None**	Trade from *FireRed/LeafGreen*
SAPPHIRE	Rarity: **None**	Trade from *FireRed/LeafGreen*
FIRERED	Rarity: **Evolve**	Evolve Pidgeotto
LEAFGREEN	Rarity: **Evolve**	Evolve Pidgeotto
COLOSSEUM	Rarity: **None**	Trade from *FireRed/LeafGreen*
EMERALD	Rarity: **None**	Trade from *FireRed/LeafGreen*
XD	Rarity: **Evolve**	Evolve Pidgeotto

MOVES

Level	Attack	Type	Power	ACC	PP	Level	Attack	Type	Power	ACC	PP
—	Tackle	Normal	35	95	35	20	Whirlwind	Normal	—	100	20
—	Sand-Attack	Ground	—	100	15	27	Wing Attack	Flying	60	100	35
—	Gust	Flying	40	100	35	34	Featherdance	Flying	—	100	15
—	Quick Attack	Normal	40	100	30	48	Agility	Psychic	—	—	30
						62	Mirror Move	Flying	—	—	20

TM/HM

TM/HM#	Name	Type	Power	ACC	PP	TM/HM#	Name	Type	Power	ACC	PP
TM06	Toxic	Poison	—	85	10	TM40	Aerial Ace	Flying	60	—	20
TM10	Hidden Power	Normal	—	100	15	TM42	Facade	Normal	70	100	20
TM11	Sunny Day	Fire	—	—	5	TM43	Secret Power	Normal	70	100	20
TM15	Hyper Beam	Normal	150	90	5	TM44	Rest	Psychic	—	—	10
TM17	Protect	Normal	—	—	10	TM45	Attract	Normal	—	100	15
TM18	Rain Dance	Water	—	—	5	TM46	Thief	Dark	40	100	10
TM21	Frustration	Normal	—	100	20	TM47	Steel Wing	Steel	70	90	25
TM27	Return	Normal	—	100	20	HM02	Fly	Flying	70	95	15
TM32	Double Team	Normal	—	—	15						

MOVE TUTOR

FireRed/LeafGreen and Emerald Only

Double-Edge	Mimic	Substitute

PRIMA OFFICIAL GAME GUIDE

Pokémon Pocket Pokédex

019 Rattata™

NORMAL

GENERAL INFO

SPECIES:	Mouse Pokémon
HEIGHT:	1'00"
WEIGHT:	8 lbs.
ABILITY 1:	Run Away

Allows Rattata to run away from wild Pokémon.

ABILITY 2: Guts

When Rattata has a status condition, its attack power multiplies by 1.5.

STATS

EVOLUTIONS

LV20

LOCATION[S]:

RUBY	Rarity: **None**	Trade from *FireRed/LeafGreen*
SAPPHIRE	Rarity: **None**	Trade from *FireRed/LeafGreen*
FIRERED	Rarity: **None**	Routes 1, 2, 4, 9, 17, 18, 22, Pokémon Mansion
LEAFGREEN	Rarity: **None**	Routes 1, 2, 4, 9, 17, 18, 22, Pokémon Mansion
COLOSSEUM	Rarity: **None**	Trade from *FireRed/LeafGreen*
EMERALD	Rarity: **None**	Trade from *FireRed/LeafGreen*
XD	Rarity: **None**	Trade from *FireRed/LeafGreen*

MOVES

Level	Attack	Type	Power	ACC	PP
—	Tackle	Normal	35	95	35
—	Tail Whip	Normal	—	100	30
7	Quick Attack	Normal	40	100	30
13	Hyper Fang	Normal	80	90	15
20	Focus Energy	Normal	—	—	30
27	Pursuit	Dark	40	100	20
34	Super Fang	Normal	—	90	10
41	Endeavor	Normal	—	100	5

TM/HM

TM/HM#	Name	Type	Power	ACC	PP
TM06	Toxic	Poison	—	85	10
TM10	Hidden Power	Normal	—	100	15
TM11	Sunny Day	Fire	—	—	5
TM12	Taunt	Dark	—	100	20
TM13	Ice Beam	Ice	95	100	10
TM14	Blizzard	Ice	120	70	5
TM17	Protect	Normal	—	—	10
TM18	Rain Dance	Water	—	—	5
TM21	Frustration	Normal	—	100	20
TM23	Iron Tail	Steel	75	75	15
TM24	Thunderbolt	Electric	95	100	15
TM25	Thunder	Electric	120	70	10
TM27	Return	Normal	—	100	20
TM28	Dig	Ground	60	100	10
TM30	Shadow Ball	Ghost	80	100	15
TM32	Double Team	Normal	—	—	15
TM34	Shock Wave	Electric	60	—	20
TM42	Facade	Normal	70	100	20
TM43	Secret Power	Normal	70	100	20
TM44	Rest	Psychic	—	—	10
TM45	Attract	Normal	—	100	15
TM46	Thief	Dark	40	100	10
HM01	Cut	Normal	50	95	30
HM06	Rock Smash	Fighting	20	100	15

EGG MOVES*

Name	Type	Power	ACC	PP
Bite	Dark	60	100	25
Counter	Fighting	—	100	20
Flame Wheel	Fire	60	100	25
Fury Swipes	Normal	18	80	15
Reversal	Fighting	—	100	15
Screech	Normal	—	85	40
Swagger	Normal	—	90	15
Uproar	Normal	50	100	10

*Learned Via Breeding

MOVE TUTOR
FireRed/LeafGreen and Emerald Only

Body Slam*	Substitute	Thunder Wave*
Mimic	Counter*	Double-Edge

*Battle Frontier tutor move (*Emerald*)

020 Raticate ™

`NORMAL`

GENERAL INFO

SPECIES: Mouse Pokémon
HEIGHT: 2'04"
WEIGHT: 41 lbs.
ABILITY 1: Run Away
Allows Raticate to run away from wild Pokémon.

ABILITY 2: Guts
When Raticate has a status condition, its attack power multiplies by 1.5.

STATS

EVOLUTIONS

LV20

LOCATION[S]:

RUBY	Rarity: **None**	Trade from *FireRed/LeafGreen*
SAPPHIRE	Rarity: **None**	Trade from *FireRed/LeafGreen*
FIRERED	Rarity: **Rare**	Route 17, Route 18, Pokémon Mansion
LEAFGREEN	Rarity: **Rare**	Route 17, Route 18, Pokémon Mansion
COLOSSEUM	Rarity: **None**	Trade from *FireRed/LeafGreen*
EMERALD	Rarity: **None**	Trade from *FireRed/LeafGreen*
XD	Rarity: **Only One**	Citadark Island (Capture from Furgy)

MOVES

Level	Attack	Type	Power	ACC	PP	Level	Attack	Type	Power	ACC	PP
—	Tackle	Normal	35	95	35	20	Scary Face	Normal	—	90	10
—	Tail Whip	Normal	—	100	30	30	Pursuit	Dark	40	100	20
—	Quick Attack	Normal	40	100	30	40	Super Fang	Normal	—	90	10
13	Hyper Fang	Normal	80	90	15	50	Endeavor	Normal	—	100	5

TM/HM

TM/HM#	Name	Type	Power	ACC	PP	TM/HM#	Name	Type	Power	ACC	PP
TM05	Roar	Normal	—	100	20	TM27	Return	Normal	—	100	20
TM06	Toxic	Poison	—	85	10	TM28	Dig	Ground	60	100	10
TM10	Hidden Power	Normal	—	100	15	TM30	Shadow Ball	Ghost	80	100	15
TM11	Sunny Day	Fire	—	—	5	TM32	Double Team	Normal	—	—	15
TM12	Taunt	Dark	—	100	20	TM34	Shock Wave	Electric	60	—	20
TM13	Ice Beam	Ice	95	100	10	TM42	Facade	Normal	70	100	20
TM14	Blizzard	Ice	120	70	5	TM43	Secret Power	Normal	70	100	20
TM15	Hyper Beam	Normal	150	90	5	TM44	Rest	Psychic	—	—	10
TM17	Protect	Normal	—	—	10	TM45	Attract	Normal	—	100	15
TM18	Rain Dance	Water	—	—	5	TM46	Thief	Dark	40	100	10
TM21	Frustration	Normal	—	100	20	HM01	Cut	Normal	50	95	30
TM23	Iron Tail	Steel	75	75	15	HM04	Strength	Normal	80	100	20
TM24	Thunderbolt	Electric	95	100	15	HM06	Rock Smash	Fighting	20	100	15
TM25	Thunder	Electric	120	70	10						

MOVE TUTOR

FireRed/LeafGreen and Emerald Only

Body Slam*	Substitute	Thunder Wave*
Mimic	Counter*	Double-Edge

*Battle Frontier tutor move (*Emerald*)

021 Spearow™

NORMAL | FLYING

GENERAL INFO

SPECIES: Tiny Bird Pokémon
HEIGHT: 1'00"
WEIGHT: 4 lbs.
ABILITY: Keen Eye

Protects Spearow from having its Accuracy lowered.

STATS

EVOLUTIONS

LV20

LOCATION[s]:

RUBY	Rarity: **None**	Trade from *FireRed/LeafGreen*
SAPPHIRE	Rarity: **None**	Trade from *FireRed/LeafGreen*
FIRERED	Rarity: **Common**	Routes 3, 4, 9, 10, 11, 17, 22, 23, One Island, Two Island, Six Island, Seven Island
LEAFGREEN	Rarity: **Common**	Routes 3, 4, 9, 10, 11, 17, 22, 23, One Island, Two Island, Six Island, Seven Island
COLOSSEUM	Rarity: **None**	Trade from *FireRed/LeafGreen*
EMERALD	Rarity: **None**	Trade from *FireRed/LeafGreen*
XD	Rarity: **Only One**	Phenac City (Capture from Cipher Peon Ezin)

MOVES

Level	Attack	Type	Power	ACC	PP		Level	Attack	Type	Power	ACC	PP
—	Peck	Flying	35	100	35		19	Pursuit	Dark	40	100	20
—	Growl	Normal	—	100	40		25	Aerial Ace	Flying	60	—	20
7	Leer	Normal	—	100	30		31	Mirror Move	Flying	—	—	20
13	Fury Attack	Normal	15	85	20		37	Drill Peck	Flying	80	100	20
							43	Agility	Psychic	—	—	30

TM/HM

TM/HM#	Name	Type	Power	ACC	PP		TM/HM#	Name	Type	Power	ACC	PP
TM06	Toxic	Poison	—	85	10		TM40	Aerial Ace	Flying	60	—	20
TM10	Hidden Power	Normal	—	100	15		TM42	Facade	Normal	70	100	20
TM11	Sunny Day	Fire	—	—	5		TM43	Secret Power	Normal	70	100	20
TM17	Protect	Normal	—	—	10		TM44	Rest	Psychic	—	—	10
TM18	Rain Dance	Water	—	—	5		TM45	Attract	Normal	—	100	15
TM21	Frustration	Normal	—	100	20		TM46	Thief	Dark	40	100	10
TM27	Return	Normal	—	100	20		TM47	Steel Wing	Steel	70	90	25
TM32	Double Team	Normal	—	—	15		HM02	Fly	Flying	70	95	15

EGG MOVES*

Name	Type	Power	ACC	PP
Astonish	Ghost	30	100	15
Faint Attack	Dark	60	—	20
False Swipe	Normal	40	100	40
Quick Attack	Normal	40	100	30
Scary Face	Normal	—	90	10
Sky Attack	Flying	140	90	5
Tri Attack	Normal	80	100	10

*Learned Via Breeding

MOVE TUTOR

FireRed/LeafGreen and Emerald Only

Mimic	Substitute	Double-Edge

022 Fearow™

NORMAL   FLYING

GENERAL INFO

SPECIES: Beak Pokémon
HEIGHT: 3'11"
WEIGHT: 84 lbs.
ABILITY: Keen Eye

Protects Fearow from having its Accuracy lowered.

STATS

HP, ATK, DEF, SP ATK, SP DEF, SPEED

EVOLUTIONS

LV20

LOCATION(s):

RUBY	Rarity: **None**	Trade from *FireRed/LeafGreen*
SAPPHIRE	Rarity: **None**	Trade from *FireRed/LeafGreen*
FIRERED	Rarity: **Rare**	Evolve Spearow, One Island, Two Island, Six Island, Seven Island, Routes 17, 18, 23
LEAFGREEN	Rarity: **Rare**	Evolve Spearow, One Island, Two Island, Six Island, Seven Island, Routes 17, 18, 23
COLOSSEUM	Rarity: **None**	Trade from *FireRed/LeafGreen*
EMERALD	Rarity: **None**	Trade from *FireRed/LeafGreen*
XD	Rarity: **Evolve**	Evolve Spearow

MOVES

Level	Attack	Type	Power	ACC	PP
—	Peck	Flying	35	100	35
—	Growl	Normal	—	100	40
—	Leer	Normal	—	100	30
—	Fury Attack	Normal	15	85	20
26	Pursuit	Dark	40	100	20
32	Mirror Move	Flying	—	—	20
40	Drill Peck	Flying	80	100	20
47	Agility	Psychic	—	—	30

TM/HM

TM/HM#	Name	Type	Power	ACC	PP
TM06	Toxic	Poison	—	85	10
TM10	Hidden Power	Normal	—	100	15
TM11	Sunny Day	Fire	—	—	5
TM15	Hyper Beam	Normal	150	90	5
TM17	Protect	Normal	—	—	10
TM18	Rain Dance	Water	—	—	5
TM21	Frustration	Normal	—	100	20
TM27	Return	Normal	—	100	20
TM32	Double Team	Normal	—	—	15
TM40	Aerial Ace	Flying	60	—	20
TM42	Facade	Normal	70	100	20
TM43	Secret Power	Normal	70	100	20
TM44	Rest	Psychic	—	—	10
TM45	Attract	Normal	—	100	15
TM46	Thief	Dark	40	100	10
TM47	Steel Wing	Steel	70	90	25
HM02	Fly	Flying	70	95	15

MOVE TUTOR

FireRed/LeafGreen and Emerald Only

Double-Edge	Mimic	Substitute

023 Ekans™

POISON

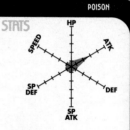

GENERAL INFO

SPECIES: Snake Pokémon
HEIGHT: 6'07"
WEIGHT: 15 lbs.
ABILITY 1: Shed Skin
Ekans only has status effects for one turn. Has a 30% chance of success.
ABILITY 2: Intimidate
Lowers an opponent's Attack when Ekans is brought into battle.

STATS

EVOLUTIONS

LV22

LOCATION[s]:

RUBY	Rarity: **None**	Trade from *FireRed/LeafGreen*
SAPPHIRE	Rarity: **None**	Trade from *FireRed/LeafGreen*
FIRERED	Rarity: **Common**	Routes 4, 8, 9, 10, 11, 23
LEAFGREEN	Rarity: **None**	Trade from *FireRed/LeafGreen*
COLOSSEUM	Rarity: **None**	Trade from *FireRed/LeafGreen*
EMERALD	Rarity: **None**	Trade from *FireRed/LeafGreen*
XD	Rarity: **None**	Trade from *FireRed/LeafGreen*

MOVES

Level	Attack	Type	Power	ACC	PP
—	Wrap	Normal	15	85	20
—	Leer	Normal	—	100	30
8	Poison Sting	Poison	15	100	35
13	Bite	Dark	60	100	25
20	Glare	Normal	—	75	30

Level	Attack	Type	Power	ACC	PP
25	Screech	Normal	—	85	40
32	Acid	Poison	40	100	30
37	Stockpile	Normal	—	—	10
37	Swallow	Normal	—	—	10
37	Spit Up	Normal	100	100	10
44	Haze	Ice	—	—	30

TM/HM

TM/HM#	Name	Type	Power	ACC	PP
TM06	Toxic	Poison	—	85	10
TM10	Hidden Power	Normal	—	100	15
TM11	Sunny Day	Fire	—	—	5
TM17	Protect	Normal	—	—	10
TM18	Rain Dance	Water	—	—	5
TM19	Giga Drain	Grass	60	100	5
TM21	Frustration	Normal	—	100	20
TM23	Iron Tail	Steel	75	75	15
TM26	Earthquake	Ground	100	100	10
TM27	Return	Normal	—	100	20
TM28	Dig	Ground	60	100	10

TM/HM#	Name	Type	Power	ACC	PP
TM32	Double Team	Normal	—	—	15
TM36	Sludge Bomb	Poison	90	100	10
TM41	Torment	Dark	—	100	15
TM42	Facade	Normal	70	100	20
TM43	Secret Power	Normal	70	100	20
TM44	Rest	Psychic	—	—	10
TM45	Attract	Normal	—	100	15
TM46	Thief	Dark	40	100	10
TM49	Snatch	Dark	—	100	10
HM04	Strength	Normal	80	100	20

EGG MOVES*

Name	Type	Power	ACC	PP
Beat Up	Dark	10	100	10
Poison Fang	Poison	50	100	15
Pursuit	Dark	40	100	20
Slam	Normal	80	75	20
Spite	Ghost	—	100	10

*Learned Via Breeding

MOVE TUTOR

FireRed/LeafGreen and Emerald Only

Body Slam*	Mimic	Rock Slide*
Double-Edge	Substitute	

*Battle Frontier tutor move (*Emerald*).

024 Arbok™

POISON

GENERAL INFO

SPECIES: Cobra Pokémon
HEIGHT: 11'06"
WEIGHT: 143 lbs.
ABILITY 1: Shed Skin
Arbok only has status effects for one turn. Has a 30% chance of success.

ABILITY 2: Intimidate
Lowers an opponent's Attack when Arbok is brought into battle.

STATS

EVOLUTIONS

LV22

LOCATION[s]:

Game	Rarity	Location
RUBY	**None**	Trade from *FireRed/LeafGreen*
SAPPHIRE	**None**	Trade from *FireRed/LeafGreen*
FIRERED	**Common**	Evolve Ekans, Route 23, Victory Road
LEAFGREEN	**None**	Trade from *FireRed*
COLOSSEUM	**None**	Trade from *FireRed/LeafGreen*
EMERALD	**None**	Trade from *FireRed/LeafGreen*
XD	**Only One**	Cipher Key Lair (Capture from Cipher Peon Smarton)

MOVES

Level	Attack	Type	Power	ACC	PP	Level	Attack	Type	Power	ACC	PP
—	Wrap	Normal	15	85	20	28	Screech	Normal	—	85	40
—	Leer	Normal	—	100	30	38	Acid	Poison	40	100	30
—	Poison Sting	Poison	15	100	35	46	Stockpile	Normal	—	—	10
—	Bite	Dark	60	100	25	46	Swallow	Normal	—	—	10
20	Glare	Normal	—	75	30	46	Spit Up	Normal	100	100	10
						56	Haze	Ice	—	—	30

TM/HM

TM/HM#	Name	Type	Power	ACC	PP	TM/HM#	Name	Type	Power	ACC	PP
TM06	Toxic	Poison	—	85	10	TM28	Dig	Ground	60	100	10
TM10	Hidden Power	Normal	—	100	15	TM32	Double Team	Normal	—	—	15
TM11	Sunny Day	Fire	—	—	5	TM36	Sludge Bomb	Poison	90	100	10
TM15	Hyper Beam	Normal	150	90	5	TM41	Torment	Dark	—	100	15
TM17	Protect	Normal	—	—	10	TM42	Facade	Normal	70	100	20
TM18	Rain Dance	Water	—	—	5	TM43	Secret Power	Normal	70	100	20
TM19	Giga Drain	Grass	60	100	5	TM44	Rest	Psychic	—	—	10
TM21	Frustration	Normal	—	100	20	TM45	Attract	Normal	—	100	15
TM23	Iron Tail	Steel	75	75	15	TM46	Thief	Dark	40	100	10
TM26	Earthquake	Ground	100	100	10	TM49	Snatch	Dark	—	100	10
TM27	Return	Normal	—	100	20	HM04	Strength	Normal	80	100	20

MOVE TUTOR

FireRed/LeafGreen and Emerald Only

Body Slam*	Mimic	Rock Slide*
Double-Edge	Substitute	

*Battle Frontier tutor move (*Emerald*)

025 Pikachu™

ELECTRIC

GENERAL INFO
SPECIES: Mouse Pokémon
HEIGHT: 1'04"
WEIGHT: 13 lbs.
ABILITY: Static

An opponent has a 30% chance of being paralyzed if it strikes Pikachu.

STATS

EVOLUTIONS

FRIENDSHIP   THUNDER STONE

LOCATION(s):

RUBY	Rarity: **Rare**	Safari Zone
SAPPHIRE	Rarity: **Rare**	Safari Zone
FIRERED	Rarity: **Rare**	Viridian Forest, Power Plant
LEAFGREEN	Rarity: **Rare**	Viridian Forest, Power Plant
COLOSSEUM	Rarity: **None**	Trade from Ruby/Sapphire/FireRed/LeafGreen
EMERALD	Rarity: **Rare**	Safari Zone
XD	Rarity: **None**	Trade from Ruby/Sapphire/FireRed/LeafGreen

MOVES

Level	Attack	Type	Power	ACC	PP	Level	Attack	Type	Power	ACC	PP
—	Thundershock	Electric	40	100	30	15	Double Team	Normal	—	—	15
—	Growl	Normal	—	100	40	20	Slam	Normal	80	75	20
6	Tail Whip	Normal	—	100	30	26	Thunderbolt	Electric	95	100	15
8	Thunder Wave	Electric	—	100	20	33	Agility	Psychic	—	—	30
11	Quick Attack	Normal	40	100	30	41	Thunder	Electric	120	70	10
						50	Light Screen	Psychic	—	—	30

TM/HM

TM/HM#	Name	Type	Power	ACC	PP	TM/HM#	Name	Type	Power	ACC	PP
TM01	Focus Punch	Fighting	150	100	20	TM28	Dig	Ground	60	100	10
TM06	Toxic	Poison	—	85	10	TM31	Brick Break	Fighting	75	100	15
TM10	Hidden Power	Normal	—	100	15	TM32	Double Team	Normal	—	—	15
TM16	Light Screen	Psychic	—	—	30	TM34	Shock Wave	Electric	60	—	20
TM17	Protect	Normal	—	—	10	TM42	Facade	Normal	70	100	20
TM18	Rain Dance	Water	—	—	5	TM43	Secret Power	Normal	70	100	20
TM21	Frustration	Normal	—	100	20	TM44	Rest	Psychic	—	—	10
TM23	Iron Tail	Steel	75	75	15	TM45	Attract	Normal	—	100	15
TM24	Thunderbolt	Electric	95	100	15	HM04	Strength	Normal	80	100	20
TM25	Thunder	Electric	120	70	10	HM05	Flash	Normal	—	70	20
TM27	Return	Normal	—	100	20	HM06	Rock Smash	Fighting	20	100	15

MOVE TUTOR
FireRed/LeafGreen and Emerald Only

Body Slam*	Substitute	Counter*
Double-Edge	Mega Punch*	Seismic Toss*
Mimic	Mega Kick*	Thunder Wave*

Emerald Only

Defense Curl*	Rollout	Swift*
Dynamicpunch	Sleep Talk	Thunderpunch*
Endure*	Snore*	
Mud-Slap*	Swagger	

*Battle Frontier tutor move (*Emerald*)

026 Raichu™

ELECTRIC

GENERAL INFO

SPECIES: Mouse Pokémon
HEIGHT: 2'07"
WEIGHT: 66 lbs.
ABILITY: Static

An opponent has a 30% chance of being paralyzed if it strikes Raichu.

STATS

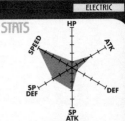

EVOLUTIONS

FRIENDSHIP   THUNDER STONE

LOCATION(s):

RUBY	Rarity: **Rare**	Evolve Pikachu
SAPPHIRE	Rarity: **Evolve**	Evolve Pikachu
FIRERED	Rarity: **Evolve**	Evolve Pikachu
LEAFGREEN	Rarity: **Evolve**	Evolve Pikachu
COLOSSEUM	Rarity: **None**	Evolve Pikachu
EMERALD	Rarity: **Rare**	Evolve Pikachu
XD	Rarity: **None**	Evolve Pikachu

MOVES

Level	Attack	Type	Power	ACC	PP	Level	Attack	Type	Power	ACC	PP
—	Thundershock	Electric	40	100	30	—	Quick Attack	Normal	40	100	30
—	Tail Whip	Normal	—	100	30	—	Thunderbolt	Electric	95	100	15

TM/HM

TM/HM#	Name	Type	Power	ACC	PP	TM/HM#	Name	Type	Power	ACC	PP
TM01	Focus Punch	Fighting	150	100	20	TM28	Dig	Ground	60	100	10
TM06	Toxic	Poison	—	85	10	TM31	Brick Break	Fighting	75	100	15
TM10	Hidden Power	Normal	—	100	15	TM32	Double Team	Normal	—	—	15
TM15	Hyper Beam	Normal	150	90	5	TM34	Shock Wave	Electric	60	—	20
TM16	Light Screen	Psychic	—	—	30	TM42	Facade	Normal	70	100	20
TM17	Protect	Normal	—	—	10	TM43	Secret Power	Normal	70	100	20
TM18	Rain Dance	Water	—	—	5	TM44	Rest	Psychic	—	—	10
TM21	Frustration	Normal	—	100	20	TM45	Attract	Normal	—	100	15
TM23	Iron Tail	Steel	75	75	15	TM46	Thief	Dark	40	100	10
TM24	Thunderbolt	Electric	95	100	15	HM04	Strength	Normal	80	100	20
TM25	Thunder	Electric	120	70	10	HM05	Flash	Normal	—	70	20
TM27	Return	Normal	—	100	20	HM06	Rock Smash	Fighting	20	100	15

MOVE TUTOR

FireRed/LeafGreen and Emerald Only

Body Slam*	Substitute	Counter*
Double-Edge	Mega Punch*	Seismic Toss*
Mimic	Mega Kick*	Thunder Wave*

Emerald Only

Defense Curl*	Rollout	Swift*
Dynamicpunch*	Sleep Talk	Thunderpunch*
Endure*	Snore*	
Mud-Slap*	Swagger	

*Battle Frontier tutor move (*Emerald*)

Pocket Pokédex

027 Sandshrew™

GROUND

GENERAL INFO
SPECIES: Mouse Pokémon
HEIGHT: 2'00"
WEIGHT: 26 lbs.
ABILITY: Sand Veil

During a sandstorm, Sandshrew gains the ability to evade more moves.

STATS

EVOLUTIONS

LV22

LOCATION[s]:

RUBY	Rarity: **Common**	Route 111	
SAPPHIRE	Rarity: **Common**	Route 111	
FIRERED	Rarity: **None**	Trade from *Ruby/Sapphire/LeafGreen*	
LEAFGREEN	Rarity: **Rare**	Routes 4, 8, 9, 10, 11, 23	
COLOSSEUM	Rarity: **None**	Trade from *Ruby/Sapphire/LeafGreen*	
EMERALD	Rarity: **Common**	Route 111, Mirage Tower	
XD	Rarity: **Common**	Rock Poké Spot	

MOVES

Level	Attack	Type	Power	ACC	PP
—	Scratch	Normal	40	100	35
6	Defense Curl	Normal	—	—	40
11	Sand-Attack	Ground	—	100	15
17	Poison Sting	Poison	15	100	35

Level	Attack	Type	Power	ACC	PP
23	Slash	Normal	70	100	20
30	Swift	Normal	60	—	20
37	Fury Swipes	Normal	18	80	15
45	Sand Tomb	Ground	15	70	15
53	Sandstorm	Rock	—	—	10

TM/HM

TM/HM#	Name	Type	Power	ACC	PP
TM01	Focus Punch	Fighting	150	100	20
TM06	Toxic	Poison	—	85	10
TM10	Hidden Power	Normal	—	100	15
TM11	Sunny Day	Fire	—	—	5
TM17	Protect	Normal	—	—	10
TM21	Frustration	Normal	—	100	20
TM23	Iron Tail	Steel	75	75	15
TM26	Earthquake	Ground	100	100	10
TM27	Return	Normal	—	100	20
TM28	Dig	Ground	60	100	10
TM31	Brick Break	Fighting	75	100	15

TM/HM#	Name	Type	Power	ACC	PP
TM32	Double Team	Normal	—	—	15
TM37	Sandstorm	Ground	—	—	10
TM39	Rock Tomb	Rock	50	80	10
TM40	Aerial Ace	Flying	60	—	20
TM42	Facade	Normal	70	100	20
TM43	Secret Power	Normal	70	100	20
TM44	Rest	Psychic	—	—	10
TM45	Attract	Normal	—	100	15
TM46	Thief	Dark	40	100	10
HM01	Cut	Normal	50	95	30
HM04	Strength	Normal	80	100	20
HM06	Rock Smash	Fighting	20	100	15

EGG MOVES*

Name	Type	Power	ACC	PP
Counter	Fighting	—	100	20
Crush Claw	Normal	75	95	10
Flail	Normal	—	100	15
Rapid Spin	Normal	20	100	40
Rock Slide	Rock	75	90	10
Safeguard	Normal	—	—	25
Swords Dance	Normal	—	—	30
Metal Claw	Steel	50	95	35

*Learned Via Breeding

MOVE TUTOR
FireRed/LeafGreen and Emerald Only

Body Slam*	Substitute	Counter*
Double-Edge	Swords Dance*	Seismic Toss*
Mimic	Rock Slide*	

Emerald Only

Defense Curl*	Mud-Slap*	Swagger
Dynamicpunch	Rollout	Swift*
Endure*	Sleep Talk	
Fury Cutter	Snore*	

*Battle Frontier tutor move (*Emerald*)

028 Sandslash™

GENERAL INFO

SPECIES: Mouse Pokémon
HEIGHT: 3'03"
WEIGHT: 65 lbs.
ABILITY: Sand Veil

During a sandstorm, Sandslash gains the ability to evade more moves.

STATS

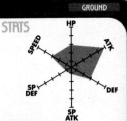

EVOLUTIONS

LV22

LOCATION[s]:

RUBY	Rarity: **Evolve**	Evolve Sandshrew
SAPPHIRE	Rarity: **Evolve**	Evolve Sandshrew
FIRERED	Rarity: **None**	Trade from *Ruby/Sapphire/LeafGreen*
LEAFGREEN	Rarity: **Rare**	Route 23, Victory Road
COLOSSEUM	Rarity: **None**	Trade from *Ruby/Sapphire/LeafGreen*
EMERALD	Rarity: **Evolve**	Evolve Sandshrew
XD	Rarity: **Evolve**	Evolve Sandshrew

MOVES

Level	Attack	Type	Power	ACC	PP	Level	Attack	Type	Power	ACC	PP
—	Scratch	Normal	40	100	35	24	Slash	Normal	70	100	20
—	Defense Curl	Normal	—	—	40	33	Swift	Normal	60	—	20
—	Sand Attack	Ground	—	100	15	42	Fury Swipes	Normal	18	80	15
17	Poison Sting	Poison	15	100	35	52	Sand Tomb	Ground	15	70	15
						62	Sandstorm	Rock	—	—	10

TM/HM

TM/HM#	Name	Type	Power	ACC	PP	TM/HM#	Name	Type	Power	ACC	PP
TM01	Focus Punch	Fighting	150	100	20	TM32	Double Team	Normal	—	—	15
TM06	Toxic	Poison	—	85	10	TM37	Sandstorm	Ground	—	—	10
TM10	Hidden Power	Normal	—	100	15	TM39	Rock Tomb	Rock	50	80	10
TM11	Sunny Day	Fire	—	—	5	TM40	Aerial Ace	Flying	60	—	20
TM15	Hyper Beam	Normal	150	90	5	TM42	Facade	Normal	70	100	20
TM17	Protect	Normal	—	—	10	TM43	Secret Power	Normal	70	100	20
TM21	Frustration	Normal	—	100	20	TM44	Rest	Psychic	—	—	10
TM23	Iron Tail	Steel	75	75	15	TM45	Attract	Normal	—	100	15
TM26	Earthquake	Ground	100	100	10	TM46	Thief	Dark	40	100	10
TM27	Return	Normal	—	100	20	HM01	Cut	Normal	50	95	30
TM28	Dig	Ground	60	100	10	HM04	Strength	Normal	80	100	20
TM31	Brick Break	Fighting	75	100	15	HM06	Rock Smash	Fighting	20	100	15

MOVE TUTOR

FireRed/LeafGreen and Emerald Only

Body Slam*	Substitute	Counter*
Double-Edge	Swords Dance*	Seismic Toss*
Mimic	Rock Slide*	

Emerald Only

Defense Curl*	Mud-Slap*	Swagger
Dynamicpunch	Rollout	Swift*
Endure*	Sleep Talk	
Fury Cutter	Snore*	

*Battle Frontier tutor move (*Emerald*)

PRIMA OFFICIAL GAME GUIDE

029 Nidoran ♀ ™

POISON

GENERAL INFO

SPECIES: Poison Pin Pokémon
HEIGHT: 1'04"
WEIGHT: 15 lbs.
ABILITY: Poison Point

If an opponent is striking Nidoran♀, it has a 30% chance of being poisoned.

STATS

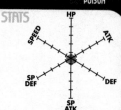

EVOLUTIONS

LV16 MOON STONE

LOCATION[s]:

RUBY	Rarity: **None**	Trade from *FireRed/LeafGreen*
SAPPHIRE	Rarity: **None**	Trade from *FireRed/LeafGreen*
FIRERED	Rarity: **Common**	Route 3, Safari Zone
LEAFGREEN	Rarity: **Common**	Route 3, Safari Zone
COLOSSEUM	Rarity: **None**	Trade from *FireRed/LeafGreen*
EMERALD	Rarity: **None**	Trade from *FireRed/LeafGreen*
XD	Rarity: **None**	Trade from *FireRed/LeafGreen*

MOVES

Level	Attack	Type	Power	ACC	PP	Level	Attack	Type	Power	ACC	PP
—	Scratch	Normal	40	100	35	20	Bite	Dark	60	100	25
—	Growl	Normal	—	100	40	23	Helping Hand	Normal	—	100	20
8	Tail Whip	Normal	—	100	30	30	Fury Swipes	Normal	18	80	15
12	Double Kick	Fighting	30	100	30	38	Flatter	Dark	—	100	15
17	Poison Sting	Poison	15	100	35	47	Crunch	Dark	80	100	15

TM/HM

TM/HM#	Name	Type	Power	ACC	PP	TM/HM#	Name	Type	Power	ACC	PP
TM03	Water Pulse	Water	60	95	20	TM28	Dig	Ground	60	100	10
TM06	Toxic	Poison	—	85	10	TM32	Double Team	Normal	—	—	15
TM10	Hidden Power	Normal	—	100	15	TM34	Shock Wave	Electric	60	—	20
TM11	Sunny Day	Fire	—	—	5	TM36	Sludge Bomb	Poison	90	100	10
TM13	Ice Beam	Ice	95	100	10	TM40	Aerial Ace	Flying	60	—	20
TM14	Blizzard	Ice	120	70	5	TM42	Facade	Normal	70	100	20
TM17	Protect	Normal	—	—	10	TM43	Secret Power	Normal	70	100	20
TM18	Rain Dance	Water	—	—	5	TM44	Rest	Psychic	—	—	10
TM21	Frustration	Normal	—	100	20	TM45	Attract	Normal	—	100	15
TM23	Iron Tail	Steel	75	75	15	TM46	Thief	Dark	40	100	10
TM24	Thunderbolt	Electric	95	100	15	HM01	Cut	Normal	50	95	30
TM25	Thunder	Electric	120	70	10	HM04	Strength	Normal	80	100	20
TM27	Return	Normal	—	100	20	HM06	Rock Smash	Fighting	20	100	15

EGG MOVES*

Name	Type	Power	ACC	PP
Beat Up	Dark	10	100	10
Charm	Normal	—	100	20
Counter	Fighting	—	100	20
Disable	Normal	—	55	20
Focus Energy	Normal	—	—	30
Supersonic	Normal	—	55	20
Take Down	Normal	90	85	20

*Learned Via Breeding

MOVE TUTOR

FireRed/LeafGreen and Emerald Only

Body Slam*	Mimic	Counter*
Double-Edge	Substitute	Rock Slide*

*Battle Frontier tutor move (*Emerald*)

030 Nidorina™

POISON

GENERAL INFO

SPECIES: Poison Pin Pokémon
HEIGHT: 2'07"
WEIGHT: 44 lbs.
ABILITY: Poison Point

If an opponent is striking Nidorina, it has a 30% chance of being poisoned.

STATS

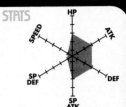

EVOLUTIONS

LV16   MOON STONE

LOCATION[s]:

RUBY	Rarity: **None**	Trade from *FireRed/LeafGreen*
SAPPHIRE	Rarity: **None**	Trade from *FireRed/LeafGreen*
FIRERED	Rarity: **Rare**	Safari Zone
LEAFGREEN	Rarity: **Rare**	Safari Zone
COLOSSEUM	Rarity: **None**	Trade from *FireRed/LeafGreen*
EMERALD	Rarity: **None**	Trade from *FireRed/LeafGreen*
XD	Rarity: **None**	Trade from *FireRed/LeafGreen*

MOVES

Level	Attack	Type	Power	ACC	PP	Level	Attack	Type	Power	ACC	PP
—	Scratch	Normal	40	100	35	22	Bite	Dark	60	100	25
—	Growl	Normal	—	100	40	26	Helping Hand	Normal	—	100	20
8	Tail Whip	Normal	—	100	30	34	Fury Swipes	Normal	18	80	15
12	Double Kick	Fighting	30	100	30	43	Flatter	Normal	—	100	15
18	Poison Sting	Poison	15	100	35	53	Crunch	Dark	80	100	15

TM/HM

TM/HM#	Name	Type	Power	ACC	PP	TM/HM#	Name	Type	Power	ACC	PP
TM03	Water Pulse	Water	60	95	20	TM28	Dig	Ground	60	100	10
TM06	Toxic	Poison	—	85	10	TM32	Double Team	Normal	—	—	15
TM10	Hidden Power	Normal	—	100	15	TM34	Shock Wave	Electric	60	—	20
TM11	Sunny Day	Fire	—	—	5	TM36	Sludge Bomb	Poison	90	100	10
TM13	Ice Beam	Ice	95	100	10	TM40	Aerial Ace	Flying	60	—	20
TM14	Blizzard	Ice	120	70	5	TM42	Facade	Normal	70	100	20
TM17	Protect	Normal	—	—	10	TM43	Secret Power	Normal	70	100	20
TM18	Rain Dance	Water	—	—	5	TM44	Rest	Psychic	—	—	10
TM21	Frustration	Normal	—	100	20	TM45	Attract	Normal	—	100	15
TM23	Iron Tail	Steel	75	75	15	TM46	Thief	Dark	40	100	10
TM24	Thunderbolt	Electric	95	100	15	HM01	Cut	Normal	50	95	30
TM25	Thunder	Electric	120	70	10	HM04	Strength	Normal	80	100	20
TM27	Return	Normal	—	100	20	HM06	Rock Smash	Fighting	20	100	15

MOVE TUTOR

FireRed/LeafGreen and Emerald Only

Body Slam*	Mimic	Counter*
Double-Edge	Substitute	

*Battle Frontier tutor move (*Emerald*)

031 Nidoqueen™

POISON | GROUND

GENERAL INFO
SPECIES: Drill Pokémon
HEIGHT: 4'03"
WEIGHT: 132 lbs.
ABILITY: Poison Point
If an opponent is striking Nidoqueen, it has a 30% chance of being poisoned.

STATS

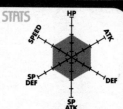

EVOLUTIONS

LV16 | MOON STONE

LOCATION[s]:

RUBY	Rarity: **None**	Trade from *FireRed/LeafGreen*
SAPPHIRE	Rarity: **None**	Trade from *FireRed/LeafGreen*
FIRERED	Rarity: **Evolve**	Evolve Nidorina
LEAFGREEN	Rarity: **Evolve**	Evolve Nidorina
COLOSSEUM	Rarity: **None**	Trade from *FireRed/LeafGreen*
EMERALD	Rarity: **None**	Trade from *FireRed/LeafGreen*
XD	Rarity: **None**	Trade from *FireRed/LeafGreen*

MOVES

Level	Attack	Type	Power	ACC	PP	Level	Attack	Type	Power	ACC	PP
—	Scratch	Normal	40	100	35	—	Poison Sting	Poison	15	100	35
—	Tail Whip	Normal	—	100	30	22	Body Slam*	Normal	85	100	15
—	Double Kick	Fighting	30	100	30	43	Superpower	Fighting	120	100	5

TM/HM

TM/HM#	Name	Type	Power	ACC	PP	TM/HM#	Name	Type	Power	ACC	PP
TM01	Focus Punch	Fighting	150	100	20	TM31	Brick Break	Fighting	75	100	15
TM03	Water Pulse	Water	60	95	20	TM32	Double Team	Normal	—	—	15
TM05	Roar	Normal	—	100	20	TM34	Shock Wave	Electric	60	—	20
TM06	Toxic	Poison	—	85	10	TM35	Flamethrower	Fire	95	100	15
TM10	Hidden Power	Normal	—	100	15	TM36	Sludge Bomb	Poison	90	100	10
TM11	Sunny Day	Fire	—	—	5	TM37	Sandstorm	Ground	—	—	10
TM12	Taunt	Dark	—	100	20	TM38	Fire Blast	Fire	120	85	5
TM13	Ice Beam	Ice	95	100	10	TM39	Rock Tomb	Rock	50	80	10
TM14	Blizzard	Ice	120	70	5	TM40	Aerial Ace	Flying	60	—	20
TM15	Hyper Beam	Normal	150	90	5	TM41	Torment	Dark	—	100	15
TM17	Protect	Normal	—	—	10	TM42	Facade	Normal	70	100	20
TM18	Rain Dance	Water	—	—	5	TM43	Secret Power	Normal	70	100	20
TM21	Frustration	Normal	—	100	20	TM44	Rest	Psychic	—	—	10
TM23	Iron Tail	Steel	75	75	15	TM45	Attract	Normal	—	100	15
TM24	Thunderbolt	Electric	95	100	15	TM46	Thief	Dark	40	100	10
TM25	Thunder	Electric	120	70	10	HM01	Cut	Normal	50	95	30
TM26	Earthquake	Ground	100	100	10	HM03	Surf	Water	95	100	15
TM27	Return	Normal	—	100	20	HM04	Strength	Normal	80	100	20
TM28	Dig	Ground	60	100	10	HM06	Rock Smash	Fighting	20	100	15
TM30	Shadow Ball	Ghost	80	100	15						

MOVE TUTOR
FireRed/LeafGreen and Emerald Only

Body Slam*	Substitute	Seismic Toss*
Double-Edge	Mega Punch*	Counter*
Mimic	Mega Kick*	Rock Slide*

*Battle Frontier tutor move (*Emerald*)

032 Nidoran♂ ™

GENERAL INFO

SPECIES: Poison Pin Pokémon
HEIGHT: 1'08"
WEIGHT: 20 lbs.
ABILITY: Poison Point

If an opponent is striking Nidoran♂, it has a 30% chance of being poisoned.

STATS

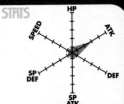

EVOLUTIONS

LV16   MOON STONE

LOCATION[S]:

RUBY	Rarity: **None**	Trade from *FireRed/LeafGreen*
SAPPHIRE	Rarity: **None**	Trade from *FireRed/LeafGreen*
FIRERED	Rarity: **Common**	Route 3, Safari Zone
LEAFGREEN	Rarity: **Rare**	Route 3, Safari Zone
COLOSSEUM	Rarity: **None**	Trade from *FireRed/LeafGreen*
EMERALD	Rarity: **None**	Trade from *FireRed/LeafGreen*
XD	Rarity: **None**	Trade from *FireRed/LeafGreen*

MOVES

Level	Attack	Type	Power	ACC	PP		Level	Attack	Type	Power	ACC	PP
—	Leer	Normal	—	100	30		20	Horn Attack	Normal	65	100	25
—	Peck	Flying	35	100	35		23	Helping Hand	Normal	—	100	20
8	Focus Energy	Normal	—	—	30		30	Fury Attack	Normal	15	85	20
12	Double Kick	Fighting	30	100	30		38	Flatter	Dark	—	100	15
17	Poison Sting	Poison	15	100	35		47	Horn Drill	Normal	—	30	5

TM/HM

TM/HM#	Name	Type	Power	ACC	PP		TM/HM#	Name	Type	Power	ACC	PP
TM03	Water Pulse	Water	60	95	20		TM27	Return	Normal	—	100	20
TM06	Toxic	Poison	—	85	10		TM28	Dig	Ground	60	100	10
TM10	Hidden Power	Normal	—	100	15		TM32	Double Team	Normal	—	—	15
TM11	Sunny Day	Fire	—	—	5		TM34	Shock Wave	Electric	60	—	20
TM13	Ice Beam	Ice	95	100	10		TM36	Sludge Bomb	Poison	90	100	10
TM14	Blizzard	Ice	120	70	5		TM42	Facade	Normal	70	100	20
TM17	Protect	Normal	—	—	10		TM43	Secret Power	Normal	70	100	20
TM18	Rain Dance	Water	—	—	5		TM44	Rest	Psychic	—	—	10
TM21	Frustration	Normal	—	100	20		TM45	Attract	Normal	—	100	15
TM23	Iron Tail	Steel	75	75	15		TM46	Thief	Dark	40	100	10
TM24	Thunderbolt	Electric	95	100	15		HM01	Cut	Normal	50	95	30
TM25	Thunder	Electric	120	70	10		HM04	Strength	Normal	80	100	20
							HM06	Rock Smash	Fighting	20	100	15

EGG MOVES*

Name	Type	Power	ACC	PP
Beat Up	Dark	10	100	10
Counter	Fighting	—	100	20
Disable	Normal	—	55	20
Focus Energy	Normal	—	—	30
Supersonic	Normal	—	55	20
Take Down	Normal	90	85	20
Amnesia	Psychic	—	—	20
Confusion	Psychic	50	100	25

*Learned Via Breeding

MOVE TUTOR
FireRed/LeafGreen and Emerald Only

Body Slam*	Mimic	Counter*
Double-Edge	Substitute	

*Battle Frontier tutor move (*Emerald*)

033 Nidorino™

POISON

GENERAL INFO

SPECIES: Poison Pin Pokémon
HEIGHT: 2'11"
WEIGHT: 43 lbs.
ABILITY: Poison Point

If an opponent is striking Nidorino, it has a 30% chance of being poisoned.

STATS

EVOLUTIONS

LV16   MOON STONE

LOCATION[s]:

RUBY	Rarity: **None**	Trade from *FireRed/LeafGreen*
SAPPHIRE	Rarity: **None**	Trade from *FireRed/LeafGreen*
FIRERED	Rarity: **Rare**	Safari Zone
LEAFGREEN	Rarity: **Rare**	Safari Zone
COLOSSEUM	Rarity: **None**	Trade from *FireRed/LeafGreen*
EMERALD	Rarity: **None**	Trade from *FireRed/LeafGreen*
XD	Rarity: **None**	Trade from *FireRed/LeafGreen*

MOVES

Level	Attack	Type	Power	ACC	PP	Level	Attack	Type	Power	ACC	PP
—	Leer	Normal	—	100	30	22	Horn Attack	Normal	65	100	25
—	Peck	Flying	35	100	35	26	Helping Hand	Normal	—	100	20
8	Focus Energy	Normal	—	—	30	34	Fury Attack	Normal	15	85	20
12	Double Kick	Fighting	30	100	30	43	Flatter	Dark	—	100	15
18	Poison Sting	Poison	15	100	35	53	Horn Drill	Normal	—	30	5

TM/HM

TM/HM#	Name	Type	Power	ACC	PP	TM/HM#	Name	Type	Power	ACC	PP
TM03	Water Pulse	Water	60	95	20	TM27	Return	Normal	—	100	20
TM06	Toxic	Poison	—	85	10	TM28	Dig	Ground	60	100	10
TM10	Hidden Power	Normal	—	100	15	TM32	Double Team	Normal	—	—	15
TM11	Sunny Day	Fire	—	—	5	TM34	Shock Wave	Electric	60	—	20
TM13	Ice Beam	Ice	95	100	10	TM36	Sludge Bomb	Poison	90	100	10
TM14	Blizzard	Ice	120	70	5	TM42	Facade	Normal	70	100	20
TM17	Protect	Normal	—	—	10	TM43	Secret Power	Normal	70	100	20
TM18	Rain Dance	Water	—	—	5	TM44	Rest	Psychic	—	—	10
TM21	Frustration	Normal	—	100	20	TM45	Attract	Normal	—	100	15
TM23	Iron Tail	Steel	75	75	15	TM46	Thief	Dark	40	100	10
TM24	Thunderbolt	Electric	95	100	15	HM01	Cut	Normal	50	95	30
TM25	Thunder	Electric	120	70	10	HM04	Strength	Normal	80	100	20
						HM06	Rock Smash	Fighting	20	100	15

MOVE TUTOR

FireRed/LeafGreen and Emerald Only

Body Slam*	Mimic	Substitute
Double-Edge	Counter*	

*Battle Frontier tutor move (*Emerald*)

034 Nidoking™

POISON | GROUND

GENERAL INFO

SPECIES: Drill Pokémon
HEIGHT: 4'07"
WEIGHT: 137 lbs.
ABILITY: Poison Point
If an opponent is striking Nidoking, it has a 30% chance of being poisoned.

STATS

(Stat hexagon: HP, ATK, DEF, SP ATK, SP DEF, SPEED)

EVOLUTIONS

  LV16 MOON STONE

LOCATION(s):

RUBY	Rarity:	None	Trade from *FireRed/LeafGreen*
SAPPHIRE	Rarity:	None	Trade from *FireRed/LeafGreen*
FIRERED	Rarity:	Evolve	Evolve Nidorino
LEAFGREEN	Rarity:	Evolve	Evolve Nidorino
COLOSSEUM	Rarity:	None	Trade from *FireRed/LeafGreen*
EMERALD	Rarity:	None	Trade from *FireRed/LeafGreen*
XD	Rarity:	None	Trade from *FireRed/LeafGreen*

MOVES

Level	Attack	Type	Power	ACC	PP
—	Poison Sting	Poison	15	100	35
—	Double Kick	Fighting	30	100	30
—	Peck	Flying	35	100	35
—	Focus Energy	Normal	—	—	30
22	Thrash	Normal	90	100	20
43	Megahorn	Bug	120	85	10

TM/HM

TM/HM#	Name	Type	Power	ACC	PP
TM01	Focus Punch	Fighting	150	100	20
TM03	Water Pulse	Water	60	95	20
TM05	Roar	Normal	—	100	20
TM06	Toxic	Poison	—	85	10
TM10	Hidden Power	Normal	—	100	15
TM11	Sunny Day	Fire	—	—	5
TM12	Taunt	Dark	—	100	20
TM13	Ice Beam	Ice	95	100	10
TM14	Blizzard	Ice	120	70	5
TM15	Hyper Beam	Normal	150	90	5
TM17	Protect	Normal	—	—	10
TM18	Rain Dance	Water	—	—	5
TM21	Frustration	Normal	—	100	20
TM23	Iron Tail	Steel	75	75	15
TM24	Thunderbolt	Electric	95	100	15
TM25	Thunder	Electric	120	70	10
TM26	Earthquake	Ground	100	100	10
TM27	Return	Normal	—	100	20
TM28	Dig	Ground	60	100	10
TM30	Shadow Ball	Ghost	80	100	15
TM31	Brick Break	Fighting	75	100	15
TM32	Double Team	Normal	—	—	15
TM34	Shock Wave	Electric	60	—	20
TM35	Flamethrower	Fire	95	100	15
TM36	Sludge Bomb	Poison	90	100	10
TM37	Sandstorm	Ground	—	—	10
TM38	Fire Blast	Fire	120	85	5
TM39	Rock Tomb	Rock	50	80	10
TM41	Torment	Dark	—	100	15
TM42	Facade	Normal	70	100	20
TM43	Secret Power	Normal	70	100	20
TM44	Rest	Psychic	—	—	10
TM45	Attract	Normal	—	100	15
TM46	Thief	Dark	40	100	10
HM01	Cut	Normal	50	95	30
HM03	Surf	Water	95	100	15
HM04	Strength	Normal	80	100	15
HM06	Rock Smash	Fighting	20	100	15

MOVE TUTOR
FireRed/LeafGreen and Emerald Only

Body Slam*	Mega Kick*	Counter*
Double-Edge	Mimic	Seismic Toss*
Mega Punch*	Substitute	Rock Slide*

*Battle Frontier tutor move (*Emerald*)

035 Clefairy™

NORMAL

GENERAL INFO

SPECIES: Fairy Pokémon
HEIGHT: 2'00"
WEIGHT: 17 lbs.
ABILITY: Cute Charm
If an opponent is striking Clefairy, it has a 30% chance of being attracted.

STATS

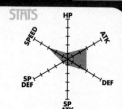

EVOLUTIONS

FRIENDSHIP   MOON STONE

LOCATION[s]:

RUBY	Rarity: **None**	Trade from *FireRed/LeafGreen*
SAPPHIRE	Rarity: **None**	Trade from *FireRed/LeafGreen*
FIRERED	Rarity: **Rare**	Mt. Moon
LEAFGREEN	Rarity: **Rare**	Mt. Moon
COLOSSEUM	Rarity: **None**	Trade from *FireRed/LeafGreen*
EMERALD	Rarity: **None**	Trade from *FireRed/LeafGreen*
XD	Rarity: **None**	Trade from *FireRed/LeafGreen*

MOVES

Level	Attack	Type	Power	ACC	PP		Level	Attack	Type	Power	ACC	PP
—	Pound	Normal	40	100	35		21	Minimize	Normal	—	—	20
—	Growl	Normal	—	100	40		25	Defense Curl	Normal	—	—	40
5	Encore	Normal	—	100	5		29	Metronome	Normal	—	—	10
9	Sing	Normal	—	55	15		33	Cosmic Power	Normal	—	—	20
13	Doubleslap	Normal	15	85	10		37	Moonlight	Normal	—	—	5
17	Follow Me	Normal	—	100	20		41	Light Screen	Psychic	—	—	30
							45	Meteor Mash	Steel	100	85	10

TM/HM

TM/HM#	Name	Type	Power	ACC	PP		TM/HM#	Name	Type	Power	ACC	PP
TM01	Focus Punch	Fighting	150	100	20		TM27	Return	Normal	—	100	20
TM03	Water Pulse	Water	60	95	20		TM28	Dig	Ground	60	100	10
TM04	Calm Mind	Psychic	—	—	20		TM29	Psychic	Psychic	90	100	10
TM06	Toxic	Poison	—	85	10		TM30	Shadow Ball	Ghost	80	100	15
TM10	Hidden Power	Normal	—	100	15		TM31	Brick Break	Fighting	75	100	15
TM11	Sunny Day	Fire	—	—	5		TM32	Double Team	Normal	—	—	15
TM13	Ice Beam	Ice	95	100	10		TM33	Reflect	Normal	—	—	20
TM14	Blizzard	Ice	120	70	5		TM34	Shock Wave	Electric	60	—	20
TM16	Light Screen	Psychic	—	—	30		TM35	Flamethrower	Fire	95	100	15
TM17	Protect	Normal	—	—	10		TM38	Fire Blast	Fire	120	85	5
TM18	Rain Dance	Water	—	—	5		TM42	Facade	Normal	70	100	20
TM20	Safeguard	Normal	—	—	25		TM43	Secret Power	Normal	70	100	20
TM21	Frustration	Normal	—	100	20		TM44	Rest	Psychic	—	—	10
TM22	Solarbeam	Grass	120	100	10		TM45	Attract	Normal	—	100	15
TM23	Iron Tail	Steel	75	75	15		TM49	Snatch	Dark	—	100	10
TM24	Thunderbolt	Electric	95	100	15		HM04	Strength	Normal	80	100	20
TM25	Thunder	Electric	120	70	10		HM05	Flash	Normal	—	70	20

MOVE TUTOR

FireRed/LeafGreen and Emerald Only

Body Slam	Mimic	Seismic Toss*
Double-Edge	Substitute	Thunder Wave*
Mega Punch*	Metronome	Dream Eater*
Mega Kick*	Counter*	Softboiled

*Battle Frontier tutor move (*Emerald*)

036 Clefable™

NORMAL

GENERAL INFO
SPECIES: Fairy Pokémon
HEIGHT: 4'03"
WEIGHT: 88 lbs.
ABILITY: Cute Charm

If an opponent is striking Clefable, it has a 30% chance of being attracted.

STATS

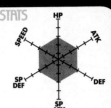

EVOLUTIONS

FRIENDSHIP   MOON STONE

LOCATION[s]:

RUBY	Rarity: **None**	Trade from *FireRed/LeafGreen*
SAPPHIRE	Rarity: **None**	Trade from *FireRed/LeafGreen*
FIRERED	Rarity: **Evolve**	Evolve Clefairy
LEAFGREEN	Rarity: **Evolve**	Evolve Clefairy
COLOSSEUM	Rarity: **None**	Trade from *FireRed/LeafGreen*
EMERALD	Rarity: **None**	Trade from *FireRed/LeafGreen*
XD	Rarity: **None**	Trade from *FireRed/LeafGreen*

MOVES

Level	Attack	Type	Power	ACC	PP		Level	Attack	Type	Power	ACC	PP
—	Sing	Normal	—	55	15		—	Minimize	Normal	—	—	20
—	Doubleslap	Normal	15	85	10		—	Metronome	Normal	—	—	10

TM/HM

TM/HM#	Name	Type	Power	ACC	PP		TM/HM#	Name	Type	Power	ACC	PP
TM01	Focus Punch	Fighting	150	100	20		TM27	Return	Normal	—	100	20
TM03	Water Pulse	Water	60	95	20		TM28	Dig	Ground	60	100	10
TM04	Calm Mind	Psychic	—	—	20		TM29	Psychic	Psychic	90	100	10
TM06	Toxic	Poison	—	85	10		TM30	Shadow Ball	Ghost	80	100	15
TM10	Hidden Power	Normal	—	100	15		TM31	Brick Break	Fighting	75	100	15
TM11	Sunny Day	Fire	—	—	5		TM32	Double Team	Normal	—	—	15
TM13	Ice Beam	Ice	95	100	10		TM33	Reflect	Normal	—	—	20
TM14	Blizzard	Ice	120	70	5		TM34	Shock Wave	Electric	60	—	20
TM15	Hyper Beam	Normal	150	90	5		TM35	Flamethrower	Fire	95	100	15
TM16	Light Screen	Psychic	—	—	30		TM38	Fire Blast	Fire	120	85	5
TM17	Protect	Normal	—	—	10		TM42	Facade	Normal	70	100	20
TM18	Rain Dance	Water	—	—	5		TM43	Secret Power	Normal	70	100	20
TM20	Safeguard	Normal	—	—	25		TM44	Rest	Psychic	—	—	10
TM21	Frustration	Normal	—	100	20		TM45	Attract	Normal	—	100	15
TM22	Solarbeam	Grass	120	100	10		TM49	Snatch	Dark	—	100	10
TM23	Iron Tail	Steel	75	75	15		HM04	Strength	Normal	80	100	20
TM24	Thunderbolt	Electric	95	100	15		HM05	Flash	Normal	—	70	20
TM25	Thunder	Electric	120	70	10							

MOVE TUTOR
FireRed/LeafGreen and Emerald Only

Body Slam*	Mimic	Seismic Toss*
Double-Edge	Substitute	Thunder Wave*
Mega Punch*	Metronome	Dream Eater*
Mega Kick*	Counter*	Softboiled

*Battle Frontier tutor move (*Emerald*)

PRIMA OFFICIAL GAME GUIDE

037 Vulpix™

FIRE

GENERAL INFO
SPECIES: Fox Pokémon
HEIGHT: 2'00"
WEIGHT: 22 lbs.
ABILITY: Flash Fire

Enhances its Fire-type moves and protects Vulpix from being damaged by Fire-type moves.

STATS

HP
SPEED
ATK
SP DEF
DEF
SP ATK

EVOLUTIONS

FIRE STONE

LOCATION(s):

RUBY	Rarity: **Common**	Mt. Pyre
SAPPHIRE	Rarity: **Common**	Mt. Pyre
FIRERED	Rarity: **None**	Trade from *Ruby/Sapphire/LeafGreen*
LEAFGREEN	Rarity: **Common**	Pokémon Mansion, Route 7, Route 8
COLOSSEUM	Rarity: **None**	Trade from *Ruby/Sapphire/LeafGreen*
EMERALD	Rarity: **Common**	Mt. Pyre
XD	Rarity: **Only One**	Pyrite Town (Capture from Cipher Peon Mesin)

MOVES

Level	Attack	Type	Power	ACC	PP
—	Ember	Fire	40	100	25
5	Tail Whip	Normal	—	100	30
9	Roar	Normal	—	100	20
13	Quick Attack	Normal	40	100	30
17	Will-O-Wisp	Fire	—	75	15

Level	Attack	Type	Power	ACC	PP
21	Confuse Ray	Ghost	—	100	10
25	Imprison	Psychic	—	100	15
29	Flamethrower	Fire	95	100	15
33	Safeguard	Normal	—	—	25
37	Grudge	Ghost	—	100	5
41	Fire Spin	Fire	15	70	15

TM/HM

TM/HM#	Name	Type	Power	ACC	PP
TM05	Roar	Normal	—	100	20
TM06	Toxic	Poison	—	85	10
TM10	Hidden Power	Normal	—	100	15
TM11	Sunny Day	Fire	—	—	5
TM17	Protect	Normal	—	—	10
TM20	Safeguard	Normal	—	—	25
TM21	Frustration	Normal	—	100	20
TM23	Iron Tail	Steel	75	75	15
TM27	Return	Normal	—	100	20

TM/HM#	Name	Type	Power	ACC	PP
TM28	Dig	Ground	60	100	10
TM32	Double Team	Normal	—	—	15
TM35	Flamethrower	Fire	95	100	15
TM38	Fire Blast	Fire	120	85	5
TM42	Facade	Normal	70	100	20
TM43	Secret Power	Normal	70	100	20
TM44	Rest	Psychic	—	—	10
TM45	Attract	Normal	—	100	15
TM50	Overheat	Fire	140	90	5

EGG MOVES*

Name	Type	Power	ACC	PP
Faint Attack	Dark	60	—	20
Hypnosis	Psychic	—	60	20
Flail	Normal	—	100	15
Disable	Normal	—	55	20
Howl	Normal	—	—	40
Psych Up	Normal	—	—	10
Heat Wave	Fire	100	90	10
Spite	Ghost	—	100	10

*Learned Via Breeding

MOVE TUTOR
FireRed/LeafGreen and Emerald Only

Body Slam*	Mimic	Substitute
Double-Edge		

Emerald Only

Endure*	Snore*	Swift*
Sleep Talk	Swagger	

*Battle Frontier tutor move (*Emerald*)

038 Ninetales™

FIRE

GENERAL INFO

SPECIES: Fox Pokémon
HEIGHT: 3'07"
WEIGHT: 44 lbs.
ABILITY: Flash Fire

Enhances its Fire-type moves and protects Ninetales from being damaged by Fire-type moves.

STATS

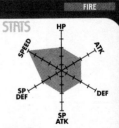

EVOLUTIONS

FIRE STONE

LOCATION(s):

RUBY	Rarity: **Evolve**	Evolve Vulpix
SAPPHIRE	Rarity: **Evolve**	Evolve Vulpix
FIRERED	Rarity: **None**	Trade from *Ruby/Sapphire/LeafGreen*
LEAFGREEN	Rarity: **Evolve**	Evolve Vulpix
COLOSSEUM	Rarity: **None**	Trade from *Ruby/Sapphire/LeafGreen*
EMERALD	Rarity: **Evolve**	Evolve Vulpix
XD	Rarity: **Evolve**	Evolve Vulpix

MOVES

Level	Attack	Type	Power	ACC	PP	Level	Attack	Type	Power	ACC	PP
—	Ember	Fire	40	100	25	—	Confuse Ray	Ghost	—	100	10
—	Quick Attack	Normal	40	100	30	—	Safeguard	Normal	—	—	25
						45	Fire Spin	Fire	15	70	15

TM/HM

TM/HM#	Name	Type	Power	ACC	PP	TM/HM#	Name	Type	Power	ACC	PP
TM05	Roar	Normal	—	100	20	TM28	Dig	Ground	60	100	10
TM06	Toxic	Poison	—	85	10	TM32	Double Team	Normal	—	—	15
TM10	Hidden Power	Normal	—	100	15	TM35	Flamethrower	Fire	95	100	15
TM11	Sunny Day	Fire	—	—	5	TM38	Fire Blast	Fire	120	85	5
TM15	Hyper Beam	Normal	150	90	5	TM42	Facade	Normal	70	100	20
TM17	Protect	Normal	—	—	10	TM43	Secret Power	Normal	70	100	20
TM20	Safeguard	Normal	—	—	25	TM44	Rest	Psychic	—	—	10
TM21	Frustration	Normal	—	100	20	TM45	Attract	Normal	—	100	15
TM23	Iron Tail	Steel	75	75	15	TM50	Overheat	Fire	140	90	5
TM27	Return	Normal	—	100	20						

MOVE TUTOR

FireRed/LeafGreen and Emerald Only

Body Slam*	Mimic	Substitute
Double-Edge		

Emerald Only

Endure*	Snore*	Swift*
Sleep Talk	Swagger	

*Battle Frontier tutor move (*Emerald*)

039 Jigglypuff™

NORMAL

GENERAL INFO

SPECIES: Balloon Pokémon
HEIGHT: 1'08"
WEIGHT: 12 lbs.
ABILITY: Cute Charm
If an opponent is striking Jigglypuff, it has a 30% chance of being attracted.

STATS

EVOLUTIONS

FRIENDSHIP   MOON STONE

LOCATION(s):

RUBY	Rarity: **Common**	Route 115
SAPPHIRE	Rarity: **Common**	Route 115
FIRERED	Rarity: **Rare**	Route 3
LEAFGREEN	Rarity: **Rare**	Route 3
COLOSSEUM	Rarity: **None**	Trade from *Ruby/Sapphire/FireRed/LeafGreen*
EMERALD	Rarity: **Common**	Route 115
XD	Rarity: **None**	Trade from *Ruby/Sapphire/FireRed/LeafGreen*

MOVES

Level	Attack	Type	Power	ACC	PP
—	Sing	Normal	—	55	15
4	Defense Curl	Normal	—	—	40
9	Pound	Normal	40	100	35
14	Disable	Normal	—	55	20
19	Rollout	Rock	30	90	20

Level	Attack	Type	Power	ACC	PP
24	Doubleslap	Normal	15	85	10
29	Rest	Psychic	—	—	10
34	Body Slam	Normal	85	100	15
39	Mimic	Normal	—	100	10
44	Hyper Voice	Normal	90	100	10
49	Double-Edge	Normal	120	100	15

TM/HM

TM/HM#	Name	Type	Power	ACC	PP
TM01	Focus Punch	Fighting	150	100	20
TM03	Water Pulse	Water	60	95	20
TM06	Toxic	Poison	—	85	10
TM10	Hidden Power	Normal	—	100	15
TM11	Sunny Day	Fire	—	—	5
TM13	Ice Beam	Ice	95	100	10
TM14	Blizzard	Ice	120	70	5
TM16	Light Screen	Psychic	—	—	30
TM17	Protect	Normal	—	—	10
TM18	Rain Dance	Water	—	—	5
TM20	Safeguard	Normal	—	—	25
TM21	Frustration	Normal	—	100	20
TM22	Solarbeam	Grass	120	100	10
TM24	Thunderbolt	Electric	95	100	15
TM25	Thunder	Electric	120	70	10
TM27	Return	Normal	—	100	20

TM/HM#	Name	Type	Power	ACC	PP
TM28	Dig	Ground	60	100	10
TM29	Psychic	Psychic	90	100	10
TM30	Shadow Ball	Ghost	80	100	15
TM31	Brick Break	Fighting	75	100	15
TM32	Double Team	Normal	—	—	15
TM33	Reflect	Normal	—	—	20
TM34	Shock Wave	Electric	60	—	20
TM35	Flamethrower	Fire	95	100	15
TM38	Fire Blast	Fire	120	85	5
TM42	Facade	Normal	70	100	20
TM43	Secret Power	Normal	70	100	20
TM44	Rest	Psychic	—	—	10
TM45	Attract	Normal	—	100	15
TM49	Snatch	Dark	—	100	10
HM04	Strength	Normal	80	100	20
HM05	Flash	Normal	—	70	20

MOVE TUTOR

FireRed/LeafGreen and Emerald Only

Body Slam*	Mimic	Thunder Wave*
Double-Edge	Substitute	Dream Eater*
Mega Punch*	Counter*	
Mega Kick*	Seismic Toss*	

*Battle Frontier tutor move (*Emerald*)

Emerald Only

Defense Curl*	Metronome	Snore*
Dynamicpunch*	Mud-Slap*	Swagger
Endure*	Psych Up*	Thunderpunch*
Fire Punch*	Rollout	
Ice Punch*	Sleep Talk	

040 Wigglytuff™

NORMAL

GENERAL INFO

SPECIES: Balloon Pokémon
HEIGHT: 3'03"
WEIGHT: 26 lbs.
ABILITY: Cute Charm

If an opponent is striking Wigglytuff, it has a 30% chance of being attracted.

STATS

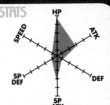

EVOLUTIONS

FRIENDSHIP   MOON STONE

LOCATION(s):

RUBY	Rarity: **Evolve**	Evolve Jigglypuff
SAPPHIRE	Rarity: **Evolve**	Evolve Jigglypuff
FIRERED	Rarity: **Evolve**	Evolve Jigglypuff
LEAFGREEN	Rarity: **Evolve**	Evolve Jigglypuff
COLOSSEUM	Rarity: **None**	Trade from *Ruby/Sapphire/FireRed/LeafGreen*
EMERALD	Rarity: **Evolve**	Evolve Jigglypuff
XD	Rarity: **None**	Trade from *Ruby/Sapphire/FireRed/LeafGreen*

MOVES

Level	Attack	Type	Power	ACC	PP	Level	Attack	Type	Power	ACC	PP
—	Sing	Normal	—	55	15	—	Disable	Normal	—	55	20
—	Defense Curl	Normal	—	—	40	—	Doubleslap	Normal	15	85	10

TM/HM

TM/HM#	Name	Type	Power	ACC	PP	TM/HM#	Name	Type	Power	ACC	PP
TM01	Focus Punch	Fighting	150	100	20	TM27	Return	Normal	—	100	20
TM03	Water Pulse	Water	60	95	20	TM28	Dig	Ground	60	100	10
TM06	Toxic	Poison	—	85	10	TM29	Psychic	Psychic	90	100	10
TM10	Hidden Power	Normal	—	100	15	TM30	Shadow Ball	Ghost	80	100	15
TM11	Sunny Day	Fire	—	—	5	TM31	Brick Break	Fighting	75	100	15
TM13	Ice Beam	Ice	95	100	10	TM32	Double Team	Normal	—	—	15
TM14	Blizzard	Ice	120	70	5	TM33	Reflect	Normal	—	—	20
TM15	Hyper Beam	Normal	150	90	5	TM34	Shock Wave	Electric	60	—	20
TM16	Light Screen	Psychic	—	—	30	TM35	Flamethrower	Fire	95	100	15
TM17	Protect	Normal	—	—	10	TM38	Fire Blast	Fire	120	85	5
TM18	Rain Dance	Water	—	—	5	TM42	Facade	Normal	70	100	20
TM20	Safeguard	Normal	—	—	25	TM43	Secret Power	Normal	70	100	20
TM21	Frustration	Normal	—	100	20	TM44	Rest	Psychic	—	—	10
TM22	Solarbeam	Grass	120	100	10	TM45	Attract	Normal	—	100	15
TM24	Thunderbolt	Electric	95	100	15	TM49	Snatch	Dark	—	100	10
TM25	Thunder	Electric	120	70	10	HM04	Strength	Normal	80	100	15
						HM05	Flash	Normal	—	70	20

MOVE TUTOR

FireRed/LeafGreen and Emerald Only

Body Slam*	Mimic	Thunder Wave*
Double-Edge	Substitute	Dream Eater*
Mega Punch*	Counter*	
Mega Kick*	Seismic Toss*	

*Battle Frontier tutor move (*Emerald*)

Emerald Only

Defense Curl*	Metronome	Snore*
Dynamicpunch	Mud-Slap*	Swagger
Endure*	Psych Up*	Thunderpunch*
Fire Punch*	Rollout	
Ice Punch*	Sleep Talk	

041 Zubat™

POISON   FLYING

GENERAL INFO
SPECIES: Bat Pokémon
HEIGHT: 2'07"
WEIGHT: 17 lbs.
ABILITY: Inner Focus
Zubat no longer flinches.

STATS
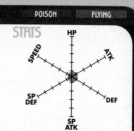

EVOLUTIONS

LV22   FRIENDSHIP

LOCATION(s):

	Rarity:	
RUBY	Common	Cave of Origin, Granite Cave, Shoal Cave, Seafloor Cavern, Victory Road, Meteor Falls
SAPPHIRE	Common	Cave of Origin, Granite Cave, Shoal Cave, Seafloor Cavern, Victory Road, Meteor Falls
FIRERED	Common	Five Island, Mt. Moon, Rock Tunnel, Victory Road
LEAFGREEN	Common	Five Island, Mt. Moon, Rock Tunnel, Victory Road
COLOSSEUM	None	Trade from Ruby/Sapphire/FireRed/LeafGreen
EMERALD	Common	Altering Cave, Cave of Origin, Granite Cave, Shoal Cave, Seafloor Cavern, Meteor Falls
XD	Common	Cave Poké Spot

MOVES

Level	Attack	Type	Power	ACC	PP
—	Leech Life	Bug	20	100	15
6	Astonish	Ghost	30	100	15
11	Supersonic	Normal	—	55	20
16	Bite	Dark	60	100	25
21	Wing Attack	Flying	60	100	35

Level	Attack	Type	Power	ACC	PP
26	Confuse Ray	Ghost	—	100	10
31	Air Cutter	Flying	55	95	25
36	Mean Look	Normal	—	100	5
41	Poison Fang	Poison	50	100	15
46	Haze	Ice	—	—	30

TM/HM

TM/HM#	Name	Type	Power	ACC	PP
TM06	Toxic	Poison	—	85	10
TM10	Hidden Power	Normal	—	100	15
TM11	Sunny Day	Fire	—	—	5
TM12	Taunt	Dark	—	100	20
TM17	Protect	Normal	—	—	10
TM18	Rain Dance	Water	—	—	5
TM19	Giga Drain	Grass	60	100	5
TM21	Frustration	Normal	—	100	20
TM27	Return	Normal	—	100	20
TM30	Shadow Ball	Ghost	80	100	15
TM32	Double Team	Normal	—	—	15

TM/HM#	Name	Type	Power	ACC	PP
TM36	Sludge Bomb	Poison	90	100	10
TM40	Aerial Ace	Flying	60	—	20
TM41	Torment	Dark	—	100	15
TM42	Facade	Normal	70	100	20
TM43	Secret Power	Normal	70	100	20
TM44	Rest	Psychic	—	—	10
TM45	Attract	Normal	—	100	15
TM46	Thief	Dark	40	100	10
TM47	Steel Wing	Steel	70	90	25
TM49	Snatch	Dark	—	100	10

EGG MOVES*

Name	Type	Power	ACC	PP
Quick Attack	Normal	40	100	30
Pursuit	Dark	40	100	20
Faint Attack	Dark	60	—	20
Whirlwind	Normal	—	100	20
Curse	Normal	—	—	—

*Learned Via Breeding

MOVE TUTOR
FireRed/LeafGreen and Emerald Only

Double-Edge	Mimic	Substitute

Emerald Only

Endure*	Snore*	Swift*
Sleep Talk	Swagger	

*Battle Frontier tutor move (*Emerald*)

042 Golbat™

POISON　FLYING

GENERAL INFO
SPECIES: Bat Pokémon
HEIGHT: 5'03"
WEIGHT: 121 lbs.
ABILITY: Inner Focus
Golbat no longer flinches.

STATS
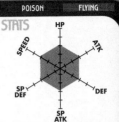

EVOLUTIONS

LV22　FRIENDSHIP

LOCATION[s]:

RUBY	Rarity: **Common**	Evolve Zubat, Cave of Origin, Granite Cave, Shoal Cave, Seafloor Cavern, Victory Road, Meteor Falls
SAPPHIRE	Rarity: **Common**	Evolve Zubat, Cave of Origin, Granite Cave, Shoal Cave, Seafloor Cavern, Victory Road, Meteor Falls
FIRERED	Rarity: **Rare**	Evolve Zubat, Five Island, Seafoam Islands, Victory Road
LEAFGREEN	Rarity: **Rare**	Evolve Zubat, Five Island, Seafoam Islands, Victory Road
COLOSSEUM	Rarity: **None**	Trade from *Ruby/Sapphire/FireRed/LeafGreen*
EMERALD	Rarity: **Common**	Evolve Zubat, Cave of Origin, Granite Cave, Shoal Cave, Seafloor Cavern, Victory Road, Meteor Falls, Sky Pillar
XD	Rarity: **Evolve**	Evolve Zubat

MOVES

Level	Attack	Type	Power	ACC	PP	Level	Attack	Type	Power	ACC	PP
—	Leech Life	Bug	20	100	15	21	Wing Attack	Flying	60	100	35
—	Screech	Normal	—	85	40	28	Confuse Ray	Ghost	—	100	10
—/6	Astonish	Ghost	30	100	15	35	Air Cutter	Flying	55	95	25
—/11	Supersonic	Normal	—	55	20	42	Mean Look	Normal	—	100	5
16	Bite	Dark	60	100	25	49	Poison Fang	Poison	50	100	15
						56	Haze	Ice	—	—	30

= Emerald Only

TM/HM

TM/HM#	Name	Type	Power	ACC	PP	TM/HM#	Name	Type	Power	ACC	PP
TM06	Toxic	Poison	—	85	10	TM32	Double Team	Normal	—	—	15
TM10	Hidden Power	Normal	—	100	15	TM36	Sludge Bomb	Poison	90	100	10
TM11	Sunny Day	Fire	—	—	5	TM40	Aerial Ace	Flying	60	—	20
TM12	Taunt	Dark	—	100	20	TM41	Torment	Dark	—	100	15
TM15	Hyper Beam	Normal	150	90	5	TM42	Facade	Normal	70	100	20
TM17	Protect	Normal	—	—	10	TM43	Secret Power	Normal	70	100	20
TM18	Rain Dance	Water	—	—	5	TM44	Rest	Psychic	—	—	10
TM19	Giga Drain	Grass	60	100	5	TM45	Attract	Normal	—	100	15
TM21	Frustration	Normal	—	100	20	TM46	Thief	Dark	40	100	10
TM27	Return	Normal	—	100	20	TM47	Steel Wing	Steel	70	90	25
TM30	Shadow Ball	Ghost	80	100	15	TM49	Snatch	Dark	—	100	10

MOVE TUTOR
FireRed/LeafGreen and Emerald Only
Double-Edge　Mimic　Substitute

Emerald Only
Endure*　Snore*　Swift*
Sleep Talk　Swagger
*Battle Frontier tutor move (*Emerald*)

043 Oddish™

POISON | GRASS

GENERAL INFO
SPECIES: Weed Pokémon
HEIGHT: 1'08"
WEIGHT: 12 lbs.
ABILITY: Chlorophyll
Oddish's Speed is doubled when the sunlight is strong.

STATS

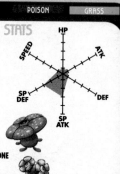

EVOLUTIONS

LV21

LEAF STONE

SUN STONE

LOCATION[s]:

RUBY	Rarity: **Rare**	Routes 110, 117, 119, 120, 121, 123, Safari Zone
SAPPHIRE	Rarity: **Rare**	Routes 110, 117, 119, 120, 121, 123, Safari Zone
FIRERED	Rarity: **Rare**	Two Island, Three Island, Six Island, Routes 5, 6, 7, 12, 13, 14, 15, 24, 25
LEAFGREEN	Rarity: **None**	Trade from *Ruby/Sapphire/FireRed*
COLOSSEUM	Rarity: **None**	Trade from *Ruby/Sapphire/FireRed/LeafGreen*
EMERALD	Rarity: **Common**	Routes 110, 117, 119, 120, 121, 123, Safari Zone
XD	Rarity: **None**	Trade from *Ruby/Sapphire/FireRed*

MOVES

Level	Attack	Type	Power	ACC	PP		Level	Attack	Type	Power	ACC	PP
—	Absorb	Grass	20	100	20		18	Sleep Powder	Grass	—	75	15
7	Sweet Scent	Normal	—	100	20		23	Acid	Poison	40	100	30
14	Poisonpowder	Poison	—	75	35		32	Moonlight	Normal	—	—	5
16	Stun Spore	Grass	—	75	30		39	Petal Dance	Grass	70	100	20

TM/HM

TM/HM#	Name	Type	Power	ACC	PP		TM/HM#	Name	Type	Power	ACC	PP
TM06	Toxic	Poison	—	85	10		TM32	Double Team	Normal	—	—	15
TM09	Bullet Seed	Grass	10	100	30		TM36	Sludge Bomb	Poison	90	100	10
TM10	Hidden Power	Normal	—	100	15		TM42	Facade	Normal	70	100	20
TM11	Sunny Day	Fire	—	—	5		TM43	Secret Power	Normal	70	100	20
TM17	Protect	Normal	—	—	10		TM44	Rest	Psychic	—	—	10
TM19	Giga Drain	Grass	60	100	5		TM45	Attract	Normal	—	100	15
TM21	Frustration	Normal	—	100	20		HM01	Cut	Normal	50	95	30
TM22	Solarbeam	Grass	120	100	10		HM05	Flash	Normal	—	70	20
TM27	Return	Normal	—	100	20							

EGG MOVES*

Name	Type	Power	ACC	PP
Charm	Normal	—	100	20
Flail	Normal	—	100	15
Ingrain	Grass	—	100	20
Razor Leaf	Grass	55	95	25
Synthesis	Grass	—	—	5
Swords Dance	Normal	—	—	30

*Learned Via Breeding

MOVE TUTOR

FireRed/LeafGreen and Emerald Only

Double-Edge	Substitute	Swords Dance*
Mimic		

Emerald Only

Endure*	Snore*	Swagger
Sleep Talk		

*Battle Frontier tutor move (*Emerald*)

044 Gloom ™

POISON | GRASS

GENERAL INFO

SPECIES: Weed Pokémon
HEIGHT: 2'07"
WEIGHT: 19 lbs.
ABILITY: Chlorophyll

Gloom's Speed is doubled when the sunlight is strong.

STATS

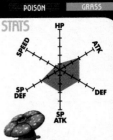

EVOLUTIONS

LV21

LEAF STONE

SUN STONE

LOCATION[s]:

RUBY	Rarity: **Rare**	Evolve Oddish, Route 121, Route 123, Safari Zone
SAPPHIRE	Rarity: **Rare**	Evolve Oddish, Route 121, Route 123, Safari Zone
FIRERED	Rarity: **Rare**	Evolve Oddish, Two Island, Three Island, Six Island, Routes 12, 13, 14, 15
LEAFGREEN	Rarity: **None**	Evolve Oddish, Trade from *Ruby/Sapphire/FireRed*
COLOSSEUM	Rarity: **None**	Trade from *Ruby/Sapphire*
EMERALD	Rarity: **Rare**	Evolve Oddish, Route 121, Route 123, Safari Zone
XD	Rarity: **None**	Trade from *Ruby/Sapphire/FireRed*

MOVES

Level	Attack	Type	Power	ACC	PP	Level	Attack	Type	Power	ACC	PP
—	Absorb	Grass	20	100	20	18	Sleep Powder	Grass	—	75	15
—	Sweet Scent	Normal	—	100	20	24	Acid	Poison	40	100	30
—	Poisonpowder	Poison	—	75	35	35	Moonlight	Normal	—	—	5
16	Stun Spore	Grass	—	75	30	44	Petal Dance	Grass	70	100	20

TM/HM

TM/HM#	Name	Type	Power	ACC	PP	TM/HM#	Name	Type	Power	ACC	PP
TM06	Toxic	Poison	—	85	10	TM32	Double Team	Normal	—	—	15
TM09	Bullet Seed	Grass	10	100	30	TM36	Sludge Bomb	Poison	90	100	10
TM10	Hidden Power	Normal	—	100	15	TM42	Facade	Normal	70	100	20
TM11	Sunny Day	Fire	—	—	5	TM43	Secret Power	Normal	70	100	20
TM17	Protect	Normal	—	—	10	TM44	Rest	Psychic	—	—	10
TM19	Giga Drain	Grass	60	100	5	TM45	Attract	Normal	—	100	15
TM21	Frustration	Normal	—	100	20	HM01	Cut	Normal	50	95	30
TM22	Solarbeam	Grass	120	100	10	HM05	Flash	Normal	—	70	20
TM27	Return	Normal	—	100	20						

MOVE TUTOR

FireRed/LeafGreen and Emerald Only

Double-Edge	Substitute	Swords Dance*
Mimic		

Emerald Only

Endure*	Snore*	Swagger
Sleep Talk		

*Battle Frontier tutor move (*Emerald*)

045 Vileplume™

POISON · GRASS

GENERAL INFO

SPECIES: Flower Pokémon
HEIGHT: 3'11"
WEIGHT: 41 lbs.
ABILITY: Chlorophyll
Gloom's Speed is doubled when the sunlight is strong.

STATS

HP · ATK · DEF · SP ATK · SP DEF · SPEED

EVOLUTIONS

LV21 · LEAF STONE

LOCATION[s]:

RUBY	Rarity: **Evolve**	Evolve Gloom
SAPPHIRE	Rarity: **Evolve**	Evolve Gloom
FIRERED	Rarity: **Evolve**	Evolve Gloom
LEAFGREEN	Rarity: **Evolve**	Evolve Gloom, Trade from *Ruby/Sapphire/FireRed*
COLOSSEUM	Rarity: **None**	Trade from *Ruby/Sapphire/FireRed*
EMERALD	Rarity: **Evolve**	Evolve Gloom
XD	Rarity: **None**	Trade from *Ruby/Sapphire/FireRed*

MOVES

Level	Attack	Type	Power	ACC	PP	Level	Attack	Type	Power	ACC	PP
—	Absorb	Grass	20	100	20	—	Stun Spore	Grass	—	75	30
—	Aromatherapy	Grass	—	—	5	—	Mega Drain	Grass	40	100	10
						44	Petal Dance	Grass	70	100	20

TM/HM

TM/HM#	Name	Type	Power	ACC	PP	TM/HM#	Name	Type	Power	ACC	PP
TM06	Toxic	Poison	—	85	10	TM27	Return	Normal	—	100	20
TM09	Bullet Seed	Grass	10	100	30	TM32	Double Team	Normal	—	—	15
TM10	Hidden Power	Normal	—	100	15	TM36	Sludge Bomb	Poison	90	100	10
TM11	Sunny Day	Fire	—	—	5	TM42	Facade	Normal	70	100	20
TM15	Hyper Beam	Normal	150	90	5	TM43	Secret Power	Normal	70	100	20
TM17	Protect	Normal	—	—	10	TM44	Rest	Psychic	—	—	10
TM19	Giga Drain	Grass	60	100	5	TM45	Attract	Normal	—	100	15
TM21	Frustration	Normal	—	100	20	HM01	Cut	Normal	50	95	30
TM22	Solarbeam	Grass	120	100	10	HM05	Flash	Normal	—	70	20

MOVE TUTOR

FireRed/LeafGreen and Emerald Only

Body Slam*	Mimic	Swords Dance*
Double-Edge	Substitute	

Emerald Only

Endure*	Snore*	Swagger
Sleep Talk		

*Battle Frontier tutor move (*Emerald*)

046 Paras™

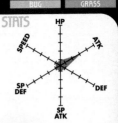

BUG   GRASS

GENERAL INFO

SPECIES: Mushroom Pokémon
HEIGHT: 1'00"
WEIGHT: 12 lbs.
ABILITY: Effect Spore

An opponent has a 10% chance of being paralyzed, poisoned, or put to sleep if it hits Paras.

STATS

HP / ATK / DEF / SP ATK / SP DEF / SPEED

EVOLUTIONS

LV24

LOCATION[s]:

RUBY	Rarity: **None**	Trade from *FireRed/LeafGreen*
SAPPHIRE	Rarity: **None**	Trade from *FireRed/LeafGreen*
FIRERED	Rarity: **Common**	Mt. Moon, Safari Zone
LEAFGREEN	Rarity: **Common**	Mt. Moon, Safari Zone
COLOSSEUM	Rarity: **None**	Trade from *FireRed/LeafGreen*
EMERALD	Rarity: **None**	Trade from *FireRed/LeafGreen*
XD	Rarity: **Only One**	Cipher Key Lair (Capture from Cipher Peon Humah)

MOVES

Level	Attack	Type	Power	ACC	PP
—	Scratch	Normal	40	100	35
7	Stun Spore	Grass	—	75	30
13	Poisonpowder	Poison	—	75	35
19	Leech Life	Bug	20	100	15

Level	Attack	Type	Power	ACC	PP
25	Spore	Grass	—	100	15
31	Slash	Normal	70	100	20
37	Growth	Normal	—	—	40
43	Giga Drain	Grass	60	100	5
49	Aromatherapy	Grass	—	—	5

TM/HM

TM/HM#	Name	Type	Power	ACC	PP
TM06	Toxic	Poison	—	85	10
TM09	Bullet Seed	Grass	10	100	30
TM10	Hidden Power	Normal	—	100	15
TM11	Sunny Day	Fire	—	—	5
TM17	Protect	Normal	—	—	10
TM19	Giga Drain	Grass	60	100	5
TM21	Frustration	Normal	—	100	20
TM22	Solarbeam	Grass	120	100	10
TM27	Return	Normal	—	100	20
TM28	Dig	Ground	60	100	10
TM32	Double Team	Normal	—	—	15

TM/HM#	Name	Type	Power	ACC	PP
TM36	Sludge Bomb	Poison	90	100	10
TM40	Aerial Ace	Flying	60	—	20
TM42	Facade	Normal	70	100	20
TM43	Secret Power	Normal	70	100	20
TM44	Rest	Psychic	—	—	10
TM45	Attract	Normal	—	100	15
TM46	Thief	Dark	40	100	10
HM01	Cut	Normal	50	95	30
HM05	Flash	Normal	—	70	20
HM06	Rock Smash	Fighting	20	100	15

EGG MOVES*

Name	Type	Power	ACC	PP
Counter	Fighting	—	100	20
False Swipe	Normal	40	100	40
Flail	Normal	—	100	15
Light Screen	Psychic	—	—	30
Psybeam	Psychic	65	100	20
Pursuit	Dark	40	100	20
Screech	Normal	—	85	40
Sweet Scent	Normal	—	100	20

*Learned Via Breeding

MOVE TUTOR

FireRed/LeafGreen and Emerald Only

Body Slam*	Mimic	Swords Dance
Double-Edge	Substitute	Counter*

*Battle Frontier tutor move (*Emerald*)

047 Parasect™

BUG GRASS

GENERAL INFO
SPECIES: Mushroom Pokémon
HEIGHT: 3'03"
WEIGHT: 65 lbs.
ABILITY: Effect Spore

An opponent has a 10% chance of being paralyzed, poisoned, or put to sleep if it hits Parasect.

STATS

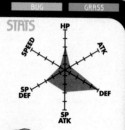

EVOLUTIONS

LV24

LOCATION(s):

RUBY	Rarity: **None**	Trade from *FireRed/LeafGreen*
SAPPHIRE	Rarity: **None**	Trade from *FireRed/LeafGreen*
FIRERED	Rarity: **Rare**	Evolve Paras, Safari Zone
LEAFGREEN	Rarity: **Rare**	Evolve Paras, Safari Zone
COLOSSEUM	Rarity: **None**	Trade from *FireRed/LeafGreen*
EMERALD	Rarity: **None**	Trade from *FireRed/LeafGreen*
XD	Rarity: **Evolve**	Evolve Paras

MOVES

Level	Attack	Type	Power	ACC	PP	Level	Attack	Type	Power	ACC	PP
—	Scratch	Normal	40	100	35	27	Spore	Grass	—	100	15
—	Stun Spore	Grass	—	75	30	35	Slash	Normal	70	100	20
—	Poisonpowder	Poison	—	75	35	43	Growth	Normal	—	—	40
19	Leech Life	Bug	20	100	15	51	Giga Drain	Grass	60	100	5
						59	Aromatherapy	Grass	—	—	5

TM/HM

TM/HM#	Name	Type	Power	ACC	PP	TM/HM#	Name	Type	Power	ACC	PP
TM06	Toxic	Poison	—	85	10	TM32	Double Team	Normal	—	—	10
TM09	Bullet Seed	Grass	10	100	30	TM36	Sludge Bomb	Poison	90	100	10
TM10	Hidden Power	Normal	—	100	15	TM40	Aerial Ace	Flying	60	—	20
TM11	Sunny Day	Fire	—	—	5	TM42	Facade	Normal	70	100	20
TM15	Hyper Beam	Normal	150	90	5	TM43	Secret Power	Normal	70	100	20
TM17	Protect	Normal	—	—	10	TM44	Rest	Psychic	—	—	10
TM19	Giga Drain	Grass	60	100	5	TM45	Attract	Normal	—	100	15
TM21	Frustration	Normal	—	100	20	TM46	Thief	Dark	40	100	10
TM22	Solarbeam	Grass	120	100	10	HM01	Cut	Normal	50	95	30
TM27	Return	Normal	—	100	20	HM05	Flash	Normal	—	70	20
TM28	Dig	Ground	60	100	10	HM06	Rock Smash	Fighting	20	100	15

MOVE TUTOR
FireRed/LeafGreen and Emerald Only

Body Slam*	Mimic	Swords Dance
Double-Edge	Substitute	Counter*

*Battle Frontier tutor move (*Emerald*)

048 Venonat™

BUG   POISON

GENERAL INFO
SPECIES: Insect Pokémon
HEIGHT: 3'03"
WEIGHT: 33 lbs.
ABILITY: Compoundeyes
Raises Venonat's Accuracy by 30%.

STATS

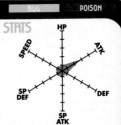

EVOLUTIONS

LV31

LOCATION(s):

RUBY	Rarity: **None**	Trade from *FireRed/LeafGreen*
SAPPHIRE	Rarity: **None**	Trade from *FireRed/LeafGreen*
FIRERED	Rarity: **Common**	Three Island, Routes 12, 13, 14, 15, Safari Zone
LEAFGREEN	Rarity: **Common**	Three Island, Routes 12, 13, 14, 15, Safari Zone
COLOSSEUM	Rarity: **None**	Trade from *FireRed/LeafGreen*
EMERALD	Rarity: **None**	Trade from *FireRed/LeafGreen*
XD	Rarity: **None**	Trade from *FireRed/LeafGreen*

MOVES

Level	Attack	Type	Power	ACC	PP
—	Tackle	Normal	35	95	35
—	Disable	Normal	—	55	20
—	Foresight	Normal	—	100	40
9	Supersonic	Normal	—	55	20
17	Confusion	Psychic	50	100	25

Level	Attack	Type	Power	ACC	PP
20	Poisonpowder	Poison	—	75	35
25	Leech Life	Bug	20	100	15
28	Stun Spore	Grass	—	75	30
33	Psybeam	Psychic	65	100	20
36	Sleep Powder	Grass	—	75	15
41	Psychic	Psychic	90	100	10

TM/HM

TM/HM#	Name	Type	Power	ACC	PP
TM06	Toxic	Poison	—	85	10
TM10	Hidden Power	Normal	—	100	15
TM11	Sunny Day	Fire	—	—	5
TM17	Protect	Normal	—	—	10
TM19	Giga Drain	Grass	60	100	5
TM21	Frustration	Normal	—	100	20
TM22	Solarbeam	Grass	120	100	10
TM27	Return	Normal	—	100	20
TM29	Psychic	Psychic	90	100	10

TM/HM#	Name	Type	Power	ACC	PP
TM32	Double Team	Normal	—	—	15
TM36	Sludge Bomb	Poison	90	100	10
TM42	Facade	Normal	70	100	20
TM43	Secret Power	Normal	70	100	20
TM44	Rest	Psychic	—	—	10
TM45	Attract	Normal	—	100	15
TM46	Thief	Dark	40	100	10
TM48	Skill Swap	Psychic	—	100	10
HM05	Flash	Normal	—	70	20

EGG MOVES*

Name	Type	Power	ACC	PP
Baton Pass	Normal	—	—	40
Giga Drain	Grass	60	100	5
Screech	Normal	—	85	40
Signal Beam	Bug	75	100	15

*Learned Via Breeding

MOVE TUTOR
FireRed/LeafGreen and Emerald Only

Double-Edge	Mimic	Substitute

*Battle Frontier tutor move (*Emerald*)

049 Venomoth™

BUG | POISON

GENERAL INFO
SPECIES: Poison Moth Pokémon
HEIGHT: 4'11"
WEIGHT: 28 lbs.
ABILITY: Shield Dust
Protects Venomoth from being struck by extra effects of moves.

STATS

EVOLUTIONS

LV31

LOCATION(s):

RUBY	**Rarity: None**	Trade from *FireRed/LeafGreen*
SAPPHIRE	**Rarity: None**	Trade from *FireRed/LeafGreen*
FIRERED	**Rarity: Rare**	Three Island, Safari Zone
LEAFGREEN	**Rarity: Rare**	Three Island, Safari Zone
COLOSSEUM	**Rarity: None**	Trade from *FireRed/LeafGreen*
EMERALD	**Rarity: None**	Trade from *FireRed/LeafGreen*
XD	**Rarity: Only One**	Cipher Key Lair (Capture from Cipher Peon Angic)

MOVES

Level	Attack	Type	Power	ACC	PP	Level	Attack	Type	Power	ACC	PP
—	Tackle	Normal	35	95	35	20	Poison Powder	Poison	—	75	35
—	Disable	Normal	—	55	20	25	Leech Life	Bug	20	100	15
—	Foresight	Normal	—	100	40	28	Stun Spore	Grass	—	75	30
—	Silver Wind	Bug	60	100	5	31	Gust	Flying	40	100	35
—	Supersonic	Normal	—	55	20	36	Psybeam	Psychic	65	100	20
17	Confusion	Psychic	50	100	25	42	Sleep Powder	Grass	—	75	15
						52	Psychic	Psychic	90	100	10

TM/HM

TM/HM#	Name	Type	Power	ACC	PP	TM/HM#	Name	Type	Power	ACC	PP
TM06	Toxic	Poison	—	85	10	TM32	Double Team	Normal	—	—	15
TM10	Hidden Power	Normal	—	100	15	TM36	Sludge Bomb	Poison	90	100	10
TM11	Sunny Day	Fire	—	—	5	TM40	Aerial Ace	Flying	60	—	20
TM15	Hyper Beam	Normal	150	90	5	TM42	Facade	Normal	70	100	20
TM17	Protect	Normal	—	—	10	TM43	Secret Power	Normal	70	100	20
TM19	Giga Drain	Grass	60	100	5	TM44	Rest	Psychic	—	—	10
TM21	Frustration	Normal	—	100	20	TM45	Attract	Normal	—	100	15
TM22	Solarbeam	Grass	120	100	10	TM46	Thief	Dark	40	100	10
TM27	Return	Normal	—	100	20	TM48	Skill Swap	Psychic	—	100	10
TM29	Psychic	Psychic	90	100	10	HM05	Flash	Normal	—	70	20

MOVE TUTOR
FireRed/LeafGreen and Emerald Only

Double-Edge	Mimic	Substitute

*Battle Frontier tutor move (*Emerald*)

050 Diglett™

GROUND

GENERAL INFO

SPECIES: Mole Pokémon
HEIGHT: 0'08"
WEIGHT: 2 lbs.
ABILITY 1: Sand Veil
During a sandstorm, Diglett is able to evade more moves.
ABILITY 2: Arena Trap
Opponent cannot escape battle.

STATS

HP / SPEED / ATK / SP DEF / DEF / SP ATK

EVOLUTIONS

LV26

LOCATION[s]:

RUBY	**Rarity: None**	Trade from *FireRed/LeafGreen*
SAPPHIRE	**Rarity: None**	Trade from *FireRed/LeafGreen*
FIRERED	**Rarity: Common**	Diglett's Cave
LEAFGREEN	**Rarity: Common**	Diglett's Cave
COLOSSEUM	**Rarity: None**	Trade from *FireRed/LeafGreen*
EMERALD	**Rarity: None**	Trade from *FireRed/LeafGreen*
XD	**Rarity: None**	Trade from *FireRed/LeafGreen*

MOVES

Level	Attack	Type	Power	ACC	PP
—	Scratch	Normal	40	100	35
—	Sand-Attack	Ground	—	100	15
5	Growl	Normal	—	100	40
9	Magnitude	Ground	—	100	30
17	Dig	Ground	60	100	10

Level	Attack	Type	Power	ACC	PP
21	Fury Swipes	Normal	18	80	15
25	Mud-Slap	Ground	20	100	10
33	Slash	Normal	70	100	20
41	Earthquake	Ground	100	100	10
49	Fissure	Ground	—	30	5

TM/HM

TM/HM#	Name	Type	Power	ACC	PP
TM06	Toxic	Poison	—	85	10
TM10	Hidden Power	Normal	—	100	15
TM11	Sunny Day	Fire	—	—	5
TM17	Protect	Normal	—	—	10
TM21	Frustration	Normal	—	100	20
TM26	Earthquake	Ground	100	100	10
TM27	Return	Normal	—	100	20
TM28	Dig	Ground	60	100	10
TM32	Double Team	Normal	—	—	15
TM36	Sludge Bomb	Poison	90	100	10

TM/HM#	Name	Type	Power	ACC	PP
TM39	Rock Tomb	Rock	50	80	10
TM40	Aerial Ace	Flying	60	—	20
TM42	Facade	Normal	70	100	20
TM43	Secret Power	Normal	70	100	20
TM44	Rest	Psychic	—	—	10
TM45	Attract	Normal	—	100	15
TM46	Thief	Dark	40	100	10
HM01	Cut	Normal	50	95	30
HM06	Rock Smash	Fighting	20	100	15

EGG MOVES*

Name	Type	Power	ACC	PP
Ancientpower	Rock	60	100	5
Beat Up	Dark	10	100	10
Faint Attack	Dark	60	—	20
Pursuit	Dark	40	100	20
Rock Slide	Rock	75	90	10
Screech	Normal	—	85	40
Uproar	Normal	50	100	10

*Learned Via Breeding

MOVE TUTOR

FireRed/LeafGreen and Emerald Only

Body Slam*	Mimic	Substitute
Double-Edge	Rock Slide*	

*Battle Frontier tutor move (*Emerald*)

051 Dugtrio™

GROUND

GENERAL INFO

SPECIES: Mole Pokémon
HEIGHT: 2'04"
WEIGHT: 73 lbs.
ABILITY 1: Sand Veil
During a sandstorm, Dugtrio is able to evade more moves.
ABILITY 2: Arena Trap
Opponent cannot escape battle.

STATS

(Stats radar chart: HP, ATK, DEF, SP ATK, SP DEF, SPEED)

EVOLUTIONS

LV26

LOCATION[s]:

RUBY	Rarity: **None**	Trade from *FireRed/LeafGreen*
SAPPHIRE	Rarity: **None**	Trade from *FireRed/LeafGreen*
FIRERED	Rarity: **Rare**	Diglett's Cave
LEAFGREEN	Rarity: **Rare**	Diglett's Cave
COLOSSEUM	Rarity: **None**	Trade from *FireRed/LeafGreen*
EMERALD	Rarity: **None**	Trade from *FireRed/LeafGreen*
XD	Rarity: **Only One**	Citadark Island (Capture from Cipher Admin Kolax)

MOVES

Level	Attack	Type	Power	ACC	PP	Level	Attack	Type	Power	ACC	PP
—	Scratch	Normal	40	100	35	21	Fury Swipes	Normal	18	80	15
—	Sand-Attack	Ground	—	100	15	25	Mud-Slap	Ground	20	100	10
—	Tri Attack	Normal	80	100	10	26	Sand Tomb	Ground	15	70	15
—	Growl	Normal	—	100	40	38	Slash	Normal	70	100	20
9	Magnitude	Ground	—	100	30	51	Earthquake	Ground	100	100	10
17	Dig	Ground	60	100	10	64	Fissure	Ground	—	30	5

TM/HM

TM/HM#	Name	Type	Power	ACC	PP	TM/HM#	Name	Type	Power	ACC	PP
TM06	Toxic	Poison	—	85	10	TM36	Sludge Bomb	Poison	90	100	10
TM10	Hidden Power	Normal	—	100	15	TM39	Rock Tomb	Rock	50	80	10
TM11	Sunny Day	Fire	—	—	5	TM40	Aerial Ace	Flying	60	—	20
TM15	Hyper Beam	Normal	150	90	5	TM42	Facade	Normal	70	100	20
TM17	Protect	Normal	—	—	10	TM43	Secret Power	Normal	70	100	20
TM21	Frustration	Normal	—	100	20	TM44	Rest	Psychic	—	—	10
TM26	Earthquake	Ground	100	100	10	TM45	Attract	Normal	—	100	15
TM27	Return	Normal	—	100	20	TM46	Thief	Dark	40	100	10
TM28	Dig	Ground	60	100	10	HM01	Cut	Normal	50	95	30
TM32	Double Team	Normal	—	—	15	HM06	Rock Smash	Fighting	20	100	15

MOVE TUTOR

FireRed/LeafGreen and Emerald Only

Body Slam*	Mimic	Substitute
Double-Edge	Rock Slide*	

*Battle Frontier tutor move (*Emerald*)

052 Meowth™

NORMAL

GENERAL INFO

SPECIES: Scratch Cat Pokémon
HEIGHT: 1'04"
WEIGHT: 9 lbs.
ABILITY: Pickup

Allows Meowth to take items from opponent, and while walking in the wild.

STATS

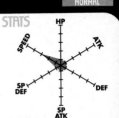

EVOLUTIONS

LV28

LOCATION(s):

	Rarity	
RUBY	**None**	Trade from *FireRed/LeafGreen*
SAPPHIRE	**None**	Trade from *FireRed/LeafGreen*
FIRERED	**Common**	Routes 5–8, Islands One, Two, Three, Five, Six, Seven
LEAFGREEN	**Common**	Routes 5–8, Islands One, Two, Three, Five, Six, Seven
COLOSSEUM	**None**	Trade from *FireRed/LeafGreen*
EMERALD	**Only One**	Battle Frontier
XD	**Only One**	Phenac City (Capture from Cipher Peon Fostin)

MOVES

Level	Attack	Type	Power	ACC	PP
—	Scratch	Normal	40	100	35
—	Growl	Normal	—	100	40
10	Bite	Dark	60	100	25
18	Pay Day	Normal	40	100	20
25	Faint Attack	Dark	60	—	20

Level	Attack	Type	Power	ACC	PP
31	Screech	Normal	—	85	40
36	Fury Swipes	Normal	18	80	15
40	Slash	Normal	70	100	20
43	Fake Out	Normal	40	100	10
45	Swagger	Normal	—	90	15

TM/HM

TM/HM#	Name	Type	Power	ACC	PP
TM03	Water Pulse	Water	60	95	20
TM06	Toxic	Poison	—	85	10
TM10	Hidden Power	Normal	—	100	15
TM11	Sunny Day	Fire	—	—	5
TM12	Taunt	Dark	—	100	20
TM17	Protect	Normal	—	—	10
TM18	Rain Dance	Water	—	—	5
TM21	Frustration	Normal	—	100	20
TM23	Iron Tail	Steel	75	75	15
TM24	Thunderbolt	Electric	95	100	15
TM25	Thunder	Electric	120	70	10
TM27	Return	Normal	—	100	20
TM28	Dig	Ground	60	100	10

TM/HM#	Name	Type	Power	ACC	PP
TM30	Shadow Ball	Ghost	80	100	15
TM32	Double Team	Normal	—	—	15
TM34	Shock Wave	Electric	60	—	20
TM40	Aerial Ace	Flying	60	—	20
TM41	Torment	Dark	—	100	15
TM42	Facade	Normal	70	100	20
TM43	Secret Power	Normal	70	100	20
TM44	Rest	Psychic	—	—	10
TM45	Attract	Normal	—	100	15
TM46	Thief	Dark	40	100	10
TM49	Snatch	Dark	—	100	10
HM01	Cut	Normal	50	95	30
HM05	Flash	Normal	—	70	20

EGG MOVES*

Name	Type	Power	ACC	PP
Amnesia	Psychic	—	—	20
Assist	Normal	—	100	20
Charm	Normal	—	100	20
Hypnosis	Psychic	—	60	20
Psych Up	Normal	—	—	10
Spite	Ghost	—	100	10

*Learned Via Breeding

MOVE TUTOR
FireRed/LeafGreen and Emerald Only

Body Slam*	Mimic	Substitute
Double-Edge	Dream Eater*	

*Battle Frontier tutor move (*Emerald*)

PRIMA OFFICIAL GAME GUIDE

053 Persian™

NORMAL

GENERAL INFO
SPECIES: Classy Cat Pokémon
HEIGHT: 3'03"
WEIGHT: 71 lbs.
ABILITY: Limber
Prevents Persian from being paralyzed.

STATS

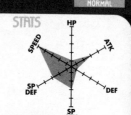

EVOLUTIONS

 ▶

LV28

LOCATION[s]:

RUBY	Rarity: **None**	Trade from *FireRed/LeafGreen*
SAPPHIRE	Rarity: **None**	Trade from *FireRed/LeafGreen*
FIRERED	Rarity: **Rare**	Evolve Meowth, Islands One, Two, Three, Five, Six, Seven
LEAFGREEN	Rarity: **Rare**	Evolve Meowth, Islands One, Two, Three, Five, Six, Seven
COLOSSEUM	Rarity: **None**	Trade from *FireRed/LeafGreen*
EMERALD	Rarity: **None**	Trade from *FireRed/LeafGreen*
XD	Rarity: **Evolve**	Evolve Meowth

MOVES

Level	Attack	Type	Power	ACC	PP	Level	Attack	Type	Power	ACC	PP
—	Scratch	Normal	40	100	35	34	Screech	Normal	—	85	40
—	Growl	Normal	—	100	40	42	Fury Swipes	Normal	18	80	15
—	Bite	Dark	60	100	25	49	Slash	Normal	70	100	20
18	Pay Day	Normal	40	100	20	55	Fake Out	Normal	40	100	10
25	Faint Attack	Dark	60	—	20	61	Swagger	Normal	—	90	15

TM/HM

TM/HM#	Name	Type	Power	ACC	PP	TM/HM#	Name	Type	Power	ACC	PP
TM03	Water Pulse	Water	60	95	20	TM28	Dig	Ground	60	100	10
TM05	Roar	Normal	—	100	20	TM30	Shadow Ball	Ghost	80	100	15
TM06	Toxic	Poison	—	85	10	TM32	Double Team	Normal	—	—	15
TM10	Hidden Power	Normal	—	100	15	TM34	Shock Wave	Electric	—	—	20
TM11	Sunny Day	Fire	—	—	5	TM40	Aerial Ace	Flying	60	—	20
TM12	Taunt	Dark	—	100	20	TM41	Torment	Dark	—	100	15
TM15	Hyper Beam	Normal	150	90	5	TM42	Facade	Normal	70	100	20
TM17	Protect	Normal	—	—	10	TM43	Secret Power	Normal	70	100	20
TM18	Rain Dance	Water	—	—	5	TM44	Rest	Psychic	—	—	10
TM21	Frustration	Normal	—	100	20	TM45	Attract	Normal	—	100	15
TM23	Iron Tail	Steel	75	75	15	TM46	Thief	Dark	40	100	10
TM24	Thunderbolt	Electric	95	100	15	TM49	Snatch	Dark	—	100	10
TM25	Thunder	Electric	120	70	10	HM01	Cut	Normal	50	95	30
TM27	Return	Normal	—	100	20	HM05	Flash	Normal	—	70	20

MOVE TUTOR
FireRed/LeafGreen and Emerald Only

Body Slam*	Mimic	Substitute
Double-Edge	Dream Eater*	

*Battle Frontier tutor move (*Emerald*)

054 Psyduck™

WATER

GENERAL INFO

SPECIES: Duck Pokémon
HEIGHT: 2'07"
WEIGHT: 43 lbs.
ABILITY 1: Damp
Prevents the opponent from using Selfdestruct or Explosion when Psyduck is in battle.
ABILITY 2: Cloud Nine
Prevents weather effects on all Pokémon while Psyduck is in that battle.

STATS

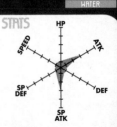

EVOLUTIONS

LV33

LOCATION[S]:

RUBY	Rarity: **Common**	Safari Zone
SAPPHIRE	Rarity: **Common**	Safari Zone
FIRERED	Rarity: **Common**	Routes 4, 6, 10, 11, 13, 19, 21, 24, Seafoam Islands, Safari Zone, Fuchsia City, Islands One, Two, Three, Five, Six, Seven
LEAFGREEN	Rarity: **None**	Trade from *Ruby/Sapphire/FireRed*
COLOSSEUM	Rarity: **None**	Trade from *Ruby/Sapphire/FireRed*
EMERALD	Rarity: **Common**	Safari Zone
XD	Rarity: **None**	Trade from *Ruby/Sapphire/FireRed*

MOVES

Level	Attack	Type	Power	ACC	PP
—	Water Sport	Water	—	100	15
—	Scratch	Normal	40	100	35
5	Tail Whip	Normal	—	100	30
10	Disable	Normal	—	55	20

Level	Attack	Type	Power	ACC	PP
16	Confusion	Psychic	50	100	25
23	Screech	Normal	—	85	40
31	Psych Up	Normal	—	—	10
40	Fury Swipes	Normal	18	80	15
50	Hydro Pump	Water	120	80	5

TM/HM

TM/HM#	Name	Type	Power	ACC	PP
TM01	Focus Punch	Fighting	150	100	20
TM03	Water Pulse	Water	60	95	20
TM04	Calm Mind	Psychic	—	—	20
TM06	Toxic	Poison	—	85	10
TM07	Hail	Ice	—	—	10
TM10	Hidden Power	Normal	—	100	15
TM13	Ice Beam	Ice	95	100	10
TM14	Blizzard	Ice	120	70	5
TM17	Protect	Normal	—	—	10
TM18	Rain Dance	Water	—	—	5
TM21	Frustration	Normal	—	100	20
TM23	Iron Tail	Steel	75	75	15
TM27	Return	Normal	—	100	20
TM28	Dig	Ground	60	100	10

TM/HM#	Name	Type	Power	ACC	PP
TM31	Brick Break	Fighting	75	100	15
TM32	Double Team	Normal	—	—	15
TM40	Aerial Ace	Flying	60	—	20
TM42	Facade	Normal	70	100	20
TM43	Secret Power	Normal	70	100	20
TM44	Rest	Psychic	—	—	10
TM45	Attract	Normal	—	100	15
HM03	Surf	Water	95	100	15
HM04	Strength	Normal	80	100	20
HM05	Flash	Normal	—	70	20
HM06	Rock Smash	Fighting	20	100	15
HM07	Waterfall	Water	80	100	15
HM08	Dive	Water	60	100	10

EGG MOVES*

Name	Type	Power	ACC	PP
Hypnosis	Psychic	—	60	20
Psybeam	Psychic	65	100	20
Foresight	Normal	—	100	40
Light Screen	Psychic	—	—	30
Future Sight	Psychic	80	90	15
Psychic	Psychic	90	100	10
Refresh	Normal	—	100	20
Cross Chop	Fighting	100	80	5

*Learned Via Breeding

MOVE TUTOR
FireRed/LeafGreen and Emerald Only

Body Slam*	Mega Kick*	Counter*
Double-Edge	Mimic	Seismic Toss*
Mega Punch*	Substitute	

Emerald Only

Dynamicpunch	Mud-Slap*	Swagger
Endure*	Psych Up*	Swift*
Ice Punch*	Sleep Talk	
Icy Wind*	Snore*	

*Battle Frontier tutor move (*Emerald*)

055 Golduck™

WATER

GENERAL INFO

SPECIES: Duck Pokémon
HEIGHT: 5'07"
WEIGHT: 169 lbs.
ABILITY 1: Damp

Prevents the opponent from using Selfdestruct or Explosion when Golduck is in battle.

ABILITY 2: Cloud Nine

Prevents weather effects on all Pokémon while Golduck is in that battle.

STATS

EVOLUTIONS

LV33

LOCATION(s):

RUBY	Rarity: **Rare**	Safari Zone
SAPPHIRE	Rarity: **Rare**	Safari Zone
FIRERED	Rarity: **Rare**	Two Island, Three Island, Seafoam Island
LEAFGREEN	Rarity: **None**	Trade from *Ruby/Sapphire/FireRed*
COLOSSEUM	Rarity: **None**	Trade from *Ruby/Sapphire/FireRed*
EMERALD	Rarity: **Rare**	Safari Zone
XD	Rarity: **Only One**	Citadark Island (Capture from Navigator Abson)

MOVES

Level	Attack	Type	Power	ACC	PP
—	Water Sport	Water	—	100	15
—	Scratch	Normal	40	100	35
—/5	Tail Whip	Normal	—	100	30
—/10	Disable	Normal	—	55	20

Level	Attack	Type	Power	ACC	PP
16	Confusion	Psychic	50	100	25
23	Screech	Normal	—	85	40
31	Psych Up	Normal	—	—	10
44	Fury Swipes	Normal	18	80	15
58	Hydro Pump	Water	120	80	5

 # = Emerald Only

TM/HM

TM/HM#	Name	Type	Power	ACC	PP
TM01	Focus Punch	Fighting	150	100	20
TM03	Water Pulse	Water	60	95	20
TM04	Calm Mind	Psychic	—	—	20
TM06	Toxic	Poison	—	85	10
TM07	Hail	Ice	—	—	10
TM10	Hidden Power	Normal	—	100	15
TM13	Ice Beam	Ice	95	100	10
TM14	Blizzard	Ice	120	70	5
TM15	Hyper Beam	Normal	150	90	5
TM17	Protect	Normal	—	—	10
TM18	Rain Dance	Water	—	—	5
TM21	Frustration	Normal	—	100	20
TM23	Iron Tail	Steel	75	75	15
TM27	Return	Normal	—	100	20

TM/HM#	Name	Type	Power	ACC	PP
TM28	Dig	Ground	60	100	10
TM31	Brick Break	Fighting	75	100	15
TM32	Double Team	Normal	—	—	15
TM40	Aerial Ace	Flying	60	—	20
TM42	Facade	Normal	70	100	20
TM43	Secret Power	Normal	70	100	20
TM44	Rest	Psychic	—	—	10
TM45	Attract	Normal	—	100	15
HM03	Surf	Water	95	100	15
HM04	Strength	Normal	80	100	15
HM05	Flash	Normal	—	70	20
HM06	Rock Smash	Fighting	20	100	15
HM07	Waterfall	Water	80	100	15
HM08	Dive	Water	60	100	10

MOVE TUTOR

FireRed/LeafGreen and Emerald Only

Body Slam*	Mega Kick*	Counter*	
Double-Edge	Mimic	Seismic Toss*	
Mega Punch*	Substitute		

Emerald Only

Dynamicpunch	Icy Wind*	Snore*
Endure*	Mud-Slap*	Swagger
Fury Cutter*	Psych Up*	Swift*
Ice Punch*	Sleep Talk	

*Battle Frontier tutor move (Emerald)

056 Mankey™

GENERAL INFO

SPECIES: Pig Monkey Pokémon
HEIGHT: 1'08"
WEIGHT: 62 lbs.
ABILITY: Vital Spirit

Protects Mankey from being put to sleep.

STATS

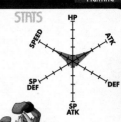

EVOLUTIONS

LV28

LOCATION[s]:

RUBY	Rarity: **None**	Trade from *FireRed/LeafGreen*
SAPPHIRE	Rarity: **None**	Trade from *FireRed/LeafGreen*
FIRERED	Rarity: **Common**	Routes 3, 4, 22, 23, Rock Tunnel
LEAFGREEN	Rarity: **Common**	Routes 3, 4, 22, 23, Rock Tunnel
COLOSSEUM	Rarity: **None**	Trade from *FireRed/LeafGreen*
EMERALD	Rarity: **None**	Trade from *FireRed/LeafGreen*
XD	Rarity: **None**	Trade from *FireRed/LeafGreen*

MOVES

Level	Attack	Type	Power	ACC	PP	Level	Attack	Type	Power	ACC	PP
—	Scratch	Normal	40	100	35	21	Focus Energy	Normal	—	—	30
—	Leer	Normal	—	100	30	26	Seismic Toss	Fighting	—	100	20
6	Low Kick	Fighting	—	100	20	31	Cross Chop	Fighting	100	80	5
11	Karate Chop	Fighting	50	100	25	36	Swagger	Normal	—	90	15
16	Fury Swipes	Normal	18	80	15	41	Screech	Normal	—	85	40
						46	Thrash	Normal	90	100	20

TM/HM

TM/HM#	Name	Type	Power	ACC	PP	TM/HM#	Name	Type	Power	ACC	PP
TM01	Focus Punch	Fighting	150	100	20	TM28	Dig	Ground	60	100	10
TM06	Toxic	Poison	—	85	10	TM31	Brick Break	Fighting	75	100	15
TM08	Bulk Up	Fighting	—	—	20	TM32	Double Team	Normal	—	—	15
TM10	Hidden Power	Normal	—	100	15	TM39	Rock Tomb	Rock	50	80	10
TM11	Sunny Day	Fire	—	—	5	TM40	Aerial Ace	Flying	60	—	20
TM12	Taunt	Dark	—	100	20	TM42	Facade	Normal	70	100	20
TM17	Protect	Normal	—	—	10	TM43	Secret Power	Normal	70	100	20
TM18	Rain Dance	Water	—	—	5	TM44	Rest	Psychic	—	—	10
TM21	Frustration	Normal	—	100	20	TM45	Attract	Normal	—	100	15
TM23	Iron Tail	Steel	75	75	15	TM46	Thief	Dark	40	100	10
TM24	Thunderbolt	Electric	95	100	15	TM50	Overheat	Fire	140	90	5
TM25	Thunder	Electric	120	70	10	HM04	Strength	Normal	80	100	20
TM26	Earthquake	Ground	100	100	10	HM06	Rock Smash	Fighting	20	100	15
TM27	Return	Normal	—	100	20						

EGG MOVES*

Name	Type	Power	ACC	PP
Beat Up	Dark	10	100	10
Foresight	Normal	—	100	40
Counter	Fighting	—	100	20
Meditate	Psychic	—	—	40
Revenge	Fighting	60	100	10
Reversal	Fighting	—	100	15
Rock Slide	Rock	75	90	10
Smellingsalt	Normal	60	100	10

*Learned Via Breeding

MOVE TUTOR

FireRed/LeafGreen and Emerald Only

Body Slam*	Mimic	Counter*
Double-Edge	Substitute	Metronome
Mega Punch*	Seismic Toss*	
Mega Kick*	Rock Slide*	

*Battle Frontier tutor move (*Emerald*)

PRIMA OFFICIAL GAME GUIDE

057 Primeape™

FIGHTING

GENERAL INFO
SPECIES: Pig Monkey Pokémon
HEIGHT: 3'03"
WEIGHT: 71 lbs.
ABILITY: Vital Spirit
Protects Primeape from being put to sleep.

STATS

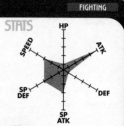

EVOLUTIONS

LV28

LOCATION(s):

RUBY	Rarity: **None**	Trade from *FireRed/LeafGreen*
SAPPHIRE	Rarity: **None**	Trade from *FireRed/LeafGreen*
FIRERED	Rarity: **Common**	Route 23, Victory Road
LEAFGREEN	Rarity: **Common**	Route 23, Victory Road
COLOSSEUM	Rarity: **None**	Trade from *FireRed/LeafGreen*
EMERALD	Rarity: **None**	Trade from *FireRed/LeafGreen*
XD	Rarity: **Only One**	Cipher Key Lair (Capture from Cipher Admin Gorigan)

MOVES

Level	Attack	Type	Power	ACC	PP		Level	Attack	Type	Power	ACC	PP
—	Scratch	Normal	40	100	35		21	Focus Energy	Normal	—	—	30
—	Leer	Normal	—	100	30		26	Seismic Toss	Fighting	—	100	20
—	Low Kick	Fighting	—	100	20		28	Rage	Normal	20	100	20
—	Rage	Normal	20	100	20		35	Cross Chop	Fighting	100	80	5
11	Karate Chop	Fighting	50	100	25		44	Swagger	Normal	—	90	15
16	Fury Swipes	Normal	18	80	15		53	Screech	Normal	—	85	40
							62	Thrash	Normal	90	100	20

TM/HM

TM/HM#	Name	Type	Power	ACC	PP		TM/HM#	Name	Type	Power	ACC	PP
TM01	Focus Punch	Fighting	150	100	20		TM27	Return	Normal	—	100	20
TM06	Toxic	Poison	—	85	10		TM28	Dig	Ground	60	100	10
TM08	Bulk Up	Fighting	—	—	20		TM31	Brick Break	Fighting	75	100	15
TM10	Hidden Power	Normal	—	100	15		TM32	Double Team	Normal	—	—	15
TM11	Sunny Day	Fire	—	—	5		TM39	Rock Tomb	Rock	50	80	10
TM12	Taunt	Dark	—	100	20		TM40	Aerial Ace	Flying	60	—	20
TM15	Hyper Beam	Normal	150	90	5		TM42	Facade	Normal	70	100	20
TM17	Protect	Normal	—	—	10		TM43	Secret Power	Normal	70	100	20
TM18	Rain Dance	Water	—	—	5		TM44	Rest	Psychic	—	—	10
TM21	Frustration	Normal	—	100	20		TM45	Attract	Normal	—	100	15
TM23	Iron Tail	Steel	75	75	15		TM46	Thief	Dark	40	100	10
TM24	Thunderbolt	Electric	95	100	15		TM50	Overheat	Fire	140	90	5
TM25	Thunder	Electric	120	70	10		HM04	Strength	Normal	80	100	20
TM26	Earthquake	Ground	100	100	10		HM06	Rock Smash	Fighting	20	100	15

MOVE TUTOR
FireRed/LeafGreen and Emerald Only

Body Slam*	Mimic	Counter*
Double-Edge	Substitute	Metronome
Mega Punch*	Seismic Toss*	
Mega Kick*	Rock Slide*	

*Battle Frontier tutor move (*Emerald*)

058 Growlithe™

FIRE

GENERAL INFO

SPECIES: Puppy Pokémon
HEIGHT: 2'04"
WEIGHT: 42 lbs.
ABILITY 1: Flash Fire
Raises the power of Growlithe's Fire-type attacks and prevents it from being damaged by Fire-type attacks.

ABILITY 2: Intimidate
The opponent's attack power lowers when Growlithe goes into battle.

STATS

HP · ATK · DEF · SP ATK · SP DEF · SPEED

EVOLUTIONS

 ▶

FIRE STONE

LOCATION(s):

RUBY	**Rarity: None**	Trade from *FireRed*
SAPPHIRE	**Rarity: None**	Trade from *FireRed*
FIRERED	**Rarity: Rare**	Route 7, Route 8, Pokémon Mansion
LEAFGREEN	**Rarity: None**	Trade from *FireRed*
COLOSSEUM	**Rarity: None**	Trade from *FireRed*
EMERALD	**Rarity: None**	Trade from *FireRed*
XD	**Rarity: Only One**	Cipher Key Lair (Capture from Cipher Peon Humah)

MOVES

Level	Attack	Type	Power	ACC	PP	Level	Attack	Type	Power	ACC	PP
—	Bite	Dark	60	100	25	25	Take Down	Normal	90	85	20
—	Roar	Normal	—	100	20	31	Flame Wheel	Fire	60	100	25
7	Ember	Fire	40	100	25	37	Helping Hand	Normal	—	100	20
13	Leer	Normal	—	100	30	43	Agility	Psychic	—	—	30
19	Odor Sleuth	Normal	—	100	40	49	Flamethrower	Fire	95	100	15

TM/HM

TM/HM#	Name	Type	Power	ACC	PP	TM/HM#	Name	Type	Power	ACC	PP
TM05	Roar	Normal	—	100	20	TM38	Fire Blast	Fire	120	85	5
TM06	Toxic	Poison	—	85	10	TM40	Aerial Ace	Flying	60	—	20
TM10	Hidden Power	Normal	—	100	15	TM42	Facade	Normal	70	100	20
TM11	Sunny Day	Fire	—	—	5	TM43	Secret Power	Normal	70	100	20
TM17	Protect	Normal	—	—	10	TM44	Rest	Psychic	—	—	10
TM21	Frustration	Normal	—	100	20	TM45	Attract	Normal	—	100	15
TM23	Iron Tail	Steel	75	75	15	TM46	Thief	Dark	40	100	10
TM27	Return	Normal	—	100	20	TM50	Overheat	Fire	140	90	5
TM28	Dig	Ground	60	100	10	HM04	Strength	Normal	80	100	20
TM32	Double Team	Normal	—	—	15	HM06	Rock Smash	Fighting	20	100	15
TM35	Flamethrower	Fire	95	100	15						

EGG MOVES*

Name	Type	Power	ACC	PP
Body Slam	Normal	85	100	15
Crunch	Dark	80	100	15
Fire Spin	Fire	15	70	15
Heat Wave	Fire	100	90	10
Howl	Normal	—	—	40
Safeguard	Normal	—	—	25
Thrash	Normal	90	100	20

*Learned Via Breeding

MOVE TUTOR
FireRed/LeafGreen and Emerald Only

Body Slam*	Mimic	Substitute
Double-Edge		

*Battle Frontier tutor move (*Emerald*)

Pokémon Pocket Pokédex

059 Arcanine™

FIRE

GENERAL INFO

SPECIES:	Legendary Pokémon
HEIGHT:	6'03"
WEIGHT:	342 lbs.
ABILITY 1:	Flash Fire

Raises the power of Arcanine's Fire-type Attacks and prevents it from being damaged by Fire-type attacks.

ABILITY 2: Intimidate

The opponent's attack power lowers when Arcanine goes into battle.

STATS

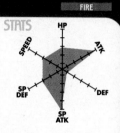

EVOLUTIONS

FIRE STONE

LOCATION[s]:

RUBY	Rarity: **None**	Trade from *FireRed*
SAPPHIRE	Rarity: **None**	Trade from *FireRed*
FIRERED	Rarity: **Evolve**	Evolve Growlithe
LEAFGREEN	Rarity: **None**	Trade from *FireRed*
COLOSSEUM	Rarity: **None**	Trade from *FireRed*
EMERALD	Rarity: **None**	Trade from *FireRed*
XD	Rarity: **Evolve**	Evolve Growlithe

MOVES

Level	Attack	Type	Power	ACC	PP	Level	Attack	Type	Power	ACC	PP
—	Bite	Dark	60	100	25	—	Ember	Fire	40	100	25
—	Roar	Normal	—	100	20	—	Odor Sleuth	Normal	—	100	40
						49	Extremespeed	Normal	80	100	5

TM/HM

TM/HM#	Name	Type	Power	ACC	PP	TM/HM#	Name	Type	Power	ACC	PP
TM05	Roar	Normal	—	100	20	TM35	Flamethrower	Fire	95	100	15
TM06	Toxic	Poison	—	85	10	TM38	Fire Blast	Fire	120	85	5
TM10	Hidden Power	Normal	—	100	15	TM40	Aerial Ace	Flying	60	—	20
TM11	Sunny Day	Fire	—	—	5	TM42	Facade	Normal	70	100	20
TM15	Hyper Beam	Normal	150	90	5	TM43	Secret Power	Normal	70	100	20
TM17	Protect	Normal	—	—	10	TM44	Rest	Psychic	—	—	10
TM21	Frustration	Normal	—	100	20	TM45	Attract	Normal	—	100	15
TM23	Iron Tail	Steel	75	75	15	TM46	Thief	Dark	40	100	10
TM27	Return	Normal	—	100	20	TM50	Overheat	Fire	140	90	5
TM28	Dig	Ground	60	100	10	HM04	Strength	Normal	80	100	20
TM32	Double Team	Normal	—	—	15	HM06	Rock Smash	Fighting	20	100	15

MOVE TUTOR

FireRed/LeafGreen and Emerald Only

Body Slam*	Mimic	Substitute
Double-Edge		

*Battle Frontier tutor move (*Emerald*)

060 Poliwag™

WATER

GENERAL INFO

SPECIES: Tadpole Pokémon
HEIGHT: 2'00"
WEIGHT: 27 lbs.
ABILITY 1: Damp
No one can use Selfdestruct or Explosion while Poliwag is in battle.

ABILITY 2: Water Absorb
When a Water-type attack hits Poliwag, it gains 1/4 of its HPs back.

STATS

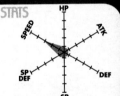

EVOLUTIONS

WATER STONE

LV25

TRADE WITH KING'S ROCK

LOCATION(s):

RUBY	Rarity: **None**	Trade from *FireRed/LeafGreen*
SAPPHIRE	Rarity: **None**	Trade from *FireRed/LeafGreen*
FIRERED	Rarity: **Common**	Two Island, Four Island, Six Island, Viridian City, Safari Zone
LEAFGREEN	Rarity: **Common**	Two Island, Four Island, Six Island, Viridian City, Safari Zone
COLOSSEUM	Rarity: **None**	Trade from *FireRed/LeafGreen*
EMERALD	Rarity: **None**	Trade from *FireRed/LeafGreen*
XD	Rarity: **None**	Trade from *FireRed/LeafGreen*

MOVES

Level	Attack	Type	Power	ACC	PP	Level	Attack	Type	Power	ACC	PP
—	Bubble	Water	20	100	30	25	Rain Dance	Water	—	—	5
7	Hypnosis	Psychic	—	60	20	31	Body Slam	Normal	85	100	15
13	Water Gun	Water	40	100	25	37	Belly Drum	Normal	—	—	10
19	Doubleslap	Normal	15	85	10	43	Hydro Pump	Water	120	80	5

TM/HM

TM/HM#	Name	Type	Power	ACC	PP	TM/HM#	Name	Type	Power	ACC	PP
TM03	Water Pulse	Water	60	95	20	TM29	Psychic	Psychic	90	100	10
TM06	Toxic	Poison	—	85	10	TM32	Double Team	Normal	—	—	15
TM07	Hail	Ice	—	—	10	TM42	Facade	Normal	70	100	20
TM10	Hidden Power	Normal	—	100	15	TM43	Secret Power	Normal	70	100	20
TM13	Ice Beam	Ice	95	100	10	TM44	Rest	Psychic	—	—	10
TM14	Blizzard	Ice	120	70	5	TM45	Attract	Normal	—	100	15
TM17	Protect	Normal	—	—	10	TM46	Thief	Dark	40	100	10
TM18	Rain Dance	Water	—	—	5	HM03	Surf	Water	95	100	15
TM21	Frustration	Normal	—	100	20	HM07	Waterfall	Water	80	100	15
TM27	Return	Normal	—	100	20	HM08	Dive	Water	60	100	10
TM28	Dig	Ground	60	100	10						

EGG MOVES*

Name	Type	Power	ACC	PP
Bubblebeam	Water	65	100	20
Haze	Ice	—	—	30
Ice Ball	Ice	30	90	20
Mind Reader	Normal	—	100	5
Mist	Ice	—	—	30
Water Sport	Water	—	100	15
Bounce	Flying	85	85	5

*Learned Via Breeding

MOVE TUTOR
FireRed/LeafGreen and Emerald Only

Body Slam*	Mimic	Substitute
Double-Edge		

*Battle Frontier tutor move (*Emerald*)

Prima **OFFICIAL GAME GUIDE**

061 Poliwhirl™

WATER

GENERAL INFO

SPECIES: Tadpole Pokémon
HEIGHT: 3'03"
WEIGHT: 44 lbs.
ABILITY 1: Damp
No one can use Selfdestruct or Explosion while Poliwhirl is in battle.

ABILITY 2: Water Absorb
When a Water-type attack hits Poliwhirl, it gains 1/4 of its HPs back.

STATS

EVOLUTIONS

LV25

WATER STONE

TRADE WITH KING'S ROCK

LOCATION(s):

RUBY	Rarity: **None**	Trade from *FireRed/LeafGreen*
SAPPHIRE	Rarity: **None**	Trade from *FireRed/LeafGreen*
FIRERED	Rarity: **Rare**	Two Island, Six Island
LEAFGREEN	Rarity: **Rare**	Two Island, Six Island
COLOSSEUM	Rarity: **None**	Trade from *FireRed/LeafGreen*
EMERALD	Rarity: **None**	Trade from *FireRed/LeafGreen*
XD	Rarity: **None**	Trade from *FireRed/LeafGreen*

MOVES

Level	Attack	Type	Power	ACC	PP	Level	Attack	Type	Power	ACC	PP
—	Bubble	Water	20	100	30	27	Rain Dance	Water	—	—	5
—	Hypnosis	Psychic	—	60	20	35	Body Slam	Normal	85	100	15
—	Water Gun	Water	40	100	25	43	Belly Drum	Normal	—	—	10
19	Doubleslap	Normal	15	85	10	51	Hydro Pump	Water	120	80	5

TM/HM

TM/HM#	Name	Type	Power	ACC	PP	TM/HM#	Name	Type	Power	ACC	PP
TM01	Focus Punch	Fighting	150	100	20	TM29	Psychic	Psychic	90	100	10
TM03	Water Pulse	Water	60	95	20	TM31	Brick Break	Fighting	75	100	15
TM06	Toxic	Poison	—	85	10	TM32	Double Team	Normal	—	—	15
TM07	Hail	Ice	—	—	10	TM42	Facade	Normal	70	100	20
TM10	Hidden Power	Normal	—	100	15	TM43	Secret Power	Normal	70	100	20
TM13	Ice Beam	Ice	95	100	10	TM44	Rest	Psychic	—	—	10
TM14	Blizzard	Ice	120	70	5	TM45	Attract	Normal	—	100	15
TM17	Protect	Normal	—	—	10	TM46	Thief	Dark	40	100	10
TM18	Rain Dance	Water	—	—	5	HM03	Surf	Water	95	100	15
TM21	Frustration	Normal	—	100	20	HM04	Strength	Normal	80	100	20
TM26	Earthquake	Ground	100	100	10	HM06	Rock Smash	Fighting	20	100	15
TM27	Return	Normal	—	100	20	HM07	Waterfall	Water	80	100	15
TM28	Dig	Ground	60	100	10	HM08	Dive	Water	60	100	10

MOVE TUTOR
FireRed/LeafGreen and Emerald Only

Body Slam*	Mega Kick*	Substitute
Double-Edge	Metronome	Counter*
Mega Punch*	Mimic	Seismic Toss*

*Battle Frontier tutor move (*Emerald*)

062 Poliwrath™

WATER | FIGHTING

GENERAL INFO

SPECIES: Tadpole Pokémon
HEIGHT: 4'03"
WEIGHT: 119 lbs.
ABILITY 1: Damp
No one can use Selfdestruct or Explosion while Poliwrath is in battle.

ABILITY 2: Water Absorb
When a Water-type attack hits Poliwrath, it gains 1/4 of its HPs back.

STATS

(Radar chart: HP, ATK, DEF, SP ATK, SP DEF, SPEED)

EVOLUTIONS

  LV25   WATER STONE

LOCATION[s]:

RUBY	Rarity: **None**	Trade from *FireRed/LeafGreen*	
SAPPHIRE	Rarity: **None**	Trade from *FireRed/LeafGreen*	
FIRERED	Rarity: **Evolve**	Evolve Poliwhirl	
LEAFGREEN	Rarity: **Evolve**	Evolve Poliwhirl	
COLOSSEUM	Rarity: **None**	Trade from *FireRed/LeafGreen*	
EMERALD	Rarity: **None**	Trade from *FireRed/LeafGreen*	
XD	Rarity: **Only One**	Citadark Island (Capture from Cipher Admin Gorigan)	

MOVES

Level	Attack	Type	Power	ACC	PP	Level	Attack	Type	Power	ACC	PP
—	Hypnosis	Psychic	—	60	20	—	Doubleslap	Normal	15	85	10
—	Water Gun	Water	40	100	25	—	Submission	Fighting	80	80	25
						51	Mind Reader	Normal	—	100	5

TM/HM

TM/HM#	Name	Type	Power	ACC	PP	TM/HM#	Name	Type	Power	ACC	PP
TM01	Focus Punch	Fighting	150	100	20	TM29	Psychic	Psychic	90	100	10
TM03	Water Pulse	Water	60	95	20	TM31	Brick Break	Fighting	75	100	15
TM06	Toxic	Poison	—	85	10	TM32	Double Team	Normal	—	—	15
TM07	Hail	Ice	—	—	10	TM39	Rock Tomb	Rock	50	80	10
TM08	Bulk Up	Fighting	—	—	20	TM42	Facade	Normal	70	100	20
TM10	Hidden Power	Normal	—	100	15	TM43	Secret Power	Normal	70	100	20
TM13	Ice Beam	Ice	95	100	10	TM44	Rest	Psychic	—	—	10
TM14	Blizzard	Ice	120	70	5	TM45	Attract	Normal	—	100	15
TM15	Hyper Beam	Normal	150	90	5	TM46	Thief	Dark	40	100	10
TM17	Protect	Normal	—	—	10	HM03	Surf	Water	95	100	15
TM18	Rain Dance	Water	—	—	5	HM04	Strength	Normal	80	100	20
TM21	Frustration	Normal	—	100	20	HM06	Rock Smash	Fighting	20	100	15
TM26	Earthquake	Ground	100	100	10	HM07	Waterfall	Water	80	100	15
TM27	Return	Normal	—	100	20	HM08	Dive	Water	60	100	10
TM28	Dig	Ground	60	100	10						

MOVE TUTOR
FireRed/LeafGreen and Emerald Only

Body Slam*	Mega Kick*	Substitute
Double-Edge	Metronome	Counter*
Mega Punch*	Mimic	Seismic Toss*

*Battle Frontier tutor move (*Emerald*)

063 Abra™

PSYCHIC

GENERAL INFO

SPECIES: Psi Pokémon
HEIGHT: 2'11"
WEIGHT: 43 lbs.
ABILITY 1: Synchronize
When an opponent inflicts a Poison, Paralyze, or Burn condition on Abra, it receives the same status ailment.
ABILITY 2: Inner Focus
Prevents Abra from flinching.

STATS

EVOLUTIONS

LV16 — EVOLVE VIA TRADE

LOCATION(s):

RUBY	Rarity: **Common**	Granite Cave
SAPPHIRE	Rarity: **Common**	Granite Cave
FIRERED	Rarity: **Rare**	Route 24, Route 25
LEAFGREEN	Rarity: **Rare**	Route 24, Route 25
COLOSSEUM	Rarity: **None**	Trade from Ruby/Sapphire/FireRed/LeafGreen
EMERALD	Rarity: **Common**	Granite Cave, Route 116
XD	Rarity: **None**	Trade from Ruby/Sapphire/FireRed/LeafGreen

MOVES

Level	Attack	Type	Power	ACC	PP
—	Teleport	Psychic	—	—	20

TM/HM

TM/HM#	Name	Type	Power	ACC	PP
TM01	Focus Punch	Fighting	150	100	20
TM04	Calm Mind	Psychic	—	—	20
TM06	Toxic	Poison	—	85	10
TM10	Hidden Power	Normal	—	100	15
TM11	Sunny Day	Fire	—	—	5
TM12	Taunt	Dark	—	100	20
TM16	Light Screen	Psychic	—	—	30
TM17	Protect	Normal	—	—	10
TM18	Rain Dance	Water	—	—	5
TM20	Safeguard	Normal	—	—	25
TM21	Frustration	Normal	—	100	20
TM23	Iron Tail	Steel	75	75	15
TM27	Return	Normal	—	100	20
TM29	Psychic	Psychic	90	100	10

TM/HM#	Name	Type	Power	ACC	PP
TM30	Shadow Ball	Ghost	80	100	15
TM32	Double Team	Normal	—	—	15
TM33	Reflect	Normal	—	—	20
TM34	Shock Wave	Electric	60	—	20
TM41	Torment	Dark	—	100	15
TM42	Facade	Normal	70	100	20
TM43	Secret Power	Normal	70	100	20
TM44	Rest	Psychic	—	—	10
TM45	Attract	Normal	—	100	15
TM46	Thief	Dark	40	100	10
TM48	Skill Swap	Psychic	—	100	10
TM49	Snatch	Dark	—	100	10
HM05	Flash	Normal	—	70	20

EGG MOVES*

Name	Type	Power	ACC	PP
Encore	Normal	—	100	5
Knock Off	Dark	20	100	20
Fire Punch	Fire	75	100	15
Thunderpunch	Electric	75	100	15
Ice Punch	Ice	75	100	15
Barrier	Psychic	—	—	30

*Learned Via Breeding

MOVE TUTOR

FireRed/LeafGreen and Emerald Only

Body Slam*	Mimic	Dream Eater*
Double-Edge	Substitute	Thunder Wave*
Mega Punch*	Counter*	
Mega Kick*	Seismic Toss*	

Emerald Only

Dynamicpunch*	Metronome	Swagger
Endure*	Psych Up*	Thunderpunch*
Fire Punch*	Sleep Talk	
Ice Punch*	Snore*	

*Battle Frontier tutor move (*Emerald*)

064 Kadabra™

PSYCHIC

GENERAL INFO

SPECIES: Psi Pokémon
HEIGHT: 4'03"
WEIGHT: 125 lbs.
ABILITY 1: Synchronize
When an opponent inflicts a Poison, Paralyze, or Burn condition on Kadabra, it receives the same status ailment.

ABILITY 2: Inner Focus
Prevents Kadabra from flinching.

STATS

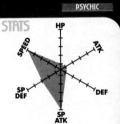

EVOLUTIONS

LV16 — EVOLVE VIA TRADE

LOCATION(S):

RUBY	Rarity: **Evolve**	Evolve Abra
SAPPHIRE	Rarity: **Evolve**	Evolve Abra
FIRERED	Rarity: **Rare**	Cerulean Cave
LEAFGREEN	Rarity: **Rare**	Cerulean Cave
COLOSSEUM	Rarity: **None**	Trade from *Ruby/Sapphire/FireRed/LeafGreen*
EMERALD	Rarity: **Evolve**	Evolve Abra
XD	Rarity: **None**	Trade from *Ruby/Sapphire/FireRed/LeafGreen*

MOVES

Level	Attack	Type	Power	ACC	PP
—	Teleport	Psychic	—	—	20
—	Kinesis	Psychic	—	80	15
—/16	Confusion	Psychic	50	100	25
18	Disable	Normal	—	55	20
21	Psybeam	Psychic	65	100	20
23	Reflect	Psychic	—	—	20

Level	Attack	Type	Power	ACC	PP
25	Recover	Normal	—	—	20
30	Future Sight	Psychic	80	90	15
33	Role Play	Psychic	—	100	10
36	Psychic	Psychic	90	100	10
43	Trick	Psychic	—	100	10

= *Emerald Only*

TM/HM

TM/HM#	Name	Type	Power	ACC	PP
TM01	Focus Punch	Fighting	150	100	20
TM04	Calm Mind	Psychic	—	—	20
TM06	Toxic	Poison	—	85	10
TM10	Hidden Power	Normal	—	100	15
TM11	Sunny Day	Fire	—	—	5
TM12	Taunt	Dark	—	100	20
TM16	Light Screen	Psychic	—	—	30
TM17	Protect	Normal	—	—	10
TM18	Rain Dance	Water	—	—	5
TM20	Safeguard	Normal	—	—	25
TM21	Frustration	Normal	—	100	20
TM23	Iron Tail	Steel	75	75	15
TM27	Return	Normal	—	100	20
TM29	Psychic	Psychic	90	100	10

TM/HM#	Name	Type	Power	ACC	PP
TM30	Shadow Ball	Ghost	80	100	15
TM32	Double Team	Normal	—	—	15
TM33	Reflect	Normal	—	—	20
TM34	Shock Wave	Electric	60	—	20
TM41	Torment	Dark	—	100	15
TM42	Facade	Normal	70	100	20
TM43	Secret Power	Normal	70	100	20
TM44	Rest	Psychic	—	—	10
TM45	Attract	Normal	—	100	15
TM46	Thief	Dark	40	100	10
TM48	Skill Swap	Psychic	—	100	10
TM49	Snatch	Dark	—	100	10
HM05	Flash	Normal	—	70	20

MOVE TUTOR

FireRed/LeafGreen and Emerald Only

Body Slam*	Mimic
Double-Edge	Substitute
Mega Punch*	Counter*
Mega Kick*	Seismic Toss*

Dream Eater*
Thunder Wave*

Emerald Only

Dynamicpunch*	Metronome	Swagger
Endure*	Psych Up*	Thunderpunch*
Fire Punch*	Sleep Talk	
Ice Punch*	Snore*	

*Battle Frontier tutor move (*Emerald*)

065 Alakazam™

PSYCHIC

GENERAL INFO

SPECIES: Psi Pokémon
HEIGHT: 4'11"
WEIGHT: 106 lbs.

ABILITY 1:Synchronize
When an opponent inflicts a Poison, Paralyze, or Burn condition on Alakazam, it receives the same status ailment.

ABILITY 2:Inner Focus
Prevents Alakazam from flinching.

STATS

EVOLUTIONS

LV16

EVOLVE VIA TRADING

LOCATION(s):

RUBY	Rarity: **Evolve**	Evolve Kadabra	
SAPPHIRE	Rarity: **Evolve**	Evolve Kadabra	
FIRERED	Rarity: **Evolve**	Evolve Kadabra	
LEAFGREEN	Rarity: **Evolve**	Evolve Kadabra	
COLOSSEUM	Rarity: **None**	Trade from *Ruby/Sapphire/FireRed/LeafGreen*	
EMERALD	Rarity: **Evolve**	Evolve Kadabra	
XD	Rarity: **None**	Trade from *Ruby/Sapphire/FireRed/LeafGreen*	

MOVES

Level	Attack	Type	Power	ACC	PP
—	Teleport	Psychic	—	—	20
—	Kinesis	Psychic	—	80	15
—/16	Confusion	Psychic	50	100	25
18	Disable	Normal	—	55	20
21	Psybeam	Psychic	65	100	20

Level	Attack	Type	Power	ACC	PP
23	Reflect	Psychic	—	—	20
25	Recover	Normal	—	—	20
30	Future Sight	Psychic	80	90	15
33	Calm Mind	Psychic	—	—	20
36	Psychic	Psychic	90	100	10
43	Trick	Psychic	—	100	10

 # = Emerald Only

TM/HM

TM/HM#	Name	Type	Power	ACC	PP
TM01	Focus Punch	Fighting	150	100	20
TM04	Calm Mind	Psychic	—	—	20
TM06	Toxic	Poison	—	85	10
TM10	Hidden Power	Normal	—	100	15
TM11	Sunny Day	Fire	—	—	5
TM12	Taunt	Dark	—	100	20
TM15	Hyper Beam	Normal	150	90	5
TM16	Light Screen	Psychic	—	—	30
TM17	Protect	Normal	—	—	10
TM18	Rain Dance	Water	—	—	5
TM20	Safeguard	Normal	—	—	25
TM21	Frustration	Normal	—	100	20
TM23	Iron Tail	Steel	75	75	15
TM27	Return	Normal	—	100	20

TM/HM#	Name	Type	Power	ACC	PP
TM29	Psychic	Psychic	90	100	10
TM30	Shadow Ball	Ghost	80	100	15
TM32	Double Team	Normal	—	—	15
TM33	Reflect	Normal	—	—	20
TM34	Shock Wave	Electric	60	—	20
TM41	Torment	Dark	—	100	15
TM42	Facade	Normal	70	100	20
TM43	Secret Power	Normal	70	100	20
TM44	Rest	Psychic	—	—	10
TM45	Attract	Normal	—	100	15
TM46	Thief	Dark	40	100	10
TM48	Skill Swap	Psychic	—	100	10
TM49	Snatch	Dark	—	100	10
HM05	Flash	Normal	—	70	20

MOVE TUTOR

FireRed/LeafGreen and Emerald Only

Body Slam*	Mimic	Dream Eater*
Double-Edge	Substitute	Thunder Wave*
Mega Punch*	Counter*	
Mega Kick*	Seismic Toss*	

Emerald Only

Dynamicpunch	Metronome	Swagger
Endure*	Psych Up*	Thunderpunch*
Fire Punch*	Sleep Talk*	
Ice Punch*	Snore*	

*Battle Frontier tutor move (*Emerald*)

066 Machop™

FIGHTING

GENERAL INFO

SPECIES: Superpower Pokémon
HEIGHT: 2'07"
WEIGHT: 43 lbs.
ABILITY: Guts

When Machop has a status condition, its attack power multiplies by 1.5.

STATS

EVOLUTIONS

LV28

EVOLVE VIA TRADING

LOCATION[s]:

RUBY	Rarity: **Common**	Route 112, Jagged Pass, Fiery Path
SAPPHIRE	Rarity: **Common**	Route 112, Jagged Pass, Fiery Path
FIRERED	Rarity: **Common**	One Island, Rock Tunnel, Victory Road
LEAFGREEN	Rarity: **Common**	One Island, Rock Tunnel, Victory Road
COLOSSEUM	Rarity: **None**	Trade from *Ruby/Sapphire/FireRed/LeafGreen*
EMERALD	Rarity: **Rare**	Jagged Pass, Fiery Path
XD	Rarity: **None**	Trade from *Ruby/Sapphire/FireRed/LeafGreen*

MOVES

Level	Attack	Type	Power	ACC	PP
—	Low Kick	Fighting	—	100	20
—	Leer	Normal	—	100	30
7	Focus Energy	Normal	—	—	30
13	Karate Chop	Fighting	50	100	25
19	Seismic Toss	Fighting	—	100	20
22	Foresight	Normal	—	100	40

Level	Attack	Type	Power	ACC	PP
25	Revenge	Fighting	60	100	10
31	Vital Throw	Fighting	70	100	10
37	Submission	Fighting	80	80	25
40	Cross Chop	Fighting	100	80	5
43	Scary Face	Normal	—	90	10
49	Dynamicpunch	Fighting	100	50	5

TM/HM

TM/HM#	Name	Type	Power	ACC	PP
TM01	Focus Punch	Fighting	150	100	20
TM06	Toxic	Poison	—	85	10
TM08	Bulk Up	Fighting	—	—	20
TM10	Hidden Power	Normal	—	100	15
TM11	Sunny Day	Fire	—	—	5
TM17	Protect	Normal	—	—	10
TM18	Rain Dance	Water	—	—	5
TM21	Frustration	Normal	—	100	20
TM26	Earthquake	Ground	100	100	10
TM27	Return	Normal	—	100	20
TM28	Dig	Ground	60	100	10
TM31	Brick Break	Fighting	75	100	15

TM/HM#	Name	Type	Power	ACC	PP
TM32	Double Team	Normal	—	—	15
TM35	Flamethrower	Fire	95	100	15
TM38	Fire Blast	Fire	120	85	5
TM39	Rock Tomb	Rock	50	80	10
TM42	Facade	Normal	70	100	20
TM43	Secret Power	Normal	70	100	20
TM44	Rest	Psychic	—	—	10
TM45	Attract	Normal	—	100	15
TM46	Thief	Dark	40	100	10
HM04	Strength	Normal	80	100	15
HM06	Rock Smash	Fighting	20	100	15

EGG MOVES*

Name	Type	Power	ACC	PP
Light Screen	Psychic	—	—	30
Meditate	Psychic	—	—	40
Encore	Normal	—	100	5
Smellingsalt	Normal	60	100	10
Counter	Fighting	—	100	20
Rock Slide	Rock	75	90	10
Rolling Kick	Fighting	60	85	10

*Learned Via Breeding

MOVE TUTOR

FireRed/LeafGreen and Emerald Only

Body Slam*	Mega Kick*	Counter*
Double-Edge	Mimic	Seismic Toss*
Mega Punch*	Substitute	Rock Slide*

Emerald Only

Defense Curl*	Ice Punch*	Snore*
Dynamicpunch	Metronome	Swagger
Endure*	Mud-Slap*	Thunderpunch*
Fire Punch*	Sleep Talk	

*Battle Frontier tutor move (*Emerald*)

067 Machoke™

FIGHTING

GENERAL INFO

SPECIES: Superpower Pokémon
HEIGHT: 4'01"
WEIGHT: 155 lbs.
ABILITY: Guts

When Machoke has a status condition, its attack power multiplies by 1.5.

STATS

EVOLUTIONS

LV28   EVOLVE VIA TRADING

LOCATION[S]:

RUBY	Rarity: **Evolve**	Evolve Machop
SAPPHIRE	Rarity: **Evolve**	Evolve Machop
FIRERED	Rarity: **Rare**	Cerulean Cave, Victory Road, One Island
LEAFGREEN	Rarity: **Rare**	Cerulean Cave, Victory Road, One Island
COLOSSEUM	Rarity: **None**	Trade from *Ruby/Sapphire/FireRed/LeafGreen*
EMERALD	Rarity: **Evolve**	Evolve Machop
XD	Rarity: **None**	Trade from *Ruby/Sapphire/FireRed/LeafGreen*

MOVES

Level	Attack	Type	Power	ACC	PP		Level	Attack	Type	Power	ACC	PP
—	Low Kick	Fighting	—	100	20		25	Revenge	Fighting	60	100	10
—	Leer	Normal	—	100	30		33	Vital Throw	Fighting	70	100	10
—/7	Focus Energy	Normal	—	—	30		41	Submission	Fighting	80	80	25
13	Karate Chop	Fighting	50	100	25		46	Cross Chop	Fighting	100	80	5
19	Seismic Toss	Fighting	—	100	20		51	Scary Face	Normal	—	90	10
22	Foresight	Normal	—	100	40		59	Dynamicpunch	Fighting	100	50	5

TM/HM

TM/HM#	Name	Type	Power	ACC	PP		TM/HM#	Name	Type	Power	ACC	PP
TM01	Focus Punch	Fighting	150	100	20		TM32	Double Team	Normal	—	—	15
TM06	Toxic	Poison	—	85	10		TM35	Flamethrower	Fire	95	100	15
TM08	Bulk Up	Fighting	—	—	20		TM38	Fire Blast	Fire	120	85	5
TM10	Hidden Power	Normal	—	100	15		TM39	Rock Tomb	Rock	50	80	10
TM11	Sunny Day	Fire	—	—	5		TM42	Facade	Normal	70	100	20
TM17	Protect	Normal	—	—	10		TM43	Secret Power	Normal	70	100	20
TM18	Rain Dance	Water	—	—	5		TM44	Rest	Psychic	—	—	10
TM21	Frustration	Normal	—	100	20		TM45	Attract	Normal	—	100	15
TM26	Earthquake	Ground	100	100	10		TM46	Thief	Dark	40	100	10
TM27	Return	Normal	—	100	20		HM04	Strength	Normal	80	100	20
TM28	Dig	Ground	60	100	10		HM06	Rock Smash	Fighting	20	100	15
TM31	Brick Break	Fighting	75	100	15							

MOVE TUTOR

FireRed/LeafGreen and Emerald Only

Body Slam*	Mega Kick*	Counter*
Double-Edge*	Mimic	Seismic Toss*
Mega Punch*	Substitute	Rock Slide*

Emerald Only

Dynamicpunch	Metronome	Swagger
Endure*	Mud-Slap*	Thunderpunch*
Fire Punch*	Sleep Talk	
Ice Punch*	Snore*	

*Battle Frontier tutor move (*Emerald*)

068 Machamp™

FIGHTING

GENERAL INFO
SPECIES: Superpower Pokémon
HEIGHT: 5'03"
WEIGHT: 287 lbs.
ABILITY: Guts

When Machamp has a status condition, its attack power multiplies by 1.5.

STATS

EVOLUTIONS

LV28 — EVOLVE VIA TRADING

LOCATION(s):

RUBY	Rarity:	Evolve	Evolve Machoke
SAPPHIRE	Rarity:	Evolve	Evolve Machoke
FIRERED	Rarity:	Evolve	Evolve Machoke
LEAFGREEN	Rarity:	Evolve	Evolve Machoke
COLOSSEUM	Rarity:	None	Trade from *Ruby/Sapphire/FireRed/LeafGreen*
EMERALD	Rarity:	Evolve	Evolve Machoke
XD	Rarity:	None	Trade from *Ruby/Sapphire/FireRed/LeafGreen*

MOVES

Level	Attack	Type	Power	ACC	PP
—	Low Kick	Fighting	—	100	20
—	Leer	Normal	—	100	30
—/#	Focus Energy	Normal	—	—	30
13	Karate Chop	Fighting	50	100	25
19	Seismic Toss	Fighting	—	100	20
22	Foresight	Normal	—	100	40

Level	Attack	Type	Power	ACC	PP
25	Revenge	Fighting	60	100	10
33	Vital Throw	Fighting	70	100	10
41	Submission	Fighting	80	80	25
46	Cross Chop	Fighting	100	80	5
51	Scary Face	Normal	—	90	10
59	Dynamicpunch	Fighting	100	50	5

 # = Emerald Only

TM/HM

TM/HM#	Name	Type	Power	ACC	PP
TM01	Focus Punch	Fighting	150	100	20
TM06	Toxic	Poison	—	85	10
TM08	Bulk Up	Fighting	—	—	20
TM10	Hidden Power	Normal	—	100	15
TM11	Sunny Day	Fire	—	—	5
TM15	Hyper Beam	Normal	150	90	5
TM17	Protect	Normal	—	—	10
TM18	Rain Dance	Water	—	—	5
TM21	Frustration	Normal	—	100	20
TM26	Earthquake	Ground	100	100	10
TM27	Return	Normal	—	100	20
TM28	Dig	Ground	60	100	10

TM/HM#	Name	Type	Power	ACC	PP
TM31	Brick Break	Fighting	75	100	15
TM32	Double Team	Normal	—	—	15
TM35	Flamethrower	Fire	95	100	15
TM38	Fire Blast	Fire	120	85	5
TM39	Rock Tomb	Rock	50	80	10
TM42	Facade	Normal	70	100	20
TM43	Secret Power	Normal	70	100	20
TM44	Rest	Psychic	—	—	10
TM45	Attract	Normal	—	100	15
TM46	Thief	Dark	40	100	10
HM04	Strength	Normal	80	100	20
HM06	Rock Smash	Fighting	20	100	15

MOVE TUTOR

FireRed/LeafGreen and Emerald Only

Body Slam*	Mega Kick*	Counter*
Double-Edge	Mimic	Seismic Toss*
Mega Punch*	Substitute	Rock Slide*

Emerald Only

Dynamicpunch	Metronome	Swagger
Endure*	Mud-Slap*	Thunderpunch*
Fire Punch*	Sleep Talk	
Ice Punch*	Snore*	

Battle Frontier tutor move (Emerald)

069 Bellsprout™

GRASS   POISON

GENERAL INFO

SPECIES: Flower Pokémon
HEIGHT: 2'04"
WEIGHT: 9 lbs.
ABILITY: Chlorophyll

When the sunlight is strong, Bellsprout's Speed doubles.

STATS

EVOLUTIONS

 ► LV21 ► LEAF STONE

LOCATION(s):

Game	Rarity	Location
RUBY	Rarity: **None**	Trade from *LeafGreen*
SAPPHIRE	Rarity: **None**	Trade from *LeafGreen*
FIRERED	Rarity: **None**	Trade from *LeafGreen*
LEAFGREEN	Rarity: **Common**	Two Island, Three Island, Six Island, Routes 5, 6, 7, 12, 13, 14, 15
COLOSSEUM	Rarity: **None**	Trade from *LeafGreen*
EMERALD	Rarity: **None**	Trade from *LeafGreen*
XD	Rarity: **None**	Trade from *LeafGreen*

MOVES

Level	Attack	Type	Power	ACC	PP
—	Vine Whip	Grass	35	100	10
6	Growth	Normal	—	—	40
11	Wrap	Normal	15	85	20
15	Sleep Powder	Grass	—	75	15
17	Poisonpowder	Poison	—	75	35
19	Stun Spore	Grass	—	75	30
23	Acid	Poison	40	100	30
30	Sweet Scent	Normal	—	100	20
37	Razor Leaf	Grass	55	95	25
45	Slam	Normal	80	75	20

TM/HM

TM/HM#	Name	Type	Power	ACC	PP
TM06	Toxic	Poison	—	85	10
TM09	Bullet Seed	Grass	10	100	30
TM10	Hidden Power	Normal	—	100	15
TM11	Sunny Day	Fire	—	—	5
TM17	Protect	Normal	—	—	10
TM19	Giga Drain	Grass	60	100	5
TM21	Frustration	Normal	—	100	20
TM22	Solarbeam	Grass	120	100	10
TM27	Return	Normal	—	100	20
TM32	Double Team	Normal	—	—	15
TM36	Sludge Bomb	Poison	90	100	10
TM42	Facade	Normal	70	100	20
TM43	Secret Power	Normal	70	100	20
TM44	Rest	Psychic	—	—	10
TM45	Attract	Normal	—	100	15
TM46	Thief	Dark	40	100	10
HM01	Cut	Normal	50	95	30
HM05	Flash	Normal	—	70	20

EGG MOVES*

Name	Type	Power	ACC	PP
Encore	Normal	—	100	5
Ingrain	Grass	—	100	20
Leech Life	Bug	20	100	15
Magical Leaf	Grass	60	—	20
Reflect	Psychic	—	—	20
Swords Dance	Normal	—	—	30
Synthesis	Grass	—	—	5

*Learned Via Breeding

MOVE TUTOR

FireRed/LeafGreen and Emerald Only

Double-Edge	Substitute	Swords Dance*
Mimic		

*Battle Frontier tutor move (*Emerald*)

070 Weepinbell™

 GRASS POISON

GENERAL INFO

SPECIES: Flycatcher Pokémon
HEIGHT: 3'03"
WEIGHT: 14 lbs.
ABILITY: Chlorophyll

When the sunlight is strong, Weepinbell's Speed doubles.

STATS

HP, ATK, DEF, SP ATK, SP DEF, SPEED

EVOLUTIONS

  LV21 LEAF STONE

LOCATION[s]:

RUBY	Rarity: **None**	Trade from *LeafGreen*
SAPPHIRE	Rarity: **None**	Trade from *LeafGreen*
FIRERED	Rarity: **None**	Trade from *LeafGreen*
LEAFGREEN	Rarity: **Rare**	Evolve Bellsprout, Two Island, Three Island, Six Island, Routes 12, 13, 14, 15
COLOSSEUM	Rarity: **None**	Trade from *LeafGreen*
EMERALD	Rarity: **None**	Trade from *LeafGreen*
XD	Rarity: **Only One**	Cipher Key Lair (Capture from Cipher Peon Angic)

MOVES

Level	Attack	Type	Power	ACC	PP	Level	Attack	Type	Power	ACC	PP
—	Vine Whip	Grass	35	100	10	19	Stun Spore	Grass	—	75	30
—	Growth	Normal	—	—	40	24	Acid	Poison	40	100	30
—	Wrap	Normal	15	85	20	33	Sweet Scent	Normal	—	100	20
15	Sleep Powder	Grass	—	75	15	42	Razor Leaf	Grass	55	95	25
17	Poison Powder	Poison	—	75	35	54	Slam	Normal	80	75	20

TM/HM

TM/HM#	Name	Type	Power	ACC	PP	TM/HM#	Name	Type	Power	ACC	PP
TM06	Toxic	Poison	—	85	10	TM32	Double Team	Normal	—	—	15
TM09	Bullet Seed	Grass	10	100	30	TM36	Sludge Bomb	Poison	90	100	10
TM10	Hidden Power	Normal	—	100	15	TM42	Facade	Normal	70	100	20
TM11	Sunny Day	Fire	—	—	5	TM43	Secret Power	Normal	70	100	20
TM17	Protect	Normal	—	—	10	TM44	Rest	Psychic	—	—	10
TM19	Giga Drain	Grass	60	100	5	TM45	Attract	Normal	—	100	15
TM21	Frustration	Normal	—	100	20	TM46	Thief	Dark	40	100	10
TM22	Solarbeam	Grass	120	100	10	HM01	Cut	Normal	50	95	30
TM27	Return	Normal	—	100	20	HM05	Flash	Normal	—	70	20

MOVE TUTOR

FireRed/LeafGreen and Emerald Only

Double-Edge	Substitute	Swords Dance*
Mimic		

*Battle Frontier tutor move (*Emerald*)

071 Victreebel™

GRASS   POISON

GENERAL INFO

SPECIES: Flycatcher Pokémon
HEIGHT: 5'07"
WEIGHT: 34 lbs.
ABILITY: Chlorophyll

When the sunlight is strong,
Victreebel's Speed doubles.

STATS

HP
SPEED
ATK
SP DEF
DEF
SP ATK

EVOLUTIONS

LV21   LEAF STONE

LOCATION[s]:

RUBY	**Rarity: None**	Trade from *LeafGreen*
SAPPHIRE	**Rarity: None**	Trade from *LeafGreen*
FIRERED	**Rarity: None**	Trade from *LeafGreen*
LEAFGREEN	**Rarity: Evolve**	Evolve Weepinbell
COLOSSEUM	**Rarity: None**	Trade from *LeafGreen*
EMERALD	**Rarity: None**	Trade from *LeafGreen*
XD	**Rarity: Evolve**	Evolve Weepinbell

MOVES

Level	Attack	Type	Power	ACC	PP		Level	Attack	Type	Power	ACC	PP
—	Stockpile	Normal	—	—	10		—	Sleep Powder	Grass	—	75	15
—	Spit Up	Normal	100	100	10		—	Razor Leaf	Grass	55	95	25
—	Swallow	Normal	—	—	10		—	Vine Whip	Grass	35	100	10
							—	Sweet Scent	Normal	—	100	20

TM/HM

TM/HM#	Name	Type	Power	ACC	PP		TM/HM#	Name	Type	Power	ACC	PP
TM06	Toxic	Poison	—	85	10		TM32	Double Team	Normal	—	—	15
TM09	Bullet Seed	Grass	10	100	30		TM36	Sludge Bomb	Poison	90	100	10
TM10	Hidden Power	Normal	—	100	15		TM42	Facade	Normal	70	100	20
TM11	Sunny Day	Fire	—	—	5		TM43	Secret Power	Normal	70	100	20
TM15	Hyper Beam	Normal	150	90	5		TM44	Rest	Psychic	—	—	10
TM17	Protect	Normal	—	—	10		TM45	Attract	Normal	—	100	15
TM19	Giga Drain	Grass	60	100	5		TM46	Thief	Dark	40	100	10
TM21	Frustration	Normal	—	100	20		HM01	Cut	Normal	50	95	30
TM22	Solarbeam	Grass	120	100	10		HM05	Flash	Normal	—	70	20
TM27	Return	Normal	—	100	20							

MOVE TUTOR

FireRed/LeafGreen and Emerald Only

Body Slam*	Mimic	Swords Dance*
Double-Edge	Substitute	

*Battle Frontier tutor move (*Emerald*)

072 Tentacool™

WATER   POISON

GENERAL INFO

SPECIES: Jellyfish Pokémon
HEIGHT: 2'11"
WEIGHT: 100 lbs.
ABILITY 1: Clear Body
Protects Tentacool from having its stats lowered.
ABILITY 2: Liquid Ooze
Damages opponents when they absorb HPs from Tentacool.

STATS

EVOLUTIONS

LV30

LOCATION[s]:

RUBY	Rarity: **Common**	Slateport City, Pacifidlog Town, Ever Grande City, Mossdeep City, Lilycove City, Dewford Town, Shoal Cave, Seafloor Cavern, Abandoned Ship, Sootopolis City, Routes 103, 105-110, 115, 118, 119, 121-134
SAPPHIRE	Rarity: **Common**	Slateport City, Pacifidlog Town, Ever Grande City, Mossdeep City, Lilycove City, Dewford Town, Shoal Cave, Seafloor Cavern, Abandoned Ship, Sootopolis City, Routes 103, 105-110, 115, 118, 119, 121-134
FIRERED	Rarity: **Common**	One Island, Three Island, Five Island, Six Island, Seven Island, Routes 4, 10, 11, 12, 13, 19, 20, 21, 24, Cerulean City, Vermilion City
LEAFGREEN	Rarity: **Common**	One Island, Three Island, Five Island, Six Island, Seven Island, Routes 4, 10, 11, 12, 13, 19, 20, 21, 24, Cerulean City, Vermilion City
COLOSSEUM	Rarity: **None**	Trade from *Ruby/Sapphire/FireRed/LeafGreen*
EMERALD	Rarity: **Common**	Routes 103, 105–110, 115, 118, 119, 121–134, Abandoned Ship, Dewford Town, Ever Grande City, Lilycove City, Mossdeep City, Pacifidlog Town, Seafloor Cavern, Shoal Cave, Slateport City, Sootopolis City
XD	Rarity: **None**	Trade from *Ruby/Sapphire/FireRed/LeafGreen*

MOVES

Level	Attack	Type	Power	ACC	PP	Level	Attack	Type	Power	ACC	PP
—	Poison Sting	Poison	15	100	35	25	Bubblebeam	Water	65	100	20
6	Supersonic	Normal	—	55	20	30	Wrap	Normal	15	85	20
12	Constrict	Normal	10	100	35	36	Barrier	Psychic	—	—	30
19	Acid	Poison	40	100	30	43	Screech	Normal	—	85	40
						49	Hydro Pump	Water	120	80	5

TM/HM

TM/HM#	Name	Type	Power	ACC	PP	TM/HM#	Name	Type	Power	ACC	PP
TM03	Water Pulse	Water	60	95	20	TM32	Double Team	Normal	—	—	15
TM06	Toxic	Poison	—	85	10	TM36	Sludge Bomb	Poison	90	100	10
TM07	Hail	Ice	—	—	10	TM42	Facade	Normal	70	100	20
TM10	Hidden Power	Normal	—	100	15	TM43	Secret Power	Normal	70	100	20
TM13	Ice Beam	Ice	95	100	10	TM44	Rest	Psychic	—	—	10
TM14	Blizzard	Ice	120	70	5	TM45	Attract	Normal	—	100	15
TM17	Protect	Normal	—	—	10	TM46	Thief	Dark	40	100	10
TM18	Rain Dance	Water	—	—	5	HM01	Cut	Normal	50	95	30
TM19	Giga Drain	Grass	60	100	5	HM03	Surf	Water	95	100	15
TM21	Frustration	Normal	—	100	20	HM07	Waterfall	Water	80	100	15
TM27	Return	Normal	—	100	20	HM08	Dive	Water	60	100	10

EGG MOVES*

Name	Type	Power	ACC	PP
Mirror Coat	Psychic	—	100	20
Safeguard	Normal	—	—	25
Confuse Ray	Ghost	—	100	10
Aurora Beam	Ice	65	100	20
Rapid Spin	Normal	20	100	40
Haze	Ice	—	—	30

*Learned Via Breeding

MOVE TUTOR

FireRed/LeafGreen and Emerald Only

Double-Edge	Substitute	Swords Dance*
Mimic		

Emerald Only

Endure*	Sleep Talk	Swagger
Icy Wind*	Snore*	

*Battle Frontier tutor move (*Emerald*)

073 Tentacruel™

WATER   POISON

GENERAL INFO
SPECIES: Jellyfish Pokémon
HEIGHT: 5'03"
WEIGHT: 121 lbs.
ABILITY 1: Clear Body
Protects Tentacruel from having its stats lowered.
ABILITY 2: Liquid Ooze
Damages opponents when they absorb HPs from Tentacruel.

STATS

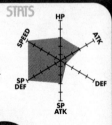

EVOLUTIONS

 ▶

LV30

LOCATION[s]:

RUBY	Rarity: **Rare**	Abandoned Ship	
SAPPHIRE	Rarity: **Rare**	Abandoned Ship	
FIRERED	Rarity: **Rare**	Evolve Tentacool, Islands One, Three, Five, Six, Seven	
LEAFGREEN	Rarity: **Common**	Evolve Tentacool, Islands One, Three, Five, Six, Seven	
COLOSSEUM	Rarity: **None**	Trade from *Ruby/Sapphire/FireRed/LeafGreen*	
EMERALD	Rarity: **Rare**	Evolve Tentacool, Abandoned Ship	
XD	Rarity: **None**	Trade from *Ruby/Sapphire/FireRed/LeafGreen*	

MOVES

Level	Attack	Type	Power	ACC	PP
—	Poison Sting	Poison	15	100	35
—/6	Supersonic	Normal	—	55	20
—/12	Constrict	Normal	10	100	35
19	Acid	Poison	40	100	30

Level	Attack	Type	Power	ACC	PP
25	Bubblebeam	Water	65	100	20
30	Wrap	Normal	15	85	20
38	Barrier	Psychic	—	—	30
47	Screech	Normal	—	85	40
55	Hydro Pump	Water	120	80	5

= *Emerald* Only

TM/HM

TM/HM#	Name	Type	Power	ACC	PP
TM03	Water Pulse	Water	60	95	20
TM06	Toxic	Poison	—	85	10
TM07	Hail	Ice	—	—	10
TM10	Hidden Power	Normal	—	100	15
TM13	Ice Beam	Ice	95	100	10
TM14	Blizzard	Ice	120	70	5
TM15	Hyper Beam	Normal	150	90	5
TM17	Protect	Normal	—	—	10
TM18	Rain Dance	Water	—	—	5
TM19	Giga Drain	Grass	60	100	5
TM21	Frustration	Normal	—	100	20

TM/HM#	Name	Type	Power	ACC	PP
TM27	Return	Normal	—	100	20
TM32	Double Team	Normal	—	—	15
TM36	Sludge Bomb	Poison	90	100	10
TM42	Facade	Normal	70	100	20
TM43	Secret Power	Normal	70	100	20
TM44	Rest	Psychic	—	—	10
TM45	Attract	Normal	—	100	15
TM46	Thief	Dark	40	100	10
HM01	Cut	Normal	50	95	30
HM03	Surf	Water	95	100	15
HM07	Waterfall	Water	80	100	15
HM08	Dive	Water	60	100	10

MOVE TUTOR

FireRed/LeafGreen and Emerald Only

Double-Edge	Substitute	Swords Dance*
Mimic		

Emerald Only

Endure*	Sleep Talk*	Swagger
Icy Wind*	Snore*	

*Battle Frontier tutor move (*Emerald*)

074 Geodude™

ROCK | GROUND

GENERAL INFO

SPECIES: Rock Pokémon
HEIGHT: 1'04"
WEIGHT: 44 lbs.
ABILITY 1: Rock Head
Protects Geodude from receiving recoil damage from Submission, Take Down, and Double-Edge.
ABILITY 2: Sturdy
Prevents Geodude from receiving a one hit KO.

STATS

HP · ATK · DEF · SP ATK · SP DEF · SPEED

EVOLUTIONS

LV25 · EVOLVE VIA TRADE

LOCATION(s):

RUBY	Rarity: **Common**	Route 111, Route 114, Victory Road, Safari Zone, Granite Cave
SAPPHIRE	Rarity: **Common**	Route 111, Route 114, Victory Road, Safari Zone, Granite Cave
FIRERED	Rarity: **Common**	One Island, Seven Island, Victory Road, Mt. Moon, Rock Tunnel
LEAFGREEN	Rarity: **Common**	One Island, Seven Island, Victory Road, Mt. Moon, Rock Tunnel
COLOSSEUM	Rarity: **None**	Trade from *Ruby/Sapphire/FireRed/LeafGreen*
EMERALD	Rarity: **Common**	Route 111, Route 114, Granite Cave, Magma Hideout, Victory Road, Safari Zone, Cerulean Cave, One Island, Seven Island
XD	Rarity: **None**	Trade from *Ruby/Sapphire/FireRed/LeafGreen*

MOVES

Level	Attack	Type	Power	ACC	PP	Level	Attack	Type	Power	ACC	PP
—	Tackle	Normal	35	95	35	21	Selfdestruct	Normal	200	100	5
—	Defense Curl	Normal	—	—	40	26	Rollout	Rock	30	90	20
6	Mud Sport	Ground	—	—	15	31	Rock Blast	Rock	25	80	10
11	Rock Throw	Rock	50	90	15	36	Earthquake	Ground	100	100	10
16	Magnitude	Ground	—	100	30	41	Explosion	Normal	250	100	5
						46	Double-Edge	Normal	120	100	15

TM/HM

TM/HM#	Name	Type	Power	ACC	PP	TM/HM#	Name	Type	Power	ACC	PP
TM01	Focus Punch	Fighting	150	100	20	TM35	Flamethrower	Fire	95	100	15
TM06	Toxic	Poison	—	85	10	TM37	Sandstorm	Ground	—	—	10
TM10	Hidden Power	Normal	—	100	15	TM38	Fire Blast	Fire	120	85	5
TM11	Sunny Day	Fire	—	—	5	TM39	Rock Tomb	Rock	50	80	10
TM17	Protect	Normal	—	—	10	TM42	Facade	Normal	70	100	20
TM21	Frustration	Normal	—	100	20	TM43	Secret Power	Normal	70	100	20
TM26	Earthquake	Ground	100	100	10	TM44	Rest	Psychic	—	—	10
TM27	Return	Normal	—	100	20	TM45	Attract	Normal	—	100	15
TM28	Dig	Ground	60	100	10	HM04	Strength	Normal	80	100	20
TM31	Brick Break	Fighting	75	100	15	HM06	Rock Smash	Fighting	20	100	15
TM32	Double Team	Normal	—	—	15						

EGG MOVES*

Name	Type	Power	ACC	PP
Rock Slide	Rock	75	90	10
Block	Normal	—	100	5
Mega Punch	Normal	80	85	20

*Learned Via Breeding

MOVE TUTOR

FireRed/LeafGreen and Emerald Only

Body Slam*	Mega Punch*	Counter*
Double-Edge	Mimic	Seismic Toss*
Explosion	Substitute	Rock Slide*

Emerald Only

Defense Curl*	Metronome	Snore*
Dynamicpunch	Mud-Slap*	Swagger
Endure*	Rollout	
Fire Punch*	Sleep Talk	

*Battle Frontier tutor move (*Emerald*)

075 Graveler™

ROCK | GROUND

GENERAL INFO
SPECIES: Rock Pokémon
HEIGHT: 3'03"
WEIGHT: 232 lbs.
ABILITY 1: Rock Head
Protects Graveler from receiving recoil damage from Submission, Take Down, and Double-Edge.
ABILITY 2: Sturdy
Prevents Graveler from receiving a one hit KO.

STATS

EVOLUTIONS

LV25 | EVOLVE VIA TRADE

LOCATION[s]:

RUBY	Rarity: **Common**	Victory Road	
SAPPHIRE	Rarity: **Common**	Victory Road	
FIRERED	Rarity: **Rare**	Cerulean Cave	
LEAFGREEN	Rarity: **Rare**	Cerulean Cave	
COLOSSEUM	Rarity: **None**	Trade from *Ruby/Sapphire/FireRed/LeafGreen*	
EMERALD	Rarity: **Common**	Evolve Geodude, Magma Hideout, Victory Road	
XD	Rarity: **None**	Trade from *Ruby/Sapphire/FireRed/LeafGreen*	

MOVES

Level	Attack	Type	Power	ACC	PP
—	Tackle	Normal	35	95	35
—	Defense Curl	Normal	—	—	40
—/6	Mud Sport	Ground	—	100	15
—/11	Rock Throw	Rock	50	90	15
16	Magnitude	Ground	—	100	30

Level	Attack	Type	Power	ACC	PP
21	Selfdestruct	Normal	200	100	5
29	Rollout	Rock	30	90	20
37	Rock Blast	Rock	25	80	10
45	Earthquake	Ground	100	100	10
53	Explosion	Normal	250	100	5
62	Double-Edge	Normal	120	100	15

 # = Emerald Only

TM/HM

TM/HM#	Name	Type	Power	ACC	PP
TM01	Focus Punch	Fighting	150	100	20
TM06	Toxic	Poison	—	85	10
TM10	Hidden Power	Normal	—	100	15
TM11	Sunny Day	Fire	—	—	5
TM17	Protect	Normal	—	—	10
TM21	Frustration	Normal	—	100	20
TM26	Earthquake	Ground	100	100	10
TM27	Return	Normal	—	100	20
TM28	Dig	Ground	60	100	10
TM31	Brick Break	Fighting	75	100	15
TM32	Double Team	Normal	—	—	15

TM/HM#	Name	Type	Power	ACC	PP
TM35	Flamethrower	Fire	95	100	15
TM37	Sandstorm	Ground	—	—	10
TM38	Fire Blast	Fire	120	85	5
TM39	Rock Tomb	Rock	50	80	10
TM42	Facade	Normal	70	100	20
TM43	Secret Power	Normal	70	100	20
TM44	Rest	Psychic	—	—	10
TM45	Attract	Normal	—	100	15
HM04	Strength	Normal	80	100	20
HM06	Rock Smash	Fighting	20	100	15

MOVE TUTOR

FireRed/LeafGreen and Emerald Only

Body Slam*	Mega Punch*	Counter*
Double-Edge*	Mimic	Seismic Toss*
Explosion	Substitute	Rock Slide*

Emerald Only

Defense Curl*	Metronome	Snore*
Dynamicpunch	Mud-Slap*	Swagger
Endure*	Rollout	
Fire Punch*	Sleep Talk	

*Battle Frontier tutor move (Emerald)

076 Golem™

ROCK GROUND

GENERAL INFO

SPECIES: Megaton Pokémon
HEIGHT: 4'07"
WEIGHT: 662 lbs.
ABILITY 1: Rock Head
Protects Golem from receiving recoil damage from Submission, Take Down, and Double-Edge.
ABILITY 2: Sturdy
Prevents Golem from receiving a one hit KO.

STATS

EVOLUTIONS

LV25 | EVOLVE VIA TRADE

LOCATION[s]:

RUBY	Rarity: **Trade**	Evolve Graveler
SAPPHIRE	Rarity: **Trade**	Evolve Graveler
FIRERED	Rarity: **Evolve**	Evolve Graveler
LEAFGREEN	Rarity: **Evolve**	Evolve Graveler
COLOSSEUM	Rarity: **None**	Trade from Ruby/Sapphire/FireRed/LeafGreen
EMERALD	Rarity: **Evolve**	Evolve Graveler
XD	Rarity: **None**	Trade from Ruby/Sapphire/FireRed/LeafGreen

MOVES

Level	Attack	Type	Power	ACC	PP
—	Tackle	Normal	35	95	35
—	Defense Curl	Normal	—	—	40
—/6	Mud Sport	Ground	—	100	15
—/11	Rock Throw	Rock	50	90	15
16	Magnitude	Ground	—	100	30

Level	Attack	Type	Power	ACC	PP
21	Selfdestruct	Normal	200	100	5
29	Rollout	Rock	30	90	20
37	Rock Blast	Rock	25	80	10
45	Earthquake	Ground	100	100	10
53	Explosion	Normal	250	100	5
62	Double-Edge	Normal	120	100	15

= Emerald Only

TM/HM

TM/HM#	Name	Type	Power	ACC	PP
TM01	Focus Punch	Fighting	150	100	20
TM05	Roar	Normal	—	100	20
TM06	Toxic	Poison	—	85	10
TM10	Hidden Power	Normal	—	100	15
TM11	Sunny Day	Fire	—	—	5
TM15	Hyper Beam	Normal	150	90	5
TM17	Protect	Normal	—	—	10
TM21	Frustration	Normal	—	100	20
TM26	Earthquake	Ground	100	100	10
TM27	Return	Normal	—	100	20
TM28	Dig	Ground	60	100	10
TM31	Brick Break	Fighting	75	100	15

TM/HM#	Name	Type	Power	ACC	PP
TM32	Double Team	Normal	—	—	15
TM35	Flamethrower	Fire	95	100	15
TM37	Sandstorm	Ground	—	—	10
TM38	Fire Blast	Fire	120	85	5
TM39	Rock Tomb	Rock	50	80	10
TM42	Facade	Normal	70	100	20
TM43	Secret Power	Normal	70	100	20
TM44	Rest	Psychic	—	—	10
TM45	Attract	Normal	—	100	15
HM04	Strength	Normal	80	100	20
HM06	Rock Smash	Fighting	20	100	15

MOVE TUTOR

FireRed/LeafGreen and Emerald Only

Body Slam*	Mega Kick*	Seismic Toss*
Double-Edge	Mimic	Rock Slide*
Explosion	Substitute	
Mega Punch*	Counter*	

Emerald Only

Defense Curl*	Fury Cutter	Sleep Talk
Dynamicpunch	Metronome	Snore*
Endure*	Mud-Slap*	Swagger
Fire Punch*	Rollout	

*Battle Frontier tutor move (Emerald)

Pocket Pokédex

077 Ponyta™

FIRE

GENERAL INFO

SPECIES: Fire Horse Pokémon
HEIGHT: 3'03"
WEIGHT: 66 lbs.
ABILITY 1: Flash Fire
Raises Ponyta's Fire-type attacks; prevents Fire-type Attacks from damaging Ponyta.

ABILITY 2: Run Away
Allows Ponyta to escape from wild Pokémon.

STATS

EVOLUTIONS

LV40

LOCATION(s):

RUBY	Rarity: None	Trade from *FireRed/LeafGreen*
SAPPHIRE	Rarity: None	Trade from *FireRed/LeafGreen*
FIRERED	Rarity: Common	One Island
LEAFGREEN	Rarity: Common	One Island
COLOSSEUM	Rarity: None	Trade from *Ruby/Sapphire/FireRed/LeafGreen*
EMERALD	Rarity: None	Trade from *FireRed/LeafGreen*
XD	Rarity: None	Trade from *Ruby/Sapphire/FireRed/LeafGreen*

MOVES

Level	Attack	Type	Power	ACC	PP	Level	Attack	Type	Power	ACC	PP
—	Quick Attack	Normal	40	100	30	25	Fire Spin	Fire	15	70	15
5	Growl	Normal	—	100	40	31	Take Down	Normal	90	85	20
9	Tail Whip	Normal	—	100	30	38	Agility	Psychic	—	—	30
14	Ember	Fire	40	100	25	45	Bounce	Flying	85	85	5
19	Stomp	Normal	65	100	20	53	Fire Blast	Fire	120	85	5

TM/HM

TM/HM#	Name	Type	Power	ACC	PP	TM/HM#	Name	Type	Power	ACC	PP
TM06	Toxic	Poison	—	85	10	TM35	Flamethrower	Fire	95	100	15
TM10	Hidden Power	Normal	—	100	15	TM38	Fire Blast	Fire	120	85	5
TM11	Sunny Day	Fire	—	—	5	TM42	Facade	Normal	70	100	20
TM17	Protect	Normal	—	—	10	TM43	Secret Power	Normal	70	100	20
TM21	Frustration	Normal	—	100	20	TM44	Rest	Psychic	—	—	10
TM22	Solarbeam	Grass	120	100	10	TM45	Attract	Normal	—	100	15
TM23	Iron Tail	Steel	75	75	15	TM50	Overheat	Fire	140	90	5
TM27	Return	Normal	—	100	20	HM04	Strength	Normal	80	100	20
TM32	Double Team	Normal	—	—	15						

EGG MOVES*

Name	Type	Power	ACC	PP
Charm	Normal	—	100	20
Double Kick	Fighting	30	100	30
Double-Edge	Normal	120	100	15
Flame Wheel	Fire	60	100	25
Hypnosis	Psychic	—	60	20
Thrash	Normal	90	100	20

*Learned Via Breeding

MOVE TUTOR

FireRed/LeafGreen and Emerald Only

Body Slam*	Mimic	Substitute
Double-Edge		

*Battle Frontier tutor move (*Emerald*)

078 Rapidash™

FIRE

GENERAL INFO

SPECIES: Fire Horse Pokémon
HEIGHT: 5'07"
WEIGHT: 209 lbs.
ABILITY 1: Flash Fire
Raises Rapidash's Fire-type attacks; prevents Fire-type Attacks from damaging Rapidash.
ABILITY 2: Run Away
Allows Rapidash to escape from wild Pokémon.

STATS

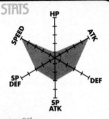

EVOLUTIONS

LV40

LOCATION[s]:

RUBY	Rarity: **None**	Trade Ponyta
SAPPHIRE	Rarity: **None**	Trade Ponyta
FIRERED	Rarity: **Rare**	Evolve Ponyta, One Island
LEAFGREEN	Rarity: **Rare**	Evolve Ponyta, One Island
COLOSSEUM	Rarity: **None**	Trade from *FireRed/LeafGreen*
EMERALD	Rarity: **None**	Trade from *FireRed/LeafGreen*
XD	Rarity: **Only One**	Citadark Island (Capture from Cipher Peon Kolest)

MOVES

Level	Attack	Type	Power	ACC	PP	Level	Attack	Type	Power	ACC	PP
—	Quick Attack	Normal	40	100	30	25	Fire Spin	Fire	15	70	15
—	Growl	Normal	—	100	40	31	Take Down	Normal	90	85	20
—	Tail Whip	Normal	—	100	30	38	Agility	Psychic	—	—	30
—	Ember	Fire	40	100	25	40	Fury Attack	Normal	15	85	20
19	Stomp	Normal	65	100	20	50	Bounce	Flying	85	85	5
						63	Fire Blast	Fire	120	85	5

TM/HM

TM/HM#	Name	Type	Power	ACC	PP	TM/HM#	Name	Type	Power	ACC	PP
TM06	Toxic	Poison	—	85	10	TM32	Double Team	Normal	—	—	15
TM10	Hidden Power	Normal	—	100	15	TM35	Flamethrower	Fire	95	100	15
TM11	Sunny Day	Fire	—	—	5	TM38	Fire Blast	Fire	120	85	5
TM15	Hyper Beam	Normal	150	90	5	TM42	Facade	Normal	70	100	20
TM17	Protect	Normal	—	—	10	TM43	Secret Power	Normal	70	100	20
TM21	Frustration	Normal	—	100	20	TM44	Rest	Psychic	—	—	10
TM22	Solarbeam	Grass	120	100	10	TM45	Attract	Normal	—	100	15
TM23	Iron Tail	Steel	75	75	15	TM50	Overheat	Fire	140	90	5
TM27	Return	Normal	—	100	20	HM04	Strength	Normal	80	100	20

MOVE TUTOR

FireRed/LeafGreen and Emerald Only

Body Slam*	Mimic	Substitute
Double-Edge		

*Battle Frontier tutor move (*Emerald*)

079 Slowpoke™

WATER | PSYCHIC

GENERAL INFO

SPECIES: Dopey Pokémon
HEIGHT: 3'11"
WEIGHT: 79 lbs.
ABILITY 1: Oblivious
Prevents Slowpoke from being attracted.
ABILITY 2: Own Tempo
Prevents Slowpoke from being confused.

STATS

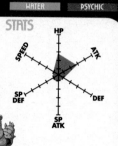

EVOLUTIONS

LV37

KING'S ROCK

LOCATION[s]:

RUBY	Rarity: **None**	Trade from *LeafGreen*
SAPPHIRE	Rarity: **None**	Trade from *LeafGreen*
FIRERED	Rarity: **None**	Trade from LeafGreen
LEAFGREEN	Rarity: **Common**	Islands One, Two, Three, Four, Five, Six, Seven, Routes 4, 10, 11, 12, 13, 14, 19, 20, 21, 24, 25, Fuchsia City, Vermilion City, Viridian City, Safari Zone
COLOSSEUM	Rarity: **None**	Trade from *LeafGreen*
EMERALD	Rarity: **None**	Trade from *LeafGreen*
XD	Rarity: **None**	Trade from *LeafGreen*

MOVES

Level	Attack	Type	Power	ACC	PP	Level	Attack	Type	Power	ACC	PP
—	Curse	—	—	—	10	17	Confusion	Psychic	50	100	25
—	Tackle	Normal	35	95	35	24	Disable	Normal	—	55	20
—	Yawn	Normal	—	100	10	29	Headbutt	Normal	70	100	15
6	Growl	Normal	—	100	40	36	Amnesia	Psychic	—	—	20
13	Water Gun	Water	40	100	25	40	Psychic	Psychic	90	100	10
						47	Psych Up	Normal	—	—	10

TM/HM

TM/HM#	Name	Type	Power	ACC	PP	TM/HM#	Name	Type	Power	ACC	PP
TM03	Water Pulse	Water	60	95	20	TM28	Dig	Ground	60	100	10
TM04	Calm Mind	Psychic	—	—	20	TM29	Psychic	Psychic	90	100	10
TM06	Toxic	Poison	—	85	10	TM30	Shadow Ball	Ghost	80	100	15
TM07	Hail	Ice	—	—	10	TM32	Double Team	Normal	—	—	15
TM10	Hidden Power	Normal	—	100	15	TM35	Flamethrower	Fire	95	100	15
TM11	Sunny Day	Fire	—	—	5	TM38	Fire Blast	Fire	120	85	5
TM13	Ice Beam	Ice	95	100	10	TM42	Facade	Normal	70	100	20
TM14	Blizzard	Ice	120	70	5	TM43	Secret Power	Normal	70	100	20
TM17	Protect	Normal	—	—	10	TM44	Rest	Psychic	—	—	10
TM18	Rain Dance	Water	—	—	5	TM45	Attract	Normal	—	100	15
TM20	Safeguard	Normal	—	—	25	TM48	Skill Swap	Psychic	—	100	10
TM21	Frustration	Normal	—	100	20	HM03	Surf	Water	95	100	15
TM23	Iron Tail	Steel	75	75	15	HM04	Strength	Normal	80	100	20
TM26	Earthquake	Ground	100	100	10	HM05	Flash	Normal	—	70	20
TM27	Return	Normal	—	100	20	HM08	Dive	Water	60	100	10

EGG MOVES*

Name	Type	Power	ACC	PP
Belly Drum	Normal	—	—	10
Future Sight	Psychic	80	90	15
Mud Sport	Ground	—	100	15
Safeguard	Normal	—	—	25
Sleep Talk	Normal	—	—	10
Snore	Normal	40	100	15
Stomp	Normal	65	100	20

*Learned Via Breeding

MOVE TUTOR

FireRed/LeafGreen and Emerald Only

Body Slam*	Mimic	Dream Eater*
Double-Edge	Substitute	Thunder Wave*

*Battle Frontier tutor move (*Emerald*)

080 Slowbro™

GENERAL INFO

SPECIES: Hermit Crab Pokémon
HEIGHT: 5'03"
WEIGHT: 173 lbs.
ABILITY 1: Oblivious
Prevents Slowbro from being attracted.
ABILITY 2: Own Tempo
Prevents Slowbro from being confused.

STATS

EVOLUTIONS

LV37

LOCATION(S):

RUBY	Rarity: **None**	Trade from *LeafGreen*
SAPPHIRE	Rarity: **None**	Trade from *LeafGreen*
FIRERED	Rarity: **None**	Trade from *LeafGreen*
LEAFGREEN	Rarity: **Rare**	Two Island, Three Island, Seafoam Islands
COLOSSEUM	Rarity: **None**	Trade from *LeafGreen*
EMERALD	Rarity: **None**	Trade from *LeafGreen*
XD	Rarity: **None**	Trade from *LeafGreen*

MOVES

Level	Attack	Type	Power	ACC	PP
—	Curse	—	—	—	10
—	Tackle	Normal	35	95	35
—	Yawn	Normal	—	100	10
—	Growl	Normal	—	100	40
13	Water Gun	Water	40	100	25
17	Confusion	Psychic	50	100	25
24	Disable	Normal	—	55	20
29	Headbutt	Normal	70	100	15
36	Amnesia	Psychic	—	—	20
37	Withdraw	Normal	—	—	40
44	Psychic	Psychic	90	100	10
55	Psych Up	Normal	—	—	10

TM/HM

TM/HM#	Name	Type	Power	ACC	PP
TM01	Focus Punch	Fighting	150	100	20
TM03	Water Pulse	Water	60	95	20
TM04	Calm Mind	Psychic	—	—	20
TM06	Toxic	Poison	—	85	10
TM07	Hail	Ice	—	—	10
TM10	Hidden Power	Normal	—	100	15
TM11	Sunny Day	Fire	—	—	5
TM13	Ice Beam	Ice	95	100	10
TM14	Blizzard	Ice	120	70	5
TM15	Hyper Beam	Normal	150	90	5
TM17	Protect	Normal	—	—	10
TM18	Rain Dance	Water	—	—	5
TM20	Safeguard	Normal	—	—	25
TM21	Frustration	Normal	—	100	20
TM23	Iron Tail	Steel	75	75	15
TM26	Earthquake	Ground	100	100	10
TM27	Return	Normal	—	100	20
TM28	Dig	Ground	60	100	10
TM29	Psychic	Psychic	90	100	10
TM30	Shadow Ball	Ghost	80	100	15
TM31	Brick Break	Fighting	75	100	15
TM32	Double Team	Normal	—	—	15
TM35	Flamethrower	Fire	95	100	15
TM38	Fire Blast	Fire	120	85	5
TM42	Facade	Normal	70	100	20
TM43	Secret Power	Normal	70	100	20
TM44	Rest	Psychic	—	—	10
TM45	Attract	Normal	—	100	15
TM48	Skill Swap	Psychic	—	100	10
HM03	Surf	Water	95	100	15
HM04	Strength	Normal	80	100	20
HM05	Flash	Normal	—	70	20
HM06	Rock Smash	Fighting	20	100	15
HM08	Dive	Water	60	100	10

MOVE TUTOR

FireRed/LeafGreen and Emerald Only

Body Slam*	Mimic	Dream Eater*
Double-Edge	Substitute	Thunder Wave*
Mega Punch*	Counter*	
Mega Kick*	Seismic Toss*	

*Battle Frontier tutor move (*Emerald*)

PRIMA OFFICIAL GAME GUIDE

081 Magnemite™

ELECTRIC | STEEL

GENERAL INFO
SPECIES: Magnet Pokémon
HEIGHT: 1'00"
WEIGHT: 13 lbs.
ABILITY 1: Magnet Pull
Other Steel-types cannot escape while Magnemite is in battle.
ABILITY 2: Sturdy
A one hit KO cannot hit Magnemite.

STATS

EVOLUTIONS

LV30

LOCATION(s):

RUBY	Rarity: **Common**	New Mauville
SAPPHIRE	Rarity: **Common**	New Mauville
FIRERED	Rarity: **Common**	Power Plant
LEAFGREEN	Rarity: **Common**	Power Plant
COLOSSEUM	Rarity: **None**	Trade from *Ruby/Sapphire/FireRed/LeafGreen*
EMERALD	Rarity: **Common**	New Mauville
XD	Rarity: **None**	Trade from *Ruby/Sapphire/FireRed/LeafGreen*

MOVES

Level	Attack	Type	Power	ACC	PP
—	Metal Sound	Steel	—	85	40
—	Tackle	Normal	35	95	35
6	Thundershock	Electric	40	100	30
11	Supersonic	Normal	—	55	20
16	Sonicboom	Normal	—	90	20

Level	Attack	Type	Power	ACC	PP
21	Thunder Wave	Electric	—	100	20
26	Spark	Electric	65	100	20
32	Lock-on	Normal	—	100	5
38	Swift	Normal	60	—	20
44	Screech	Normal	—	85	40
50	Zap Cannon	Electric	100	50	5

TM/HM

TM/HM#	Name	Type	Power	ACC	PP
TM06	Toxic	Poison	—	85	10
TM10	Hidden Power	Normal	—	100	15
TM11	Sunny Day	Fire	—	—	5
TM17	Protect	Normal	—	—	10
TM18	Rain Dance	Water	—	—	5
TM21	Frustration	Normal	—	100	20
TM24	Thunderbolt	Electric	95	100	15
TM25	Thunder	Electric	120	70	10

TM/HM#	Name	Type	Power	ACC	PP
TM27	Return	Normal	—	100	20
TM32	Double Team	Normal	—	—	15
TM33	Reflect	Normal	—	—	20
TM34	Shock Wave	Electric	60	—	20
TM42	Facade	Normal	70	100	20
TM43	Secret Power	Normal	70	100	20
TM44	Rest	Psychic	—	—	10
HM05	Flash	Normal	—	70	20

EGG MOVES*

Name	Type	Power	ACC	PP
None				

*Learned Via Breeding

MOVE TUTOR
FireRed/LeafGreen and Emerald Only

Double-Edge	Substitute	Thunder Wave*
Mimic		

Emerald Only

Endure*	Sleep Talk	Swagger
Rollout	Snore*	Swift*

*Battle Frontier tutor move (*Emerald*)

082 Magneton ™

ELECTRIC **STEEL**

GENERAL INFO

SPECIES: Magnet Pokémon
HEIGHT: 3'03"
WEIGHT: 132 lbs.
ABILITY 1: Magnet Pull
Other Steel-types cannot escape while Magneton is in battle.
ABILITY 2: Sturdy
A one hit KO cannot hit Magneton.

STATS

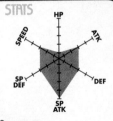

EVOLUTIONS

LV30

LOCATION(S):

RUBY	Rarity: **Rare**	Evolve from Magnemite, New Mauville
SAPPHIRE	Rarity: **Rare**	Evolve from Magnemite, New Mauville
FIRERED	Rarity: **Common**	Evolve from Magnemite, Power Plant, Cerulean Cave
LEAFGREEN	Rarity: **Common**	Evolve from Magnemite, Power Plant, Cerulean Cave
COLOSSEUM	Rarity: **None**	Trade from *Ruby/Sapphire/FireRed/LeafGreen*
EMERALD	Rarity: **Rare**	Evolve from Magnemite, New Mauville
XD	Rarity: **Only One**	Cipher Key Lair (Capture from Snidle)

MOVES

Level	Attack	Type	Power	ACC	PP		Level	Attack	Type	Power	ACC	PP
—	Metal Sound	Steel	—	85	40		26	Spark	Electric	65	100	20
—	Tackle	Normal	35	95	35		35	Lock-on	Normal	—	100	5
—/6	Thundershock	Electric	40	100	30		44	Tri Attack	Normal	80	100	10
—/11	Supersonic	Normal	—	55	20		53	Screech	Normal	—	85	40
16	Sonicboom	Normal	—	90	20		62	Zap Cannon	Electric	100	50	5
21	Thunder Wave	Electric	—	100	20		# = Emerald Only					

TM/HM

TM/HM#	Name	Type	Power	ACC	PP		TM/HM#	Name	Type	Power	ACC	PP
TM06	Toxic	Poison	—	85	10		TM27	Return	Normal	—	100	20
TM10	Hidden Power	Normal	—	100	15		TM32	Double Team	Normal	—	—	15
TM11	Sunny Day	Fire	—	—	5		TM33	Reflect	Normal	—	—	20
TM15	Hyper Beam	Normal	150	90	5		TM34	Shock Wave	Electric	60	—	20
TM17	Protect	Normal	—	—	10		TM42	Facade	Normal	70	100	20
TM18	Rain Dance	Water	—	—	5		TM43	Secret Power	Normal	70	100	20
TM21	Frustration	Normal	—	100	20		TM44	Rest	Psychic	—	—	10
TM24	Thunderbolt	Electric	95	100	15		HM05	Flash	Normal	—	70	20
TM25	Thunder	Electric	120	70	10							

EGG MOVES*

Name	Type	Power	ACC	PP
None				

*Learned Via Breeding

MOVE TUTOR

FireRed/LeafGreen and Emerald Only

Double-Edge	Substitute	Thunder Wave*
Mimic		

Emerald Only

Endure*	Sleep Talk	Swagger
Rollout	Snore*	Swift*

*Battle Frontier tutor move (Emerald)

PRIMA OFFICIAL GAME GUIDE

083 Farfetch'd™

GENERAL INFO
SPECIES: Wild Duck Pokémon
HEIGHT: 2'07"
WEIGHT: 33 lbs.
ABILITY 1: Keen Eye
Prevents Farfetch'd from having its accuracy lowered.
ABILITY 2: Inner Focus
Prevents Farfetch'd from flinching.

STATS

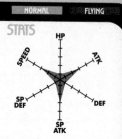

EVOLUTIONS

DOES NOT EVOLVE

LOCATION[s]:

RUBY	Rarity: **None**	Trade from *FireRed/LeafGreen*
SAPPHIRE	Rarity: **None**	Trade from *FireRed/LeafGreen*
FIRERED	Rarity: **Only One**	Trade for Spearow in Vermilion City
LEAFGREEN	Rarity: **Only One**	Trade for Spearow in Vermilion City
COLOSSEUM	Rarity: **None**	Trade from *Ruby/Sapphire/FireRed/LeafGreen*
EMERALD	Rarity: **None**	Trade from *FireRed/LeafGreen*
XD	Rarity: **Only One**	Citadark Island (Capture from Cipher Admin Lovrina)

MOVES

Level	Attack	Type	Power	ACC	PP	Level	Attack	Type	Power	ACC	PP
—	Peck	Flying	35	100	35	26	Fury Cutter	Bug	10	95	20
6	Sand-Attack	Ground	—	100	15	31	Swords Dance	Normal	—	—	30
11	Leer	Normal	—	100	30	36	Agility	Psychic	—	—	30
16	Fury Attack	Normal	15	85	20	41	Slash	Normal	70	100	20
21	Knock Off	Dark	20	100	20	46	False Swipe	Normal	40	100	40

TM/HM

TM/HM#	Name	Type	Power	ACC	PP	TM/HM#	Name	Type	Power	ACC	PP
TM06	Toxic	Poison	—	85	10	TM42	Facade	Normal	70	100	20
TM10	Hidden Power	Normal	—	100	15	TM43	Secret Power	Normal	70	100	20
TM11	Sunny Day	Fire	—	—	5	TM44	Rest	Psychic	—	—	10
TM17	Protect	Normal	—	—	10	TM45	Attract	Normal	—	100	15
TM21	Frustration	Normal	—	100	20	TM46	Thief	Dark	40	100	10
TM23	Iron Tail	Steel	75	75	15	TM47	Steel Wing	Steel	70	90	25
TM27	Return	Normal	—	100	20	HM01	Cut	Normal	50	95	30
TM32	Double Team	Normal	—	—	15	HM02	Fly	Flying	70	95	15
TM40	Aerial Ace	Flying	60	—	20						

EGG MOVES*

Name	Type	Power	ACC	PP
Curse	—	—	—	10
Featherdance	Flying	—	100	15
Flail	Normal	—	100	15
Foresight	Normal	—	—	40
Mirror Move	Flying	—	—	20
Quick Attack	Normal	40	100	30
Steel Wing	Steel	70	90	25
Whirlwind	Normal	—	100	20

*Learned Via Breeding

MOVE TUTOR
FireRed/LeafGreen and Emerald Only

Body Slam*	Mimic	Substitute
Double-Edge	Swords Dance*	

*Battle Frontier tutor move (*Emerald*)

084 Doduo™

NORMAL   FLYING

GENERAL INFO

SPECIES: Twin Bird Pokémon
HEIGHT: 4'07"
WEIGHT: 86 lbs.
ABILITY 1: Run Away
Allows Doduo to escape from wild Pokémon.
ABILITY 2: Early Bird
Allows Doduo to wake up earlier when put to sleep.

STATS

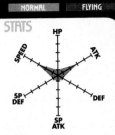

HP, ATK, DEF, SP ATK, SP DEF, SPEED

EVOLUTIONS

LV31

LOCATION[s]:

RUBY	Rarity: **Common**	Safari Zone
SAPPHIRE	Rarity: **Common**	Safari Zone
FIRERED	Rarity: **Common**	Route 16, Route 17, Route 18, Safari Zone
LEAFGREEN	Rarity: **Common**	Route 16, Route 17, Route 18, Safari Zone
COLOSSEUM	Rarity: **None**	Trade from *Ruby/Sapphire/FireRed/LeafGreen*
EMERALD	Rarity: **Common**	Safari Zone
XD	Rarity: **None**	Trade from *Ruby/Sapphire/FireRed/LeafGreen*

MOVES

Level	Attack	Type	Power	ACC	PP
—	Peck	Flying	35	100	35
—	Growl	Normal	—	100	40
9	Pursuit	Dark	40	100	20
13	Fury Attack	Normal	15	85	20
21	Tri Attack	Normal	80	100	10
25	Rage	Normal	20	100	20
33	Uproar	Normal	50	100	10
37	Drill Peck	Flying	80	100	20
45	Agility	Psychic	—	—	30

TM/HM

TM/HM#	Name	Type	Power	ACC	PP
TM06	Toxic	Poison	—	85	10
TM10	Hidden Power	Normal	—	100	15
TM11	Sunny Day	Fire	—	—	5
TM17	Protect	Normal	—	—	10
TM21	Frustration	Normal	—	100	20
TM27	Return	Normal	—	100	20
TM32	Double Team	Normal	—	—	15
TM40	Aerial Ace	Flying	60	—	20
TM42	Facade	Normal	70	100	20
TM43	Secret Power	Normal	70	100	20
TM44	Rest	Psychic	—	—	10
TM45	Attract	Normal	—	100	15
TM46	Thief	Dark	40	100	10
TM47	Steel Wing	Steel	70	90	25
HM02	Fly	Flying	70	95	15

EGG MOVES*

Name	Type	Power	ACC	PP
Quick Attack	Normal	40	100	30
Supersonic	Normal	—	55	20
Haze	Ice	—	—	30
Endeavor	Normal	—	100	5
Faint Attack	Dark	60	—	20
Flail	Normal	—	100	15

*Learned Via Breeding

MOVE TUTOR

FireRed/LeafGreen and Emerald Only

Body Slam*	Mimic	Substitute
Double-Edge		

Emerald Only

Endure*	Sleep Talk	Swagger
Mud-Slap*	Snore*	Swift*

*Battle Frontier tutor move (*Emerald*)

085 Dodrio™

NORMAL   FLYING

GENERAL INFO

SPECIES: Triple Bird Pokémon
HEIGHT: 5'11"
WEIGHT: 188 lbs.
ABILITY 1: Run Away
Allows Dodrio to escape from wild Pokémon.
ABILITY 2: Early Bird
Allows Dodrio to wake up earlier when put to sleep.

STATS

(radar chart: HP, ATK, DEF, SP ATK, SP DEF, SPEED)

EVOLUTIONS

LV31

LOCATION(s):

RUBY	Rarity: **Rare**	Evolve Doduo, Safari Zone
SAPPHIRE	Rarity: **Rare**	Evolve Doduo, Safari Zone
FIRERED	Rarity: **Evolve**	Evolve Doduo
LEAFGREEN	Rarity: **Evolve**	Evolve Doduo
COLOSSEUM	Rarity: **None**	Trade from Ruby/Sapphire/FireRed/LeafGreen
EMERALD	Rarity: **Rare**	Evolve Doduo, Safari Zone
XD	Rarity: **Only One**	Citadark Island (Capture from Cipher Peon Furgy)

MOVES

Level	Attack	Type	Power	ACC	PP
—	Peck	Flying	35	100	35
—	Growl	Normal	—	100	40
—	Pursuit	Dark	40	100	20
—	Fury Attack	Normal	15	85	20
21	Tri Attack	Normal	80	100	10

Level	Attack	Type	Power	ACC	PP
25	Rage	Normal	20	100	20
38	Uproar	Normal	50	100	10
47	Drill Peck	Flying	80	100	20
50/60	Agility	Psychic	—	—	30

= *Emerald* Only

TM/HM

TM/HM#	Name	Type	Power	ACC	PP
TM06	Toxic	Poison	—	85	10
TM10	Hidden Power	Normal	—	100	15
TM11	Sunny Day	Fire	—	—	5
TM12	Taunt	Dark	—	100	20
TM15	Hyper Beam	Normal	150	90	5
TM17	Protect	Normal	—	—	10
TM21	Frustration	Normal	—	100	20
TM27	Return	Normal	—	100	20
TM32	Double Team	Normal	—	—	15

TM/HM#	Name	Type	Power	ACC	PP
TM40	Aerial Ace	Flying	60	—	20
TM41	Torment	Dark	—	100	15
TM42	Facade	Normal	70	100	20
TM43	Secret Power	Normal	70	100	20
TM44	Rest	Psychic	—	—	10
TM45	Attract	Normal	—	100	15
TM46	Thief	Dark	40	100	10
TM47	Steel Wing	Steel	70	90	25
HM02	Fly	Flying	70	95	15

MOVE TUTOR

FireRed/LeafGreen and Emerald Only

Body Slam*	Mimic	Substitute
Double-Edge		

Emerald Only

Endure*	Sleep Talk	Swagger
Mud-Slap*	Snore*	Swift*

*Battle Frontier tutor move (*Emerald*)

086 Seel™

WATER

GENERAL INFO

SPECIES: Sea Lion Pokémon
HEIGHT: 3'07"
WEIGHT: 198 lbs.
ABILITY: Thick Fat

Effects of an opponent's Ice- and Fire-type moves used on Seel are halved.

STATS

HP · ATK · DEF · SP ATK · SP DEF · SPEED

EVOLUTIONS

 ▶

LV34

LOCATION[s]:

RUBY	Rarity: **None**	Trade from *FireRed/LeafGreen*
SAPPHIRE	Rarity: **None**	Trade from *FireRed/LeafGreen*
FIRERED	Rarity: **Common**	Seafoam Islands
LEAFGREEN	Rarity: **Common**	Seafoam Islands
COLOSSEUM	Rarity: **None**	Trade from *FireRed/LeafGreen*
EMERALD	Rarity: **None**	Trade from *FireRed/LeafGreen*
XD	Rarity: **Only One**	Phenac City (Capture from Cipher Peon Egrog)

MOVES

Level	Attack	Type	Power	ACC	PP	Level	Attack	Type	Power	ACC	PP
—	Headbutt	Normal	70	100	15	29	Rest	Psychic	—	—	10
9	Growl	Normal	—	100	40	37	Take Down	Normal	90	85	20
17	Icy Wind	Ice	55	95	15	41	Ice Beam	Ice	—	95	100	10
21	Aurora Beam	Ice	65	100	20	49	Safeguard	Normal	—	—	25

TM/HM

TM/HM#	Name	Type	Power	ACC	PP	TM/HM#	Name	Type	Power	ACC	PP
TM03	Water Pulse	Water	60	95	20	TM27	Return	Normal	—	100	20
TM06	Toxic	Poison	—	85	10	TM32	Double Team	Normal	—	—	15
TM07	Hail	Ice	—	—	10	TM42	Facade	Normal	70	100	20
TM10	Hidden Power	Normal	—	100	15	TM43	Secret Power	Normal	70	100	20
TM13	Ice Beam	Ice	95	100	10	TM44	Rest	Psychic	—	—	10
TM14	Blizzard	Ice	120	70	5	TM45	Attract	Normal	—	100	15
TM17	Protect	Normal	—	—	10	TM46	Thief	Dark	40	100	10
TM18	Rain Dance	Water	—	—	5	HM03	Surf	Water	95	100	15
TM20	Safeguard	Normal	—	—	25	HM07	Waterfall	Water	80	100	15
TM21	Frustration	Normal	—	100	20	HM08	Dive	Water	60	100	10

EGG MOVES*

Name	Type	Power	ACC	PP
Disable	Normal	—	55	20
Encore	Normal	—	100	5
Fake Out	Normal	40	100	10
Horn Drill	Normal	—	30	5
Icicle Spear	Ice	10	100	30
Lick	Ghost	20	100	30
Perish Song	Normal	—	—	5
Slam	Normal	80	75	20

*Learned Via Breeding

MOVE TUTOR

FireRed/LeafGreen and Emerald Only

Body Slam*	Mimic	Substitute
Double-Edge		

*Battle Frontier tutor move (*Emerald*)

PRIMA OFFICIAL GAME GUIDE

087 Dewgong™

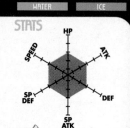

WATER | ICE

GENERAL INFO
SPECIES: Sea Lion Pokémon
HEIGHT: 5'07"
WEIGHT: 265 lbs.
ABILITY: Thick Fat

Effects of an opponent's Ice- and Fire-type moves used on Dewgong are halved.

STATS

EVOLUTIONS

LV34

LOCATION(s):

RUBY	Rarity: **None**	Trade from *FireRed/LeafGreen*
SAPPHIRE	Rarity: **None**	Trade from *FireRed/LeafGreen*
FIRERED	Rarity: **Rare**	Evolve Seel, Seafoam Islands
LEAFGREEN	Rarity: **Rare**	Evolve Seel, Seafoam Islands
COLOSSEUM	Rarity: **None**	Trade from *FireRed/LeafGreen*
EMERALD	Rarity: **None**	Trade from *FireRed/LeafGreen*
XD	Rarity: **Evolve**	Evolve Seel

MOVES

Level	Attack	Type	Power	ACC	PP	Level	Attack	Type	Power	ACC	PP
—	Signal Beam	Bug	75	100	15	29	Rest	Psychic	—	—	10
—	Headbutt	Normal	70	100	15	34	Sheer Cold	Ice	—	30	5
—	Growl	Normal	—	100	40	42	Take Down	Normal	90	85	20
—	Icy Wind	Ice	55	95	15	51	Ice Beam	Ice	95	100	10
—	Aurora Beam	Ice	65	100	20	64	Safeguard	Normal	—	—	25

TM/HM

TM/HM#	Name	Type	Power	ACC	PP	TM/HM#	Name	Type	Power	ACC	PP
TM03	Water Pulse	Water	60	95	20	TM27	Return	Normal	—	100	20
TM06	Toxic	Poison	—	85	10	TM32	Double Team	Normal	—	—	15
TM07	Hail	Ice	—	—	10	TM42	Facade	Normal	70	100	20
TM10	Hidden Power	Normal	—	100	15	TM43	Secret Power	Normal	70	100	20
TM13	Ice Beam	Ice	95	100	10	TM44	Rest	Psychic	—	—	10
TM14	Blizzard	Ice	120	70	5	TM45	Attract	Normal	—	100	15
TM15	Hyper Beam	Normal	150	90	5	TM46	Thief	Dark	40	100	10
TM17	Protect	Normal	—	—	10	HM03	Surf	Water	95	100	15
TM18	Rain Dance	Water	—	—	5	HM07	Waterfall	Water	80	100	15
TM20	Safeguard	Normal	—	—	25	HM08	Dive	Water	60	100	10
TM21	Frustration	Normal	—	100	20						

MOVE TUTOR
FireRed/LeafGreen and Emerald Only

Body Slam*	Mimic	Substitute
Double-Edge		

*Battle Frontier tutor move (*Emerald*)

088 Grimer™

POISON

GENERAL INFO

SPECIES: Sludge Pokémon
HEIGHT: 2'11"
WEIGHT: 66 lbs.
ABILITY 1: Stench
When Grimer is in the first slot, the chances of running into a wild Pokémon decrease.

ABILITY 2: Sticky Hold
Prevents an opponent from stealing a Held Item Grimer may have.

STATS

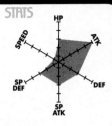

EVOLUTIONS

LV38

LOCATION(s):

RUBY	Rarity: **Rare**	Fiery Path
SAPPHIRE	Rarity: **Rare**	Fiery Path
FIRERED	Rarity: **Common**	Pokémon Mansion
LEAFGREEN	Rarity: **Common**	Pokémon Mansion
COLOSSEUM	Rarity: **None**	Trade from Ruby/Sapphire/FireRed/LeafGreen
EMERALD	Rarity: **Rare**	Fiery Path
XD	Rarity: **Only One**	Phenac City (Capture from Cipher Peon Faltly)

MOVES

Level	Attack	Type	Power	ACC	PP	Level	Attack	Type	Power	ACC	PP
—	Poison Gas	Poison	—	55	40	19	Minimize	Normal	—	—	20
—	Pound	Normal	40	100	35	26	Screech	Normal	—	85	40
4	Harden	Normal	—	—	30	34	Acid Armor	Poison	—	—	40
8	Disable	Normal	—	55	20	43	Sludge Bomb	Poison	90	100	10
13	Sludge	Poison	65	100	20	53	Memento	Dark	—	100	10

TM/HM

TM/HM#	Name	Type	Power	ACC	PP	TM/HM#	Name	Type	Power	ACC	PP
TM06	Toxic	Poison	—	85	10	TM32	Double Team	Normal	—	—	15
TM10	Hidden Power	Normal	—	100	15	TM34	Shock Wave	Electric	60	—	20
TM11	Sunny Day	Fire	—	—	5	TM35	Flamethrower	Fire	95	100	15
TM12	Taunt	Dark	—	100	20	TM36	Sludge Bomb	Poison	90	100	10
TM17	Protect	Normal	—	—	10	TM38	Fire Blast	Fire	120	85	5
TM18	Rain Dance	Water	—	—	5	TM39	Rock Tomb	Rock	50	80	10
TM19	Giga Drain	Grass	60	100	5	TM41	Torment	Dark	—	100	15
TM21	Frustration	Normal	—	100	20	TM42	Facade	Normal	70	100	20
TM24	Thunderbolt	Electric	95	100	15	TM43	Secret Power	Normal	70	100	20
TM25	Thunder	Electric	120	70	10	TM44	Rest	Psychic	—	—	10
TM27	Return	Normal	—	100	20	TM45	Attract	Normal	—	100	15
TM28	Dig	Ground	60	100	10	TM46	Thief	Dark	40	100	10

EGG MOVES*

Name	Type	Power	ACC	PP
Haze	Ice	—	—	30
Mean Look	Normal	—	100	5
Imprison	Psychic	—	100	15
Curse	—	—	—	10
Shadow Punch	Ghost	60	—	20
Explosion	Normal	250	100	5
Lick	Ghost	20	100	30

*Learned Via Breeding

MOVE TUTOR

FireRed/LeafGreen and Emerald Only

Body Slam*	Substitute	Explosion
Mimic		

Emerald Only

Dynamic Punch	Ice Punch*	Snore*
Endure*	Mud-Slap*	Swagger
Fire Punch*	Sleep Talk	Thunderpunch*

*Battle Frontier tutor move (*Emerald*)

089 Muk™

POISON

GENERAL INFO

SPECIES: Sludge Pokémon
HEIGHT: 3'11"
WEIGHT: 66 lbs.
ABILITY 1: Stench
When Muk is in the first slot, the chances of running into a wild Pokémon decrease.
ABILITY 2: Sticky Hold
Prevents an opponent from stealing a Held Item Muk may have.

STATS

EVOLUTIONS

LV38

LOCATION(S):

RUBY	Rarity: **Evolve**	Evolve Grimer
SAPPHIRE	Rarity: **Evolve**	Evolve Grimer
FIRERED	Rarity: **Evolve**	Evolve Grimer
LEAFGREEN	Rarity: **Rare**	Evolve Grimer, Pokémon Mansion
COLOSSEUM	Rarity: **None**	Trade from *Ruby/Sapphire/FireRed/LeafGreen*
EMERALD	Rarity: **Evolve**	Evolve Grimer
XD	Rarity: **Evolve**	Evolve Grimer

MOVES

Level	Attack	Type	Power	ACC	PP	Level	Attack	Type	Power	ACC	PP
—	Poison Gas	Poison	—	55	40	19	Minimize	Normal	—	—	20
—	Pound	Normal	40	100	35	26	Screech	Normal	—	85	40
—	Harden	Normal	—	—	30	34	Acid Armor	Poison	—	—	40
8	Disable	Normal	—	55	20	47	Sludge Bomb	Poison	90	100	10
13	Sludge	Poison	65	100	20	61	Memento	Dark	—	100	10

TM/HM

TM/HM#	Name	Type	Power	ACC	PP	TM/HM#	Name	Type	Power	ACC	PP
TM01	Focus Punch	Fighting	150	100	20	TM32	Double Team	Normal	—	—	15
TM06	Toxic	Poison	—	85	10	TM34	Shock Wave	Electric	60	—	20
TM10	Hidden Power	Normal	—	100	15	TM35	Flamethrower	Fire	95	100	15
TM11	Sunny Day	Fire	—	—	5	TM36	Sludge Bomb	Poison	90	100	10
TM12	Taunt	Dark	—	100	20	TM38	Fire Blast	Fire	120	85	5
TM15	Hyper Beam	Normal	150	90	5	TM39	Rock Tomb	Rock	50	80	10
TM17	Protect	Normal	—	—	10	TM41	Torment	Dark	—	100	15
TM18	Rain Dance	Water	—	—	5	TM42	Facade	Normal	70	100	20
TM19	Giga Drain	Grass	60	100	5	TM43	Secret Power	Normal	70	100	20
TM21	Frustration	Normal	—	100	20	TM44	Rest	Psychic	—	—	10
TM24	Thunderbolt	Electric	95	100	15	TM45	Attract	Normal	—	100	15
TM25	Thunder	Electric	120	70	10	TM46	Thief	Dark	40	100	10
TM27	Return	Normal	—	100	20	HM04	Strength	Normal	80	100	20
TM28	Dig	Ground	60	100	10	HM06	Rock Smash	Fighting	20	100	15
TM31	Brick Break	Fighting	75	100	15						

MOVE TUTOR

FireRed/LeafGreen and Emerald Only

Body Slam*	Substitute	Explosion
Mimic		

Emerald Only

Dynamic Punch	Ice Punch*	Snore*
Endure*	Mud-Slap*	Swagger
Fire Punch*	Sleep Talk	Thunderpunch*

*Battle Frontier tutor move (*Emerald*)

090 Shellder™

WATER

GENERAL INFO

SPECIES: Bivalve Pokémon
HEIGHT: 1'00"
WEIGHT: 9 lbs.
ABILITY: Shell Armor

Protects Shellder from being struck by critical hits.

STATS

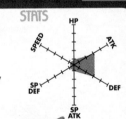

EVOLUTIONS

WATER STONE

LOCATION(s):

RUBY	Rarity: **None**	Trade from *FireRed*
SAPPHIRE	Rarity: **None**	Trade from *FireRed*
FIRERED	Rarity: **Common**	One Island, Five Island, Vermilion City
LEAFGREEN	Rarity: **None**	Trade from *FireRed*
COLOSSEUM	Rarity: **None**	Trade from *FireRed*
EMERALD	Rarity: **None**	Trade from *FireRed*
XD	Rarity: **Only One**	Cipher Key Lair (Capture from Cipher Peon Gorog)

MOVES

Level	Attack	Type	Power	ACC	PP	Level	Attack	Type	Power	ACC	PP
—	Tackle	Normal	35	95	35	22	Aurora Beam	Ice	65	100	20
—	Withdraw	Normal	—	—	40	29	Protect	Normal	—	—	10
8	Icicle Spear	Ice	10	100	30	36	Leer	Normal	—	100	30
15	Supersonic	Normal	—	55	20	43	Clamp	Water	35	75	10
						50	Ice Beam	Ice	95	100	10

TM/HM

TM/HM#	Name	Type	Power	ACC	PP	TM/HM#	Name	Type	Power	ACC	PP
TM03	Water Pulse	Water	60	95	20	TM27	Return	Normal	—	100	20
TM06	Toxic	Poison	—	85	10	TM32	Double Team	Normal	—	—	15
TM07	Hail	Ice	—	—	10	TM42	Facade	Normal	70	100	20
TM10	Hidden Power	Normal	—	100	15	TM43	Secret Power	Normal	70	100	20
TM13	Ice Beam	Ice	95	100	10	TM44	Rest	Psychic	—	—	10
TM14	Blizzard	Ice	120	70	5	TM45	Attract	Normal	—	100	15
TM17	Protect	Normal	—	—	10	HM03	Surf	Water	95	100	15
TM18	Rain Dance	Water	—	—	5	HM08	Dive	Water	60	100	10
TM21	Frustration	Normal	—	100	20						

EGG MOVES*

Name	Type	Power	ACC	PP
Barrier	Psychic	—	—	30
Bubblebeam	Water	65	100	20
Icicle Spear	Ice	10	100	30
Rapid Spin	Normal	20	100	40
Screech	Normal	—	85	40

*Learned Via Breeding

MOVE TUTOR
FireRed/LeafGreen and Emerald Only

Double-Edge	Explosion	Substitute
Mimic		

*Battle Frontier tutor move (*Emerald*)

PRIMA OFFICIAL GAME GUIDE

091 Cloyster™

WATER | ICE

GENERAL INFO
SPECIES: Bivalve Pokémon
HEIGHT: 4'11"
WEIGHT: 292 lbs.
ABILITY: Shell Armor
Protects Cloyster from being struck by critical hits.

STATS

HP
SPEED
ATK
SP DEF
DEF
SP ATK

EVOLUTIONS

WATER STONE

LOCATION[s]:

RUBY	Rarity: **None**	Trade from *FireRed*
SAPPHIRE	Rarity: **None**	Trade from *FireRed*
FIRERED	Rarity: **Evolve**	Evolve Shellder
LEAFGREEN	Rarity: **None**	Trade from *FireRed*
COLOSSEUM	Rarity: **None**	Trade from *FireRed*
EMERALD	Rarity: **None**	Trade from *FireRed*
XD	Rarity: **Evolve**	Evolve Shellder

MOVES

Level	Attack	Type	Power	ACC	PP	Level	Attack	Type	Power	ACC	PP
—	Withdraw	Normal	—	—	40	—	Protect	Normal	—	—	10
—	Supersonic	Normal	—	55	20	36	Spikes	Ground	—	—	20
—	Aurora Beam	Ice	65	100	20	43	Spike Cannon	Normal	20	100	15

TM/HM

TM/HM#	Name	Type	Power	ACC	PP	TM/HM#	Name	Type	Power	ACC	PP
TM03	Water Pulse	Water	60	95	20	TM27	Return	Normal	—	100	20
TM06	Toxic	Poison	—	85	10	TM32	Double Team	Normal	—	—	15
TM07	Hail	Ice	—	—	10	TM41	Torment	Dark	—	100	15
TM10	Hidden Power	Normal	—	100	15	TM42	Facade	Normal	70	100	20
TM13	Ice Beam	Ice	95	100	10	TM43	Secret Power	Normal	70	100	20
TM14	Blizzard	Ice	120	70	5	TM44	Rest	Psychic	—	—	10
TM15	Hyper Beam	Normal	150	90	5	TM45	Attract	Normal	—	100	15
TM17	Protect	Normal	—	—	10	HM03	Surf	Water	95	100	15
TM18	Rain Dance	Water	—	—	5	HM08	Dive	Water	60	100	10
TM21	Frustration	Normal	—	100	20						

MOVE TUTOR
FireRed/LeafGreen and Emerald Only

Double-Edge	Explosion	Substitute
Mimic		

*Battle Frontier tutor move (*Emerald*)

092 Gastly

GHOST POISON

GENERAL INFO
SPECIES: Gas Pokémon
HEIGHT: 4'03"
WEIGHT: .02 lbs.
ABILITY: Levitate
Protects Gastly from Ground-type attacks.

STATS
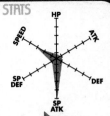

EVOLUTIONS

LV25 EVOLVE VIA TRADE

LOCATION(s):

RUBY	Rarity: **None**	Trade from *FireRed/LeafGreen*
SAPPHIRE	Rarity: **None**	Trade from *FireRed/LeafGreen*
FIRERED	Rarity: **Common**	Pokémon Tower
LEAFGREEN	Rarity: **Common**	Pokémon Tower
COLOSSEUM	Rarity: **None**	Trade from *FireRed/LeafGreen*
EMERALD	Rarity: **None**	Trade from *FireRed/LeafGreen*
XD	Rarity: **None**	Trade from *FireRed/LeafGreen*

MOVES

Level	Attack	Type	Power	ACC	PP
—	Lick	Ghost	20	100	30
—	Hypnosis	Psychic	—	60	20
8	Spite	Ghost	—	100	10
13	Curse	—	—	—	10
16	Night Shade	Ghost	—	100	15
21	Confuse Ray	Ghost	—	100	10
28	Dream Eater	Psychic	100	100	15
33	Destiny Bond	Ghost	—	—	5
36	Shadow Ball	Ghost	80	100	15
41	Nightmare	Ghost	—	100	15
48	Mean Look	Normal	—	100	5

TM/HM

TM/HM#	Name	Type	Power	ACC	PP
TM06	Toxic	Poison	—	85	10
TM10	Hidden Power	Normal	—	100	15
TM11	Sunny Day	Fire	—	—	5
TM12	Taunt	Dark	—	100	20
TM17	Protect	Normal	—	—	10
TM18	Rain Dance	Water	—	—	5
TM19	Giga Drain	Grass	60	100	5
TM21	Frustration	Normal	—	100	20
TM24	Thunderbolt	Electric	95	100	15
TM27	Return	Normal	—	100	20
TM29	Psychic	Psychic	90	100	10
TM30	Shadow Ball	Ghost	80	100	15
TM32	Double Team	Normal	—	—	15
TM36	Sludge Bomb	Poison	90	100	10
TM41	Torment	Dark	—	100	15
TM42	Facade	Normal	70	100	20
TM43	Secret Power	Normal	70	100	20
TM44	Rest	Psychic	—	—	10
TM45	Attract	Normal	—	100	15
TM46	Thief	Dark	40	100	10
TM48	Skill Swap	Psychic	—	100	10
TM49	Snatch	Dark	—	100	10

EGG MOVES*

Name	Type	Power	ACC	PP
Astonish	Ghost	30	100	15
Explosion	Normal	250	100	5
Grudge	Ghost	—	100	5
Haze	Ice	—	—	30
Perish Song	Normal	—	—	5
Psywave	Psychic	—	80	15
Will-O-Wisp	Fire	—	75	15

*Learned Via Breeding

MOVE TUTOR
FireRed/LeafGreen and Emerald Only

Mimic	Dream Eater*	Substitute
Explosion		

*Battle Frontier tutor move (*Emerald*)

093 Haunter™

GHOST | POISON

GENERAL INFO

SPECIES: Gas Pokémon
HEIGHT: 5'03"
WEIGHT: .02 lbs.
ABILITY: Levitate

Protects Haunter from Ground-type attacks.

STATS

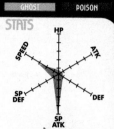

EVOLUTIONS

LV25 | EVOLVE VIA TRADE

LOCATION(s):

RUBY	Rarity: **None**	Trade from *FireRed/LeafGreen*
SAPPHIRE	Rarity: **None**	Trade from *FireRed/LeafGreen*
FIRERED	Rarity: **Common**	Evolve Gastly, Five Island, Pokémon Tower
LEAFGREEN	Rarity: **Common**	Evolve Gastly, Five Island, Pokémon Tower
COLOSSEUM	Rarity: **None**	Trade from *FireRed/LeafGreen*
EMERALD	Rarity: **None**	Trade from *FireRed/LeafGreen*
XD	Rarity: **None**	Trade from *FireRed/LeafGreen*

MOVES

Level	Attack	Type	Power	ACC	PP	Level	Attack	Type	Power	ACC	PP
—	Lick	Ghost	20	100	30	25	Shadow Punch	Ghost	60	—	20
—	Hypnosis	Psychic	—	60	20	31	Dream Eater	Psychic	100	100	15
—	Spite	Ghost	—	100	10	39	Destiny Bond	Ghost	—	—	5
13	Curse	—	—	—	10	45	Shadow Ball	Ghost	80	100	15
16	Night Shade	Ghost	—	100	15	53	Nightmare	Ghost	—	100	15
21	Confuse Ray	Ghost	—	100	10	64	Mean Look	Normal	—	100	5

TM/HM

TM/HM#	Name	Type	Power	ACC	PP	TM/HM#	Name	Type	Power	ACC	PP
TM06	Toxic	Poison	—	85	10	TM30	Shadow Ball	Ghost	80	100	15
TM10	Hidden Power	Normal	—	100	15	TM32	Double Team	Normal	—	—	15
TM11	Sunny Day	Fire	—	—	5	TM36	Sludge Bomb	Poison	90	100	10
TM12	Taunt	Dark	—	100	20	TM41	Torment	Dark	—	100	15
TM17	Protect	Normal	—	—	10	TM42	Facade	Normal	70	100	20
TM18	Rain Dance	Water	—	—	5	TM43	Secret Power	Normal	70	100	20
TM19	Giga Drain	Grass	60	100	5	TM44	Rest	Psychic	—	—	10
TM21	Frustration	Normal	—	100	20	TM45	Attract	Normal	—	100	15
TM24	Thunderbolt	Electric	95	100	15	TM46	Thief	Dark	40	100	10
TM27	Return	Normal	—	100	20	TM48	Skill Swap	Psychic	—	100	10
TM29	Psychic	Psychic	90	100	10	TM49	Snatch	Dark	—	100	10

MOVE TUTOR

FireRed/LeafGreen and Emerald Only

Mimic	Dream Eater*	Substitute
Explosion		

*Battle Frontier tutor move (*Emerald*)

094 Gengar ™

GHOST   POISON

GENERAL INFO
SPECIES: Shadow Pokémon
HEIGHT: 4'11"
WEIGHT: 89 lbs.
ABILITY: Levitate
Protects Gengar from Ground-type attacks.

STATS

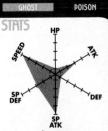

EVOLUTIONS

LV25   EVOLVE VIA TRADE

LOCATION[s]:

RUBY	Rarity: **None**	Trade from *FireRed/LeafGreen*
SAPPHIRE	Rarity: **None**	Trade from *FireRed/LeafGreen*
FIRERED	Rarity: **Evolve**	Evolve Haunter
LEAFGREEN	Rarity: **Evolve**	Evolve Haunter
COLOSSEUM	Rarity: **None**	Trade from *FireRed/LeafGreen*
EMERALD	Rarity:	Trade from *FireRed/LeafGreen*
XD	Rarity: **None**	Trade from *FireRed/LeafGreen*

MOVES

Level	Attack	Type	Power	ACC	PP
—	Lick	Ghost	20	100	30
—	Hypnosis	Psychic	—	60	20
—	Spite	Ghost	—	100	10
13	Curse	—	—	—	10
16	Night Shade	Ghost	—	100	15
21	Confuse Ray	Ghost	—	100	10
25	Shadow Punch	Ghost	60	—	20
31	Dream Eater	Psychic	100	100	15
39	Destiny Bond	Ghost	—	—	5
45	Shadow Ball	Ghost	80	100	15
53	Nightmare	Ghost	—	100	15
64	Mean Look	Normal	—	100	5

TM/HM

TM/HM#	Name	Type	Power	ACC	PP
TM01	Focus Punch	Fighting	150	100	20
TM06	Toxic	Poison	—	85	10
TM10	Hidden Power	Normal	—	100	15
TM11	Sunny Day	Fire	—	—	5
TM12	Taunt	Dark	—	100	20
TM15	Hyper Beam	Normal	150	90	5
TM17	Protect	Normal	—	—	10
TM18	Rain Dance	Water	—	—	5
TM19	Giga Drain	Grass	60	100	5
TM21	Frustration	Normal	—	100	20
TM24	Thunderbolt	Electric	95	100	15
TM25	Thunder	Electric	120	70	10
TM27	Return	Normal	—	100	20
TM29	Psychic	Psychic	90	100	10
TM30	Shadow Ball	Ghost	80	100	15
TM31	Brick Break	Fighting	75	100	15
TM32	Double Team	Normal	—	—	15
TM36	Sludge Bomb	Poison	90	100	10
TM41	Torment	Dark	—	100	15
TM42	Facade	Normal	70	100	20
TM43	Secret Power	Normal	70	100	20
TM44	Rest	Psychic	—	—	10
TM45	Attract	Normal	—	100	15
TM46	Thief	Dark	40	100	10
TM48	Skill Swap	Psychic	—	—	10
TM49	Snatch	Dark	—	100	10
HM04	Strength	Normal	80	100	20
HM06	Rock Smash	Fighting	20	100	15

MOVE TUTOR
FireRed/LeafGreen and Emerald Only

Body Slam*	Metronome	Seismic Toss*
Explosion	Mimic	Dream Eater*
Mega Punch*	Substitute	Double-Edge
Mega Kick*	Counter*	

*Battle Frontier tutor move (*Emerald*)

095 Onix™

ROCK | GROUND

GENERAL INFO

SPECIES: Rock Snake Pokémon
HEIGHT: 28'10"
WEIGHT: 463 lbs.
ABILITY 1: Sturdy
Prevents a one hit KO from hitting Onix.
ABILITY 2: Rock Head
Prevents Onix from receiving recoil damage.

STATS

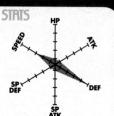

EVOLUTIONS

 ▶

TRADE WITH METAL COAT

LOCATION[s]:

RUBY	Rarity: **None**	Trade from *FireRed/LeafGreen*
SAPPHIRE	Rarity: **None**	Trade from *FireRed/LeafGreen*
FIRERED	Rarity: **Common**	Victory Road, Rock Tunnel, Seven Island
LEAFGREEN	Rarity: **Common**	Victory Road, Rock Tunnel, Seven Island
COLOSSEUM	Rarity: **None**	Trade from *FireRed/LeafGreen*
EMERALD	Rarity: **None**	Trade from *FireRed/LeafGreen*
XD	Rarity: **None**	Trade from *FireRed/LeafGreen*

MOVES

Level	Attack	Type	Power	ACC	PP	Level	Attack	Type	Power	ACC	PP
—	Tackle	Normal	35	95	35	30	Dragonbreath	Dragon	60	100	20
—	Screech	Normal	—	85	40	34	Sandstorm	Rock	—	—	10
8	Bind	Normal	15	75	20	41	Slam	Normal	80	75	20
12	Rock Throw	Rock	50	90	15	45	Iron Tail	Steel	100	75	15
19	Harden	Normal	—	—	30	52	Sand Tomb	Ground	15	70	15
23	Rage	Normal	20	100	20	56	Double-Edge	Normal	120	100	15

TM/HM

TM/HM#	Name	Type	Power	ACC	PP	TM/HM#	Name	Type	Power	ACC	PP
TM05	Roar	Normal	—	100	20	TM32	Double Team	Normal	—	—	15
TM06	Toxic	Poison	—	85	10	TM37	Sandstorm	Ground	—	—	10
TM10	Hidden Power	Normal	—	100	15	TM39	Rock Tomb	Rock	50	80	10
TM11	Sunny Day	Fire	—	—	5	TM41	Torment	Dark	—	100	15
TM12	Taunt	Dark	—	100	20	TM42	Facade	Normal	70	100	20
TM17	Protect	Normal	—	—	10	TM43	Secret Power	Normal	70	100	20
TM21	Frustration	Normal	—	100	20	TM44	Rest	Psychic	—	—	10
TM23	Iron Tail	Steel	75	75	15	TM45	Attract	Normal	—	100	15
TM26	Earthquake	Ground	100	100	10	HM04	Strength	Normal	80	100	20
TM27	Return	Normal	—	100	20	HM06	Rock Smash	Fighting	20	100	15
TM28	Dig	Ground	60	100	10						

EGG MOVES*

Name	Type	Power	ACC	PP
Block	Normal	—	100	5
Explosion	Normal	250	100	5
Flail	Normal	—	100	15
Rock Slide	Rock	75	90	10

*Learned Via Breeding

MOVE TUTOR

FireRed/LeafGreen and Emerald Only

Body Slam*	Mimic	Substitute
Double-Edge	Explosion	Rock Slide*

*Battle Frontier tutor move (*Emerald*)

096 Drowzee™

PSYCHIC

GENERAL INFO

SPECIES: Hypnosis Pokémon
HEIGHT: 3'03"
WEIGHT: 71 lbs.
ABILITY: Insomnia
Protects Drowzee from an opponent's sleep attack.

STATS

EVOLUTIONS

LV26

LOCATION(s):

RUBY	Rarity: **None**	Trade from *FireRed/LeafGreen*
SAPPHIRE	Rarity: **None**	Trade from *FireRed/LeafGreen*
FIRERED	Rarity: **Common**	Three Island, Route 11
LEAFGREEN	Rarity: **Common**	Three Island, Route 11
COLOSSEUM	Rarity: **None**	Trade from *FireRed/LeafGreen*
EMERALD	Rarity: **None**	Trade from *FireRed/LeafGreen*
XD	Rarity: **None**	Trade from *FireRed/LeafGreen*

MOVES

Level	Attack	Type	Power	ACC	PP		Level	Attack	Type	Power	ACC	PP
—	Pound	Normal	40	100	35		21	Poison Gas	Poison	—	55	40
—	Hypnosis	Psychic	—	60	20		27	Mediate	Psychic	—	—	40
7	Disable	Normal	—	55	20		31	Psychic	Psychic	90	100	10
11	Confusion	Psychic	50	100	25		37	Psych Up	Normal	—	—	10
17	Headbutt	Normal	70	100	15		41	Swagger	Normal	—	90	15
							47	Future Sight	Psychic	80	90	15

TM/HM

TM/HM#	Name	Type	Power	ACC	PP		TM/HM#	Name	Type	Power	ACC	PP
TM01	Focus Punch	Fighting	150	100	20		TM30	Shadow Ball	Ghost	80	100	15
TM04	Calm Mind	Psychic	—	—	20		TM31	Brick Break	Fighting	75	100	15
TM06	Toxic	Poison	—	85	10		TM32	Double Team	Normal	—	—	15
TM10	Hidden Power	Normal	—	100	15		TM33	Reflect	Normal	—	—	20
TM11	Sunny Day	Fire	—	—	5		TM41	Torment	Dark	—	100	15
TM12	Taunt	Dark	—	100	20		TM42	Facade	Normal	70	100	20
TM16	Light Screen	Psychic	—	—	30		TM43	Secret Power	Normal	70	100	20
TM17	Protect	Normal	—	—	10		TM44	Rest	Psychic	—	—	10
TM18	Rain Dance	Water	—	—	5		TM45	Attract	Normal	—	100	15
TM20	Safeguard	Normal	—	—	25		TM46	Thief	Dark	40	100	10
TM21	Frustration	Normal	—	100	20		TM48	Skill Swap	Psychic	—	100	10
TM27	Return	Normal	—	100	20		TM49	Snatch	Dark	—	100	10
TM29	Psychic	Psychic	90	100	10		HM05	Flash	Normal	—	70	20

EGG MOVES*

Name	Type	Power	ACC	PP
Assist	Normal	—	100	20
Barrier	Psychic	—	—	30
Fire Punch	Fire	75	100	15
Thunderpunch	Electric	75	100	15
Ice Punch	Ice	75	100	15
Role Play	Psychic	—	100	10

*Learned Via Breeding

MOVE TUTOR
FireRed/LeafGreen and Emerald Only

Body Slam*	Metronome	Counter*
Double-Edge	Mimic	Seismic Toss*
Mega Punch*	Substitute	Thunder Wave*
Mega Kick*	Dream Eater*	

*Battle Frontier tutor move (*Emerald*)

097 Hypno™

PSYCHIC

GENERAL INFO

SPECIES: Hypnosis Pokémon
HEIGHT: 5'03"
WEIGHT: 167 lbs.
ABILITY: Insomnia

Protects Hypno from an opponent's sleep attack.

STATS

(Stat chart showing: HP, ATK, DEF, SP ATK, SP DEF, SPEED)

EVOLUTIONS

LV26

LOCATION(s):

RUBY	Rarity: **None**	Trade from *FireRed/LeafGreen*	
SAPPHIRE	Rarity: **None**	Trade from *FireRed/LeafGreen*	
FIRERED	Rarity: **Common**	Three Island	
LEAFGREEN	Rarity: **Common**	Three Island	
COLOSSEUM	Rarity: **None**	Trade from *FireRed/LeafGreen*	
EMERALD	Rarity: **None**	Trade from *FireRed/LeafGreen*	
XD	Rarity: **Only One**	Cipher Key Lair (Capture from Cipher Admin Gorigan)	

MOVES

Level	Attack	Type	Power	ACC	PP	Level	Attack	Type	Power	ACC	PP
—	Nightmare	Ghost	—	100	15	21	Poison Gas	Poison	—	55	40
—	Pound	Normal	40	100	35	29	Mediate	Psychic	—	—	40
—	Hypnosis	Psychic	—	60	20	35	Psychic	Psychic	90	100	10
—	Disable	Normal	—	55	20	43	Psych Up	Normal	—	—	10
—	Confusion	Psychic	50	100	25	49	Swagger	Normal	—	90	15
17	Headbutt	Normal	70	100	15	57	Future Sight	Psychic	80	90	15

TM/HM

TM/HM#	Name	Type	Power	ACC	PP	TM/HM#	Name	Type	Power	ACC	PP
TM01	Focus Punch	Fighting	150	100	20	TM30	Shadow Ball	Ghost	80	100	15
TM04	Calm Mind	Psychic	—	—	20	TM31	Brick Break	Fighting	75	100	15
TM06	Toxic	Poison	—	85	10	TM32	Double Team	Normal	—	—	15
TM10	Hidden Power	Normal	—	100	15	TM33	Reflect	Normal	—	—	20
TM11	Sunny Day	Fire	—	—	5	TM41	Torment	Dark	—	100	15
TM12	Taunt	Dark	—	100	20	TM42	Facade	Normal	70	100	20
TM15	Hyper Beam	Normal	150	90	5	TM43	Secret Power	Normal	70	100	20
TM16	Light Screen	Psychic	—	—	30	TM44	Rest	Psychic	—	—	10
TM17	Protect	Normal	—	—	10	TM45	Attract	Normal	—	100	15
TM18	Rain Dance	Water	—	—	5	TM46	Thief	Dark	40	100	10
TM20	Safeguard	Normal	—	—	25	TM48	Skill Swap	Psychic	—	100	10
TM21	Frustration	Normal	—	100	20	TM49	Snatch	Dark	—	100	10
TM27	Return	Normal	—	100	20	HM05	Flash	Normal	—	70	20
TM29	Psychic	Psychic	90	100	10						

MOVE TUTOR
FireRed/LeafGreen and Emerald Only

Body Slam*	Metronome	Seismic Toss*
Double-Edge	Mimic	Dream Eater*
Mega Punch*	Substitute	Thunder Wave*
Mega Kick*	Counter*	

*Battle Frontier tutor move (*Emerald*)

098 Krabby™

WATER

GENERAL INFO

SPECIES: River Crab Pokémon
HEIGHT: 1'04"
WEIGHT: 14 lbs.
ABILITY: Shell Armor
Protects Krabby from critical hits.
ABILITY 2: Hyper Cutter
Prevents effects that reduce the Pokémon's attack power.

STATS

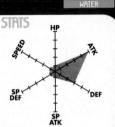

EVOLUTIONS

LV28

LOCATION[s]:

RUBY	Rarity: **None**	Trade from *FireRed/LeafGreen*
SAPPHIRE	Rarity: **None**	Trade from *FireRed/LeafGreen*
FIRERED	Rarity: **Common**	Islands One, Three, Four, Five, Six, Seven, Routes 4, 10, 11, 12, 13, 19, 20, 21, 24, Cerulean City, Vermilion City
LEAFGREEN	Rarity: **Common**	Islands One, Three, Four, Five, Six, Seven, Routes 4, 10, 11, 12, 13, 19, 20, 21, 24, Cerulean City, Vermilion City
COLOSSEUM	Rarity: **None**	Trade from *FireRed/LeafGreen*
EMERALD	Rarity: **None**	Trade from *FireRed/LeafGreen*
XD	Rarity: **None**	Trade from *FireRed/LeafGreen*

MOVES

Level	Attack	Type	Power	ACC	PP
—	Bubble	Water	20	100	30
5	Leer	Normal	—	100	30
12	Vicegrip	Normal	55	100	30
16	Harden	Normal	—	—	30
23	Mud Shot	Ground	55	95	15

Level	Attack	Type	Power	ACC	PP
27	Stomp	Normal	65	100	20
34	Guillotine	Normal	—	30	5
38	Protect	Normal	—	—	10
45	Crabhammer	Water	90	85	10
49	Flail	Normal	—	100	15

TM/HM

TM/HM#	Name	Type	Power	ACC	PP
TM03	Water Pulse	Water	60	95	20
TM06	Toxic	Poison	—	85	10
TM07	Hail	Ice	—	—	10
TM10	Hidden Power	Normal	—	100	15
TM13	Ice Beam	Ice	95	100	10
TM14	Blizzard	Ice	120	70	5
TM17	Protect	Normal	—	—	10
TM18	Rain Dance	Water	—	—	5
TM21	Frustration	Normal	—	100	20
TM27	Return	Normal	—	100	20
TM28	Dig	Ground	60	100	10
TM32	Double Team	Normal	—	—	15

TM/HM#	Name	Type	Power	ACC	PP
TM39	Rock Tomb	Rock	50	80	10
TM42	Facade	Normal	70	100	20
TM43	Secret Power	Normal	70	100	20
TM44	Rest	Psychic	—	—	10
TM45	Attract	Normal	—	100	15
TM46	Thief	Dark	40	100	10
HM01	Cut	Normal	50	95	30
HM03	Surf	Water	95	100	15
HM04	Strength	Normal	80	100	20
HM06	Rock Smash	Fighting	20	100	15
HM08	Dive	Water	60	100	10

EGG MOVES*

Move	Type	Power	ACC	PP
Amnesia	Psychic	—	—	20
Dig	Ground	60	100	10
Flail	Normal	—	100	15
Haze	Ice	—	—	30
Knock Off	Dark	20	100	20
Slam	Normal	80	75	20
Swords Dance	Normal	—	—	30

*Learned Via Breeding

MOVE TUTOR
FireRed/LeafGreen and Emerald Only

Body Slam*	Mimic	Substitute
Double-Edge	Swords Dance*	

*Battle Frontier tutor move (*Emerald*)

PRIMA OFFICIAL GAME GUIDE

099 Kingler™

GENERAL INFO

SPECIES: Pincer Pokémon
HEIGHT: 4'03"
WEIGHT: 132 lbs.
ABILITY: Shell Armor
Protects Kingler from critical hits.

ABILITY 2: Hyper Cutter
Prevents effects that reduce the Pokémon's attack power.

STATS

EVOLUTIONS

LV28

LOCATION[s]:

RUBY	Rarity: **None**	Trade from *FireRed/LeafGreen*
SAPPHIRE	Rarity: **None**	Trade from *FireRed/LeafGreen*
FIRERED	Rarity: **Rare**	Evolve Krabby
LEAFGREEN	Rarity: **Rare**	Evolve Krabby, Islands One, Three, Five, Six, Seven, Routes 19–21
COLOSSEUM	Rarity: **None**	Trade from *FireRed/LeafGreen*
EMERALD	Rarity: **None**	Trade from *FireRed/LeafGreen*
XD	Rarity: **None**	Trade from *FireRed/LeafGreen*

MOVES

Level	Attack	Type	Power	ACC	PP		Level	Attack	Type	Power	ACC	PP
—	Metal Claw	Steel	50	95	35		23	Mud Shot	Ground	55	95	15
—	Bubble	Water	20	100	30		27	Stomp	Normal	65	100	20
—	Leer	Normal	—	100	30		38	Guillotine	Normal	—	30	5
—	Vicegrip	Normal	55	100	30		42	Protect	Normal	—	—	10
—	Harden	Normal	—	—	30		57	Crabhammer	Water	90	85	10
							65	Flail	Normal	—	100	15

TM/HM

TM/HM#	Name	Type	Power	ACC	PP		TM/HM#	Name	Type	Power	ACC	PP
TM03	Water Pulse	Water	60	95	20		TM32	Double Team	Normal	—	—	15
TM06	Toxic	Poison	—	85	10		TM39	Rock Tomb	Rock	50	80	10
TM07	Hail	Ice	—	—	10		TM42	Facade	Normal	70	100	20
TM10	Hidden Power	Normal	—	100	15		TM43	Secret Power	Normal	70	100	20
TM13	Ice Beam	Ice	95	100	10		TM44	Rest	Psychic	—	—	10
TM14	Blizzard	Ice	120	70	5		TM45	Attract	Normal	—	100	15
TM15	Hyper Beam	Normal	150	90	5		TM46	Thief	Dark	40	100	10
TM17	Protect	Normal	—	—	10		HM01	Cut	Normal	50	95	30
TM18	Rain Dance	Water	—	—	5		HM03	Surf	Water	95	100	15
TM21	Frustration	Normal	—	100	20		HM04	Strength	Normal	80	100	20
TM27	Return	Normal	—	100	20		HM06	Rock Smash	Fighting	20	100	15
TM28	Dig	Ground	60	100	10		HM08	Dive	Water	60	100	10

MOVE TUTOR

FireRed/LeafGreen and Emerald Only

Body Slam*	Mimic	Substitute
Double-Edge	Swords Dance*	

*Battle Frontier tutor move (*Emerald*)

100 Voltorb™

ELECTRIC

GENERAL INFO

SPECIES: Ball Pokémon
HEIGHT: 1'08"
WEIGHT: 23 lbs.
ABILITY 1: Soundproof

Prevents Grasswhistle, Growl, Heal Bell, Hyper Voice, Metal Sound, Perish Song, Roar, Screech, Sing, Snore, Supersonic, and Uproar from hitting Voltorb.

ABILITY 2: Static

The opponent has a 30% chance of being paralyzed if a physical attack hits Voltorb.

STATS

(radar chart: HP, ATK, DEF, SP ATK, SP DEF, SPEED)

EVOLUTIONS

 ▶

LV30

LOCATION[S]:

RUBY	Rarity: **Common**	New Mauville
SAPPHIRE	Rarity: **Common**	New Mauville
FIRERED	Rarity: **Common**	Power Plant, Route 10
LEAFGREEN	Rarity: **Common**	Power Plant, Route 10
COLOSSEUM	Rarity: **None**	Trade from Ruby/Sapphire
EMERALD	Rarity: **Common**	New Mauville
XD	Rarity: **Only One**	Cave Poké Spot (Capture from Miror B.)

MOVES

Level	Attack	Type	Power	ACC	PP
—	Charge	Electric	—	100	20
—	Tackle	Normal	35	95	35
8	Screech	Normal	—	85	40
15	Sonicboom	Normal	—	90	20
21	Spark	Electric	65	100	20

Level	Attack	Type	Power	ACC	PP
27	Selfdestruct	Normal	200	100	5
32	Rollout	Rock	30	90	20
37	Light Screen	Psychic	—	—	30
42	Swift	Normal	60	—	20
46	Explosion	Normal	250	100	5
49	Mirror Coat	Psychic	—	100	20

TM/HM

TM/HM#	Name	Type	Power	ACC	PP
TM06	Toxic	Poison	—	85	10
TM10	Hidden Power	Normal	—	100	15
TM12	Taunt	Dark	—	100	20
TM16	Light Screen	Psychic	—	—	30
TM17	Protect	Normal	—	—	10
TM18	Rain Dance	Water	—	—	5
TM21	Frustration	Normal	—	100	20
TM24	Thunderbolt	Electric	95	100	15
TM25	Thunder	Electric	120	70	10

TM/HM#	Name	Type	Power	ACC	PP
TM27	Return	Normal	—	100	20
TM32	Double Team	Normal	—	—	15
TM34	Shock Wave	Electric	60	—	20
TM41	Torment	Dark	—	100	15
TM42	Facade	Normal	70	100	20
TM43	Secret Power	Normal	70	100	20
TM44	Rest	Psychic	—	—	10
TM46	Thief	Dark	40	100	10
HM05	Flash	Normal	—	70	20

EGG MOVES*

Move	Type	Power	ACC	PP
None				

*Learned Via Breeding

MOVE TUTOR

FireRed/LeafGreen and Emerald Only

Explosion	Substitute	Thunder Wave*
Mimic		

Emerald Only

Endure*	Sleep Talk	Swagger
Rollout	Snore*	Swift*

*Battle Frontier tutor move (Emerald)

PRIMA OFFICIAL GAME GUIDE

101 Electrode™

ELECTRIC

GENERAL INFO
SPECIES: Ball Pokémon
HEIGHT: 3'11"
WEIGHT: 147 lbs.
ABILITY 1: Soundproof

Prevents Electrode from being hit by Grasswhistle, Growl, Heal Bell, Hyper Voice, Metal Sound, Perish Song, Roar, Screech, Sing, Snore, Supersonic, and Uproar.

ABILITY 2: Static
The opponent has a 30% chance of being paralyzed if a physical attack hits Electrode.

STATS

EVOLUTIONS

LV30

LOCATION(s):

RUBY	Rarity: **Rare**	New Mauville (Fake Poké Ball), Team Aqua/Team Magma Base	
SAPPHIRE	Rarity: **Rare**	New Mauville (Fake Poké Ball), Team Aqua/Team Magma Base (Fake Poké Ball)	
FIRERED	Rarity: **Rare**	Cerulean Cave	
LEAFGREEN	Rarity: **Rare**	Cerulean Cave	
COLOSSEUM	Rarity: **None**	Trade from Ruby/Sapphire/FireRed/LeafGreen	
EMERALD	Rarity: **Rare**	Aqua Hideout, New Mauville	
XD	Rarity: **Evolve**	Evolve Voltorb	

MOVES

Level	Attack	Type	Power	ACC	PP
—	Charge	Electric	—	100	20
—	Tackle	Normal	35	95	35
—/8	Screech	Normal	—	85	40
—/15	Sonicboom	Normal	—	90	20
21	Spark	Electric	65	100	20
27	Selfdestruct	Normal	200	100	5

Level	Attack	Type	Power	ACC	PP
34	Rollout	Rock	30	90	20
41	Light Screen	Psychic	—	—	30
48	Swift	Normal	60	—	20
54	Explosion	Normal	250	100	5
59	Mirror Coat	Psychic	—	100	20
# = Emerald Only					

TM/HM

TM/HM#	Name	Type	Power	ACC	PP
TM06	Toxic	Poison	—	85	10
TM10	Hidden Power	Normal	—	100	15
TM12	Taunt	Dark	—	100	20
TM15	Hyper Beam	Normal	150	90	5
TM16	Light Screen	Psychic	—	—	30
TM17	Protect	Normal	—	—	10
TM18	Rain Dance	Water	—	—	5
TM21	Frustration	Normal	—	100	20
TM24	Thunderbolt	Electric	95	100	15
TM25	Thunder	Electric	120	70	10

TM/HM#	Name	Type	Power	ACC	PP
TM27	Return	Normal	—	100	20
TM32	Double Team	Normal	—	—	15
TM34	Shock Wave	Electric	60	—	20
TM41	Torment	Dark	—	100	15
TM42	Facade	Normal	70	100	20
TM43	Secret Power	Normal	70	100	20
TM44	Rest	Psychic	—	—	10
TM46	Thief	Dark	40	100	10
HM05	Flash	Normal	—	70	20

EGG MOVES*

Move	Type	Power	ACC	PP
None				

*Learned Via Breeding

MOVE TUTOR
FireRed/LeafGreen and Emerald Only

Explosion	Substitute	Thunder Wave*
Mimic		

Emerald Only

Endure*	Sleep Talk	Swagger
Rollout	Snore*	Swift*

*Battle Frontier tutor move (Emerald)

Exeggcute™

GRASS | PSYCHIC

GENERAL INFO

SPECIES: Egg Pokémon
HEIGHT: 1'04"
WEIGHT: 6 lbs.
ABILITY: Chlorophyll

When the sunlight is strong, Exeggcute's Speed doubles.

STATS

EVOLUTIONS

EVOLVE WITH LEAF STONE

LOCATION(s):

RUBY	Rarity: **None**	Trade from *FireRed/LeafGreen*
SAPPHIRE	Rarity: **None**	Trade from *FireRed/LeafGreen*
FIRERED	Rarity: **Common**	Safari Zone
LEAFGREEN	Rarity: **Common**	Safari Zone
COLOSSEUM	Rarity: **None**	Trade from *FireRed/LeafGreen*
EMERALD	Rarity: **None**	Trade from *FireRed/LeafGreen*
XD	Rarity: **None**	Trade from *FireRed/LeafGreen*

MOVES

Level	Attack	Type	Power	ACC	PP	Level	Attack	Type	Power	ACC	PP
—	Barrage	Normal	12	85	20	19	Confusion	Psychic	50	100	25
—	Hypnosis	Psychic	—	60	20	25	Stun Spore	Grass	—	75	30
—	Uproar	Normal	50	100	10	31	Poisonpowder	Poison	—	75	35
7	Reflect	Psychic	—	—	20	37	Sleep Powder	Grass	—	75	15
13	Leech Seed	Grass	—	90	10	43	Solarbeam	Grass	120	100	10

TM/HM

TM/HM#	Name	Type	Power	ACC	PP	TM/HM#	Name	Type	Power	ACC	PP
TM06	Toxic	Poison	—	85	10	TM32	Double Team	Normal	—	—	15
TM09	Bullet Seed	Grass	10	100	30	TM33	Reflect	Normal	—	—	20
TM10	Hidden Power	Normal	—	100	15	TM36	Sludge Bomb	Poison	90	100	10
TM11	Sunny Day	Fire	—	—	5	TM42	Facade	Normal	70	100	20
TM16	Light Screen	Psychic	—	—	30	TM43	Secret Power	Normal	70	100	20
TM17	Protect	Normal	—	—	10	TM44	Rest	Psychic	—	—	10
TM19	Giga Drain	Grass	60	100	5	TM45	Attract	Normal	—	100	15
TM21	Frustration	Normal	—	100	20	TM46	Thief	Dark	40	100	10
TM22	Solarbeam	Grass	120	100	10	TM48	Skill Swap	Psychic	—	100	10
TM27	Return	Normal	—	100	20	HM04	Strength	Normal	80	100	20
TM29	Psychic	Psychic	90	100	10	HM05	Flash	Normal	—	70	20

EGG MOVES*

Move	Type	Power	ACC	PP
Ancientpower	Rock	60	100	5
Curse	—	—	—	10
Ingrain	Grass	—	100	20
Moonlight	Normal	—	—	5
Psych Up	Normal	—	—	10
Reflect	Psychic	—	—	20
Synthesis	Grass	—	—	5

*Learned Via Breeding

MOVE TUTOR

FireRed/LeafGreen and Emerald Only

Double-Edge	Mimic	Substitute
Explosion	Dream Eater*	

*Battle Frontier tutor move (*Emerald*)

103 Exeggutor™

GRASS   PSYCHIC

GENERAL INFO
SPECIES: Coconut Pokémon
HEIGHT: 6'07"
WEIGHT: 265 lbs.
ABILITY: Chlorophyll
When the sunlight is strong, Exeggutor's Speed doubles.

STATS

Radar chart with axes: HP, ATK, DEF, SP ATK, SP DEF, SPEED

EVOLUTIONS

EVOLVE WITH LEAF STONE

LOCATION[S]:

Game	Rarity	Location
RUBY	Rarity: **None**	Trade from *FireRed/LeafGreen*
SAPPHIRE	Rarity: **None**	Trade from *FireRed/LeafGreen*
FIRERED	Rarity: **Evolve**	Evolve Exeggcute
LEAFGREEN	Rarity: **Evolve**	Evolve Exeggcute
COLOSSEUM	Rarity: **None**	Trade from *FireRed/LeafGreen*
EMERALD	Rarity: **None**	Trade from *FireRed/LeafGreen*
XD	Rarity: **Only One**	Citadark Island (Capture from Master Greevil)

MOVES

Level	Attack	Type	Power	ACC	PP		Level	Attack	Type	Power	ACC	PP
—	Barrage	Normal	12	85	20		—	Confusion	Psychic	50	100	25
—	Hypnosis	Psychic	—	60	20		19	Stomp	Normal	65	100	20
							31	Egg Bomb	Normal	100	75	10

TM/HM

TM/HM#	Name	Type	Power	ACC	PP		TM/HM#	Name	Type	Power	ACC	PP
TM06	Toxic	Poison	—	85	10		TM32	Double Team	Normal	—	—	15
TM09	Bullet Seed	Grass	10	100	30		TM33	Reflect	Normal	—	—	20
TM10	Hidden Power	Normal	—	100	15		TM36	Sludge Bomb	Poison	90	100	10
TM11	Sunny Day	Fire	—	—	5		TM42	Facade	Normal	70	100	20
TM15	Hyper Beam	Normal	150	90	5		TM43	Secret Power	Normal	70	100	20
TM16	Light Screen	Psychic	—	—	30		TM44	Rest	Psychic	—	—	10
TM17	Protect	Normal	—	—	10		TM45	Attract	Normal	—	100	15
TM19	Giga Drain	Grass	60	100	5		TM46	Thief	Dark	40	100	10
TM21	Frustration	Normal	—	100	20		TM48	Skill Swap	Psychic	—	100	10
TM22	Solarbeam	Grass	120	100	10		HM04	Strength	Normal	80	100	20
TM27	Return	Normal	—	100	20		HM05	Flash	Normal	—	70	20
TM29	Psychic	Psychic	90	100	10							

MOVE TUTOR
FireRed/LeafGreen and Emerald Only

Double-Edge	Mimic	Substitute
Explosion	Dream Eater*	

*Battle Frontier tutor move (*Emerald*)

104 Cubone™

GROUND

GENERAL INFO

SPECIES: Lonely Pokémon
HEIGHT: 1'04"
WEIGHT: 14 lbs.
ABILITY 1: Lightningrod

All Electric-type attacks go toward Cubone during a 2-on-2 battle.

ABILITY 2: Rock Head

Protects Cubone from recoil damage.

STATS

HP / ATK / DEF / SP ATK / SP DEF / SPEED

EVOLUTIONS

 ▶

LV28

LOCATION[s]:

RUBY	Rarity: None		Trade from *FireRed/LeafGreen*
SAPPHIRE	Rarity: None		Trade from *FireRed/LeafGreen*
FIRERED	Rarity: Rare		Pokémon Tower, Seven Island
LEAFGREEN	Rarity: Rare		Pokémon Tower, Seven Island
COLOSSEUM	Rarity: None		Trade from *FireRed/LeafGreen*
EMERALD	Rarity: None		Trade from *FireRed/LeafGreen*
XD	Rarity: None		Trade from *FireRed/LeafGreen*

MOVES

Level	Attack	Type	Power	ACC	PP		Level	Attack	Type	Power	ACC	PP
—	Growl	Normal	—	100	40		25	Bonemerang	Ground	50	90	10
5	Tail Whip	Normal	—	100	30		29	Rage	Normal	20	100	20
9	Bone Club	Ground	65	85	20		33	False Swipe	Normal	40	100	40
13	Headbutt	Normal	70	100	15		37	Thrash	Normal	90	100	20
17	Leer	Normal	—	100	30		41	Bone Rush	Ground	25	80	10
21	Focus Energy	Normal	—	—	30		45	Double-Edge	Normal	120	100	15

TM/HM

TM/HM#	Name	Type	Power	ACC	PP		TM/HM#	Name	Type	Power	ACC	PP
TM01	Focus Punch	Fighting	150	100	20		TM32	Double Team	Normal	—	—	15
TM06	Toxic	Poison	—	85	10		TM35	Flamethrower	Fire	95	100	15
TM10	Hidden Power	Normal	—	100	15		TM37	Sandstorm	Ground	—	—	10
TM11	Sunny Day	Fire	—	—	5		TM38	Fire Blast	Fire	120	85	5
TM13	Ice Beam	Ice	95	100	10		TM39	Rock Tomb	Rock	50	80	10
TM14	Blizzard	Ice	120	70	5		TM40	Aerial Ace	Flying	60	—	20
TM17	Protect	Normal	—	—	10		TM42	Facade	Normal	70	100	20
TM21	Frustration	Normal	—	100	20		TM43	Secret Power	Normal	70	100	20
TM23	Iron Tail	Steel	75	75	15		TM44	Rest	Psychic	—	—	10
TM26	Earthquake	Ground	100	100	10		TM45	Attract	Normal	—	100	15
TM27	Return	Normal	—	100	20		TM46	Thief	Dark	40	100	10
TM28	Dig	Ground	60	100	10		HM04	Strength	Normal	80	100	20
TM31	Brick Break	Fighting	75	100	15		HM06	Rock Smash	Fighting	20	100	15

EGG MOVES*

Move	Type	Power	ACC	PP
Ancientpower	Rock	60	100	5
Belly Drum	Normal	—	—	10
Perish Song	Normal	—	—	5
Rock Slide	Rock	75	90	10
Screech	Normal	—	85	40
Skull Bash	Normal	100	100	15
Swords Dance	Normal	—	—	30

*Learned Via Breeding

MOVE TUTOR

FireRed/LeafGreen and Emerald Only

Body Slam*	Mimic	Seismic Toss*
Double-Edge	Substitute	Rock Slide*
Mega Punch*	Swords Dance*	
Mega Kick*	Counter*	

*Battle Frontier tutor move (*Emerald*)

105 Marowak™

GROUND

GENERAL INFO

SPECIES: Bone Keeper Pokémon
HEIGHT: 3'03"
WEIGHT: 99 lbs.
ABILITY 1: Lightningrod

All Electric-type attacks go toward Marowak during a 2-on-2 battle.

ABILITY 2: Rock Head

Protects Marowak from recoil damage.

STATS

HP · SPEED · ATK · DEF · SP DEF · SP ATK

EVOLUTIONS

 ▶

LV28

LOCATION[s]:

RUBY	Rarity: **None**	Trade from *FireRed/LeafGreen*
SAPPHIRE	Rarity: **None**	Trade from *FireRed/LeafGreen*
FIRERED	Rarity: **Rare**	Victory Road, Seven Island
LEAFGREEN	Rarity: **Rare**	Victory Road, Seven Island
COLOSSEUM	Rarity: **None**	Trade from *FireRed/LeafGreen*
EMERALD	Rarity: **None**	Trade from *FireRed/LeafGreen*
XD	Rarity: **Only One**	Citadark Island (Capture from Cipher Admin Eldes)

MOVES

Level	Attack	Type	Power	ACC	PP	Level	Attack	Type	Power	ACC	PP
—	Growl	Normal	—	100	40	25	Bonemerang	Ground	50	90	10
—	Tail Whip	Normal	—	100	30	32	Rage	Normal	20	100	20
—	Bone Club	Ground	65	85	20	39	False Swipe	Normal	40	100	40
—	Headbutt	Normal	70	100	15	46	Thrash	Normal	90	100	20
17	Leer	Normal	—	100	30	53	Bone Rush	Ground	25	80	10
21	Focus Energy	Normal	—	—	30	61	Double-Edge	Normal	120	100	15

TM/HM

TM/HM#	Name	Type	Power	ACC	PP	TM/HM#	Name	Type	Power	ACC	PP
TM01	Focus Punch	Fighting	150	100	20	TM32	Double Team	Normal	—	—	15
TM06	Toxic	Poison	—	85	10	TM35	Flamethrower	Fire	95	100	15
TM10	Hidden Power	Normal	—	100	15	TM37	Sandstorm	Ground	—	—	10
TM11	Sunny Day	Fire	—	—	5	TM38	Fire Blast	Fire	120	85	5
TM13	Ice Beam	Ice	95	100	10	TM39	Rock Tomb	Rock	50	80	10
TM14	Blizzard	Ice	120	70	5	TM40	Aerial Ace	Flying	60	—	20
TM15	Hyper Beam	Normal	150	90	5	TM42	Facade	Normal	70	100	20
TM17	Protect	Normal	—	—	10	TM43	Secret Power	Normal	70	100	20
TM21	Frustration	Normal	—	100	20	TM44	Rest	Psychic	—	—	10
TM23	Iron Tail	Steel	75	75	15	TM45	Attract	Normal	—	100	15
TM26	Earthquake	Ground	100	100	10	TM46	Thief	Dark	40	100	10
TM27	Return	Normal	—	100	20	HM04	Strength	Normal	80	100	20
TM28	Dig	Ground	60	100	10	HM06	Rock Smash	Fighting	20	100	15
TM31	Brick Break	Fighting	75	100	15						

MOVE TUTOR

FireRed/LeafGreen and Emerald Only

Body Slam*	Mimic	Seismic Toss*
Double-Edge*	Substitute	Rock Slide*
Mega Punch*	Swords Dance*	
Mega Kick*	Counter*	

*Battle Frontier tutor move (*Emerald*)

106 Hitmonlee™

FIGHTING

GENERAL INFO
SPECIES: Kicking Pokémon
HEIGHT: 4'11"
WEIGHT: 110 lbs.
ABILITY: Limber
Protects Hitmonlee from being paralyzed.

STATS

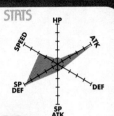

EVOLUTIONS

LV20
ATTACK>DEFENSE

LOCATION[s]:

RUBY	Rarity: **None**	Trade from *FireRed/LeafGreen*
SAPPHIRE	Rarity: **None**	Trade from *FireRed/LeafGreen*
FIRERED	Rarity: **Only One**	Fighting Gym in Saffron City
LEAFGREEN	Rarity: **Only One**	Fighting Gym in Saffron City
COLOSSEUM	Rarity: **None**	Trade from *FireRed/LeafGreen*
EMERALD	Rarity: **None**	Trade from *FireRed/LeafGreen*
XD	Rarity: **Only One**	Citadark Island (Capture from Cipher Peon Petro)

MOVES

Level	Attack	Type	Power	ACC	PP	Level	Attack	Type	Power	ACC	PP
—	Revenge	Fighting	60	100	10	21	Focus Energy	Normal	—	—	30
—	Double-Kick	Fighting	30	100	30	26	Hi Jump Kick	Fighting	85	90	20
6	Mediate	Psychic	—	—	40	31	Mind Reader	Normal	—	100	5
11	Rolling Kick	Fight	60	85	15	36	Foresight	Normal	—	100	40
16	Jump Kick	Fight	70	95	25	41	Endure	Normal	—	—	10
20	Brick Break	Fighting	75	100	15	46	Mega Kick	Normal	120	75	5
21	Focus Energy	Normal	—	—	30	51	Reversal	Fighting	—	100	15

TM/HM

TM/HM#	Name	Type	Power	ACC	PP	TM/HM#	Name	Type	Power	ACC	PP
TM01	Focus Punch	Fighting	150	100	20	TM31	Brick Break	Fighting	75	100	15
TM06	Toxic	Poison	—	85	10	TM32	Double Team	Normal	—	—	15
TM08	Bulk Up	Fighting	—	—	20	TM39	Rock Tomb	Rock	50	80	10
TM10	Hidden Power	Normal	—	100	15	TM42	Facade	Normal	70	100	20
TM11	Sunny Day	Fire	—	—	5	TM43	Secret Power	Normal	70	100	20
TM17	Protect	Normal	—	—	10	TM44	Rest	Psychic	—	—	10
TM18	Rain Dance	Water	—	—	5	TM45	Attract	Normal	—	100	15
TM21	Frustration	Normal	—	100	20	TM46	Thief	Dark	40	100	10
TM26	Earthquake	Ground	100	100	10	HM04	Strength	Normal	80	100	15
TM27	Return	Normal	—	100	20	HM06	Rock Smash	Fighting	20	100	15

MOVE TUTOR
FireRed/LeafGreen and Emerald Only

Body Slam*	Metronome	Seismic Toss*
Double-Edge	Mimic	Rock Slide*
Mega Punch*	Substitute	
Mega Kick*	Counter*	

*Battle Frontier tutor move (*Emerald*)

107 Hitmonchan™

FIGHTING

GENERAL INFO
SPECIES: Punching Pokémon
HEIGHT: 4'7"
WEIGHT: 111 lbs.
ABILITY: Keen Eye
Prevents Hitmonchan from having its Accuracy lowered.

STATS

EVOLUTIONS

LV20
ATTACK<DEFENSE

LOCATION(s):

RUBY	Rarity: **None**	Trade from *FireRed/LeafGreen*
SAPPHIRE	Rarity: **None**	Trade from *FireRed/LeafGreen*
FIRERED	Rarity: **Only One**	Fighting Gym in Saffron City
LEAFGREEN	Rarity: **Only One**	Fighting Gym in Saffron City
COLOSSEUM	Rarity: **None**	Trade from *FireRed/LeafGreen*
EMERALD	Rarity: **None**	Trade from *FireRed/LeafGreen*
XD	Rarity: **Only One**	Citadark Island (Capture from Cipher Peon Karbon)

MOVES

Level	Attack	Type	Power	ACC	PP	Level	Attack	Type	Power	ACC	PP
—	Comet Punch	Normal	18	85	15	26	Ice Punch	Ice	75	100	15
—	Revenge	Fighting	60	100	10	26	Thunderpunch	Electric	75	100	15
7	Agility	Psychic	—	—	30	32	Sky Uppercut	Fighting	85	90	15
13	Pursuit	Dark	40	100	20	38	Mega Punch	Normal	80	85	20
20	Mach Punch	Fighting	40	100	30	44	Detect	Fight	—	—	5
26	Fire Punch	Fire	75	100	15	50	Counter	Fighting	—	100	20

TM/HM

TM/HM#	Name	Type	Power	ACC	PP	TM/HM#	Name	Type	Power	ACC	PP
TM01	Focus Punch	Fighting	150	100	20	TM31	Brick Break	Fighting	75	100	15
TM06	Toxic	Poison	—	85	10	TM32	Double Team	Normal	—	—	15
TM08	Bulk Up	Fighting	—	—	20	TM39	Rock Tomb	Rock	50	80	10
TM10	Hidden Power	Normal	—	100	15	TM42	Facade	Normal	70	100	20
TM11	Sunny Day	Fire	—	—	5	TM43	Secret Power	Normal	70	100	20
TM17	Protect	Normal	—	—	10	TM44	Rest	Psychic	—	—	10
TM18	Rain Dance	Water	—	—	5	TM45	Attract	Normal	—	100	15
TM21	Frustration	Normal	—	100	20	TM46	Thief	Dark	40	100	10
TM26	Earthquake	Ground	100	100	10	HM04	Strength	Normal	80	100	20
TM27	Return	Normal	—	100	20	HM06	Rock Smash	Fighting	20	100	15

MOVE TUTOR
FireRed/LeafGreen and Emerald Only

Body Slam*	Metronome	Seismic Toss*
Double-Edge	Mimic	Rock Slide*
Mega Punch*	Substitute	
Mega Kick*	Counter*	

*Battle Frontier tutor move (*Emerald*)

108 Lickitung™

GENERAL INFO

SPECIES: Licking Pokémon
HEIGHT: 3'11"
WEIGHT: 144 lbs.
ABILITY 1: Oblivious
Prevents Lickitung from being attracted.
ABILITY 2: Own Tempo
Prevents Lickitung from being confused.

STATS

EVOLUTIONS

DOES NOT EVOLVE

LOCATION[s]:

RUBY	Rarity: **None**	Trade from *FireRed/LeafGreen*	
SAPPHIRE	Rarity: **None**	Trade from *FireRed/LeafGreen*	
FIRERED	Rarity: **Only One**	Trade for Golduck (Route 18)	
LEAFGREEN	Rarity: **Only One**	Trade for Slowbro (Route 18)	
COLOSSEUM	Rarity: **None**	Trade from *FireRed/LeafGreen*	
EMERALD	Rarity: **None**	Trade from *FireRed/LeafGreen*	
XD	Rarity: **Only One**	Citadark Island (Capture from Cipher Peon Geftal)	

MOVES

Level	Attack	Type	Power	ACC	PP	Level	Attack	Type	Power	ACC	PP
—	Lick	Ghost	20	100	30	29	Wrap	Normal	15	85	20
7	Supersonic	Normal	—	55	20	34	Disable	Normal	—	55	20
12	Defense Curl	Normal	—	—	40	40	Slam	Normal	80	75	20
18	Knock Off	Dark	20	100	20	45	Screech	Normal	—	85	40
23	Stomp	Normal	65	100	20	51	Refresh	Normal	—	100	20

TM/HM

TM/HM#	Name	Type	Power	ACC	PP	TM/HM#	Name	Type	Power	ACC	PP
TM01	Focus Punch	Fighting	150	100	20	TM30	Shadow Ball	Ghost	80	100	15
TM03	Water Pulse	Water	60	95	20	TM31	Brick Break	Fighting	75	100	15
TM06	Toxic	Poison	—	85	10	TM32	Double Team	Normal	—	—	15
TM10	Hidden Power	Normal	—	100	15	TM34	Shock Wave	Electric	60	—	20
TM11	Sunny Day	Fire	—	—	5	TM35	Flamethrower	Fire	95	100	15
TM13	Ice Beam	Ice	95	100	10	TM37	Sandstorm	Ground	—	—	10
TM14	Blizzard	Ice	120	70	5	TM38	Fire Blast	Fire	120	85	5
TM15	Hyper Beam	Normal	150	90	5	TM39	Rock Tomb	Rock	50	80	10
TM17	Protect	Normal	—	—	10	TM42	Facade	Normal	70	100	20
TM18	Rain Dance	Water	—	—	5	TM43	Secret Power	Normal	70	100	20
TM21	Frustration	Normal	—	100	20	TM44	Rest	Psychic	—	—	10
TM22	Solarbeam	Grass	120	100	10	TM45	Attract	Normal	—	100	15
TM23	Iron Tail	Steel	75	75	15	TM46	Thief	Dark	40	100	10
TM24	Thunderbolt	Electric	95	100	15	HM01	Cut	Normal	50	95	30
TM25	Thunder	Electric	120	70	10	HM03	Surf	Water	95	100	15
TM26	Earthquake	Ground	100	100	10	HM04	Strength	Normal	80	100	15
TM27	Return	Normal	—	100	20	HM06	Rock Smash	Fighting	20	100	15
TM28	Dig	Ground	60	100	10						

EGG MOVES*

Name	Type	Power	ACC	PP
Belly Drum	Normal	—	—	10
Body Slam	Normal	85	100	15
Curse	—	—	—	10
Magnitude	Ground	—	100	30
Sleep Talk	Normal	—	—	10
Smellingsalt	Normal	60	100	10
Snore	Normal	40	100	15
Substitute	Normal	—	—	10

*Learned Via Breeding

MOVE TUTOR

FireRed/LeafGreen and Emerald Only

Body Slam*	Mimic	Seismic Toss*
Double-Edge	Substitute	Rock Slide*
Mega Punch*	Swords Dance*	Dream Eater*
Mega Kick*	Counter*	

*Battle Frontier tutor move (*Emerald*)

109 Koffing™

POISON

GENERAL INFO

SPECIES: Poison Gas Pokémon
HEIGHT: 2'00"
WEIGHT: 2 lbs.
ABILITY: Levitate

Protects Koffing from being hit by Ground-type attacks.

STATS

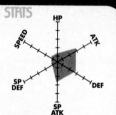

EVOLUTIONS

LV35

LOCATION[s]:

RUBY	Rarity: **Common**	Fiery Path
SAPPHIRE	Rarity: **Common**	Fiery Path
FIRERED	Rarity: **Common**	Pokémon Mansion
LEAFGREEN	Rarity: **Common**	Pokémon Mansion
COLOSSEUM	Rarity: **None**	Trade from *Ruby/Sapphire/FireRed/LeafGreen*
EMERALD	Rarity: **Common**	Fiery Path
XD	Rarity: **None**	Trade from *Ruby/Sapphire/FireRed/LeafGreen*

MOVES

Level	Attack	Type	Power	ACC	PP		Level	Attack	Type	Power	ACC	PP
—	Poison Gas	Poison	—	55	40		25	Smokescreen	Normal	—	100	20
—	Tackle	Normal	35	95	35		33	Haze	Ice	—	—	30
9	Smog	Poison	20	70	20		41	Explosion	Normal	250	100	5
17	Selfdestruct	Normal	200	100	5		45	Destiny Bond	Ghost	—	—	5
21	Sludge	Poison	65	100	20		49	Memento	Dark	—	100	10

TM/HM

TM/HM#	Name	Type	Power	ACC	PP		TM/HM#	Name	Type	Power	ACC	PP
TM06	Toxic	Poison	—	85	10		TM34	Shock Wave	Electric	60	—	20
TM10	Hidden Power	Normal	—	100	15		TM35	Flamethrower	Fire	95	100	15
TM11	Sunny Day	Fire	—	—	5		TM36	Sludge Bomb	Poison	90	100	10
TM12	Taunt	Dark	—	100	20		TM38	Fire Blast	Fire	120	85	5
TM17	Protect	Normal	—	—	10		TM41	Torment	Dark	—	100	15
TM18	Rain Dance	Water	—	—	5		TM42	Facade	Normal	70	100	20
TM21	Frustration	Normal	—	100	20		TM43	Secret Power	Normal	70	100	20
TM24	Thunderbolt	Electric	95	100	15		TM44	Rest	Psychic	—	—	10
TM25	Thunder	Electric	120	70	10		TM45	Attract	Normal	—	100	15
TM27	Return	Normal	—	100	20		TM46	Thief	Dark	40	100	10
TM30	Shadow Ball	Ghost	80	100	15		HM05	Flash	Normal	—	70	20
TM32	Double Team	Normal	—	—	15							

EGG MOVES*

Name	Type	Power	ACC	PP
Screech	Normal	—	85	40
Psywave	Psychic	—	80	15
Destiny Bond	Ghost	—	—	5
Will-O-Wisp	Fire	—	75	15
Psybeam	Psychic	65	100	20
Pain Split	Normal	—	100	10

*Learned Via Breeding

MOVE TUTOR

FireRed/LeafGreen and Emerald Only

Mimic	Substitute	Explosion

Emerald Only

Endure*	Sleep Talk	Swagger
Rollout	Snore*	

*Battle Frontier tutor move (*Emerald*)

110 Weezing™

POISON

GENERAL INFO

SPECIES: Poison Gas Pokémon
HEIGHT: 3'11"
WEIGHT: 21 lbs.
ABILITY: Levitate

Protects Weezing from being hit by Ground-type attacks.

STATS

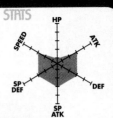

EVOLUTIONS

LV35

LOCATION(s):

RUBY	Rarity: **Evolve**	Evolve Koffing
SAPPHIRE	Rarity: **Evolve**	Evolve Koffing
FIRERED	Rarity: **Rare**	Evolve Koffing, Pokémon Mansion
LEAFGREEN	Rarity: **Evolve**	Evolve Koffing
COLOSSEUM	Rarity: **None**	Trade from *Ruby/Sapphire/FireRed/LeafGreen*
EMERALD	Rarity: **Evolve**	Evolve Koffing
XD	Rarity: **None**	Trade from *Ruby/Sapphire/FireRed/LeafGreen*

MOVES

Level	Attack	Type	Power	ACC	PP	Level	Attack	Type	Power	ACC	PP
—	Poison Gas	Poison	—	55	40	25	Smokescreen	Normal	—	100	20
—	Tackle	Normal	35	95	35	33	Haze	Ice	—	—	30
—	Smog	Poison	20	70	20	44	Explosion	Normal	250	100	5
—	Selfdestruct	Normal	200	100	5	51	Destiny Bond	Ghost	—	—	5
21	Sludge	Poison	65	100	20	58	Memento	Dark	—	100	10

TM/HM

TM/HM#	Name	Type	Power	ACC	PP	TM/HM#	Name	Type	Power	ACC	PP
TM06	Toxic	Poison	—	85	10	TM32	Double Team	Normal	—	—	15
TM10	Hidden Power	Normal	—	100	15	TM34	Shock Wave	Electric	60	—	20
TM11	Sunny Day	Fire	—	—	5	TM35	Flamethrower	Fire	95	100	15
TM12	Taunt	Dark	—	100	20	TM36	Sludge Bomb	Poison	90	100	10
TM15	Hyper Beam	Normal	150	90	5	TM38	Fire Blast	Fire	120	85	5
TM17	Protect	Normal	—	—	10	TM41	Torment	Dark	—	100	15
TM18	Rain Dance	Water	—	—	5	TM42	Facade	Normal	70	100	20
TM21	Frustration	Normal	—	100	20	TM43	Secret Power	Normal	70	100	20
TM24	Thunderbolt	Electric	95	100	15	TM44	Rest	Psychic	—	—	10
TM25	Thunder	Electric	120	70	10	TM45	Attract	Normal	—	100	15
TM27	Return	Normal	—	100	20	TM46	Thief	Dark	40	100	10
TM30	Shadow Ball	Ghost	80	100	15	HM05	Flash	Normal	—	70	20

MOVE TUTOR

FireRed/LeafGreen and Emerald Only

Mimic	Substitute	Explosion

Emerald Only

Endure*	Sleep Talk	Swagger
Rollout	Snore*	

*Battle Frontier tutor move (*Emerald*)

111 Rhyhorn™

GROUND   ROCK

GENERAL INFO
SPECIES: Spikes Pokémon
HEIGHT: 3'03"
WEIGHT: 254 lbs.
ABILITY 1: Rock Head
Prevents Rhyhorn from taking recoil damage from Submission, Take Down, and Double-Edge.
ABILITY 2: Lightningrod
In a 2-on-2 battle, Electric-type moves attack Rhyhorn.

STATS
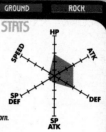

EVOLUTIONS

LV42

LOCATION(s):

RUBY	Rarity: **Common**	Safari Zone	
SAPPHIRE	Rarity: **Common**	Safari Zone	
FIRERED	Rarity: **Rare**	Safari Zone	
LEAFGREEN	Rarity: **Rare**	Safari Zone	
COLOSSEUM	Rarity: **None**	Trade from *Ruby/Sapphire/FireRed/LeafGreen*	
EMERALD	Rarity: **Common**	Safari Zone	
XD	Rarity: **None**	Trade from *Ruby/Sapphire/FireRed/LeafGreen*	

MOVES

Level	Attack	Type	Power	ACC	PP
—	Horn Attack	Normal	65	100	25
—	Tail Whip	Normal	—	100	30
10	Stomp	Normal	65	100	20
15	Fury Attack	Normal	15	85	20
24	Scary Face	Normal	—	90	10
29	Rock Blast	Rock	25	80	10
38	Horn Drill	Normal	—	30	5
43	Take Down	Normal	90	85	20
52	Earthquake	Ground	100	100	10
57	Megahorn	Bug	120	85	10

TM/HM

TM/HM#	Name	Type	Power	ACC	PP
TM05	Roar	Normal	—	100	20
TM06	Toxic	Poison	—	85	10
TM10	Hidden Power	Normal	—	100	15
TM11	Sunny Day	Fire	—	—	5
TM13	Ice Beam	Ice	95	100	10
TM14	Blizzard	Ice	120	70	5
TM17	Protect	Normal	—	—	10
TM18	Rain Dance	Water	—	—	5
TM21	Frustration	Normal	—	100	20
TM23	Iron Tail	Steel	75	75	15
TM24	Thunderbolt	Electric	95	100	15
TM25	Thunder	Electric	120	70	10
TM26	Earthquake	Ground	100	100	10
TM27	Return	Normal	—	100	20
TM28	Dig	Ground	60	100	10
TM32	Double Team	Normal	—	—	15
TM34	Shock Wave	Electric	60	—	20
TM35	Flamethrower	Fire	95	100	15
TM37	Sandstorm	Normal	—	—	10
TM38	Fire Blast	Fire	120	85	5
TM39	Rock Tomb	Rock	50	80	10
TM42	Facade	Normal	70	100	20
TM43	Secret Power	Normal	70	100	20
TM44	Rest	Psychic	—	—	10
TM45	Attract	Normal	—	100	15
TM46	Thief	Dark	40	100	10
HM04	Strength	Normal	80	100	20
HM06	Rock Smash	Fighting	20	100	15

EGG MOVES*

Name	Type	Power	ACC	PP
Crunch	Dark	80	100	15
Reversal	Fighting	—	100	15
Rock Slide	Rock	75	90	10
Counter	Fighting	—	100	20
Magnitude	Ground	—	100	30
Swords Dance	Normal	—	—	30
Curse	—	—	—	10
Crush Claw	Normal	75	95	10

*Learned Via Breeding

MOVE TUTOR
FireRed/LeafGreen and Emerald Only

Body Slam*	Substitute	Rock Slide*
Double-Edge	Swords Dance*	
Mimic	Counter*	

Emerald Only

Endure*	Mud-Slap*	Sleep Talk
Icy Wind*	Rollout	Swagger

*Battle Frontier tutor move (*Emerald*)

112 Rhydon™

GROUND   ROCK

GENERAL INFO

SPECIES: Drill Pokémon
HEIGHT: 6'03"
WEIGHT: 265 lbs.
ABILITY 1: Rock Head
Prevents Rhydon from taking recoil damage from Submission, Take Down, and Double-Edge.
ABILITY 2: Lightningrod
In a 2-on-2 battle, Electric-type moves attack Rhydon.

STATS

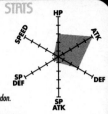

EVOLUTIONS

LV42

LOCATION[s]:

RUBY	Rarity: **Evolve**	Evolve Rhyhorn
SAPPHIRE	Rarity: **Evolve**	Evolve Rhyhorn
FIRERED	Rarity: **Evolve**	Evolve Rhyhorn
LEAFGREEN	Rarity: **Evolve**	Evolve Rhyhorn
COLOSSEUM	Rarity: **None**	Trade from *Ruby/Sapphire/FireRed/LeafGreen*
EMERALD	Rarity: **Evolve**	Evolve Rhyhorn
XD	Rarity: **Only One**	Citadark Island (Capture from Master Greevil)

MOVES

Level	Attack	Type	Power	ACC	PP	Level	Attack	Type	Power	ACC	PP
—	Horn Attack	Normal	65	100	25	29	Rock Blast	Rock	25	80	10
—	Tail Whip	Normal	—	100	30	38	Horn Drill	Normal	—	30	5
—	Stomp	Normal	65	100	20	46	Take Down	Normal	90	85	20
—	Fury Attack	Normal	15	85	20	58	Earthquake	Ground	100	100	10
24	Scary Face	Normal	—	90	10	66	Megahorn	Bug	120	85	10

TM/HM

TM/HM#	Name	Type	Power	ACC	PP	TM/HM#	Name	Type	Power	ACC	PP
TM01	Focus Punch	Fighting	150	100	20	TM31	Brick Break	Fighting	75	100	15
TM05	Roar	Normal	—	100	20	TM32	Double Team	Normal	—	—	15
TM06	Toxic	Poison	—	85	10	TM34	Shock Wave	Electric	60	—	20
TM10	Hidden Power	Normal	—	100	15	TM35	Flamethrower	Fire	95	100	15
TM11	Sunny Day	Fire	—	—	5	TM37	Sandstorm	Ground	—	—	10
TM13	Ice Beam	Ice	95	100	10	TM38	Fire Blast	Fire	120	85	5
TM14	Blizzard	Ice	120	70	5	TM39	Rock Tomb	Rock	50	80	10
TM15	Hyper Beam	Normal	150	90	5	TM42	Facade	Normal	70	100	20
TM17	Protect	Normal	—	—	10	TM43	Secret Power	Normal	70	100	20
TM18	Rain Dance	Water	—	—	5	TM44	Rest	Psychic	—	—	10
TM21	Frustration	Normal	—	100	20	TM45	Attract	Normal	—	100	15
TM23	Iron Tail	Steel	75	75	15	TM46	Thief	Dark	40	100	10
TM24	Thunderbolt	Electric	95	100	15	HM01	Cut	Normal	50	95	30
TM25	Thunder	Electric	120	70	10	HM03	Surf	Water	95	100	15
TM26	Earthquake	Ground	100	100	10	HM04	Strength	Normal	80	100	15
TM27	Return	Normal	—	100	20	HM06	Rock Smash	Fighting	20	100	15
TM28	Dig	Ground	60	100	10						

MOVE TUTOR
FireRed/LeafGreen and Emerald Only

Body Slam*	Mimic	Swords Dance*
Double-Edge	Substitute	Rock Slide*
Mega Punch*	Counter*	
Mega Kick*	Seismic Toss*	

Emerald Only

Dynamicpunch*	Icy Wind*	Snore*
Endure*	Mud-Slap*	Swagger
Fire Punch*	Rollout	Thunderpunch*
Fury Cutter	Sleep Talk	

*Battle Frontier tutor move (*Emerald*)

113 Chansey™

NORMAL

GENERAL INFO

SPECIES: Egg Pokémon
HEIGHT: 3'07"
WEIGHT: 76 lbs.
ABILITY 1: Natural Cure
Any status problem is cured when Chansey is switched out.
ABILITY 2: Serene Grace
When Chansey is in battle, the chances of extra effects occurring are doubled.

STATS

EVOLUTIONS

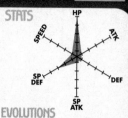

(FRIENDSHIP)

LOCATION[s]:

RUBY	Rarity: **None**	Trade from *FireRed/LeafGreen*
SAPPHIRE	Rarity: **None**	Trade from *FireRed/LeafGreen*
FIRERED	Rarity: **Rare**	Safari Zone
LEAFGREEN	Rarity: **Rare**	Safari Zone
COLOSSEUM	Rarity: **None**	Trade from *FireRed/LeafGreen*
EMERALD	Rarity: **None**	Trade from *FireRed/LeafGreen*
XD	Rarity: **Only One**	Citadark Island (Capture from Cipher Peon Leden)

MOVES

Level	Attack	Type	Power	ACC	PP	Level	Attack	Type	Power	ACC	PP
—	Pound	Normal	40	100	35	23	Minimize	Normal	—	—	20
—	Growl	Normal	—	100	40	29	Sing	Normal	—	55	15
5	Tail Whip	Normal	—	100	30	35	Egg Bomb	Normal	100	75	10
9	Refresh	Normal	—	100	20	41	Defense Curl	Normal	—	—	40
13	Softboiled	Normal	—	100	10	49	Light Screen	Psychic	—	—	30
17	Doubleslap	Normal	15	85	10	57	Double-Edge	Normal	120	100	15

TM/HM

TM/HM#	Name	Type	Power	ACC	PP	TM/HM#	Name	Type	Power	ACC	PP
TM01	Focus Punch	Fighting	150	100	20	TM27	Return	Normal	—	100	20
TM03	Water Pulse	Water	60	95	20	TM29	Psychic	Psychic	90	100	10
TM04	Calm Mind	Psychic	—	—	20	TM30	Shadow Ball	Ghost	80	100	15
TM06	Toxic	Poison	—	85	10	TM31	Brick Break	Fighting	75	100	15
TM07	Hail	Ice	—	—	10	TM32	Double Team	Normal	—	—	15
TM10	Hidden Power	Normal	—	100	15	TM34	Shock Wave	Electric	60	—	20
TM11	Sunny Day	Fire	—	—	5	TM35	Flamethrower	Fire	95	100	15
TM13	Ice Beam	Ice	95	100	10	TM37	Sandstorm	Ground	—	—	10
TM14	Blizzard	Ice	120	70	5	TM38	Fire Blast	Fire	120	85	5
TM15	Hyper Beam	Normal	150	90	5	TM39	Rock Tomb	Rock	50	80	10
TM16	Light Screen	Psychic	—	—	30	TM42	Facade	Normal	70	100	20
TM17	Protect	Normal	—	—	10	TM43	Secret Power	Normal	70	100	20
TM18	Rain Dance	Water	—	—	5	TM44	Rest	Psychic	—	—	10
TM20	Safeguard	Normal	—	—	25	TM45	Attract	Normal	—	100	15
TM21	Frustration	Normal	—	100	20	TM48	Skill Swap	Psychic	—	100	10
TM22	Solarbeam	Grass	120	100	10	TM49	Snatch	Dark	—	100	10
TM23	Iron Tail	Steel	75	75	15	HM04	Strength	Normal	80	100	15
TM24	Thunderbolt	Electric	95	100	15	HM05	Flash	Normal	—	70	20
TM25	Thunder	Electric	120	70	10	HM06	Rock Smash	Fighting	20	100	15
TM26	Earthquake	Ground	100	100	10						

EGG MOVES*

Name	Type	Power	ACC	PP
Aromatherapy	Grass	—	—	5
Heal Bell	Normal	—	—	5
Metronome	Normal	—	—	10
Present	Normal	—	90	15
Substitute	Normal	—	—	10

*Learned Via Breeding

MOVE TUTOR

FireRed/LeafGreen and Emerald Only

Body Slam*	Metronome	Counter*
Double-Edge	Mimic	Seismic Toss*
Mega Punch*	Softboiled	Dream Eater*
Mega Kick*	Substitute	Thunder Wave

*Battle Frontier tutor move (*Emerald*)

114 Tangela™

GRASS

GENERAL INFO

SPECIES: Vine Pokémon
HEIGHT: 3'03"
WEIGHT: 77 lbs.
ABILITY: Chlorophyll

When the sunlight is strong, Tangela's Speed doubles.

STATS

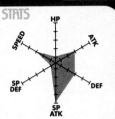

EVOLUTIONS

DOES NOT EVOLVE

LOCATION[s]:

RUBY	Rarity: **None**	Trade from *FireRed/LeafGreen*
SAPPHIRE	Rarity: **None**	Trade from *FireRed/LeafGreen*
FIRERED	Rarity: **Rare**	Route 21, One Island
LEAFGREEN	Rarity: **Rare**	Route 21, One Island
COLOSSEUM	Rarity: **None**	Trade from *FireRed/LeafGreen*
EMERALD	Rarity: **None**	Trade from *FireRed/LeafGreen*
XD	Rarity: **Only One**	Cipher Key Lair (Capture from Cipher Peon Targ)

MOVES

Level	Attack	Type	Power	ACC	PP
—	Constrict	Normal	10	100	35
—	Ingrain	Grass	—	100	20
4	Sleep Powder	Grass	—	75	15
10	Absorb	Grass	20	100	10
13	Growth	Normal	—	—	40
19	Poisonpowder	Poison	—	75	35

Level	Attack	Type	Power	ACC	PP
22	Vine Whip	Grass	35	100	10
28	Bind	Normal	15	75	20
31	Mega Drain	Grass	40	100	10
37	Stun Spore	Grass	—	75	30
40	Slam	Normal	80	75	20
46	Tickle	Normal	—	100	20

TM/HM

TM/HM#	Name	Type	Power	ACC	PP
TM06	Toxic	Poison	—	85	10
TM09	Bullet Seed	Grass	10	100	30
TM10	Hidden Power	Normal	—	100	15
TM11	Sunny Day	Fire	—	—	5
TM15	Hyper Beam	Normal	150	90	5
TM17	Protect	Normal	—	—	10
TM19	Giga Drain	Grass	60	100	5
TM21	Frustration	Normal	—	100	20
TM22	Solarbeam	Grass	120	100	10
TM27	Return	Normal	—	100	20

TM/HM#	Name	Type	Power	ACC	PP
TM32	Double Team	Normal	—	—	15
TM36	Sludge Bomb	Poison	90	100	10
TM42	Facade	Normal	70	100	20
TM43	Secret Power	Normal	70	100	20
TM44	Rest	Psychic	—	—	10
TM45	Attract	Normal	—	100	15
TM46	Thief	Dark	40	100	10
HM01	Cut	Normal	50	95	30
HM05	Flash	Normal	—	70	20
HM06	Rock Smash	Fighting	20	100	15

EGG MOVES*

Name	Type	Power	ACC	PP
Amnesia	Psychic	—	—	20
Confusion	Psychic	50	100	25
Flail	Normal	—	100	15
Leech Seed	Grass	—	90	10
Mega Drain	Grass	40	100	10
Nature Power	Normal	—	95	20
Reflect	Psychic	—	—	20

*Learned Via Breeding

MOVE TUTOR

FireRed/LeafGreen and Emerald Only

Body Slam*	Mimic	Swords Dance
Double-Edge	Substitute	

*Battle Frontier tutor move (*Emerald*)

115 Kangaskhan™

NORMAL

GENERAL INFO
SPECIES: Parent Pokémon
HEIGHT: 7'03"
WEIGHT: 176 lbs.
ABILITY: Early Bird
Allows Kangaskhan to wake up earlier when put to sleep.

EVOLUTIONS

DOES NOT EVOLVE

STATS

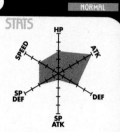

LOCATION[s]:

RUBY	Rarity: **None**	Trade from *FireRed/LeafGreen*
SAPPHIRE	Rarity: **None**	Trade from *FireRed/LeafGreen*
FIRERED	Rarity: **Rare**	Safari Zone
LEAFGREEN	Rarity: **Rare**	Safari Zone
COLOSSEUM	Rarity: **None**	Trade from *FireRed/LeafGreen*
EMERALD	Rarity: **None**	Trade from *FireRed/LeafGreen*
XD	Rarity: **Only One**	Citadark Island (Capture from Cipher Peon Litnar)

MOVES

Level	Attack	Type	Power	ACC	PP		Level	Attack	Type	Power	ACC	PP
—	Comet Punch	Normal	18	85	15		25	Mega Punch	Normal	80	85	20
—	Leer	Normal	—	100	30		31	Rage	Normal	20	100	20
7	Bite	Dark	60	100	25		37	Endure	Normal	—	—	10
13	Tail Whip	Normal	—	100	30		43	Dizzy Punch	Normal	70	100	10
19	Fake Out	Normal	40	100	10		49	Reversal	Fighting	—	100	15

TM/HM

TM/HM#	Name	Type	Power	ACC	PP		TM/HM#	Name	Type	Power	ACC	PP
TM01	Focus Punch	Fighting	150	100	20		TM28	Dig	Ground	60	100	10
TM03	Water Pulse	Water	60	95	20		TM31	Brick Break	Fighting	75	100	15
TM05	Roar	Normal	—	100	20		TM32	Double Team	Normal	—	—	15
TM06	Toxic	Poison	—	85	10		TM34	Shock Wave	Electric	60	—	20
TM07	Hail	Ice	—	—	10		TM35	Flamethrower	Fire	95	100	15
TM10	Hidden Power	Normal	—	100	15		TM37	Sandstorm	Ground	—	—	10
TM11	Sunny Day	Fire	—	—	5		TM38	Fire Blast	Fire	120	85	5
TM13	Ice Beam	Ice	95	100	10		TM39	Rock Tomb	Rock	50	80	10
TM14	Blizzard	Ice	120	70	5		TM40	Aerial Ace	Flying	60	—	20
TM15	Hyper Beam	Normal	150	90	5		TM42	Facade	Normal	70	100	20
TM17	Protect	Normal	—	—	10		TM43	Secret Power	Normal	70	100	20
TM18	Rain Dance	Water	—	—	5		TM44	Rest	Psychic	—	—	10
TM21	Frustration	Normal	—	100	20		TM45	Attract	Normal	—	100	15
TM22	Solarbeam	Grass	120	100	10		TM46	Thief	Dark	40	100	10
TM23	Iron Tail	Steel	75	75	15		HM01	Cut	Normal	50	95	30
TM24	Thunderbolt	Electric	95	100	15		HM03	Surf	Water	40	100	15
TM25	Thunder	Electric	120	100	10		HM04	Strength	Normal	80	100	20
TM26	Earthquake	Ground	100	100	10		HM06	Rock Smash	Fighting	20	100	15
TM27	Return	Normal	—	100	20							

EGG MOVES*

Name	Type	Power	ACC	PP
Counter	Fighting	—	100	20
Crush Claw	Normal	75	95	10
Disable	Normal	—	55	20
Focus Energy	Normal	—	—	30
Foresight	Normal	—	100	40
Safeguard	Normal	—	—	25
Stomp	Normal	65	100	20
Substitute	Normal	—	—	10

*Learned Via Breeding

MOVE TUTOR
FireRed/LeafGreen and Emerald Only

Body Slam*	Mega Kick*	Counter*
Double-Edge	Mimic	Seismic Toss*
Mega Punch*	Substitute	Rock Slide*

*Battle Frontier tutor move (*Emerald*)

116 Horsea ™

WATER

GENERAL INFO

SPECIES: Dragon Pokémon
HEIGHT: 1'04"
WEIGHT: 18 lbs.
ABILITY: Swift Swim

Increases Horsea's Speed when it's raining.

STATS

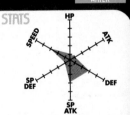

EVOLUTIONS

LV32

TRADE WITH
DRAGON SCALE

LOCATION(s):

RUBY	Rarity: **Common**	Routes 132, 133, 134 (Super Rod)
SAPPHIRE	Rarity: **Common**	Routes 132, 133, 134 (Super Rod)
FIRERED	Rarity: **Common**	Routes 4, 10, 12, 13, 19, 20, 21, 24, Vermilion City
LEAFGREEN	Rarity: **Common**	Routes 4, 10, 12, 13, 19, 20, 21, 24, Vermilion City
COLOSSEUM	Rarity: **None**	Trade from *Ruby/Sapphire/FireRed/LeafGreen*
EMERALD	Rarity: **Common**	Routes 132, 133, 134, Pacifidlog Town
XD	Rarity: **None**	Trade from *Ruby/Sapphire/FireRed/LeafGreen*

MOVES

Level	Attack	Type	Power	ACC	PP
—	Bubble	Water	20	100	30
8	Smokescreen	Normal	—	100	20
15	Leer	Normal	—	100	30
22	Water Gun	Water	40	100	25

Level	Attack	Type	Power	ACC	PP
29	Twister	Dragon	40	100	20
36	Agility	Psychic	—	—	30
43	Hydro Pump	Water	120	80	5
50	Dragon Dance	Dragon	—	—	20

TM/HM

TM/HM#	Name	Type	Power	ACC	PP
TM03	Water Pulse	Water	60	95	20
TM06	Toxic	Poison	—	85	10
TM07	Hail	Ice	—	—	10
TM10	Hidden Power	Normal	—	100	15
TM13	Ice Beam	Ice	95	100	10
TM14	Blizzard	Ice	120	70	5
TM17	Protect	Normal	—	—	10
TM18	Rain Dance	Water	—	—	5
TM21	Frustration	Normal	—	100	20

TM/HM#	Name	Type	Power	ACC	PP
TM27	Return	Normal	—	100	20
TM32	Double Team	Normal	—	—	15
TM42	Facade	Normal	70	100	20
TM43	Secret Power	Normal	70	100	20
TM44	Rest	Psychic	—	—	10
TM45	Attract	Normal	—	100	15
HM03	Surf	Water	95	100	15
HM07	Waterfall	Water	80	100	15
HM08	Dive	Water	60	100	10

EGG MOVES*

Name	Type	Power	ACC	PP
Flail	Normal	—	100	15
Aurora Beam	Ice	65	100	20
Disable	Normal	—	55	20
Dragon Rage	Dragon	—	100	10
Dragonbreath	Dragon	60	100	20
Octazooka	Water	65	85	10
Bounce	Flying	85	85	5

*Learned Via Breeding

MOVE TUTOR

FireRed/LeafGreen and Emerald Only

Double-Edge	Mimic	Substitute

Emerald Only

Endure*	Sleep Talk	Swagger
Icy Wind*	Snore*	Swift*

*Battle Frontier tutor move (*Emerald*)

PRIMA OFFICIAL GAME GUIDE

117 Seadra™

WATER

GENERAL INFO
SPECIES: Dragon Pokémon
HEIGHT: 3'11"
WEIGHT: 55 lbs.
ABILITY: Poison Point

The opponent has a 30% chance of being poisoned if Seadra is directly hit.

STATS

EVOLUTIONS

LV32 TRADE WITH DRAGON SCALE

LOCATION(s):

RUBY	Rarity: **Evolve**	Evolve Horsea
SAPPHIRE	Rarity: **Evolve**	Evolve Horsea
FIRERED	Rarity: **Rare**	Evolve Horsea, Islands One, Three, Five, Six, Seven, Routes 19–21
LEAFGREEN	Rarity: **Evolve**	Evolve Horsea
COLOSSEUM	Rarity: **None**	Trade from *Ruby/Sapphire/FireRed/LeafGreen*
EMERALD	Rarity: **Evolve**	Evolve Horsea
XD	Rarity: **None**	Trade from *Ruby/Sapphire/FireRed/LeafGreen*

MOVES

Level	Attack	Type	Power	ACC	PP
—	Bubble	Water	20	100	30
—	Smokescreen	Normal	—	100	20
—	Leer	Normal	—	100	30
—	Water Gun	Water	40	100	25
29	Twister	Dragon	40	100	20
40	Agility	Psychic	—	—	30
51	Hydro Pump	Water	120	80	5
62	Dragon Dance	Dragon	—	—	20

TM/HM

TM/HM#	Name	Type	Power	ACC	PP
TM03	Water Pulse	Water	60	95	20
TM06	Toxic	Poison	—	85	10
TM07	Hail	Ice	—	—	10
TM10	Hidden Power	Normal	—	100	15
TM13	Ice Beam	Ice	95	100	10
TM14	Blizzard	Ice	120	70	5
TM15	Hyper Beam	Normal	150	90	5
TM17	Protect	Normal	—	—	10
TM18	Rain Dance	Water	—	—	5
TM21	Frustration	Normal	—	100	20
TM27	Return	Normal	—	100	20
TM32	Double Team	Normal	—	—	15
TM42	Facade	Normal	70	100	20
TM43	Secret Power	Normal	70	100	20
TM44	Rest	Psychic	—	—	10
TM45	Attract	Normal	—	100	15
HM03	Surf	Water	95	100	15
HM07	Waterfall	Water	80	100	15
HM08	Dive	Water	60	100	10

MOVE TUTOR
FireRed/LeafGreen and Emerald Only

Double-Edge	Mimic	Substitute

Emerald Only

Endure*	Sleep Talk	Swagger
Icy Wind*	Snore*	Swift*

*Battle Frontier tutor move (*Emerald*)

118 Goldeen™

GENERAL INFO

SPECIES: Goldfish Pokémon
HEIGHT: 2'00"
WEIGHT: 33 lbs.
ABILITY 1: Swift Swim
Doubles Goldeen's Speed when it's raining.
ABILITY 2: Water Veil
Protects Goldeen from being burned.

STATS

HP
SPEED
ATK
SP DEF
DEF
SP ATK

EVOLUTIONS

LV33

LOCATION[s]:

RUBY	Rarity: **Common**	Routes 102, 111, 114, 117, 120, Petalburg City, Victory Road, Meteor Falls, Safari Zone
SAPPHIRE	Rarity: **Common**	Routes 102, 111, 114, 117, 120, Petalburg City, Victory Road, Meteor Falls, Safari Zone
FIRERED	Rarity: **Common**	Viridian City, Cerulean Cave, Islands Two, Three, Four, Six, Safari Zone
LEAFGREEN	Rarity: **Common**	Viridian City, Cerulean Cave, Islands Two, Three, Four, Six, Safari Zone
COLOSSEUM	Rarity: **None**	Trade from *Ruby/Sapphire/FireRed/LeafGreen*
EMERALD	Rarity: **Common**	Routes 102, 111, 114, 117, 120, Meteor Falls, Safari Zone, Victory Road
XD	Rarity: **None**	Trade from *Ruby/Sapphire/FireRed/LeafGreen*

MOVES

Level	Attack	Type	Power	ACC	PP		Level	Attack	Type	Power	ACC	PP
—	Peck	Flying	35	100	35		29	Fury Attack	Normal	15	85	20
—	Tail Whip	Normal	—	100	30		38	Waterfall	Water	80	100	15
—	Water Sport	Water	—	100	15		43	Horn Drill	Normal	—	30	5
10	Supersonic	Normal	—	55	20		52	Agility	Psychic	—	—	30
15	Horn Attack	Normal	65	100	25		57	Megahorn*	Bug	120	85	10
24	Flail	Normal	—	100	15							

*Not Available in Emerald

TM/HM

TM/HM#	Name	Type	Power	ACC	PP		TM/HM#	Name	Type	Power	ACC	PP
TM03	Water Pulse	Water	60	95	20		TM27	Return	Normal	—	100	20
TM06	Toxic	Poison	—	85	10		TM32	Double Team	Normal	—	—	15
TM07	Hail	Ice	—	—	10		TM42	Facade	Normal	70	100	20
TM10	Hidden Power	Normal	—	100	15		TM43	Secret Power	Normal	70	100	20
TM13	Ice Beam	Ice	95	100	10		TM44	Rest	Psychic	—	—	10
TM14	Blizzard	Ice	120	70	5		TM45	Attract	Normal	—	100	15
TM17	Protect	Normal	—	—	10		HM03	Surf	Water	95	100	15
TM18	Rain Dance	Water	—	—	5		HM07	Waterfall	Water	80	100	15
TM21	Frustration	Normal	—	100	20		HM08	Dive	Water	60	100	10

EGG MOVES*

Name	Type	Power	ACC	PP
Psybeam	Psychic	65	100	20
Hydro Pump	Water	120	80	5
Sleep Talk	Normal	—	—	10
Mud Sport	Ground	—	100	15
Haze	Ice	—	—	30

*Learned Via Breeding

MOVE TUTOR
FireRed/LeafGreen and Emerald Only

Double-Edge	Mimic	Substitute

Emerald Only

Endure*	Sleep Talk	Swagger
Icy Wind*	Snore*	Swift*

*Battle Frontier tutor move (*Emerald*)

PRIMA OFFICIAL GAME GUIDE

119 Seaking™

WATER

GENERAL INFO
SPECIES: Goldfish Pokémon
HEIGHT: 4'03"
WEIGHT: 86 lbs.
ABILITY 1: Swift Swim
Doubles Seaking's Speed when it's raining.
ABILITY 2: Water Veil
Protects Seaking from being burned.

STATS
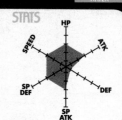

EVOLUTIONS

LV33

LOCATION(s):

RUBY	Rarity: **Common**	Evolve Goldeen, Safari Zone
SAPPHIRE	Rarity: **Common**	Evolve Goldeen, Safari Zone
FIRERED	Rarity: **Rare**	Evolve Goldeen, Three Island, Safari Zone, Fuchsia City
LEAFGREEN	Rarity: **Rare**	Evolve Goldeen, Three Island, Safari Zone, Fuchsia City
COLOSSEUM	Rarity: **None**	Trade from *Ruby/Sapphire/FireRed/LeafGreen*
EMERALD	Rarity: **Common**	Evolve Goldeen, Safari Zone
XD	Rarity: **None**	Trade from *Ruby/Sapphire/FireRed/LeafGreen*

MOVES

Level	Attack	Type	Power	ACC	PP	Level	Attack	Type	Power	ACC	PP
—	Peck	Flying	35	100	35	29	Fury Attack	Normal	15	85	20
—	Tail Whip	Normal	—	100	30	41	Waterfall	Water	80	100	15
—	Water Sport	Water	—	100	15	49	Horn Drill	Normal	—	30	5
—/10	Supersonic	Normal	—	55	20	61	Agility	Psychic	—	—	30
15	Horn Attack	Normal	65	100	25	69	Megahorn*	Bug	120	85	10
24	Flail	Normal	—	100	15						

 # = Emerald Only *Not Available in Emerald

TM/HM

TM/HM#	Name	Type	Power	ACC	PP	TM/HM#	Name	Type	Power	ACC	PP
TM03	Water Pulse	Water	60	95	20	TM27	Return	Normal	—	100	20
TM06	Toxic	Poison	—	85	10	TM32	Double Team	Normal	—	—	15
TM07	Hail	Ice	—	—	10	TM42	Facade	Normal	70	100	20
TM10	Hidden Power	Normal	—	100	15	TM43	Secret Power	Normal	70	100	20
TM13	Ice Beam	Ice	95	100	10	TM44	Rest	Psychic	—	—	10
TM14	Blizzard	Ice	120	70	5	TM45	Attract	Normal	—	100	15
TM15	Hyper Beam	Normal	150	90	5	HM03	Surf	Water	95	100	15
TM17	Protect	Normal	—	—	10	HM07	Waterfall	Water	80	100	15
TM18	Rain Dance	Water	—	—	5	HM08	Dive	Water	60	100	10
TM21	Frustration	Normal	—	100	20						

MOVE TUTOR
FireRed/LeafGreen and Emerald Only

Double-Edge	Mimic	Substitute

Emerald Only

Endure*	Sleep Talk	Swagger
Icy Wind*	Snore*	Swift*

*Battle Frontier tutor move (Emerald)

130

120 Staryu™

WATER

GENERAL INFO

SPECIES: Star Shape Pokémon
HEIGHT: 2'07"
WEIGHT: 76 lbs.
ABILITY 1: Illuminate

When Staryu is in the first slot, the chances of running into a wild Pokémon increase.

ABILITY 2: Natural Cure

When Staryu gets switched out, whatever status condition it had is cured.

STATS

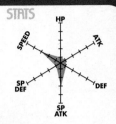

EVOLUTIONS

WATER STONE

LOCATION[s]:

RUBY	Rarity: **Common**	Lilycove City (Super Rod)
SAPPHIRE	Rarity: **Common**	Lilycove City (Super Rod)
FIRERED	Rarity: **None**	Trade from *Ruby/Sapphire/LeafGreen*
LEAFGREEN	Rarity: **Common**	One Island, Five Island, Pallet Town, Vermilion City (Fish)
COLOSSEUM	Rarity: **None**	Trade from *Ruby/Sapphire/LeafGreen*
EMERALD	Rarity: **Common**	Lilycove City (Super Rod)
XD	Rarity: **None**	Trade from *Ruby/Sapphire/LeafGreen*

MOVES

Level	Attack	Type	Power	ACC	PP		Level	Attack	Type	Power	ACC	PP
—	Tackle	Normal	35	95	35		24	Swift	Normal	60	—	20
—	Harden	Normal	—	—	30		28	Bubblebeam	Water	65	100	20
6	Water Gun	Water	40	100	25		33	Minimize	Normal	—	—	20
10	Rapid Spin	Normal	20	100	40		37	Light Screen	Psychic	—	—	30
15	Recover	Normal	—	—	20		42	Cosmic Power	Normal	—	—	20
19	Camouflage	Normal	—	100	20		46	Hydro Pump	Water	120	80	5

TM/HM

TM/HM#	Name	Type	Power	ACC	PP		TM/HM#	Name	Type	Power	ACC	PP
TM03	Water Pulse	Water	60	95	20		TM27	Return	Normal	—	100	20
TM06	Toxic	Poison	—	85	10		TM29	Psychic	Psychic	90	100	10
TM07	Hail	Ice	—	—	10		TM32	Double Team	Normal	—	—	15
TM10	Hidden Power	Normal	—	100	15		TM33	Reflect	Normal	—	—	20
TM13	Ice Beam	Ice	95	100	10		TM42	Facade	Normal	70	100	20
TM14	Blizzard	Ice	120	70	5		TM43	Secret Power	Normal	70	100	20
TM16	Light Screen	Psychic	—	—	30		TM44	Rest	Psychic	—	—	10
TM17	Protect	Normal	—	—	10		HM03	Surf	Water	95	100	15
TM18	Rain Dance	Water	—	—	5		HM05	Flash	Normal	—	70	20
TM21	Frustration	Normal	—	100	20		HM07	Waterfall	Water	80	100	15
TM24	Thunderbolt	Electric	95	100	15		HM08	Dive	Water	60	100	10
TM25	Thunder	Electric	120	70	10							

EGG MOVES*

Name	Type	Power	ACC	PP
None				

*Learned Via Breeding

MOVE TUTOR

FireRed/LeafGreen and Emerald Only

Double-Edge	Substitute	Thunder Wave*
Mimic		

Emerald Only

Endure*	Sleep Talk	Swift*
Icy Wind*	Snore*	
Psych Up*	Swagger	

*Battle Frontier tutor move (Emerald)

121 Starmie™

GENERAL INFO

SPECIES: Mysterious Pokémon
HEIGHT: 3'07"
WEIGHT: 176 lbs.
ABILITY 1: Illuminate
When Starmie is in the first slot, the chances of running into a wild Pokémon increase.

ABILITY 2: Natural Cure
When Starmie gets switched out, whatever status condition it had is cured.

STATS

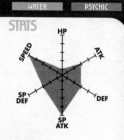

EVOLUTIONS

WATER STONE

LOCATION[s]:

RUBY	Rarity: **Evolve**	Evolve Staryu
SAPPHIRE	Rarity: **Evolve**	Evolve Staryu
FIRERED	Rarity: **None**	Trade from *Ruby/Sapphire/LeafGreen*
LEAFGREEN	Rarity: **Evolve**	Evolve Staryu
COLOSSEUM	Rarity: **None**	Trade from *Ruby/Sapphire/LeafGreen*
EMERALD	Rarity: **Evolve**	Evolve Staryu
XD	Rarity: **Only One**	Citadark Island (Capture from Cipher Admin Snattle)

MOVES

Level	Attack	Type	Power	ACC	PP		Level	Attack	Type	Power	ACC	PP
—	Water Gun	Water	40	100	25		—	Recover	Normal	—	—	20
—	Rapid Spin	Normal	20	100	40		—	Swift	Normal	60	—	20
							33	Confuse Ray	Ghost	—	100	10

TM/HM

TM/HM#	Name	Type	Power	ACC	PP		TM/HM#	Name	Type	Power	ACC	PP
TM03	Water Pulse	Water	60	95	20		TM27	Return	Normal	—	100	20
TM06	Toxic	Poison	—	85	10		TM29	Psychic	Psychic	90	100	10
TM07	Hail	Ice	—	—	10		TM32	Double Team	Normal	—	—	15
TM10	Hidden Power	Normal	—	100	15		TM33	Reflect	Normal	—	—	20
TM13	Ice Beam	Ice	95	100	10		TM42	Facade	Normal	70	100	20
TM14	Blizzard	Ice	120	70	5		TM43	Secret Power	Normal	70	100	20
TM15	Hyper Beam	Normal	150	90	5		TM44	Rest	Psychic	—	—	10
TM16	Light Screen	Psychic	—	—	30		TM48	Skill Swap	Psychic	—	100	10
TM17	Protect	Normal	—	—	10		HM03	Surf	Water	95	100	15
TM18	Rain Dance	Water	—	—	5		HM05	Flash	Normal	—	70	20
TM21	Frustration	Normal	—	100	20		HM07	Waterfall	Water	80	100	15
TM24	Thunderbolt	Electric	95	100	15		HM08	Dive	Water	60	100	10
TM25	Thunder	Electric	120	70	10							

EGG MOVES*

Name	Type	Power	ACC	PP
None				

*Learned Via Breeding

MOVE TUTOR
FireRed/LeafGreen and Emerald Only

Double-Edge	Substitute	Thunder Wave*
Mimic	Dream Eater*	

Emerald Only

Endure*	Sleep Talk	Swift*
Icy Wind*	Snore*	
Psych Up*	Swagger	

*Battle Frontier tutor move (*Emerald*)

122 Mr. Mime™

PSYCHIC

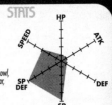

GENERAL INFO

SPECIES: Barrier Pokémon
HEIGHT: 4'03"
WEIGHT: 123 lbs.
ABILITY: Soundproof
Prevents Mr. Mime from being hit by Grasswhistle, Growl, Heal Bell, Hyper Voice, Metal Sound, Perish Song, Roar, Screech, Sing, Snore, Supersonic, and Uproar.

STATS

(Stat chart: HP, ATK, DEF, SP ATK, SP DEF, SPEED)

EVOLUTIONS

DOES NOT EVOLVE

LOCATION[S]:

RUBY	Rarity: **None**	Trade from *FireRed/LeafGreen*
SAPPHIRE	Rarity: **None**	Trade from *FireRed/LeafGreen*
FIRERED	Rarity: **Only One**	Trade for Abra on Route 2
LEAFGREEN	Rarity: **Only One**	Trade for Abra on Route 2
COLOSSEUM	Rarity: **None**	Trade from *FireRed/LeafGreen*
EMERALD	Rarity: **None**	Trade from *FireRed/LeafGreen*
XD	Rarity: **Only One**	Citadark Island (Capture from Cipher Admin Gorigan)

MOVES

Level	Attack	Type	Power	ACC	PP
—	Barrier	Psychic	—	—	30
5	Confusion	Psychic	50	100	25
8	Substitute	Normal	—	—	10
12	Mediate	Psychic	—	—	40
15	Doubleslap	Normal	15	85	10
19	Light Screen	Psychic	—	—	30
19	Reflect	Psychic	—	—	20
22	Magical Leaf	Grass	60	—	20

Level	Attack	Type	Power	ACC	PP
26	Encore	Normal	—	100	5
29	Psybeam	Psychic	65	100	20
33	Recycle	Normal	—	100	10
36	Trick	Psychic	—	100	10
40	Role Play	Psychic	—	100	10
43	Psychic	Psychic	90	100	10
47	Baton Pass	Normal	—	—	40
50	Safeguard	Normal	—	—	25

TM/HM

TM/HM#	Name	Type	Power	ACC	PP
TM01	Focus Punch	Fighting	150	100	20
TM04	Calm Mind	Psychic	—	—	20
TM06	Toxic	Poison	—	85	10
TM10	Hidden Power	—	—	100	15
TM11	Sunny Day	Fire	—	—	5
TM12	Taunt	Dark	—	100	20
TM15	Hyper Beam	Normal	150	90	5
TM16	Light Screen	Psychic	—	—	30
TM17	Protect	Normal	—	—	10
TM18	Rain Dance	Water	—	—	5
TM20	Safeguard	Normal	—	—	25
TM21	Frustration	Normal	—	100	20
TM22	Solarbeam	Grass	120	100	10
TM24	Thunderbolt	Electric	95	100	15
TM25	Thunder	Electric	120	70	10
TM27	Return	Normal	—	100	20

TM/HM#	Name	Type	Power	ACC	PP
TM29	Psychic	Psychic	90	100	10
TM30	Shadow Ball	Ghost	80	100	15
TM31	Brick Break	Fighting	75	100	15
TM32	Double Team	Normal	—	—	15
TM33	Reflect	Normal	—	—	20
TM34	Shock Wave	Electric	60	—	20
TM41	Torment	Dark	—	100	15
TM42	Facade	Normal	70	100	20
TM43	Secret Power	Normal	70	100	20
TM44	Rest	Psychic	—	—	10
TM45	Attract	Normal	—	100	15
TM46	Thief	Dark	40	100	10
TM48	Skill Swap	Psychic	—	100	10
TM49	Snatch	Dark	—	100	10
HM05	Flash	Normal	—	70	20

EGG MOVES*

Name	Type	Power	ACC	PP
Fake Out	Normal	40	100	10
Future Sight	Psychic	80	90	15
Hypnosis	Psychic	—	60	20
Mimic	Normal	—	100	10
Psych Up	Normal	—	—	10
Trick	Psychic	—	100	10

*Learned Via Breeding

MOVE TUTOR

FireRed/LeafGreen and Emerald Only

Body Slam*	Mimic	Seismic Toss*
Double-Edge	Metronome	Dream Eater*
Mega Punch*	Substitute	Thunder Wave*
Mega Kick*	Counter*	

*Battle Frontier tutor move (*Emerald*)

PRIMA OFFICIAL GAME GUIDE

123 Scyther™

BUG FLYING

GENERAL INFO
SPECIES: Mantis Pokémon
HEIGHT: 4'11"
WEIGHT: 124 lbs.
ABILITY: Swarm
Multiplies Scyther's Bug-type Moves when HPs are low.

STATS

EVOLUTIONS

TRADE WITH
METAL COAT

LOCATION(s):

RUBY	Rarity: **None**	Trade from *FireRed*
SAPPHIRE	Rarity: **None**	Trade from *FireRed*
FIRERED	Rarity: **Rare**	Safari Zone
LEAFGREEN	Rarity: **None**	Trade from *FireRed*
COLOSSEUM	Rarity: **None**	Trade from *FireRed*
EMERALD	Rarity: **None**	Trade from *FireRed*
XD	Rarity: **Only One**	Citadark Island (Capture from Cipher Peon Leden)

MOVES

Level	Attack	Type	Power	ACC	PP	Level	Attack	Type	Power	ACC	PP
—	Quick Attack	Normal	40	100	30	21	Agility	Psychic	—	—	30
—	Leer	Normal	—	100	30	26	Wing Attack	Flying	60	100	35
6	Focus Energy	Normal	—	—	30	31	Slash	Normal	70	100	20
11	Pursuit	Dark	40	100	20	36	Swords Dance	Normal	—	—	30
16	False Swipe	Normal	40	100	40	41	Double Team	Normal	—	—	15
						46	Fury Cutter	Bug	10	95	20

TM/HM

TM/HM#	Name	Type	Power	ACC	PP	TM/HM#	Name	Type	Power	ACC	PP
TM06	Toxic	Poison	—	85	10	TM40	Aerial Ace	Flying	60	—	20
TM10	Hidden Power	Normal	—	100	15	TM42	Facade	Normal	70	100	20
TM11	Sunny Day	Fire	—	—	5	TM43	Secret Power	Normal	70	100	20
TM15	Hyper Beam	Normal	150	90	5	TM44	Rest	Psychic	—	—	10
TM17	Protect	Normal	—	—	10	TM45	Attract	Normal	—	100	15
TM18	Rain Dance	Water	—	—	5	TM46	Thief	Dark	40	100	10
TM21	Frustration	Normal	—	100	20	TM47	Steel Wing	Steel	70	90	25
TM27	Return	Normal	—	100	20	HM01	Cut	Normal	50	95	30
TM32	Double Team	Normal	—	—	15	HM06	Rock Smash	Fighting	20	100	15

EGG MOVES*

Name	Type	Power	ACC	PP
Baton Pass	Normal	—	—	40
Counter	Fighting	—	100	20
Endure	Normal	—	—	10
Light Screen	Psychic	—	—	30
Reversal	Fighting	—	100	15
Safeguard	Normal	—	—	25
Silver Wind	Bug	60	100	5

*Learned Via Breeding

MOVE TUTOR
FireRed/LeafGreen and Emerald Only

Double-Edge	Substitute	Counter*
Mimic	Swords Dance*	

*Battle Frontier tutor move (*Emerald*)

124 Jynx™

| ICE | PSYCHIC |

GENERAL INFO

SPECIES: Human Shape Pokémon
HEIGHT: 4'07"
WEIGHT: 90 lbs.
ABILITY: Oblivious
Prevents Jynx from being attracted.

STATS

Stat chart showing HP, ATK, DEF, SP ATK, SP DEF, SPEED

EVOLUTIONS

LV30

LOCATION[S]:

RUBY	Rarity: **None**	Trade from *FireRed/LeafGreen*
SAPPHIRE	Rarity: **None**	Trade from *FireRed/LeafGreen*
FIRERED	Rarity: **Only One**	Trade for Poliwhirl in Cerulean City
LEAFGREEN	Rarity: **Only One**	Trade for Poliwhirl in Cerulean City
COLOSSEUM	Rarity: **None**	Trade from *FireRed/LeafGreen*
EMERALD	Rarity: **None**	Trade from *FireRed/LeafGreen*
XD	Rarity: **None**	Trade from *FireRed/LeafGreen*

MOVES

Level	Attack	Type	Power	ACC	PP
—	Pound	Normal	40	100	35
—	Lick	Ghost	20	100	30
—	Lovely Kiss	Normal	—	75	10
—	Powder Snow	Ice	40	100	25
21	Doubleslap	Normal	15	85	10

Level	Attack	Type	Power	ACC	PP
25	Ice Punch	Ice	75	100	15
35	Mean Look	Normal	—	100	5
41	Fake Tears	Dark	—	100	20
51	Body Slam	Normal	85	100	15
57	Perish Song	Normal	—	—	5
67	Blizzard	Ice	120	70	5

TM/HM

TM/HM#	Name	Type	Power	ACC	PP
TM01	Focus Punch	Fighting	150	100	20
TM03	Water Pulse	Water	60	95	20
TM04	Calm Mind	Psychic	—	—	20
TM06	Toxic	Poison	—	85	10
TM07	Hail	Ice	—	—	10
TM10	Hidden Power	Normal	—	100	15
TM12	Taunt	Dark	—	100	20
TM13	Ice Beam	Ice	95	100	10
TM14	Blizzard	Ice	120	70	5
TM15	Hyper Beam	Normal	150	90	5
TM16	Light Screen	Psychic	—	—	30
TM17	Protect	Normal	—	—	10
TM18	Rain Dance	Water	—	—	5
TM21	Frustration	Normal	—	100	20

TM/HM#	Name	Type	Power	ACC	PP
TM27	Return	Normal	—	100	20
TM29	Psychic	Psychic	90	100	10
TM30	Shadow Ball	Ghost	80	100	15
TM31	Brick Break	Fighting	75	100	15
TM32	Double Team	Normal	—	—	15
TM33	Reflect	Normal	—	—	20
TM41	Torment	Dark	—	100	15
TM42	Facade	Normal	70	100	20
TM43	Secret Power	Normal	70	100	20
TM44	Rest	Psychic	—	—	10
TM45	Attract	Normal	—	100	15
TM46	Thief	Dark	40	100	10
TM48	Skill Swap	Psychic	—	100	10
HM05	Flash	Normal	—	70	20

MOVE TUTOR
FireRed/LeafGreen and Emerald Only

Body Slam*	Metronome	Seismic Toss*
Double-Edge	Mimic	Dream Eater*
Mega Punch*	Substitute	
Mega Kick*	Counter*	

*Battle Frontier tutor move (*Emerald*)

125 Electabuzz™

ELECTRIC

GENERAL INFO
SPECIES: Electric Pokémon
HEIGHT: 3'07"
WEIGHT: 66 lbs.
ABILITY: Static

An opponent has a 30% chance of being paralyzed when it directly strikes Electabuzz.

STATS

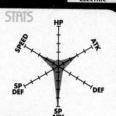

EVOLUTIONS

 ►

LV30

LOCATION[s]:

RUBY	Rarity: **None**	Trade from *FireRed*
SAPPHIRE	Rarity: **None**	Trade from *FireRed*
FIRERED	Rarity: **Rare**	Power Plant
LEAFGREEN	Rarity: **None**	Trade from *FireRed*
COLOSSEUM	Rarity: **None**	Trade from *FireRed*
EMERALD	Rarity: **None**	Trade from *FireRed*
XD	Rarity: **Only One**	Citadark Island (Capture from Cipher Admin Ardos)

MOVES

Level	Attack	Type	Power	ACC	PP
—	Quick Attack	Normal	40	100	30
—	Leer	Normal	—	100	30
—	Thunderpunch	Electric	75	100	15
17	Light Screen	Psychic	—	—	30
25	Swift	Normal	60	—	20
36	Screech	Normal	—	85	40
47	Thunderbolt	Electric	95	100	15
58	Thunder	Electric	120	70	10

TM/HM

TM/HM#	Name	Type	Power	ACC	PP
TM01	Focus Punch	Fighting	150	100	20
TM06	Toxic	Poison	—	85	10
TM10	Hidden Power	Normal	—	100	15
TM15	Hyper Beam	Normal	150	90	5
TM16	Light Screen	Psychic	—	—	30
TM17	Protect	Normal	—	—	10
TM18	Rain Dance	Water	—	—	5
TM21	Frustration	Normal	—	100	20
TM23	Iron Tail	Steel	75	75	15
TM24	Thunderbolt	Electric	95	100	15
TM25	Thunder	Electric	120	70	10
TM27	Return	Normal	—	100	20
TM29	Psychic	Psychic	90	100	10
TM31	Brick Break	Fighting	75	100	15
TM32	Double Team	Normal	—	—	15
TM34	Shock Wave	Electric	60	—	20
TM42	Facade	Normal	70	100	20
TM43	Secret Power	Normal	70	100	20
TM44	Rest	Psychic	—	—	10
TM45	Attract	Normal	—	100	15
TM46	Thief	Dark	40	100	10
HM04	Strength	Normal	80	100	20
HM05	Flash	Normal	—	70	20
HM06	Rock Smash	Fighting	20	100	15

MOVE TUTOR
FireRed/LeafGreen and Emerald Only

Body Slam*	Mega Kick*	Counter*
Double-Edge	Mimic	Seismic Toss*
Mega Punch*	Substitute	Thunder Wave*

*Battle Frontier tutor move (*Emerald*)

126 Magmar™

FIRE

GENERAL INFO

SPECIES: Spitfire Pokémon
HEIGHT: 4'03"
WEIGHT: 98 lbs.
ABILITY: Flame Body
If Magmar is struck directly, the opponent has a 30% chance of being burned.

STATS

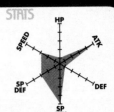

EVOLUTIONS

LV30

LOCATION[s]:

Game	Rarity	Location
RUBY	Rarity: **None**	Trade from *LeafGreen*
SAPPHIRE	Rarity: **None**	Trade from *LeafGreen*
FIRERED	Rarity: **None**	Trade from *LeafGreen*
LEAFGREEN	Rarity: **Rare**	One Island
COLOSSEUM	Rarity: **None**	Trade from *LeafGreen*
EMERALD	Rarity: **None**	Trade from *LeafGreen*
XD	Rarity: **Only One**	Citadark Island (Capture from Cipher Peon Grupel)

MOVES

Level	Attack	Type	Power	ACC	PP	Level	Attack	Type	Power	ACC	PP
—	Ember	Fire	40	100	25	25	Smokescreen	Normal	—	100	20
—	Leer	Normal	—	100	30	33	Sunny Day	Fire	—	—	5
—	Smog	Poison	20	70	20	41	Flamethrower	Fire	95	100	15
—	Fire Punch	Fire	75	100	15	49	Confuse Ray	Ghost	—	100	10
						57	Fire Blast	Fire	120	85	5

TM/HM

TM/HM#	Name	Type	Power	ACC	PP	TM/HM#	Name	Type	Power	ACC	PP
TM01	Focus Punch	Fighting	150	100	20	TM32	Double Team	Normal	—	—	15
TM06	Toxic	Poison	—	85	10	TM35	Flamethrower	Fire	95	100	15
TM10	Hidden Power	Normal	—	100	15	TM38	Fire Blast	Fire	120	85	5
TM11	Sunny Day	Fire	—	—	5	TM42	Facade	Normal	70	100	20
TM15	Hyper Beam	Normal	150	90	5	TM43	Secret Power	Normal	70	100	20
TM17	Protect	Normal	—	—	10	TM44	Rest	Psychic	—	—	10
TM21	Frustration	Normal	—	100	20	TM45	Attract	Normal	—	100	15
TM23	Iron Tail	Steel	75	75	15	TM46	Thief	Dark	40	100	10
TM27	Return	Normal	—	100	20	HM04	Strength	Normal	80	100	20
TM29	Psychic	Psychic	90	100	10	HM06	Rock Smash	Fighting	20	100	15
TM31	Brick Break	Fighting	75	100	15						

MOVE TUTOR

FireRed/LeafGreen and Emerald Only

Body Slam*	Mega Kick*	Counter*
Double-Edge	Mimic	Seismic Toss*
Mega Punch*	Substitute	

*Battle Frontier tutor move (*Emerald*)

PRIMA OFFICIAL GAME GUIDE

127 Pinsir™

BUG

GENERAL INFO
SPECIES: Stag Beetle Pokémon
HEIGHT: 4'11"
WEIGHT: 121 lbs.
ABILITY: Hyper Cutter
Pinsir's attack power cannot be decreased.

STATS

EVOLUTIONS

DOES NOT EVOLVE

LOCATION(s):

RUBY	Rarity: **Rare**	Safari Zone
SAPPHIRE	Rarity: **Rare**	Safari Zone
FIRERED	Rarity: **None**	Trade from *Ruby/Sapphire/LeafGreen*
LEAFGREEN	Rarity: **Rare**	Safari Zone
COLOSSEUM	Rarity: **None**	Trade from *Ruby/Sapphire/LeafGreen*
EMERALD	Rarity: **Rare**	Safari Zone
XD	Rarity: **Only One**	Citadark Island (Capture from Cipher Peon Grupel)

MOVES

Level	Attack	Type	Power	ACC	PP
—	Vicegrip	Normal	55	100	30
—	Focus Energy	Normal	—	—	30
7	Bind	Normal	15	75	20
13	Seismic Toss	Fighting	—	100	20
19	Harden	Normal	—	—	30

Level	Attack	Type	Power	ACC	PP
25	Revenge	Fighting	60	100	10
31	Brick Break	Fighting	75	100	15
37	Guillotine	Normal	—	30	5
43	Submission	Fighting	80	80	25
49	Swords Dance	Normal	—	—	30

TM/HM

TM/HM#	Name	Type	Power	ACC	PP
TM01	Focus Punch	Fighting	150	100	20
TM06	Toxic	Poison	—	85	10
TM08	Bulk Up	Fighting	—	—	20
TM10	Hidden Power	Normal	—	100	15
TM11	Sunny Day	Fire	—	—	5
TM15	Hyper Beam	Normal	150	90	5
TM17	Protect	Normal	—	—	10
TM18	Rain Dance	Water	—	—	5
TM21	Frustration	Normal	—	100	20
TM26	Earthquake	Ground	100	100	10
TM27	Return	Normal	—	100	20
TM28	Dig	Ground	60	100	10

TM/HM#	Name	Type	Power	ACC	PP
TM31	Brick Break	Fighting	75	100	15
TM32	Double Team	Normal	—	—	15
TM39	Rock Tomb	Rock	50	80	10
TM42	Facade	Normal	70	100	20
TM43	Secret Power	Normal	70	100	20
TM44	Rest	Psychic	—	—	10
TM45	Attract	Normal	—	100	15
TM46	Thief	Dark	40	100	10
HM01	Cut	Normal	50	95	30
HM04	Strength	Normal	80	100	20
HM06	Rock Smash	Fighting	20	100	15

EGG MOVES*

Name	Type	Power	ACC	PP
Fury Attack	Normal	15	85	20
False Swipe	Normal	40	100	40
Faint Attack	Dark	60	—	20
Flail	Normal	—	100	15

*Learned Via Breeding

MOVE TUTOR
FireRed/LeafGreen and Emerald Only

Body Slam*	Substitute	Rock Slide*
Double-Edge	Swords Dance*	
Mimic	Seismic Toss*	

Emerald Only

Endure*	Sleep Talk	Swagger
Fury Cutter	Snore*	

*Battle Frontier tutor move (Emerald)

128 Tauros™

GENERAL INFO

SPECIES: **Wild Bull Pokémon**
HEIGHT: **4'07"**
WEIGHT: **195 lbs.**
ABILITY: **Intimidate**

An opponent's Attack decreases when Tauros is summoned into battle.

STATS

EVOLUTIONS

DOES NOT EVOLVE

LOCATION[s]:

RUBY	Rarity: **None**	Trade from *FireRed/LeafGreen*
SAPPHIRE	Rarity: **None**	Trade from *FireRed/LeafGreen*
FIRERED	Rarity: **Rare**	Safari Zone
LEAFGREEN	Rarity: **Rare**	Safari Zone
COLOSSEUM	Rarity: **None**	Trade from *FireRed/LeafGreen*
EMERALD	Rarity: **None**	Trade from *FireRed/LeafGreen*
XD	Rarity: **Only One**	Citadark Island (Capture from Master Greevil)

MOVES

Level	Attack	Type	Power	ACC	PP	Level	Attack	Type	Power	ACC	PP
—	Tackle	Normal	35	95	35	19	Pursuit	Dark	40	100	20
—	Tail Whip	Normal	—	100	30	26	Swagger	Normal	—	90	15
4	Rage	Normal	20	100	20	34	Rest	Psychic	—	—	10
8	Horn Attack	Normal	65	100	25	43	Thrash	Normal	90	100	20
13	Scary Face	Normal	—	90	10	53	Take Down	Normal	90	85	20

TM/HM

TM/HM#	Name	Type	Power	ACC	PP	TM/HM#	Name	Type	Power	ACC	PP
TM03	Water Pulse	Water	60	95	20	TM27	Return	Normal	—	100	20
TM06	Toxic	Poison	—	85	10	TM32	Double Team	Normal	—	—	15
TM10	Hidden Power	Normal	—	100	15	TM34	Shock Wave	Electric	60	—	20
TM11	Sunny Day	Fire	—	—	5	TM35	Flamethrower	Fire	95	100	15
TM13	Ice Beam	Ice	95	100	10	TM37	Sandstorm	Ground	—	—	10
TM14	Blizzard	Ice	120	70	5	TM38	Fire Blast	Fire	120	85	5
TM15	Hyper Beam	Normal	150	90	5	TM39	Rock Tomb	Rock	50	80	10
TM17	Protect	Normal	—	—	10	TM42	Facade	Normal	70	100	20
TM18	Rain Dance	Water	—	—	5	TM43	Secret Power	Normal	70	100	20
TM21	Frustration	Normal	—	100	20	TM44	Rest	Psychic	—	—	10
TM22	Solarbeam	Grass	120	100	10	TM45	Attract	Normal	—	100	15
TM23	Iron Tail	Steel	75	75	15	HM03	Surf	Water	95	100	15
TM24	Thunderbolt	Electric	95	100	15	HM04	Strength	Normal	80	100	20
TM25	Thunder	Electric	120	70	10	HM06	Rock Smash	Fighting	20	100	15
TM26	Earthquake	Ground	100	100	10						

EGG MOVES*

Name	Type	Power	ACC	PP
None				

*Learned Via Breeding

MOVE TUTOR

FireRed/LeafGreen and Emerald Only

Body Slam*	Mimic	Substitute
Double-Edge		

*Battle Frontier tutor move (*Emerald*)

129 Magikarp™

GENERAL INFO

SPECIES: Fish Pokémon
HEIGHT: 2'11"
WEIGHT: 22 lbs.
ABILITY: Swift Swim

Increases Magikarp's Speed when it's raining.

STATS

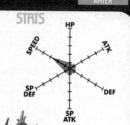

EVOLUTIONS

LV20

LOCATION[s]:

RUBY	Rarity: **Common**	All Fishing Holes
SAPPHIRE	Rarity: **Common**	All Fishing Holes
FIRERED	Rarity: **Common**	All Fishing Holes
LEAFGREEN	Rarity: **Common**	All Fishing Holes
COLOSSEUM	Rarity: **None**	Trade from *Ruby/Sapphire/FireRed/LeafGreen*
EMERALD	Rarity: **Common**	All Fishing Holes
XD	Rarity: **None**	Trade from *Ruby/Sapphire/FireRed/LeafGreen*

MOVES

Level	Attack	Type	Power	ACC	PP
—	Splash	Normal	—	—	40
15	Tackle	Normal	35	95	35
30	Flail	Normal	—	100	15

TM/HM

TM/HM#	Name	Type	Power	ACC	PP
None					

EGG MOVES*

Name	Type	Power	ACC	PP
None				

*Learned Via Breeding

MOVE TUTOR
FireRed/LeafGreen and Emerald Only

None

130 Gyarados™

WATER | FLYING

GENERAL INFO
SPECIES: Atrocious Pokémon
HEIGHT: 21'04"
WEIGHT: 518 lbs.
ABILITY: Intimidate
When Gyarados enters battle, the opponent's Attack lowers.

STATS

EVOLUTIONS

LV20

LOCATION(s):

RUBY	Rarity: **Common**	Sootopolis City
SAPPHIRE	Rarity: **Common**	Sootopolis City
FIRERED	Rarity: **Common**	All Fishing Holes
LEAFGREEN	Rarity: **Common**	All Fishing Holes
COLOSSEUM	Rarity: **None**	Trade from *Ruby/Sapphire/FireRed/LeafGreen*
EMERALD	Rarity: **Rare**	Sootopolis City
XD	Rarity: **None**	Trade from *Ruby/Sapphire/FireRed/LeafGreen*

MOVES

Level	Attack	Type	Power	ACC	PP
—	Thrash	Normal	90	100	20
20	Bite	Dark	60	100	25
25	Dragon Rage	Dragon	—	100	10
30	Leer	Normal	—	100	30

Level	Attack	Type	Power	ACC	PP
35	Twister	Dragon	40	100	20
40	Hydro Pump	Water	120	80	5
45	Rain Dance	Water	—	—	5
50	Dragon Dance	Dragon	—	—	20
55	Hyper Beam	Normal	150	90	5

TM/HM

TM/HM#	Name	Type	Power	ACC	PP
TM03	Water Pulse	Water	60	95	20
TM05	Roar	Normal	—	100	20
TM06	Toxic	Poison	—	85	10
TM07	Hail	Ice	—	—	10
TM10	Hidden Power	Normal	—	100	15
TM12	Taunt	Dark	—	100	20
TM13	Ice Beam	Ice	95	100	10
TM14	Blizzard	Ice	120	70	5
TM15	Hyper Beam	Normal	150	90	5
TM17	Protect	Normal	—	—	10
TM18	Rain Dance	Water	—	—	5
TM21	Frustration	Normal	—	100	20
TM24	Thunderbolt	Electric	95	100	15
TM25	Thunder	Electric	120	70	10
TM26	Earthquake	Ground	100	100	10

TM/HM#	Name	Type	Power	ACC	PP
TM27	Return	Normal	—	100	20
TM32	Double Team	Normal	—	—	15
TM35	Flamethrower	Fire	95	100	15
TM37	Sandstorm	Ground	—	—	10
TM38	Fire Blast	Fire	120	85	5
TM41	Torment	Dark	—	100	15
TM42	Facade	Normal	70	100	20
TM43	Secret Power	Normal	70	100	20
TM44	Rest	Psychic	—	—	10
TM45	Attract	Normal	—	100	15
HM03	Surf	Water	95	100	15
HM04	Strength	Normal	80	100	20
HM06	Rock Smash	Fighting	20	100	15
HM07	Waterfall	Water	80	100	15
HM08	Dive	Water	60	100	10

MOVE TUTOR
FireRed/LeafGreen and Emerald Only

Body Slam* | Mimic | Thunder Wave*
Double-Edge | Substitute

Emerald Only

Endure* | Sleep Talk | Swagger
Icy Wind* | Snore*

*Battle Frontier tutor move (*Emerald*)

131 Lapras™

WATER | ICE

GENERAL INFO

SPECIES: Transport Pokémon
HEIGHT: 8'02"
WEIGHT: 485 lbs.
ABILITY 1: Water Absorb
Lapras gets 1/4 HPs back when a Water-type attack hits it.
ABILITY 2: Shell Armor
Protects Lapras from being hit by a critical hit.

STATS

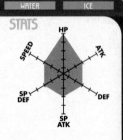

EVOLUTIONS

DOES NOT EVOLVE

LOCATION[s]:

RUBY	Rarity: **None**	Trade from *FireRed/LeafGreen*
SAPPHIRE	Rarity: **None**	Trade from *FireRed/LeafGreen*
FIRERED	Rarity: **Rare**	Sylph Co., Four Island
LEAFGREEN	Rarity: **Rare**	Sylph Co., Four Island
COLOSSEUM	Rarity: **None**	Trade from *FireRed/LeafGreen*
EMERALD	Rarity: **None**	Trade from *FireRed/LeafGreen*
XD	Rarity: **Only One**	Citadark Island (Capture from Cipher Admin Eldes)

MOVES

Level	Attack	Type	Power	ACC	PP		Level	Attack	Type	Power	ACC	PP
—	Water Gun	Water	40	100	25		25	Perish Song	Normal	—	—	5
—	Growl	Normal	—	100	40		31	Ice Beam	Ice	95	100	10
—	Sing	Normal	—	55	15		37	Rain Dance	Water	—	—	5
7	Mist	Ice	—	—	30		43	Safeguard	Normal	—	—	25
13	Body Slam	Normal	85	100	15		49	Hydro Pump	Water	120	80	5
19	Confuse Ray	Ghost	—	100	10		55	Sheer Cold	Ice	—	30	5

TM/HM

TM/HM#	Name	Type	Power	ACC	PP		TM/HM#	Name	Type	Power	ACC	PP
TM03	Water Pulse	Water	60	95	20		TM25	Thunder	Electric	120	70	10
TM05	Roar	Normal	—	100	20		TM27	Return	Normal	—	100	20
TM06	Toxic	Poison	—	85	10		TM29	Psychic	Psychic	90	100	10
TM07	Hail	Ice	—	—	10		TM32	Double Team	Normal	—	—	15
TM10	Hidden Power	Normal	—	100	15		TM34	Shock Wave	Electric	60	—	20
TM13	Ice Beam	Ice	95	100	10		TM42	Facade	Normal	70	100	20
TM14	Blizzard	Ice	120	70	5		TM43	Secret Power	Normal	70	100	20
TM15	Hyper Beam	Normal	150	90	5		TM44	Rest	Psychic	—	—	10
TM17	Protect	Normal	—	—	10		TM45	Attract	Normal	—	100	15
TM18	Rain Dance	Water	—	—	5		HM03	Surf	Water	95	100	15
TM20	Safeguard	Normal	—	—	25		HM04	Strength	Normal	80	100	20
TM21	Frustration	Normal	—	100	20		HM06	Rock Smash	Fighting	20	100	15
TM23	Iron Tail	Steel	75	75	15		HM07	Waterfall	Water	80	100	15
TM24	Thunderbolt	Electric	95	100	15		HM08	Dive	Water	60	100	10

EGG MOVES*

Name	Type	Power	ACC	PP
Curse	—	—	—	10
Dragon Dance	Dragon	—	—	20
Foresight	Normal	—	100	40
Horn Drill	Normal	—	30	5
Refresh	Normal	—	100	20
Sleep Talk	Normal	—	—	10
Substitute	Normal	—	—	10
Tickle	Normal	—	100	20

*Learned Via Breeding

MOVE TUTOR
FireRed/LeafGreen and Emerald Only

Body Slam*	Mimic	Substitute
Double-Edge	Dream Eater*	

*Battle Frontier tutor move (*Emerald*)

132 Ditto™

NORMAL

GENERAL INFO

SPECIES: Transform Pokémon
HEIGHT: 1'00"
WEIGHT: 9 lbs.
ABILITY: Limber
Protects Ditto from being paralyzed.

STATS

HP · ATK · DEF · SP ATK · SP DEF · SPEED

EVOLUTIONS

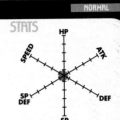

DOES NOT EVOLVE

LOCATION[s]:

Game	Rarity	Location
RUBY	Rarity: **None**	Trade from *FireRed/LeafGreen*
SAPPHIRE	Rarity: **None**	Trade from *FireRed/LeafGreen*
FIRERED	Rarity: **Common**	Cerulean Cave, Pokémon Mansion, Route 13, Route 14
LEAFGREEN	Rarity: **Common**	Cerulean Cave, Pokémon Mansion, Route 13, Route 14
COLOSSEUM	Rarity: **None**	Trade from *FireRed/LeafGreen*
EMERALD	Rarity: **None**	Trade from *FireRed/LeafGreen*
XD	Rarity: **None**	Trade from *FireRed/LeafGreen*

MOVES

Level	Attack	Type	Power	ACC	PP
—	Transform	Normal	—	—	10

TM/HM

TM/HM#	Name	Type	Power	ACC	PP
None					

EGG MOVES*

Name	Type	Power	ACC	PP
None				

*Learned Via Breeding

MOVE TUTOR
FireRed/LeafGreen and Emerald Only

None

PRIMA OFFICIAL GAME GUIDE

133 Eevee™

NORMAL

GENERAL INFO
SPECIES: Evolution Pokémon
HEIGHT: 1'00"
WEIGHT: 14 lbs.
ABILITY: Run Away
Allows Eevee to escape from any wild Pokémon.

STATS

EVOLUTIONS

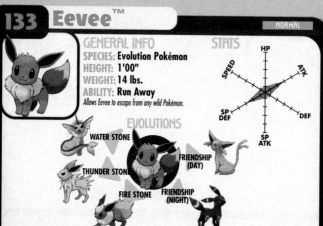

WATER STONE
THUNDER STONE
FIRE STONE
FRIENDSHIP (DAY)
FRIENDSHIP (NIGHT)

LOCATION[s]:

RUBY	Rarity: **None**	Trade from *FireRed/LeafGreen*
SAPPHIRE	Rarity: **None**	Trade from *FireRed/LeafGreen*
FIRERED	Rarity: **Only One**	Celadon Mansion Top Floor
LEAFGREEN	Rarity: **Only One**	Celadon Mansion Top Floor
COLOSSEUM	Rarity: **None**	Trade from *FireRed/LeafGreen*
EMERALD	Rarity: **None**	Trade from *FireRed/LeafGreen*
XD	Rarity: **Only One**	Starter Pokémon

MOVES

Level	Attack	Type	Power	ACC	PP	Level	Attack	Type	Power	ACC	PP
—	Tackle	Normal	35	95	35	16	Growl	Normal	—	100	40
—	Tail Whip	Normal	—	100	30	23	Quick Attack	Normal	40	100	30
—	Helping Hand	Normal	—	100	20	30	Bite	Dark	60	100	25
8	Sand-Attack	Ground	—	100	15	36	Baton Pass	Normal	—	—	40
						42	Take Down	Normal	90	85	20

TM/HM

TM/HM#	Name	Type	Power	ACC	PP	TM/HM#	Name	Type	Power	ACC	PP
TM06	Toxic	Poison	—	85	10	TM28	Dig	Ground	60	100	10
TM10	Hidden Power	Normal	—	100	15	TM30	Shadow Ball	Ghost	80	100	15
TM11	Sunny Day	Fire	—	—	5	TM32	Double Team	Normal	—	—	15
TM17	Protect	Normal	—	—	10	TM42	Facade	Normal	70	100	20
TM18	Rain Dance	Water	—	—	5	TM43	Secret Power	Normal	70	100	20
TM21	Frustration	Normal	—	100	20	TM44	Rest	Psychic	—	—	10
TM23	Iron Tail	Steel	75	75	15	TM45	Attract	Normal	—	100	15
TM27	Return	Normal	—	100	20						

EGG MOVES*

Name	Type	Power	ACC	PP
Charm	Normal	—	100	20
Curse	—	—	—	10
Endure	Normal	—	—	10
Flail	Normal	—	100	15
Tickle	Normal	—	100	20
Wish	Normal	—	—	10

*Learned Via Breeding

MOVE TUTOR
FireRed/LeafGreen and Emerald Only

Body Slam*   Mimic   Substitute
Double-Edge

*Battle Frontier tutor move (*Emerald*)

134 Vaporeon™

GENERAL INFO

SPECIES: Bubble Jet Pokémon
HEIGHT: 3'03"
WEIGHT: 64 lbs.
ABILITY: Water Absorb
When hit by Water-type attacks, Vaporeon gets 1/4 HPs back.

STATS

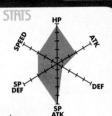

EVOLUTIONS

WATER STONE

LOCATION[s]:

RUBY	Rarity: **None**	Trade from *FireRed/LeafGreen*
SAPPHIRE	Rarity: **None**	Trade from *FireRed/LeafGreen*
FIRERED	Rarity: **None**	Evolve Eevee
LEAFGREEN	Rarity: **None**	Evolve Eevee
COLOSSEUM	Rarity: **None**	Trade from *FireRed/LeafGreen*
EMERALD	Rarity: **None**	Trade from *FireRed/LeafGreen*
XD	Rarity: **Evolve**	Evolve Eevee

MOVES

Level	Attack	Type	Power	ACC	PP
—	Tackle	Normal	35	95	35
—	Tail Whip	Normal	—	100	30
—	Helping Hand	Normal	—	100	20
8	Sand-Attack	Ground	—	100	15
16	Water Gun	Water	40	100	25
23	Quick Attack	Normal	40	100	30
30	Bite	Dark	60	100	25
36	Aurora Beam	Ice	65	100	20
42	Haze	Ice	—	—	30
47	Acid Armor	Poison	—	—	40
52	Hydro Pump	Water	120	80	5

TM/HM

TM/HM#	Name	Type	Power	ACC	PP
TM03	Water Pulse	Water	60	95	20
TM05	Roar	Normal	—	100	20
TM06	Toxic	Poison	—	85	10
TM07	Hail	Ice	—	—	10
TM10	Hidden Power	Normal	—	100	15
TM11	Sunny Day	Fire	—	—	5
TM13	Ice Beam	Ice	95	100	10
TM14	Blizzard	Ice	120	70	5
TM15	Hyper Beam	Normal	150	90	5
TM17	Protect	Normal	—	—	10
TM18	Rain Dance	Water	—	—	5
TM21	Frustration	Normal	—	100	20
TM23	Iron Tail	Steel	75	75	15
TM27	Return	Normal	—	100	20
TM28	Dig	Ground	60	100	10
TM30	Shadow Ball	Ghost	80	100	15
TM32	Double Team	Normal	—	—	15
TM42	Facade	Normal	70	100	20
TM43	Secret Power	Normal	70	100	20
TM44	Rest	Psychic	—	—	10
TM45	Attract	Normal	—	100	15
HM03	Surf	Water	95	100	15
HM07	Waterfall	Water	80	100	15
HM08	Dive	Water	60	100	10

MOVE TUTOR

FireRed/LeafGreen and Emerald Only

Body Slam*	Mimic	Substitute
Double-Edge		

*Battle Frontier tutor move (*Emerald*)

135 Jolteon™

ELECTRIC

GENERAL INFO
SPECIES: Lightning Pokémon
HEIGHT: 2'07"
WEIGHT: 54 lbs.
ABILITY: Volt Absorb
When struck by an Electric-type attack, Jolteon receives 1/4 HPs back.

STATS
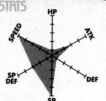

EVOLUTIONS
 ▶

THUNDER STONE

LOCATION(s):

RUBY	Rarity: **None**	Trade from *FireRed/LeafGreen*	
SAPPHIRE	Rarity: **None**	Trade from *FireRed/LeafGreen*	
FIRERED	Rarity: **None**	Evolve Eevee	
LEAFGREEN	Rarity: **None**	Evolve Eevee	
COLOSSEUM	Rarity: **None**	Trade from *FireRed/LeafGreen*	
EMERALD	Rarity: **None**	Trade from *FireRed/LeafGreen*	
XD	Rarity: **Evolve**	Evolve Eevee	

MOVES

Level	Attack	Type	Power	ACC	PP	Level	Attack	Type	Power	ACC	PP
—	Tackle	Normal	35	95	35	23	Quick Attack	Normal	40	100	30
—	Tail Whip	Normal	—	100	30	30	Double Kick	Fighting	30	100	30
—	Helping Hand	Normal	—	100	20	36	Pin Missile	Bug	14	85	20
8	Sand-Attack	Ground	—	100	15	42	Thunder Wave	Electric	—	100	20
16	Thundershock	Electric	40	100	30	47	Agility	Psychic	—	—	30
						52	Thunder	Electric	120	70	10

TM/HM

TM/HM#	Name	Type	Power	ACC	PP	TM/HM#	Name	Type	Power	ACC	PP
TM05	Roar	Normal	—	100	20	TM27	Return	Normal	—	100	20
TM06	Toxic	Poison	—	85	10	TM28	Dig	Ground	60	100	10
TM10	Hidden Power	Normal	—	100	15	TM30	Shadow Ball	Ghost	80	100	15
TM11	Sunny Day	Fire	—	—	5	TM32	Double Team	Normal	—	—	15
TM15	Hyper Beam	Normal	150	90	5	TM34	Shock Wave	Electric	60	—	20
TM17	Protect	Normal	—	—	10	TM42	Facade	Normal	70	100	20
TM18	Rain Dance	Water	—	—	5	TM43	Secret Power	Normal	70	100	20
TM21	Frustration	Normal	—	100	20	TM44	Rest	Psychic	—	—	10
TM23	Iron Tail	Steel	75	75	15	TM45	Attract	Normal	—	100	15
TM24	Thunderbolt	Electric	95	100	15	HM05	Flash	Normal	—	70	20
TM25	Thunder	Electric	120	70	10						

MOVE TUTOR
FireRed/LeafGreen and Emerald Only

Body Slam*	Mimic	Thunder Wave*
Double-Edge	Substitute	

*Battle Frontier tutor move (*Emerald*)

136 Flareon™

FIRE

GENERAL INFO

SPECIES: Flame Pokémon
HEIGHT: 2'11"
WEIGHT: 55 lbs.
ABILITY: Flash Fire

Enhances its Fire-type moves and protects Flareon from being damaged by Fire-Type moves.

STATS

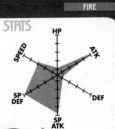

EVOLUTIONS

FIRE STONE

LOCATION[S]:

RUBY	Rarity: **None**	Trade from *FireRed/LeafGreen*
SAPPHIRE	Rarity: **None**	Trade from *FireRed/LeafGreen*
FIRERED	Rarity: **None**	Evolve Eevee
LEAFGREEN	Rarity: **None**	Evolve Eevee
COLOSSEUM	Rarity: **None**	Trade from *FireRed/LeafGreen*
EMERALD	Rarity: **None**	Trade from *FireRed/LeafGreen*
XD	Rarity: **Evolve**	Evolve Eevee

MOVES

Level	Attack	Type	Power	ACC	PP	Level	Attack	Type	Power	ACC	PP
—	Tackle	Normal	35	95	35	23	Quick Attack	Normal	40	100	30
—	Tail Whip	Normal	—	100	30	30	Bite	Dark	60	100	25
—	Helping Hand	Normal	—	100	20	36	Fire Spin	Fire	15	70	15
8	Sand-Attack	Ground	—	100	15	42	Smog	Poison	20	70	20
16	Ember	Fire	40	100	25	47	Leer	Normal	—	100	30
						52	Flamethrower	Fire	95	100	15

TM/HM

TM/HM#	Name	Type	Power	ACC	PP	TM/HM#	Name	Type	Power	ACC	PP
TM05	Roar	Normal	—	100	20	TM28	Dig	Ground	60	100	10
TM06	Toxic	Poison	—	85	10	TM30	Shadow Ball	Ghost	80	100	15
TM10	Hidden Power	Normal	—	100	15	TM32	Double Team	Normal	—	—	15
TM11	Sunny Day	Fire	—	—	5	TM35	Flamethrower	Fire	95	100	15
TM15	Hyper Beam	Normal	150	90	5	TM38	Fire Blast	Fire	120	85	5
TM17	Protect	Normal	—	—	10	TM42	Facade	Normal	70	100	20
TM18	Rain Dance	Water	—	—	5	TM43	Secret Power	Normal	70	100	20
TM21	Frustration	Normal	—	100	20	TM44	Rest	Psychic	—	—	10
TM23	Iron Tail	Steel	75	75	15	TM45	Attract	Normal	—	100	15
TM27	Return	Normal	—	100	20	TM50	Overheat	Fire	140	90	5

MOVE TUTOR

FireRed/LeafGreen and Emerald Only

Body Slam*	Mimic	Substitute
Double-Edge		

*Battle Frontier tutor move (*Emerald*)

137 Porygon™

NORMAL

GENERAL INFO

SPECIES: **Virtual Pokémon**
HEIGHT: **2'07"**
WEIGHT: **80 lbs.**
ABILITY: **Trace**
Allows Porygon to copy the opponent's ability.

STATS

HP · ATK · DEF · SP ATK · SP DEF · SPEED

EVOLUTIONS

TRADE WITH UP-GRADE

LOCATION[s]:

RUBY	Rarity: **None**	Trade from *FireRed/LeafGreen*
SAPPHIRE	Rarity: **None**	Trade from *FireRed/LeafGreen*
FIRERED	Rarity: **Common**	Game Corner: 9,999 Coins
LEAFGREEN	Rarity: **Common**	Game Corner: 6,500 Coins
COLOSSEUM	Rarity: **None**	Trade from *FireRed/LeafGreen*
EMERALD	Rarity: **None**	Trade from *FireRed/LeafGreen*
XD	Rarity: **None**	Trade from *FireRed/LeafGreen*

MOVES

Level	Attack	Type	Power	ACC	PP
—	Tackle	Normal	35	95	35
—	Conversion	Normal	—	—	30
—	Conversion 2	Normal	—	—	30
9	Agility	Psychic	—	—	30
12	Psybeam	Psychic	65	100	20
20	Recover	Normal	—	—	20
24	Sharpen	Normal	—	—	30
32	Lock-on	Normal	—	100	5
36	Tri Attack	Normal	80	100	10
44	Recycle	Normal	—	100	10
48	Zap Cannon	Electric	100	50	5

TM/HM

TM/HM#	Name	Type	Power	ACC	PP
TM06	Toxic	Poison	—	85	10
TM10	Hidden Power	Normal	—	100	15
TM11	Sunny Day	Fire	—	—	5
TM13	Ice Beam	Ice	95	100	10
TM14	Blizzard	Ice	120	70	5
TM15	Hyper Beam	Normal	150	90	5
TM17	Protect	Normal	—	—	10
TM18	Rain Dance	Water	—	—	5
TM21	Frustration	Normal	—	100	20
TM22	Solarbeam	Grass	120	100	10
TM23	Iron Tail	Steel	75	75	15
TM24	Thunderbolt	Electric	95	100	15
TM25	Thunder	Electric	120	70	10
TM27	Return	Normal	—	100	20
TM29	Psychic	Psychic	90	100	10
TM30	Shadow Ball	Ghost	80	100	15
TM32	Double Team	Normal	—	—	15
TM34	Shock Wave	Electric	60	—	20
TM40	Aerial Ace	Flying	60	—	20
TM42	Facade	Normal	70	100	20
TM43	Secret Power	Normal	70	100	20
TM44	Rest	Psychic	—	—	10
TM46	Thief	Dark	40	100	10
HM05	Flash	Normal	—	70	20

EGG MOVES*

Name	Type	Power	ACC	PP
None				

*Learned Via Breeding

MOVE TUTOR
FireRed/LeafGreen and Emerald Only

Double-Edge	Substitute	Dream Eater*
Mimic	Thunder Wave*	

*Battle Frontier tutor move (*Emerald*)

138 Omanyte™

ROCK   WATER

GENERAL INFO

SPECIES: Spiral Pokémon
HEIGHT: 1'04"
WEIGHT: 17 lbs.
ABILITY 1: Swift Swim
Increases Omanyte's Speed when it's raining.
ABILITY 2: Shell Armor
Prevents Omanyte from receiving critical hits.

STATS

EVOLUTIONS

LV40

LOCATION[s]:

RUBY	Rarity: None	Trade from *FireRed/LeafGreen*
SAPPHIRE	Rarity: None	Trade from *FireRed/LeafGreen*
FIRERED	Rarity: Only One	Revive from Helix Fossil
LEAFGREEN	Rarity: Only One	Revive from Helix Fossil
COLOSSEUM	Rarity: None	Trade from *FireRed/LeafGreen*
EMERALD	Rarity: None	Trade from *FireRed/LeafGreen*
XD	Rarity: None	Trade from *FireRed/LeafGreen*

MOVES

Level	Attack	Type	Power	ACC	PP
—	Withdraw	Normal	—	—	40
—	Constrict	Normal	10	100	35
13	Bite	Dark	60	100	25
19	Water Gun	Water	40	100	25
25	Mud Shot	Ground	55	95	15

Level	Attack	Type	Power	ACC	PP
31	Leer	Normal	—	100	30
37	Protect	Normal	—	—	10
43	Tickle	Normal	—	100	20
49	Ancientpower	Rock	60	100	5
55	Hydro Pump	Water	120	80	5

TM/HM

TM/HM#	Name	Type	Power	ACC	PP
TM03	Water Pulse	Water	60	95	20
TM06	Toxic	Poison	—	85	10
TM07	Hail	Ice	—	—	10
TM10	Hidden Power	Normal	—	100	15
TM13	Ice Beam	Ice	95	100	10
TM14	Blizzard	Ice	120	70	5
TM17	Protect	Normal	—	—	10
TM18	Rain Dance	Water	—	—	5
TM21	Frustration	Normal	—	100	20
TM27	Return	Normal	—	100	20
TM32	Double Team	Normal	—	—	15

TM/HM#	Name	Type	Power	ACC	PP
TM37	Sandstorm	Ground	—	—	10
TM39	Rock Tomb	Rock	50	80	10
TM42	Facade	Normal	70	100	20
TM43	Secret Power	Normal	70	100	20
TM44	Rest	Psychic	—	—	10
TM45	Attract	Normal	—	100	15
TM46	Thief	Dark	40	100	10
HM03	Surf	Water	95	100	15
HM06	Rock Smash	Fighting	20	100	15
HM07	Waterfall	Water	80	100	15
HM08	Dive	Water	60	100	10

EGG MOVES*

Name	Type	Power	ACC	PP
Aurora Beam	Ice	65	100	20
Bubblebeam	Water	65	100	20
Haze	Ice	—	—	30
Rock Slide	Rock	75	90	10
Slam	Normal	80	75	20
Spikes	Ground	—	—	20
Supersonic	Normal	—	55	20

*Learned Via Breeding

MOVE TUTOR

FireRed/LeafGreen and Emerald Only

Body Slam*	Mimic	Rock Slide*
Double-Edge	Substitute	

*Battle Frontier tutor move (*Emerald*)

139 Omastar™

ROCK | WATER

GENERAL INFO

SPECIES: Spiral Pokémon
HEIGHT: 3'03"
WEIGHT: 77 lbs.
ABILITY 1: Swift Swim
Increases Omastar's Speed when it's raining.
ABILITY 2: Shell Armor
Prevents Omastar from receiving critical hits.

STATS

EVOLUTIONS

LV40

LOCATION(s):

RUBY	Rarity: **None**	Trade from *FireRed/LeafGreen*
SAPPHIRE	Rarity: **None**	Trade from *FireRed/LeafGreen*
FIRERED	Rarity: **None**	Evolve Omanyte
LEAFGREEN	Rarity: **None**	Evolve Omanyte
COLOSSEUM	Rarity: **None**	Trade from *FireRed/LeafGreen*
EMERALD	Rarity: **None**	Trade from *FireRed/LeafGreen*
XD	Rarity: **None**	Trade from *FireRed/LeafGreen*

MOVES

Level	Attack	Type	Power	ACC	PP
—	Withdraw	Normal	—	—	40
—	Constrict	Normal	10	100	35
—	Bite	Dark	60	100	25
—	Water Gun	Water	40	100	25
25	Mud Shot	Ground	55	95	15

Level	Attack	Type	Power	ACC	PP
31	Leer	Normal	—	100	30
37	Protect	Normal	—	—	10
40	Spike Cannon	Normal	20	100	15
46	Tickle	Normal	—	100	20
55	Ancientpower	Rock	60	100	5
65	Hydro Pump	Water	120	80	5

TM/HM

TM/HM#	Name	Type	Power	ACC	PP
TM03	Water Pulse	Water	60	95	20
TM06	Toxic	Poison	—	85	10
TM07	Hail	Ice	—	—	10
TM10	Hidden Power	Normal	—	100	15
TM13	Ice Beam	Ice	95	100	10
TM14	Blizzard	Ice	120	70	5
TM15	Hyper Beam	Normal	150	90	5
TM17	Protect	Normal	—	—	10
TM18	Rain Dance	Water	—	—	5
TM21	Frustration	Normal	—	100	20
TM27	Return	Normal	—	100	20
TM32	Double Team	Normal	—	—	15

TM/HM#	Name	Type	Power	ACC	PP
TM37	Sandstorm	Ground	—	—	10
TM39	Rock Tomb	Rock	50	80	10
TM42	Facade	Normal	70	100	20
TM43	Secret Power	Normal	70	100	20
TM44	Rest	Psychic	—	—	10
TM45	Attract	Normal	—	100	15
TM46	Thief	Dark	40	100	10
HM03	Surf	Water	95	100	15
HM06	Rock Smash	Fighting	20	100	15
HM07	Waterfall	Water	80	100	15
HM08	Dive	Water	60	100	10

MOVE TUTOR

FireRed/LeafGreen and Emerald Only

Body Slam*	Mimic	Rock Slide*
Double-Edge	Substitute	Seismic Toss*

*Battle Frontier tutor move (*Emerald*)

140 Kabuto™

ROCK   WATER

GENERAL INFO
SPECIES: Shellfish Pokémon
HEIGHT: 1'08"
WEIGHT: 25 lbs.
ABILITY 1: Swift Swim
Increases Kabuto's Speed when it's raining.
ABILITY 2: Battle Armor
Prevents Kabuto from receiving critical hits.

STATS

EVOLUTIONS

LV40

LOCATION[S]:

RUBY	Rarity: None	Trade from *FireRed/LeafGreen*
SAPPHIRE	Rarity: None	Trade from *FireRed/LeafGreen*
FIRERED	Rarity: Only One	Revive from Dome Fossil
LEAFGREEN	Rarity: Only One	Revive from Dome Fossil
COLOSSEUM	Rarity: None	Trade from *FireRed/LeafGreen*
EMERALD	Rarity: None	Trade from *FireRed/LeafGreen*
XD	Rarity: None	Trade from *FireRed/LeafGreen*

MOVES

Level	Attack	Type	Power	ACC	PP
—	Scratch	Normal	40	100	35
—	Harden	Normal	—	—	30
13	Absorb	Grass	20	100	20
19	Leer	Normal	—	100	30
25	Mud Shot	Ground	55	95	15

Level	Attack	Type	Power	ACC	PP
31	Sand-Attack	Ground	—	100	15
37	Endure	Normal	—	—	10
43	Metal Sound	Steel	—	85	40
49	Mega Drain	Grass	40	100	10
55	Ancientpower	Rock	60	100	5

TM/HM

TM/HM#	Name	Type	Power	ACC	PP
TM03	Water Pulse	Water	60	95	20
TM06	Toxic	Poison	—	85	10
TM07	Hail	Ice	—	—	10
TM10	Hidden Power	Normal	—	100	15
TM13	Ice Beam	Ice	95	100	10
TM14	Blizzard	Ice	120	70	5
TM17	Protect	Normal	—	—	10
TM18	Rain Dance	Water	—	—	5
TM19	Giga Drain	Grass	60	100	5
TM21	Frustration	Normal	—	100	20
TM27	Return	Normal	—	100	20
TM28	Dig	Ground	60	100	10

TM/HM#	Name	Type	Power	ACC	PP
TM32	Double Team	Normal	—	—	15
TM37	Sandstorm	Normal	—	—	10
TM39	Rock Tomb	Rock	50	80	10
TM40	Aerial Ace	Flying	60	—	20
TM42	Facade	Normal	70	100	20
TM43	Secret Power	Normal	70	100	20
TM44	Rest	Psychic	—	—	10
TM45	Attract	Normal	—	100	15
TM46	Thief	Dark	40	100	10
HM03	Surf	Water	95	100	15
HM06	Rock Smash	Fighting	20	100	15
HM07	Waterfall	Water	80	100	15

EGG MOVES*

Name	Type	Power	ACC	PP
Aurora Beam	Ice	65	100	20
Bubblebeam	Water	65	100	20
Confuse Ray	Ghost	—	100	10
Dig	Ground	60	100	10
Flail	Normal	—	100	15
Knock Off	Dark	20	100	20
Rapid Spin	Normal	20	100	40

*Learned Via Breeding

MOVE TUTOR
FireRed/LeafGreen and Emerald Only

Body Slam*	Mimic	Rock Slide*
Double-Edge	Substitute	

*Battle Frontier tutor move (*Emerald*)

141 Kabutops™

ROCK | WATER

GENERAL INFO

SPECIES: Shellfish Pokémon
HEIGHT: 4'03"
WEIGHT: 89 lbs.
ABILITY 1: Swift Swim
Increases Kabutops's Speed when it's raining.
ABILITY 2: Battle Armor
Prevents Kabutops from receiving critical hits.

STATS

EVOLUTIONS

LV40

LOCATION[s]:

RUBY	Rarity: **None**	Trade from *FireRed/LeafGreen*
SAPPHIRE	Rarity: **None**	Trade from *FireRed/LeafGreen*
FIRERED	Rarity: **Evolve**	Evolve Kabuto
LEAFGREEN	Rarity: **Evolve**	Evolve Kabuto
COLOSSEUM	Rarity: **None**	Trade from *FireRed/LeafGreen*
EMERALD	Rarity: **None**	Trade from *FireRed/LeafGreen*
XD	Rarity: **None**	Trade from *FireRed/LeafGreen*

MOVES

Level	Attack	Type	Power	ACC	PP	Level	Attack	Type	Power	ACC	PP
—	Fury Cutter	Bug	10	95	20	31	Sand Attack	Ground	—	100	15
—	Scratch	Normal	40	100	35	37	Endure	Normal	—	—	10
—	Harden	Normal	—	—	30	40	Slash	Normal	70	100	20
—	Absorb	Grass	20	100	20	46	Metal Sound	Steel	—	85	40
—	Leer	Normal	—	100	30	55	Mega Drain	Grass	40	100	10
25	Mud Shot	Ground	55	95	15	65	Ancientpower	Rock	60	100	5

TM/HM

TM/HM#	Name	Type	Power	ACC	PP	TM/HM#	Name	Type	Power	ACC	PP
TM03	Water Pulse	Water	60	95	20	TM32	Double Team	Normal	—	—	15
TM06	Toxic	Poison	—	85	10	TM37	Sandstorm	Ground	—	—	10
TM07	Hail	Ice	—	—	10	TM39	Rock Tomb	Rock	50	80	10
TM10	Hidden Power	Normal	—	100	15	TM40	Aerial Ace	Flying	60	—	20
TM13	Ice Beam	Ice	95	100	10	TM42	Facade	Normal	70	100	20
TM14	Blizzard	Ice	120	70	5	TM43	Secret Power	Normal	70	100	20
TM15	Hyper Beam	Normal	150	90	5	TM44	Rest	Psychic	—	—	10
TM17	Protect	Normal	—	—	10	TM45	Attract	Normal	—	100	15
TM18	Rain Dance	Water	—	—	5	TM46	Thief	Dark	40	100	10
TM19	Giga Drain	Grass	60	100	5	HM01	Cut	Normal	50	95	30
TM21	Frustration	Normal	—	100	20	HM03	Surf	Water	95	100	15
TM27	Return	Normal	—	100	20	HM06	Rock Smash	Fighting	20	100	15
TM28	Dig	Ground	60	100	10	HM07	Waterfall	Water	80	100	15
TM31	Brick Break	Fighting	75	100	15	HM08	Dive	Water	60	100	10

MOVE TUTOR

FireRed/LeafGreen and Emerald Only

Body Slam*	Mimic	Seismic Toss*
Double-Edge	Substitute	Rock Slide*
Mega Kick*	Swords Dance*	

*Battle Frontier tutor move (*Emerald*)

142 Aerodactyl™

ROCK   FLYING

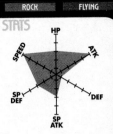

GENERAL INFO

SPECIES: Fossil Pokémon
HEIGHT: 5'11"
WEIGHT: 130 lbs.
ABILITY 1: Pressure
When an opponent damages Aerodactyl, it uses 2 PPs for that move.
ABILITY 2: Rock Head
Aerodactyl doesn't take recoil damage.

STATS

EVOLUTIONS

DOES NOT EVOLVE

LOCATION(s):

	Rarity	
RUBY	**None**	Trade from *FireRed/LeafGreen*
SAPPHIRE	**None**	Trade from *FireRed/LeafGreen*
FIRERED	**Only One**	Revive the Old Amber (Found in Pewter Museum)
LEAFGREEN	**Only One**	Revive the Old Amber (Found in Pewter Museum)
COLOSSEUM	**None**	Trade from *FireRed/LeafGreen*
EMERALD	**None**	Trade from *FireRed/LeafGreen*
XD	**None**	Trade from *FireRed/LeafGreen*

MOVES

Level	Attack	Type	Power	ACC	PP
—	Wing Attack	Flying	60	100	35
8	Agility	Psychic	—	—	30
15	Bite	Dark	60	100	25
22	Supersonic	Normal	—	55	20
29	Ancientpower	Rock	60	100	5
36	Scary Face	Normal	—	90	10
43	Take Down	Normal	90	85	20
50	Hyper Beam	Normal	150	90	5

TM/HM

TM/HM#	Name	Type	Power	ACC	PP
TM02	Dragon Claw	Dragon	80	100	15
TM05	Roar	Normal	—	100	20
TM06	Toxic	Poison	—	85	10
TM10	Hidden Power	Normal	—	100	15
TM11	Sunny Day	Fire	—	—	5
TM12	Taunt	Dark	—	100	20
TM15	Hyper Beam	Normal	150	90	5
TM17	Protect	Normal	—	—	10
TM18	Rain Dance	Water	—	—	5
TM21	Frustration	Normal	—	100	20
TM23	Iron Tail	Steel	75	75	15
TM26	Earthquake	Ground	100	100	10
TM27	Return	Normal	—	100	20
TM32	Double Team	Normal	—	—	15
TM35	Flamethrower	Fire	95	100	15
TM37	Sandstorm	Ground	—	—	10
TM38	Fire Blast	Fire	120	85	5
TM39	Rock Tomb	Rock	50	80	10
TM40	Aerial Ace	Flying	60	—	20
TM41	Torment	Dark	—	100	15
TM42	Facade	Normal	70	100	20
TM43	Secret Power	Normal	70	100	20
TM44	Rest	Psychic	—	—	10
TM45	Attract	Normal	—	100	15
TM46	Thief	Dark	40	100	10
TM47	Steel Wing	Steel	70	90	25
HM02	Fly	Flying	70	95	15
HM04	Strength	Normal	80	100	20
HM06	Rock Smash	Fighting	20	100	15

EGG MOVES*

Name	Type	Power	ACC	PP
Curse	—	—	—	10
Dragonbreath	Dragon	60	100	20
Foresight	Normal	—	100	40
Pursuit	Dark	40	100	20
Steel Wing	Steel	70	90	25
Whirlwind	Normal	—	100	20

*Learned Via Breeding

MOVE TUTOR

FireRed/LeafGreen and Emerald Only

Double-Edge	Substitute	Rock Slide*
Mimic		

*Battle Frontier tutor move (*Emerald*)

143 Snorlax™

NORMAL

GENERAL INFO

SPECIES: Sleeping Pokémon
HEIGHT: 6'11"
WEIGHT: 1014 lbs.
ABILITY 1: Immunity
Prevents Snorlax from being poisoned.
ABILITY 2: Thick Fat
Fire-type and Ice-type attacks are half the damage on Snorlax.

STATS

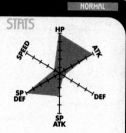

EVOLUTIONS

DOES NOT EVOLVE

LOCATION(s):

RUBY	Rarity:	**None**	Trade from *FireRed/LeafGreen*
SAPPHIRE	Rarity:	**None**	Trade from *FireRed/LeafGreen*
FIRERED	Rarity:	**Only Two**	Route 12, Route 16
LEAFGREEN	Rarity:	**Only Two**	Route 12, Route 16
COLOSSEUM	Rarity:	**None**	Trade from *FireRed/LeafGreen*
EMERALD	Rarity:	**None**	Trade from *FireRed/LeafGreen*
XD	Rarity:	**Only One**	Citadark Island (Capture from Cipher Peon Ardos)

MOVES

Level	Attack	Type	Power	ACC	PP
—	Tackle	Normal	35	95	35
5	Amnesia	Psychic	—	—	20
9	Defense Curl	Normal	—	—	40
13	Belly Drum	Normal	—	—	10
17	Headbutt	Normal	70	100	15
21	Yawn	Normal	—	100	10
25	Rest	Psychic	—	—	10

Level	Attack	Type	Power	ACC	PP
29	Snore	Normal	40	100	15
33	Body Slam	Normal	85	100	15
37	Sleep Talk	Normal	—	—	10
41	Block	Normal	—	100	5
45	Covet	Normal	40	100	40
49	Rollout	Rock	30	90	20
53	Hyper Beam	Normal	150	90	5

TM/HM

TM/HM#	Name	Type	Power	ACC	PP
TM01	Focus Punch	Fighting	150	100	20
TM03	Water Pulse	Water	60	95	20
TM06	Toxic	Poison	—	85	10
TM10	Hidden Power	Normal	—	100	15
TM11	Sunny Day	Fire	—	—	5
TM13	Ice Beam	Ice	95	100	10
TM14	Blizzard	Ice	120	70	5
TM15	Hyper Beam	Normal	150	90	5
TM17	Protect	Normal	—	—	10
TM18	Rain Dance	Water	—	—	5
TM21	Frustration	Normal	—	100	20
TM22	Solarbeam	Grass	120	100	10
TM24	Thunderbolt	Electric	95	100	15
TM25	Thunder	Electric	120	70	10
TM26	Earthquake	Ground	100	100	10
TM27	Return	Normal	—	100	20

TM/HM#	Name	Type	Power	ACC	PP
TM29	Psychic	Psychic	90	100	10
TM30	Shadow Ball	Ghost	80	100	15
TM31	Brick Break	Fighting	75	100	15
TM32	Double Team	Normal	—	—	15
TM34	Shock Wave	Electric	60	—	20
TM35	Flamethrower	Fire	95	100	15
TM37	Sandstorm	Ground	—	—	10
TM38	Fire Blast	Fire	120	85	5
TM39	Rock Tomb	Rock	50	80	10
TM42	Facade	Normal	70	100	20
TM43	Secret Power	Normal	70	100	20
TM44	Rest	Psychic	—	—	10
TM45	Attract	Normal	—	100	15
HM03	Surf	Water	95	100	15
HM04	Strength	Normal	80	100	20

EGG MOVES*

Name	Type	Power	ACC	PP
Charm	Normal	—	100	20
Curse	—	—	—	10
Double-Edge	Normal	120	100	15
Fissure	Ground	—	30	5
Lick	Ghost	20	100	30
Substitute	Normal	—	—	10

*Learned Via Breeding

MOVE TUTOR
FireRed/LeafGreen and Emerald Only

Body Slam*	Mimic	Seismic Toss*
Double-Edge	Substitute	Rock Slide*
Mega Punch*	Metronome	
Mega Kick*	Counter*	

*Battle Frontier tutor move (*Emerald*)

144 Articuno™

ICE | FLYING

GENERAL INFO

SPECIES: Freeze Pokémon
HEIGHT: 5'07"
WEIGHT: 122 lbs.
ABILITY: Pressure
Opponent uses 2 PPs for damage inflicted against Articuno.

STATS

(radar chart: HP, ATK, DEF, SP ATK, SP DEF, SPEED)

EVOLUTIONS

DOES NOT EVOLVE

LOCATION(S):

Game	Rarity	Location
RUBY	Rarity: None	Trade from *FireRed/LeafGreen*
SAPPHIRE	Rarity: None	Trade from *FireRed/LeafGreen*
FIRERED	Rarity: Only One	Seafoam Islands
LEAFGREEN	Rarity: Only One	Seafoam Islands
COLOSSEUM	Rarity: None	Trade from *FireRed/LeafGreen*
EMERALD	Rarity: None	Trade from *FireRed/LeafGreen*
XD	Rarity: Only One	Citadark Island (Capture from Master Greevil)

MOVES

Level	Attack	Type	Power	ACC	PP
—	Gust	Flying	40	100	35
—	Powder Snow	Ice	40	100	25
13	Mist	Ice	—	—	30
25	Agility	Psychic	—	—	30

Level	Attack	Type	Power	ACC	PP
37	Mind Reader	Normal	—	100	5
49	Ice Beam	Ice	95	100	10
61	Reflect	Psychic	—	—	20
73	Blizzard	Ice	120	70	5
85	Sheer Cold	Ice	—	30	5

TM/HM

TM/HM#	Name	Type	Power	ACC	PP
TM03	Water Pulse	Water	60	95	20
TM05	Roar	Normal	—	100	20
TM06	Toxic	Poison	—	85	10
TM07	Hail	Ice	—	—	10
TM10	Hidden Power	Normal	—	100	15
TM11	Sunny Day	Fire	—	—	5
TM13	Ice Beam	Ice	95	100	10
TM14	Blizzard	Ice	120	70	5
TM15	Hyper Beam	Normal	150	90	5
TM17	Protect	Normal	—	—	10
TM18	Rain Dance	Water	—	—	5
TM21	Frustration	Normal	—	100	20

TM/HM#	Name	Type	Power	ACC	PP
TM27	Return	Normal	—	100	20
TM32	Double Team	Normal	—	—	15
TM33	Reflect	Normal	—	—	20
TM37	Sandstorm	Ground	—	—	10
TM40	Aerial Ace	Flying	60	—	20
TM42	Facade	Normal	70	100	20
TM43	Secret Power	Normal	70	100	20
TM44	Rest	Psychic	—	—	10
TM47	Steel Wing	Steel	70	90	25
HM02	Fly	Flying	70	95	15
HM06	Rock Smash	Fighting	20	100	15

EGG MOVES*

Name	Type	Power	ACC	PP
None				

*Learned Via Breeding

MOVE TUTOR

FireRed/LeafGreen and Emerald Only

Double-Edge	Mimic	Substitute

*Battle Frontier tutor move (*Emerald*)

145 Zapdos™

ELECTRIC | FLYING

GENERAL INFO

SPECIES: Electric Pokémon
HEIGHT: 5'03"
WEIGHT: 116 lbs.
ABILITY: Pressure
Opponent uses 2 PPs for damage inflicted against Zapdos.

STATS

EVOLUTIONS

DOES NOT EVOLVE

LOCATION(s):

RUBY	Rarity: **None**	Trade from *FireRed/LeafGreen*
SAPPHIRE	Rarity: **None**	Trade from *FireRed/LeafGreen*
FIRERED	Rarity: **Only One**	Power Plant
LEAFGREEN	Rarity: **Only One**	Power Plant
COLOSSEUM	Rarity: **None**	Trade from *FireRed/LeafGreen*
EMERALD	Rarity: **None**	Trade from *FireRed/LeafGreen*
XD	Rarity: **Only One**	Citadark Island (Capture from Master Greevil)

MOVES

Level	Attack	Type	Power	ACC	PP
—	Thundershock	Electric	40	100	30
—	Peck	Flying	35	100	35
13	Thunder Wave	Electric	—	100	20
25	Agility	Psychic	—	—	30

Level	Attack	Type	Power	ACC	PP
37	Detect	Fight	—	—	5
49	Drill Peck	Flying	80	100	20
61	Charge	Electric	—	100	20
73	Light Screen	Psychic	—	—	30
85	Thunder	Electric	120	70	10

TM/HM

TM/HM#	Name	Type	Power	ACC	PP
TM05	Roar	Normal	—	100	20
TM06	Toxic	Poison	—	85	10
TM10	Hidden Power	Normal	—	100	15
TM11	Sunny Day	Fire	—	—	5
TM15	Hyper Beam	Normal	150	90	5
TM16	Light Screen	Psychic	—	—	30
TM17	Protect	Normal	—	—	10
TM18	Rain Dance	Water	—	—	5
TM21	Frustration	Normal	—	100	20
TM24	Thunderbolt	Electric	95	100	15
TM25	Thunder	Electric	120	70	10
TM27	Return	Normal	—	100	20

TM/HM#	Name	Type	Power	ACC	PP
TM32	Double Team	Normal	—	—	15
TM34	Shock Wave	Electric	60	—	20
TM37	Sandstorm	Ground	—	—	10
TM40	Aerial Ace	Flying	60	—	20
TM42	Facade	Normal	70	100	20
TM43	Secret Power	Normal	70	100	20
TM44	Rest	Psychic	—	—	10
TM47	Steel Wing	Steel	70	90	25
HM02	Fly	Flying	70	95	15
HM05	Flash	Normal	—	70	20
HM06	Rock Smash	Fighting	20	100	15

EGG MOVES*

Name	Type	Power	ACC	PP
None				

*Learned Via Breeding

MOVE TUTOR

FireRed/LeafGreen and Emerald Only

Double-Edge	Substitute	Thunder Wave*
Mimic		

*Battle Frontier tutor move (*Emerald*)

146 Moltres™

FIRE | FLYING

GENERAL INFO

SPECIES: Flame Pokémon
HEIGHT: 6'07"
WEIGHT: 132 lbs.
ABILITY: Pressure
Opponent uses 2 PPs for damage inflicted against Moltres.

STATS

HP, SPEED, ATK, DEF, SP ATK, SP DEF

EVOLUTIONS

DOES NOT EVOLVE

LOCATION(s):

RUBY	Rarity: **None**	Trade from *FireRed/LeafGreen*
SAPPHIRE	Rarity: **None**	Trade from *FireRed/LeafGreen*
FIRERED	Rarity: **Only One**	One Island
LEAFGREEN	Rarity: **Only One**	One Island
COLOSSEUM	Rarity: **None**	Trade from *FireRed/LeafGreen*
EMERALD	Rarity: **None**	Trade from *FireRed/LeafGreen*
XD	Rarity: **Only One**	Citadark Island (Capture from Master Greevil)

MOVES

Level	Attack	Type	Power	ACC	PP
—	Wing Attack	Flying	60	100	35
—	Ember	Fire	40	100	25
13	Fire Spin	Fire	15	70	15
25	Agility	Psychic	—	—	30

Level	Attack	Type	Power	ACC	PP
37	Endure	Normal	—	—	10
49	Flamethrower	Fire	95	100	15
61	Safeguard	Normal	—	—	25
73	Heat Wave	Fire	100	90	10
85	Sky Attack	Flying	140	90	5

TM/HM

TM/HM#	Name	Type	Power	ACC	PP
TM05	Roar	Normal	—	100	20
TM06	Toxic	Poison	—	85	10
TM10	Hidden Power	Normal	—	100	15
TM11	Sunny Day	Fire	—	—	5
TM15	Hyper Beam	Normal	150	90	5
TM17	Protect	Normal	—	—	10
TM18	Rain Dance	Water	—	—	5
TM20	Safeguard	Normal	—	—	25
TM21	Frustration	Normal	—	100	20
TM27	Return	Normal	—	100	20
TM32	Double Team	Normal	—	—	15

TM/HM#	Name	Type	Power	ACC	PP
TM35	Flamethrower	Fire	95	100	15
TM37	Sandstorm	Ground	—	—	10
TM38	Fire Blast	Fire	120	85	5
TM40	Aerial Ace	Flying	60	—	20
TM42	Facade	Normal	70	100	20
TM43	Secret Power	Normal	70	100	20
TM44	Rest	Psychic	—	—	10
TM47	Steel Wing	Steel	70	90	25
TM50	Overheat	Fire	140	90	5
HM02	Fly	Flying	70	95	15
HM06	Rock Smash	Fighting	20	100	15

EGG MOVES*

Name	Type	Power	ACC	PP
None				

*Learned Via Breeding

MOVE TUTOR

FireRed/LeafGreen and Emerald Only

Double-Edge	Mimic	Substitute

*Battle Frontier tutor move (*Emerald*)

147 Dratini™

DRAGON

GENERAL INFO

SPECIES: Dragon Pokémon
HEIGHT: 5'11"
WEIGHT: 7 lbs.
ABILITY: Shed Skin
Status effects only last one turn on Dratini. Has a 30% chance of success.

STATS

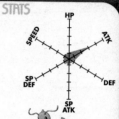

EVOLUTIONS

LV30   LV55

LOCATION[s]:

RUBY	Rarity: **None**	Trade from *FireRed/LeafGreen*
SAPPHIRE	Rarity: **None**	Trade from *FireRed/LeafGreen*
FIRERED	Rarity: **Rare**	Safari Zone
LEAFGREEN	Rarity: **Rare**	Safari Zone
COLOSSEUM	Rarity: **None**	Trade from *FireRed/LeafGreen*
EMERALD	Rarity: **None**	Trade from *FireRed/LeafGreen*
XD	Rarity: **None**	Trade from *FireRed/LeafGreen*

MOVES

Level	Attack	Type	Power	ACC	PP
—	Wrap	Normal	15	85	20
—	Leer	Normal	—	100	30
8	Thunder Wave	Electric	—	100	20
15	Twister	Dragon	40	100	20
22	Dragon Rage	Dragon	—	100	10

Level	Attack	Type	Power	ACC	PP
29	Slam	Normal	80	75	20
36	Agility	Psychic	—	—	30
43	Safeguard	Normal	—	—	25
50	Outrage	Dragon	90	100	15
57	Hyper Beam	Normal	150	90	5

TM/HM

TM/HM#	Name	Type	Power	ACC	PP
TM03	Water Pulse	Water	60	95	20
TM06	Toxic	Poison	—	85	10
TM07	Hail	Ice	—	—	10
TM10	Hidden Power	Normal	—	100	15
TM11	Sunny Day	Fire	—	—	5
TM13	Ice Beam	Ice	95	100	10
TM14	Blizzard	Ice	120	70	5
TM15	Hyper Beam	Normal	150	90	5
TM17	Protect	Normal	—	—	10
TM18	Rain Dance	Water	—	—	5
TM20	Safeguard	Normal	—	—	25
TM21	Frustration	Normal	—	100	20
TM23	Iron Tail	Steel	75	75	15

TM/HM#	Name	Type	Power	ACC	PP
TM24	Thunderbolt	Electric	95	100	15
TM25	Thunder	Electric	120	70	10
TM27	Return	Normal	—	100	20
TM32	Double Team	Normal	—	—	15
TM34	Shock Wave	Electric	60	—	20
TM35	Flamethrower	Fire	95	100	15
TM38	Fire Blast	Fire	120	85	5
TM42	Facade	Normal	70	100	20
TM43	Secret Power	Normal	70	100	20
TM44	Rest	Psychic	—	—	10
TM45	Attract	Normal	—	100	15
HM03	Surf	Water	95	100	15
HM07	Waterfall	Water	80	100	15

EGG MOVES*

Name	Type	Power	ACC	PP
Dragon Dance	Dragon	—	—	20
Dragonbreath	Dragon	60	100	20
Haze	Ice	—	—	30
Light Screen	Psychic	—	—	30
Mist	Ice	—	—	30
Supersonic	Normal	—	55	20

*Learned Via Breeding

MOVE TUTOR

FireRed/LeafGreen and Emerald Only

Body Slam*	Mimic	Thunder Wave*
Double-Edge	Substitute	

*Battle Frontier tutor move (*Emerald*)

148 Dragonair™

DRAGON

GENERAL INFO

SPECIES: Dragon Pokémon
HEIGHT: 13'01"
WEIGHT: 36 lbs.
ABILITY: Shed Skin
Status effects only last one turn on Dragonair. Has a 30% chance of success.

STATS

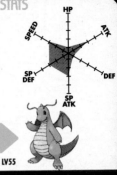

EVOLUTIONS

 ▶ ▶

LV30   LV55

LOCATION[s]:

RUBY	Rarity: **None**	Trade from *FireRed/LeafGreen*
SAPPHIRE	Rarity: **None**	Trade from *FireRed/LeafGreen*
FIRERED	Rarity: **Rare**	Evolve Dratini, Safari Zone
LEAFGREEN	Rarity: **Rare**	Evolve Dratini, Safari Zone
COLOSSEUM	Rarity: **None**	Trade from *FireRed/LeafGreen*
EMERALD	Rarity: **None**	Trade from *FireRed/LeafGreen*
XD	Rarity: **None**	Trade from *FireRed/LeafGreen*

MOVES

Level	Attack	Type	Power	ACC	PP	Level	Attack	Type	Power	ACC	PP
—	Wrap	Normal	15	85	20	29	Slam	Normal	80	75	20
—	Leer	Normal	—	100	30	38	Agility	Psychic	—	—	30
—	Thunder Wave	Electric	—	100	20	47	Safeguard	Normal	—	—	25
—	Twister	Dragon	40	100	20	56	Outrage	Dragon	90	100	15
22	Dragon Rage	Dragon	—	100	10	65	Hyper Beam	Normal	150	90	5

TM/HM

TM/HM#	Name	Type	Power	ACC	PP	TM/HM#	Name	Type	Power	ACC	PP
TM03	Water Pulse	Water	60	95	20	TM24	Thunderbolt	Electric	95	100	15
TM06	Toxic	Poison	—	85	10	TM25	Thunder	Electric	120	70	10
TM07	Hail	Ice	—	—	10	TM27	Return	Normal	—	100	20
TM10	Hidden Power	Normal	—	100	15	TM32	Double Team	Normal	—	—	15
TM11	Sunny Day	Fire	—	—	5	TM34	Shock Wave	Electric	60	—	20
TM13	Ice Beam	Ice	95	100	10	TM35	Flamethrower	Fire	95	100	15
TM14	Blizzard	Ice	120	70	5	TM38	Fire Blast	Fire	120	85	5
TM15	Hyper Beam	Normal	150	90	5	TM42	Facade	Normal	70	100	20
TM17	Protect	Normal	—	—	10	TM43	Secret Power	Normal	70	100	20
TM18	Rain Dance	Water	—	—	5	TM44	Rest	Psychic	—	—	10
TM20	Safeguard	Normal	—	—	25	TM45	Attract	Normal	—	100	15
TM21	Frustration	Normal	—	100	20	HM03	Surf	Water	95	100	15
TM23	Iron Tail	Steel	75	75	15	HM07	Waterfall	Water	80	100	15

MOVE TUTOR

FireRed/LeafGreen and Emerald Only

Body Slam*	Mimic	Thunder Wave*
Double-Edge	Substitute	

*Battle Frontier tutor move (*Emerald*)

149 Dragonite™

DRAGON	FLYING

GENERAL INFO
SPECIES: Dragon Pokémon
HEIGHT: 7'03"
WEIGHT: 463 lbs.
ABILITY: Inner Focus
Prevents Dragonite from flinching.

STATS
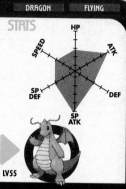

EVOLUTIONS

LV30   LV55

LOCATION[s]:

	Rarity	
RUBY	**None**	Trade from *FireRed/LeafGreen*
SAPPHIRE	**None**	Trade from *FireRed/LeafGreen*
FIRERED	**None**	Evolve Dragonair
LEAFGREEN	**None**	Evolve Dragonair
COLOSSEUM	**None**	Trade from *FireRed/LeafGreen*
EMERALD	**None**	Trade from *FireRed/LeafGreen*
XD	**Only One**	Capture from Miror B. after shutting down the Cipher Key Lair

MOVES

Level	Attack	Type	Power	ACC	PP
—	Wrap	Normal	15	85	20
—	Leer	Normal	—	100	30
—	Thunder Wave	Electric	—	100	20
—	Twister	Dragon	40	100	20
22	Dragon Rage	Dragon	—	100	10

Level	Attack	Type	Power	ACC	PP
29	Slam	Normal	80	75	20
38	Agility	Psychic	—	—	30
47	Safeguard	Normal	—	—	25
55	Wing Attack	Flying	60	100	35
61	Outrage	Dragon	90	100	15
75	Hyper Beam	Normal	150	90	5

TM/HM

TM/HM#	Name	Type	Power	ACC	PP
TM01	Focus Punch	Fighting	150	100	20
TM02	Dragon Claw	Dragon	80	100	15
TM03	Water Pulse	Water	60	95	20
TM05	Roar	Normal	—	100	20
TM06	Toxic	Poison	—	85	10
TM07	Hail	Ice	—	—	10
TM10	Hidden Power	Normal	—	100	15
TM11	Sunny Day	Fire	—	—	5
TM13	Ice Beam	Ice	95	100	10
TM14	Blizzard	Ice	120	70	5
TM15	Hyper Beam	Normal	150	90	5
TM17	Protect	Normal	—	—	10
TM18	Rain Dance	Water	—	—	5
TM20	Safeguard	Normal	—	—	25
TM21	Frustration	Normal	—	100	20
TM23	Iron Tail	Steel	75	75	15
TM24	Thunderbolt	Electric	95	100	15
TM25	Thunder	Electric	120	70	10
TM26	Earthquake	Ground	100	100	10
TM27	Return	Normal	—	100	20

TM/HM#	Name	Type	Power	ACC	PP
TM31	Brick Break	Fighting	75	100	15
TM32	Double Team	Normal	—	—	15
TM34	Shock Wave	Electric	60	—	20
TM35	Flamethrower	Fire	95	100	15
TM37	Sandstorm	Ground	—	—	10
TM38	Fire Blast	Fire	120	85	5
TM39	Rock Tomb	Rock	50	80	10
TM40	Aerial Ace	Flying	60	—	20
TM42	Facade	Normal	70	100	20
TM43	Secret Power	Normal	70	100	20
TM44	Rest	Psychic	—	—	10
TM45	Attract	Normal	—	100	15
TM47	Steel Wing	Steel	70	90	25
HM01	Cut	Normal	50	95	30
HM02	Fly	Flying	70	95	15
HM03	Surf	Water	95	100	15
HM04	Strength	Normal	80	100	20
HM06	Rock Smash	Fighting	20	100	15
HM07	Waterfall	Water	80	100	15
HM08	Dive	Water	60	100	10

EGG MOVES*

Name	Type	Power	ACC	PP
Dragon Dance	Dragon	—	—	20
Dragonbreath	Dragon	60	100	20
Haze	Ice	—	—	30
Light Screen	Psychic	—	—	30
Mist	Ice	—	—	30
Supersonic	Normal	—	55	20

*Learned Via Breeding

MOVE TUTOR
FireRed/LeafGreen and Emerald Only

Body Slam	Mimic	Thunder Wave*
Double-Edge	Substitute	

*Battle Frontier tutor move (*Emerald*)

150 Mewtwo™

PSYCHIC

GENERAL INFO

SPECIES: Genetic Pokémon
HEIGHT: 6'07"
WEIGHT: 269 lbs.
ABILITY: Pressure
Opponent uses 2 PPs for damage inflicted against Mewtwo.

STATS

EVOLUTIONS

DOES NOT EVOLVE

LOCATION(s):

Game	Rarity	Location
RUBY	Rarity: None	Trade from *FireRed/LeafGreen*
SAPPHIRE	Rarity: None	Trade from *FireRed/LeafGreen*
FIRERED	Rarity: Only One	Cerulean Cave
LEAFGREEN	Rarity: Only One	Cerulean Cave
COLOSSEUM	Rarity: None	Trade from *FireRed/LeafGreen*
EMERALD	Rarity: None	Trade from *FireRed/LeafGreen*
XD	Rarity: None	Trade from *FireRed/LeafGreen*

MOVES

Level	Attack	Type	Power	ACC	PP
—	Confusion	Psychic	50	100	25
—	Disable	Normal	—	55	20
11	Barrier	Psychic	—	—	30
22	Mist	Ice	—	—	30
33	Swift	Normal	60	—	20
44	Recover	Normal	—	—	20
55	Safeguard	Normal	—	—	25
66	Psychic	Psychic	90	100	10
77	Psych Up	Normal	—	—	10
88	Future Sight	Psychic	80	90	15
99	Amnesia	Psychic	—	—	20

TM/HM

TM/HM#	Name	Type	Power	ACC	PP
TM01	Focus Punch	Fighting	150	100	20
TM03	Water Pulse	Water	60	95	20
TM04	Calm Mind	Psychic	—	—	20
TM06	Toxic	Poison	—	85	10
TM07	Hail	Ice	—	—	10
TM08	Bulk Up	Fighting	—	—	20
TM10	Hidden Power	Normal	—	100	15
TM11	Sunny Day	Fire	—	—	5
TM12	Taunt	Dark	—	100	20
TM13	Ice Beam	Ice	95	100	10
TM14	Blizzard	Ice	120	70	5
TM15	Hyper Beam	Normal	150	90	5
TM16	Light Screen	Psychic	—	—	30
TM17	Protect	Normal	—	—	10
TM18	Rain Dance	Water	—	—	5
TM20	Safeguard	Normal	—	—	25
TM21	Frustration	Normal	—	100	20
TM22	Solarbeam	Grass	120	100	10
TM23	Iron Tail	Steel	75	75	15
TM24	Thunderbolt	Electric	95	100	15
TM25	Thunder	Electric	120	70	10
TM26	Earthquake	Ground	100	100	10
TM27	Return	Normal	—	100	20
TM29	Psychic	Psychic	90	100	10
TM30	Shadow Ball	Ghost	80	100	15
TM31	Brick Break	Fighting	75	100	15
TM32	Double Team	Normal	—	—	15
TM33	Reflect	Normal	—	—	20
TM34	Shock Wave	Electric	60	—	20
TM35	Flamethrower	Fire	95	100	15
TM37	Sandstorm	Ground	—	—	10
TM38	Fire Blast	Fire	120	85	5
TM39	Rock Tomb	Rock	50	80	10
TM40	Aerial Ace	Flying	60	—	20
TM41	Torment	Dark	—	100	15
TM42	Facade	Normal	70	100	20
TM43	Secret Power	Normal	70	100	20
TM44	Rest	Psychic	—	—	10
TM48	Skill Swap	Psychic	—	100	10
TM49	Snatch	Dark	—	100	10
HM04	Strength	Normal	80	100	20
HM05	Flash	Normal	—	70	20
HM06	Rock Smash	Fighting	20	100	15

EGG MOVES*

Name	Type	Power	ACC	PP
None				

*Learned Via Breeding

MOVE TUTOR
FireRed/LeafGreen and Emerald Only

Body Slam*
Double-Edge
Mega Punch*
Mega Kick*

Mimic
Metronome
Substitute
Counter*

Seismic Toss*
Dream Eater*
Thunder Wave*

*Battle Frontier tutor move (*Emerald*)

151 Mew™

note This character has not been released in the United States.

POKÉMON FACTS

Bulbasaur always has its lunch with it, thanks to the photosynthetic bulb on its back.

POKÉMON FACTS

As if the stench from a Grimer wasn't bad enough, it also leaves bits of itself behind as it slides about the ground, which gradually become new Grimer.

152 Chikorita™

GRASS

GENERAL INFO
SPECIES: Leaf Pokémon
HEIGHT: 2'11"
WEIGHT: 14 lbs.
ABILITY: Overgrow
When Chikorita's HPs are very low, its Grass-type attacks are multiplied by 1.5.

STATS

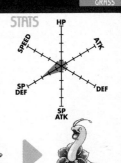

EVOLUTIONS

  LV16 LV32

LOCATION(s):

RUBY	Rarity:	None	Trade Bayleef or Meganium from *Colosseum* then breed
SAPPHIRE	Rarity:	None	Trade Bayleef or Meganium from *Colosseum* then breed
FIRERED	Rarity:	None	Trade Bayleef or Meganium from *Colosseum* then breed
LEAFGREEN	Rarity:	None	Trade Bayleef or Meganium from *Colosseum* then breed
COLOSSEUM	Rarity:	Breed	Breed in *Ruby/Sapphire/FireRed/LeafGreen* then trade back to *Colosseum*
EMERALD	Rarity:	Only One	Trade Bayleef or Meganium from *Colosseum* then breed, Littleroot Town
XD	Rarity:	Only One	Complete Mt. Battle in Story mode

MOVES

Level	Attack	Type	Power	ACC	PP	Level	Attack	Type	Power	ACC	PP
—	Tackle	Normal	35	95	35	22	Synthesis	Grass	—	—	5
—	Growl	Normal	—	100	40	29	Body Slam	Normal	85	100	15
8	Razor Leaf	Grass	55	95	25	36	Light Screen	Psychic	—	—	30
12	Reflect	Psychic	—	—	20	43	Safeguard	Normal	—	—	25
15	Poisonpowder	Poison	—	75	35	50	Solarbeam	Grass	120	100	10

TM/HM

TM/HM#	Name	Type	Power	ACC	PP	TM/HM#	Name	Type	Power	ACC	PP
TM06	Toxic	Poison	—	85	10	TM23	Iron Tail	Steel	75	75	15
TM09	Bullet Seed	Grass	10	100	30	TM27	Return	Normal	—	100	20
TM10	Hidden Power	Normal	—	100	15	TM32	Double Team	Normal	—	—	15
TM11	Sunny Day	Fire	—	—	5	TM33	Reflect	Normal	—	—	20
TM16	Light Screen	Psychic	—	—	30	TM42	Facade	Normal	70	100	20
TM17	Protect	Normal	—	—	10	TM43	Secret Power	Normal	70	100	20
TM19	Giga Drain	Grass	60	100	5	TM44	Rest	Psychic	—	—	10
TM20	Safeguard	Normal	—	—	25	TM45	Attract	Normal	—	100	15
TM21	Frustration	Normal	—	100	20	HM01	Cut	Normal	50	95	30
TM22	Solarbeam	Grass	120	100	10	HM05	Flash	Normal	—	70	20

EGG MOVES*

Name	Type	Power	ACC	PP
Ancientpower	Rock	60	100	5
Counter	Fighting	—	100	20
Flail	Normal	—	100	15
Grasswhistle	Grass	—	55	15
Ingrain	Grass	—	100	20
Leech Seed	Grass	—	90	10
Nature Power	Normal	—	95	20
Vine Whip	Grass	35	100	10

*Learned Via Breeding

MOVE TUTOR
FireRed/LeafGreen and Emerald Only

Body Slam*	Mimic	Swords Dance*
Double-Edge	Substitute	Counter*

*Battle Frontier tutor move (*Emerald*)

153 Bayleef™

GRASS

GENERAL INFO
SPECIES: Leaf Pokémon
HEIGHT: 3'11"
WEIGHT: 35 lbs.
ABILITY: Overgrow
When Bayleef's HPs are very low, its Grass-type attacks are multiplied by 1.5.

STATS
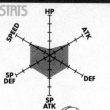

EVOLUTIONS

LV16   LV32

LOCATION(s):

RUBY	Rarity: **None**	Trade from *Colosseum*
SAPPHIRE	Rarity: **None**	Trade from *Colosseum*
FIRERED	Rarity: **None**	Trade from *Colosseum*
LEAFGREEN	Rarity: **None**	Trade from *Colosseum*
COLOSSEUM	Rarity: **Only One**	Obtained from Mystery Troop Verde in Phenac City
EMERALD	Rarity: **None**	Trade from *Colosseum*
XD	Rarity: **Evolve**	Evolve Chikorita

MOVES

Level	Attack	Type	Power	ACC	PP	Level	Attack	Type	Power	ACC	PP
—	Tackle	Normal	35	95	35	23	Synthesis	Grass	—	—	5
—	Growl	Normal	—	100	40	31	Body Slam	Normal	85	100	15
—	Razor Leaf	Grass	55	95	25	39	Light Screen	Psychic	—	—	30
—	Reflect	Psychic	—	—	20	47	Safeguard	Normal	—	—	25
15	Poisonpowder	Poison	—	75	35	55	Solarbeam	Grass	120	100	10

TM/HM

TM/HM#	Name	Type	Power	ACC	PP	TM/HM#	Name	Type	Power	ACC	PP
TM06	Toxic	Poison	—	85	10	TM27	Return	Normal	—	100	20
TM09	Bullet Seed	Grass	10	100	30	TM32	Double Team	Normal	—	—	15
TM10	Hidden Power	Normal	—	100	15	TM33	Reflect	Normal	—	—	20
TM11	Sunny Day	Fire	—	—	5	TM42	Facade	Normal	70	100	20
TM16	Light Screen	Psychic	—	—	30	TM43	Secret Power	Normal	70	100	20
TM17	Protect	Normal	—	—	10	TM44	Rest	Psychic	—	—	10
TM19	Giga Drain	Grass	60	100	5	TM45	Attract	Normal	—	100	15
TM20	Safeguard	Normal	—	—	25	HM01	Cut	Normal	50	95	30
TM21	Frustration	Normal	—	100	20	HM04	Strength	Normal	80	100	15
TM22	Solarbeam	Grass	120	100	10	HM05	Flash	Normal	—	70	20
TM23	Iron Tail	Steel	75	75	15	HM06	Rock Smash	Fighting	20	100	15

MOVE TUTOR
FireRed/LeafGreen and Emerald Only

Body Slam*	Mimic	Swords Dance*
Double-Edge	Substitute	Counter*

*Battle Frontier tutor move (*Emerald*)

154 Meganium™

GRASS

GENERAL INFO
SPECIES: Herb Pokémon
HEIGHT: 5'11"
WEIGHT: 222 lbs.
ABILITY: Overgrow
When Meganium's HPs are very low, its Grass-type attacks are multiplied by 1.5.

STATS

EVOLUTIONS

LV16 LV32

LOCATION(s):

RUBY	Rarity: **None**	Trade from *Colosseum*
SAPPHIRE	Rarity: **None**	Trade from *Colosseum*
FIRERED	Rarity: **None**	Trade from *Colosseum*
LEAFGREEN	Rarity: **None**	Trade from *Colosseum*
COLOSSEUM	Rarity: **Evolve**	Evolve Bayleef
EMERALD	Rarity: **Evolve**	Evolve Bayleef
XD	Rarity: **Evolve**	Evolve Bayleef

MOVES

Level	Attack	Type	Power	ACC	PP
—	Tackle	Normal	35	95	35
—	Growl	Normal	—	100	40
—	Razor Leaf	Grass	55	95	25
—	Reflect	Psychic	—	—	20
15	Poisonpowder	Poison	—	75	35

Level	Attack	Type	Power	ACC	PP
23	Synthesis	Grass	—	—	5
31	Body Slam	Normal	85	100	15
41	Light Screen	Psychic	—	—	30
51	Safeguard	Normal	—	—	25
61	Solarbeam	Grass	120	100	10

TM/HM

TM/HM#	Name	Type	Power	ACC	PP
TM06	Toxic	Poison	—	85	10
TM09	Bullet Seed	Grass	10	100	30
TM10	Hidden Power	Normal	—	100	15
TM11	Sunny Day	Fire	—	—	5
TM15	Hyper Beam	Normal	150	90	5
TM16	Light Screen	Psychic	—	—	30
TM17	Protect	Normal	—	—	10
TM19	Giga Drain	Grass	60	100	5
TM20	Safeguard	Normal	—	—	25
TM21	Frustration	Normal	—	100	20
TM22	Solarbeam	Grass	120	100	10
TM23	Iron Tail	Steel	75	75	15

TM/HM#	Name	Type	Power	ACC	PP
TM26	Earthquake	Ground	100	100	10
TM27	Return	Normal	—	100	20
TM32	Double Team	Normal	—	—	15
TM33	Reflect	Normal	—	—	20
TM42	Facade	Normal	70	100	20
TM43	Secret Power	Normal	70	100	20
TM44	Rest	Psychic	—	—	10
TM45	Attract	Normal	—	100	15
HM01	Cut	Normal	50	95	30
HM04	Strength	Normal	80	100	20
HM05	Flash	Normal	—	70	20
HM06	Rock Smash	Fighting	20	100	15

MOVE TUTOR
FireRed/LeafGreen and Emerald Only

Body Slam*	Mimic	Swords Dance*
Double-Edge	Substitute	Counter*

*Battle Frontier tutor move (*Emerald*)

PRIMA OFFICIAL GAME GUIDE

155 Cyndaquil™

FIRE

GENERAL INFO
SPECIES: Fire Mouse Pokémon
HEIGHT: 1'08"
WEIGHT: 17 lbs.
ABILITY: Blaze
When Cyndaquil's HPs are very low, its Fire-type attacks are multiplied by 1.5.

STATS

EVOLUTIONS

LV14   LV36

LOCATION[s]:

RUBY	Rarity: **None**	Trade Quilava or Typhlosion from *Colosseum* then breed
SAPPHIRE	Rarity: **None**	Trade Quilava or Typhlosion from *Colosseum* then breed
FIRERED	Rarity: **None**	Trade Quilava or Typhlosion from *Colosseum* then breed
LEAFGREEN	Rarity: **None**	Trade Quilava or Typhlosion from *Colosseum* then breed
COLOSSEUM	Rarity: **Breed**	Breed in *Ruby/Sapphire/FireRed/LeafGreen* then trade back to *Colosseum*
EMERALD	Rarity: **Only One**	Trade Quilava or Typhlosion from *Colosseum* then breed, Littleroot Town
XD	Rarity: **Only One**	Reward from Battlus for climbing Mt. Battle without switching Pokémon

MOVES

Level	Attack	Type	Power	ACC	PP
—	Tackle	Normal	35	95	35
—	Leer	Normal	—	100	30
6	Smokescreen	Normal	—	100	20
12	Ember	Fire	40	100	25

Level	Attack	Type	Power	ACC	PP
19	Quick Attack	Normal	40	100	30
27	Flame Wheel	Fire	60	100	25
36	Swift	Normal	60	—	20
46	Flamethrower	Fire	95	100	15

TM/HM

TM/HM#	Name	Type	Power	ACC	PP
TM06	Toxic	Poison	—	85	10
TM10	Hidden Power	Normal	—	100	15
TM11	Sunny Day	Fire	—	—	5
TM17	Protect	Normal	—	—	10
TM21	Frustration	Normal	—	100	20
TM27	Return	Normal	—	100	20
TM28	Dig	Ground	60	100	10
TM32	Double Team	Normal	—	—	15
TM35	Flamethrower	Fire	95	100	15

TM/HM#	Name	Type	Power	ACC	PP
TM38	Fire Blast	Fire	120	85	5
TM40	Aerial Ace	Flying	60	—	20
TM42	Facade	Normal	70	100	20
TM43	Secret Power	Normal	70	100	20
TM44	Rest	Psychic	—	—	10
TM45	Attract	Normal	—	100	15
TM50	Overheat	Fire	140	90	5
HM01	Cut	Normal	50	95	30

EGG MOVES*

Name	Type	Power	ACC	PP
Covet	Normal	40	100	40
Crush Claw	Normal	75	95	10
Foresight	Normal	—	100	40
Fury Swipes	Normal	18	80	15
Howl	Normal	—	—	40
Quick Attack	Normal	40	100	30
Reversal	Fighting	—	100	15
Thrash	Normal	90	100	20

*Learned Via Breeding

MOVE TUTOR
FireRed/LeafGreen and Emerald Only

Body Slam*	Mimic	Substitute
Double-Edge		

*Battle Frontier tutor move (*Emerald*)

156 Quilava™

FIRE

GENERAL INFO

SPECIES: Volcano Pokémon
HEIGHT: 2'11"
WEIGHT: 42 lbs.
ABILITY: Blaze
When Quilava's HPs are very low, its Fire-type attacks are multiplied by 1.5.

STATS

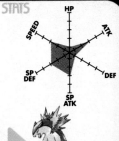

HP · ATK · DEF · SP ATK · SP DEF · SPEED

EVOLUTIONS

LV14   LV36

LOCATION(s):

RUBY	Rarity: **None**	Trade from *Colosseum*
SAPPHIRE	Rarity: **None**	Trade from *Colosseum*
FIRERED	Rarity: **None**	Trade from *Colosseum*
LEAFGREEN	Rarity: **None**	Trade from *Colosseum*
COLOSSEUM	Rarity: **Only One**	Phenac City
EMERALD	Rarity: **None**	Trade from *Colosseum*
XD	Rarity: **Evolve**	Evolve Cyndaquil

MOVES

Level	Attack	Type	Power	ACC	PP	Level	Attack	Type	Power	ACC	PP
—	Tackle	Normal	35	95	35	21	Quick Attack	Normal	40	100	30
—	Leer	Normal	—	100	30	31	Flame Wheel	Fire	60	100	25
—	Smokescreen	Normal	—	100	20	42	Swift	Normal	60	—	20
12	Ember	Fire	40	100	25	54	Flamethrower	Fire	95	100	15

TM/HM

TM/HM#	Name	Type	Power	ACC	PP	TM/HM#	Name	Type	Power	ACC	PP
TM01	Focus Punch	Fighting	150	100	20	TM35	Flamethrower	Fire	95	100	15
TM05	Roar	Normal	—	100	20	TM38	Fire Blast	Fire	120	85	5
TM06	Toxic	Poison	—	85	10	TM40	Aerial Ace	Flying	60	—	20
TM10	Hidden Power	Normal	—	100	15	TM42	Facade	Normal	70	100	20
TM11	Sunny Day	Fire	—	—	5	TM43	Secret Power	Normal	70	100	20
TM17	Protect	Normal	—	—	10	TM44	Rest	Psychic	—	—	10
TM21	Frustration	Normal	—	100	20	TM45	Attract	Normal	—	100	15
TM27	Return	Normal	—	100	20	TM50	Overheat	Fire	140	90	5
TM28	Dig	Ground	60	100	10	HM01	Cut	Normal	50	95	30
TM31	Brick Break	Fighting	75	100	15	HM04	Strength	Normal	80	100	20
TM32	Double Team	Normal	—	—	15	HM06	Rock Smash	Fighting	20	100	15

MOVE TUTOR

FireRed/LeafGreen and Emerald Only

Body Slam*	Mimic	Substitute
Double-Edge		

*Battle Frontier tutor move (*Emerald*)

157 Typhlosion™

FIRE

GENERAL INFO
SPECIES: Volcano Pokémon
HEIGHT: 5'07"
WEIGHT: 175 lbs.
ABILITY: Blaze
When Typhlosion's HPs are very low, its Fire-type attacks are multiplied by 1.5.

STATS

EVOLUTIONS

LV14   LV36

LOCATION[s]:

RUBY	Rarity: **None**	Trade from *Colosseum*
SAPPHIRE	Rarity: **None**	Trade from *Colosseum*
FIRERED	Rarity: **None**	Trade from *Colosseum*
LEAFGREEN	Rarity: **None**	Trade from *Colosseum*
COLOSSEUM	Rarity: **Evolve**	Evolve Quilava
EMERALD	Rarity: **Evolve**	Evolve Quilava
XD	Rarity: **Evolve**	Evolve Quilava

MOVES

Level	Attack	Type	Power	ACC	PP	Level	Attack	Type	Power	ACC	PP
—	Tackle	Normal	35	95	35	21	Quick Attack	Normal	40	100	30
—	Leer	Normal	—	100	30	31	Flame Wheel	Fire	60	100	25
—	Smokescreen	Normal	—	100	20	45	Swift	Normal	60	—	20
—	Ember	Fire	40	100	25	60	Flamethrower	Fire	95	100	15

TM/HM

TM/HM#	Name	Type	Power	ACC	PP	TM/HM#	Name	Type	Power	ACC	PP
TM01	Focus Punch	Fighting	150	100	20	TM32	Double Team	Normal	—	—	15
TM05	Roar	Normal	—	100	20	TM35	Flamethrower	Fire	95	100	15
TM06	Toxic	Poison	—	85	10	TM38	Fire Blast	Fire	120	85	5
TM10	Hidden Power	Normal	—	100	15	TM40	Aerial Ace	Flying	60	—	20
TM11	Sunny Day	Fire	—	—	5	TM42	Facade	Normal	70	100	20
TM15	Hyper Beam	Normal	150	90	5	TM43	Secret Power	Normal	70	100	20
TM17	Protect	Normal	—	—	10	TM44	Rest	Psychic	—	—	10
TM21	Frustration	Normal	—	100	20	TM45	Attract	Normal	—	100	15
TM26	Earthquake	Ground	100	100	10	TM50	Overheat	Fire	140	90	5
TM27	Return	Normal	—	100	20	HM01	Cut	Normal	50	95	30
TM28	Dig	Ground	60	100	10	HM04	Strength	Normal	80	100	20
TM31	Brick Break	Fighting	75	100	15	HM06	Rock Smash	Fighting	20	100	15

MOVE TUTOR
FireRed/LeafGreen and Emerald Only

Body Slam*	Mega Kick*	Counter*
Double-Edge	Mimic	Seismic Toss*
Mega Punch*	Substitute	Rock Slide*

*Battle Frontier tutor move (*Emerald*)

158 Totodile™

WATER

GENERAL INFO
SPECIES: Big Jaw Pokémon
HEIGHT: 2'00"
WEIGHT: 21 lbs.
ABILITY: Torrent

When Totodile's HPs are very low, its Water-type attacks are multiplied by 1.5.

STATS

HP, SPEED, ATK, DEF, SP ATK, SP DEF

EVOLUTIONS

  LV18 LV30

LOCATION[s]:

RUBY	**Rarity: None**	Trade Croconaw or Feraligatr from *Colosseum* then breed
SAPPHIRE	**Rarity: None**	Trade Croconaw or Feraligatr from *Colosseum* then breed
FIRERED	**Rarity: None**	Trade Croconaw or Feraligatr from *Colosseum* then breed
LEAFGREEN	**Rarity: None**	Trade Croconaw or Feraligatr from *Colosseum* then breed
COLOSSEUM	**Rarity: None**	Breed in *Ruby/Sapphire/FireRed/LeafGreen* then trade back to *Colosseum*
EMERALD	**Rarity: Only One**	Trade Croconaw or Feraligatr from *Colosseum* then breed, Littleroot Town
XD	**Rarity: Only One**	Reward from Battlus for climbing Mt. Battle without switching Pokémon

MOVES

Level	Attack	Type	Power	ACC	PP		Level	Attack	Type	Power	ACC	PP
—	Scratch	Normal	40	100	35		20	Bite	Dark	60	100	25
—	Leer	Normal	—	100	30		27	Scary Face	Normal	—	90	10
7	Rage	Normal	20	100	20		35	Slash	Normal	70	100	20
13	Water Gun	Water	40	100	25		43	Screech	Normal	—	85	40
							52	Hydro Pump	Water	120	80	5

TM/HM

TM/HM#	Name	Type	Power	ACC	PP		TM/HM#	Name	Type	Power	ACC	PP
TM01	Focus Punch	Fighting	150	100	20		TM28	Dig	Ground	60	100	10
TM03	Water Pulse	Water	60	95	20		TM31	Brick Break	Fighting	75	100	15
TM06	Toxic	Poison	—	85	10		TM32	Double Team	Normal	—	—	15
TM07	Hail	Ice	—	—	10		TM40	Aerial Ace	Flying	60	—	20
TM10	Hidden Power	Normal	—	100	15		TM42	Facade	Normal	70	100	20
TM13	Ice Beam	Ice	95	100	10		TM43	Secret Power	Normal	70	100	20
TM14	Blizzard	Ice	120	70	5		TM44	Rest	Psychic	—	—	10
TM17	Protect	Normal	—	—	10		TM45	Attract	Normal	—	100	15
TM18	Rain Dance	Water	—	—	5		HM01	Cut	Normal	50	95	30
TM21	Frustration	Normal	—	100	20		HM03	Surf	Water	95	100	15
TM23	Iron Tail	Steel	75	75	15		HM07	Waterfall	Water	80	100	15
TM27	Return	Normal	—	100	20		HM08	Dive	Water	60	100	10

EGG MOVES*

Name	Type	Power	ACC	PP
Ancientpower	Rock	60	100	5
Crunch	Dark	80	100	15
Dragon Claw	Dragon	80	100	15
Hydro Pump	Water	120	80	5
Mud Sport	Ground	—	100	15
Rock Slide	Rock	75	90	10
Thrash	Normal	90	100	20
Water Sport	Water	—	100	15

*Learned Via Breeding

MOVE TUTOR
FireRed/LeafGreen and Emerald Only

Body Slam*	Mimic	Seismic Toss*
Double-Edge	Substitute	Rock Slide*
Mega Punch*	Swords Dance*	
Mega Kick*	Counter*	

*Battle Frontier tutor move (*Emerald*)

PRIMA OFFICIAL GAME GUIDE

159 Croconaw™

WATER

GENERAL INFO

SPECIES: Big Jaw Pokémon
HEIGHT: 3'07"
WEIGHT: 55 lbs.
ABILITY: Torrent

When Croconaw's HPs are very low, its Water-type attacks are multiplied by 1.5.

STATS

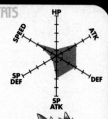

EVOLUTIONS

LV18   LV30

LOCATION(s):

RUBY	Rarity: **None**	Trade from *Colosseum*
SAPPHIRE	Rarity: **None**	Trade from *Colosseum*
FIRERED	Rarity: **None**	Trade from *Colosseum*
LEAFGREEN	Rarity: **None**	Trade from *Colosseum*
COLOSSEUM	Rarity: **Only One**	Phenac City
EMERALD	Rarity: **None**	Trade from *Colosseum*
XD	Rarity: **Evolve**	Evolve Totodile

MOVES

Level	Attack	Type	Power	ACC	PP		Level	Attack	Type	Power	ACC	PP
—	Scratch	Normal	40	100	35		21	Bite	Dark	60	100	25
—	Leer	Normal	—	100	30		28	Scary Face	Normal	—	90	10
—	Rage	Normal	20	100	20		37	Slash	Normal	70	100	20
13	Water Gun	Water	40	100	25		45	Screech	Normal	—	85	40
							55	Hydro Pump	Water	120	80	5

TM/HM

TM/HM#	Name	Type	Power	ACC	PP		TM/HM#	Name	Type	Power	ACC	PP
TM01	Focus Punch	Fighting	150	100	20		TM31	Brick Break	Fighting	75	100	15
TM03	Water Pulse	Water	60	95	20		TM32	Double Team	Normal	—	—	15
TM05	Roar	Normal	—	100	20		TM40	Aerial Ace	Flying	60	—	20
TM06	Toxic	Poison	—	85	10		TM42	Facade	Normal	70	100	20
TM07	Hail	Ice	—	—	10		TM43	Secret Power	Normal	70	100	20
TM10	Hidden Power	Normal	—	100	15		TM44	Rest	Psychic	—	—	10
TM13	Ice Beam	Ice	95	100	10		TM45	Attract	Normal	—	100	15
TM14	Blizzard	Ice	120	70	5		HM01	Cut	Normal	50	95	30
TM17	Protect	Normal	—	—	10		HM03	Surf	Water	95	100	15
TM18	Rain Dance	Water	—	5		HM04	Strength	Normal	80	100	20
TM21	Frustration	Normal	—	100	20		HM06	Rock Smash	Fighting	20	100	15
TM23	Iron Tail	Steel	75	75	15		HM07	Waterfall	Water	80	100	15
TM27	Return	Normal	—	100	20		HM08	Dive	Water	60	100	10
TM28	Dig	Ground	60	100	10							

MOVE TUTOR

FireRed/LeafGreen and Emerald Only

Body Slam*	Mimic	Seismic Toss*
Double-Edge	Substitute	Rock Slide*
Mega Punch*	Swords Dance*	
Mega Kick*	Counter*	

*Battle Frontier tutor move (*Emerald*)

160 Feraligatr™

WATER

GENERAL INFO
SPECIES: Big Jaw Pokémon
HEIGHT: 7'07"
WEIGHT: 196 lbs.
ABILITY: Torrent

When Feraligatr's HPs are very low, its Water-type attacks are multiplied by 1.5.

STATS

EVOLUTIONS

LV18   LV30

LOCATION[S]:

RUBY	Rarity: **None**	Trade from *Colosseum*
SAPPHIRE	Rarity: **None**	Trade from *Colosseum*
FIRERED	Rarity: **None**	Trade from *Colosseum*
LEAFGREEN	Rarity: **None**	Trade from *Colosseum*
COLOSSEUM	Rarity: **Evolve**	Evolve Croconaw
EMERALD	Rarity: **Evolve**	Evolve Croconaw
XD	Rarity: **Evolve**	Evolve Croconaw

MOVES

Level	Attack	Type	Power	ACC	PP
—	Scratch	Normal	40	100	35
—	Leer	Normal	—	100	30
—	Rage	Normal	20	100	20
—	Water Gun	Water	40	100	25

Level	Attack	Type	Power	ACC	PP
21	Bite	Dark	60	100	25
28	Scary Face	Normal	—	90	10
38	Slash	Normal	70	100	20
47	Screech	Normal	—	85	40
58	Hydro Pump	Water	120	80	5

TM/HM

TM/HM#	Name	Type	Power	ACC	PP
TM01	Focus Punch	Fighting	150	100	20
TM02	Dragon Claw	Dragon	80	100	15
TM03	Water Pulse	Water	60	95	20
TM05	Roar	Normal	—	100	20
TM06	Toxic	Poison	—	85	10
TM07	Hail	Ice	—	—	10
TM10	Hidden Power	Normal	—	100	15
TM13	Ice Beam	Ice	95	100	10
TM14	Blizzard	Ice	120	70	5
TM15	Hyper Beam	Normal	150	90	5
TM17	Protect	Normal	—	—	10
TM18	Rain Dance	Water	—	—	5
TM21	Frustration	Normal	—	100	20
TM23	Iron Tail	Steel	75	75	15
TM26	Earthquake	Ground	100	100	10

TM/HM#	Name	Type	Power	ACC	PP
TM27	Return	Normal	—	100	20
TM28	Dig	Ground	60	100	10
TM31	Brick Break	Fighting	75	100	15
TM32	Double Team	Normal	—	—	15
TM40	Aerial Ace	Flying	60	—	20
TM42	Facade	Normal	70	100	20
TM43	Secret Power	Normal	70	100	20
TM44	Rest	Psychic	—	—	10
TM45	Attract	Normal	—	100	15
HM01	Cut	Normal	50	95	30
HM03	Surf	Water	95	100	15
HM04	Strength	Normal	80	100	20
HM06	Rock Smash	Fight	20	100	15
HM07	Waterfall	Water	80	100	15
HM08	Dive	Water	60	100	10

MOVE TUTOR
FireRed/LeafGreen and Emerald Only

Body Slam*	Mimic	Seismic Toss*
Double-Edge	Substitute	Rock Slide*
Mega Punch*	Swords Dance*	
Mega Kick*	Counter*	

*Battle Frontier tutor move (*Emerald*)

161 Sentret™

NORMAL

GENERAL INFO

SPECIES: Scout Pokémon
HEIGHT: 2'07"
WEIGHT: 13 lbs.
ABILITY 1: Run Away
Allows Sentret to escape from wild Pokémon.
ABILITY 2: Keen Eye
Protects Sentret from having its Accuracy lowered.

STATS

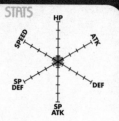

EVOLUTIONS

LV15

LOCATION[s]:

RUBY	Rarity: **None**	Trade from *FireRed/LeafGreen*
SAPPHIRE	Rarity: **None**	Trade from *FireRed/LeafGreen*
FIRERED	Rarity: **Common**	Five Island, Six Island, Seven Island
LEAFGREEN	Rarity: **Common**	Five Island, Six Island, Seven Island
COLOSSEUM	Rarity: **Breed**	Trade from *FireRed/LeafGreen*
EMERALD	Rarity: **None**	Trade from *FireRed/LeafGreen*
XD	Rarity: **None**	Trade from *FireRed/LeafGreen*

MOVES

Level	Attack	Type	Power	ACC	PP	Level	Attack	Type	Power	ACC	PP
—	Scratch	Normal	40	100	35	17	Helping Hand	Normal	—	100	20
4	Defense Curl	Normal	—	—	40	24	Slam	Normal	80	75	20
7	Quick Attack	Normal	40	100	30	31	Follow Me	Normal	—	100	20
12	Fury Swipes	Normal	18	80	15	40	Rest	Psychic	—	—	10
						49	Amnesia	Psychic	—	—	20

TM/HM

TM/HM#	Name	Type	Power	ACC	PP	TM/HM#	Name	Type	Power	ACC	PP
TM01	Focus Punch	Fighting	150	100		TM28	Dig	Ground	60	100	10
TM03	Water Pulse	Water	60	95	20	TM30	Shadow Ball	Ghost	80	100	15
TM06	Toxic	Poison	—	85	10	TM31	Brick Break	Fighting	75	100	15
TM10	Hidden Power	Normal	—	100	15	TM32	Double Team	Normal	—	—	15
TM11	Sunny Day	Fire	—	—	5	TM34	Shock Wave	Electric	60	—	20
TM13	Ice Beam	Ice	95	100	10	TM35	Flamethrower	Fire	95	100	15
TM17	Protect	Normal	—	—	10	TM42	Facade	Normal	70	100	20
TM18	Rain Dance	Water	—	—	5	TM43	Secret Power	Normal	70	100	20
TM21	Frustration	Normal	—	100	20	TM44	Rest	Psychic	—	—	10
TM22	Solarbeam	Grass	120	100	10	TM45	Attract	Normal	—	100	15
TM23	Iron Tail	Steel	75	75	15	TM46	Thief	Dark	40	100	10
TM24	Thunderbolt	Electric	95	100	15	HM01	Cut	Normal	50	95	30
TM27	Return	Normal	—	100	20	HM03	Surf	Water	95	100	15

EGG MOVES*

Name	Type	Power	ACC	PP
Assist	Normal	—	100	20
Double-Edge	Normal	120	100	15
Focus Energy	Normal	—	—	30
Pursuit	Dark	40	100	20
Reversal	Fighting	—	100	15
Slash	Normal	70	100	20
Substitute	Normal	—	—	10
Trick	Psychic	—	100	10

*Learned Via Breeding

MOVE TUTOR

FireRed/LeafGreen and Emerald Only

Body Slam*	Mimic	Substitute
Double-Edge		

*Battle Frontier tutor move (*Emerald*)

162 Furret™

NORMAL

GENERAL INFO

SPECIES: Long Body Pokémon
HEIGHT: 5'11"
WEIGHT: 72 lbs.
ABILITY 1: Run Away
Allows Furret to escape from wild Pokémon.
ABILITY 2: Keen Eye
Protects Furret from having its Accuracy lowered.

STATS

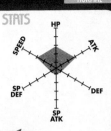

EVOLUTIONS

LV15

LOCATION(s):

RUBY	Rarity: **None**	Evolve Sentret
SAPPHIRE	Rarity: **None**	Evolve Sentret
FIRERED	Rarity: **Evolve**	Evolve Sentret
LEAFGREEN	Rarity: **Evolve**	Evolve Sentret
COLOSSEUM	Rarity: **Only One**	Pyrite Town
EMERALD	Rarity: **None**	Trade from *Colosseum*
XD	Rarity: **None**	Trade from *FireRed/LeafGreen*

MOVES

Level	Attack	Type	Power	ACC	PP	Level	Attack	Type	Power	ACC	PP
—	Scratch	Normal	40	100	35	19	Helping Hand	Normal	—	100	20
—	Defense Curl	Normal	—	—	40	28	Slam	Normal	80	75	20
—	Quick Attack	Normal	40	100	30	37	Follow Me	Normal	—	100	20
12	Fury Swipes	Normal	18	80	15	48	Rest	Psychic	—	—	10
						59	Amnesia	Psychic	—	—	20

TM/HM

TM/HM#	Name	Type	Power	ACC	PP	TM/HM#	Name	Type	Power	ACC	PP
TM01	Focus Punch	Fighting	150	100	20	TM28	Dig	Ground	60	100	10
TM03	Water Pulse	Water	60	95	20	TM30	Shadow Ball	Ghost	80	100	15
TM06	Toxic	Poison	—	85	10	TM31	Brick Break	Fighting	75	100	15
TM10	Hidden Power	Normal	—	100	15	TM32	Double Team	Normal	—	—	15
TM11	Sunny Day	Fire	—	—	5	TM34	Shock Wave	Electric	60	—	20
TM13	Ice Beam	Ice	95	100	10	TM35	Flamethrower	Fire	95	100	15
TM14	Blizzard	Ice	120	70	5	TM42	Facade	Normal	70	100	20
TM15	Hyper Beam	Normal	150	90	5	TM43	Secret Power	Normal	70	100	20
TM17	Protect	Normal	—	—	10	TM44	Rest	Psychic	—	—	10
TM18	Rain Dance	Water	—	—	5	TM45	Attract	Normal	—	100	15
TM21	Frustration	Normal	—	100	20	TM46	Thief	Dark	40	100	10
TM22	Solarbeam	Grass	120	100	10	HM01	Cut	Normal	50	95	30
TM23	Iron Tail	Steel	75	75	15	HM03	Surf	Water	95	100	15
TM24	Thunderbolt	Electric	95	100	15	HM04	Strength	Normal	80	100	20
TM25	Thunder	Electric	120	70	10	HM06	Rock Smash	Fighting	20	100	15
TM27	Return	Normal	—	100	20						

MOVE TUTOR

FireRed/LeafGreen and Emerald Only

Body Slam*	Mimic	Substitute
Double-Edge		

*Battle Frontier tutor move (*Emerald*)

163 Hoothoot™

NORMAL   FLYING

GENERAL INFO
SPECIES: Owl Pokémon
HEIGHT: 2'04"
WEIGHT: 47 lbs.
ABILITY 1: Insomnia
Prevents Hoothoot from being put to sleep.
ABILITY 2: Keen Eye
Protects Hoothoot from having its Accuracy lowered.

STATS

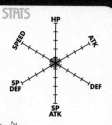

HP
SPEED   ATK
SP DEF   DEF
SP ATK

EVOLUTIONS

LV20

LOCATION[s]:

RUBY	Rarity: **None**	Trade Noctowl from *Colosseum*, then breed
SAPPHIRE	Rarity: **None**	Trade Noctowl from *Colosseum*, then breed
FIRERED	Rarity: **None**	Trade Noctowl from *Colosseum*, then breed
LEAFGREEN	Rarity: **None**	Trade Noctowl from *Colosseum*, then breed
COLOSSEUM	Rarity: **Breed**	Breed Noctowl in *Ruby/Sapphire/FireRed/LeafGreen* then trade back
EMERALD	Rarity: **Rare**	Safari Zone
XD	Rarity: **None**	Trade Noctowl from *Colosseum*, then breed

MOVES

Level	Attack	Type	Power	ACC	PP
—	Tackle	Normal	35	95	35
—	Growl	Normal	—	100	40
6	Foresight	Normal	—	100	40
11	Peck	Flying	35	100	35

Level	Attack	Type	Power	ACC	PP
16	Hypnosis	Psychic	—	60	20
22	Reflect	Psychic	—	—	20
28	Take Down	Normal	90	85	20
34	Confusion	Psychic	50	100	25
48	Dream Eater	Psychic	100	100	15

TM/HM

TM/HM#	Name	Type	Power	ACC	PP
TM06	Toxic	Poison	—	85	10
TM10	Hidden Power	Normal	—	100	15
TM11	Sunny Day	Fire	—	—	5
TM17	Protect	Normal	—	—	10
TM18	Rain Dance	Water	—	—	5
TM21	Frustration	Normal	—	100	20
TM27	Return	Normal	—	100	20
TM29	Psychic	Psychic	90	100	10
TM30	Shadow Ball	Ghost	80	100	15
TM32	Double Team	Normal	—	—	15

TM/HM#	Name	Type	Power	ACC	PP
TM33	Reflect	Normal	—	—	20
TM40	Aerial Ace	Flying	60	—	20
TM42	Facade	Normal	70	100	20
TM43	Secret Power	Normal	70	100	20
TM44	Rest	Psychic	—	—	10
TM45	Attract	Normal	—	100	15
TM46	Thief	Dark	40	100	10
TM47	Steel Wing	Steel	70	90	25
HM02	Fly	Flying	70	95	15
HM05	Flash	Normal	—	70	20

EGG MOVES*

Name	Type	Power	ACC	PP
Featherdance	Flying	—	100	15
Faint Attack	Dark	60	—	20
Mirror Move	Flying	—	—	20
Sky Attack	Flying	140	90	5
Supersonic	Normal	—	55	20
Whirlwind	Normal	—	100	20
Wing Attack	Flying	60	100	35

*Learned Via Breeding

MOVE TUTOR
FireRed/LeafGreen and Emerald Only

Double-Edge	Dream Eater*	Substitute
Mimic		

*Battle Frontier tutor move (*Emerald*)

164 Noctowl™

NORMAL · FLYING

GENERAL INFO

SPECIES: Owl Pokémon
HEIGHT: 5'03"
WEIGHT: 90 lbs.
ABILITY 1: Insomnia
Prevents Noctowl from being put to sleep.
ABILITY 2: Keen Eye
Protects Noctowl from having its Accuracy lowered.

STATS

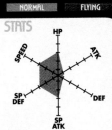

EVOLUTIONS

LV20

LOCATION[S]:

RUBY	Rarity: **None**	Trade from *Colosseum*
SAPPHIRE	Rarity: **None**	Trade from *Colosseum*
FIRERED	Rarity: **None**	Trade from *Colosseum*
LEAFGREEN	Rarity: **None**	Trade from *Colosseum*
COLOSSEUM	Rarity: **Only One**	Pyrite Town
EMERALD	Rarity: **Evolve**	Evolve Hoothoot
XD	Rarity: **None**	Trade from *Colosseum*

MOVES

Level	Attack	Type	Power	ACC	PP	Level	Attack	Type	Power	ACC	PP
—	Tackle	Normal	35	95	35	16	Hypnosis	Psychic	—	60	20
—	Growl	Normal	—	100	40	25	Reflect	Psychic	—	—	20
—	Foresight	Normal	—	100	40	33	Take Down	Normal	90	85	20
—	Peck	Flying	35	100	35	41	Confusion	Psychic	50	100	25
						57	Dream Eater	Psychic	100	100	15

TM/HM

TM/HM#	Name	Type	Power	ACC	PP	TM/HM#	Name	Type	Power	ACC	PP
TM06	Toxic	Poison	—	85	10	TM33	Reflect	Normal	—	—	20
TM10	Hidden Power	Normal	—	100	15	TM40	Aerial Ace	Flying	60	—	20
TM11	Sunny Day	Fire	—	—	5	TM42	Facade	Normal	70	100	20
TM15	Hyper Beam	Normal	150	90	5	TM43	Secret Power	Normal	70	100	20
TM17	Protect	Normal	—	—	10	TM44	Rest	Psychic	—	—	10
TM18	Rain Dance	Water	—	—	5	TM45	Attract	Normal	—	100	15
TM21	Frustration	Normal	—	100	20	TM46	Thief	Dark	40	100	10
TM27	Return	Normal	—	100	20	TM47	Steel Wing	Steel	70	90	25
TM29	Psychic	Psychic	90	100	10	HM02	Fly	Flying	70	95	15
TM30	Shadow Ball	Ghost	80	100	15	HM05	Flash	Normal	—	70	20
TM32	Double Team	Normal	—	—	15						

MOVE TUTOR
FireRed/LeafGreen and Emerald Only

Double-Edge	Dream Eater*	Substitute
Mimic		

*Battle Frontier tutor move (*Emerald*)

165 Ledyba™

BUG   FLYING

GENERAL INFO

SPECIES: Five Star Pokémon
HEIGHT: 3'03"
WEIGHT: 24 lbs.
ABILITY 1: Early Bird
Allows Ledyba to wake up earlier when put to sleep.
ABILITY 2: Swarm
When Ledyba's HPs are low, its Bug-type moves are multiplied by 1.5.

STATS

EVOLUTIONS

LV18

LOCATION[s]:

RUBY	Rarity: **None**	Trade from *FireRed/LeafGreen*
SAPPHIRE	Rarity: **None**	Trade from *FireRed/LeafGreen*
FIRERED	Rarity: **Rare**	Six Island
LEAFGREEN	Rarity: **Rare**	Six Island
COLOSSEUM	Rarity: **Breed**	Breed Ledian in *Ruby/Sapphire/FireRed/LeafGreen* then trade back
EMERALD	Rarity: **Rare**	Safari Zone
XD	Rarity: **Only One**	Gateon Port (Capture from Casual Guy Cyle)

MOVES

Level	Attack	Type	Power	ACC	PP	Level	Attack	Type	Power	ACC	PP
—	Tackle	Normal	35	95	35	22	Safeguard	Normal	—	—	25
8	Supersonic	Normal	—	55	20	29	Baton Pass	Normal	—	—	40
15	Comet Punch	Normal	18	85	15	36	Swift	Normal	60	—	20
22	Light Screen	Psychic	—	—	30	43	Agility	Psychic	—	—	30
22	Reflect	Psychic	—	—	20	50	Double-Edge	Normal	120	100	15

TM/HM

TM/HM#	Name	Type	Power	ACC	PP	TM/HM#	Name	Type	Power	ACC	PP
TM01	Focus Punch	Fighting	150	100	20	TM28	Dig	Ground	60	100	10
TM06	Toxic	Poison	—	85	10	TM31	Brick Break	Fighting	75	100	15
TM10	Hidden Power	Normal	—	100	15	TM32	Double Team	Normal	—	—	15
TM11	Sunny Day	Fire	—	—	5	TM33	Reflect	Normal	—	—	20
TM16	Light Screen	Psychic	—	—	30	TM40	Aerial Ace	Flying	60	—	20
TM17	Protect	Normal	—	—	10	TM42	Facade	Normal	70	100	20
TM19	Giga Drain	Grass	60	100	5	TM43	Secret Power	Normal	70	100	20
TM20	Safeguard	Normal	—	—	25	TM44	Rest	Psychic	—	—	10
TM21	Frustration	Normal	—	100	20	TM45	Attract	Normal	—	100	15
TM22	Solarbeam	Grass	120	100	10	TM46	Thief	Dark	40	100	10
TM27	Return	Normal	—	100	20	HM05	Flash	Normal	—	70	20

EGG MOVES*

Name	Type	Power	ACC	PP
Bide	Normal	—	100	10
Psybeam	Psychic	65	100	20
Silver Wind	Bug	60	100	5

*Learned Via Breeding

MOVE TUTOR
FireRed/LeafGreen and Emerald Only

Double-Edge	Substitute	Mega Punch*
Mimic	Swords Dance*	

*Battle Frontier tutor move (*Emerald*)

166 Ledian™

BUG   FLYING

GENERAL INFO

SPECIES: Five Star Pokémon
HEIGHT: 4'07"
WEIGHT: 79 lbs.

ABILITY 1: Early Bird
Allows Ledian to wake up earlier when put to sleep.

ABILITY 2: Swarm
When Ledian's HPs are low, its Bug-type moves are multiplied by 1.5.

STATS

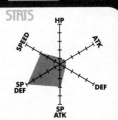

EVOLUTIONS

LV18

LOCATION[s]:

RUBY	Rarity: **Evolve**	Trade from *Colosseum*
SAPPHIRE	Rarity: **Evolve**	Trade from *Colosseum*
FIRERED	Rarity: **Evolve**	Trade from *Colosseum*
LEAFGREEN	Rarity: **Evolve**	Trade from *Colosseum*
COLOSSEUM	Rarity: **Only One**	The Under
EMERALD	Rarity: **Evolve**	Evolve Ledyba
XD	Rarity: **Evolve**	Evolve Ledyba

MOVES

Level	Attack	Type	Power	ACC	PP	Level	Attack	Type	Power	ACC	PP
—	Tackle	Normal	35	95	35	24	Safeguard	Normal	—	—	25
—	Supersonic	Normal	—	55	20	33	Baton Pass	Normal	—	—	40
15	Comet Punch	Normal	18	85	15	42	Swift	Normal	60	—	20
24	Light Screen	Psychic	—	—	30	51	Agility	Psychic	—	—	30
24	Reflect	Psychic	—	—	20	60	Double-Edge	Normal	120	100	15

TM/HM

TM/HM#	Name	Type	Power	ACC	PP	TM/HM#	Name	Type	Power	ACC	PP
TM01	Focus Punch	Fighting	150	100	20	TM28	Dig	Ground	60	100	10
TM06	Toxic	Poison	—	85	10	TM31	Brick Break	Fighting	75	100	15
TM10	Hidden Power	Normal	—	100	15	TM32	Double Team	Normal	—	—	15
TM11	Sunny Day	Fire	—	—	5	TM33	Reflect	Normal	—	—	20
TM15	Hyper Beam	Normal	150	90	5	TM40	Aerial Ace	Flying	60	—	20
TM16	Light Screen	Psychic	—	—	30	TM42	Facade	Normal	70	100	20
TM17	Protect	Normal	—	—	10	TM43	Secret Power	Normal	70	100	20
TM19	Giga Drain	Grass	60	100	5	TM44	Rest	Psychic	—	—	10
TM20	Safeguard	Normal	—	—	25	TM45	Attract	Normal	—	100	15
TM21	Frustration	Normal	—	100	20	TM46	Thief	Dark	40	100	10
TM22	Solarbeam	Grass	120	100	10	HM05	Flash	Normal	—	70	20
TM27	Return	Normal	—	100	20						

MOVE TUTOR

FireRed/LeafGreen and Emerald Only

Double-Edge	Substitute	Mega Punch*
Mimic	Swords Dance*	

*Battle Frontier tutor move (*Emerald*)

PRIMA OFFICIAL GAME GUIDE

167 Spinarak™

BUG   POISON

GENERAL INFO
SPECIES: **String Spit Pokémon**
HEIGHT: **1'08"**
WEIGHT: **19 lbs.**
ABILITY 1: **Insomnia**
Prevents Spinarak from being put to sleep.
ABILITY 2: **Swarm**
When Spinarak's HPs are low, its Bug-type moves are multiplied by 1.5.

STATS

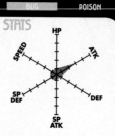

EVOLUTIONS

LV22

LOCATION(s):

RUBY	Rarity: **None**	Trade from FireRed/LeafGreen
SAPPHIRE	Rarity: **None**	Trade from FireRed/LeafGreen
FIRERED	Rarity: **Rare**	Six Island
LEAFGREEN	Rarity: **Rare**	Six Island
COLOSSEUM	Rarity: **None**	Breed Ariados in Ruby/Sapphire/FireRed/LeafGreen then trade back
EMERALD	Rarity: **Rare**	Safari Zone
XD	Rarity: **Only One**	Cipher Lab (Capture from Cipher Peon Nexir)

MOVES

Level	Attack	Type	Power	ACC	PP	Level	Attack	Type	Power	ACC	PP
—	Poison Sting	Poison	15	100	35	23	Leech Life	Bug	20	100	15
—	String Shot	Bug	—	95	40	30	Fury Swipes	Normal	18	80	15
6	Scary Face	Normal	—	90	10	37	Spider Web	Bug	—	100	10
11	Constrict	Normal	10	100	35	45	Agility	Psychic	—	—	30
17	Night Shade	Ghost	—	100	15	53	Psychic	Psychic	90	100	10

TM/HM

TM/HM#	Name	Type	Power	ACC	PP	TM/HM#	Name	Type	Power	ACC	PP
TM06	Toxic	Poison	—	85	10	TM29	Psychic	Psychic	90	100	10
TM10	Hidden Power	Normal	—	100	15	TM32	Double Team	Normal	—	—	15
TM11	Sunny Day	Fire	—	—	5	TM36	Sludge Bomb	Poison	90	100	10
TM17	Protect	Normal	—	—	10	TM42	Facade	Normal	70	100	20
TM19	Giga Drain	Grass	60	100	5	TM43	Secret Power	Normal	70	100	20
TM21	Frustration	Normal	—	100	20	TM44	Rest	Psychic	—	—	10
TM22	Solarbeam	Grass	120	100	10	TM45	Attract	Normal	—	100	15
TM27	Return	Normal	—	100	20	TM46	Thief	Dark	40	100	10
TM28	Dig	Ground	60	100	10	HM05	Flash	Normal	—	70	20

EGG MOVES*

Name	Type	Power	ACC	PP
Baton Pass	Normal	—	—	40
Disable	Normal	—	55	20
Psybeam	Psychic	65	100	20
Pursuit	Dark	40	100	20
Signal Beam	Bug	75	100	15
Sonicboom	Normal	—	90	20

*Learned Via Breeding

MOVE TUTOR
FireRed/LeafGreen and Emerald Only

Body Slam*	Mimic	Substitute
Double-Edge		

*Battle Frontier tutor move (*Emerald*)

168 Ariados™

BUG POISON

GENERAL INFO

SPECIES: Long Leg Pokémon
HEIGHT: 3'07"
WEIGHT: 74 lbs.
ABILITY 1: Insomnia
Prevents Ariados from being put to sleep.
ABILITY 2: Swarm
When Ariados's HPs are low, its Bug-type moves are multiplied by 1.5.

STATS

EVOLUTIONS

LV22

LOCATION(s):

RUBY	Rarity: **Evolve**	Trade from *FireRed/LeafGreen/Colosseum*
SAPPHIRE	Rarity: **Evolve**	Trade from *FireRed/LeafGreen/Colosseum*
FIRERED	Rarity: **Evolve**	Evolve Spinarak
LEAFGREEN	Rarity: **Evolve**	Evolve Spinarak
COLOSSEUM	Rarity: **Only One**	Shadow Pokémon Lab
EMERALD	Rarity: **Evolve**	Evolve Spinarak
XD	Rarity: **Evolve**	Evolve Spinarak

MOVES

Level	Attack	Type	Power	ACC	PP
—	Poison Sting	Poison	15	100	35
—	String Shot	Bug	—	95	40
—	Scary Face	Normal	—	90	10
—	Constrict	Normal	10	100	35
17	Night Shade	Ghost	—	100	15

Level	Attack	Type	Power	ACC	PP
25	Leech Life	Bug	20	100	15
34	Fury Swipes	Normal	18	80	15
43	Spider Web	Bug	—	100	10
53	Agility	Psychic	—	—	30
63	Psychic	Psychic	90	100	10

TM/HM

TM/HM#	Name	Type	Power	ACC	PP
TM06	Toxic	Poison	—	85	10
TM10	Hidden Power	Normal	—	100	15
TM11	Sunny Day	Fire	—	—	5
TM15	Hyper Beam	Normal	150	90	5
TM17	Protect	Normal	—	—	10
TM19	Giga Drain	Grass	60	100	5
TM21	Frustration	Normal	—	100	20
TM22	Solarbeam	Grass	120	100	10
TM27	Return	Normal	—	100	20
TM28	Dig	Ground	60	100	10

TM/HM#	Name	Type	Power	ACC	PP
TM29	Psychic	Psychic	90	100	10
TM32	Double Team	Normal	—	—	15
TM36	Sludge Bomb	Poison	90	100	10
TM42	Facade	Normal	70	100	20
TM43	Secret Power	Normal	70	100	20
TM44	Rest	Psychic	—	—	10
TM45	Attract	Normal	—	100	15
TM46	Thief	Dark	40	100	10
HM05	Flash	Normal	—	70	20

MOVE TUTOR

FireRed/LeafGreen and Emerald Only

Body Slam*	Mimic	Substitute
Double-Edge		

*Battle Frontier tutor move (*Emerald*)

169 Crobat™

POISON   FLYING

GENERAL INFO

SPECIES: Bat Pokémon
HEIGHT: 5'11"
WEIGHT: 165 lbs.
ABILITY: Inner Focus
Prevents Crobat from flinching.

STATS

EVOLUTIONS

LV22   FRIENDSHIP

LOCATION(s):

RUBY	Rarity: **Evolve**	Evolve Golbat
SAPPHIRE	Rarity: **Evolve**	Evolve Golbat
FIRERED	Rarity: **Evolve**	Evolve Golbat
LEAFGREEN	Rarity: **Evolve**	Evolve Golbat
COLOSSEUM	Rarity: **None**	Trade from *Ruby/Sapphire/FireRed/LeafGreen*
EMERALD	Rarity: **Evolve**	Evolve Golbat
XD	Rarity: **Evolve**	Evolve Golbat

MOVES

Level	Attack	Type	Power	ACC	PP
—	Leech Life	Bug	20	100	15
—	Screech	Normal	—	85	40
—/6	Astonish	Ghost	30	100	15
—/11	Supersonic	Normal	—	55	20
16	Bite	Dark	60	100	25
21	Wing Attack	Flying	60	100	35

Level	Attack	Type	Power	ACC	PP
28	Confuse Ray	Ghost	—	100	10
35	Air Cutter	Flying	55	95	25
42	Mean Look	Normal	—	100	5
49	Poison Fang	Poison	50	100	15
56	Haze	Ice	—	—	30

= *Emerald* Only

TM/HM

TM/HM#	Name	Type	Power	ACC	PP
TM06	Toxic	Poison	—	85	10
TM10	Hidden Power	Normal	—	100	15
TM11	Sunny Day	Fire	—	—	5
TM12	Taunt	Dark	—	100	20
TM15	Hyper Beam	Normal	150	90	5
TM17	Protect	Normal	—	—	10
TM18	Rain Dance	Water	—	—	5
TM19	Giga Drain	Grass	60	100	5
TM21	Frustration	Normal	—	100	20
TM27	Return	Normal	—	100	20
TM30	Shadow Ball	Ghost	80	100	15
TM32	Double Team	Normal	—	—	15

TM/HM#	Name	Type	Power	ACC	PP
TM36	Sludge Bomb	Poison	90	100	10
TM40	Aerial Ace	Flying	60	—	20
TM41	Torment	Dark	—	100	15
TM42	Facade	Normal	70	100	20
TM43	Secret Power	Normal	70	100	20
TM44	Rest	Psychic	—	—	10
TM45	Attract	Normal	—	100	15
TM46	Thief	Dark	40	100	10
TM47	Steel Wing	Steel	70	90	25
TM49	Snatch	Dark	—	100	10
HM02	Fly	Flying	70	95	15

MOVE TUTOR

FireRed/LeafGreen and Emerald Only

Double-Edge	Mimic	Substitute

Emerald Only

Endure*	Snore*	Swift*
Sleep Talk	Swagger	

*Battle Frontier tutor move (*Emerald*)

170 Chinchou

ELECTRIC | WATER

GENERAL INFO

SPECIES: Angler Pokémon
HEIGHT: 1'08"
WEIGHT: 26 lbs.
ABILITY 1: Volt Absorb
Chinchou's HPs are restored every time it gets struck by an Electric-type attack.

ABILITY 2: Illuminate
When Chinchou is in the first Slot, the chances of running into a wild Pokémon increase.

STATS

EVOLUTIONS

LV 27

LOCATION(s):

RUBY	Rarity: **Common**	Route 124, Route 126
SAPPHIRE	Rarity: **Common**	Route 124, Route 126
FIRERED	Rarity: **None**	Trade from *Ruby/Sapphire*
LEAFGREEN	Rarity: **None**	Trade from *Ruby/Sapphire*
COLOSSEUM	Rarity: **None**	Trade from *Ruby/Sapphire*
EMERALD	Rarity: **Common**	Route 124, Route 126
XD	Rarity: **None**	Trade from *Ruby/Sapphire*

MOVES

Level	Attack	Type	Power	ACC	PP
—	Bubble	Water	20	100	30
—	Thunder Wave	Electric	—	100	20
5	Supersonic	Normal	—	55	20
13	Flail	Normal	—	100	15
17	Water Gun	Water	40	100	25

Level	Attack	Type	Power	ACC	PP
25	Spark	Electric	65	100	20
29	Confuse Ray	Ghost	—	100	10
37	Take Down	Normal	90	85	20
41	Hydro Pump	Water	120	80	5
49	Charge	Electric	—	100	20

TM/HM

TM/HM#	Name	Type	Power	ACC	PP
TM03	Water Pulse	Water	60	95	20
TM06	Toxic	Poison	—	85	10
TM07	Hail	Ice	—	—	10
TM10	Hidden Power	Normal	—	100	15
TM13	Ice Beam	Ice	95	100	10
TM14	Blizzard	Ice	120	70	5
TM17	Protect	Normal	—	—	10
TM18	Rain Dance	Water	—	—	5
TM21	Frustration	Normal	—	100	20
TM24	Thunderbolt	Electric	95	100	15
TM25	Thunder	Electric	120	70	10

TM/HM#	Name	Type	Power	ACC	PP
TM27	Return	Normal	—	100	20
TM32	Double Team	Normal	—	—	15
TM34	Shock Wave	Electric	60	—	20
TM42	Facade	Normal	70	100	20
TM43	Secret Power	Normal	70	100	20
TM44	Rest	Psychic	—	—	10
TM45	Attract	Normal	—	100	15
HM03	Surf	Water	95	100	15
HM05	Flash	Normal	—	70	20
HM07	Waterfall	Water	80	100	15
HM08	Dive	Water	60	100	10

EGG MOVES*

Name	Type	Power	ACC	PP
Flail	Normal	—	100	15
Screech	Normal	—	85	40
Amnesia	Psychic	—	—	20

*Learned Via Breeding

MOVE TUTOR

FireRed/LeafGreen and Emerald Only

Double-Edge	Substitute	Thunder Wave*
Mimic		

Emerald Only

Endure*	Snore*	Swagger
Sleep Talk		

*Battle Frontier tutor move (*Emerald*)

171 Lanturn™

ELECTRIC | WATER

GENERAL INFO

SPECIES: Light Pokémon
HEIGHT: 3'11"
WEIGHT: 50 lbs.
ABILITY 1: Volt Absorb
Lanturn's HPs are restored every time it gets struck by an Electric-type attack.
ABILITY 2: Illuminate
When Lanturn is in the first slot, the chances of running into a wild Pokémon increase.

STATS

EVOLUTIONS

LV 27

LOCATION[s]:

RUBY	Rarity: **Evolve**	Evolve Chinchou
SAPPHIRE	Rarity: **Evolve**	Evolve Chinchou
FIRERED	Rarity: **None**	Trade from *Ruby/Sapphire*
LEAFGREEN	Rarity: **None**	Trade from *Ruby/Sapphire*
COLOSSEUM	Rarity: **None**	Trade from *Ruby/Sapphire*
EMERALD	Rarity: **Evolve**	Evolve Chinchou
XD	Rarity: **None**	Trade from *Ruby/Sapphire*

MOVES

Level	Attack	Type	Power	ACC	PP	Level	Attack	Type	Power	ACC	PP
—	Bubble	Water	20	100	30	25	Spark	Electric	65	100	20
—	Thunder Wave	Electric	—	100	20	32	Confuse Ray	Ghost	—	100	10
—	Supersonic	Normal	—	55	20	43	Take Down	Normal	90	85	20
13	Flail	Normal	—	100	15	50	Hydro Pump	Water	120	80	5
17	Water Gun	Water	40	100	25	61	Charge	Electric	—	100	20

TM/HM

TM/HM#	Name	Type	Power	ACC	PP	TM/HM#	Name	Type	Power	ACC	PP
TM03	Water Pulse	Water	60	95	20	TM27	Return	Normal	—	100	20
TM06	Toxic	Poison	—	85	10	TM32	Double Team	Normal	—	—	15
TM07	Hail	Ice	—	—	10	TM34	Shock Wave	Electric	60	—	20
TM10	Hidden Power	Normal	—	100	15	TM42	Facade	Normal	70	100	20
TM13	Ice Beam	Ice	95	100	10	TM43	Secret Power	Normal	70	100	20
TM14	Blizzard	Ice	120	70		TM44	Rest	Psychic	—	—	10
TM15	Hyper Beam	Normal	150	90	5	TM45	Attract	Normal	—	100	15
TM17	Protect	Normal	—	—	10	HM03	Surf	Water	95	100	15
TM18	Rain Dance	Water	—	—	5	HM05	Flash	Normal	—	70	20
TM21	Frustration	Normal	—	100	20	HM07	Waterfall	Water	80	100	15
TM24	Thunderbolt	Electric	95	100	15	HM08	Dive	Water	60	100	10
TM25	Thunder	Electric	120	70	10						

MOVE TUTOR

FireRed/LeafGreen and Emerald Only

Double-Edge	Substitute	Thunder Wave*
Mimic		

Emerald Only

Endure*	Snore*	Swagger
Sleep Talk		

*Battle Frontier tutor move (*Emerald*)

172 Pichu™

ELECTRIC

GENERAL INFO

SPECIES: Tiny Mouse Pokémon
HEIGHT: 1'00"
WEIGHT: 4 lbs.
ABILITY: Static

An opponent has a 30% chance of being paralyzed if Pichu is hit directly.

STATS

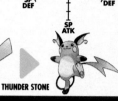

EVOLUTIONS

PICHU → PIKACHU **FRIENDSHIP** → RAICHU **THUNDER STONE**

LOCATION[s]:

RUBY	Rarity: **Breed**	Breed Pikachu	
SAPPHIRE	Rarity: **Breed**	Breed Pikachu	
FIRERED	Rarity: **Breed**	Breed Pikachu	
LEAFGREEN	Rarity: **Breed**	Breed Pikachu	
COLOSSEUM	Rarity: **None**	Trade from *Ruby/Sapphire/FireRed/LeafGreen*	
EMERALD	Rarity: **Breed**	Breed Pikachu	
XD	Rarity: **None**	Trade from *Ruby/Sapphire/FireRed/LeafGreen*	

MOVES

Level	Attack	Type	Power	ACC	PP	Level	Attack	Type	Power	ACC	PP
—	Thundershock	Electric	40	100	30	6	Tail Whip	Normal	—	100	30
—	Charm	Normal	—	100	20	8	Thunder Wave	Electric	—	100	20
						11	Sweet Kiss	Normal	—	75	10

TM/HM

TM/HM#	Name	Type	Power	ACC	PP	TM/HM#	Name	Type	Power	ACC	PP
TM06	Toxic	Poison	—	85	10	TM27	Return	Normal	—	100	20
TM10	Hidden Power	Normal	—	100	15	TM32	Double Team	Normal	—	—	15
TM16	Light Screen	Psychic	—	—	30	TM34	Shock Wave	Electric	60	—	20
TM17	Protect	Normal	—	—	10	TM42	Facade	Normal	70	100	20
TM18	Rain Dance	Water	—	—	5	TM43	Secret Power	Normal	70	100	20
TM21	Frustration	Normal	—	100	20	TM44	Rest	Psychic	—	—	10
TM23	Iron Tail	Steel	75	75	15	TM45	Attract	Normal	—	100	15
TM24	Thunderbolt	Electric	95	100	15	HM05	Flash	Normal	—	70	20
TM25	Thunder	Electric	120	70	10						

EGG MOVES*

Name	Type	Power	ACC	PP
Reversal	Fighting	—	100	15
Bide	Normal	—	100	10
Encore	Normal	—	100	5
Doubleslap	Normal	15	85	10
Charge	Electric	—	100	20
Present	Normal	—	90	15
Wish	Normal	—	100	10

*Learned Via Breeding

MOVE TUTOR

FireRed/LeafGreen and Emerald Only

Body Slam*	Mega Kick*	Counter*
Double-Edge	Mimic	Seismic Toss*
Mega Punch*	Substitute	Thunder Wave*

Emerald Only

Defense Curl*	Mud-Slap*	Snore*
Endure*	Rollout	Swagger
Metronome	Sleep Talk	Swift*

*Battle Frontier tutor move (*Emerald*)

173 Cleffa™

NORMAL

GENERAL INFO
SPECIES: Star Shape Pokémon
HEIGHT: 1'0"
WEIGHT: 7 lbs.
ABILITY: Cute Charm

If an opponent physically strikes Cleffa, it has a 30% chance of becoming attracted to it.

STATS

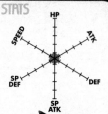

EVOLUTIONS

FRIENDSHIP   MOON STONE

LOCATION[s]:

RUBY	Rarity: **None**	Trade from *FireRed/LeafGreen*
SAPPHIRE	Rarity: **None**	Trade from *FireRed/LeafGreen*
FIRERED	Rarity: **Breed**	Breed Clefairy
LEAFGREEN	Rarity: **Breed**	Breed Clefairy
COLOSSEUM	Rarity: **None**	Trade from *FireRed/LeafGreen*
EMERALD	Rarity: **None**	Trade from *FireRed/LeafGreen*
XD	Rarity: **None**	Trade from *FireRed/LeafGreen*

MOVES

Level	Attack	Type	Power	ACC	PP	Level	Attack	Type	Power	ACC	PP
—	Pound	Normal	40	100	35	8	Sing	Normal	—	55	15
—	Charm	Normal	—	100	20	13	Sweet Kiss	Normal	—	75	10
4	Encore	Normal	—	100	5	17	Magical Leaf	Grass	60	—	20

TM/HM

TM/HM#	Name	Type	Power	ACC	PP	TM/HM#	Name	Type	Power	ACC	PP
TM03	Water Pulse	Water	60	95	20	TM29	Psychic	Psychic	90	100	10
TM06	Toxic	Poison	—	85	10	TM30	Shadow Ball	Ghost	80	100	15
TM10	Hidden Power	Normal	—	100	15	TM32	Double Team	Normal	—	—	15
TM11	Sunny Day	Fire	—	—	5	TM33	Reflect	Normal	—	—	20
TM16	Light Screen	Psychic	—	—	30	TM34	Shock Wave	Electric	60	—	20
TM17	Protect	Normal	—	—	10	TM35	Flamethrower	Fire	95	100	15
TM18	Rain Dance	Water	—	—	5	TM38	Fire Blast	Fire	120	85	5
TM20	Safeguard	Normal	—	—	25	TM42	Facade	Normal	70	100	20
TM21	Frustration	Normal	—	100	20	TM43	Secret Power	Normal	70	100	20
TM22	Solarbeam	Grass	120	100	10	TM44	Rest	Psychic	—	—	10
TM23	Iron Tail	Steel	75	75	15	TM45	Attract	Normal	—	100	15
TM27	Return	Normal	—	100	20	HM05	Flash	Normal	—	70	20
TM28	Dig	Ground	60	100	10						

EGG MOVES*

Name	Type	Power	ACC	PP
Amnesia	Psychic	—	—	20
Belly Drum	Normal	—	—	10
Metronome	Normal	—	—	10
Mimic	Normal	—	100	10
Present	Normal	—	90	15
Substitute	Normal	—	—	10
Wish	Normal	—	100	10
Bounce	Flying	85	85	5

*Learned Via Breeding

MOVE TUTOR
FireRed/LeafGreen and Emerald Only

Body Slam*	Metronome	Seismic Toss*
Double-Edge	Mimic	Dream Eater*
Mega Punch*	Substitute	Thunder Wave*
Mega Kick*	Counter*	Softboiled

*Battle Frontier tutor move (*Emerald*)

174 Igglybuff™

NORMAL

GENERAL INFO

SPECIES: Balloon Pokémon
HEIGHT: 1'00"
WEIGHT: 2 lbs.
ABILITY: Cute Charm

If an opponent physically strikes Igglybuff, it has a 30% chance of becoming attracted to it.

STATS

EVOLUTIONS

FRIENDSHIP   MOON STONE

LOCATION(S):

RUBY	Rarity: **Breed**	Breed Jigglypuff
SAPPHIRE	Rarity: **Breed**	Breed Jigglypuff
FIRERED	Rarity: **Breed**	Breed Jigglypuff
LEAFGREEN	Rarity: **Breed**	Breed Jigglypuff
COLOSSEUM	Rarity: **None**	Trade from *Ruby/Sapphire/FireRed/LeafGreen*
EMERALD	Rarity: **Breed**	Breed Jigglypuff
XD	Rarity: **None**	Trade from *Ruby/Sapphire/FireRed/LeafGreen*

MOVES

Level	Attack	Type	Power	ACC	PP	Level	Attack	Type	Power	ACC	PP
—	Charm	Normal	—	100	20	4	Defense Curl	Normal	—	—	40
—	Sing	Normal	—	55	15	9	Pound	Normal	40	100	35
						14	Sweet Kiss	Normal	—	75	10

TM/HM

TM/HM#	Name	Type	Power	ACC	PP	TM/HM#	Name	Type	Power	ACC	PP
TM03	Water Pulse	Water	60	95	20	TM29	Psychic	Psychic	90	100	10
TM06	Toxic	Poison	—	85	10	TM30	Shadow Ball	Ghost	80	100	15
TM10	Hidden Power	Normal	.	100	15	TM32	Double Team	Normal	—	—	15
TM11	Sunny Day	Fire	—	—	5	TM33	Reflect	Normal	—	—	20
TM16	Light Screen	Psychic	—	—	30	TM34	Shock Wave	Electric	60	—	20
TM17	Protect	Normal	—	—	10	TM35	Flamethrower	Fire	95	100	15
TM18	Rain Dance	Water	—	—	5	TM38	Fire Blast	Fire	120	85	5
TM20	Safeguard	Normal	—	—	25	TM42	Facade	Normal	70	100	20
TM21	Frustration	Normal	—	100	20	TM43	Secret Power	Normal	70	100	20
TM22	Solarbeam	Grass	120	100	10	TM44	Rest	Psychic	—	—	10
TM27	Return	Normal	—	100	20	TM45	Attract	Normal	—	100	15
TM28	Dig	Ground	60	100	10	HM05	Flash	Normal	—	70	20

EGG MOVES*

Name	Type	Power	ACC	PP
Faint Attack	Dark	60	—	20
Fake Tears	Dark	—	100	20
Perish Song	Normal	—	—	5
Present	Normal	—	90	15
Wish	Normal	—	100	10

*Learned Via Breeding

MOVE TUTOR
FireRed/LeafGreen and Emerald Only

Body Slam*	Mimic	Dream Eater*
Double-Edge	Substitute	Thunder Wave*
Mega Punch*	Seismic Toss*	
Mega Kick*	Counter*	

Emerald Only

Defense Curl*	Mud-Slap*	Sleep Talk
Endure*	Psych Up*	Snore*
Icy Wind*	Rollout	Swagger

*Battle Frontier tutor move (*Emerald*)

175 Togepi ™

NORMAL

GENERAL INFO

SPECIES: Spike Ball Pokémon
HEIGHT: 1'00"
WEIGHT: 3 lbs.
ABILITY 1: Serene Grace

Togepi's attacks that inflict extra status effects have twice the chance of occurring.

ABILITY 2: Hustle

Multiplies Togepi's attacks by 1.5, but lowers its Accuracy to 80%.

STATS

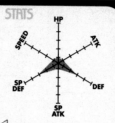

EVOLUTIONS

FRIENDSHIP

LOCATION[s]:

RUBY	Rarity: **None**	Trade from *FireRed/LeafGreen*
SAPPHIRE	Rarity: **None**	Trade from *FireRed/LeafGreen*
FIRERED	Rarity: **Only One**	Five Island (Old Man on Western Island)
LEAFGREEN	Rarity: **Only One**	Five Island (Old Man on Western Island)
COLOSSEUM	Rarity: **None**	Trade from *FireRed/LeafGreen*
EMERALD	Rarity: **None**	Trade from *FireRed/LeafGreen*
XD	Rarity: **Only One**	Outskirt Stand (Receive from Hordel)

MOVES

Level	Attack	Type	Power	ACC	PP		Level	Attack	Type	Power	ACC	PP
—	Growl	Normal	—	100	40		21	Ancientpower	Rock	60	100	5
—	Charm	Normal	—	100	20		25	Follow Me	Normal	—	100	20
9	Sweet Kiss	Normal	—	75	10		29	Wish	Normal	—	100	10
13	Yawn	Normal	—	100	10		33	Safeguard	Normal	—	—	25
17	Encore	Normal	—	100	5		37	Double-Edge	Normal	120	100	15
							41	Baton Pass	Normal	—	—	40

TM/HM

TM/HM#	Name	Type	Power	ACC	PP		TM/HM#	Name	Type	Power	ACC	PP
TM03	Water Pulse	Water	60	95	20		TM30	Shadow Ball	Ghost	80	100	15
TM06	Toxic	Poison	—	85	10		TM32	Double Team	Normal	—	—	15
TM10	Hidden Power	Normal	—	100	15		TM33	Reflect	Normal	—	—	20
TM11	Sunny Day	Fire	—	—	5		TM34	Shock Wave	Electric	60	—	20
TM16	Light Screen	Psychic	—	—	30		TM35	Flamethrower	Fire	95	100	15
TM17	Protect	Normal	—	—	10		TM38	Fire Blast	Fire	120	85	5
TM18	Rain Dance	Water	—	—	5		TM42	Facade	Normal	70	100	20
TM20	Safeguard	Normal	—	—	25		TM43	Secret Power	Normal	70	100	20
TM21	Frustration	Normal	—	100	20		TM44	Rest	Psychic	—	—	10
TM22	Solarbeam	Grass	120	100	10		TM45	Attract	Normal	—	100	15
TM27	Return	Normal	—	100	20		HM05	Flash	Normal	—	70	20
TM29	Psychic	Psychic	90	100	10		HM06	Rock Smash	Fighting	20	100	15

EGG MOVES*

Name	Type	Power	ACC	PP
Foresight	Normal	—	100	40
Future Sight	Psychic	80	90	15
Mirror Move	Flying	—	—	20
Peck	Flying	35	100	35
Present	Normal	—	90	15
Psych Up	Normal	—	—	10
Substitute	Normal	—	—	10

*Learned Via Breeding

MOVE TUTOR

FireRed/LeafGreen and Emerald Only

Body Slam*	Metronome	Seismic Toss*
Double-Edge	Mimic	Dream Eater*
Mega Punch*	Substitute	Thunder Wave*
Mega Kick*	Counter*	Softboiled

*Battle Frontier tutor move (Emerald)

176 Togetic™

NORMAL

GENERAL INFO

SPECIES: Happiness Pokémon
HEIGHT: 2'00"
WEIGHT: 7 lbs.
ABILITY 1: Serene Grace
Togetic's attacks that inflict extra status effects have twice the chance of occurring.

ABILITY 2: Hustle
Multiplies Togetic's attacks by 1.5, but lowers its Accuracy to 80%.

STATS

EVOLUTIONS

FRIENDSHIP

LOCATION(S):

Game	Rarity	Location
RUBY	Rarity: **None**	Trade from *FireRed/LeafGreen/Colosseum*
SAPPHIRE	Rarity: **None**	Trade from *FireRed/LeafGreen/Colosseum*
FIRERED	Rarity: **Evolve**	Evolve Togepi
LEAFGREEN	Rarity: **Evolve**	Evolve Togepi
COLOSSEUM	Rarity: **Only One**	Obtained from Fake Artist in Outskirt Stand
EMERALD	Rarity: **None**	Trade from *FireRed/LeafGreen/Colosseum*
XD	Rarity: **Evolve**	Evolve Togepi

MOVES

Level	Attack	Type	Power	ACC	PP		Level	Attack	Type	Power	ACC	PP
—	Magical Leaf	Grass	60	—	20		17	Encore	Normal	—	100	5
—	Growl	Normal	—	100	40		21	Ancientpower	Rock	60	100	5
—	Charm	Normal	—	100	20		25	Follow Me	Normal	—	100	20
—	Metronome	Normal	—	—	10		29	Wish	Normal	—	100	10
—	Sweet Kiss	Normal	—	75	10		33	Safeguard	Normal	—	—	25
13	Yawn	Normal	—	100	10		37	Double-Edge	Normal	120	100	15
							41	Baton Pass	Normal	—	—	40

TM/HM

TM/HM#	Name	Type	Power	ACC	PP		TM/HM#	Name	Type	Power	ACC	PP
TM01	Focus Punch	Fighting	150	100	20		TM31	Brick Break	Fighting	75	100	15
TM03	Water Pulse	Water	60	95	20		TM32	Double Team	Normal	—	—	15
TM06	Toxic	Poison	—	85	10		TM33	Reflect	Normal	—	—	20
TM10	Hidden Power	Normal	—	100	15		TM34	Shock Wave	Electric	60	—	20
TM11	Sunny Day	Fire	—	—	5		TM35	Flamethrower	Fire	95	100	15
TM15	Hyper Beam	Normal	150	90	5		TM38	Fire Blast	Fire	120	85	5
TM16	Light Screen	Psychic	—	—	30		TM40	Aerial Ace	Flying	60	—	20
TM17	Protect	Normal	—	—	10		TM42	Facade	Normal	70	100	20
TM18	Rain Dance	Water	—	—	5		TM43	Secret Power	Normal	70	100	20
TM20	Safeguard	Normal	—	—	25		TM44	Rest	Psychic	—	—	10
TM21	Frustration	Normal	—	100	20		TM45	Attract	Normal	—	100	15
TM22	Solarbeam	Grass	120	100	10		TM47	Steel Wing	Steel	70	90	25
TM27	Return	Normal	—	100	20		HM02	Fly	Flying	70	95	15
TM29	Psychic	Psychic	90	100	10		HM05	Flash	Normal	—	70	20
TM30	Shadow Ball	Ghost	80	100	15		HM06	Rock Smash	Fighting	20	100	15

MOVE TUTOR

FireRed/LeafGreen and Emerald Only

Body Slam*	Metronome	Seismic Toss*
Double-Edge	Mimic	Dream Eater*
Mega Punch*	Substitute	Thunder Wave*
Mega Kick*	Counter*	Softboiled

*Battle Frontier tutor move (*Emerald*)

PRIMA OFFICIAL GAME GUIDE

177 Natu™

GENERAL INFO

SPECIES: Tiny Bird Pokémon
HEIGHT: 0'08"
WEIGHT: 4 lbs.
ABILITY 1: Synchronize
When Natu gets poisoned, burned, or paralyzed, the opponent also gets the same condition.
ABILITY 2: Early Bird
Allows Natu to wake up earlier when put to sleep.

STATS

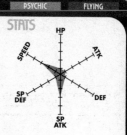

EVOLUTIONS

LV25

LOCATION[s]:

RUBY	Rarity: **Common**		Safari Zone
SAPPHIRE	Rarity: **Common**		Safari Zone
FIRERED	Rarity: **Common**		Six Island
LEAFGREEN	Rarity: **Common**		Six Island
COLOSSEUM	Rarity: **None**		Trade from *Ruby/Sapphire/FireRed/LeafGreen*
EMERALD	Rarity: **Common**		Safari Zone
XD	Rarity: **Only One**		Phenac City (Capture from Cipher Peon Elosin)

MOVES

Level	Attack	Type	Power	ACC	PP	Level	Attack	Type	Power	ACC	PP
—	Peck	Flying	35	100	35	30	Wish	Normal	—	100	10
—	Leer	Normal	—	100	30	30	Future Sight	Psychic	80	90	15
10	Night Shade	Ghost	—	100	15	40	Confuse Ray	Ghost	—	100	10
20	Teleport	Psychic	—	—	20	50	Psychic	Psychic	90	100	10

TM/HM

TM/HM#	Name	Type	Power	ACC	PP	TM/HM#	Name	Type	Power	ACC	PP
TM04	Calm Mind	Psychic	—	—	20	TM30	Shadow Ball	Ghost	80	100	15
TM06	Toxic	Poison	—	85	10	TM32	Double Team	Normal	—	—	15
TM10	Hidden Power	Normal	—	100	15	TM33	Reflect	Normal	—	—	20
TM11	Sunny Day	Fire	—	—	5	TM40	Aerial Ace	Flying	60	—	20
TM16	Light Screen	Psychic	—	—	30	TM42	Facade	Normal	70	100	20
TM17	Protect	Normal	—	—	10	TM43	Secret Power	Normal	70	100	20
TM18	Rain Dance	Water	—	—	5	TM44	Rest	Psychic	—	—	10
TM19	Giga Drain	Grass	60	100	5	TM45	Attract	Normal	—	100	15
TM21	Frustration	Normal	—	100	20	TM46	Thief	Dark	40	100	10
TM22	Solarbeam	Grass	120	100	10	TM47	Steel Wing	Steel	70	90	25
TM27	Return	Normal	—	100	20	TM48	Skill Swap	Psychic	—	100	10
TM29	Psychic	Psychic	90	100	10	HM05	Flash	Normal	—	70	20

EGG MOVES*

Name	Type	Power	ACC	PP
Haze	Ice	—	—	30
Drill Peck	Flying	80	100	20
Quick Attack	Normal	40	100	30
Steel Wing	Steel	70	90	25
Refresh	Normal	—	100	20
Featherdance	Flying	—	100	15
Psych Up	Normal	—	—	10
Faint Attack	Dark	60	—	20

*Learned Via Breeding

MOVE TUTOR

FireRed/LeafGreen and Emerald Only

Double-Edge	Substitute	Thunder Wave*
Mimic	Dream Eater*	

Emerald Only

Endure*	Sleep Talk	Swagger
Psych Up*	Snore*	Swift*

*Battle Frontier tutor move (*Emerald*)

178 Xatu™

PSYCHIC | FLYING

GENERAL INFO

SPECIES: Mystic Pokémon
HEIGHT: 4'11"
WEIGHT: 33 lbs.
ABILITY 1: Synchronize
When Xatu gets poisoned, burned, or paralyzed, the opponent also gets the same condition.
ABILITY 2: Early Bird
Allows Xatu to wake up earlier when put to sleep.

STATS

(radar chart: HP, ATK, DEF, SP ATK, SP DEF, SPEED)

EVOLUTIONS

 ▶

LV25

LOCATION[S]:

RUBY	Rarity: Rare	Safari Zone
SAPPHIRE	Rarity: Rare	Safari Zone
FIRERED	Rarity: Evolve	Evolve Natu
LEAFGREEN	Rarity: Evolve	Evolve Natu
COLOSSEUM	Rarity: None	Trade from Ruby/Sapphire/FireRed/LeafGreen
EMERALD	Rarity: Rare	Safari Zone
XD	Rarity: Evolve	Evolve Natu

MOVES

Level	Attack	Type	Power	ACC	PP	Level	Attack	Type	Power	ACC	PP
—	Peck	Flying	35	100	35	35	Wish	Normal	—	—	10
—	Leer	Normal	—	100	30	35	Future Sight	Psychic	80	90	15
10	Night Shade	Ghost	—	100	15	50	Confuse Ray	Ghost	—	100	10
20	Teleport	Psychic	—	—	20	65	Psychic	Psychic	90	100	10

TM/HM

TM/HM#	Name	Type	Power	ACC	PP	TM/HM#	Name	Type	Power	ACC	PP
TM04	Calm Mind	Psychic	—	—	20	TM30	Shadow Ball	Ghost	80	100	15
TM06	Toxic	Poison	—	85	10	TM32	Double Team	Normal	—	—	15
TM10	Hidden Power	Normal	—	100	15	TM33	Reflect	Normal	—	—	20
TM11	Sunny Day	Fire	—	—	5	TM40	Aerial Ace	Flying	60	—	20
TM15	Hyper Beam	Normal	150	90	5	TM42	Facade	Normal	70	100	20
TM16	Light Screen	Psychic	—	—	30	TM43	Secret Power	Normal	70	100	20
TM17	Protect	Normal	—	—	5	TM44	Rest	Psychic	—	—	10
TM18	Rain Dance	Water	—	—	5	TM45	Attract	Normal	—	100	15
TM19	Giga Drain	Grass	60	100	5	TM46	Thief	Dark	40	100	10
TM21	Frustration	Normal	—	100	10	TM47	Steel Wing	Steel	70	90	25
TM22	Solarbeam	Grass	120	100	10	TM48	Skill Swap	Psychic	—	100	10
TM27	Return	Normal	—	100	20	HM02	Fly	Flying	70	95	15
TM29	Psychic	Psychic	90	100	10	HM05	Flash	Normal	—	70	20

MOVE TUTOR
FireRed/LeafGreen and Emerald Only

Double-Edge	Substitute	Thunder Wave*
Mimic	Dream Eater*	

Emerald Only

Endure*	Sleep Talk*	Swagger
Psych Up*	Snore*	Swift*

*Battle Frontier tutor move (*Emerald*)

PRIMA OFFICIAL GAME GUIDE

179 Mareep™

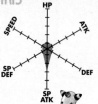

ELECTRIC

GENERAL INFO
SPECIES: Wool Pokémon
HEIGHT: 2'00"
WEIGHT: 17 lbs.
ABILITY: Static
An opponent has a 30% chance of being paralyzed if Mareep is hit directly.

STATS

EVOLUTIONS

 LV15

 LV30

LOCATION[s]:

RUBY	Rarity: **None**	Trade Flaaffy or Ampharos from *Colosseum*, then breed
SAPPHIRE	Rarity: **None**	Trade Flaaffy or Ampharos from *Colosseum*, then breed
FIRERED	Rarity: **None**	Trade Flaaffy or Ampharos from *Colosseum*, then breed
LEAFGREEN	Rarity: **None**	Trade Flaaffy or Ampharos from *Colosseum*, then breed
COLOSSEUM	Rarity: **None**	Breed in *Ruby/Sapphire/FireRed/LeafGreen*, then trade back
EMERALD	Rarity: **Common**	Safari Zone
XD	Rarity: **Only One**	Cipher Lab (Capture from Cipher Peon Yellosix)

MOVES

Level	Attack	Type	Power	ACC	PP
—	Tackle	Normal	35	95	35
—	Growl	Normal	—	100	40
9	Thundershock	Electric	40	100	30

Level	Attack	Type	Power	ACC	PP
16	Thunder Wave	Electric	—	100	20
23	Cotton Spore	Grass	—	85	40
30	Light Screen	Psychic	—	—	30
37	Thunder	Electric	120	70	10

TM/HM

TM/HM#	Name	Type	Power	ACC	PP
TM06	Toxic	Poison	—	85	10
TM10	Hidden Power	Normal	—	100	15
TM16	Light Screen	Psychic	—	—	30
TM17	Protect	Normal	—	—	10
TM18	Rain Dance	Water	—	—	5
TM21	Frustration	Normal	—	100	20
TM23	Iron Tail	Steel	75	75	15
TM24	Thunderbolt	Electric	95	100	15
TM25	Thunder	Electric	120	70	10

TM/HM#	Name	Type	Power	ACC	PP
TM27	Return	Normal	—	100	20
TM32	Double Team	Normal	—	—	15
TM34	Shock Wave	Electric	60	—	20
TM42	Facade	Normal	70	100	20
TM43	Secret Power	Normal	70	100	20
TM44	Rest	Psychic	—	—	10
TM45	Attract	Normal	—	100	15
HM05	Flash	Normal	—	70	20

EGG MOVES*

Name	Type	Power	ACC	PP
Body Slam	Normal	85	100	15
Charge	Electric	—	100	20
Odor Sleuth	Normal	—	100	40
Reflect	Psychic	—	—	20
Safeguard	Normal	—	—	25
Screech	Normal	—	85	40
Take Down	Normal	90	85	20

*Learned Via Breeding

MOVE TUTOR
FireRed/LeafGreen and Emerald Only

Body Slam*	Mimic	Thunder Wave*
Double-Edge	Substitute	

*Battle Frontier tutor move (*Emerald*)

180 Flaaffy™

ELECTRIC

GENERAL INFO

SPECIES: Wool Pokémon
HEIGHT: 2'07"
WEIGHT: 29 lbs.
ABILITY: Static
An opponent has a 30% chance of being paralyzed if Flaaffy is hit directly.

STATS

EVOLUTIONS

 ▶ LV15 ▶ LV30

LOCATION(s):

RUBY	Rarity:	**None**	Trade from *Colosseum*
SAPPHIRE	Rarity:	**None**	Trade from *Colosseum*
FIRERED	Rarity:	**Evolve**	Evolve Mareep
LEAFGREEN	Rarity:	**Evolve**	Evolve Mareep
COLOSSEUM	Rarity:	**Only One**	Pyrite Town
EMERALD	Rarity:	**Evolve**	Evolve Mareep
XD	Rarity:	**Evolve**	Evolve Mareep

MOVES

Level	Attack	Type	Power	ACC	PP	Level	Attack	Type	Power	ACC	PP
—	Tackle	Normal	35	95	35	18	Thunder Wave	Electric	—	100	20
—	Growl	Normal	—	100	40	27	Cotton Spore	Grass	—	85	40
—	Thundershock	Electric	40	100	30	36	Light Screen	Psychic	—	—	30
						45	Thunder	Electric	120	70	10

TM/HM

TM/HM#	Name	Type	Power	ACC	PP	TM/HM#	Name	Type	Power	ACC	PP
TM01	Focus Punch	Fighting	150	100	20	TM31	Brick Break	Fighting	75	100	15
TM06	Toxic	Poison	—	85	10	TM32	Double Team	Normal	—	—	15
TM10	Hidden Power	Normal	—	100	15	TM34	Shock Wave	Electric	60	—	20
TM16	Light Screen	Psychic	—	—	30	TM42	Facade	Normal	70	100	20
TM17	Protect	Normal	—	—	10	TM43	Secret Power	Normal	70	100	20
TM18	Rain Dance	Water	—	—	5	TM44	Rest	Psychic	—	—	10
TM21	Frustration	Normal	—	100	20	TM45	Attract	Normal	—	100	15
TM23	Iron Tail	Steel	75	75	15	HM04	Strength	Normal	80	100	20
TM24	Thunderbolt	Electric	95	100	15	HM05	Flash	Normal	—	70	20
TM25	Thunder	Electric	120	70	10	HM06	Rock Smash	Fighting	20	100	15
TM27	Return	Normal	—	100	20						

MOVE TUTOR

FireRed/LeafGreen and Emerald Only

Body Slam*	Mega Kick*	Counter*
Double-Edge	Mimic	Seismic Toss*
Mega Punch*	Substitute	Thunder Wave*

*Battle Frontier tutor move (*Emerald*)

PRIMA OFFICIAL GAME GUIDE

181 Amancharos™

ELECTRIC

GENERAL INFO

SPECIES: Light Pokémon
HEIGHT: 4'07"
WEIGHT: 136 lbs.
ABILITY: Static

An opponent has a 30% chance of being paralyzed if Ampharos is hit directly.

STATS

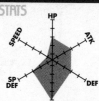

EVOLUTIONS

LV15   LV30

LOCATION[s]:

RUBY	Rarity: **Evolve**	Trade from *Colosseum*
SAPPHIRE	Rarity: **Evolve**	Trade from *Colosseum*
FIRERED	Rarity: **Evolve**	Trade from *Colosseum*
LEAFGREEN	Rarity: **Evolve**	Trade from *Colosseum*
COLOSSEUM	Rarity: **Evolve**	Evolve Flaaffy
EMERALD	Rarity: **Evolve**	Evolve Flaaffy
XD	Rarity: **Evolve**	Evolve Flaaffy

MOVES

Level	Attack	Type	Power	ACC	PP
—	Tackle	Normal	35	95	35
—	Growl	Normal	—	100	40
—	Thundershock	Electric	40	100	30
—	Thunder Wave	Electric	—	100	20

Level	Attack	Type	Power	ACC	PP
27	Cotton Spore	Grass	—	85	40
30	Thunderpunch	Electric	75	100	15
42	Light Screen	Psychic	—	—	30
57	Thunder	Electric	120	70	10

TM/HM

TM/HM#	Name	Type	Power	ACC	PP
TM01	Focus Punch	Fighting	150	100	20
TM06	Toxic	Poison	—	85	10
TM10	Hidden Power	Normal	—	100	15
TM15	Hyper Beam	Normal	150	90	5
TM16	Light Screen	Psychic	—	—	30
TM17	Protect	Normal	—	—	10
TM18	Rain Dance	Water	—	—	5
TM21	Frustration	Normal	—	100	20
TM23	Iron Tail	Steel	75	75	15
TM24	Thunderbolt	Electric	95	100	15
TM25	Thunder	Electric	120	70	10

TM/HM#	Name	Type	Power	ACC	PP
TM27	Return	Normal	—	100	20
TM31	Brick Break	Fighting	75	100	15
TM32	Double Team	Normal	—	—	15
TM34	Shock Wave	Electric	60	—	20
TM42	Facade	Normal	70	100	20
TM43	Secret Power	Normal	70	100	20
TM44	Rest	Psychic	—	—	10
TM45	Attract	Normal	—	100	15
HM04	Strength	Normal	80	100	20
HM05	Flash	Normal	—	70	20
HM06	Rock Smash	Fighting	20	100	15

MOVE TUTOR
FireRed/LeafGreen and Emerald Only

Body Slam*	Mega Kick*	Counter*
Double-Edge	Mimic	Seismic Toss*
Mega Punch*	Substitute	Thunder Wave*

*Battle Frontier tutor move (*Emerald*)

182 Bellossom™

GRASS

GENERAL INFO

SPECIES: Flower Pokémon
HEIGHT: 1'04"
WEIGHT: 13 lbs.
ABILITY: Chlorophyll
Bellossom's Speed is doubled when the sunlight is strong.

STATS

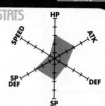

EVOLUTIONS

LV21 — SUN STONE

LOCATION(s):

RUBY	Rarity: **Evolve**	Evolve Gloom
SAPPHIRE	Rarity: **Evolve**	Evolve Gloom
FIRERED	Rarity: **Evolve**	Evolve Gloom
LEAFGREEN	Rarity: **None**	Trade from *Ruby/Sapphire/FireRed*
COLOSSEUM	Rarity: **None**	Trade from *Ruby/Sapphire/FireRed*
EMERALD	Rarity: **Evolve**	Evolve Gloom
XD	Rarity: **None**	Trade from *Ruby/Sapphire/FireRed*

MOVES

Level	Attack	Type	Power	ACC	PP		Level	Attack	Type	Power	ACC	PP
—	Absorb	Grass	20	100	20		—	Magical Leaf	Grass	60	—	20
—	Sweet Scent	Normal	—	100	20		44	Petal Dance	Grass	70	100	20
—	Stun Spore	Grass	—	75	30		55	Solarbeam	Grass	120	100	10

TM/HM

TM/HM#	Name	Type	Power	ACC	PP		TM/HM#	Name	Type	Power	ACC	PP
TM06	Toxic	Poison	—	85	10		TM27	Return	Normal	—	100	20
TM09	Bullet Seed	Grass	10	100	30		TM32	Double Team	Normal	—	—	15
TM10	Hidden Power	Normal	—	100	15		TM36	Sludge Bomb	Poison	90	100	10
TM11	Sunny Day	Fire	—	—	5		TM42	Facade	Normal	70	100	20
TM15	Hyper Beam	Normal	150	90	5		TM43	Secret Power	Normal	70	100	20
TM17	Protect	Normal	—	—	10		TM44	Rest	Psychic	—	—	10
TM19	Giga Drain	Grass	60	100	5		TM45	Attract	Normal	—	100	15
TM20	Safeguard	Normal	—	—	25		HM01	Cut	Normal	50	95	30
TM21	Frustration	Normal	—	100	20		HM05	Flash	Normal	—	70	20
TM22	Solarbeam	Grass	120	100	10							

MOVE TUTOR

FireRed/LeafGreen and Emerald Only

Double-Edge	Substitute	Swords Dance*
Mimic		

Emerald Only

Endure*	Snore*	Swagger
Sleep Talk		

*Battle Frontier tutor move (*Emerald*)

183 Marill™

WATER

GENERAL INFO
SPECIES: Aqua Mouse Pokémon
HEIGHT: 1'04"
WEIGHT: 19 lbs.
ABILITY 1: Thick Fat
When Marill is attacked by Fire-type or Ice-type attacks, the damage is reduced by half.
ABILITY 2: Huge Power
Increases the Power of Marill's attack, but power is reduced when the ability is changed.

STATS
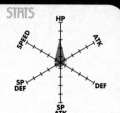

EVOLUTIONS

FRIENDSHIP

LV18

LOCATION(s):

RUBY	Rarity: **Common**	Routes 102, 111, 114, 117, 120
SAPPHIRE	Rarity: **Common**	Routes 102, 111, 114, 117, 120
FIRERED	Rarity: **None**	Trade from *Ruby/Sapphire/LeafGreen*
LEAFGREEN	Rarity: **Common**	Six Island
COLOSSEUM	Rarity: **None**	Trade from *Ruby/Sapphire/LeafGreen*
EMERALD	Rarity: **Common**	Routes 102, 104, 111, 112, 114, 117, 120, Petalburg City, Safari Zone
XD	Rarity: **None**	Trade from *Ruby/Sapphire/LeafGreen*

MOVES

Level	Attack	Type	Power	ACC	PP
—	Tackle	Normal	35	95	35
3	Defense Curl	Normal	—	—	40
6	Tail Whip	Normal	—	100	30
10	Water Gun	Water	40	100	25

Level	Attack	Type	Power	ACC	PP
15	Rollout	Rock	30	90	20
21	Bubblebeam	Water	65	100	20
28	Double-Edge	Normal	120	100	15
36	Rain Dance	Water	—	—	5
45	Hydro Pump	Water	120	80	5

TM/HM

TM/HM#	Name	Type	Power	ACC	PP
TM01	Focus Punch	Fighting	150	100	20
TM03	Water Pulse	Water	60	95	20
TM06	Toxic	Poison	—	85	10
TM07	Hail	Ice	—	—	10
TM10	Hidden Power	Normal	—	100	15
TM13	Ice Beam	Ice	95	100	10
TM14	Blizzard	Ice	120	70	5
TM17	Protect	Normal	—	—	10
TM18	Rain Dance	Water	—	—	5
TM21	Frustration	Normal	—	100	20
TM23	Iron Tail	Steel	75	75	15
TM27	Return	Normal	—	100	20

TM/HM#	Name	Type	Power	ACC	PP
TM28	Dig	Ground	60	100	10
TM31	Brick Break	Fighting	75	100	15
TM32	Double Team	Normal	—	—	15
TM42	Facade	Normal	70	100	20
TM43	Secret Power	Normal	70	100	20
TM44	Rest	Psychic	—	—	10
TM45	Attract	Normal	—	100	15
HM03	Surf	Water	95	100	15
HM04	Strength	Normal	80	100	20
HM06	Rock Smash	Fighting	20	100	15
HM07	Waterfall	Water	80	100	15
HM08	Dive	Water	60	100	10

EGG MOVES*

Name	Type	Power	ACC	PP
Light Screen	Psychic	—	—	30
Amnesia	Psychic	—	—	20
Future Sight	Psychic	80	90	15
Supersonic	Normal	—	55	20
Substitute	Normal	—	—	10
Present	Normal	—	90	15
Belly Drum	Normal	—	—	10
Perish Song	Normal	—	—	5

*Learned Via Breeding

MOVE TUTOR
FireRed/LeafGreen and Emerald Only

Body Slam*	Mega Kick*	Substitute
Double-Edge*	Mimic	Seismic Toss*
Mega Punch*		

Emerald Only

Defense Curl*	Icy Wind*	Snore*
Dynamicpunch*	Mud-Slap*	Swagger
Endure*	Rollout	Swift*
Ice Punch*	Sleep Talk	

*Battle Frontier tutor move (*Emerald*)

184 Azumarill™

WATER

GENERAL INFO

SPECIES: Aqua Rabbit Pokémon
HEIGHT: 2'07"
WEIGHT: 63 lbs.
ABILITY 1: Thick Fat
When Azumarill is attacked by Fire-type or Ice-type attacks, the damage is reduced by half.
ABILITY 2: Huge Power
Increases the Power of Azumarill's attack, but power is reduced when the ability is changed.

STATS

EVOLUTIONS

FRIENDSHIP   LV18

LOCATION[s]:

RUBY	Rarity: **Evolve**	Evolve Marill
SAPPHIRE	Rarity: **Evolve**	Evolve Marill
FIRERED	Rarity: **None**	Trade from *Ruby/Sapphire/LeafGreen*
LEAFGREEN	Rarity: **Evolve**	Evolve Marill
COLOSSEUM	Rarity: **Evolve**	Trade from *Ruby/Sapphire/LeafGreen*
EMERALD	Rarity: **Evolve**	Evolve Marill
XD	Rarity: **None**	Trade from *Ruby/Sapphire/LeafGreen*

MOVES

Level	Attack	Type	Power	ACC	PP		Level	Attack	Type	Power	ACC	PP
—	Tackle	Normal	35	95	35		24	Bubblebeam	Water	65	100	20
—/3	Defense Curl	Normal	—	—	40		34	Double-Edge	Normal	120	100	15
—/6	Tail Whip	Normal	—	100	30		45	Rain Dance	Water	—	—	5
—/10	Water Gun	Water	40	100	25		57	Hydro Pump	Water	120	80	5
15	Rollout	Rock	30	90	20		# = *Emerald Only*					

TM/HM

TM/HM#	Name	Type	Power	ACC	PP		TM/HM#	Name	Type	Power	ACC	PP
TM01	Focus Punch	Fighting	150	100	20		TM28	Dig	Ground	60	100	10
TM03	Water Pulse	Water	60	95	20		TM31	Brick Break	Fighting	75	100	15
TM06	Toxic	Poison	—	85	10		TM32	Double Team	Normal	—	—	15
TM07	Hail	Ice	—	—	10		TM42	Facade	Normal	70	100	20
TM10	Hidden Power	Normal	—	100	15		TM43	Secret Power	Normal	70	100	20
TM13	Ice Beam	Ice	95	100	10		TM44	Rest	Psychic	—	—	10
TM14	Blizzard	Ice	120	70	5		TM45	Attract	Normal	—	100	15
TM15	Hyper Beam	Normal	150	90	5		HM03	Surf	Water	95	100	15
TM17	Protect	Normal	—	—	10		HM04	Strength	Normal	80	100	20
TM18	Rain Dance	Water	—	—	5		HM06	Rock Smash	Fighting	20	100	15
TM21	Frustration	Normal	—	100	20		HM07	Waterfall	Water	80	100	15
TM23	Iron Tail	Steel	75	75	15		HM08	Dive	Water	60	100	10
TM27	Return	Normal	—	100	20							

MOVE TUTOR

FireRed/LeafGreen and Emerald Only

Body Slam*	Mega Kick*	Substitute
Double-Edge	Mimic	Seismic Toss*
Mega Punch*		

Emerald Only

Defense Curl*	Icy Wind*	Snore*
Dynamicpunch	Mud-Slap*	Swagger
Endure*	Rollout	Swift*
Ice Punch*	Sleep Talk	

*Battle Frontier tutor move (*Emerald*)

185 Sudowoodo™

ROCK

GENERAL INFO

SPECIES:	Imitation Pokémon
HEIGHT:	3'11"
WEIGHT:	84 lbs.
ABILITY 1:	**Rock Head**

Prevents Sudowoodo from receiving recoil damage.

ABILITY 2: Sturdy

Prevents Sudowoodo from receiving a one hit KO.

STATS

HP
SPEED
ATK
SP DEF
DEF
SP ATK

EVOLUTIONS

DOES NOT EVOLVE

LOCATION[s]:

RUBY	**Rarity: None**	Trade from *Colosseum/Emerald*
SAPPHIRE	**Rarity: None**	Trade from *Colosseum/Emerald*
FIRERED	**Rarity: None**	Trade from *Colosseum/Emerald*
LEAFGREEN	**Rarity: None**	Trade from *Colosseum/Emerald*
COLOSSEUM	**Rarity: Only One**	Pyrite Cave
EMERALD	**Rarity: Only One**	Battle Frontier
XD	**Rarity: None**	Trade from *Colosseum/Emerald*

MOVES

Level	Attack	Type	Power	ACC	PP	Level	Attack	Type	Power	ACC	PP
—	Rock Throw	Rock	50	90	15	25	Rock Slide	Rock	75	90	10
—	Mimic	Normal	—	100	10	33	Block	Normal	—	100	5
9	Flail	Normal	—	100	15	41	Faint Attack	Dark	60	—	20
17	Low Kick	Fighting	—	100	20	49	Slam	Normal	80	75	20
						57	Double-Edge	Normal	120	100	15

TM/HM

TM/HM#	Name	Type	Power	ACC	PP	TM/HM#	Name	Type	Power	ACC	PP
TM01	Focus Punch	Fighting	150	100	20	TM31	Brick Break	Fighting	75	100	15
TM04	Calm Mind	Psychic	—	—	20	TM32	Double Team	Normal	—	—	15
TM06	Toxic	Poison	—	85	10	TM37	Sandstorm	Ground	—	—	10
TM10	Hidden Power	Normal	—	100	15	TM39	Rock Tomb	Rock	50	80	10
TM11	Sunny Day	Fire	—	—	5	TM42	Facade	Normal	70	100	20
TM12	Taunt	Dark	—	100	20	TM43	Secret Power	Normal	70	100	20
TM17	Protect	Normal	—	—	10	TM44	Rest	Psychic	—	—	10
TM21	Frustration	Normal	—	100	20	TM45	Attract	Normal	—	100	15
TM26	Earthquake	Ground	100	100	10	TM46	Thief	Dark	40	100	10
TM27	Return	Normal	—	100	20	HM04	Strength	Normal	80	100	20
TM28	Dig	Ground	60	100	10	HM06	Rock Smash	Fighting	20	100	15

EGG MOVES*

Name	Type	Power	ACC	PP
Selfdestruct	Normal	200	100	5

*Learned Via Breeding

MOVE TUTOR

FireRed/LeafGreen and Emerald Only

Body Slam*	Mega Kick*	Seismic Toss*
Double-Edge	Mimic	Rock Slide*
Explosion	Substitute	
Mega Punch*	Counter*	

*Battle Frontier tutor move (*Emerald*)

186 Politoed™

WATER

GENERAL INFO

SPECIES: Frog Pokémon
HEIGHT: 3'07"
WEIGHT: 75 lbs.
ABILITY 1: Damp
No one can use Selfdestruct or Explosion while Politoed is in battle.
ABILITY 2: Water Absorb
Politoed gets 1/4 HPs back when hit by a Water-type attack.

STATS

HP
SPEED
ATK
SP DEF
DEF
SP ATK

EVOLUTIONS

LV25

TRADE WITH KING'S ROCK

LOCATION[s]:

RUBY	Rarity: **None**	Trade from *FireRed/LeafGreen*
SAPPHIRE	Rarity: **None**	Trade from *FireRed/LeafGreen*
FIRERED	Rarity: **Evolve**	Evolve Poliwhirl
LEAFGREEN	Rarity: **Evolve**	Evolve Poliwhirl
COLOSSEUM	Rarity: **None**	Trade from *FireRed/LeafGreen*
EMERALD	Rarity: **None**	Trade from *FireRed/LeafGreen*
XD	Rarity: **None**	Trade from *FireRed/LeafGreen*

MOVES

Level	Attack	Type	Power	ACC	PP	Level	Attack	Type	Power	ACC	PP
—	Water Gun	Water	40	100	25	—	Doubleslap	Normal	15	85	10
—	Hypnosis	Psychic	—	60	20	—	Perish Song	Normal	—	—	5
						51	Swagger	Normal	—	90	15

TM/HM

TM/HM#	Name	Type	Power	ACC	PP	TM/HM#	Name	Type	Power	ACC	PP
TM01	Focus Punch	Fighting	150	100	20	TM29	Psychic	Psychic	90	100	10
TM03	Water Pulse	Water	60	95	20	TM31	Brick Break	Fighting	75	100	15
TM06	Toxic	Poison	—	85	10	TM32	Double Team	Normal	—	—	15
TM07	Hail	Ice	—	—	10	TM42	Facade	Normal	70	100	20
TM10	Hidden Power	Normal	—	100	15	TM43	Secret Power	Normal	70	100	20
TM13	Ice Beam	Ice	95	100	10	TM44	Rest	Psychic	—	—	10
TM14	Blizzard	Ice	120	70	5	TM45	Attract	Normal	—	100	15
TM15	Hyper Beam	Normal	150	90	5	TM46	Thief	Dark	40	100	10
TM17	Protect	Normal	—	—	10	HM03	Surf	Water	95	100	15
TM18	Rain Dance	Water	—	—	5	HM04	Strength	Normal	80	100	20
TM21	Frustration	Normal	—	100	20	HM06	Rock Smash	Fighting	20	100	15
TM26	Earthquake	Ground	100	100	10	HM07	Waterfall	Water	80	100	15
TM27	Return	Normal	—	100	20	HM08	Dive	Water	60	100	10
TM28	Dig	Ground	60	100	10						

MOVE TUTOR
FireRed/LeafGreen and Emerald Only

Body Slam*	Mega Kick*	Substitute
Double-Edge	Metronome	Counter*
Mega Punch*	Mimic	Seismic Toss*

*Battle Frontier tutor move (*Emerald*)

187 Hoppip™

GRASS   FLYING

GENERAL INFO

SPECIES: Cottonweed Pokémon
HEIGHT: 1'04"
WEIGHT: 1 lb.
ABILITY: Chlorophyll
When the sunlight is strong, Hoppip's Speed is doubled.

STATS

EVOLUTIONS

LV18   LV27

LOCATION(s):

RUBY	Rarity: **None**	Trade from *FireRed/LeafGreen*
SAPPHIRE	Rarity: **None**	Trade from *FireRed/LeafGreen*
FIRERED	Rarity: **Common**	Five Island
LEAFGREEN	Rarity: **Common**	Five Island
COLOSSEUM	Rarity: **None**	Breed Skiploom in *Ruby/Sapphire/FireRed/LeafGreen*, then trade back
EMERALD	Rarity: **None**	Trade from *FireRed/LeafGreen*
XD	Rarity: **Common**	Oasis Poké Spot

MOVES

Level	Attack	Type	Power	ACC	PP
—	Splash	Normal	—	—	40
5	Synthesis	Grass	—	—	5
5	Tail Whip	Normal	—	100	30
10	Tackle	Normal	35	95	35
13	Poisonpowder	Poison	—	75	35

Level	Attack	Type	Power	ACC	PP
15	Stun Spore	Grass	—	75	30
17	Sleep Powder	Grass	—	75	15
20	Leech Seed	Grass	—	90	10
25	Cotton Spore	Grass	—	85	40
30	Mega Drain	Grass	40	100	10

TM/HM

TM/HM#	Name	Type	Power	ACC	PP
TM06	Toxic	Poison	—	85	10
TM09	Bullet Seed	Grass	10	100	30
TM10	Hidden Power	Normal	—	100	15
TM11	Sunny Day	Fire	—	—	5
TM17	Protect	Normal	—	—	10
TM19	Giga Drain	Grass	60	100	5
TM21	Frustration	Normal	—	100	20
TM22	Solarbeam	Grass	120	100	10

TM/HM#	Name	Type	Power	ACC	PP
TM27	Return	Normal	—	100	20
TM32	Double Team	Normal	—	—	15
TM40	Aerial Ace	Flying	60	—	20
TM42	Facade	Normal	70	100	20
TM43	Secret Power	Normal	70	100	20
TM44	Rest	Psychic	—	—	10
TM45	Attract	Normal	—	100	15
HM05	Flash	Normal	—	70	20

EGG MOVES*

Name	Type	Power	ACC	PP
Amnesia	Psychic	—	—	20
Confusion	Psychic	50	100	25
Double-Edge	Normal	120	100	15
Encore	Normal	—	100	5
Helping Hand	Normal	—	100	20
Psych Up	Normal	—	—	10
Reflect	Psychic	—	—	20

*Learned Via Breeding

MOVE TUTOR
FireRed/LeafGreen and Emerald Only

Double-Edge	Substitute	Swords Dance*
Mimic		

*Battle Frontier tutor move (*Emerald*)

188 Skiploom™

GRASS FLYING

GENERAL INFO

SPECIES: Cottonweed Pokémon
HEIGHT: 2'00"
WEIGHT: 2 lbs.
ABILITY: Chlorophyll
When the sunlight is strong, Skiploom's Speed is doubled.

STATS

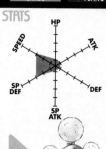

EVOLUTIONS

  LV18 LV27

LOCATION[S]:

RUBY	Rarity: **Evolve**	Trade from *FireRed/LeafGreen/Colosseum*
SAPPHIRE	Rarity: **Evolve**	Trade from *FireRed/LeafGreen/Colosseum*
FIRERED	Rarity: **Evolve**	Evolve Hoppip
LEAFGREEN	Rarity: **Evolve**	Evolve Hoppip
COLOSSEUM	Rarity: **Only One**	Pyrite Town
EMERALD	Rarity: **None**	Trade from *FireRed/LeafGreen/Colosseum*
XD	Rarity: **Evolve**	Evolve Hoppip

MOVES

Level	Attack	Type	Power	ACC	PP	Level	Attack	Type	Power	ACC	PP
—	Splash	Normal	—	—	40	15	Stun Spore	Grass	—	75	30
—	Synthesis	Grass	—	—	5	17	Sleep Powder	Grass	—	75	15
—	Tail Whip	Normal	—	100	30	22	Leech Seed	Grass	—	90	10
—	Tackle	Normal	35	95	35	29	Cotton Spore	Grass	—	85	40
13	Poisonpowder	Poison	—	75	35	36	Mega Drain	Grass	40	100	10

TM/HM

TM/HM#	Name	Type	Power	ACC	PP	TM/HM#	Name	Type	Power	ACC	PP
TM06	Toxic	Poison	—	85	10	TM27	Return	Normal	—	100	20
TM09	Bullet Seed	Grass	10	100	30	TM32	Double Team	Normal	—	—	15
TM10	Hidden Power	Normal	—	100	15	TM40	Aerial Ace	Flying	60	—	20
TM11	Sunny Day	Fire	—	—	5	TM42	Facade	Normal	70	100	20
TM17	Protect	Normal	—	—	10	TM43	Secret Power	Normal	70	100	20
TM19	Giga Drain	Grass	60	100	5	TM44	Rest	Psychic	—	—	10
TM21	Frustration	Normal	—	100	20	TM45	Attract	Normal	—	100	15
TM22	Solarbeam	Grass	120	100	10	HM05	Flash	Normal	—	70	20

MOVE TUTOR

FireRed/LeafGreen and Emerald Only

Double-Edge	Substitute	Swords Dance*
Mimic		

*Battle Frontier tutor move (*Emerald*)

189 Jumpluff™

GRASS   FLYING

GENERAL INFO

SPECIES: Cottonweed Pokémon
HEIGHT: 2'07"
WEIGHT: 7 lbs.
ABILITY: Chlorophyll
When the sunlight is strong, Jumpluff's Speed is doubled.

STATS

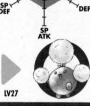

EVOLUTIONS

LV18   LV27

LOCATION[s]:

RUBY	Rarity: **Evolve**	Trade from *FireRed/LeafGreen/Colosseum*
SAPPHIRE	Rarity: **Evolve**	Trade from *FireRed/LeafGreen/Colosseum*
FIRERED	Rarity: **Evolve**	Evolve Skiploom
LEAFGREEN	Rarity: **Evolve**	Evolve Skiploom
COLOSSEUM	Rarity: **Evolve**	Evolve Skiploom
EMERALD	Rarity: **None**	Trade from *FireRed/LeafGreen/Colosseum*
XD	Rarity: **Evolve**	Evolve Skiploom

MOVES

Level	Attack	Type	Power	ACC	PP	Level	Attack	Type	Power	ACC	PP
—	Splash	Normal	—	—	40	15	Stun Spore	Grass	—	75	30
—	Synthesis	Grass	—	—	5	17	Sleep Powder	Grass	—	75	15
—	Tail Whip	Normal	—	100	30	22	Leech Seed	Grass	—	90	10
—	Tackle	Normal	35	95	35	33	Cotton Spore	Grass	—	85	40
13	Poisonpowder	Poison	—	75	35	44	Mega Drain	Grass	40	100	10

TM/HM

TM/HM#	Name	Type	Power	ACC	PP	TM/HM#	Name	Type	Power	ACC	PP
TM06	Toxic	Poison	—	85	10	TM27	Return	Normal	—	100	20
TM09	Bullet Seed	Grass	10	100	30	TM32	Double Team	Normal	—	—	15
TM10	Hidden Power	Normal	—	100	15	TM40	Aerial Ace	Flying	60	—	20
TM11	Sunny Day	Fire	—	—	5	TM42	Facade	Normal	70	100	20
TM15	Hyper Beam	Normal	150	90	5	TM43	Secret Power	Normal	70	100	20
TM17	Protect	Normal	—	—	10	TM44	Rest	Psychic	—	—	10
TM19	Giga Drain	Grass	60	100	5	TM45	Attract	Normal	—	100	15
TM21	Frustration	Normal	—	100	20	HM05	Flash	Normal	—	70	20
TM22	Solarbeam	Grass	120	100	10						

EGG MOVES*

Name	Type	Power	ACC	PP
Amnesia	Psychic	—	—	20
Confusion	Psychic	50	100	25
Double-Edge	Normal	120	100	15
Encore	Normal	—	100	5
Helping Hand	Normal	—	100	20
Psych Up	Normal	—	—	10
Refresh	Normal	—	100	20

*Learned Via Breeding

MOVE TUTOR
FireRed/LeafGreen and Emerald Only

Double-Edge	Substitute	Swords Dance*
Mimic		

*Battle Frontier tutor move (*Emerald*)

190 Aipom™

NORMAL

GENERAL INFO
SPECIES: Long Tail Pokémon
HEIGHT: 2'07"
WEIGHT: 25 lbs.
ABILITY 1: Run Away
Allows Aipom to escape from wild Pokémon.
ABILITY 2: Pickup
Attaches items when walking; allows Aipom to take opponent's item during battle.

STATS

EVOLUTIONS

DOES NOT EVOLVE

LOCATION[s]:

RUBY	Rarity: **None**	Trade from *Colosseum*
SAPPHIRE	Rarity: **None**	Trade from *Colosseum*
FIRERED	Rarity: **None**	Trade from *Colosseum*
LEAFGREEN	Rarity: **None**	Trade from *Colosseum*
COLOSSEUM	Rarity: **Only One**	Shadow Pokémon Lab
EMERALD	Rarity: **Common**	Safari Zone
XD	Rarity: **None**	Trade from *Colosseum*

MOVES

Level	Attack	Type	Power	ACC	PP
—	Scratch	Normal	40	100	35
—	Tail Whip	Normal	—	100	30
6	Sand-Attack	Ground	—	100	15
13	Astonish	Ghost	30	100	15
18	Baton Pass	Normal	—	—	40
25	Tickle	Normal	—	100	20
31	Fury Swipes	Normal	18	80	15
38	Swift	Normal	60	—	20
43	Screech	Normal	—	85	40
50	Agility	Psychic	—	—	30

TM/HM

TM/HM#	Name	Type	Power	ACC	PP
TM01	Focus Punch	Fighting	150	100	20
TM03	Water Pulse	Water	60	95	20
TM06	Toxic	Poison	—	85	10
TM10	Hidden Power	Normal	—	100	15
TM11	Sunny Day	Fire	—	—	5
TM12	Taunt	Dark	—	100	20
TM17	Protect	Normal	—	—	10
TM18	Rain Dance	Water	—	—	5
TM21	Frustration	Normal	—	100	20
TM22	Solarbeam	Grass	120	100	10
TM23	Iron Tail	Steel	75	75	15
TM24	Thunderbolt	Electric	95	100	15
TM25	Thunder	Electric	120	70	10
TM27	Return	Normal	—	100	20
TM28	Dig	Ground	60	100	10
TM30	Shadow Ball	Ghost	80	100	15
TM31	Brick Break	Fighting	75	100	15
TM32	Double Team	Normal	—	—	15
TM34	Shock Wave	Electric	60	—	20
TM40	Aerial Ace	Flying	60	—	20
TM42	Facade	Normal	70	100	20
TM43	Secret Power	Normal	70	100	20
TM44	Rest	Psychic	—	—	10
TM45	Attract	Normal	—	100	15
TM46	Thief	Dark	40	100	10
TM49	Snatch	Dark	—	100	10
HM01	Cut	Normal	50	95	30
HM04	Strength	Normal	80	100	20
HM06	Rock Smash	Fighting	20	100	15

EGG MOVES*

Name	Type	Power	ACC	PP
Agility	Psychic	—	—	30
Beat Up	Dark	10	100	10
Counter	Fighting	—	100	20
Doubleslap	Normal	15	85	10
Pursuit	Dark	40	100	20
Screech	Normal	—	85	40
Slam	Normal	80	75	20
Spite	Ghost	—	100	10

*Learned Via Breeding

MOVE TUTOR
FireRed/LeafGreen and Emerald Only

Body Slam*	Metronome	Seismic Toss*
Double-Edge*	Mimic	Dream Eater*
Mega Punch*	Substitute	Thunder Wave*
Mega Kick*	Counter*	

*Battle Frontier tutor move (*Emerald*)

191 Sunkern™

GRASS

GENERAL INFO
SPECIES: Seed Pokémon
HEIGHT: 1'00"
WEIGHT: 4 lbs.
ABILITY: Chlorophyll
Sunkern's Speed is doubled when the sunlight is strong.

STATS

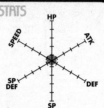

EVOLUTIONS

SUN STONE

LOCATION[S]:

RUBY	Rarity: **None**	Trade Sunflora from *Colosseum*, then breed
SAPPHIRE	Rarity: **None**	Trade Sunflora from *Colosseum*, then breed
FIRERED	Rarity: **None**	Trade Sunflora from *Colosseum*, then breed
LEAFGREEN	Rarity: **None**	Trade Sunflora from *Colosseum*, then breed
COLOSSEUM	Rarity: **Breed**	Breed in *Ruby/Sapphire/FireRed/LeafGreen* then trade back
EMERALD	Rarity: **Common**	Safari Zone
XD	Rarity: **None**	Trade Sunflora from *Colosseum*, then breed

MOVES

Level	Attack	Type	Power	ACC	PP	Level	Attack	Type	Power	ACC	PP
—	Absorb	Grass	20	100	20	25	Endeavor	Normal	—	100	5
6	Growth	Normal	—	—	40	30	Sunny Day	Fire	—	—	5
13	Mega Drain	Grass	40	100	10	37	Synthesis	Grass	—	—	5
18	Ingrain	Grass	—	100	20	42	Giga Drain	Grass	60	100	5

TM/HM

TM/HM#	Name	Type	Power	ACC	PP	TM/HM#	Name	Type	Power	ACC	PP
TM06	Toxic	Poison	—	85	10	TM27	Return	Normal	—	100	20
TM09	Bullet Seed	Grass	10	100	30	TM32	Double Team	Normal	—	—	15
TM10	Hidden Power	Normal	—	100	15	TM36	Sludge Bomb	Poison	90	100	10
TM11	Sunny Day	Fire	—	—	5	TM42	Facade	Normal	70	100	20
TM16	Light Screen	Psychic	—	—	30	TM43	Secret Power	Normal	70	100	20
TM17	Protect	Normal	—	—	10	TM44	Rest	Psychic	—	—	10
TM19	Giga Drain	Grass	60	100	5	TM45	Attract	Normal	—	100	15
TM20	Safeguard	Normal	—	—	25	HM01	Cut	Normal	50	95	30
TM21	Frustration	Normal	—	100	20	HM05	Flash	Normal	—	70	20
TM22	Solarbeam	Grass	120	100	10						

EGG MOVES*

Name	Type	Power	ACC	PP
Curse	—	—	—	10
Encore	Normal	—	100	5
Grasswhistle	Grass	—	55	15
Helping Hand	Normal	—	100	20
Leech Seed	Grass	—	90	10
Nature Power	Normal	—	95	20

*Learned Via Breeding

MOVE TUTOR
FireRed/LeafGreen and Emerald Only

Double-Edge	Substitute	Swords Dance*
Mimic		

*Battle Frontier tutor move (*Emerald*)

192 Sunflora™

GRASS

GENERAL INFO

SPECIES: Sun Pokémon
HEIGHT: 2'07"
WEIGHT: 19 lbs.
ABILITY: Chlorophyll
Sunflora's Speed is doubled when the sunlight is strong.

STATS

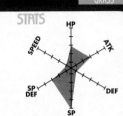

EVOLUTIONS

SUN STONE

LOCATION[s]:

RUBY	Rarity: **None**	Trade from *Colosseum*	
SAPPHIRE	Rarity: **None**	Trade from *Colosseum*	
FIRERED	Rarity: **None**	Trade from *Colosseum*	
LEAFGREEN	Rarity: **None**	Trade from *Colosseum*	
COLOSSEUM	Rarity: **Only One**	Obtained from Baila in Realgam Tower	
EMERALD	Rarity: **Evolve**	Evolve Sunkern	
XD	Rarity: **None**	Trade from *Colosseum*	

MOVES

Level	Attack	Type	Power	ACC	PP	Level	Attack	Type	Power	ACC	PP
—	Absorb	Grass	20	100	20	18	Ingrain	Grass	—	100	20
—	Pound	Normal	40	100	35	25	Bullet Seed	Grass	10	100	30
6	Growth	Normal	—	—	40	30	Sunny Day	Fire	—	—	5
13	Razor Leaf	Grass	55	95	25	37	Petal Dance	Grass	70	100	20
						42	Solarbeam	Grass	120	100	10

TM/HM

TM/HM#	Name	Type	Power	ACC	PP	TM/HM#	Name	Type	Power	ACC	PP
TM06	Toxic	Poison	—	85	10	TM22	Solarbeam	Grass	120	100	10
TM09	Bullet Seed	Grass	10	100	30	TM27	Return	Normal	—	100	20
TM10	Hidden Power	Normal	—	100	15	TM32	Double Team	Normal	—	—	15
TM11	Sunny Day	Fire	—	—	5	TM36	Sludge Bomb	Poison	90	100	10
TM15	Hyper Beam	Normal	150	90	5	TM42	Facade	Normal	70	100	20
TM16	Light Screen	Psychic	—	—	30	TM43	Secret Power	Normal	70	100	20
TM17	Protect	Normal	—	—	10	TM44	Rest	Psychic	—	—	10
TM19	Giga Drain	Grass	60	100	5	TM45	Attract	Normal	—	100	15
TM20	Safeguard	Normal	—	—	25	HM01	Cut	Normal	50	95	30
TM21	Frustration	Normal	—	100	20	HM05	Flash	Normal	—	70	20

MOVE TUTOR

FireRed/LeafGreen and Emerald Only

Double-Edge	Substitute	Swords Dance*
Mimic		

*Battle Frontier tutor move (*Emerald*)

193 Yanma™

BUG   FLYING

GENERAL INFO

SPECIES: Clear Wing Pokémon
HEIGHT: 3'11"
WEIGHT: 84 lbs.
ABILITY 1: Speed Boost
Yanma's Speed raises one level after each turn.
ABILITY 2: Compoundeyes
Yanma's Accuracy is raised by 30%.

STATS

HP
SPEED
ATK
SP DEF
DEF
SP ATK

EVOLUTIONS

DOES NOT EVOLVE

LOCATION[s]:

RUBY	Rarity: **None**	Trade from *FireRed/LeafGreen/Colosseum*
SAPPHIRE	Rarity: **None**	Trade from *FireRed/LeafGreen/Colosseum*
FIRERED	Rarity: **Rare**	Six Island
LEAFGREEN	Rarity: **Rare**	Six Island
COLOSSEUM	Rarity: **Only One**	Pyrite Town
EMERALD	Rarity: **None**	Trade from *FireRed/LeafGreen/Colosseum*
XD	Rarity: **None**	Trade from *FireRed/LeafGreen/Colosseum*

MOVES

Level	Attack	Type	Power	ACC	PP	Level	Attack	Type	Power	ACC	PP
—	Tackle	Normal	35	95	35	23	Hypnosis	Psychic	—	60	20
—	Foresight	Normal	—	100	40	28	Detect	Fight	—	—	5
6	Quick Attack	Normal	40	100	30	34	Uproar	Normal	50	100	10
12	Double Team	Normal	—	—	15	39	Wing Attack	Flying	60	100	35
17	Sonicboom	Normal	—	90	20	45	Supersonic	Normal	—	55	20
						50	Screech	Normal	—	85	40

TM/HM

TM/HM#	Name	Type	Power	ACC	PP	TM/HM#	Name	Type	Power	ACC	PP
TM06	Toxic	Poison	—	85	10	TM32	Double Team	Normal	—	—	15
TM10	Hidden Power	Normal	—	100	15	TM40	Aerial Ace	Flying	60	—	20
TM11	Sunny Day	Fire	—	—	5	TM42	Facade	Normal	70	100	20
TM17	Protect	Normal	—	—	10	TM43	Secret Power	Normal	70	100	20
TM19	Giga Drain	Grass	60	100	5	TM44	Rest	Psychic	—	—	10
TM21	Frustration	Normal	—	100	20	TM45	Attract	Normal	—	100	15
TM22	Solarbeam	Grass	120	100	10	TM46	Thief	Dark	40	100	10
TM27	Return	Normal	—	100	20	TM47	Steel Wing	Steel	70	90	25
TM29	Psychic	Psychic	90	100	10	HM05	Flash	Normal	—	70	20
TM30	Shadow Ball	Ghost	80	100	15						

EGG MOVES*

Name	Type	Power	ACC	PP
Leech Life	Bug	20	100	15
Reversal	Fighting	—	100	15
Signal Beam	Bug	75	100	15
Silver Wind	Bug	60	100	5
Whirlwind	Normal	—	100	20

*Learned Via Breeding

MOVE TUTOR

FireRed/LeafGreen and Emerald Only

Double-Edge	Substitute	Dream Eater*
Mimic		

*Battle Frontier tutor move (*Emerald*)

194 Wooper™

WATER · GROUND

GENERAL INFO

SPECIES: Water Fish Pokémon
HEIGHT: 1'04"
WEIGHT: 19 lbs.
ABILITY 1: Damp
No one can use Selfdestruct or Explosion while Wooper is in battle.
ABILITY 2: Water Absorb
Wooper gets 1/4 HPs back when hit by a Water-type attack.

STATS

HP · ATK · DEF · SP ATK · SP DEF · SPEED

EVOLUTIONS

LV20

LOCATION[s]:

RUBY	Rarity:	None	Trade from *FireRed*
SAPPHIRE	Rarity:	None	Trade from *FireRed*
FIRERED	Rarity:	Common	Six Island
LEAFGREEN	Rarity:	None	Trade from *FireRed*
COLOSSEUM	Rarity:	None	Trade from *FireRed/LeafGreen*
EMERALD	Rarity:	Common	Safari Zone
XD	Rarity:	Rare	Cave Poké Spot

MOVES

Level	Attack	Type	Power	ACC	PP
—	Water Gun	Water	40	100	25
—	Tail Whip	Normal	—	100	30
11	Slam	Normal	80	75	20
16	Mud Shot	Ground	55	95	15
21	Amnesia	Psychic	—	—	20

Level	Attack	Type	Power	ACC	PP
31	Yawn	Normal	—	—	10
36	Earthquake	Ground	100	100	10
41	Rain Dance	Water	—	—	5
51	Mist	Ice	—	—	30
51	Haze	Ice	—	—	30

TM/HM

TM/HM#	Name	Type	Power	ACC	PP
TM03	Water Pulse	Water	60	95	20
TM06	Toxic	Poison	—	85	10
TM07	Hail	Ice	—	—	10
TM10	Hidden Power	Normal	—	100	15
TM13	Ice Beam	Ice	95	100	10
TM14	Blizzard	Ice	120	70	5
TM17	Protect	Normal	—	—	10
TM18	Rain Dance	Water	—	—	5
TM21	Frustration	Normal	—	100	20
TM23	Iron Tail	Steel	75	75	15
TM26	Earthquake	Ground	100	100	10
TM27	Return	Normal	—	100	20
TM28	Dig	Ground	60	100	10

TM/HM#	Name	Type	Power	ACC	PP
TM32	Double Team	Normal	—	—	15
TM36	Sludge Bomb	Poison	90	100	10
TM37	Sandstorm	Ground	—	—	10
TM42	Facade	Normal	70	100	20
TM43	Secret Power	Normal	70	100	20
TM44	Rest	Psychic	—	—	10
TM45	Attract	Normal	—	100	15
HM03	Surf	Water	95	100	15
HM05	Flash	Normal	—	70	20
HM06	Rock Smash	Fighting	20	100	15
HM07	Waterfall	Water	80	100	15
HM08	Dive	Water	60	100	10

EGG MOVES*

Name	Type	Power	ACC	PP
Ancientpower	Rock	60	100	5
Body Slam	Normal	85	100	15
Curse	—	—	—	10
Mud Sport	Ground	—	100	15
Safeguard	Normal	—	—	25
Spit Up	Normal	100	100	10
Swallow	Normal	—	—	10
Stockpile	Normal	—	—	10

*Learned Via Breeding

MOVE TUTOR
FireRed/LeafGreen and Emerald Only

Body Slam*	Mimic	Substitute
Double-Edge		

*Battle Frontier tutor move (*Emerald*)

195 Quagsire™

WATER | GROUND

GENERAL INFO

SPECIES: Water Fish Pokémon
HEIGHT: 4'07"
WEIGHT: 165 lbs.
ABILITY 1: Damp
No one can use Selfdestruct or Explosion while Quagsire is in battle.
ABILITY 2: Water Absorb
Quagsire gets 1/4 HPs back when hit by a Water-type attack.

STATS

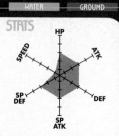

EVOLUTIONS

LV20

LOCATION(s):

RUBY	Rarity: **Evolve**	Trade from *FireRed/Colosseum*
SAPPHIRE	Rarity: **Evolve**	Trade from *FireRed/Colosseum*
FIRERED	Rarity: **Evolve**	Evolve Wooper
LEAFGREEN	Rarity: **None**	Trade from *FireRed/Colosseum*
COLOSSEUM	Rarity: **Only One**	Pyrite Town
EMERALD	Rarity: **Rare**	Safari Zone
XD	Rarity: **Evolve**	Evolve Wooper

MOVES

Level	Attack	Type	Power	ACC	PP		Level	Attack	Type	Power	ACC	PP
—	Water Gun	Water	40	100	25		35	Yawn	Normal	—	100	10
—	Tail Whip	Normal	—	100	30		42	Earthquake	Ground	100	100	10
11	Slam	Normal	80	75	20		49	Rain Dance	Water	—	—	5
16	Mud Shot	Ground	55	95	15		61	Mist	Ice	—	—	30
23	Amnesia	Psychic	—	—	20		61	Haze	Ice	—	—	30

TM/HM

TM/HM#	Name	Type	Power	ACC	PP		TM/HM#	Name	Type	Power	ACC	PP
TM01	Focus Punch	Fighting	150	100	20		TM31	Brick Break	Fighting	75	100	15
TM03	Water Pulse	Water	60	95	20		TM32	Double Team	Normal	—	—	15
TM06	Toxic	Poison	—	85	10		TM36	Sludge Bomb	Poison	90	100	10
TM07	Hail	Ice	—	—	10		TM37	Sandstorm	Ground	—	—	10
TM10	Hidden Power	Normal	—	100	15		TM39	Rock Tomb	Rock	50	80	10
TM13	Ice Beam	Ice	95	100	10		TM42	Facade	Normal	70	100	20
TM14	Blizzard	Ice	120	70	5		TM43	Secret Power	Normal	70	100	20
TM15	Hyper Beam	Normal	150	90	5		TM44	Rest	Psychic	—	—	10
TM17	Protect	Normal	—	—	10		TM45	Attract	Normal	—	100	15
TM18	Rain Dance	Water	—	—	5		HM03	Surf	Water	95	100	15
TM21	Frustration	Normal	—	100	20		HM04	Strength	Normal	80	100	20
TM23	Iron Tail	Steel	75	75	15		HM05	Flash	Normal	—	70	20
TM26	Earthquake	Ground	100	100	10		HM06	Rock Smash	Fighting	20	100	15
TM27	Return	Normal	—	100	20		HM07	Waterfall	Water	80	100	15
TM28	Dig	Ground	60	100	10		HM08	Dive	Water	60	100	10

MOVE TUTOR
FireRed/LeafGreen and Emerald Only

Body Slam*	Mega Kick*	Counter*
Double-Edge	Mimic	Seismic Toss*
Mega Punch*	Substitute	

*Battle Frontier tutor move (*Emerald*)

196 Espeon™

GENERAL INFO

SPECIES: Sun Pokémon
HEIGHT: 2'11"
WEIGHT: 58 lbs.
ABILITY: Synchronize

When Espeon is hit by Poison, Paralyze, or Burn, the opponent receives the same.

STATS

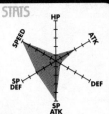

EVOLUTIONS

FRIENDSHIP (DAY)

LOCATION[s]:

	Rarity:	
RUBY	**Evolve**	Evolve Eevee
SAPPHIRE	**Evolve**	Evolve Eevee
FIRERED	**Evolve**	Trade from *Ruby/Sapphire/Colosseum*
LEAFGREEN	**Evolve**	Trade from *Ruby/Sapphire/Colosseum*
COLOSSEUM	**Only One**	Starter Pokémon in *Colosseum*
EMERALD	**None**	Trade from *Ruby/Sapphire/Colosseum*
XD	**Evolve**	Evolve Eevee

MOVES

Level	Attack	Type	Power	ACC	PP	Level	Attack	Type	Power	ACC	PP
—	Tackle	Normal	35	95	35	23	Quick Attack	Normal	40	100	30
—	Tail Whip	Normal	—	100	30	30	Swift	Normal	60	—	20
—	Helping Hand	Normal	—	100	20	36	Psybeam	Psychic	65	100	20
8	Sand-Attack	Ground	—	100	15	42	Psych Up	Normal	—	—	10
16	Confusion	Psychic	50	100	25	47	Psychic	Psychic	90	100	10
						52	Morning Sun	Normal	—	—	5

TM/HM

TM/HM#	Name	Type	Power	ACC	PP	TM/HM#	Name	Type	Power	ACC	PP
TM04	Calm Mind	Psychic	—	—	20	TM29	Psychic	Psychic	90	100	10
TM06	Toxic	Poison	—	85	10	TM30	Shadow Ball	Ghost	80	100	15
TM10	Hidden Power	Normal	—	100	15	TM32	Double Team	Normal	—	—	15
TM11	Sunny Day	Fire	—	—	5	TM33	Reflect	Normal	—	—	20
TM15	Hyper Beam	Normal	150	90	5	TM42	Facade	Normal	70	100	20
TM16	Light Screen	Psychic	—	—	30	TM43	Secret Power	Normal	70	100	20
TM17	Protect	Normal	—	—	10	TM44	Rest	Psychic	—	—	10
TM18	Rain Dance	Water	—	—	5	TM45	Attract	Normal	—	100	15
TM21	Frustration	Normal	—	100	20	TM48	Skill Swap	Psychic	—	100	10
TM23	Iron Tail	Steel	75	75	15	HM01	Cut	Normal	50	95	30
TM27	Return	Normal	—	100	20	HM05	Flash	Normal	—	70	20
TM28	Dig	Ground	60	100	10						

MOVE TUTOR

FireRed/LeafGreen and Emerald Only

Body Slam*	Mimic	Substitute
Double-Edge	Dream Eater*	

*Battle Frontier tutor move (*Emerald*)

197 Umbreon™

DARK

GENERAL INFO

SPECIES: Moonlight Pokémon
HEIGHT: 3'03"
WEIGHT: 60 lbs.
ABILITY: Synchronize
When Umbreon is hit by Poison, Paralyze, or Burn, the opponent receives the same.

STATS

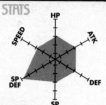

EVOLUTIONS

 ▶

FRIENDSHIP (NIGHT)

LOCATION[s]:

RUBY	Rarity: **Evolve**	Evolve Eevee
SAPPHIRE	Rarity: **Evolve**	Evolve Eevee
FIRERED	Rarity: **Evolve**	Trade from *Ruby/Sapphire/Colosseum*
LEAFGREEN	Rarity: **Evolve**	Trade from *Ruby/Sapphire/Colosseum*
COLOSSEUM	Rarity: **Only One**	Starter Pokémon in *Colosseum*
EMERALD	Rarity: **None**	Trade from *Ruby/Sapphire/Colosseum*
XD	Rarity: **Evolve**	Evolve Eevee

MOVES

Level	Attack	Type	Power	ACC	PP
—	Tackle	Normal	35	95	35
—	Tail Whip	Normal	—	100	30
—	Helping Hand	Normal	—	100	20
8	Sand-Attack	Ground	—	100	15
16	Pursuit	Dark	40	100	20

Level	Attack	Type	Power	ACC	PP
23	Quick Attack	Normal	40	100	30
30	Confuse Ray	Ghost	—	100	10
36	Faint Attack	Dark	60	—	20
42	Mean Look	Normal	—	100	5
47	Screech	Normal	—	85	40
52	Moonlight	Normal	—	—	5

TM/HM

TM/HM#	Name	Type	Power	ACC	PP
TM06	Toxic	Poison	—	85	10
TM10	Hidden Power	Normal	—	100	15
TM11	Sunny Day	Fire	—	—	5
TM12	Taunt	Dark	—	100	20
TM15	Hyper Beam	Normal	150	90	5
TM17	Protect	Normal	—	—	10
TM18	Rain Dance	Water	—	—	5
TM21	Frustration	Normal	—	100	20
TM23	Iron Tail	Steel	75	75	15
TM27	Return	Normal	—	100	20
TM28	Dig	Ground	60	100	10

TM/HM#	Name	Type	Power	ACC	PP
TM29	Psychic	Psychic	90	100	10
TM30	Shadow Ball	Ghost	80	100	15
TM32	Double Team	Normal	—	—	15
TM41	Torment	Dark	—	100	15
TM42	Facade	Normal	70	100	20
TM43	Secret Power	Normal	70	100	20
TM44	Rest	Psychic	—	—	10
TM45	Attract	Normal	—	100	15
TM49	Snatch	Dark	—	100	10
HM01	Cut	Normal	50	95	30
HM05	Flash	Normal	—	70	20

MOVE TUTOR

FireRed/LeafGreen and Emerald Only

Body Slam*	Mimic	Substitute
Double-Edge	Dream Eater*	

*Battle Frontier tutor move (*Emerald*)

198 Murkrow™

DARK | FLYING

GENERAL INFO

SPECIES: Darkness Pokémon
HEIGHT: 1'08"
WEIGHT: 5 lbs.
ABILITY: Insomnia
Prevents Murkrow from being put to sleep.

STATS

HP
SPEED
ATK
SP DEF
DEF
SP ATK

EVOLUTIONS

DOES NOT EVOLVE

LOCATION(s):

RUBY	Rarity:	None	Trade from *FireRed/Colosseum*
SAPPHIRE	Rarity:	None	Trade from *FireRed/Colosseum*
FIRERED	Rarity:	Rare	Five Island
LEAFGREEN	Rarity:	None	Trade from *FireRed/Colosseum*
COLOSSEUM	Rarity:	Only One	Shadow Pokémon Lab
EMERALD	Rarity:	None	Trade from *FireRed/Colosseum*
XD	Rarity:	None	Trade from *FireRed/Colosseum*

MOVES

Level	Attack	Type	Power	ACC	PP	Level	Attack	Type	Power	ACC	PP
—	Peck	Flying	35	100	35	27	Night Shade	Ghost	—	100	15
9	Astonish	Ghost	30	100	15	35	Faint Attack	Dark	60	—	20
14	Pursuit	Dark	40	100	20	40	Taunt	Dark	—	100	20
22	Haze	Ice	—	—	30	48	Mean Look	Normal	—	100	5

TM/HM

TM/HM#	Name	Type	Power	ACC	PP	TM/HM#	Name	Type	Power	ACC	PP
TM04	Calm Mind	Psychic	—	—	20	TM40	Aerial Ace	Flying	60	—	20
TM06	Toxic	Poison	—	85	10	TM41	Torment	Dark	—	100	15
TM10	Hidden Power	Normal	—	100	15	TM42	Facade	Normal	70	100	20
TM11	Sunny Day	Fire	—	—	5	TM43	Secret Power	Normal	70	100	20
TM12	Taunt	Dark	—	100	20	TM44	Rest	Psychic	—	—	10
TM17	Protect	Normal	—	—	10	TM45	Attract	Normal	—	100	15
TM18	Rain Dance	Water	—	—	5	TM46	Thief	Dark	40	100	10
TM21	Frustration	Normal	—	100	20	TM47	Steel Wing	Steel	70	90	25
TM27	Return	Normal	—	100	20	TM49	Snatch	Dark	—	100	10
TM30	Shadow Ball	Ghost	80	100	15	HM02	Fly	Flying	70	95	15
TM32	Double Team	Normal	—	—	15						

EGG MOVES*

Name	Type	Power	ACC	PP
Confuse Ray	Ghost	—	100	10
Drill Peck	Flying	80	100	20
Featherdance	Flying	—	100	15
Mirror Move	Flying	—	—	20
Perish Song	Normal	—	—	5
Sky Attack	Flying	140	90	5
Whirlwind	Normal	—	100	20
Wing Attack	Flying	60	100	35

*Learned Via Breeding

MOVE TUTOR
FireRed/LeafGreen and Emerald Only

Double-Edge	Dream Eater*	Thunder Wave*
Mimic	Substitute	

*Battle Frontier tutor move (*Emerald*)

199 Slowking™

WATER   PSYCHIC

GENERAL INFO
SPECIES: Royal Pokémon
HEIGHT: 6'07"
WEIGHT: 175 lbs.
ABILITY 1: Oblivious
Prevents Slowking from being attracted.
ABILITY 2: Own Tempo
Prevents Slowking from being Confused.

STATS

HP, ATK, DEF, SP ATK, SP DEF, SPEED

EVOLUTIONS

KING'S ROCK

LOCATION(s):

RUBY	Rarity: **None**	Evolve Slowpoke, Trade from *LeafGreen*
SAPPHIRE	Rarity: **None**	Evolve Slowpoke, Trade from *LeafGreen*
FIRERED	Rarity: **None**	Trade from *LeafGreen*
LEAFGREEN	Rarity: **Evolve**	Evolve Slowpoke
COLOSSEUM	Rarity: **None**	Trade from *LeafGreen*
EMERALD	Rarity: **None**	Trade from *LeafGreen*
XD	Rarity: **None**	Trade from *LeafGreen*

MOVES

Level	Attack	Type	Power	ACC	PP	Level	Attack	Type	Power	ACC	PP
—	Curse	—	—	—	10	17	Confusion	Psychic	50	100	25
—	Tackle	Normal	35	95	35	24	Disable	Normal	—	55	20
—	Yawn	Normal	—	100	10	29	Headbutt	Normal	70	100	15
6	Growl	Normal	—	100	40	36	Swagger	Normal	—	90	15
13	Water Gun	Water	40	100	25	40	Psychic	Psychic	90	100	10
						47	Psych Up	Normal	—	—	10

TM/HM

TM/HM#	Name	Type	Power	ACC	PP	TM/HM#	Name	Type	Power	ACC	PP
TM01	Focus Punch	Fighting	150	100	20	TM28	Dig	Ground	60	100	10
TM03	Water Pulse	Water	60	95	20	TM29	Psychic	Psychic	90	100	10
TM04	Calm Mind	Psychic	—	—	20	TM30	Shadow Ball	Ghost	80	100	15
TM06	Toxic	Poison	—	85	10	TM31	Brick Break	Fighting	75	100	15
TM07	Hail	Ice	—	—	10	TM32	Double Team	Normal	—	—	15
TM10	Hidden Power	Normal	—	100	15	TM35	Flamethrower	Fire	95	100	15
TM11	Sunny Day	Fire	—	—	5	TM38	Fire Blast	Fire	120	85	5
TM13	Ice Beam	Ice	95	100	10	TM42	Facade	Normal	70	100	20
TM14	Blizzard	Ice	120	70	5	TM43	Secret Power	Normal	70	100	20
TM15	Hyper Beam	Normal	150	90	5	TM44	Rest	Psychic	—	—	10
TM17	Protect	Normal	—	—	10	TM45	Attract	Normal	—	100	15
TM18	Rain Dance	Water	—	—	5	TM48	Skill Swap	Psychic	—	100	10
TM20	Safeguard	Normal	—	—	25	HM03	Surf	Water	95	100	15
TM21	Frustration	Normal	—	100	20	HM04	Strength	Normal	80	100	15
TM23	Iron Tail	Steel	75	75	15	HM05	Flash	Normal	—	70	20
TM26	Earthquake	Ground	100	100	10	HM06	Rock Smash	Fighting	20	100	15
TM27	Return	Normal	—	100	20	HM08	Dive	Water	60	100	10

MOVE TUTOR
FireRed/LeafGreen and Emerald Only

Body Slam*	Mimic	Dream Eater*
Double-Edge	Substitute	Thunder Wave*
Mega Punch*	Counter*	
Mega Kick*	Seismic Toss*	

*Battle Frontier tutor move (*Emerald*)

200 Misdreavus™

GHOST

GENERAL INFO

SPECIES: Screech Pokémon
HEIGHT: 2'04"
WEIGHT: 2 lbs.
ABILITY: Levitate

Prevents Misdreavus from being hit by Ground-type attacks.

STATS

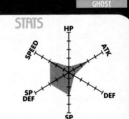

EVOLUTIONS

DOES NOT EVOLVE

LOCATION[s]:

Game	Rarity	Location
RUBY	Rarity: **None**	Trade from *Colosseum/LeafGreen*
SAPPHIRE	Rarity: **None**	Trade from *Colosseum/LeafGreen*
FIRERED	Rarity: **None**	Trade from *Colosseum/LeafGreen*
LEAFGREEN	Rarity: **Common**	Five Island
COLOSSEUM	Rarity: **Only One**	Pyrite Town
EMERALD	Rarity: **None**	Trade from *Colosseum/LeafGreen*
XD	Rarity: **None**	Trade from *Colosseum/LeafGreen*

MOVES

Level	Attack	Type	Power	ACC	PP
—	Growl	Normal	—	100	40
—	Psywave	Psychic	—	80	15
6	Spite	Ghost	—	100	10
11	Astonish	Ghost	30	100	15
17	Confuse Ray	Ghost	—	100	10

Level	Attack	Type	Power	ACC	PP
23	Mean Look	Normal	—	100	5
30	Psybeam	Psychic	65	100	20
37	Pain Split	Normal	—	100	20
45	Perish Song	Normal	—	—	5
53	Grudge	Ghost	—	100	5

TM/HM

TM/HM#	Name	Type	Power	ACC	PP
TM04	Calm Mind	Psychic	—	—	20
TM06	Toxic	Poison	—	85	10
TM10	Hidden Power	Normal	—	100	15
TM11	Sunny Day	Fire	—	—	5
TM12	Taunt	Dark	—	100	20
TM17	Protect	Normal	—	—	10
TM18	Rain Dance	Water	—	—	5
TM21	Frustration	Normal	—	100	20
TM24	Thunderbolt	Electric	95	100	15
TM25	Thunder	Electric	120	70	10
TM27	Return	Normal	—	100	20
TM29	Psychic	Psychic	90	100	10
TM30	Shadow Ball	Ghost	80	100	15

TM/HM#	Name	Type	Power	ACC	PP
TM32	Double Team	Normal	—	—	15
TM34	Shock Wave	Electric	60	—	20
TM40	Aerial Ace	Flying	60	—	20
TM41	Torment	Dark	—	100	15
TM42	Facade	Normal	70	100	20
TM43	Secret Power	Normal	70	100	20
TM44	Rest	Psychic	—	—	10
TM45	Attract	Normal	—	100	15
TM46	Thief	Dark	40	100	10
TM48	Skill Swap	Psychic	—	100	10
TM49	Snatch	Dark	—	100	10
HM05	Flash	Normal	—	70	20

EGG MOVES*

Name	Type	Power	ACC	PP
Destiny Bond	Ghost	—	—	5
Imprison	Psychic	—	100	15
Psych Up	Normal	—	—	10
Screech	Normal	—	85	40

*Learned Via Breeding

MOVE TUTOR

FireRed/LeafGreen and Emerald Only

Double-Edge	Dream Eater*	Thunder Wave*
Mimic	Substitute	

*Battle Frontier tutor move (*Emerald*)

201 Unown™

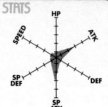

PSYCHIC

GENERAL INFO
SPECIES: Symbol Pokémon
HEIGHT: 1'08"
WEIGHT: 11 lbs.
ABILITY: Levitate
Prevents Unown from being hit by Ground-type moves.

STATS

HP
SPEED
ATK
SP DEF
DEF
SP ATK

EVOLUTIONS

DOES NOT EVOLVE

LOCATION[s]:

RUBY	Rarity: None		Trade from *FireRed/LeafGreen*
SAPPHIRE	Rarity: None		Trade from *FireRed/LeafGreen*
FIRERED	Rarity: Common		Ruins of Seven Island
LEAFGREEN	Rarity: Common		Ruins of Seven Island
COLOSSEUM	Rarity: None		Trade from *FireRed/LeafGreen*
EMERALD	Rarity: None		Trade from *FireRed/LeafGreen*
XD	Rarity: None		Trade from *FireRed/LeafGreen*

MOVES

Level	Attack	Type	Power	ACC	PP
—	Hidden Power	Normal	—	100	15

TM/HM

TM/HM# Name	Type	Power	ACC	PP
None				

EGG MOVES*

Name	Type	Power	ACC	PP
None				

*Learned Via Breeding

MOVE TUTOR
FireRed/LeafGreen and Emerald Only

None

202 Wobbuffet™

GENERAL INFO
SPECIES: Patient Pokémon
HEIGHT: 4'03"
WEIGHT: 63 lbs.
ABILITY: Shadow Tag

An opponent cannot escape while Wobbuffet is in battle.

STATS

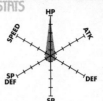

EVOLUTIONS

LV15

LOCATION[s]:

RUBY	Rarity: **Common**	Safari Zone
SAPPHIRE	Rarity: **Common**	Safari Zone
FIRERED	Rarity: **Common**	Six Island
LEAFGREEN	Rarity: **Common**	Six Island
COLOSSEUM	Rarity: **None**	Trade from *Ruby/Sapphire*
EMERALD	Rarity: **Common**	Safari Zone
XD	Rarity: **None**	Trade from *Ruby/Sapphire/Emerald*

MOVES

Level	Attack	Type	Power	ACC	PP
—	Counter	Fighting	—	100	20
—	Mirror Coat	Psychic	—	100	20
—	Safeguard	Normal	—	—	25
—	Destiny Bond	Ghost	—	—	5

TM/HM

TM/HM#	Name	Type	Power	ACC	PP
None					

EGG MOVES*

Name	Type	Power	ACC	PP
None				

*Learned Via Breeding

MOVE TUTOR
FireRed/LeafGreen and Emerald Only

None

PRIMA OFFICIAL GAME GUIDE

203 Girafarig™

NORMAL | PSYCHIC

GENERAL INFO

SPECIES: Long Neck Pokémon
HEIGHT: 4'11"
WEIGHT: 91 lbs.
ABILITY 1: Inner Focus
Prevents Girafarig from flinching.
ABILITY 2: Early Bird
Allows Girafarig to wake up sooner when put to sleep.

STATS

EVOLUTIONS

DOES NOT EVOLVE

LOCATION[s]:

RUBY	Rarity: **Common**	Safari Zone
SAPPHIRE	Rarity: **Common**	Safari Zone
FIRERED	Rarity: **None**	Trade from *Ruby/Sapphire*
LEAFGREEN	Rarity: **None**	Trade from *Ruby/Sapphire*
COLOSSEUM	Rarity: **None**	Trade from *Ruby/Sapphire*
EMERALD	Rarity: **Common**	Safari Zone
XD	Rarity: **None**	Trade from *Ruby/Sapphire*

MOVES

Level	Attack	Type	Power	ACC	PP		Level	Attack	Type	Power	ACC	PP
—	Tackle	Normal	35	95	35		25	Odor Sleuth	Normal	—	100	40
—	Growl	Normal	—	100	40		31	Agility	Psychic	—	—	30
7	Astonish	Ghost	30	100	15		37	Baton Pass	Normal	—	—	40
13	Confusion	Psychic	50	100	25		43	Psybeam	Psychic	65	100	20
19	Stomp	Normal	65	100	20		49	Crunch	Dark	80	100	15

TM/HM

TM/HM#	Name	Type	Power	ACC	PP		TM/HM#	Name	Type	Power	ACC	PP
TM04	Calm Mind	Psychic	—	—	20		TM30	Shadow Ball	Ghost	80	100	15
TM06	Toxic	Poison	—	85	10		TM32	Double Team	Normal	—	—	15
TM10	Hidden Power	Normal	—	100	15		TM33	Reflect	Normal	—	—	20
TM11	Sunny Day	Fire	—	—	5		TM34	Shock Wave	Electric	60	—	20
TM16	Light Screen	Psychic	—	—	30		TM42	Facade	Normal	70	100	20
TM17	Protect	Normal	—	—	10		TM43	Secret Power	Normal	70	100	20
TM18	Rain Dance	Water	—	—	5		TM44	Rest	Psychic	—	—	10
TM21	Frustration	Normal	—	100	20		TM45	Attract	Normal	—	100	15
TM23	Iron Tail	Steel	75	75	15		TM46	Thief	Dark	40	100	10
TM24	Thunderbolt	Electric	95	100	15		TM48	Skill Swap	Psychic	—	100	10
TM25	Thunder	Electric	120	70	10		HM04	Strength	Normal	80	100	20
TM26	Earthquake	Ground	100	100	10		HM05	Flash	Normal	—	70	20
TM27	Return	Normal	—	100	20		HM06	Rock Smash	Fighting	20	100	15
TM29	Psychic	Psychic	90	100	10							

EGG MOVES*

Name	Type	Power	ACC	PP
Take Down	Normal	90	85	20
Amnesia	Psychic	—	—	20
Foresight	Normal	—	100	40
Future Sight	Psychic	80	90	15
Psych Up	Normal	—	—	10
Magic Coat	Psychic	—	100	15
Beat Up	Dark	10	100	10
Wish	Normal	—	100	10

*Learned Via Breeding

MOVE TUTOR
FireRed/LeafGreen and Emerald Only

Body Slam*	Mimic	Thunder Wave*
Double-Edge	Substitute	Dream Eater*

Emerald Only

Endure*	Sleep Talk	Swagger
Mud-Slap*	Snore*	Swift*
Psych Up*		

*Battle Frontier tutor move (*Emerald*)

204 Pineco

GENERAL INFO

SPECIES: Bagworm Pokémon
HEIGHT: 2'00"
WEIGHT: 16 lbs.
ABILITY: Sturdy
Prevents Pineco from being hit by a one hit KO.

STATS

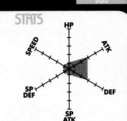

EVOLUTIONS

LV31

LOCATION[S]:

RUBY	Rarity: **None**	Trade from *Colosseum*
SAPPHIRE	Rarity: **None**	Trade from *Colosseum*
FIRERED	Rarity: **None**	Trade from *Colosseum*
LEAFGREEN	Rarity: **None**	Trade from *Colosseum*
COLOSSEUM	Rarity: **Breed**	Must Breed Forretress
EMERALD	Rarity: **Common**	Safari Zone
XD	Rarity: **Only One**	Phenac City (Capture from Cipher Peon Gonrag)

MOVES

Level	Attack	Type	Power	ACC	PP		Level	Attack	Type	Power	ACC	PP
—	Tackle	Normal	35	95	35		22	Rapid Spin	Normal	20	100	40
—	Protect	Normal	—	—	10		29	Bide	Normal	—	100	10
8	Selfdestruct	Normal	200	100	5		36	Explosion	Normal	250	100	5
15	Take Down	Normal	90	85	20		43	Spikes	Ground	—	—	20
							50	Double-Edge	Normal	120	100	15

TM/HM

TM/HM#	Name	Type	Power	ACC	PP		TM/HM#	Name	Type	Power	ACC	PP
TM06	Toxic	Poison	—	85	10		TM28	Dig	Ground	60	100	10
TM10	Hidden Power	Normal	—	100	15		TM32	Double Team	Normal	—	—	15
TM11	Sunny Day	Fire	—	—	5		TM33	Reflect	Normal	—	—	20
TM16	Light Screen	Psychic	—	—	30		TM37	Sandstorm	Ground	—	—	10
TM17	Protect	Normal	—	—	10		TM42	Facade	Normal	70	100	20
TM19	Giga Drain	Grass	60	100	5		TM43	Secret Power	Normal	70	100	20
TM21	Frustration	Normal	—	100	20		TM44	Rest	Psychic	—	—	10
TM22	Solarbeam	Grass	120	100	10		TM45	Attract	Normal	—	100	15
TM26	Earthquake	Ground	100	100	10		HM04	Strength	Normal	80	100	20
TM27	Return	Normal	—	100	20		HM06	Rock Smash	Fighting	20	100	15

EGG MOVES*

Name	Type	Power	ACC	PP
Counter	Fighting	—	100	20
Flail	Normal	—	100	15
Pin Missile	Bug	14	85	20
Reflect	Psychic	—	—	20
Sand Tomb	Ground	15	70	15
Swift	Normal	60	—	20

*Learned Via Breeding

MOVE TUTOR
FireRed/LeafGreen and Emerald Only

Body Slam*	Substitute	Rock Slide*
Double-Edge	Counter*	Explosion
Mimic		

*Battle Frontier tutor move (*Emerald*)

205 Forretress™

GENERAL INFO

SPECIES: Bagworm Pokémon
HEIGHT: 3'11"
WEIGHT: 277 lbs.
ABILITY: Sturdy
Prevents Forretress from being hit by a one hit KO.

STATS

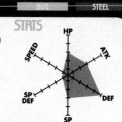

EVOLUTIONS

LV31

LOCATION[s]:

RUBY	Rarity: **None**	Evolve Pineco, Obtain in *Colosseum*
SAPPHIRE	Rarity: **None**	Evolve Pineco, Obtain in *Colosseum*
FIRERED	Rarity: **None**	Trade from *Colosseum*
LEAFGREEN	Rarity: **None**	Trade from *Colosseum*
COLOSSEUM	Rarity: **Only One**	Shadow Pokémon Lab
EMERALD	Rarity: **Evolve**	Evolve Pineco, Trade from *Colosseum*
XD	Rarity: **Evolve**	Evolve Pineco

MOVES

Level	Attack	Type	Power	ACC	PP		Level	Attack	Type	Power	ACC	PP
—	Tackle	Normal	35	95	35		29	Bide	Normal	—	100	10
—	Protect	Normal	—	—	10		31	Zap Cannon	Electric	100	50	5
—	Selfdestruct	Normal	200	100	5		39	Explosion	Normal	250	100	5
15	Take Down	Normal	90	85	20		49	Spikes	Ground	—	—	20
22	Rapid Spin	Normal	20	100	40		59	Double-Edge	Normal	120	100	15

TM/HM

TM/HM#	Name	Type	Power	ACC	PP		TM/HM#	Name	Type	Power	ACC	PP
TM06	Toxic	Poison	—	85	10		TM28	Dig	Ground	60	100	10
TM10	Hidden Power	Normal	—	100	15		TM32	Double Team	Normal	—	—	15
TM11	Sunny Day	Fire	—	—	5		TM33	Reflect	Normal	—	—	20
TM15	Hyper Beam	Normal	150	90	5		TM37	Sandstorm	Ground	—	—	10
TM16	Light Screen	Psychic	—	—	30		TM42	Facade	Normal	70	100	20
TM17	Protect	Normal	—	—	10		TM43	Secret Power	Normal	70	100	20
TM19	Giga Drain	Grass	60	100	5		TM44	Rest	Psychic	—	—	10
TM21	Frustration	Normal	—	100	20		TM45	Attract	Normal	—	100	15
TM22	Solarbeam	Grass	120	100	10		HM04	Strength	Normal	80	100	20
TM26	Earthquake	Ground	100	100	10		HM06	Rock Smash	Fighting	20	100	15
TM27	Return	Normal	—	100	20							

MOVE TUTOR
FireRed/LeafGreen and Emerald Only

Body Slam*	Substitute	Rock Slide*
Double-Edge	Counter*	Explosion
Mimic		

*Battle Frontier tutor move (*Emerald*)

206 Dunsparce™

NORMAL

GENERAL INFO
SPECIES: Land Snake Pokémon
HEIGHT: 4'11"
WEIGHT: 31 lbs.
ABILITY 1: Run Away
Dunsparce can escape from wild Pokémon.
ABILITY 2: Serene Grace
When Dunsparce is in battle, attacks with extra effects have two times the chance of happening.

STATS

HP · ATK · DEF · SP ATK · SP DEF · SPEED

EVOLUTIONS

DOES NOT EVOLVE

LOCATION[s]:

RUBY	Rarity: **None**	Obtain in *Colosseum*
SAPPHIRE	Rarity: **None**	Obtain in *Colosseum*
FIRERED	Rarity: **Common**	Three Island
LEAFGREEN	Rarity: **Common**	Three Island
COLOSSEUM	Rarity: **Only One**	Pyrite Cave
EMERALD	Rarity: **None**	Trade from *FireRed/LeafGreen/Colosseum*
XD	Rarity: **None**	Trade from *FireRed/LeafGreen/Colosseum*

MOVES

Level	Attack	Type	Power	ACC	PP
—	Rage	Normal	20	100	20
4	Defense Curl	Normal	—	—	40
11	Yawn	Normal	—	100	10
14	Glare	Normal	—	75	30
21	Rollout	Rock	30	90	20

Level	Attack	Type	Power	ACC	PP
24	Spite	Ghost	—	100	10
31	Pursuit	Dark	40	100	20
34	Screech	Normal	—	85	40
41	Take Down	Normal	90	85	20
44	Flail	Normal	—	100	15
51	Endeavor	Normal	—	100	5

TM/HM

TM/HM#	Name	Type	Power	ACC	PP
TM03	Water Pulse	Water	60	95	20
TM04	Calm Mind	Psychic	—	—	20
TM06	Toxic	Poison	—	85	10
TM10	Hidden Power	Normal	—	100	15
TM11	Sunny Day	Fire	—	—	5
TM13	Ice Beam	Ice	95	100	10
TM14	Blizzard	Ice	120	70	5
TM17	Protect	Normal	—	—	10
TM18	Rain Dance	Water	—	—	5
TM21	Frustration	Normal	—	100	20
TM22	Solarbeam	Grass	120	100	10
TM23	Iron Tail	Steel	75	75	15
TM24	Thunderbolt	Electric	95	100	15
TM25	Thunder	Electric	120	70	10
TM26	Earthquake	Ground	100	100	10
TM27	Return	Normal	—	100	20

TM/HM#	Name	Type	Power	ACC	PP
TM28	Dig	Ground	60	100	10
TM30	Shadow Ball	Ghost	80	100	15
TM31	Brick Break	Fighting	75	100	15
TM32	Double Team	Normal	—	—	15
TM34	Shock Wave	Electric	60	—	20
TM35	Flamethrower	Fire	95	100	15
TM38	Fire Blast	Fire	120	85	5
TM39	Rock Tomb	Rock	50	80	10
TM42	Facade	Normal	70	100	20
TM43	Secret Power	Normal	70	100	20
TM44	Rest	Psychic	—	—	10
TM45	Attract	Normal	—	100	15
TM46	Thief	Dark	40	100	10
HM04	Strength	Normal	80	100	20
HM06	Rock Smash	Fighting	20	100	15

EGG MOVES*

Name	Type	Power	ACC	PP
Ancientpower	Rock	60	100	5
Astonish	Ghost	30	100	15
Bide	Normal	—	100	10
Bite	Dark	60	100	25
Curse	—	—	—	10
Headbutt	Normal	70	100	15
Rock Slide	Rock	75	90	10

*Learned Via Breeding

MOVE TUTOR
FireRed/LeafGreen and Emerald Only

Body Slam*	Substitute	Dream Eater*
Double-Edge	Counter*	Rock Slide*
Mimic	Thunder Wave*	

*Battle Frontier tutor move (*Emerald*)

207 Gligar™

GROUND | FLYING

GENERAL INFO

SPECIES: Flyscorpion Pokémon
HEIGHT: 3'07"
WEIGHT: 143 lbs.
ABILITY 1: Sand Veil
During a sandstorm, Gligar is able to evade more moves.
ABILITY 2: Hyper Cutter
Prevents Gligar from having its Attack lowered.

STATS

EVOLUTIONS

DOES NOT EVOLVE

LOCATION[s]:

RUBY	Rarity: **None**	Obtain in *Colosseum*
SAPPHIRE	Rarity: **None**	Obtain in *Colosseum*
FIRERED	Rarity: **None**	Trade from *Colosseum*
LEAFGREEN	Rarity: **None**	Trade from *Colosseum*
COLOSSEUM	Rarity: **Only One**	The Under
EMERALD	Rarity: **Rare**	Safari Zone
XD	Rarity: **Rare**	Rock Poké Spot

MOVES

Level	Attack	Type	Power	ACC	PP	Level	Attack	Type	Power	ACC	PP
—	Poison Sting	Poison	15	100	35	28	Faint Attack	Dark	60	—	20
6	Sand Attack	Ground	—	100	15	36	Slash	Normal	70	100	20
13	Harden	Normal	—	—	30	44	Screech	Normal	—	85	40
20	Quick Attack	Normal	40	100	30	52	Guillotine	Normal	—	30	5

TM/HM

TM/HM#	Name	Type	Power	ACC	PP	TM/HM#	Name	Type	Power	ACC	PP
TM06	Toxic	Poison	—	85	10	TM37	Sandstorm	Ground	—	—	10
TM10	Hidden Power	Normal	—	100	15	TM39	Rock Tomb	Rock	50	80	10
TM11	Sunny Day	Fire	—	—	5	TM40	Aerial Ace	Flying	60	—	20
TM17	Protect	Normal	—	—	10	TM42	Facade	Normal	70	100	20
TM18	Rain Dance	Water	—	—	5	TM43	Secret Power	Normal	70	100	20
TM21	Frustration	Normal	—	100	20	TM44	Rest	Psychic	—	—	10
TM23	Iron Tail	Steel	75	75	15	TM45	Attract	Normal	—	100	15
TM26	Earthquake	Ground	100	100	10	TM46	Thief	Dark	40	100	10
TM27	Return	Normal	—	100	20	TM47	Steel Wing	Steel	70	90	25
TM28	Dig	Ground	60	100	10	HM01	Cut	Normal	50	95	30
TM32	Double Team	Normal	—	—	10	HM04	Strength	Normal	80	100	20
TM36	Sludge Bomb	Poison	90	100	1	HM06	Rock Smash	Fighting	20	100	15

EGG MOVES*

Name	Type	Power	ACC	PP
Counter	Fighting	—	100	20
Metal Claw	Steel	50	95	35
Sand Tomb	Ground	15	70	15
Wing Attack	Flying	60	100	35

*Learned Via Breeding

MOVE TUTOR

FireRed/LeafGreen and Emerald Only

Double-Edge	Counter*	Swords Dance*
Mimic	Dream Eater*	
Substitute	Rock Slide*	

*Battle Frontier tutor move (*Emerald*)

208 Steelix™

STEEL | GROUND

GENERAL INFO

SPECIES: Iron Snake Pokémon
HEIGHT: 30'02"
WEIGHT: 882 lbs.
ABILITY 1: Sturdy
Prevents a one hit KO from hitting Steelix.
ABILITY 2: Rock Head
Prevents Steelix from receiving recoil damage.

STATS

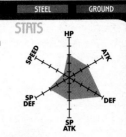

EVOLUTIONS

TRADE WITH METAL COAT

LOCATION(S):

RUBY	Rarity: None	Evolve Onix
SAPPHIRE	Rarity: None	Evolve Onix
FIRERED	Rarity: None	Evolve Onix
LEAFGREEN	Rarity: None	Evolve Onix
COLOSSEUM	Rarity: None	Trade from FireRed/LeafGreen
EMERALD	Rarity: None	Trade from FireRed/LeafGreen
XD	Rarity: None	Trade from FireRed/LeafGreen

MOVES

Level	Attack	Type	Power	ACC	PP	Level	Attack	Type	Power	ACC	PP
—	Tackle	Normal	35	95	35	30	Dragonbreath	Dragon	60	100	20
—	Screech	Normal	—	85	40	34	Sandstorm	Rock	—	—	10
8	Bind	Normal	15	75	20	41	Slam	Normal	80	75	20
12	Rock Throw	Rock	50	90	15	45	Iron Tail	Steel	100	75	15
19	Harden	Normal	—	—	30	52	Crunch	Dark	80	100	15
23	Rage	Normal	20	100	20	56	Double-Edge	Normal	120	100	15

TM/HM

TM/HM#	Name	Type	Power	ACC	PP	TM/HM#	Name	Type	Power	ACC	PP
TM05	Roar	Normal	—	100	20	TM32	Double Team	Normal	—	—	15
TM06	Toxic	Poison	—	85	10	TM37	Sandstorm	Ground	—	—	10
TM10	Hidden Power	Normal	—	100	15	TM39	Rock Tomb	Rock	50	80	10
TM11	Sunny Day	Fire	—	—	5	TM41	Torment	Dark	—	100	15
TM12	Taunt	Dark	—	100	20	TM42	Facade	Normal	70	100	20
TM15	Hyper Beam	Normal	150	90	5	TM43	Secret Power	Normal	70	100	20
TM17	Protect	Normal	—	—	10	TM44	Rest	Psychic	—	—	10
TM21	Frustration	Normal	—	100	20	TM45	Attract	Normal	—	100	15
TM23	Iron Tail	Steel	75	75	15	HM01	Cut	Normal	50	95	30
TM26	Earthquake	Ground	100	100	10	HM04	Strength	Normal	80	100	20
TM27	Return	Normal	—	100	20	HM06	Rock Smash	Fighting	20	100	15
TM28	Dig	Ground	60	100	10						

MOVE TUTOR

FireRed/LeafGreen and Emerald Only

Body Slam*	Explosion	Substitute
Double-Edge	Mimic	Rock Slide*

*Battle Frontier tutor move (*Emerald*)

209 Snubbull™

NORMAL

GENERAL INFO
SPECIES: Fairy Pokémon
HEIGHT: 2'00"
WEIGHT: 17 lbs.
ABILITY 1: Intimidate
When Snubbull is sent into battle, it lowers the opponent's Attack.
ABILITY 2: Run Away
Allows Snubbull to escape from wild Pokémon.

STATS

EVOLUTIONS

 LV23

LOCATION[s]:

RUBY	Rarity: **None**	Obtain in *Colosseum*
SAPPHIRE	Rarity: **None**	Obtain in *Colosseum*
FIRERED	Rarity: **None**	Trade Granbull from *Colosseum*, then Breed
LEAFGREEN	Rarity: **None**	Trade Granbull from *Colosseum*, then Breed
COLOSSEUM	Rarity: **Breed**	Breed Granbull
EMERALD	Rarity: **Rare**	Safari Zone
XD	Rarity: **None**	Obtain in *Colosseum*

MOVES

Level	Attack	Type	Power	ACC	PP	Level	Attack	Type	Power	ACC	PP
—	Tackle	Normal	35	95	35	19	Lick	Ghost	20	100	30
—	Scary Face	Normal	—	90	10	26	Roar	Normal	—	100	20
4	Tail Whip	Normal	—	100	30	34	Rage	Normal	20	100	20
8	Charm	Normal	—	100	20	43	Take Down	Normal	90	85	20
13	Bite	Dark	60	100	25	53	Crunch	Dark	80	100	15

TM/HM

TM/HM#	Name	Type	Power	ACC	PP	TM/HM#	Name	Type	Power	ACC	PP
TM01	Focus Punch	Fighting	150	100	20	TM30	Shadow Ball	Ghost	80	100	15
TM03	Water Pulse	Water	60	95	20	TM31	Brick Break	Fighting	75	100	15
TM05	Roar	Normal	—	100	20	TM32	Double Team	Normal	—	—	10
TM06	Toxic	Poison	—	85	10	TM34	Shock Wave	Electric	60	—	20
TM08	Bulk Up	Fighting	—	—	20	TM35	Flamethrower	Fire	95	100	15
TM10	Hidden Power	Normal	—	100	15	TM36	Sludge Bomb	Poison	90	100	10
TM11	Sunny Day	Fire	—	—	5	TM38	Fire Blast	Fire	120	85	5
TM12	Taunt	Dark	—	100	20	TM41	Torment	Dark	—	100	15
TM17	Protect	Normal	—	—	10	TM42	Facade	Normal	70	100	20
TM18	Rain Dance	Water	—	—	5	TM43	Secret Power	Normal	70	100	20
TM21	Frustration	Normal	—	100	20	TM44	Rest	Psychic	—	—	10
TM22	Solarbeam	Grass	120	100	10	TM45	Attract	Normal	—	100	15
TM24	Thunderbolt	Electric	95	100	15	TM46	Thief	Dark	40	100	10
TM25	Thunder	Electric	120	70	10	TM50	Overheat	Fire	140	90	5
TM26	Earthquake	Ground	100	100	10	HM04	Strength	Normal	80	100	20
TM27	Return	Normal	—	100	20	HM06	Rock Smash	Fighting	20	100	15
TM28	Dig	Ground	60	100	10						

EGG MOVES*

Name	Type	Power	ACC	PP
Crunch	Dark	80	100	15
Faint Attack	Dark	60	—	20
Heal Bell	Normal	—	—	5
Metronome	Normal	—	—	10
Present	Normal	—	90	15
Reflect	Psychic	—	—	20
Smellingsalt	Normal	60	100	10
Snore	Normal	40	100	15

*Learned Via Breeding

MOVE TUTOR
FireRed/LeafGreen and Emerald Only

- Body Slam*
- Double-Edge
- Mega Punch*
- Mega Kick*
- Mimic
- Substitute
- Metronome
- Counter*
- Seismic Toss*
- Thunder Wave*

*Battle Frontier tutor move (*Emerald*)

210 Granbull™

NORMAL

GENERAL INFO

SPECIES: Fairy Pokémon
HEIGHT: 4'07"
WEIGHT: 107 lbs.
ABILITY: Intimidate
When Granbull is sent into battle, it lowers the opponent's Attack.

STATS

HP / ATK / DEF / SP ATK / SP DEF / SPEED

EVOLUTIONS

LV23

LOCATION(S):

RUBY	Rarity: **None**	Evolve Snubbull or Obtain in *Colosseum*
SAPPHIRE	Rarity: **None**	Evolve Snubbull or Obtain in *Colosseum*
FIRERED	Rarity: **None**	Trade from *Colosseum*
LEAFGREEN	Rarity: **None**	Trade from *Colosseum*
COLOSSEUM	Rarity: **Only one**	Shadow Pokémon Lab
EMERALD	Rarity: **Evolve**	Evolve Snubbull, Trade from *Colosseum*
XD	Rarity: **None**	Trade from *Colosseum*

MOVES

Level	Attack	Type	Power	ACC	PP	Level	Attack	Type	Power	ACC	PP
—	Scary Face	Normal	—	90	10	19	Lick	Ghost	20	100	30
—	Tackle	Normal	35	95	35	28	Roar	Normal	—	100	20
4	Tail Whip	Normal	—	100	30	38	Rage	Normal	20	100	20
8	Charm	Normal	—	100	20	49	Take Down	Normal	90	85	20
13	Bite	Dark	60	100	25	61	Crunch	Dark	80	100	15

TM/HM

TM/HM#	Name	Type	Power	ACC	PP	TM/HM#	Name	Type	Power	ACC	PP
TM01	Focus Punch	Fighting	150	100	20	TM28	Dig	Ground	60	100	10
TM03	Water Pulse	Water	60	95	20	TM30	Shadow Ball	Ghost	80	100	15
TM05	Roar	Normal	—	100	20	TM31	Brick Break	Fighting	75	100	15
TM06	Toxic	Poison	—	85	10	TM32	Double Team	Normal	—	—	15
TM08	Bulk Up	Fighting	—	—	20	TM34	Shock Wave	Electric	60	—	20
TM10	Hidden Power	Normal	—	100	15	TM35	Flamethrower	Fire	95	100	15
TM11	Sunny Day	Fire	—	—	5	TM36	Sludge Bomb	Poison	90	100	10
TM12	Taunt	Dark	—	100	20	TM38	Fire Blast	Fire	120	85	5
TM15	Hyper Beam	Normal	150	90	5	TM39	Rock Tomb	Rock	50	80	10
TM17	Protect	Normal	—	—	10	TM41	Torment	Dark	—	100	15
TM18	Rain Dance	Water	—	—	5	TM42	Facade	Normal	70	100	20
TM21	Frustration	Normal	—	100	20	TM43	Secret Power	Normal	70	100	20
TM22	Solarbeam	Grass	120	100	10	TM44	Rest	Psychic	—	—	10
TM23	Iron Tail	Steel	75	75	15	TM45	Attract	Normal	—	100	15
TM24	Thunderbolt	Electric	95	100	15	TM46	Thief	Dark	40	100	10
TM25	Thunder	Electric	120	70	10	TM50	Overheat	Fire	140	90	5
TM26	Earthquake	Ground	100	100	10	HM04	Strength	Normal	80	100	20
TM27	Return	Normal	—	100	20	HM06	Rock Smash	Fighting	20	100	15

MOVE TUTOR

FireRed/LeafGreen and Emerald Only

Body Slam*	Mimic	Seismic Toss*
Double-Edge*	Substitute	Thunder Wave*
Mega Punch*	Metronome	Rock Slide*
Mega Kick*	Counter*	

*Battle Frontier tutor move (*Emerald*)

211 Qwilfish™

WATER   POISON

GENERAL INFO
SPECIES: Balloon Pokémon
HEIGHT: 1'08"
WEIGHT: 9 lbs.
ABILITY 1: Swift Swim
Increases Qwilfish's Speed when it's raining.
ABILITY 2: Poison Point
When Qwilfish is hit directly, the opponent has a 30% chance of being poisoned.

STATS
HP, SPEED, ATK, DEF, SP DEF, SP ATK

EVOLUTIONS

DOES NOT EVOLVE

LOCATION(s):

RUBY	Rarity: **None**	Obtain in *Colosseum*
SAPPHIRE	Rarity: **None**	Obtain in *Colosseum*
FIRERED	Rarity: **Common**	Five Island, Six Island, Seven Island
LEAFGREEN	Rarity: **None**	Trade from *FireRed/Colosseum*
COLOSSEUM	Rarity: **Only One**	Pyrite Town
EMERALD	Rarity: **None**	Trade from *FireRed/Colosseum*
XD	Rarity: **None**	Trade from *FireRed/Colosseum*

MOVES

Level	Attack	Type	Power	ACC	PP
—	Tackle	Normal	35	95	35
—	Poison Sting	Poison	15	100	35
—	Spikes	Ground	—	—	20
9	Harden	Normal	—	—	30
9	Minimize	Normal	—	—	20

Level	Attack	Type	Power	ACC	PP
13	Water Gun	Water	40	100	25
21	Pin Missile	Bug	14	85	20
25	Revenge	Fighting	60	100	10
33	Take Down	Normal	90	85	20
37	Hydro Pump	Water	120	80	5
45	Destiny Bond	Ghost	—	—	5

TM/HM

TM/HM#	Name	Type	Power	ACC	PP
TM03	Water Pulse	Water	60	95	20
TM06	Toxic	Poison	—	85	10
TM07	Hail	Ice	—	—	10
TM10	Hidden Power	Normal	—	100	15
TM13	Ice Beam	Ice	95	100	10
TM14	Blizzard	Ice	120	70	5
TM17	Protect	Normal	—	—	10
TM18	Rain Dance	Water	—	—	5
TM21	Frustration	Normal	—	100	20
TM27	Return	Normal	—	100	20
TM30	Shadow Ball	Ghost	80	100	15

TM/HM#	Name	Type	Power	ACC	PP
TM32	Double Team	Normal	—	—	15
TM34	Shock Wave	Electric	60	—	20
TM36	Sludge Bomb	Poison	90	100	10
TM42	Facade	Normal	70	100	20
TM43	Secret Power	Normal	70	100	20
TM44	Rest	Psychic	—	—	10
TM45	Attract	Normal	—	100	15
HM03	Surf	Water	95	100	15
HM07	Waterfall	Water	80	100	15
HM08	Dive	Water	60	100	10

EGG MOVES*

Name	Type	Power	ACC	PP
Astonish	Ghost	30	100	15
Bubblebeam	Water	65	100	20
Flail	Normal	—	100	15
Haze	Ice	—	—	30
Supersonic	Normal	—	55	20

*Learned Via Breeding

MOVE TUTOR
FireRed/LeafGreen and Emerald Only

Body Slam*	Mimic	Thunder Wave*
Double-Edge	Substitute	Swords Dance*

*Battle Frontier tutor move (*Emerald*)

212 Scizor™

BUG | STEEL

GENERAL INFO

SPECIES: Scissors Pokémon
HEIGHT: 5'11"
WEIGHT: 260 lbs.
ABILITY: Swarm
When Scizor's HPs are low, its Bug-type moves are multiplied by 1.5.

STATS

EVOLUTIONS

TRADE WITH METAL COAT

LOCATION(S):

RUBY	Rarity: **None**	Trade from *FireRed*
SAPPHIRE	Rarity: **None**	Trade from *FireRed*
FIRERED	Rarity: **None**	Evolve Scyther
LEAFGREEN	Rarity: **None**	Trade from *FireRed*
COLOSSEUM	Rarity: **None**	Trade from *FireRed*
EMERALD	Rarity: **None**	Trade from *FireRed*
XD	Rarity: **None**	Trade from *FireRed*

MOVES

Level	Attack	Type	Power	ACC	PP
—	Quick Attack	Normal	40	100	30
—	Leer	Normal	—	100	30
6	Focus Energy	Normal	—	—	30
11	Pursuit	Dark	40	100	20
16	False Swipe	Normal	40	100	40

Level	Attack	Type	Power	ACC	PP
21	Agility	Psychic	—	—	30
26	Metal Claw	Steel	50	95	35
31	Slash	Normal	70	100	20
36	Swords Dance	Normal	—	—	30
41	Iron Defense	Steel	—	—	15
46	Fury Cutter	Bug	10	95	20

TM/HM

TM/HM#	Name	Type	Power	ACC	PP
TM06	Toxic	Poison	—	85	10
TM10	Hidden Power	Normal	—	100	15
TM11	Sunny Day	Fire	—	—	5
TM15	Hyper Beam	Normal	150	90	5
TM17	Protect	Normal	—	—	10
TM18	Rain Dance	Water	—	—	5
TM21	Frustration	Normal	—	100	20
TM27	Return	Normal	—	100	20
TM32	Double Team	Normal	—	—	15
TM37	Sandstorm	Ground	—	—	10

TM/HM#	Name	Type	Power	ACC	PP
TM40	Aerial Ace	Flying	60	—	20
TM42	Facade	Normal	70	100	20
TM43	Secret Power	Normal	70	100	20
TM44	Rest	Psychic	—	—	10
TM45	Attract	Normal	—	100	15
TM46	Thief	Dark	40	100	10
TM47	Steel Wing	Steel	70	90	25
HM01	Cut	Normal	50	95	30
HM04	Strength	Normal	80	100	20
HM06	Rock Smash	Fighting	20	100	15

MOVE TUTOR
FireRed/LeafGreen and Emerald Only

Double-Edge	Substitute	Counter*
Mimic	Swords Dance*	

*Battle Frontier tutor move (*Emerald*)

213 Shuckle™

BUG ROCK

GENERAL INFO

SPECIES: Mold Pokémon
HEIGHT: 2'00"
WEIGHT: 45 lbs.
ABILITY: Sturdy
Prevents Shuckle from being hit by a one hit KO.

STATS

EVOLUTIONS

DOES NOT EVOLVE

LOCATION(s):

RUBY	Rarity: **None**	Obtain in *Colosseum*
SAPPHIRE	Rarity: **None**	Obtain in *Colosseum*
FIRERED	Rarity: **None**	Trade from *Colosseum*
LEAFGREEN	Rarity: **None**	Trade from *Colosseum*
COLOSSEUM	Rarity: **Only One**	The Under
EMERALD	Rarity: **Common**	Safari Zone
XD	Rarity: **None**	Trade from *Colosseum*

MOVES

Level	Attack	Type	Power	ACC	PP		Level	Attack	Type	Power	ACC	PP
—	Constrict	Normal	10	100	35		14	Encore	Normal	—	100	5
—	Withdraw	Normal	—	—	40		23	Safeguard	Normal	—	—	25
9	Wrap	Normal	15	85	20		28	Bide	Normal	—	100	10
							37	Rest	Psychic	—	—	10

TM/HM

TM/HM#	Name	Type	Power	ACC	PP		TM/HM#	Name	Type	Power	ACC	PP
TM06	Toxic	Poison	—	85	10		TM36	Sludge Bomb	Poison	90	100	10
TM10	Hidden Power	Normal	—	100	15		TM37	Sandstorm	Ground	—	—	10
TM11	Sunny Day	Fire	—	—	5		TM39	Rock Tomb	Rock	50	80	10
TM17	Protect	Normal	—	—	10		TM42	Facade	Normal	70	100	20
TM20	Safeguard	Normal	—	—	25		TM43	Secret Power	Normal	70	100	20
TM21	Frustration	Normal	—	100	20		TM44	Rest	Psychic	—	—	10
TM26	Earthquake	Ground	100	100	10		TM45	Attract	Normal	—	100	15
TM27	Return	Normal	—	100	20		HM04	Strength	Normal	80	100	15
TM28	Dig	Ground	60	100	10		HM05	Flash	Normal	—	70	20
TM32	Double Team	Normal	—	—	15		HM06	Rock Smash	Fighting	20	100	15

EGG MOVES*

Name	Type	Power	ACC	PP
Sweet Scent	Normal	—	100	2

*Learned Via Breeding

MOVE TUTOR

FireRed/LeafGreen and Emerald Only

Body Slam*	Mimic	Substitute
Double-Edge	Rock Slide*	

*Battle Frontier tutor move (*Emerald*)

214 Heracross™

BUG | **FIGHTING**

GENERAL INFO

SPECIES: Single Horn Pokémon
HEIGHT: 4'11"
WEIGHT: 119 lbs
ABILITY 1: Swarm
When Heracross's HPs are low, its Bug-type moves are multiplied by 1.5.
ABILITY 2: Guts
When Heracross has a status condition, its attack power is multiplied by 1.5.

STATS

HP · ATK · DEF · SP ATK · SP DEF · SPEED

EVOLUTIONS

DOES NOT EVOLVE

LOCATION(s):

RUBY	Rarity: **Rare**	Safari Zone
SAPPHIRE	Rarity: **Rare**	Safari Zone
FIRERED	Rarity: **Rare**	Six Island
LEAFGREEN	Rarity: **Rare**	Six Island
COLOSSEUM	Rarity: **Only one**	Realgam Tower
EMERALD	Rarity: **Rare**	Safari Zone
XD	Rarity: **None**	Trade from *Ruby/Sapphire/FireRed/LeafGreen/Colosseum*

MOVES

Level	Attack	Type	Power	ACC	PP
—	Tackle	Normal	35	95	35
—	Leer	Normal	—	100	30
6	Horn Attack	Normal	65	100	25
11	Endure	Normal	—	—	10
17	Fury Attack	Normal	15	85	20

Level	Attack	Type	Power	ACC	PP
23	Brick Break	Fighting	75	100	15
30	Counter	Fighting	—	100	20
37	Take Down	Normal	90	85	20
45	Reversal	Fighting	—	100	15
53	Megahorn	Bug	120	85	10

TM/HM

TM/HM#	Name	Type	Power	ACC	PP
TM01	Focus Punch	Fighting	150	100	20
TM06	Toxic	Poison	—	85	10
TM08	Bulk Up	Fighting	—	—	20
TM10	Hidden Power	Normal	—	100	15
TM11	Sunny Day	Fire	—	—	5
TM15	Hyper Beam	Normal	150	90	5
TM17	Protect	Normal	—	—	10
TM18	Rain Dance	Water	—	—	5
TM21	Frustration	Normal	—	100	20
TM26	Earthquake	Ground	100	100	10
TM27	Return	Normal	—	100	20
TM28	Dig	Ground	60	100	10

TM/HM#	Name	Type	Power	ACC	PP
TM31	Brick Break	Fighting	75	100	15
TM32	Double Team	Normal	—	—	15
TM39	Rock Tomb	Rock	50	80	10
TM42	Facade	Normal	70	100	20
TM43	Secret Power	Normal	70	100	20
TM44	Rest	Psychic	—	—	10
TM45	Attract	Normal	—	100	15
TM46	Thief	Dark	40	100	10
HM01	Cut	Normal	50	95	30
HM04	Strength	Normal	80	100	20
HM06	Rock Smash	Fighting	20	100	15

EGG MOVES*

Name	Type	Power	ACC	PP
Harden	Normal	—	—	30
False Swipe	Normal	40	100	40
Bide	Normal	15	75	20
Flail	Normal	—	100	15

*Learned Via Breeding

MOVE TUTOR

FireRed/LeafGreen and Emerald Only

Body Slam*	Substitute	Rock Slide*
Double-Edge	Counter*	Swords Dance*
Mimic	Seismic Toss*	

Emerald Only

Endure*	Sleep Talk	Swagger
Mud-Slap*	Snore*	Swift*

*Battle Frontier tutor move (*Emerald*)

PRIMA OFFICIAL GAME GUIDE

215 Sneasel™

DARK   ICE

GENERAL INFO

SPECIES: Sharp Claw Pokémon
HEIGHT: 2'11"
WEIGHT: 62 lbs.
ABILITY 1: Inner Focus
Prevents Sneasel from flinching.
ABILITY 2: Keen Eye
Prevents Sneasel from having its Accuracy lowered.

STATS

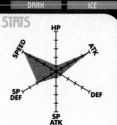

EVOLUTIONS

DOES NOT EVOLVE

LOCATION(s):

RUBY	Rarity: **None**	Obtain in *Colosseum*
SAPPHIRE	Rarity: **None**	Obtain in *Colosseum*
FIRERED	Rarity: **None**	Trade from *LeafGreen/Colosseum*
LEAFGREEN	Rarity: **Rare**	Four Island
COLOSSEUM	Rarity: **Only One**	The Under
EMERALD	Rarity: **None**	Trade from *LeafGreen/Colosseum*
XD	Rarity: **None**	Trade from *LeafGreen/Colosseum*

MOVES

Level	Attack	Type	Power	ACC	PP	Level	Attack	Type	Power	ACC	PP
—	Scratch	Normal	40	100	35	29	Fury Swipes	Normal	18	80	15
—	Leer	Normal	—	100	30	36	Agility	Psychic	—	—	30
—	Taunt	Dark	—	100	20	43	Icy Wind	Ice	55	95	15
8	Quick Attack	Normal	40	100	30	50	Slash	Normal	70	100	20
15	Screech	Normal	—	85	40	57	Beat Up	Dark	10	100	10
22	Faint Attack	Dark	60	—	20	64	Metal Claw	Steel	50	95	35

TM/HM

TM/HM#	Name	Type	Power	ACC	PP	TM/HM#	Name	Type	Power	ACC	PP
TM01	Focus Punch	Fighting	150	100	20	TM30	Shadow Ball	Ghost	80	100	15
TM04	Calm Mind	Psychic	—	—	20	TM31	Brick Break	Fighting	75	100	15
TM06	Toxic	Poison	—	85	10	TM32	Double Team	Normal	—	—	15
TM07	Hail	Ice	—	—	10	TM40	Aerial Ace	Flying	60	—	20
TM10	Hidden Power	Normal	—	100	15	TM41	Torment	Dark	—	100	15
TM11	Sunny Day	Fire	—	—	5	TM42	Facade	Normal	70	100	20
TM12	Taunt	Dark	—	100	20	TM43	Secret Power	Normal	70	100	20
TM13	Ice Beam	Ice	95	100	10	TM44	Rest	Psychic	—	—	10
TM14	Blizzard	Ice	120	70	5	TM45	Attract	Normal	—	100	15
TM17	Protect	Normal	—	—	10	TM46	Thief	Dark	40	100	10
TM18	Rain Dance	Water	—	—	5	TM49	Snatch	Dark	—	100	10
TM21	Frustration	Normal	—	100	20	HM01	Cut	Normal	50	95	30
TM23	Iron Tail	Steel	75	75	15	HM03	Surf	Water	95	100	15
TM27	Return	Normal	—	100	20	HM04	Strength	Normal	80	100	20
TM28	Dig	Ground	60	100	10	HM06	Rock Smash	Fighting	20	100	15

EGG MOVES*

Name	Type	Power	ACC	PP
Bite	Dark	60	100	25
Counter	Fighting	—	100	20
Crush Claw	Normal	75	95	10
Fake Out	Normal	40	100	10
Foresight	Normal	—	100	40
Reflect	Psychic	—	—	20
Spite	Ghost	—	100	10

*Learned Via Breeding

MOVE TUTOR

FireRed/LeafGreen and Emerald Only

Double-Edge	Substitute	Dream Eater*
Mimic	Counter*	Swords Dance*

*Battle Frontier tutor move (*Emerald*)

216 Teddiursa™

GENERAL INFO

SPECIES: Little Bear Pokémon
HEIGHT: 2'00"
WEIGHT: 19 lbs.
ABILITY: Pickup
Allows Teddiursa to take items from an opponent.

STATS

EVOLUTIONS

LV30

LOCATION(s):

RUBY	Rarity: **None**	Obtain in *Colosseum*
SAPPHIRE	Rarity: **None**	Obtain in *Colosseum*
FIRERED	Rarity: **None**	Trade Ursaring from *Colosseum* then breed
LEAFGREEN	Rarity: **None**	Trade Ursaring from *Colosseum* then breed
COLOSSEUM	Rarity: **Breed**	Breed in *Ruby/Sapphire/FireRed/LeafGreen* then trade back
EMERALD	Rarity: **Common**	Safari Zone
XD	Rarity: **Only One**	Pokémon HQ (Capture from Cipher Peon Naps)

MOVES

Level	Attack	Type	Power	ACC	PP	Level	Attack	Type	Power	ACC	PP
—	Scratch	Normal	40	100	35	25	Faint Attack	Dark	60	—	20
—	Leer	Normal	—	100	30	31	Rest	Psychic	—	—	10
7	Lick	Ghost	20	100	30	37	Slash	Normal	70	100	20
13	Fury Swipes	Normal	18	80	15	43	Snore	Normal	40	100	15
19	Fake Tears	Dark	—	100	20	49	Thrash	Normal	90	100	20

TM/HM

TM/HM#	Name	Type	Power	ACC	PP	TM/HM#	Name	Type	Power	ACC	PP
TM01	Focus Punch	Fighting	150	100	20	TM31	Brick Break	Fighting	75	100	15
TM05	Roar	Normal	—	100	20	TM32	Double Team	Normal	—	—	15
TM06	Toxic	Poison	—	85	10	TM40	Aerial Ace	Flying	60	—	20
TM08	Bulk Up	Fighting	—	—	20	TM41	Torment	Dark	—	100	15
TM10	Hidden Power	Normal	—	100	15	TM42	Facade	Normal	70	100	20
TM11	Sunny Day	Fire	—	—	5	TM43	Secret Power	Normal	70	100	20
TM12	Taunt	Dark	—	100	20	TM44	Rest	Psychic	—	—	10
TM17	Protect	Normal	—	—	10	TM45	Attract	Normal	—	100	15
TM18	Rain Dance	Water	—	—	5	TM46	Thief	Dark	40	100	10
TM21	Frustration	Normal	—	100	20	HM01	Cut	Normal	50	95	30
TM26	Earthquake	Ground	100	100	10	HM04	Strength	Normal	80	100	20
TM27	Return	Normal	—	100	20	HM06	Rock Smash	Fighting	20	100	15
TM28	Dig	Ground	60	100	10						

EGG MOVES*

Name	Type	Power	ACC	PP
Counter	Fighting	—	100	20
Crunch	Dark	80	100	15
Fake Tears	Dark	—	100	20
Metal Claw	Steel	50	95	35
Seismic Toss	Fighting	—	100	20
Sleep Talk	Normal	—	—	10
Take Down	Normal	90	85	20
Yawn	Normal	—	100	10

*Learned Via Breeding

MOVE TUTOR
FireRed/LeafGreen and Emerald Only

Body Slam*	Mimic	Seismic Toss*
Double-Edge*	Substitute	Swords Dance*
Mega Punch*	Metronome	
Mega Kick*	Counter*	

*Battle Frontier tutor move (*Emerald*)

217 Ursaring™

NORMAL

GENERAL INFO

SPECIES: Hibernator Pokémon
HEIGHT: 5'11"
WEIGHT: 277 lbs.
ABILITY: Guts

When Ursaring has a status condition, its attack power is multiplied by 1.5.

STATS

EVOLUTIONS

LV30

LOCATION(s):

RUBY	Rarity: **None**	Trade from *Colosseum/Emerald*
SAPPHIRE	Rarity: **None**	Trade from *Colosseum/Emerald*
FIRERED	Rarity: **None**	Trade from *Colosseum/Emerald*
LEAFGREEN	Rarity: **None**	Trade from *Colosseum/Emerald*
COLOSSEUM	Rarity: **Only One**	Snagem Hideout
EMERALD	Rarity: **Evolve**	Evolve Teddiursa
XD	Rarity: **Evolve**	Evolve Teddiursa

MOVES

Level	Attack	Type	Power	ACC	PP	Level	Attack	Type	Power	ACC	PP
—	Scratch	Normal	40	100	35	25	Faint Attack	Dark	60	—	20
—	Leer	Normal	—	100	30	31	Rest	Psychic	—	—	10
—	Lick	Ghost	20	100	30	37	Slash	Normal	70	100	20
—	Fury Swipes	Normal	18	80	15	43	Snore	Normal	40	100	15
19	Fake Tears	Dark	—	100	20	49	Thrash	Normal	90	100	20

TM/HM

TM/HM#	Name	Type	Power	ACC	PP	TM/HM#	Name	Type	Power	ACC	PP
TM01	Focus Punch	Fighting	150	100	20	TM31	Brick Break	Fighting	75	100	15
TM05	Roar	Normal	—	100	20	TM32	Double Team	Normal	—	—	15
TM06	Toxic	Poison	—	85	10	TM39	Rock Tomb	Rock	50	80	10
TM08	Bulk Up	Fighting	—	—	20	TM40	Aerial Ace	Flying	60	—	20
TM10	Hidden Power	Normal	—	100	15	TM41	Torment	Dark	—	100	15
TM11	Sunny Day	Fire	—	—	5	TM42	Facade	Normal	70	100	20
TM12	Taunt	Dark	—	100	20	TM43	Secret Power	Normal	70	100	20
TM15	Hyper Beam	Normal	150	90	5	TM44	Rest	Psychic	—	—	10
TM17	Protect	Normal	—	—	10	TM45	Attract	Normal	—	100	15
TM18	Rain Dance	Water	—	—	5	TM46	Thief	Dark	40	100	10
TM21	Frustration	Normal	—	100	20	HM01	Cut	Normal	50	95	30
TM26	Earthquake	Ground	100	100	10	HM04	Strength	Normal	80	100	20
TM27	Return	Normal	—	100	20	HM06	Rock Smash	Fighting	20	100	15
TM28	Dig	Ground	60	100	10						

MOVE TUTOR

FireRed/LeafGreen and Emerald Only

Body Slam*	Mimic	Seismic Toss*
Double-Edge	Substitute	Swords Dance*
Mega Punch*	Metronome	Rock Slide*
Mega Kick*	Counter*	

*Battle Frontier tutor move (*Emerald*)

218 Slugma™

FIRE

GENERAL INFO

SPECIES: Lava Pokémon
HEIGHT: 2'04"
WEIGHT: 77 lbs.
ABILITY 1: Magma Armor
Slugma cannot be frozen.
ABILITY 2: Flame Body
An opponent has a 30% chance of being burned if it attacks Slugma.

STATS

HP · ATK · DEF · SP ATK · SP DEF · SPEED

EVOLUTIONS

 ▶

LV38

LOCATION[s]:

RUBY	Rarity: **Common**	Fiery Path
SAPPHIRE	Rarity: **Common**	Fiery Path
FIRERED	Rarity: **Common**	One Island
LEAFGREEN	Rarity: **Common**	One Island
COLOSSEUM	Rarity: **Only One**	Pyrite Town
EMERALD	Rarity: **Common**	Route 113, Fiery Path
XD	Rarity: **None**	Trade from *Ruby/Sapphire/FireRed/LeafGreen/Colosseum*

MOVES

Level	Attack	Type	Power	ACC	PP
—	Yawn	Normal	—	100	10
—	Smog	Poison	20	70	20
8	Ember	Fire	40	100	25
15	Rock Throw	Rock	50	90	15

Level	Attack	Type	Power	ACC	PP
22	Harden	Normal	—	—	30
29	Amnesia	Psychic	—	—	20
36	Flamethrower	Fire	95	100	15
43	Rock Slide	Rock	75	90	10
50	Body Slam	Normal	85	100	15

TM/HM

TM/HM#	Name	Type	Power	ACC	PP
TM06	Toxic	Poison	—	85	10
TM10	Hidden Power	Normal	—	100	15
TM11	Sunny Day	Fire	—	—	5
TM16	Light Screen	Psychic	—	—	30
TM17	Protect	Normal	—	—	10
TM21	Frustration	Normal	—	100	20
TM27	Return	Normal	—	100	20
TM32	Double Team	Normal	—	—	15
TM33	Reflect	Normal	—	—	20

TM/HM#	Name	Type	Power	ACC	PP
TM35	Flamethrower	Fire	95	100	15
TM38	Fire Blast	Fire	120	85	5
TM42	Facade	Normal	70	100	20
TM43	Secret Power	Normal	70	100	20
TM44	Rest	Psychic	—	—	10
TM45	Attract	Normal	—	100	15
TM50	Overheat	Fire	140	90	5
HM06	Rock Smash	Fighting	20	100	15

EGG MOVES*

Name	Type	Power	ACC	PP
Acid Armor	Poison	—	—	4

*Learned Via Breeding

MOVE TUTOR

FireRed/LeafGreen and Emerald Only

Body Slam*	Mimic	Rock Slide*
Double-Edge	Substitute	

Emerald Only

Defense Curl*	Rollout	Swagger
Endure*	Sleep Talk	
Mud-Slap*	Snore*	

*Battle Frontier tutor move (*Emerald*)

219 Magcargo™

FIRE   ROCK

GENERAL INFO

SPECIES: Lava Pokémon
HEIGHT: 2'07"
WEIGHT: 121 lbs.
ABILITY 1: Magma Armor
Magcargo cannot be frozen.
ABILITY 2: Flame Body
An opponent has a 30% chance of being burned if it attacks Magcargo.

STATS

EVOLUTIONS

LV38

LOCATION[s]:

RUBY	Rarity: **None**	Evolve Slugma
SAPPHIRE	Rarity: **None**	Evolve Slugma
FIRERED	Rarity: **None**	Evolve Slugma, One Island
LEAFGREEN	Rarity: **None**	Evolve Slugma, One Island
COLOSSEUM	Rarity: **None**	Evolve Slugma
EMERALD	Rarity: **Evolve**	Evolve Slugma
XD	Rarity: **Only One**	Citadark Island (Capture from Cipher Peon Kolest)

MOVES

Level	Attack	Type	Power	ACC	PP	Level	Attack	Type	Power	ACC	PP
—	Yawn	Normal	—	100	10	22	Harden	Normal	—	—	30
—	Smog	Poison	20	70	20	29	Amnesia	Psychic	—	—	20
—	Ember	Fire	40	100	25	36	Flamethrower	Fire	95	100	15
—	Rock Throw	Rock	50	90	15	48	Rock Slide	Rock	75	90	10
						60	Body Slam	Normal	85	100	15

TM/HM

TM/HM#	Name	Type	Power	ACC	PP	TM/HM#	Name	Type	Power	ACC	PP
TM06	Toxic	Poison	—	85	10	TM35	Flamethrower	Fire	95	100	15
TM10	Hidden Power	Normal	—	100	15	TM37	Sandstorm	Ground	—	—	10
TM11	Sunny Day	Fire	—	—	5	TM38	Fire Blast	Fire	120	85	5
TM15	Hyper Beam	Normal	150	90	5	TM39	Rock Tomb	Rock	50	80	10
TM16	Light Screen	Psychic	—	—	30	TM42	Facade	Normal	70	100	20
TM17	Protect	Normal	—	—	10	TM43	Secret Power	Normal	70	100	20
TM21	Frustration	Normal	—	100	20	TM44	Rest	Psychic	—	—	10
TM26	Earthquake	Ground	100	100	10	TM45	Attract	Normal	—	100	15
TM27	Return	Normal	—	100	20	TM50	Overheat	Fire	140	90	5
TM32	Double Team	Normal	—	—	15	HM04	Strength	Normal	80	100	20
TM33	Reflect	Normal	—	—	20	HM06	Rock Smash	Fighting	20	100	15

MOVE TUTOR
FireRed/LeafGreen and Emerald Only

Body Slam*	Mimic	Rock Slide*
Double-Edge	Substitute	

Emerald Only

Defense Curl*	Rollout	Swagger
Endure*	Sleep Talk	
Mud-Slap*	Snore*	

*Battle Frontier tutor move (*Emerald*)

220 Swinub™

ICE | GROUND

GENERAL INFO
SPECIES: Pig Pokémon
HEIGHT: 1'04"
WEIGHT: 14 lbs.
ABILITY: Oblivious
Prevents Swinub from being attracted.

STATS

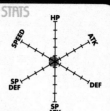

EVOLUTIONS

LV33

LOCATION[s]:

RUBY	Rarity: **None**	Trade from *FireRed/LeafGreen*
SAPPHIRE	Rarity: **None**	Trade from *FireRed/LeafGreen*
FIRERED	Rarity: **None**	Four Island
LEAFGREEN	Rarity: **None**	Four Island
COLOSSEUM	Rarity: **None**	Trade from *FireRed/LeafGreen*
EMERALD	Rarity: **None**	Trade from *FireRed/LeafGreen*
XD	Rarity: **Only One**	Phenac City (Capture from Cipher Peon Greck)

MOVES

Level	Attack	Type	Power	ACC	PP
—	Tackle	Normal	35	95	35
—	Odor Sleuth	Normal	—	100	40
10	Powder Snow	Ice	40	100	25
19	Endure	Normal	—	—	10

Level	Attack	Type	Power	ACC	PP
28	Take Down	Normal	90	85	20
37	Mist	Ice	—	—	30
46	Blizzard	Ice	120	70	5
55	Amnesia	Psychic	—	—	20

TM/HM

TM/HM#	Name	Type	Power	ACC	PP
TM05	Roar	Normal	—	100	20
TM06	Toxic	Poison	—	85	10
TM07	Hail	Ice	—	—	10
TM10	Hidden Power	Normal	—	100	15
TM13	Ice Beam	Ice	95	100	10
TM14	Blizzard	Ice	120	70	5
TM16	Light Screen	Psychic	—	—	30
TM17	Protect	Normal	—	—	10
TM18	Rain Dance	Water	—	—	5
TM21	Frustration	Normal	—	100	20
TM26	Earthquake	Ground	100	100	10
TM27	Return	Normal	—	100	20

TM/HM#	Name	Type	Power	ACC	PP
TM28	Dig	Ground	60	100	10
TM32	Double Team	Normal	—	—	15
TM33	Reflect	Normal	—	—	20
TM37	Sandstorm	Ground	—	—	10
TM39	Rock Tomb	Rock	50	80	10
TM42	Facade	Normal	70	100	20
TM43	Secret Power	Normal	70	100	20
TM44	Rest	Psychic	—	—	10
TM45	Attract	Normal	—	100	15
HM04	Strength	Normal	80	100	20
HM06	Rock Smash	Fighting	20	100	15

EGG MOVES*

Name	Type	Power	ACC	PP
Ancientpower	Rock	60	100	5
Bite	Dark	60	100	25
Body Slam	Normal	85	100	15
Double-Edge	Normal	120	100	15
Icicle Spear	Ice	15	100	30
Mud Shot	Ground	55	95	15
Rock Slide	Rock	75	90	10
Take Down	Normal	90	85	20

*Learned Via Breeding

MOVE TUTOR
FireRed/LeafGreen and Emerald Only

Body Slam*	Mimic	Substitute
Double-Edge	Rock Slide*	

*Battle Frontier tutor move (*Emerald*)

221 Piloswine™

ICE   GROUND

GENERAL INFO

SPECIES: Swine Pokémon
HEIGHT: 3'07"
WEIGHT: 123 lbs.
ABILITY: Oblivious
Prevents Piloswine from being attracted.

STATS

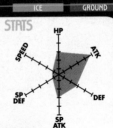

EVOLUTIONS

LV33

LOCATION[s]:

RUBY	Rarity: **None**	Trade from *FireRed/LeafGreen/Colosseum*
SAPPHIRE	Rarity: **None**	Trade from *FireRed/LeafGreen/Colosseum*
FIRERED	Rarity: **None**	Evolve Swinub
LEAFGREEN	Rarity: **None**	Evolve Swinub
COLOSSEUM	Rarity: **Only One**	Snatched from Bodybuilder Lonia in The Under
EMERALD	Rarity: **None**	Trade from *FireRed/LeafGreen/Colosseum*
XD	Rarity: **Evolve**	Evolve Swinub

MOVES

Level	Attack	Type	Power	ACC	PP	Level	Attack	Type	Power	ACC	PP
—	Horn Attack	Normal	65	100	25	28	Take Down	Normal	90	85	20
—	Odor Sleuth	Normal	—	100	40	33	Fury Attack	Normal	15	85	20
—	Powder Snow	Ice	40	100	25	42	Mist	Ice	—	—	30
—	Endure	Normal	—	—	10	56	Blizzard	Ice	120	70	5
						70	Amnesia	Psychic	—	—	20

TM/HM

TM/HM#	Name	Type	Power	ACC	PP	TM/HM#	Name	Type	Power	ACC	PP
TM05	Roar	Normal	—	100	20	TM27	Return	Normal	—	100	20
TM06	Toxic	Poison	—	85	10	TM28	Dig	Ground	60	100	10
TM07	Hail	Ice	—	—	10	TM32	Double Team	Normal	—	—	15
TM10	Hidden Power	Normal	—	100	15	TM33	Reflect	Normal	—	—	20
TM13	Ice Beam	Ice	95	100	10	TM37	Sandstorm	Ground	—	—	10
TM14	Blizzard	Ice	120	70	5	TM39	Rock Tomb	Rock	50	80	10
TM15	Hyper Beam	Normal	150	90	5	TM42	Facade	Normal	70	100	20
TM16	Light Screen	Psychic	—	—	30	TM43	Secret Power	Normal	70	100	20
TM17	Protect	Normal	—	—	10	TM44	Rest	Psychic	—	—	10
TM18	Rain Dance	Water	—	—	5	TM45	Attract	Normal	—	100	15
TM21	Frustration	Normal	—	100	20	HM04	Strength	Normal	80	100	20
TM26	Earthquake	Ground	100	100	10	HM06	Rock Smash	Fighting	20	100	15

MOVE TUTOR

FireRed/LeafGreen and Emerald Only

Body Slam*	Mimic	Substitute
Double-Edge*	Rock Slide*	

*Battle Frontier tutor move (*Emerald*)

222 Corsola™

WATER | ROCK

GENERAL INFO
SPECIES: Coral Pokémon
HEIGHT: 2'00"
WEIGHT: 11 lbs.
ABILITY 1: Hustle
Multiplies Corsola's attack power by 1.5, but lowers its Accuracy to 80%.
ABILITY 2: Natural Cure
Any status condition Corsola may have is cured when Corsola is switched out.

STATS

EVOLUTIONS

DOES NOT EVOLVE

LOCATION[s]:

RUBY	Rarity: **Common**	Ever Grande City, Pacifidlog Town
SAPPHIRE	Rarity: **Common**	Ever Grande City, Pacifidlog Town
FIRERED	Rarity: **None**	Trade from *Ruby/Sapphire*
LEAFGREEN	Rarity: **None**	Trade from *Ruby/Sapphire*
COLOSSEUM	Rarity: **None**	Trade from *Ruby/Sapphire*
EMERALD	Rarity: **Common**	Route 128, Ever Grande City
XD	Rarity: **None**	Trade from *Ruby/Sapphire/Emerald*

MOVES

Level	Attack	Type	Power	ACC	PP
—	Tackle	Normal	35	95	35
6	Harden	Normal	—	—	30
12	Bubble	Water	20	100	30
17	Recover	Normal	—	—	20
17	Refresh	Normal	—	100	20

Level	Attack	Type	Power	ACC	PP
23	Bubblebeam	Water	65	100	20
28	Spike Cannon	Normal	20	100	15
34	Rock Blast	Rock	25	80	10
39	Mirror Coat	Psychic	—	100	20
45	Ancientpower	Rock	60	100	5

TM/HM

TM/HM#	Name	Type	Power	ACC	PP
TM03	Water Pulse	Water	60	95	20
TM04	Calm Mind	Psychic	—	—	20
TM06	Toxic	Poison	—	85	10
TM07	Hail	Ice	—	—	10
TM10	Hidden Power	Normal	—	100	15
TM11	Sunny Day	Fire	—	—	5
TM13	Ice Beam	Ice	95	100	10
TM14	Blizzard	Ice	120	70	5
TM16	Light Screen	Psychic	—	—	30
TM17	Protect	Normal	—	—	10
TM18	Rain Dance	Water	—	—	5
TM20	Safeguard	Normal	—	—	25
TM21	Frustration	Normal	—	100	20
TM26	Earthquake	Ground	100	100	10
TM27	Return	Normal	—	100	20

TM/HM#	Name	Type	Power	ACC	PP
TM28	Dig	Ground	60	100	10
TM29	Psychic	Psychic	90	100	10
TM30	Shadow Ball	Ghost	80	100	15
TM32	Double Team	Normal	—	—	15
TM33	Reflect	Normal	—	—	20
TM37	Sandstorm	Normal	—	—	10
TM39	Rock Tomb	Rock	50	80	10
TM42	Facade	Normal	70	100	20
TM43	Secret Power	Normal	70	100	20
TM44	Rest	Psychic	—	—	10
TM45	Attract	Normal	—	100	15
HM03	Surf	Water	95	100	15
HM04	Strength	Normal	80	100	20
HM06	Rock Smash	Fighting	20	100	15

EGG MOVES*

Name	Type	Power	ACC	PP
Amnesia	Psychic	—	—	20
Rock Slide	Rock	75	90	10
Screech	Normal	—	85	40
Mist	Ice	—	—	30
Barrier	Psychic	—	—	30
Ingrain	Grass	—	100	20
Confuse Ray	Ghost	—	100	10
Icicle Spear	Ice	10	100	30

*Learned Via Breeding

MOVE TUTOR
FireRed/LeafGreen and Emerald Only

Body Slam*	Mimic	Rock Slide*
Double-Edge	Substitute	Explosion

Emerald Only

Defense Curl*	Rollout	Snore*
Endure*	Sleep Talk	Swagger
Mud-Slap*		

*Battle Frontier tutor move (*Emerald*)

PRIMA OFFICIAL GAME GUIDE

223 Remoraid™

WATER

GENERAL INFO
SPECIES: Jet Pokémon
HEIGHT: 2'00"
WEIGHT: 26 lbs.
ABILITY: Hustle

Multiplies Remoraid's attacks by 1.5, but lowers its Accuracy to 80%.

STATS

EVOLUTIONS

LV25

LOCATION[S]:

RUBY	Rarity: **None**	Obtain in *Colosseum*
SAPPHIRE	Rarity: **None**	Obtain in *Colosseum*
FIRERED	Rarity: **None**	Trade from *LeafGreen/Colosseum*
LEAFGREEN	Rarity: **Common**	Five Island
COLOSSEUM	Rarity: **Only One**	Pyrite Town
EMERALD	Rarity: **Common**	Safari Zone
XD	Rarity: **None**	Trade from *LeafGreen/Colosseum*

MOVES

Level	Attack	Type	Power	ACC	PP	Level	Attack	Type	Power	ACC	PP
—	Water Gun	Water	40	100	25	22	Bubblebeam	Water	65	100	20
11	Lock-on	Normal	—	100	5	33	Focus Energy	Normal	—	—	30
22	Psybeam	Psychic	65	100	20	44	Ice Beam	Ice	95	100	10
22	Aurora Beam	Ice	65	100	20	55	Hyper Beam	Normal	150	90	5

TM/HM

TM/HM#	Name	Type	Power	ACC	PP	TM/HM#	Name	Type	Power	ACC	PP
TM03	Water Pulse	Water	60	95	20	TM32	Double Team	Normal	—	—	15
TM06	Toxic	Poison	—	85	10	TM35	Flamethrower	Fire	95	100	15
TM10	Hidden Power	Normal	—	100	15	TM38	Fire Blast	Fire	120	85	5
TM11	Sunny Day	Fire	—	—	5	TM42	Facade	Normal	70	100	20
TM13	Ice Beam	Ice	95	100	10	TM43	Secret Power	Normal	70	100	20
TM14	Blizzard	Ice	120	70	5	TM44	Rest	Psychic	—	—	10
TM15	Hyper Beam	Normal	150	90	5	TM45	Attract	Normal	—	100	15
TM17	Protect	Normal	—	—	10	TM46	Thief	Dark	40	100	10
TM18	Rain Dance	Water	—	—	5	HM03	Surf	Water	95	100	15
TM21	Frustration	Normal	—	100	20	HM07	Waterfall	Water	80	100	15
TM27	Return	Normal	—	100	20	HM08	Dive	Water	60	100	10
TM29	Psychic	Psychic	90	100	10						

EGG MOVES*

Name	Type	Power	ACC	PP
Aurora Beam	Ice	65	100	20
Haze	Ice	—	—	30
Octazooka	Water	65	85	10
Rock Blast	Rock	25	80	10
Screech	Normal	—	85	40
Supersonic	Normal	—	55	20
Thunder Wave	Electric	—	100	20

*Learned Via Breeding

MOVE TUTOR
FireRed/LeafGreen and Emerald Only

Double-Edge	Substitute	Thunder Wave*
Mimic		

*Battle Frontier tutor move (*Emerald*)

224 Octillery™

WATER

GENERAL INFO

SPECIES: Jet Pokémon
HEIGHT: 2'11"
WEIGHT: 63 lbs.
ABILITY: Suction Cups
Protects Octillery from being switched out by Whirlwind or Roar.

STATS

EVOLUTIONS

LV25

LOCATION[s]:

RUBY	Rarity: **None**	Evolve Remoraid or Trade from *Colosseum*
SAPPHIRE	Rarity: **None**	Evolve Remoraid or Trade from *Colosseum*
FIRERED	Rarity: **None**	Trade from *LeafGreen/Colosseum*
LEAFGREEN	Rarity: **None**	Evolve Remoraid
COLOSSEUM	Rarity: **None**	Evolve Remoraid
EMERALD	Rarity: **Evolve**	Evolve Remoraid
XD	Rarity: **None**	Trade from *LeafGreen/Colosseum/Emerald*

MOVES

Level	Attack	Type	Power	ACC	PP	Level	Attack	Type	Power	ACC	PP
—	Water Gun	Water	40	100	25	22	Bubblebeam	Water	65	100	20
11	Constrict	Normal	10	100	35	25	Octazooka	Water	65	85	10
22	Psybeam	Psychic	65	100	20	38	Focus Energy	Normal	—	—	30
22	Aurora Beam	Ice	65	100	20	54	Ice Beam	Ice	95	100	10
						70	Hyper Beam	Normal	150	90	5

TM/HM

TM/HM#	Name	Type	Power	ACC	PP	TM/HM#	Name	Type	Power	ACC	PP
TM03	Water Pulse	Water	60	95	20	TM32	Double Team	Normal	—	—	15
TM06	Toxic	Poison		85	10	TM35	Flamethrower	Fire	95	100	15
TM10	Hidden Power	Normal	—	100	15	TM36	Sludge Bomb	Poison	90	100	10
TM11	Sunny Day	Fire	—	—	5	TM38	Fire Blast	Fire	120	85	5
TM13	Ice Beam	Ice	95	100	10	TM42	Facade	Normal	70	100	20
TM14	Blizzard	Ice	120	70	5	TM43	Secret Power	Normal	70	100	20
TM15	Hyper Beam	Normal	150	90	5	TM44	Rest	Psychic	—	—	10
TM17	Protect	Normal	—	—	10	TM45	Attract	Normal	—	100	15
TM18	Rain Dance	Water	—	—	5	TM46	Thief	Dark	40	100	10
TM21	Frustration	Normal	—	100	20	HM03	Surf	Water	95	100	15
TM27	Return	Normal	—	100	20	HM07	Waterfall	Water	80	100	15
TM29	Psychic	Psychic	90	100	10	HM08	Dive	Water	60	100	10

MOVE TUTOR

FireRed/LeafGreen and Emerald Only

Double-Edge	Substitute	Seismic Toss*
Mimic	Thunder Wave*	

*Battle Frontier tutor move (*Emerald*)

225 Delibird™

ICE   FLYING

GENERAL INFO

SPECIES: Delivery Pokémon
HEIGHT: 2'11"
WEIGHT: 35 lbs.
ABILITY 1: Hustle
Multiplies Delibird's attacks by 1.5, but lowers its Accuracy to 80%.
ABILITY 2: Vital Spirit
Prevents Delibird from getting a Sleep condition.

STATS

HP · ATK · DEF · SP ATK · SP DEF · SPEED

EVOLUTIONS

DOES NOT EVOLVE

LOCATION[s]:

RUBY	Rarity: **None**	Obtain in *Colosseum*
SAPPHIRE	Rarity: **None**	Obtain in *Colosseum*
FIRERED	Rarity: **Rare**	Four Island
LEAFGREEN	Rarity: **None**	Trade from *FireRed/Colosseum*
COLOSSEUM	Rarity: **Only One**	Realgam Tower
EMERALD	Rarity: **None**	Trade from *FireRed/Colosseum*
XD	Rarity: **None**	Trade from *FireRed/Colosseum*

MOVES

Level	Attack	Type	Power	ACC	PP
—	Present	Normal	—	90	15

TM/HM

TM/HM#	Name	Type	Power	ACC	PP		TM/HM#	Name	Type	Power	ACC	PP
TM01	Focus Punch	Fighting	150	100	20		TM27	Return	Normal	—	100	20
TM03	Water Pulse	Water	60	95	20		TM32	Double Team	Normal	—	—	15
TM06	Toxic	Poison	—	85	10		TM40	Aerial Ace	Flying	60	—	20
TM07	Hail	Ice	—	—	10		TM42	Facade	Normal	70	100	20
TM10	Hidden Power	Normal	—	100	15		TM43	Secret Power	Normal	70	100	20
TM13	Ice Beam	Ice	95	100	10		TM44	Rest	Psychic	—	—	10
TM14	Blizzard	Ice	120	70	5		TM45	Attract	Normal	—	100	15
TM17	Protect	Normal	—	—	10		TM46	Thief	Dark	40	100	10
TM18	Rain Dance	Water	—	—	5		HM02	Fly	Flying	70	95	15
TM21	Frustration	Normal	—	100	20							

EGG MOVES*

Name	Type	Power	ACC	PP
Aurora Beam	Ice	65	100	20
Future Sight	Psychic	80	90	15
Ice Ball	Ice	30	90	20
Quick Attack	Normal	40	100	30
Rapid Spin	Normal	20	100	40
Bounce	Flying	85	85	5

*Learned Via Breeding

MOVE TUTOR
FireRed/LeafGreen and Emerald Only

Body Slam*	Mega Kick*	Counter*
Double-Edge	Mimic	Seismic Toss*
Mega Punch*	Substitute	

*Battle Frontier tutor move (*Emerald*)

226 Mantine™

FLYING   WATER

GENERAL INFO

SPECIES: Kite Pokémon
HEIGHT: 6'11"
WEIGHT: 485 lbs.
ABILITY 1: Water Absorb
When Mantine is hit with a Water attack, it gets 1/4 of its HPs back.
ABILITY 2: Swift Swim
Increases Mantine's Speed when it's raining.

STATS

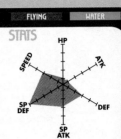

EVOLUTIONS

DOES NOT EVOLVE

LOCATION(s):

RUBY	Rarity: **None**	Obtain in *Colosseum*
SAPPHIRE	Rarity: **None**	Obtain in *Colosseum*
FIRERED	Rarity: **Common**	Trade from *LeafGreen/Colosseum*
LEAFGREEN	Rarity: **Rare**	Seven Island
COLOSSEUM	Rarity: **Only One**	Pyrite Town
EMERALD	Rarity: **None**	Trade from *LeafGreen/Colosseum*
XD	Rarity: **None**	Trade from *LeafGreen/Colosseum*

MOVES

Level	Attack	Type	Power	ACC	PP	Level	Attack	Type	Power	ACC	PP
—	Tackle	Normal	35	95	35	22	Take Down	Normal	90	85	20
—	Bubble	Water	20	100	30	29	Agility	Psychic	—	—	30
8	Supersonic	Normal	—	55	20	36	Wing Attack	Flying	60	100	35
15	Bubblebeam	Water	65	100	20	43	Water Pulse	Water	60	100	20
						50	Confuse Ray	Ghost	—	100	10

TM/HM

TM/HM#	Name	Type	Power	ACC	PP	TM/HM#	Name	Type	Power	ACC	PP
TM03	Water Pulse	Water	60	95	20	TM27	Return	Normal	—	100	20
TM06	Toxic	Poison	—	85	10	TM32	Double Team	Normal	—	—	15
TM07	Hail	Ice	—	—	10	TM40	Aerial Ace	Flying	60	—	20
TM10	Hidden Power	Normal	—	100	15	TM42	Facade	Normal	70	100	20
TM11	Sunny Day	Fire	—	—	5	TM43	Secret Power	Normal	70	100	20
TM13	Ice Beam	Ice	95	100	10	TM44	Rest	Psychic	—	—	10
TM14	Blizzard	Ice	120	70	5	TM45	Attract	Normal	—	100	15
TM17	Protect	Normal	—	—	10	HM03	Surf	Water	95	100	15
TM18	Rain Dance	Water	—	—	5	HM07	Waterfall	Water	80	100	15
TM21	Frustration	Normal	—	100	20	HM08	Dive	Water	60	100	10
TM26	Earthquake	Ground	100	100	10						

EGG MOVES*

Name	Type	Power	ACC	PP
Haze	Ice	—	—	30
Hydro Pump	Water	120	80	5
Mud Sport	Ground	—	100	15
Rock Slide	Rock	75	90	10
Slam	Normal	80	75	20
Twister	Dragon	40	100	20

*Learned Via Breeding

MOVE TUTOR
FireRed/LeafGreen and Emerald Only

Body Slam*	Mimic	Substitute
Double-Edge		

*Battle Frontier tutor move (*Emerald*)

227 Skarmory™

STEEL   FLYING

GENERAL INFO
SPECIES: Armor Bird Pokémon
HEIGHT: 5'07"
WEIGHT: 111 lbs.
ABILITY 1: Keen Eye
Skarmory's Accuracy cannot be lowered.
ABILITY 2: Sturdy
One hit KO moves have no effect.

STATS

EVOLUTIONS

DOES NOT EVOLVE

LOCATION(s):

RUBY	Rarity: **Rare**	Route 113
SAPPHIRE	Rarity: **Rare**	Route 113
FIRERED	Rarity: **Rare**	Seven Island
LEAFGREEN	Rarity: **Rare**	Trade from FireRed/Colosseum
COLOSSEUM	Rarity: **Only One**	Realgam Tower
EMERALD	Rarity: **Rare**	Route 113
XD	Rarity: **None**	Trade from Ruby/Sapphire/FireRed/LeafGreen/Colosseum

MOVES

Level	Attack	Type	Power	ACC	PP	Level	Attack	Type	Power	ACC	PP
—	Leer	Normal	—	100	30	26	Fury Attack	Normal	15	85	20
—	Peck	Flying	35	100	35	29	Air Cutter	Flying	55	95	25
10	Sand-Attack	Ground	—	100	15	32	Steel Wing	Steel	70	90	25
13	Swift	Normal	60	—	20	42	Spikes	Ground	—	—	20
16	Agility	Psychic	—	—	30	45	Metal Sound	Steel	—	85	40

TM/HM

TM/HM#	Name	Type	Power	ACC	PP	TM/HM#	Name	Type	Power	ACC	PP
TM05	Roar	Normal	—	100	20	TM41	Torment	Dark	—	100	15
TM06	Toxic	Poison	—	85	10	TM42	Facade	Normal	70	100	20
TM10	Hidden Power	Normal	—	100	15	TM43	Secret Power	Normal	70	100	20
TM11	Sunny Day	Fire	—	—	5	TM44	Rest	Psychic	—	—	10
TM12	Taunt	Dark	—	100	20	TM45	Attract	Normal	—	100	15
TM17	Protect	Normal	—	—	10	TM46	Thief	Dark	40	100	10
TM21	Frustration	Normal	—	100	20	TM47	Steel Wing	Steel	70	90	25
TM27	Return	Normal	—	100	20	HM01	Cut	Normal	50	95	30
TM32	Double Team	Normal	—	—	15	HM02	Fly	Flying	70	95	15
TM37	Sandstorm	Rock	—	—	10	HM06	Rock Smash	Fighting	20	100	15
TM40	Aerial Ace	Flying	60	—	20						

EGG MOVES*

Name	Type	Power	ACC	PP
Drill Peck	Flying	80	100	20
Pursuit	Dark	40	100	20
Sky Attack	Flying	140	90	5
Whirlwind	Normal	—	100	20
Curse	—	—	—	10

*Learned Via Breeding

MOVE TUTOR
FireRed/LeafGreen and Emerald Only

Double-Edge	Substitute	Counter*
Mimic	Rock Slide*	

Emerald Only

Endure*	Sleep Talk	Swagger
Mud-Slap*	Snore*	Swift*

*Battle Frontier tutor move (Emerald)

228 Houndour™

DARK | FIRE

GENERAL INFO

SPECIES: Dark Pokémon
HEIGHT: 2'00"
WEIGHT: 24 lbs.
ABILITY 1: Flash Fire

Boosts the power of Houndour's Fire-type attacks and prevents it from being damaged by Fire-type attacks.

ABILITY 2: Early Bird

Allows Houndour to wake up sooner when put to sleep.

STATS

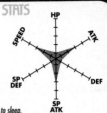

EVOLUTIONS

LV24

LOCATION(s):

RUBY	Rarity: **None**	Obtain in *Colosseum*
SAPPHIRE	Rarity: **None**	Obtain in *Colosseum*
FIRERED	Rarity: **None**	Trade Houndoom from *Colosseum* and breed
LEAFGREEN	Rarity: **None**	Trade Houndoom from *Colosseum* and breed
COLOSSEUM	Rarity: **None**	Breed Houndoom
EMERALD	Rarity: **Rare**	Safari Zone
XD	Rarity: **Only One**	Cipher Lab (Capture from Cipher Peon Resix)

MOVES

Level	Attack	Type	Power	ACC	PP
—	Leer	Normal	—	100	30
—	Ember	Fire	40	100	25
7	Howl	Normal	—	—	40
13	Smog	Poison	20	70	20
19	Roar	Normal	—	100	20
25	Bite	Dark	60	100	25
31	Odor Sleuth	Normal	—	100	40
37	Faint Attack	Dark	60	—	20
43	Flamethrower	Fire	95	100	15
49	Crunch	Dark	80	100	15

TM/HM

TM/HM#	Name	Type	Power	ACC	PP
TM05	Roar	Normal	—	100	20
TM06	Toxic	Poison	—	85	10
TM10	Hidden Power	Normal	—	100	15
TM11	Sunny Day	Fire	—	—	5
TM12	Taunt	Dark	—	100	20
TM17	Protect	Normal	—	—	10
TM21	Frustration	Normal	—	100	20
TM22	Solarbeam	Grass	120	100	10
TM23	Iron Tail	Steel	75	75	15
TM27	Return	Normal	—	100	20
TM30	Shadow Ball	Ghost	80	100	15
TM32	Double Team	Normal	—	—	15
TM35	Flamethrower	Fire	95	100	15
TM36	Sludge Bomb	Poison	90	100	10
TM38	Fire Blast	Fire	120	85	5
TM41	Torment	Dark	—	100	15
TM42	Facade	Normal	70	100	20
TM43	Secret Power	Normal	70	100	20
TM44	Rest	Psychic	—	—	10
TM45	Attract	Normal	—	100	15
TM46	Thief	Dark	40	100	10
TM49	Snatch	Dark	—	100	10
TM50	Overheat	Fire	140	90	5
HM06	Rock Smash	Fighting	20	100	15

EGG MOVES*

Name	Type	Power	ACC	PP
Beat Up	Dark	10	100	10
Counter	Fighting	—	100	10
Fire Spin	Fire	15	70	15
Pursuit	Dark	40	100	20
Rage	Normal	20	100	20
Reversal	Fighting	—	100	15
Spite	Ghost	—	100	10
Will-O-Wisp	Fire	—	75	15

*Learned Via Breeding

MOVE TUTOR

FireRed/LeafGreen and Emerald Only

Body Slam*	Mimic	Substitute
Double-Edge	Dream Eater*	Counter*

*Battle Frontier tutor move (*Emerald*)

229 Houndoom™

DARK | FIRE

GENERAL INFO

SPECIES: Dark Pokémon
HEIGHT: 4'07"
WEIGHT: 77 lbs.
ABILITY 1: Flash Fire

Boosts the power of Houndoom's Fire-type attacks and prevents it from being damaged by Fire-type attacks.

ABILITY 2: Early Bird

Allows Houndoom to wake up sooner when put to sleep.

STATS

EVOLUTIONS

LV24

LOCATION[s]:

RUBY	Rarity: **None**	Trade from *Colosseum*
SAPPHIRE	Rarity: **None**	Trade from *Colosseum*
FIRERED	Rarity: **None**	Trade from *Colosseum*
LEAFGREEN	Rarity: **None**	Trade from *Colosseum*
COLOSSEUM	Rarity: **Only One**	Realgam Tower
EMERALD	Rarity: **Evolve**	Evolve Houndour
XD	Rarity: **Evolve**	Evolve Houndour

MOVES

Level	Attack	Type	Power	ACC	PP	Level	Attack	Type	Power	ACC	PP
—	Leer	Normal	—	100	30	27	Bite	Dark	60	100	25
—	Ember	Fire	40	100	25	35	Odor Sleuth	Normal	—	100	40
—	Howl	Normal	—	—	40	43	Faint Attack	Dark	60	—	20
13	Smog	Poison	20	70	20	51	Flamethrower	Fire	95	100	15
19	Roar	Normal	—	100	20	59	Crunch	Dark	80	100	15

TM/HM

TM/HM#	Name	Type	Power	ACC	PP	TM/HM#	Name	Type	Power	ACC	PP
TM05	Roar	Normal	—	100	20	TM35	Flamethrower	Fire	95	100	15
TM06	Toxic	Poison	—	85	10	TM36	Sludge Bomb	Poison	90	100	10
TM10	Hidden Power	Normal	—	100	15	TM38	Fire Blast	Fire	120	85	5
TM11	Sunny Day	Fire	—	—	5	TM41	Torment	Dark	—	100	15
TM12	Taunt	Dark	—	100	20	TM42	Facade	Normal	70	100	20
TM15	Hyper Beam	Normal	150	90	5	TM43	Secret Power	Normal	70	100	20
TM17	Protect	Normal	—	—	10	TM44	Rest	Psychic	—	—	10
TM21	Frustration	Normal	—	100	20	TM45	Attract	Normal	—	100	15
TM22	Solarbeam	Grass	120	100	10	TM46	Thief	Dark	40	100	10
TM23	Iron Tail	Steel	75	75	15	TM49	Snatch	Dark	—	100	10
TM27	Return	Normal	—	100	20	TM50	Overheat	Fire	140	90	5
TM30	Shadow Ball	Ghost	80	100	15	HM04	Strength	Normal	80	100	20
TM32	Double Team	Normal	—	—	15	HM06	Rock Smash	Fighting	20	100	15

MOVE TUTOR
FireRed/LeafGreen and Emerald Only

Body Slam*	Mimic	Substitute
Double-Edge	Dream Eater*	Counter*

*Battle Frontier tutor move (*Emerald*)

230 Kingdra™

WATER | DRAGON

GENERAL INFO

SPECIES: Dragon Pokémon
HEIGHT: 5'11"
WEIGHT: 335 lbs.
ABILITY: Swift Swim
Doubles the Kingdra's Speed when it's raining.

STATS

EVOLUTIONS

LV24

TRADE WITH DRAGON SCALE

LOCATION(s):

RUBY	Rarity: **None**	Evolve Seadra
SAPPHIRE	Rarity: **None**	Evolve Seadra
FIRERED	Rarity: **None**	Evolve Seadra
LEAFGREEN	Rarity: **None**	Evolve Seadra
COLOSSEUM	Rarity: **None**	Trade from Ruby/Sapphire/FireRed/LeafGreen
EMERALD	Rarity: **Evolve**	Evolve Seadra
XD	Rarity: **None**	Trade from Ruby/Sapphire/FireRed/LeafGreen

MOVES

Level	Attack	Type	Power	ACC	PP	Level	Attack	Type	Power	ACC	PP
—	Bubble	Water	20	100	30	29	Twister	Dragon	40	100	20
—	Smokescreen	Normal	—	100	20	40	Agility	Psychic	—	—	30
—	Leer	Normal	—	100	30	51	Hydro Pump	Water	120	80	5
—/22	Water Gun	Water	40	100	25	62	Dragon Dance	Dragon	—	—	20

= Emerald Only

TM/HM

TM/HM#	Name	Type	Power	ACC	PP	TM/HM#	Name	Type	Power	ACC	PP
TM03	Water Pulse	Water	60	100	20	TM27	Return	Normal	—	100	20
TM06	Toxic	Poison	—	85	10	TM32	Double Team	Normal	—	—	15
TM07	Hail	Ice	—	—	10	TM42	Facade	Normal	70	100	20
TM10	Hidden Power	Normal	—	100	15	TM43	Secret Power	Normal	70	100	20
TM13	Ice Beam	Ice	95	100	10	TM44	Rest	Psychic	—	—	10
TM14	Blizzard	Ice	120	70	5	TM45	Attract	Normal	—	100	15
TM15	Hyper Beam	Normal	150	90	5	HM03	Surf	Water	95	100	15
TM17	Protect	Normal	—	—	10	HM07	Waterfall	Water	80	100	15
TM18	Rain Dance	Water	—	—	5	HM08	Dive	Water	60	100	10
TM21	Frustration	Normal	—	100	20						

MOVE TUTOR
FireRed/LeafGreen and Emerald Only

Body Slam*	Mimic	Substitute
Double-Edge		

Emerald Only

Endure*	Sleep Talk	Swagger
Icy Wind*	Snore*	Swift*

*Battle Frontier tutor move (Emerald)

231 Phanpy™

GROUND

GENERAL INFO

SPECIES: Long Nose Pokémon
HEIGHT: 1'08"
WEIGHT: 74 lbs.
ABILITY: Pickup

Allows Phanpy to pick up items from the opponent in battle. Also picks up items on roads when in a party.

STATS

EVOLUTIONS

LV25

LOCATION[s]:

RUBY	Rarity: **Common**	Safari Zone
SAPPHIRE	Rarity: **Common**	Safari Zone
FIRERED	Rarity: **Common**	Seven Island
LEAFGREEN	Rarity: **Common**	Seven Island
COLOSSEUM	Rarity: **None**	Trade from *Ruby/Sapphire/FireRed/LeafGreen*
EMERALD	Rarity: **Common**	Safari Zone
XD	Rarity: **Rare**	Oasis Poké Spot

MOVES

Level	Attack	Type	Power	ACC	PP	Level	Attack	Type	Power	ACC	PP
—	Odor Sleuth	Normal	—	100	40	17	Flail	Normal	—	100	15
—	Growl	Normal	—	100	40	25	Take Down	Normal	90	85	20
—	Tackle	Normal	35	95	35	33	Rollout	Rock	30	90	20
9	Defense Curl	Normal	—	—	40	41	Endure	Normal	—	—	10
						49	Double-Edge	Normal	120	100	15

TM/HM

TM/HM#	Name	Type	Power	ACC	PP	TM/HM#	Name	Type	Power	ACC	PP
TM05	Roar	Normal	—	100	20	TM32	Double Team	Normal	—	—	15
TM06	Toxic	Poison	—	85	10	TM37	Sandstorm	Rock	—	—	10
TM10	Hidden Power	Normal	—	100	15	TM39	Rock Tomb	Rock	50	80	10
TM11	Sunny Day	Fire	—	—	5	TM42	Facade	Normal	70	100	20
TM17	Protect	Normal	—	—	10	TM43	Secret Power	Normal	70	100	20
TM21	Frustration	Normal	—	100	20	TM44	Rest	Psychic	—	—	10
TM23	Iron Tail	Steel	100	75	15	TM45	Attract	Normal	—	100	15
TM26	Earthquake	Ground	100	100	10	HM04	Strength	Normal	80	100	15
TM27	Return	Normal	—	100	20	HM06	Rock Smash	Fighting	20	100	15

EGG MOVES*

Name	Type	Power	ACC	PP
Focus Energy	Normal	—	—	30
Body Slam	Normal	85	100	15
Ancientpower	Rock	60	100	5
Snore	Normal	40	100	15
Counter	Fighting	—	100	20
Fissure	Ground	—	30	5

*Learned Via Breeding

MOVE TUTOR
FireRed/LeafGreen and Emerald Only

Body Slam*	Mimic	Counter*
Double-Edge	Substitute	

Emerald Only

Endure*	Rollout	Snore*
Mud-Slap*	Sleep Talk	Swagger

*Battle Frontier tutor move (*Emerald*)

232 Donphan™

GROUND

GENERAL INFO

SPECIES: Armor Pokémon
HEIGHT: 3'07"
WEIGHT: 265 lbs.
ABILITY: Sturdy
One hit KO moves have no effect.

STATS

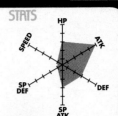

EVOLUTIONS

LV25

LOCATION[s]:

RUBY	Rarity: **Common**	Evolve Phanpy
SAPPHIRE	Rarity: **Common**	Evolve Phanpy
FIRERED	Rarity: **Common**	Evolve Phanpy
LEAFGREEN	Rarity: **Common**	Evolve Phanpy
COLOSSEUM	Rarity: **None**	Trade from *Ruby/Sapphire/FireRed/LeafGreen*
EMERALD	Rarity: **Evolve**	Evolve Phanpy
XD	Rarity: **Evolve**	Evolve Phanpy

MOVES

Level	Attack	Type	Power	ACC	PP	Level	Attack	Type	Power	ACC	PP
—	Odor Sleuth	Normal	—	100	40	17	Flail	Normal	—	100	15
—	Horn Attack	Normal	65	100	25	25	Fury Attack	Normal	15	85	20
—	Growl	Normal	—	100	40	33	Rollout	Rock	30	90	20
9	Defense Curl	Normal	—	—	40	41	Rapid Spin	Normal	20	100	40
						49	Earthquake	Ground	100	100	10

TM/HM

TM/HM#	Name	Type	Power	ACC	PP	TM/HM#	Name	Type	Power	ACC	PP
TM05	Roar	Normal	—	100	20	TM32	Double Team	Normal	—	—	15
TM06	Toxic	Poison	—	85	10	TM37	Sandstorm	Rock	—	—	10
TM10	Hidden Power	Normal	—	100	15	TM39	Rock Tomb	Rock	50	80	10
TM11	Sunny Day	Fire	—	—	5	TM42	Facade	Normal	70	100	20
TM15	Hyper Beam	Normal	150	90	5	TM43	Secret Power	Normal	70	100	20
TM17	Protect	Normal	—	—	10	TM44	Rest	Psychic	—	—	10
TM21	Frustration	Normal	—	100	20	TM45	Attract	Normal	—	100	15
TM23	Iron Tail	Steel	100	75	15	HM04	Strength	Normal	80	100	15
TM26	Earthquake	Ground	100	100	10	HM06	Rock Smash	Fighting	20	100	15
TM27	Return	Normal	—	100	20						

MOVE TUTOR

FireRed/LeafGreen and Emerald Only

Body Slam*	Mimic	Counter*
Double-Edge	Substitute	Rock Slide*

Emerald Only

Defense Curl*	Rollout	Swagger
Endure*	Sleep Talk	
Mud-Slap*	Snore*	

*Battle Frontier tutor move (*Emerald*)

233 Porygon2™

NORMAL

GENERAL INFO

SPECIES: Virtual Pokémon
HEIGHT: 2'00"
WEIGHT: 72 lbs.
ABILITY: Trace
Allows Porygon2 to copy the opponent's ability.

STATS

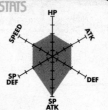

EVOLUTIONS

TRADE WITH UP-GRADE

LOCATION[s]:

RUBY	Rarity: **None**	Trade from *FireRed/LeafGreen*
SAPPHIRE	Rarity: **None**	Trade from *FireRed/LeafGreen*
FIRERED	Rarity: **None**	Evolve Porygon
LEAFGREEN	Rarity: **None**	Evolve Porygon
COLOSSEUM	Rarity: **None**	Evolve Porygon
EMERALD	Rarity: **None**	Trade from *FireRed/LeafGreen*
XD	Rarity: **None**	Trade from *FireRed/LeafGreen*

MOVES

Level	Attack	Type	Power	ACC	PP
—	Tackle	Normal	35	95	35
—	Conversion	Normal	—	—	30
—	Conversion 2	Normal	—	—	30
9	Agility	Psychic	—	—	30
12	Psybeam	Psychic	65	100	20

Level	Attack	Type	Power	ACC	PP
20	Recover	Normal	—	—	20
24	Defense Curl	Normal	—	—	40
32	Lock-on	Normal	—	100	5
36	Tri Attack	Normal	80	100	10
44	Recycle	Normal	—	—	10
48	Zap Cannon	Electric	100	50	5

TM/HM

TM/HM#	Name	Type	Power	ACC	PP
TM06	Toxic	Poison	—	85	10
TM10	Hidden Power	Normal	—	100	15
TM11	Sunny Day	Fire	—	—	5
TM13	Ice Beam	Ice	95	100	10
TM14	Blizzard	Ice	120	70	5
TM15	Hyper Beam	Normal	150	90	5
TM17	Protect	Normal	—	—	10
TM18	Rain Dance	Water	—	—	5
TM21	Frustration	Normal	—	100	20
TM22	Solarbeam	Grass	120	100	10
TM23	Iron Tail	Steel	75	75	15
TM24	Thunderbolt	Electric	95	100	15

TM/HM#	Name	Type	Power	ACC	PP
TM25	Thunder	Electric	120	70	10
TM27	Return	Normal	—	100	20
TM29	Psychic	Psychic	90	100	10
TM30	Shadow Ball	Ghost	80	100	15
TM32	Double Team	Normal	—	—	15
TM34	Shock Wave	Electric	60	—	20
TM40	Aerial Ace	Flying	60	—	20
TM42	Facade	Normal	70	100	20
TM43	Secret Power	Normal	70	100	20
TM44	Rest	Psychic	—	—	10
TM46	Thief	Dark	40	100	10
HM05	Flash	Normal	—	70	20

EGG MOVES*

Name	Type	Power	ACC	PP
None				

*Learned Via Breeding

MOVE TUTOR

FireRed/LeafGreen and Emerald Only

Double-Edge	Substitute	Dream Eater*
Mimic	Thunder Wave*	

*Battle Frontier tutor move (*Emerald*)

234 Stantler™

NORMAL

GENERAL INFO

SPECIES: Big Horn Pokémon
HEIGHT: 4'07"
WEIGHT: 157 lbs.
ABILITY: Intimidate

An opponent's Attack decreases when Stantler is summoned into battle.

STATS

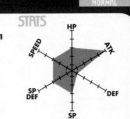

EVOLUTIONS

DOES NOT EVOLVE

LOCATION[s]:

RUBY	Rarity: **None**	Trade from *Colosseum*
SAPPHIRE	Rarity: **None**	Trade from *Colosseum*
FIRERED	Rarity: **None**	Trade from *Colosseum*
LEAFGREEN	Rarity: **None**	Trade from *Colosseum*
COLOSSEUM	Rarity: **Only One**	The Under
EMERALD	Rarity: **Rare**	Safari Zone
XD	Rarity: **None**	Trade from *Colosseum*

MOVES

Level	Attack	Type	Power	ACC	PP	Level	Attack	Type	Power	ACC	PP
—	Tackle	Normal	35	95	35	27	Sand-Attack	Ground	—	100	15
7	Leer	Normal	—	100	20	31	Role Play	Psychic	—	100	10
11	Astonish	Ghost	30	100	15	37	Take Down	Normal	90	85	20
17	Hypnosis	Psychic	—	60	20	41	Confuse Ray	Ghost	—	100	10
21	Stomp	Normal	65	100	20	47	Calm Mind	Psychic	—	—	20

TM/HM

TM/HM#	Name	Type	Power	ACC	PP	TM/HM#	Name	Type	Power	ACC	PP
TM04	Calm Mind	Psychic	—	—	20	TM27	Return	Normal	—	100	20
TM05	Roar	Normal	—	100	20	TM29	Psychic	Psychic	90	100	10
TM06	Toxic	Poison	—	85	10	TM30	Shadow Ball	Ghost	80	100	15
TM10	Hidden Power	Normal	—	100	15	TM32	Double Team	Normal	—	—	15
TM11	Sunny Day	Fire	—	—	5	TM33	Reflect	Normal	—	—	20
TM16	Light Screen	Psychic	—	—	30	TM34	Shock Wave	Electric	60	—	20
TM17	Protect	Normal	—	—	10	TM42	Facade	Normal	70	100	20
TM18	Rain Dance	Water	—	—	5	TM43	Secret Power	Normal	70	100	20
TM21	Frustration	Normal	—	100	20	TM44	Rest	Psychic	—	—	10
TM22	Solarbeam	Grass	120	100	10	TM45	Attract	Normal	—	100	15
TM23	Iron Tail	Steel	75	75	15	TM46	Thief	Dark	40	100	10
TM24	Thunderbolt	Electric	95	100	15	TM48	Skill Swap	Psychic	—	100	10
TM25	Thunder	Electric	120	70	10	HM05	Flash	Normal	—	70	20
TM26	Earthquake	Ground	100	100	10						

EGG MOVES*

Name	Type	Power	ACC	PP
Bite	Dark	60	100	25
Disable	Normal	—	55	20
Extrasensory	Psychic	80	100	30
Psych Up	Normal	—	—	10
Spite	Ghost	—	100	10
Swagger	Normal	—	90	15

*Learned Via Breeding

MOVE TUTOR

FireRed/LeafGreen and Emerald Only

Double-Edge	Substitute	Dream Eater*
Mimic	Thunder Wave*	Body Slam*

*Battle Frontier tutor move (*Emerald*)

235 Smeargle™

NORMAL

GENERAL INFO
SPECIES: Painter Pokémon
HEIGHT: 3'11"
WEIGHT: 128 lbs.
ABILITY: Own Tempo
Smeargle can't be confused.

STATS

HP · SPEED · ATK · DEF · SP DEF · SP ATK

EVOLUTIONS

DOES NOT EVOLVE

LOCATION(s):

RUBY	Rarity: **None**	Trade from *Colosseum/Emerald*
SAPPHIRE	Rarity: **None**	Trade from *Colosseum/Emerald*
FIRERED	Rarity: **None**	Trade from *Colosseum/Emerald*
LEAFGREEN	Rarity: **None**	Trade from *Colosseum/Emerald*
COLOSSEUM	Rarity: **None**	Snagem Hideout
EMERALD	Rarity: **Common**	Battle Frontier
XD	Rarity: **None**	Trade from *Colosseum/Emerald*

MOVES

Level	Attack	Type	Power	ACC	PP	Level	Attack	Type	Power	ACC	PP
—	Sketch	Normal	—	—	1	51	Sketch	Normal	—	—	1
11	Sketch	Normal	—	—	1	61	Sketch	Normal	—	—	1
21	Sketch	Normal	—	—	1	71	Sketch	Normal	—	—	1
31	Sketch	Normal	—	—	1	81	Sketch	Normal	—	—	1
41	Sketch	Normal	—	—	1	91	Sketch	Normal	—	—	1

TM/HM

TM/HM# Name	Type	Power	ACC	PP
None				

EGG MOVES*

Name	Type	Power	ACC	PP
None				

*Learned Via Breeding

MOVE TUTOR
FireRed/LeafGreen and Emerald Only

None

236 Tyrogue™

FIGHTING

GENERAL INFO
SPECIES: Scuffle Pokémon
HEIGHT: 2'04"
WEIGHT: 46 lbs.
ABILITY: Guts
When Tyrogue has a status condition, its attack power is multiplied by 1.5.

STATS

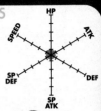

EVOLUTIONS

(ATTACK<DEFENSE) LV20

(ATTACK>DEFENSE) LV20

(ATTACK=DEFENSE) LV20

LOCATION[s]:

	Rarity	
RUBY	**None**	Trade and then breed Hitmonchan or Hitmonlee
SAPPHIRE	**None**	Trade and then breed Hitmonchan or Hitmonlee
FIRERED	**None**	Breed Hitmonchan or Hitmonlee
LEAFGREEN	**None**	Breed Hitmonchan or Hitmonlee
COLOSSEUM	**None**	Trade from *Ruby/Sapphire/FireRed/LeafGreen*
EMERALD	**None**	Trade and then breed Hitmonchan or Hitmonlee
XD	**None**	Trade from *Ruby/Sapphire/FireRed/LeafGreen*

MOVES

Level	Attack	Type	Power	ACC	PP
—	Tackle	Normal	35	95	35

TM/HM

TM/HM#	Name	Type	Power	ACC	PP	TM/HM#	Name	Type	Power	ACC	PP
TM06	Toxic	Poison	—	85	10	TM31	Brick Break	Fighting	75	100	15
TM08	Bulk Up	Fighting	—	—	20	TM32	Double Team	Normal	—	—	15
TM10	Hidden Power	Normal	—	100	15	TM42	Facade	Normal	70	100	20
TM11	Sunny Day	Fire	—	—	5	TM43	Secret Power	Normal	70	100	20
TM17	Protect	Normal	—	—	10	TM44	Rest	Psychic	—	—	10
TM18	Rain Dance	Water	—	—	5	TM45	Attract	Normal	—	100	15
TM21	Frustration	Normal	—	100	20	TM46	Thief	Dark	40	100	10
TM26	Earthquake	Ground	100	100	10	HM04	Strength	Normal	80	100	20
TM27	Return	Normal	—	100	20	HM06	Rock Smash	Fighting	20	100	15

EGG MOVES*

Name	Type	Power	ACC	PP
Mach Punch	Fighting	40	100	30
Mind Reader	Normal	—	100	5
Rapid Spin	Normal	20	100	40
Hi Jump Kick	Fighting	85	90	20

*Learned Via Breeding

MOVE TUTOR
FireRed/LeafGreen and Emerald Only

Body Slam*	Mimic	Seismic Toss*
Double-Edge	Substitute	Rock Slide*
Mega Kick*	Counter*	

*Battle Frontier tutor move (*Emerald*)

237 Hitmontop™

FIGHTING

GENERAL INFO

SPECIES: Handstand Pokémon
HEIGHT: 4'07"
WEIGHT: 105 lbs.
ABILITY: Intimidate

When Hitmontop is sent into battle, it lowers the opponent's Attack.

STATS

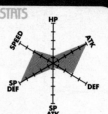

EVOLUTIONS

ATTACK=DEFENSE
LV20

LOCATION[s]:

RUBY	Rarity: **None**	Trade from *Colosseum*
SAPPHIRE	Rarity: **None**	Trade from *Colosseum*
FIRERED	Rarity: **None**	Trade from *Colosseum*
LEAFGREEN	Rarity: **None**	Trade from *Colosseum*
COLOSSEUM	Rarity: **Only One**	Agate Village
EMERALD	Rarity: **None**	Trade from *Colosseum*
XD	Rarity: **None**	Trade from *Colosseum*

MOVES

Level	Attack	Type	Power	ACC	PP	Level	Attack	Type	Power	ACC	PP
—	Rolling Kick	Fight	60	85	15	20	Triple Kick	Fight	10	90	10
—	Revenge	Fighting	60	100	10	25	Rapid Spin	Normal	20	100	40
7	Focus Energy	Normal	—	—	30	31	Counter	Fighting	—	100	20
13	Pursuit	Dark	40	100	20	37	Agility	Psychic	—	—	30
19	Quick Attack	Normal	40	100	30	43	Detect	Fight	—	—	5
						49	Endeavor	Normal	—	100	5

TM/HM

TM/HM#	Name	Type	Power	ACC	PP	TM/HM#	Name	Type	Power	ACC	PP
TM06	Toxic	Poison	—	85	10	TM31	Brick Break	Fighting	75	100	15
TM08	Bulk Up	Fighting	—	—	20	TM32	Double Team	Normal	—	—	15
TM10	Hidden Power	Normal	—	100	15	TM37	Sandstorm	Ground	—	—	10
TM11	Sunny Day	Fire	—	—	5	TM42	Facade	Normal	70	100	20
TM17	Protect	Normal	—	—	10	TM43	Secret Power	Normal	70	100	20
TM18	Rain Dance	Water	—	—	5	TM44	Rest	Psychic	—	—	10
TM21	Frustration	Normal	—	100	20	TM45	Attract	Normal	—	100	15
TM26	Earthquake	Ground	100	100	10	TM46	Thief	Dark	40	100	10
TM27	Return	Normal	—	100	20	HM04	Strength	Normal	80	100	15
TM28	Dig	Ground	60	100	10	HM06	Rock Smash	Fighting	20	100	15

MOVE TUTOR

FireRed/LeafGreen and Emerald Only

Body Slam*	Mimic	Seismic Toss*
Double-Edge	Substitute	Rock Slide*
Mega Kick*	Counter*	

*Battle Frontier tutor move (*Emerald*)

238 Smoochum™

ICE | PSYCHIC

GENERAL INFO

SPECIES: Kiss Pokémon
HEIGHT: 1'04"
WEIGHT: 14 lbs.
ABILITY: Oblivious
Prevents Smoochum from being attracted.

STATS

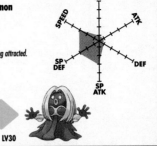

EVOLUTIONS

LV30

LOCATION(S):

RUBY	Rarity: **None**	Trade from *FireRed/LeafGreen*
SAPPHIRE	Rarity: **None**	Trade from *FireRed/LeafGreen*
FIRERED	Rarity: **None**	Breed Jynx
LEAFGREEN	Rarity: **None**	Breed Jynx
COLOSSEUM	Rarity: **None**	Trade from *FireRed/LeafGreen*
EMERALD	Rarity: **None**	Trade from *FireRed/LeafGreen*
XD	Rarity: **None**	Trade from *FireRed/LeafGreen*

MOVES

Level	Attack	Type	Power	ACC	PP	Level	Attack	Type	Power	ACC	PP
—	Pound	Normal	40	100	35	25	Sing	Normal	—	55	15
—	Lick	Ghost	20	100	30	33	Mean Look	Normal	—	100	5
9	Sweet Kiss	Normal	—	75	10	37	Fake Tears	Dark	—	100	20
13	Powder Snow	Ice	40	100	25	45	Psychic	Psychic	90	100	10
21	Confusion	Psychic	50	100	25	49	Perish Song	Normal	—	—	5
						57	Blizzard	Ice	120	70	5

TM/HM

TM/HM#	Name	Type	Power	ACC	PP	TM/HM#	Name	Type	Power	ACC	PP
TM03	Water Pulse	Water	60	95	20	TM29	Psychic	Psychic	90	100	10
TM04	Calm Mind	Psychic	—	—	20	TM30	Shadow Ball	Ghost	80	100	15
TM06	Toxic	Poison	—	85	10	TM32	Double Team	Normal	—	—	15
TM07	Hail	Ice	—	—	10	TM33	Reflect	Normal	—	—	20
TM10	Hidden Power	Normal	—	100	15	TM42	Facade	Normal	70	100	20
TM13	Ice Beam	Ice	95	100	10	TM43	Secret Power	Normal	70	100	20
TM14	Blizzard	Ice	120	70	5	TM44	Rest	Psychic	—	—	10
TM16	Light Screen	Psychic	—	—	30	TM45	Attract	Normal	—	100	15
TM17	Protect	Normal	—	—	10	TM46	Thief	Dark	40	100	10
TM18	Rain Dance	Water	—	—	5	TM48	Skill Swap	Psychic	—	100	10
TM21	Frustration	Normal	—	100	20	HM05	Flash	Normal	—	70	20
TM27	Return	Normal	—	100	20						

EGG MOVES*

Name	Type	Power	ACC	PP
Fake Out	Normal	40	100	10
Ice Punch	Ice	75	100	15
Meditate	Psychic	—	—	40
Psych Up	Normal	—	—	10
Wish	Normal	—	100	10

*Learned Via Breeding

MOVE TUTOR
FireRed/LeafGreen and Emerald Only

Body Slam*	Metronome	Seismic Toss*
Double-Edge	Mimic	Dream Eater*
Mega Punch*	Substitute	
Mega Kick*	Counter*	

*Battle Frontier tutor move (*Emerald*)

PRIMA OFFICIAL GAME GUIDE

239 Elekid™

ELECTRIC

GENERAL INFO

SPECIES: Electric Pokémon
HEIGHT: 2'00"
WEIGHT: 52 lbs.
ABILITY: Static

An opponent has a 30% chance of being paralyzed when it directly strikes Elekid.

STATS

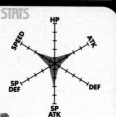

EVOLUTIONS

LV30

LOCATION[s]:

RUBY	Rarity: **None**	Trade from *FireRed/LeafGreen*
SAPPHIRE	Rarity: **None**	Trade from *FireRed/LeafGreen*
FIRERED	Rarity: **None**	Breed Electabuzz
LEAFGREEN	Rarity: **None**	Trade from *FireRed/LeafGreen*
COLOSSEUM	Rarity: **None**	Trade from *FireRed/LeafGreen*
EMERALD	Rarity: **None**	Trade from *FireRed/LeafGreen*
XD	Rarity: **Only One**	Give Hordel the Purified Togepi in trade for Elekid

MOVES

Level	Attack	Type	Power	ACC	PP	Level	Attack	Type	Power	ACC	PP
—	Quick Attack	Normal	40	100	30	25	Swift	Normal	60	—	20
—	Leer	Normal	—	100	30	33	Screech	Normal	—	85	40
9	Thunderpunch	Electric	75	100	15	41	Thunderbolt	Electric	95	100	15
17	Light Screen	Psychic	—	—	30	49	Thunder	Electric	120	70	10

TM/HM

TM/HM#	Name	Type	Power	ACC	PP	TM/HM#	Name	Type	Power	ACC	PP
TM01	Focus Punch	Fighting	150	100	20	TM31	Brick Break	Fighting	75	100	15
TM06	Toxic	Poison	—	85	10	TM32	Double Team	Normal	—	—	15
TM10	Hidden Power	Normal	—	100	15	TM34	Shock Wave	Electric	60	—	20
TM16	Light Screen	Psychic	—	—	30	TM42	Facade	Normal	70	100	20
TM17	Protect	Normal	—	—	10	TM43	Secret Power	Normal	70	100	20
TM18	Rain Dance	Water	—	—	5	TM44	Rest	Psychic	—	—	10
TM21	Frustration	Normal	—	100	20	TM45	Attract	Normal	—	100	15
TM24	Thunderbolt	Electric	95	100	15	TM46	Thief	Dark	40	100	10
TM25	Thunder	Electric	120	70	10	HM05	Flash	Normal	—	70	20
TM27	Return	Normal	—	100	20	HM06	Rock Smash	Fighting	20	100	15
TM29	Psychic	Psychic	90	100	10						

EGG MOVES*

Name	Type	Power	ACC	PP
Barrier	Psychic	—	—	30
Cross Chop	Fighting	100	80	5
Fire Punch	Fire	75	100	15
Ice Punch	Ice	75	100	15
Karate Chop	Fighting	50	100	25
Medtiate	Psychic	—	—	40
Rolling Kick	Fight	60	85	15

*Learned Via Breeding

MOVE TUTOR
FireRed/LeafGreen and Emerald Only

Body Slam*	Mega Kick*	Counter*
Double-Edge	Mimic	Seismic Toss*
Mega Punch*	Substitute	Thunder Wave*

*Battle Frontier tutor move (*Emerald*)

240 Magby™

FIRE

GENERAL INFO

SPECIES: Live Coal Pokémon
HEIGHT: 2'04"
WEIGHT: 47 lbs.
ABILITY: Flame Body
If Magby is struck directly, the opponent has a 30% chance of being burned.

STATS

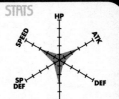

EVOLUTIONS

LV30

LOCATION[s]:

RUBY	Rarity: **None**	Trade from *LeafGreen*
SAPPHIRE	Rarity: **None**	Trade from *LeafGreen*
FIRERED	Rarity: **None**	Trade from *LeafGreen*
LEAFGREEN	Rarity: **None**	Breed Magmar
COLOSSEUM	Rarity: **None**	Trade from *LeafGreen*
EMERALD	Rarity: **None**	Trade from *LeafGreen*
XD	Rarity: **None**	Trade from *LeafGreen*

MOVES

Level	Attack	Type	Power	ACC	PP	Level	Attack	Type	Power	ACC	PP
—	Ember	Fire	40	100	25	25	Smokescreen	Normal	—	100	20
7	Leer	Normal	—	100	30	31	Sunny Day	Fire	—	—	5
13	Smog	Poison	20	70	20	37	Flamethrower	Fire	95	100	15
19	Fire Punch	Fire	75	100	15	43	Confuse Ray	Ghost	—	100	10
						49	Fire Blast	Fire	120	85	5

TM/HM

TM/HM#	Name	Type	Power	ACC	PP	TM/HM#	Name	Type	Power	ACC	PP
TM01	Focus Punch	Fighting	150	100	20	TM32	Double Team	Normal	—	—	15
TM06	Toxic	Poison	—	85	10	TM35	Flamethrower	Fire	95	100	15
TM10	Hidden Power	Normal	—	100	15	TM38	Fire Blast	Fire	120	85	5
TM11	Sunny Day	Fire	—	—	5	TM42	Facade	Normal	70	100	20
TM17	Protect	Normal	—	—	10	TM43	Secret Power	Normal	70	100	20
TM21	Frustration	Normal	—	100	20	TM44	Rest	Psychic	—	—	10
TM23	Iron Tail	Steel	75	75	15	TM45	Attract	Normal	—	100	15
TM27	Return	Normal	—	100	20	TM46	Thief	Dark	40	100	10
TM29	Psychic	Psychic	90	100	10	HM06	Rock Smash	Fighting	20	100	15
TM31	Brick Break	Fighting	75	100	15						

EGG MOVES*

Name	Type	Power	ACC	PP
Barrier	Psychic	—	—	30
Cross Chop	Fighting	100	80	5
Karate Chop	Fighting	50	100	25
Mega Punch	Normal	80	85	20
Screech	Normal	—	85	40
Thunderpunch	Electric	75	100	15

*Learned Via Breeding

MOVE TUTOR
FireRed/LeafGreen and Emerald Only

Body Slam*	Mega Kick*	Counter*
Double-Edge	Mimic	Seismic Toss*
Mega Punch*	Substitute	

*Battle Frontier tutor move (*Emerald*)

241 Miltank™

NORMAL

GENERAL INFO
SPECIES: Milk Cow Pokémon
HEIGHT: 3'11"
WEIGHT: 166 lbs.
ABILITY: Thick Fat
Miltank takes half damage on all Fire-type and Ice-type attacks.

STATS

EVOLUTIONS

DOES NOT EVOLVE

LOCATION[S]:

RUBY	Rarity: **None**	Obtain in *Colosseum/Emerald*
SAPPHIRE	Rarity: **None**	Obtain in *Colosseum/Emerald*
FIRERED	Rarity: **None**	Obtain in *Colosseum/Emerald*
LEAFGREEN	Rarity: **None**	Obtain in *Colosseum/Emerald*
COLOSSEUM	Rarity: **Only One**	Realgam Tower
EMERALD	Rarity: **Rare**	Safari Zone
XD	Rarity: **None**	Obtain in *Colosseum/Emerald*

MOVES

Level	Attack	Type	Power	ACC	PP	Level	Attack	Type	Power	ACC	PP
—	Tackle	Normal	35	95	35	19	Milk Drink	Normal	—	—	10
4	Growl	Normal	—	100	40	26	Bide	Normal	—	100	10
8	Defense Curl	Normal	—	—	40	34	Rollout	Rock	30	90	20
13	Stomp	Normal	65	100	20	43	Body Slam	Normal	85	100	15
						53	Heal Bell	Normal	—	—	5

TM/HM

TM/HM#	Name	Type	Power	ACC	PP	TM/HM#	Name	Type	Power	ACC	PP
TM01	Focus Punch	Fighting	150	100	20	TM26	Earthquake	Ground	100	100	10
TM03	Water Pulse	Water	60	95	20	TM27	Return	Normal	—	100	20
TM06	Toxic	Poison	—	85	10	TM30	Shadow Ball	Ghost	80	100	15
TM10	Hidden Power	Normal	—	100	15	TM31	Brick Break	Fighting	75	100	15
TM11	Sunny Day	Fire	—	—	5	TM32	Double Team	Normal	—	—	15
TM13	Ice Beam	Ice	95	100	10	TM34	Shock Wave	Electric	60	—	20
TM14	Blizzard	Ice	120	70	5	TM37	Sandstorm	Ground	—	—	10
TM15	Hyper Beam	Normal	150	90	5	TM39	Rock Tomb	Rock	50	80	10
TM17	Protect	Normal	—	—	10	TM42	Facade	Normal	70	100	20
TM18	Rain Dance	Water	—	—	5	TM43	Secret Power	Normal	70	100	20
TM21	Frustration	Normal	—	100	20	TM44	Rest	Psychic	—	—	10
TM22	Solarbeam	Grass	120	100	10	TM45	Attract	Normal	—	100	15
TM23	Iron Tail	Steel	75	75	15	HM03	Surf	Water	95	100	15
TM24	Thunderbolt	Electric	95	100	15	HM04	Strength	Normal	80	100	20
TM25	Thunder	Electric	120	70	10	HM06	Rock Smash	Fighting	20	100	15

EGG MOVES*

Name	Type	Power	ACC	PP
Curse	—	—	—	10
Endure	Normal	—	—	10
Helping Hand	Normal	—	100	20
Present	Normal	—	90	15
Psych Up	Normal	—	—	10
Reversal	Fighting	—	100	15
Seismic Toss	Fighting	—	100	20
Sleep Talk	Normal	—	—	10

*Learned Via Breeding

MOVE TUTOR
FireRed/LeafGreen and Emerald Only

Body Slam*	Metronome	Seismic Toss*
Double-Edge	Mimic	Rock Slide*
Mega Punch*	Substitute	Thunder Wave*
Mega Kick*	Counter*	

*Battle Frontier tutor move (*Emerald*)

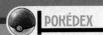

242 Blissey™

NORMAL

GENERAL INFO

SPECIES: Happiness Pokémon
HEIGHT: 4'11"
WEIGHT: 103 lbs.
ABILITY 1: Natural Cure
Any status condition is cured when Blissey is switched out.
ABILITY 2: Serene Grace
When Blissey is in battle, the chances of extra effects occurring are doubled.

STATS

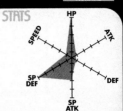

EVOLUTIONS

FRIENDSHIP

LOCATION(S):

RUBY	Rarity: None	Trade from *FireRed/LeafGreen*
SAPPHIRE	Rarity: None	Trade from *FireRed/LeafGreen*
FIRERED	Rarity: None	Evolve Chansey
LEAFGREEN	Rarity: None	Evolve Chansey
COLOSSEUM	Rarity: None	Trade from *FireRed/LeafGreen*
EMERALD	Rarity: None	Trade from *FireRed/LeafGreen*
XD	Rarity: Evolve	Evolve Chansey

MOVES

Level	Attack	Type	Power	ACC	PP	Level	Attack	Type	Power	ACC	PP
—	Pound	Normal	40	100	35	18	Minimize	Normal	—	—	20
—	Growl	Normal	—	100	40	23	Sing	Normal	—	55	15
4	Tail Whip	Normal	—	100	30	28	Egg Bomb	Normal	100	75	10
7	Refresh	Normal	—	100	20	33	Defense Curl	Normal	—	—	40
10	Softboiled	Normal	—	100	10	40	Light Screen	Psychic	—	—	30
13	Doubleslap	Normal	15	85	10	47	Double-Edge	Normal	120	100	15

TM/HM

TM/HM#	Name	Type	Power	ACC	PP	TM/HM#	Name	Type	Power	ACC	PP
TM01	Focus Punch	Fighting	150	100	20	TM26	Earthquake	Ground	100	100	10
TM03	Water Pulse	Water	60	95	20	TM27	Return	Normal	—	100	20
TM04	Calm Mind	Psychic	—	—	20	TM29	Psychic	Psychic	90	100	10
TM06	Toxic	Poison	—	85	10	TM30	Shadow Ball	Ghost	80	100	15
TM07	Hail	Ice	—	—	10	TM31	Brick Break	Fighting	75	100	15
TM10	Hidden Power	Normal	—	100	15	TM32	Double Team	Normal	—	—	15
TM11	Sunny Day	Fire	—	—	5	TM34	Shock Wave	Electric	60	—	20
TM13	Ice Beam	Ice	95	100	10	TM35	Flamethrower	Fire	95	100	15
TM14	Blizzard	Ice	120	70	5	TM37	Sandstorm	Ground	—	—	10
TM15	Hyper Beam	Normal	150	90	5	TM38	Fire Blast	Fire	120	85	5
TM16	Light Screen	Psychic	—	—	30	TM39	Rock Tomb	Rock	50	80	10
TM17	Protect	Normal	—	—	10	TM42	Facade	Normal	70	100	20
TM18	Rain Dance	Water	—	—	5	TM43	Secret Power	Normal	70	100	20
TM20	Safeguard	Normal	—	—	25	TM44	Rest	Psychic	—	—	10
TM21	Frustration	Normal	—	100	20	TM45	Attract	Normal	—	100	15
TM22	Solarbeam	Grass	120	100	10	TM48	Skill Swap	Psychic	—	100	10
TM23	Iron Tail	Steel	75	75	15	TM49	Snatch	Dark	—	100	10
TM24	Thunderbolt	Electric	95	100	15	HM04	Strength	Normal	80	100	15
TM25	Thunder	Electric	120	70	10	HM05	Flash	Normal	—	70	20
						HM06	Rock Smash	Fighting	20	100	15

MOVE TUTOR
FireRed/LeafGreen and Emerald Only

Body Slam*	Metronome	Counter*
Double-Edge	Mimic	Seismic Toss*
Mega Punch*	Softboiled	Dream Eater*
Mega Kick*	Substitute	Thunder Wave*

*Battle Frontier tutor move (*Emerald*)

PRIMA OFFICIAL GAME GUIDE

243 Raikou™

ELECTRIC

GENERAL INFO
SPECIES: Thunder Pokémon
HEIGHT: 6'03"
WEIGHT: 392 lbs.
ABILITY: Pressure
Opponent uses 2 PPs for damage inflicted against Raikou.

STATS

HP, ATK, DEF, SP ATK, SP DEF, SPEED

EVOLUTIONS

DOES NOT EVOLVE

LOCATION(s):

RUBY	**Rarity: None**	Trade from *FireRed/LeafGreen/Colosseum*
SAPPHIRE	**Rarity: None**	Trade from *FireRed/LeafGreen/Colosseum*
FIRERED	**Rarity: Only One**	Wild in Kanto (after beating Elite Four) if starter Pokémon is Squirtle
LEAFGREEN	**Rarity: Only One**	Wild in Kanto (after beating Elite Four) if starter Pokémon is Squirtle
COLOSSEUM	**Rarity: Only One**	Shadow Pokémon Lab
EMERALD	**Rarity: None**	Trade from *FireRed/LeafGreen/Colosseum*
XD	**Rarity: None**	Trade from *FireRed/LeafGreen/Colosseum*

MOVES

Level	Attack	Type	Power	ACC	PP
—	Bite	Dark	60	100	25
—	Leer	Normal	—	100	30
11	Thundershock	Electric	40	100	30
21	Roar	Normal	—	100	20
31	Quick Attack	Normal	40	100	30

Level	Attack	Type	Power	ACC	PP
41	Spark	Electric	65	100	20
51	Reflect	Psychic	—	—	20
61	Crunch	Dark	80	100	15
71	Thunder	Electric	120	70	10
81	Calm Mind	Psychic	—	—	20

TM/HM

TM/HM#	Name	Type	Power	ACC	PP
TM04	Calm Mind	Psychic	—	—	20
TM05	Roar	Normal	—	100	20
TM06	Toxic	Poison	—	85	10
TM10	Hidden Power	Normal	—	100	15
TM11	Sunny Day	Fire	—	—	5
TM15	Hyper Beam	Normal	150	90	5
TM17	Protect	Normal	—	—	10
TM18	Rain Dance	Water	—	—	5
TM21	Frustration	Normal	—	100	20
TM23	Iron Tail	Steel	75	75	15
TM24	Thunderbolt	Electric	95	100	15
TM25	Thunder	Electric	120	70	10
TM27	Return	Normal	—	100	20

TM/HM#	Name	Type	Power	ACC	PP
TM28	Dig	Ground	60	100	10
TM32	Double Team	Normal	—	—	15
TM33	Reflect	Normal	—	—	20
TM34	Shock Wave	Electric	60	—	20
TM37	Sandstorm	Ground	—	—	10
TM42	Facade	Normal	70	100	20
TM43	Secret Power	Normal	70	100	20
TM44	Rest	Psychic	—	—	10
HM01	Cut	Normal	50	95	30
HM04	Strength	Normal	80	100	20
HM05	Flash	Normal	—	70	20
HM06	Rock Smash	Fighting	20	100	15

MOVE TUTOR
FireRed/LeafGreen and Emerald Only

Body Slam*	Mimic	Substitute
Double-Edge	Thunder Wave*	

*Battle Frontier tutor move (*Emerald*)

244 Entei™

FIRE

GENERAL INFO

SPECIES: Volcano Pokémon
HEIGHT: 6'11"
WEIGHT: 437 lbs.
ABILITY: Pressure

Opponent uses 2 PPs for damage inflicted against Entei.

STATS

HP, ATK, DEF, SP ATK, SP DEF, SPEED

EVOLUTIONS

DOES NOT EVOLVE

LOCATION[s]:

RUBY	Rarity: **None**	Trade from *FireRed/LeafGreen/Colosseum*
SAPPHIRE	Rarity: **None**	Trade from *FireRed/LeafGreen/Colosseum*
FIRERED	Rarity: **Only One**	Wild in Kanto (after beating Elite Four) if starter Pokémon is Bulbasaur
LEAFGREEN	Rarity: **Only One**	Wild in Kanto (after beating Elite Four) if starter Pokémon is Bulbasaur
COLOSSEUM	Rarity: **Only One**	Mt. Battle
EMERALD	Rarity: **None**	Trade from *FireRed/LeafGreen/Colosseum*
XD	Rarity: **None**	Trade from *FireRed/LeafGreen/Colosseum*

MOVES

Level	Attack	Type	Power	ACC	PP
—	Bite	Dark	60	100	25
—	Leer	Normal	—	100	30
11	Ember	Fire	40	100	25
21	Roar	Normal	—	100	20
31	Fire Spin	Fire	15	70	15

Level	Attack	Type	Power	ACC	PP
41	Stomp	Normal	65	100	20
51	Flamethrower	Fire	95	100	15
61	Swagger	Normal	—	90	15
71	Fire Blast	Fire	120	85	5
81	Calm Mind	Psychic	—	—	20

TM/HM

TM/HM#	Name	Type	Power	ACC	PP
TM04	Calm Mind	Psychic	—	—	20
TM05	Roar	Normal	—	100	20
TM06	Toxic	Poison	—	85	10
TM10	Hidden Power	Normal	—	100	15
TM11	Sunny Day	Fire	—	—	5
TM15	Hyper Beam	Normal	150	90	5
TM17	Protect	Normal	—	—	10
TM18	Rain Dance	Water	—	—	5
TM21	Frustration	Normal	—	100	20
TM22	Solar Beam	Grass	120	100	10
TM23	Iron Tail	Steel	75	75	15
TM27	Return	Normal	—	100	20
TM28	Dig	Ground	60	100	10

TM/HM#	Name	Type	Power	ACC	PP
TM32	Double Team	Normal	—	—	15
TM33	Reflect	Normal	—	—	20
TM35	Flamethrower	Fire	95	100	15
TM37	Sandstorm	Ground	—	—	10
TM38	Fire Blast	Fire	120	85	5
TM42	Facade	Normal	70	100	20
TM43	Secret Power	Normal	70	100	20
TM44	Rest	Psychic	—	—	10
HM01	Cut	Normal	50	95	30
HM04	Strength	Normal	80	100	20
HM05	Flash	Normal	—	70	20
HM06	Rock Smash	Fighting	20	100	15

MOVE TUTOR

FireRed/LeafGreen and Emerald Only

Body Slam*	Mimic	Substitute
Double-Edge		

*Battle Frontier tutor move (*Emerald*)

245 Suicune™

WATER

GENERAL INFO

SPECIES: Aurora Pokémon
HEIGHT: 6'07"
WEIGHT: 412 lbs.
ABILITY: Pressure
Opponent uses 2 PPs for damage inflicted against Suicune.

STATS

EVOLUTIONS

DOES NOT EVOLVE

LOCATION[s]:

RUBY	Rarity: **None**	Trade from *FireRed/LeafGreen/Colosseum*
SAPPHIRE	Rarity: **None**	Trade from *FireRed/LeafGreen/Colosseum*
FIRERED	Rarity: **Only One**	Wild in Kanto (after beating Elite Four) if starter Pokémon is Charmander
LEAFGREEN	Rarity: **Only One**	Wild in Kanto (after beating Elite Four) if starter Pokémon is Charmander
COLOSSEUM	Rarity: **Only One**	The Under
EMERALD	Rarity: **None**	Trade from *FireRed/LeafGreen/Colosseum*
XD	Rarity: **None**	Trade from *FireRed/LeafGreen/Colosseum*

MOVES

Level	Attack	Type	Power	ACC	PP
—	Bite	Dark	60	100	25
—	Leer	Normal	—	100	30
11	Bubblebeam	Water	65	100	20
21	Rain Dance	Water	—	—	5
31	Gust	Flying	40	100	35

Level	Attack	Type	Power	ACC	PP
41	Aurora Beam	Ice	65	100	20
51	Mist	Ice	—	—	30
61	Mirror Coat	Psychic	—	100	20
71	Hydro Pump	Water	120	80	5
81	Calm Mind	Psychic	—	—	20

TM/HM

TM/HM#	Name	Type	Power	ACC	PP
TM03	Water Pulse	Water	60	95	20
TM04	Calm Mind	Psychic	—	—	20
TM05	Roar	Normal	—	100	20
TM06	Toxic	Poison	—	85	10
TM07	Hail	Ice	—	—	10
TM10	Hidden Power	Normal	—	100	15
TM11	Sunny Day	Fire	—	—	5
TM13	Ice Beam	Ice	95	100	10
TM14	Blizzard	Ice	120	70	5
TM15	Hyper Beam	Normal	150	90	5
TM17	Protect	Normal	—	—	10
TM18	Rain Dance	Water	—	—	5
TM21	Frustration	Normal	—	100	20
TM23	Iron Tail	Steel	75	75	15

TM/HM#	Name	Type	Power	ACC	PP
TM27	Return	Normal	—	100	20
TM28	Dig	Ground	60	100	10
TM32	Double Team	Normal	—	—	15
TM33	Reflect	Normal	—	—	20
TM37	Sandstorm	Ground	—	—	10
TM42	Facade	Normal	70	—	20
TM43	Secret Power	Normal	70	100	20
TM44	Rest	Psychic	—	—	10
HM01	Cut	Normal	50	95	30
HM03	Surf	Water	95	100	15
HM06	Rock Smash	Fighting	20	100	15
HM07	Waterfall	Water	80	100	15
HM08	Dive	Water	60	100	10

MOVE TUTOR
FireRed/LeafGreen and Emerald Only

Body Slam*	Mimic	Substitute
Double-Edge		

*Battle Frontier tutor move (*Emerald*)

246 Larvitar™

ROCK | GROUND

GENERAL INFO

SPECIES: Rock Skin Pokémon
HEIGHT: 2'00"
WEIGHT: 159 lbs.
ABILITY: Guts

When Larvitar has a status condition, its attack power is multiplied by 1.5.

STATS

EVOLUTIONS

 ▶ LV30 ▶ LV55

LOCATION[s]:

RUBY	Rarity: **None**	Trade from *FireRed/LeafGreen*
SAPPHIRE	Rarity: **None**	Trade from *FireRed/LeafGreen*
FIRERED	Rarity: **Rare**	Seven Island
LEAFGREEN	Rarity: **Rare**	Seven Island
COLOSSEUM	Rarity: **None**	Trade from *FireRed/LeafGreen*
EMERALD	Rarity: **None**	Trade from *FireRed/LeafGreen*
XD	Rarity: **Only One**	Trade from Duking

MOVES

Level	Attack	Type	Power	ACC	PP
—	Bite	Dark	60	100	25
—	Leer	Normal	—	100	30
—	Sandstorm	Rock	—	—	10
5	Screech	Normal	—	85	40
22	Rock Slide	Rock	75	90	10
29	Thrash	Normal	90	100	20
36	Scary Face	Normal	—	90	10
43	Crunch	Dark	80	100	15
50	Earthquake	Ground	100	100	10
57	Hyper Beam	Normal	150	90	5

TM/HM

TM/HM#	Name	Type	Power	ACC	PP
TM06	Toxic	Poison	—	85	10
TM10	Hidden Power	Normal	—	100	15
TM11	Sunny Day	Fire	—	—	5
TM12	Taunt	Dark	—	100	20
TM15	Hyper Beam	Normal	150	90	5
TM17	Protect	Normal	—	—	10
TM18	Rain Dance	Water	—	—	5
TM21	Frustration	Normal	—	100	20
TM26	Earthquake	Ground	100	100	10
TM27	Return	Normal	—	100	20
TM28	Dig	Ground	60	100	10
TM31	Brick Break	Fighting	75	100	15
TM32	Double Team	Normal	—	—	15
TM37	Sandstorm	Ground	—	—	10
TM41	Torment	Dark	—	100	15
TM42	Facade	Normal	70	100	20
TM43	Secret Power	Normal	70	100	20
TM44	Rest	Psychic	—	—	10
TM45	Attract	Normal	—	100	15
HM06	Rock Smash	Fighting	20	100	15

EGG MOVES*

Name	Type	Power	ACC	PP
Ancientpower	Rock	60	100	5
Curse	—	—	—	10
Dragon Dance	Dragon	—	—	20
Focus Energy	Normal	—	—	30
Outrage	Dragon	90	100	15
Pursuit	Dark	40	100	20
Stomp	Normal	65	100	20

*Learned Via Breeding

MOVE TUTOR

FireRed/LeafGreen and Emerald Only

Body Slam*	Mimic	Substitute
Double-Edge	Rock Slide*	

*Battle Frontier tutor move (*Emerald*)

PRIMA OFFICIAL GAME GUIDE

247 Pupitar™

ROCK   GROUND

GENERAL INFO

SPECIES: Hard Shell Pokémon
HEIGHT: 3'11"
WEIGHT: 335 lbs.
ABILITY: Shed Skin

Enables Pupitar to have a status effect for only one turn. Shed Skin has 30% of success.

STATS

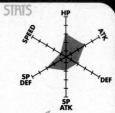

EVOLUTIONS

LV30   LV55

LOCATION(s):

RUBY	Rarity: **None**	Evolve Larvitar or Trade from *FireRed/LeafGreen*
SAPPHIRE	Rarity: **None**	Evolve Larvitar or Trade from *FireRed/LeafGreen*
FIRERED	Rarity: **Rare**	Evolve Larvitar
LEAFGREEN	Rarity: **Rare**	Evolve Larvitar
COLOSSEUM	Rarity: **None**	Evolve Larvitar
EMERALD	Rarity: **None**	Trade from *FireRed/LeafGreen*
XD	Rarity: **Evolve**	Evolve Larvitar

MOVES

Level	Attack	Type	Power	ACC	PP	Level	Attack	Type	Power	ACC	PP
—	Bite	Dark	60	100	25	29	Thrash	Normal	90	100	20
—	Leer	Normal	—	100	30	38	Scary Face	Normal	—	90	10
—	Sandstorm	Rock	—	—	10	47	Crunch	Dark	80	100	15
—	Screech	Normal	—	85	40	56	Earthquake	Ground	100	100	10
22	Rock Slide	Rock	75	90	10	56	Hyper Beam	Normal	150	90	5

TM/HM

TM/HM#	Name	Type	Power	ACC	PP	TM/HM#	Name	Type	Power	ACC	PP
TM06	Toxic	Poison	—	85	10	TM28	Dig	Ground	60	100	10
TM10	Hidden Power	Normal	—	100	15	TM31	Brick Break	Fighting	75	100	15
TM11	Sunny Day	Fire	—	—	5	TM32	Double Team	Normal	—	—	15
TM12	Taunt	Dark	—	100	20	TM37	Sandstorm	Ground	—	—	10
TM15	Hyper Beam	Normal	150	90	5	TM41	Torment	Dark	—	100	15
TM17	Protect	Normal	—	—	10	TM42	Facade	Normal	70	100	20
TM18	Rain Dance	Water	—	—	5	TM43	Secret Power	Normal	70	100	20
TM21	Frustration	Normal	—	100	20	TM44	Rest	Psychic	—	—	10
TM26	Earthquake	Ground	100	100	10	TM45	Attract	Normal	—	100	15
TM27	Return	Normal	—	100	20	HM06	Rock Smash	Fighting	20	100	15

MOVE TUTOR
FireRed/LeafGreen and Emerald Only

Body Slam*	Mimic	Substitute
Double-Edge	Rock Slide*	

*Battle Frontier tutor move (*Emerald*)

248 Tyranitar™

ROCK | DARK

GENERAL INFO

SPECIES: Armor Pokémon
HEIGHT: 6'07"
WEIGHT: 445 lbs.
ABILITY: Sand Stream
A sandstorm begins when Tyranitar enters battle.

STATS

EVOLUTIONS

  LV30 LV55

LOCATION[S]:

RUBY	Rarity: **None**	Trade from *Colosseum*
SAPPHIRE	Rarity: **None**	Trade from *Colosseum*
FIRERED	Rarity: **None**	Trade from *Colosseum*
LEAFGREEN	Rarity: **None**	Trade from *Colosseum*
COLOSSEUM	Rarity: **Only One**	Realgam Tower
EMERALD	Rarity: **None**	Trade from *FireRed/LeafGreen*
XD	Rarity: **Evolve**	Evolve Pupitar

MOVES

Level	Attack	Type	Power	ACC	PP		Level	Attack	Type	Power	ACC	PP
—	Bite	Dark	60	100	25		29	Thrash	Normal	90	100	20
—	Leer	Normal	—	100	30		38	Scary Face	Normal	—	90	10
—	Sandstorm	Rock	—	—	10		47	Crunch	Dark	80	100	15
—	Screech	Normal	—	85	40		61	Earthquake	Ground	100	100	10
22	Rock Slide	Rock	75	90	10		75	Hyper Beam	Normal	150	90	5

TM/HM

TM/HM#	Name	Type	Power	ACC	PP		TM/HM#	Name	Type	Power	ACC	PP
TM01	Focus Punch	Fighting	150	100	20		TM28	Dig	Ground	60	100	10
TM02	Dragon Claw	Dragon	80	100	15		TM31	Brick Break	Fighting	75	100	15
TM03	Water Pulse	Water	60	95	20		TM32	Double Team	Normal	—	—	15
TM05	Roar	Normal	—	100	20		TM34	Shock Wave	Electric	60	—	20
TM06	Toxic	Poison	—	85	10		TM35	Flamethrower	Fire	95	100	15
TM10	Hidden Power	Normal	—	100	15		TM37	Sandstorm	Ground	—	—	10
TM11	Sunny Day	Fire	—	—	5		TM38	Fire Blast	Fire	120	85	5
TM12	Taunt	Dark	—	100	20		TM39	Rock Tomb	Rock	50	80	10
TM13	Ice Beam	Ice	95	100	10		TM40	Aerial Ace	Flying	60	—	20
TM14	Blizzard	Ice	120	70	5		TM41	Torment	Dark	—	100	15
TM15	Hyper Beam	Normal	150	90	5		TM42	Facade	Normal	70	100	20
TM17	Protect	Normal	—	—	10		TM43	Secret Power	Normal	70	100	20
TM18	Rain Dance	Water	—	—	5		TM44	Rest	Psychic	—	—	10
TM21	Frustration	Normal	—	100	20		TM45	Attract	Normal	—	100	15
TM23	Iron Tail	Steel	75	75	15		HM01	Cut	Normal	50	95	30
TM24	Thunderbolt	Electric	95	100	15		HM03	Surf	Water	95	100	15
TM25	Thunder	Electric	120	70	10		HM04	Strength	Normal	80	100	15
TM26	Earthquake	Ground	100	100	10		HM06	Rock Smash	Fighting	20	100	15
TM27	Return	Normal	—	100	20							

MOVE TUTOR
FireRed/LeafGreen and Emerald Only

Body Slam*	Mimic	Rock Slide*
Double-Edge	Substitute	Thunder Wave*
Mega Punch*	Counter*	
Mega Kick*	Seismic Toss*	

*Battle Frontier tutor move (*Emerald*)

249 Lugia™

PSYCHIC   FLYING

GENERAL INFO

SPECIES: Diving Pokémon
HEIGHT: 17'01"
WEIGHT: 476 lbs.
ABILITY: Pressure
Opponent uses 2 PPs for damage inflicted against Lugia.

STATS

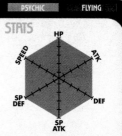

EVOLUTIONS

DOES NOT EVOLVE

LOCATION[s]:

RUBY	Rarity: **None**	Trade from *XD*	
SAPPHIRE	Rarity: **None**	Trade from *XD*	
FIRERED	Rarity: **None**	Trade from *XD*	
LEAFGREEN	Rarity: **None**	Trade from *XD*	
COLOSSEUM	Rarity: **None**	Trade from *XD*	
EMERALD	Rarity: **None**	Trade from *XD*	
XD	Rarity: **Only One**	Citadark Island (Capture from Master Greevil)	

MOVES

Level	Attack	Type	Power	ACC	PP	Level	Attack	Type	Power	ACC	PP
—	Whirlwind	Normal	—	100	20	55	Rain Dance	Water	—	—	5
11	Safeguard	Normal	—	—	25	66	Swift	Normal	60	—	20
22	Gust	Flying	40	100	35	77	Aeroblast	Flying	100	95	5
33	Recover	Normal	—	—	20	88	Ancientpower	Rock	60	100	5
44	Hydro Pump	Water	120	80	5	99	Future Sight	Psychic	80	90	15

TM/HM

TM/HM#	Name	Type	Power	ACC	PP	TM/HM#	Name	Type	Power	ACC	PP
TM03	Water Pulse	Water	60	100	20	TM24	Thunderbolt	Electric	95	100	15
TM04	Calm Mind	Psychic	—	—	20	TM25	Thunder	Electric	120	70	10
TM05	Roar	Normal	—	100	20	TM26	Earthquake	Ground	100	100	10
TM06	Toxic	Poison	—	85	10	TM27	Return	Normal	—	100	20
TM07	Hail	Ice	—	—	10	TM29	Psychic	Psychic	90	100	10
TM10	Hidden Power	Normal	—	100	15	TM30	Shadow Punch	Ghost	60	—	20
TM11	Sunny Day	Fire	—	—	5	TM32	Double Team	Normal	—	—	—
TM13	Ice Beam	Ice	95	100	10	TM33	Reflect	Psychic	—	—	20
TM14	Blizzard	Ice	120	70	5	TM34	Shockwave	Electric	60	—	20
TM15	Hyper Beam	Normal	150	90	5	TM37	Sandstorm	Ground	—	—	10
TM16	Light Screen	Psychic	—	—	30	TM40	Aerial Ace	Flying	60	—	20
TM17	Protect	Normal	—	—	10	TM42	Facade	Normal	70	100	20
TM18	Rain Dance	Water	—	—	5	TM43	Secret Power	Normal	70	100	20
TM19	Giga Drain	Ground	600	100	5	TM44	Rest	Psychic	—	—	10
TM20	Safeguard	Normal	—	—	25	TM47	Steel Wing	Steel	70	90	25
TM21	Frustration	Normal	—	100	20	TM48	Skill Swap	Psychic	—	100	10
TM23	Iron Tail	Steel	100	75	15						

250 Ho-Oh™

FIRE | FLYING

GENERAL INFO

SPECIES: Rainbow Pokémon
HEIGHT: 12'06"
WEIGHT: 439 lbs.
ABILITY: Pressure
Opponent uses 2 PPs for damage inflicted on Ho-Oh.

STATS

EVOLUTIONS

DOES NOT EVOLVE

LOCATION(S):

RUBY	Rarity: **None**	Obtain in *Colosseum*
SAPPHIRE	Rarity: **None**	Obtain in *Colosseum*
FIRERED	Rarity: **None**	Trade from *Colosseum*
LEAFGREEN	Rarity: **None**	Trade from *Colosseum*
COLOSSEUM	Rarity: **Only One**	Mt. Battle 100 Man Challenge
EMERALD	Rarity: **None**	Navel Rock
XD	Rarity: **None**	Trade from *Colosseum*

MOVES

Level	Attack	Type	Power	ACC	PP	Level	Attack	Type	Power	ACC	PP
—	Whirlwind	Normal	—	100	20	55	Sunny Day	Fire	—	—	5
11	Safeguard	Normal	—	—	25	66	Swift	Normal	60	—	20
22	Gust	Flying	40	100	35	77	Sacred Fire	Fire	100	100	5
33	Recover	Normal	—	—	20	88	Ancientpower	Rock	60	100	5
44	Fire Blast	Fire	120	85	5	99	Future Sight	Psychic	80	90	15

TM/HM

TM/HM#	Name	Type	Power	ACC	PP	TM/HM#	Name	Type	Power	ACC	PP
TM04	Calm Mind	Psychic	—	—	20	TM30	Shadow Ball	Ghost	80	100	15
TM05	Roar	Normal	—	100	20	TM32	Double Team	Normal	—	—	15
TM06	Toxic	Poison	—	85	10	TM33	Reflect	Normal	—	—	20
TM10	Hidden Power	Normal	—	100	15	TM34	Shock Wave	Electric	60	—	20
TM11	Sunny Day	Fire	—	—	5	TM35	Flamethrower	Fire	95	100	15
TM15	Hyper Beam	Normal	150	90	5	TM37	Sandstorm	Ground	—	—	10
TM16	Light Screen	Psychic	—	—	30	TM38	Fire Blast	Fire	120	85	5
TM17	Protect	Normal	—	—	10	TM40	Aerial Ace	Flying	60	—	20
TM18	Rain Dance	Water	—	—	5	TM42	Facade	Normal	70	100	20
TM19	Giga Drain	Grass	60	100	5	TM43	Secret Power	Normal	70	100	20
TM20	Safeguard	Normal	—	—	25	TM44	Rest	Psychic	—	—	10
TM21	Frustration	Normal	—	100	20	TM47	Steel Wing	Steel	70	90	25
TM22	Solarbeam	Grass	120	100	10	TM50	Overheat	Fire	140	90	5
TM24	Thunderbolt	Electric	95	100	15	HM02	Fly	Flying	70	95	15
TM25	Thunder	Electric	120	70	10	HM04	Strength	Normal	80	100	20
TM26	Earthquake	Ground	100	100	10	HM05	Flash	Normal	—	70	20
TM27	Return	Normal	—	100	20	HM06	Rock Smash	Fighting	20	100	15
TM29	Psychic	Psychic	90	100	10						

MOVE TUTOR

FireRed/LeafGreen and Emerald Only

Body Slam*	Mimic	Substitute
Double-Edge	Dream Eater*	Thunder Wave*

*Battle Frontier tutor move (*Emerald*)

251 Celebi™

GRASS · PSYCHIC

GENERAL INFO
SPECIES: Time Travel Pokémon
HEIGHT: 2'00"
WEIGHT: 11 lbs.
ABILITY: Natural Cure
If Celebi is switched out, the Status condition is gone.

STATS

EVOLUTIONS

DOES NOT EVOLVE

LOCATION[s]:

RUBY	Rarity: **None**
SAPPHIRE	Rarity: **None**
FIRERED	Rarity: **None**
LEAFGREEN	Rarity: **None**
COLOSSEUM	Rarity: **None**
EMERALD	Rarity: **None**
XD	Rarity: **None**

MOVES

Level	Attack	Type	Power	ACC	PP
—	Leech Seeds	Grass	—	90	10
—	Confusion	Psychic	50	100	25
—	Recover	Normal	—	—	20
—	Heal Bell	Normal	—	—	5
10	Safeguard	Normal	—	—	25
20	Ancient Power	Rock	60	100	5
30	Future Sight	Psychic	80	90	15
40	Baton Pass	Normal	—	—	40
50	Perish Song	Normal	—	—	5

TM/HM

TM/HM#	Name	Type	Power	ACC	PP
TM03	Water Pulse	Water	60	100	20
TM04	Calm Mind	Psychic	—	—	20
TM06	Toxic	Poison	—	85	10
TM10	Hidden Power	Normal	—	100	15
TM11	Sunny Day	Fire	—	—	5
TM15	Hyper Beam	Normal	150	90	5
TM16	Light Screen	Psychic	—	—	30
TM17	Protect	Normal	—	—	10
TM18	Rain Dance	Water	—	—	5
TM19	Giga Drain	Grass	60	100	5
TM20	Safeguard	Normal	—	—	25
TM21	Frustration	Normal	—	100	20
TM22	Solarbeam	Grass	120	100	10
TM27	Return	Normal	—	100	20
TM29	Psychic	Psychic	90	100	10
TM30	Shadow Ball	Ghost	80	100	15
TM32	Double Team	Normal	—	—	15
TM33	Reflect	Psychic	—	—	20
TM34	Shock Wave	Electric	60	—	20
TM37	Sandstorm	Rock	—	—	10
TM40	Aerial Ace	Flying	60	—	20
TM42	Facade	Normal	70	100	20
TM43	Secret Power	Normal	70	100	20
TM44	Rest	Psychic	—	—	10
TM48	Skill Swap	Psychic	—	100	10
HM01	Cut	Normal	50	95	30
HM05	Flash	Normal	—	70	20

MOVE TUTOR
FireRed/LeafGreen and Emerald Only

Dream Eater*	Mimic	Metronome
Double-Edge	Swords Dance*	Substitute

*Battle Frontier tutor move (*Emerald*)

252 Treecko™

GRASS

GENERAL INFO

SPECIES: Wood Gecko Pokémon
HEIGHT: 1'08"
WEIGHT: 11 lbs.
ABILITY: Overgrow

Treecko's Grass-type attack power is multiplied by 1.5 when its HPs get low.

STATS

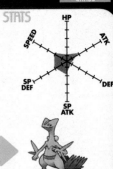

EVOLUTIONS

LV16   LV36

LOCATION[s]:

RUBY	Rarity: **Only One**	Starter Pokémon obtained from Prof. Birch on Route 101
SAPPHIRE	Rarity: **Only One**	Starter Pokémon obtained from Prof. Birch on Route 101
FIRERED	Rarity: **None**	Trade from *Ruby/Sapphire*
LEAFGREEN	Rarity: **None**	Trade from *Ruby/Sapphire*
COLOSSEUM	Rarity: **None**	Trade from *Ruby/Sapphire*
EMERALD	Rarity: **Only One**	Starter Pokémon obtained from Prof. Birch on Route 101
XD	Rarity: **None**	Trade from *Ruby/Sapphire*

MOVES

Level	Attack	Type	Power	ACC	PP		Level	Attack	Type	Power	ACC	PP
—/5	Pound	Normal	40	100	35		26	Mega Drain	Grass	40	100	10
—/5	Leer	Normal	—	100	30		31	Agility	Psychic	—	—	30
6	Absorb	Grass	20	100	20		36	Slam	Normal	80	75	20
11	Quick Attack	Normal	40	100	30		41	Detect	Fight	—	—	5
16	Pursuit	Dark	40	100	20		46	Giga Drain	Grass	60	100	5
21	Screech	Normal	—	85	40							

TM/HM

TM/HM#	Name	Type	Power	ACC	PP		TM/HM#	Name	Type	Power	ACC	PP
TM01	Focus Punch	Fighting	150	100	20		TM31	Brick Break	Fighting	75	100	15
TM06	Toxic	Poison	—	85	10		TM32	Double Team	Normal	—	—	15
TM09	Bullet Seed	Grass	10	100	30		TM39	Rock Tomb	Rock	50	80	10
TM10	Hidden Power	Normal	—	100	15		TM40	Aerial Ace	Flying	60	—	20
TM11	Sunny Day	Fire	—	—	5		TM42	Facade	Normal	70	100	20
TM17	Protect	Normal	—	—	10		TM43	Secret Power	Normal	70	100	20
TM19	Giga Drain	Grass	60	100	5		TM44	Rest	Psychic	—	—	10
TM20	Safeguard	Normal	—	—	25		TM45	Attract	Normal	—	100	15
TM21	Frustration	Normal	—	100	20		HM01	Cut	Normal	50	95	30
TM22	Solarbeam	Grass	120	100	10		HM04	Strength	Normal	80	100	20
TM23	Iron Tail	Steel	75	75	15		HM05	Flash	Normal	—	70	20
TM27	Return	Normal	—	100	20		HM06	Rock Smash	Fighting	20	100	15
TM28	Dig	Ground	60	100	10							

EGG MOVES*

Name	Type	Power	ACC	PP
Mud Sport	Ground	—	100	15
Endeavor	Normal	—	100	5
Crunch	Dark	80	100	15
Leech Seed	Grass	—	90	10
Crush Claw	Normal	75	95	10
Dragonbreath	Dragon	60	100	20

*Learned Via Breeding

MOVE TUTOR

FireRed/LeafGreen and Emerald Only

Body Slam*	Mega Kick*	Swords Dance*
Double-Edge	Mimic	Counter*
Mega Punch*	Substitute	Seismic Toss*

Emerald Only

Dynamicpunch	Mud-Slap*	Swagger
Endure*	Sleep Talk	Swift*
Fury Cutter	Snore	Thunderpunch*

*Battle Frontier tutor move (*Emerald*)

253 Grovyle™

GRASS

GENERAL INFO
SPECIES: Wood Gecko Pokémon
HEIGHT: 2'11"
WEIGHT: 48 lbs.
ABILITY: Overgrow
Grovyle's Grass-type attack power is multiplied by 1.5 when its HPs get low.

STATS

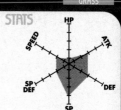

EVOLUTIONS

LV16　　　　LV36

LOCATION[s]:

RUBY	Rarity:	**Evolve**	Evolve Treecko
SAPPHIRE	Rarity:	**Evolve**	Evolve Treecko
FIRERED	Rarity:	**None**	Trade from *Ruby/Sapphire*
LEAFGREEN	Rarity:	**None**	Trade from *Ruby/Sapphire*
COLOSSEUM	Rarity:	**None**	Trade from *Ruby/Sapphire*
EMERALD	Rarity:	**Evolve**	Evolve Treecko
XD	Rarity:	**None**	Trade from *Ruby/Sapphire*

MOVES

Level	Attack	Type	Power	ACC	PP	Level	Attack	Type	Power	ACC	PP
—	Pound	Normal	40	100	35	23	Screech	Normal	—	85	40
—	Leer	Normal	—	100	30	29	Leaf Blade	Grass	70	100	15
—/6	Absorb	Grass	20	100	20	35	Agility	Psychic	—	—	30
—/11	Quick Attack	Normal	40	100	30	41	Slam	Normal	80	75	20
16	Fury Cutter	Bug	10	95	20	47	Detect	Fight	—	—	5
17	Pursuit	Dark	40	100	20	53	False Swipe	Normal	40	100	40

TM/HM

TM/HM#	Name	Type	Power	ACC	PP	TM/HM#	Name	Type	Power	ACC	PP
TM01	Focus Punch	Fighting	150	100	20	TM31	Brick Break	Fighting	75	100	15
TM06	Toxic	Poison	—	85	10	TM32	Double Team	Normal	—	—	15
TM09	Bullet Seed	Grass	10	100	30	TM39	Rock Tomb	Rock	50	80	10
TM10	Hidden Power	Normal	—	100	15	TM40	Aerial Ace	Flying	60	—	20
TM11	Sunny Day	Fire	—	—	5	TM42	Facade	Normal	70	100	20
TM17	Protect	Normal	—	—	10	TM43	Secret Power	Normal	70	100	20
TM19	Giga Drain	Grass	60	100	5	TM44	Rest	Psychic	—	—	10
TM20	Safeguard	Normal	—	—	25	TM45	Attract	Normal	—	100	15
TM21	Frustration	Normal	—	100	20	HM01	Cut	Normal	50	95	30
TM22	Solarbeam	Grass	120	100	10	HM04	Strength	Normal	80	100	20
TM23	Iron Tail	Steel	75	75	15	HM05	Flash	Normal	—	70	20
TM27	Return	Normal	—	100	20	HM06	Rock Smash	Fighting	20	100	15
TM28	Dig	Ground	60	100	10						

MOVE TUTOR

FireRed/LeafGreen and Emerald Only

Body Slam*	Mega Kick*	Swords Dance*
Double-Edge	Mimic	Counter*
Mega Punch*	Substitute	Seismic Toss*

Emerald Only

Dynamicpunch	Mud-Slap*	Swagger
Endure*	Sleep Talk	Swift*
Fury Cutter	Snore*	Thunderpunch*

*Battle Frontier tutor move (*Emerald*)

254 Sceptile™

GRASS

GENERAL INFO

SPECIES: Forest Pokémon
HEIGHT: 5'07"
WEIGHT: 115 lbs.
ABILITY: Overgrow

Sceptile's Grass-type attack power is multiplied by 1.5 when its HPs get low.

STATS

EVOLUTIONS

LV16 — LV36

LOCATION[s]:

RUBY	Rarity: **Evolve**	Evolve Grovyle	
SAPPHIRE	Rarity: **Evolve**	Evolve Grovyle	
FIRERED	Rarity: **None**	Trade from *Ruby/Sapphire*	
LEAFGREEN	Rarity: **None**	Trade from *Ruby/Sapphire*	
COLOSSEUM	Rarity: **None**	Trade from *Ruby/Sapphire*	
EMERALD	Rarity: **Evolve**	Evolve Grovyle	
XD	Rarity: **None**	Trade from *Ruby/Sapphire*	

MOVES

Level	Attack	Type	Power	ACC	PP
—	Pound	Normal	40	100	35
—	Leer	Normal	—	100	30
—/6	Absorb	Grass	20	100	25
—/11	Quick Attack	Normal	40	100	30
16	Fury Cutter	Bug	10	95	20
17	Pursuit	Dark	40	100	20
23	Screech	Normal	—	85	40
29	Leaf Blade	Grass	70	100	15
35	Agility	Psychic	—	—	30
43	Slam	Normal	80	75	20
51	Detect	Fight	—	—	5
59	False Swipe	Normal	40	100	40

TM/HM

TM/HM#	Name	Type	Power	ACC	PP
TM01	Focus Punch	Fighting	150	100	20
TM02	Dragon Claw	Dragon	80	100	15
TM05	Roar	Normal	—	100	20
TM06	Toxic	Poison	—	85	10
TM09	Bullet Seed	Grass	10	100	30
TM10	Hidden Power	Normal	—	100	15
TM11	Sunny Day	Fire	—	—	5
TM15	Hyper Beam	Normal	150	90	5
TM17	Protect	Normal	—	—	10
TM19	Giga Drain	Grass	60	100	5
TM20	Safeguard	Normal	—	—	25
TM21	Frustration	Normal	—	100	20
TM22	Solarbeam	Grass	120	100	10
TM23	Iron Tail	Steel	75	75	15
TM26	Earthquake	Ground	100	100	10
TM27	Return	Normal	—	100	20
TM28	Dig	Ground	60	100	10
TM31	Brick Break	Fighting	75	100	15
TM32	Double Team	Normal	—	—	15
TM39	Rock Tomb	Rock	50	80	10
TM40	Aerial Ace	Flying	60	—	20
TM42	Facade	Normal	70	100	20
TM43	Secret Power	Normal	70	100	20
TM44	Rest	Psychic	—	—	10
TM45	Attract	Normal	—	100	15
HM01	Cut	Normal	50	95	30
HM04	Strength	Normal	80	100	20
HM05	Flash	Normal	—	70	20
HM06	Rock Smash	Fighting	20	100	15

MOVE TUTOR

FireRed/LeafGreen and Emerald Only

Body Slam*
Double-Edge
Mega Punch*
Mega Kick*
Mimic
Substitute
Swords Dance*
Counter*
Seismic Toss*

Emerald Only

Dynamicpunch*
Endure*
Fury Cutter
Mud-Slap*
Sleep Talk
Snore*
Swagger
Swift*
Thunderpunch*

*Battle Frontier tutor move (*Emerald*)

255 Torchic™

FIRE

GENERAL INFO

SPECIES: Chick Pokémon
HEIGHT: 1'04"
WEIGHT: 6 lbs.
ABILITY: Blaze

Torchic's Fire-type attack power is multiplied by 1.5 when its HPs get low.

STATS

EVOLUTIONS

 ►  LV16 ► LV36

LOCATION[s]:

RUBY	Rarity: **Only One**	Starter Pokémon obtained from Prof. Birch on Route 101
SAPPHIRE	Rarity: **Only One**	Starter Pokémon obtained from Prof. Birch on Route 101
FIRERED	Rarity: **None**	Trade from *Ruby/Sapphire*
LEAFGREEN	Rarity: **None**	Trade from *Ruby/Sapphire*
COLOSSEUM	Rarity: **None**	Trade from *Ruby/Sapphire*
EMERALD	Rarity: **Only One**	Starter Pokémon obtained from Prof. Birch on Route 101
XD	Rarity: **None**	Trade from *Ruby/Sapphire*

MOVES

Level	Attack	Type	Power	ACC	PP
—	Scratch	Normal	40	100	35
—	Growl	Normal	—	100	40
7	Focus Energy	Normal	—	—	30
10	Ember	Fire	40	100	25
16	Peck	Flying	35	100	35

Level	Attack	Type	Power	ACC	PP
19	Sand-Attack	Ground	—	100	15
25	Fire Spin	Fire	15	70	15
28	Quick Attack	Normal	40	100	30
34	Slash	Normal	70	100	20
37	Mirror Move	Flying	—	—	20
43	Flamethrower	Fire	95	100	15

TM/HM

TM/HM#	Name	Type	Power	ACC	PP
TM06	Toxic	Poison	—	85	10
TM10	Hidden Power	Normal	—	100	15
TM11	Sunny Day	Fire	—	—	5
TM17	Protect	Normal	—	—	10
TM21	Frustration	Normal	—	100	20
TM27	Return	Normal	—	100	20
TM28	Dig	Ground	60	100	10
TM32	Double Team	Normal	—	—	15
TM35	Flamethrower	Fire	95	100	15
TM38	Fire Blast	Fire	120	85	5

TM/HM#	Name	Type	Power	ACC	PP
TM39	Rock Tomb	Rock	50	80	10
TM40	Aerial Ace	Flying	60	—	20
TM42	Facade	Normal	70	100	20
TM43	Secret Power	Normal	70	100	20
TM44	Rest	Psychic	—	—	10
TM45	Attract	Normal	—	100	15
TM50	Overheat	Fire	140	90	5
HM01	Cut	Normal	50	95	30
HM04	Strength	Normal	80	100	20
HM06	Rock Smash	Fighting	20	100	15

EGG MOVES*

Name	Type	Power	ACC	PP
Counter	Fighting	—	100	20
Reversal	Fighting	—	100	15
Endure	Normal	—	—	10
Swagger	Normal	—	90	15
Smellingsalt	Normal	60	100	10
Rock Slide	Rock	75	90	10

*Learned Via Breeding

MOVE TUTOR

FireRed/LeafGreen and Emerald Only

Body Slam*	Swords Dance*	Mega Kick*
Double-Edge*	Seismic Toss*	Counter*
Mimic	Rock Slide*	
Substitute	Mega Punch*	

Emerald Only

Endure*	Sleep Talk*	Swagger*
Mud-Slap*	Snore*	Swift*

*Battle Frontier tutor move (*Emerald*)

256 Combusken ™

FIRE **FIGHTING**

GENERAL INFO

SPECIES: Young Fowl Pokémon
HEIGHT: 2'11"
WEIGHT: 43 lbs.
ABILITY: Blaze

Combusken's Fire-type attack power is multiplied by 1.5 when its HPs get low.

STATS

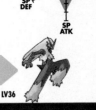

EVOLUTIONS

LV16 LV36

LOCATION[s]:

RUBY	Rarity: **Evolve**	Evolve Torchic
SAPPHIRE	Rarity: **Evolve**	Evolve Torchic
FIRERED	Rarity: **None**	Trade from *Ruby/Sapphire*
LEAFGREEN	Rarity: **None**	Trade from *Ruby/Sapphire*
COLOSSEUM	Rarity: **None**	Trade from *Ruby/Sapphire*
EMERALD	Rarity: **Evolve**	Evolve Torchic
XD	Rarity: **None**	Trade from *Ruby/Sapphire*

MOVES

Level	Attack	Type	Power	ACC	PP
—	Scratch	Normal	40	100	35
—	Growl	Normal	—	100	40
—/	Focus Energy	Normal	—	—	30
—/13	Ember	Fire	40	100	25
16	Double Kick	Fighting	30	100	30
17	Peck	Flying	35	100	35

Level	Attack	Type	Power	ACC	PP
21	Sand-Attack	Ground	—	100	15
28	Bulk Up	Fighting	—	—	20
32	Quick Attack	Normal	40	100	30
39	Slash	Normal	70	100	20
43	Mirror Move	Flying	—	—	20
50	Sky Uppercut	Fighting	85	90	15

TM/HM

TM/HM#	Name	Type	Power	ACC	PP
TM01	Focus Punch	Fighting	150	100	20
TM06	Toxic	Poison	—	85	10
TM08	Bulk Up	Fighting	—	—	20
TM10	Hidden Power	Normal	—	100	15
TM11	Sunny Day	Fire	—	—	5
TM17	Protect	Normal	—	—	10
TM21	Frustration	Normal	—	100	20
TM27	Return	Normal	—	100	20
TM28	Dig	Ground	60	100	10
TM31	Brick Break	Fighting	75	100	15
TM32	Double Team	Normal	—	—	15
TM35	Flamethrower	Fire	95	100	15

TM/HM#	Name	Type	Power	ACC	PP
TM38	Fire Blast	Fire	120	85	5
TM39	Rock Tomb	Rock	50	80	10
TM40	Aerial Ace	Flying	60	—	20
TM42	Facade	Normal	70	100	20
TM43	Secret Power	Normal	70	100	20
TM44	Rest	Psychic	—	—	10
TM45	Attract	Normal	—	100	15
TM50	Overheat	Fire	140	90	5
HM01	Cut	Normal	50	95	30
HM04	Strength	Normal	80	100	20
HM06	Rock Smash	Fighting	20	100	15

MOVE TUTOR

FireRed/LeafGreen and Emerald Only

Body Slam	Mimic	Seismic Toss
Double-Edge	Substitute	Rock Slide
Mega Punch	Swords Dance	
Mega Kick	Counter	

Emerald Only

Dynamicpunch	Fury Cutter	Swagger
Endure*	Sleep Talk	Swift*
Fire Punch*	Snore*	Thunderpunch*

*Battle Frontier tutor move (*Emerald*)

257 Blaziken™

FIRE   FIGHTING

GENERAL INFO

SPECIES: Blaze Pokémon
HEIGHT: 6'03"
WEIGHT: 116 lbs.
ABILITY: Blaze

Blaziken's Fire-type attack power is multiplied when its HPs get low.

STATS

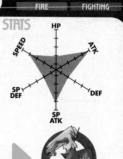

EVOLUTIONS

 ▶ LV16 ▶ LV36

LOCATION[s]:

RUBY	Rarity: **Evolve**	Evolve Combusken
SAPPHIRE	Rarity: **Evolve**	Evolve Combusken
FIRERED	Rarity: **None**	Trade from *Ruby/Sapphire*
LEAFGREEN	Rarity: **None**	Trade from *Ruby/Sapphire*
COLOSSEUM	Rarity: **None**	Trade from *Ruby/Sapphire*
EMERALD	Rarity: **Evolve**	Evolve Combusken
XD	Rarity: **None**	Trade from *Ruby/Sapphire/Emerald*

MOVES

Level	Attack	Type	Power	ACC	PP
—	Fire Punch	Fire	75	100	15
—	Scratch	Normal	40	100	35
—	Growl	Normal	—	100	40
—/17	Focus Energy	Normal	—	—	30
—/13	Ember	Fire	40	100	25
16	Double Kick	Fighting	30	100	30
17	Peck	Flying	35	100	35

Level	Attack	Type	Power	ACC	PP
21	Sand-Attack	Ground	—	100	15
28	Bulk Up	Fight	—	—	10
32	Quick Attack	Normal	40	100	30
36	Blaze Kick	Fire	85	90	10
42	Slash	Normal	70	100	20
49	Mirror Move	Flying	—	—	20
59	Sky Uppercut	Fighting	85	90	15

= Emerald Only

TM/HM

TM/HM#	Name	Type	Power	ACC	PP
TM01	Focus Punch	Fighting	150	100	20
TM05	Roar	Normal	—	100	20
TM06	Toxic	Poison	—	85	10
TM08	Bulk Up	Fighting	—	—	20
TM10	Hidden Power	Normal	—	100	15
TM11	Sunny Day	Fire	—	—	5
TM15	Hyper Beam	Normal	150	90	5
TM17	Protect	Normal	—	—	10
TM21	Frustration	Normal	—	100	20
TM26	Earthquake	Ground	100	100	10
TM27	Return	Normal	—	100	20
TM28	Dig	Ground	60	100	10
TM31	Brick Break	Fighting	75	100	15

TM/HM#	Name	Type	Power	ACC	PP
TM32	Double Team	Normal	—	—	15
TM35	Flamethrower	Fire	95	100	15
TM38	Fire Blast	Fire	120	85	5
TM39	Rock Tomb	Rock	50	80	10
TM40	Aerial Ace	Flying	60	—	20
TM42	Facade	Normal	70	100	20
TM43	Secret Power	Normal	70	100	20
TM44	Rest	Psychic	—	—	10
TM45	Attract	Normal	—	100	15
TM50	Overheat	Fire	140	90	5
HM01	Cut	Normal	50	95	30
HM04	Strength	Normal	80	100	20
HM06	Rock Smash	Fighting	20	100	15

MOVE TUTOR

FireRed/LeafGreen and Emerald Only

Body Slam*	Mimic	Seismic Toss*
Double-Edge	Substitute	Rock Slide*
Mega Punch*	Swords Dance*	
Mega Kick*	Counter*	

Emerald Only

Dynamicpunch*	Mud-Slap*	Swift*
Endure*	Sleep Talk*	Thunderpunch*
Fire Punch*	Snore*	
Fury Cutter	Swagger	

*Battle Frontier tutor move (*Emerald*)

258 Mudkip™

WATER

GENERAL INFO

SPECIES: Mud Fish Pokémon
HEIGHT: 1'04"
WEIGHT: 17 lbs.
ABILITY: Torrent

When Mudkip's HPs fall below 1/3, its Water-type attack power increases 1.5 times.

STATS

EVOLUTIONS

LV16   LV36

LOCATION[s]:

RUBY	Rarity:	Only One	Starter Pokémon obtained from Prof. Birch on Route 101
SAPPHIRE	Rarity:	Only One	Starter Pokémon obtained from Prof. Birch on Route 101
FIRERED	Rarity:	None	Trade from Ruby/Sapphire
LEAFGREEN	Rarity:	None	Trade from Ruby/Sapphire
COLOSSEUM	Rarity:	None	Trade from Ruby/Sapphire
EMERALD	Rarity:	Only One	Starter Pokémon obtained from Prof. Birch on Route 101
XD	Rarity:	None	Trade from Ruby/Sapphire/Emerald

MOVES

Level	Attack	Type	Power	ACC	PP
—	Tackle	Normal	35	95	35
—	Growl	Normal	—	100	40
6	Mud-Slap	Ground	20	100	10
10	Water Gun	Water	40	100	25
15	Bide	Normal	—	100	10
19	Foresight	Normal	—	100	40

Level	Attack	Type	Power	ACC	PP
24	Mud Sport	Ground	—	100	15
28	Take Down	Normal	90	85	20
33	Whirlpool	Water	15	70	15
37	Protect	Normal	—	—	10
42	Hydro Pump	Water	120	80	5
46	Endeavor	Normal	—	100	5

TM/HM

TM/HM#	Name	Type	Power	ACC	PP
TM03	Water Pulse	Water	60	100	20
TM06	Toxic	Poison	—	85	10
TM07	Hail	Ice	—	—	10
TM10	Hidden Power	Normal	—	100	15
TM13	Ice Beam	Ice	95	100	10
TM14	Blizzard	Ice	120	70	5
TM17	Protect	Normal	—	—	10
TM18	Rain Dance	Water	—	—	5
TM21	Frustration	Normal	—	100	20
TM23	Iron Tail	Steel	100	75	15
TM27	Return	Normal	—	100	20
TM28	Dig	Ground	60	100	10

TM/HM#	Name	Type	Power	ACC	PP
TM32	Double Team	Normal	—	—	15
TM39	Rock Tomb	Rock	50	80	10
TM42	Facade	Normal	70	100	20
TM43	Secret Power	Normal	70	100	20
TM44	Rest	Psychic	—	—	10
TM45	Attract	Normal	—	100	15
HM03	Surf	Water	95	100	15
HM04	Strength	Normal	80	100	15
HM06	Rock Smash	Fighting	20	100	15
HM07	Waterfall	Water	80	100	15
HM08	Dive	Water	60	100	10

EGG MOVES*

Name	Type	Power	ACC	PP
Refresh	Normal	—	100	20
Uproar	Normal	50	100	10
Curse	—	—	—	10
Stomp	Normal	65	100	20
Ice Ball	Ice	30	90	20
Mirror Coat	Psychic	—	100	20

*Learned Via Breeding

MOVE TUTOR

FireRed/LeafGreen and Emerald Only

Body Slam*	Mimic	Substitute
Double-Edge		

Emerald Only

Defense Curl*	Mud-Slap*	Snore*
Endure*	Rollout	Swagger
Icy Wind*	Sleep Talk	

*Battle Frontier tutor move (Emerald)

259 Marshtomp™

WATER | GROUND

GENERAL INFO

SPECIES: Mud Fish Pokémon
HEIGHT: 2'04"
WEIGHT: 63 lbs.
ABILITY: Torrent

When Marshtomp's HPs fall below 1/3, its Water-type attack power increases 1.5 times.

STATS

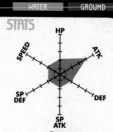

EVOLUTIONS

  LV16 LV36

LOCATION[s]:

RUBY	Rarity: **Evolve**	Evolve Mudkip
SAPPHIRE	Rarity: **Evolve**	Evolve Mudkip
FIRERED	Rarity: **None**	Trade from *Ruby/Sapphire*
LEAFGREEN	Rarity: **None**	Trade from *Ruby/Sapphire*
COLOSSEUM	Rarity: **None**	Trade from *Ruby/Sapphire*
EMERALD	Rarity: **Evolve**	Evolve Mudkip
XD	Rarity: **None**	Trade from *Ruby/Sapphire/Emerald*

MOVES

Level	Attack	Type	Power	ACC	PP	Level	Attack	Type	Power	ACC	PP
—	Tackle	Normal	35	95	35	20	Foresight	Normal	—	100	40
—	Growl	Normal	—	100	40	25	Mud Sport	Ground	—	100	15
—	Mud-Slap	Ground	20	100	10	31	Take Down	Normal	90	85	20
—	Water Gun	Water	40	100	25	37	Muddy Water	Water	95	85	10
15	Bide	Normal	—	100	10	42	Protect	Normal	—	—	10
16	Mud Shot	Ground	55	95	15	46	Earthquake	Ground	100	100	10
						53	Endeavor	Normal	—	100	5

TM/HM

TM/HM#	Name	Type	Power	ACC	PP	TM/HM#	Name	Type	Power	ACC	PP
TM03	Water Pulse	Water	60	100	20	TM28	Dig	Ground	60	100	10
TM06	Toxic	Poison	—	85	10	TM32	Double Team	Normal	—	—	15
TM07	Hail	Ice	—	—	10	TM39	Rock Tomb	Rock	50	80	10
TM10	Hidden Power	Normal	—	100	15	TM42	Facade	Normal	70	100	20
TM13	Ice Beam	Ice	95	100	10	TM43	Secret Power	Normal	70	100	20
TM14	Blizzard	Ice	120	70	5	TM44	Rest	Psychic	—	—	10
TM17	Protect	Normal	—	—	10	TM45	Attract	Normal	—	100	15
TM18	Rain Dance	Water	—	—	5	HM03	Surf	Water	95	100	15
TM21	Frustration	Normal	—	100	20	HM04	Strength	Normal	80	100	15
TM23	Iron Tail	Steel	100	75	15	HM06	Rock Smash	Fighting	20	100	15
TM26	Earthquake	Ground	100	100	10	HM07	Waterfall	Water	80	100	15
TM27	Return	Normal	—	100	20	HM08	Dive	Water	60	100	10

MOVE TUTOR

FireRed/LeafGreen and Emerald Only

Body Slam*	Mega Kick*	Counter*
Double-Edge	Mimic	Seismic Toss*
Mega Punch*	Substitute	Rock Slide*

Emerald Only

Defense Curl*	Icy Wind*	Snore*
Dynamicpunch*	Mud-Slap*	Swagger
Endure*	Rollout	
Ice Punch*	Sleep Talk	

*Battle Frontier tutor move (*Emerald*)

260 Swampert™

WATER GROUND

GENERAL INFO

SPECIES: Mud Fish Pokémon
HEIGHT: 4'11"
WEIGHT: 181 lbs.
ABILITY: Torrent

When Swampert's HPs fall below 1/3, its Water-type attack power increases 1.5 times.

STATS

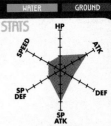

EVOLUTIONS

LV16   LV36

LOCATION[s]:

RUBY	Rarity: **Evolve**	Evolve Marshtomp
SAPPHIRE	Rarity: **Evolve**	Evolve Marshtomp
FIRERED	Rarity: **None**	Trade from *Ruby/Sapphire*
LEAFGREEN	Rarity: **None**	Trade from *Ruby/Sapphire*
COLOSSEUM	Rarity: **None**	Trade from *Ruby/Sapphire*
EMERALD	Rarity: **Evolve**	Evolve Marshtomp
XD	Rarity: **None**	Trade from *Ruby/Sapphire/Emerald*

MOVES

Level	Attack	Type	Power	ACC	PP	Level	Attack	Type	Power	ACC	PP
—	Tackle	Normal	35	95	35	20	Foresight	Normal	—	100	40
—	Growl	Normal	—	100	40	25	Mud Sport	Ground	—	100	15
—	Mud-Slap	Ground	20	100	10	31	Take Down	Normal	90	85	20
—	Water Gun	Water	40	100	25	39	Muddy Water	Water	95	85	10
15	Bide	Normal	—	100	10	46	Protect	Normal	—	—	10
16	Mud Shot	Ground	55	95	15	52	Earthquake	Ground	100	100	10
						61	Endeavor	Normal	—	100	5

TM/HM

TM/HM#	Name	Type	Power	ACC	PP	TM/HM#	Name	Type	Power	ACC	PP
TM01	Focus Punch	Fighting	150	100	20	TM27	Return	Normal	—	100	20
TM03	Water Pulse	Water	60	100	20	TM28	Dig	Ground	60	100	10
TM05	Roar	Normal	—	100	20	TM31	Brick Break	Fighting	75	100	15
TM06	Toxic	Poison	—	85	10	TM32	Double Team	Normal	—	—	15
TM07	Hail	Ice	—	—	10	TM39	Rock Tomb	Rock	50	80	10
TM10	Hidden Power	Normal	—	100	15	TM42	Facade	Normal	70	100	20
TM13	Ice Beam	Ice	95	100	10	TM43	Secret Power	Normal	70	100	20
TM14	Blizzard	Ice	120	70	5	TM44	Rest	Psychic	—	—	10
TM15	Hyper Beam	Normal	150	90	5	TM45	Attract	Normal	—	100	15
TM17	Protect	Normal	—	—	10	HM03	Surf	Water	95	100	15
TM18	Rain Dance	Water	—	—	5	HM04	Strength	Normal	80	100	15
TM21	Frustration	Normal	—	100	20	HM06	Rock Smash	Fighting	20	100	15
TM23	Iron Tail	Steel	100	75	15	HM07	Waterfall	Water	80	100	15
TM26	Earthquake	Ground	100	100	10	HM08	Dive	Water	60	100	10

MOVE TUTOR

FireRed/LeafGreen and Emerald Only

Body Slam*	Mega Kick*	Rock Slide*
Double-Edge	Mimic	Counter*
Mega Punch*	Substitute	Seismic Toss*

Emerald Only

Defense Curl*	Icy Wind*	Sleep Talk
Dynamicpunch	Mud-Slap*	Snore*
Endure*	Rollout	Swagger

*Battle Frontier tutor move (*Emerald*)

261 Poochyena™

DARK

GENERAL INFO

SPECIES: Bite Pokémon
HEIGHT: 1'08"
WEIGHT: 30 lbs.
ABILITY: Run Away

Poochyena can flee from wild Pokémon.

STATS

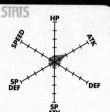

EVOLUTIONS

LV18

LOCATION(s):

RUBY	Rarity:	Common	Route 103
SAPPHIRE	Rarity:	Common	Route 103
FIRERED	Rarity:	None	Trade from *Ruby/Sapphire*
LEAFGREEN	Rarity:	None	Trade from *Ruby/Sapphire*
COLOSSEUM	Rarity:	None	Trade from *Ruby/Sapphire*
EMERALD	Rarity:	Common	Routes 101–104, 110, 116, 117, 120, 121, 123, Petalburg Woods
XD	Rarity:	Only One	Gateon Port (Capture from Bodybuilder Kilen)

MOVES

Level	Attack	Type	Power	ACC	PP	Level	Attack	Type	Power	ACC	PP
—	Tackle	Normal	35	95	35	25	Swagger	Normal	—	90	15
5	Howl	Normal	—	—	40	29	Scary Face	Normal	—	90	10
9	Sand-Attack	Ground	—	100	15	33	Take Down	Normal	90	85	20
13	Bite	Dark	60	100	25	37	Taunt	Dark	—	100	20
17	Odor Sleuth	Normal	—	100	40	41	Crunch	Dark	80	100	15
21	Roar	Normal	—	100	20	45	Thief	Dark	40	100	10

TM/HM

TM/HM#	Name	Type	Power	ACC	PP	TM/HM#	Name	Type	Power	ACC	PP
TM05	Roar	Normal	—	100	20	TM30	Shadow Ball	Ghost	60	—	20
TM06	Toxic	Poison	—	85	10	TM32	Double Team	Normal	—	—	15
TM10	Hidden Power	Normal	—	100	15	TM41	Torment	Dark	—	100	15
TM11	Sunny Day	Fire	—	—	5	TM42	Facade	Normal	70	100	20
TM12	Taunt	Dark	—	100	20	TM43	Secret Power	Normal	70	100	20
TM17	Protect	Normal	—	—	10	TM44	Rest	Psychic	—	—	10
TM18	Rain Dance	Water	—	—	5	TM45	Attract	Normal	—	100	15
TM21	Frustration	Normal	—	100	20	TM46	Thief	Dark	40	100	10
TM23	Iron Tail	Steel	100	75	15	TM49	Snatch	Dark	—	100	10
TM27	Return	Normal	—	100	20	HM06	Rock Smash	Fighting	20	100	15
TM28	Dig	Ground	60	100	10						

EGG MOVES*

Name	Type	Power	ACC	PP
Astonish	Ghost	30	100	15
Poison Fang	Poison	50	100	15
Covet	Normal	40	100	40
Leer	Normal	—	100	30
Yawn	Normal	—	100	10

*Learned Via Breeding

MOVE TUTOR

FireRed/LeafGreen and Emerald Only

Body Slam*	Mimic	Counter*
Double-Edge	Substitute	

Emerald Only

Endure*	Psych Up*	Snore*
Mud-Slap*	Sleep Talk	Swagger

*Battle Frontier tutor move (*Emerald*)

262 Mightyena™

DARK

GENERAL INFO
SPECIES: Bite Pokémon
HEIGHT: 3'03"
WEIGHT: 82 lbs.
ABILITY: Intimidate
Lowers the opponent's attack by one point at the start of a battle.

STATS

HP · SPEED · ATK · DEF · SP ATK · SP DEF

EVOLUTIONS

LV18

LOCATION(s):

RUBY	**Rarity:** Evolve		Evolve Poochyena
SAPPHIRE	**Rarity:** Evolve		Evolve Poochyena
FIRERED	**Rarity:** None		Trade from *Ruby/Sapphire*
LEAFGREEN	**Rarity:** None		Trade from *Ruby/Sapphire*
COLOSSEUM	**Rarity:** None		Trade from *Ruby/Sapphire*
EMERALD	**Rarity:** Rare		Evolve Poochyena, Routes 120, 121, 123
XD	**Rarity:** Evolve		Evolve Poochyena

MOVES

Level	Attack	Type	Power	ACC	PP	Level	Attack	Type	Power	ACC	PP
—	Tackle	Normal	35	95	35	27	Swagger	Normal	—	90	15
—	Howl	Normal	—	—	40	32	Scary Face	Normal	—	90	10
—	Sand-Attack	Ground	—	100	15	37	Take Down	Normal	90	85	20
—	Bite	Dark	60	100	25	42	Taunt	Dark	—	100	20
17	Odor Sleuth	Normal	—	100	40	47	Crunch	Dark	80	100	15
22	Roar	Normal	—	100	20	52	Thief	Dark	40	100	10

TM/HM

TM/HM#	Name	Type	Power	ACC	PP	TM/HM#	Name	Type	Power	ACC	PP
TM05	Roar	Normal	—	100	20	TM30	Shadow Ball	Ghost	60	—	20
TM06	Toxic	Poison	—	85	10	TM32	Double Team	Normal	—	—	15
TM10	Hidden Power	Normal	—	100	15	TM41	Torment	Dark	—	100	15
TM11	Sunny Day	Fire	—	—	5	TM42	Facade	Normal	70	100	20
TM12	Taunt	Dark	—	100	20	TM43	Secret Power	Normal	70	100	20
TM15	Hyper Beam	Normal	150	90	5	TM44	Rest	Psychic	—	—	10
TM17	Protect	Normal	—	—	10	TM45	Attract	Normal	—	100	15
TM18	Rain Dance	Water	—	—	5	TM46	Thief	Dark	40	100	10
TM21	Frustration	Normal	—	100	20	TM49	Snatch	Dark	—	100	10
TM23	Iron Tail	Steel	100	75	15	HM04	Strength	Normal	80	100	15
TM27	Return	Normal	—	100	20	HM06	Rock Smash	Fighting	20	100	15
TM28	Dig	Ground	60	100	10						

MOVE TUTOR

FireRed/LeafGreen and Emerald Only

Body Slam*	Mimic	Counter*
Double-Edge	Substitute	

Emerald Only

Endure*	Psych Up*	Snore*
Mud-Slap*	Sleep Talk	Swagger

*Battle Frontier tutor move (*Emerald*)

263 Zigzagoon™

NORMAL

GENERAL INFO

SPECIES: Tinyraccoon Pokémon
HEIGHT: 1'04"
WEIGHT: 39 lbs.
ABILITY: Pickup

Zigzagoon may find an item at the end of the battle.

STATS

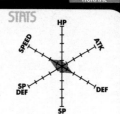

EVOLUTIONS

LV20

LOCATION(s):

RUBY	Rarity: **Common**	Routes 101, 102, 103, 104, 110
SAPPHIRE	Rarity: **Common**	Routes 101, 102, 103, 104, 110
FIRERED	Rarity: **None**	Trade from *Ruby/Sapphire*
LEAFGREEN	Rarity: **None**	Trade from *Ruby/Sapphire*
COLOSSEUM	Rarity: **None**	Trade from *Ruby/Sapphire*
EMERALD	Rarity: **Common**	Routes 101, 102, 103, 118, 119
XD	Rarity: **None**	Trade from *Ruby/Sapphire/Emerald*

MOVES

Level	Attack	Type	Power	ACC	PP	Level	Attack	Type	Power	ACC	PP
—	Tackle	Normal	35	95	35	21	Mud Sport	Ground	—	100	15
—	Growl	Normal	—	100	40	25	Pin Missile	Bug	14	85	20
5	Tail Whip	Normal	—	100	30	29	Covet	Normal	40	100	40
9	Headbutt	Normal	70	100	15	33	Flail	Normal	—	100	15
13	Sand-Attack	Ground	—	100	15	37	Rest	Psychic	—	—	10
17	Odor Sleuth	Normal	—	100	40	41	Belly Drum	Normal	—	—	10

TM/HM

TM/HM#	Name	Type	Power	ACC	PP	TM/HM#	Name	Type	Power	ACC	PP
TM03	Water Pulse	Water	60	100	20	TM28	Dig	Ground	60	100	10
TM06	Toxic	Poison	—	85	10	TM30	Shadow Ball	Ghost	60	—	20
TM10	Hidden Power	Normal	—	100	15	TM32	Double Team	Normal	—	—	15
TM11	Sunny Day	Fire	—	—	5	TM34	Shock Wave	Electric	60	—	20
TM13	Ice Beam	Ice	95	100	10	TM42	Facade	Normal	70	100	20
TM14	Blizzard	Ice	120	70	5	TM43	Secret Power	Normal	70	100	20
TM17	Protect	Normal	—	—	10	TM44	Rest	Psychic	—	—	10
TM18	Rain Dance	Water	—	—	5	TM45	Attract	Normal	—	100	15
TM21	Frustration	Normal	—	100	20	TM46	Thief	Dark	40	100	10
TM23	Iron Tail	Steel	100	75	15	HM01	Cut	Normal	50	95	30
TM24	Thunderbolt	Electric	95	100	15	HM03	Surf	Water	95	100	15
TM25	Thunder	Electric	120	70	10	HM06	Rock Smash	Fighting	20	100	15
TM27	Return	Normal	—	100	20						

EGG MOVES*

Name	Type	Power	ACC	PP
Charm	Normal	—	100	20
Pursuit	Dark	40	100	20
Substitute	Normal	—	—	10
Tickle	Normal	—	100	20
Trick	Psychic	—	100	10

*Learned Via Breeding

MOVE TUTOR

FireRed/LeafGreen and Emerald Only

Body Slam*	Mimic	Thunder Wave*
Double-Edge	Substitute	

Emerald Only

Defense Curl*	Mud-Slap*	Snore*
Endure*	Psych Up*	Swagger*
Fury Cutter*	Rollout	Swift*
Icy Wind*	Sleep Talk	

*Battle Frontier tutor move (*Emerald*)

264 Linoone™

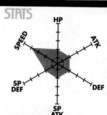

NORMAL

GENERAL INFO

SPECIES: Rushing Pokémon
HEIGHT: 1'08"
WEIGHT: 72 lbs.
ABILITY: Pickup
Linoone may find an Item at the end of the battle.

STATS

EVOLUTIONS

LV20

LOCATION[s]:

RUBY	Rarity: **Rare**	Evolve Zigzagoon, Routes 118, 119, 120, 121, 123
SAPPHIRE	Rarity: **Rare**	Evolve Zigzagoon, Routes 118, 119, 120, 121, 123
FIRERED	Rarity: **None**	Trade from *Ruby/Sapphire*
LEAFGREEN	Rarity: **None**	Trade from *Ruby/Sapphire*
COLOSSEUM	Rarity: **None**	Trade from *Ruby/Sapphire*
EMERALD	Rarity: **Rare**	Evolve Zigzagoon, Routes 118, 119
XD	Rarity: **None**	Trade from *Ruby/Sapphire/Emerald*

MOVES

Level	Attack	Type	Power	ACC	PP
—	Tackle	Normal	35	95	35
—	Growl	Normal	—	100	40
—/5	Tail Whip	Normal	—	100	30
—/9	Headbutt	Normal	70	100	15
13	Sand-Attack	Ground	—	100	15
17	Odor Sleuth	Normal	—	100	40

Level	Attack	Type	Power	ACC	PP
23	Mud Sport	Ground	—	100	15
29	Fury Swipes	Normal	18	80	15
35	Covet	Normal	40	100	40
41	Slash	Normal	70	100	20
47	Rest	Psychic	—	—	10
53	Belly Drum	Normal	—	—	10

= Emerald Only

TM/HM

TM/HM#	Name	Type	Power	ACC	PP
TM03	Water Pulse	Water	60	100	20
TM05	Roar	Normal	—	100	20
TM06	Toxic	Poison	—	85	10
TM10	Hidden Power	Normal	—	100	15
TM11	Sunny Day	Fire	—	—	5
TM13	Ice Beam	Ice	95	100	10
TM14	Blizzard	Ice	120	70	5
TM15	Hyper Beam	Normal	150	90	5
TM17	Protect	Normal	—	—	10
TM18	Rain Dance	Water	—	—	5
TM21	Frustration	Normal	—	100	20
TM23	Iron Tail	Steel	100	75	15
TM24	Thunderbolt	Electric	95	100	15
TM25	Thunder	Electric	120	70	10

TM/HM#	Name	Type	Power	ACC	PP
TM27	Return	Normal	—	100	20
TM28	Dig	Ground	60	100	10
TM30	Shadow Ball	Ghost	60	—	10
TM32	Double Team	Normal	—	—	15
TM34	Shock Wave	Electric	60	—	20
TM42	Facade	Normal	70	100	20
TM43	Secret Power	Normal	70	100	20
TM44	Rest	Psychic	—	—	10
TM45	Attract	Normal	—	100	15
TM46	Thief	Dark	40	100	10
HM01	Cut	Normal	50	95	30
HM03	Surf	Water	95	100	15
HM04	Strength	Normal	80	100	15
HM06	Rock Smash	Fighting	20	100	15

MOVE TUTOR

FireRed/LeafGreen and Emerald Only

Body Slam*	Mimic	Thunder Wave*
Double-Edge	Substitute	

Emerald Only

Defense Curl*	Mud-Slap*	Swagger
Endure*	Rollout	Swift*
Fury Cutter	Sleep Talk	
Icy Wind*	Snore*	

*Battle Frontier tutor move (*Emerald*)

265 Wurmple™

BUG

GENERAL INFO

SPECIES: Worm Pokémon
HEIGHT: 1'00"
WEIGHT: 8 lbs.
ABILITY: Shield Dust
Protects Wurmple from any additional Effects of moves.

STATS

EVOLUTIONS*

LV7 LV10

LOCATION[s]:

RUBY	Rarity: **Common**	Route 101, Route 102, Route 104, Petalburg Woods
SAPPHIRE	Rarity: **Common**	Route 101, Route 102, Route 104, Petalburg Woods
FIRERED	Rarity: **None**	Trade from *Ruby/Sapphire*
LEAFGREEN	Rarity: **None**	Trade from *Ruby/Sapphire*
COLOSSEUM	Rarity: **None**	Trade from *Ruby/Sapphire*
EMERALD	Rarity: **Common**	Route 101, Route 102, Route 104, Petalburg Woods
XD	Rarity: **None**	Trade from *Ruby/Sapphire/Emerald*

MOVES

Level	Attack	Type	Power	ACC	PP
—	Tackle	Normal	35	95	35
—	String Shot	Bug	—	95	40
5	Poison Sting	Poison	15	100	35

TM/HM

TM/HM# Name	Type	Power	ACC	PP
None				

EGG MOVES*

Name	Type	Power	ACC	PP
None				

*Learned Via Breeding

MOVE TUTOR
FireRed/LeafGreen and Emerald Only
None

266 Silcoon™

GENERAL INFO

SPECIES: Cocoon Pokémon
HEIGHT: 2'00"
WEIGHT: 22 lbs.
ABILITY: Shed Skin

Every turn, Silcoon has a 1/3 chance of recovering from a status condition.

STATS

EVOLUTIONS

 ▶ LV7 ▶ LV10

LOCATION(S):

RUBY	Rarity: **Rare**	Evolve Wurmple, Petalburg Woods
SAPPHIRE	Rarity: **Rare**	Evolve Wurmple, Petalburg Woods
FIRERED	Rarity: **None**	Trade from Ruby/Sapphire
LEAFGREEN	Rarity: **None**	Trade from Ruby/Sapphire
COLOSSEUM	Rarity: **None**	Trade from Ruby/Sapphire
EMERALD	Rarity: **Rare**	Evolve Wurmple, Petalburg Woods
XD	Rarity: **None**	Trade from Ruby/Sapphire/Emerald

MOVES

Level	Attack	Type	Power	ACC	PP
—/1	Harden	Normal	—	—	30

 # = Emerald Only

TM/HM

TM/HM#	Name	Type	Power	ACC	PP
None					

MOVE TUTOR

FireRed/LeafGreen and Emerald Only

None

PRIMA OFFICIAL GAME GUIDE

267 Beautifly™

BUG · FLYING

GENERAL INFO

SPECIES: Butterfly Pokémon
HEIGHT: 3'03"
WEIGHT: 63 lbs.
ABILITY: Swarm

When Beautifly's HPs fall below 1/3, the power of its Bug-type Moves increases 1.5 times.

STATS

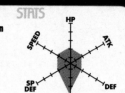

EVOLUTIONS

LV7 · LV10

LOCATION[s]:

RUBY	Rarity: **Evolve**	Evolve Silcoon
SAPPHIRE	Rarity: **Evolve**	Evolve Silcoon
FIRERED	Rarity: **None**	Trade from *Ruby/Sapphire*
LEAFGREEN	Rarity: **None**	Trade from *Ruby/Sapphire*
COLOSSEUM	Rarity: **None**	Trade from *Ruby/Sapphire*
EMERALD	Rarity: **Evolve**	Evolve Silcoon
XD	Rarity: **None**	Trade from *Ruby/Sapphire/Emerald*

MOVES

Level	Attack	Type	Power	ACC	PP	Level	Attack	Type	Power	ACC	PP
—/10	Absorb	Grass	20	100	20	27	Whirlwind	Normal	—	100	20
13	Gust	Flying	40	100	35	31	Attract	Normal	—	100	15
17	Stun Spore	Grass	—	75	30	34	Silver Wind	Bug	60	100	5
20	Morning Sun	Normal	—	—	5	38	Giga Drain	Grass	60	100	5
24	Mega Drain	Grass	40	100	10						

= *Emerald Only*

TM/HM

TM/HM#	Name	Type	Power	ACC	PP	TM/HM#	Name	Type	Power	ACC	PP
TM06	Toxic	Poison	—	85	10	TM29	Psychic	Psychic	90	100	10
TM10	Hidden Power	Normal	—	100	15	TM30	Shadow Ball	Ghost	60	—	20
TM11	Sunny Day	Fire	—	—	5	TM32	Double Team	Normal	—	—	15
TM15	Hyper Beam	Normal	150	90	5	TM40	Aerial Ace	Flying	60	—	20
TM17	Protect	Normal	—	—	10	TM42	Facade	Normal	70	100	20
TM19	Giga Drain	Grass	60	100	5	TM43	Secret Power	Normal	70	100	20
TM20	Safeguard	Normal	—	—	25	TM44	Rest	Psychic	—	—	10
TM21	Frustration	Normal	—	100	20	TM45	Attract	Normal	—	100	15
TM22	Solarbeam	Grass	120	100	10	TM46	Thief	Dark	40	100	10
TM27	Return	Normal	—	100	20	HM05	Flash	Normal	—	70	20

MOVE TUTOR

Emerald Only

Endure*	Snore*	Swift*
Sleep Talk	Swagger	

*Battle Frontier tutor move (*Emerald*)

268 Cascoon ™

GENERAL INFO
SPECIES: Cocoon Pokémon
HEIGHT: 2'04"
WEIGHT: 25 lbs.
ABILITY: Shed Skin
Every turn, Cascoon has a 1/3 chance of recovering from a status condition.

STATS

EVOLUTIONS

LV7   LV10

LOCATION(S):

RUBY	Rarity: **Rare**		Evolve Wurmple, Petalburg Woods
SAPPHIRE	Rarity: **Rare**		Evolve Wurmple, Petalburg Woods
FIRERED	Rarity: **None**		Trade from *Ruby/Sapphire*
LEAFGREEN	Rarity: **None**		Trade from *Ruby/Sapphire*
COLOSSEUM	Rarity: **None**		Trade from *Ruby/Sapphire*
EMERALD	Rarity: **Rare**		Evolve Wurmple, Petalburg Woods
XD	Rarity: **None**		Trade from *Ruby/Sapphire/Emerald*

MOVES

Level	Attack	Type	Power	ACC	PP
—//	Harden	Normal	—	—	30

= *Emerald* Only

TM/HM

TM/HM#	Name	Type	Power	ACC	PP
None					

MOVE TUTOR
FireRed/LeafGreen and Emerald Only
None

269 Dustox™

GENERAL INFO

SPECIES: Poison Moth Pokémon
HEIGHT: 3'11"
WEIGHT: 70 lbs.
ABILITY: Shield Dust

Protects Dustox from any additional effects of moves.

STATS

EVOLUTIONS*

  ▶ LV7 ▶ LV10

LOCATION(s):

RUBY	Rarity: **Evolve**	Evolve Cascoon
SAPPHIRE	Rarity: **Evolve**	Evolve Cascoon
FIRERED	Rarity: **None**	Trade from *Ruby/Sapphire*
LEAFGREEN	Rarity: **None**	Trade from *Ruby/Sapphire*
COLOSSEUM	Rarity: **None**	Trade from *Ruby/Sapphire*
EMERALD	Rarity: **Evolve**	Evolve Cascoon
XD	Rarity: **None**	Trade from *Ruby/Sapphire/Emerald*

MOVES

Level	Attack	Type	Power	ACC	PP
—/10	Confusion	Psychic	50	100	25
13	Gust	Flying	40	100	35
17	Protect	Normal	—	—	10
20	Moonlight	Normal	—	—	5
24	Psybeam	Psychic	65	100	20

Level	Attack	Type	Power	ACC	PP
27	Whirlwind	Normal	—	100	20
31	Light Screen	Psychic	—	—	30
34	Silver Wind	Bug	60	100	5
38	Toxic	Poison	—	85	10

 # = Emerald Only

TM/HM

TM/HM#	Name	Type	Power	ACC	PP
TM06	Toxic	Poison	—	85	10
TM10	Hidden Power	Normal	—	100	15
TM11	Sunny Day	Fire	—	—	5
TM15	Hyper Beam	Normal	150	90	5
TM16	Light Screen	Psychic	—	—	30
TM17	Protect	Normal	—	—	10
TM19	Giga Drain	Grass	60	100	5
TM21	Frustration	Normal	—	100	20
TM22	Solarbeam	Grass	120	100	10
TM27	Return	Normal	—	100	20
TM29	Psychic	Psychic	90	100	10

TM/HM#	Name	Type	Power	ACC	PP
TM30	Shadow Ball	Ghost	60	—	20
TM32	Double Team	Normal	—	—	15
TM36	Sludge Bomb	Poison	90	100	10
TM40	Aerial Ace	Flying	60	—	20
TM42	Facade	Normal	70	100	20
TM43	Secret Power	Normal	70	100	20
TM44	Rest	Psychic	—	—	10
TM45	Attract	Normal	—	100	15
TM46	Thief	Dark	40	100	10
HM05	Flash	Normal	—	70	20

MOVE TUTOR

Emerald Only

Endure*	Snore*	Swift*
Sleep Talk	Swagger	

*Battle Frontier tutor move (*Emerald*)

270 Lotad™

WATER GRASS

GENERAL INFO

SPECIES: Water Weed Pokémon
HEIGHT: 1'08"
WEIGHT: 6 lbs.
ABILITY 1: Swift Swim
Doubles Lotad's Speed when it is raining.
ABILITY 2: Rain Dish
Restores a few HPs every turn that it is raining.

STATS

EVOLUTIONS

LV14 WATER STONE

LOCATION(S):

RUBY	Rarity: **None**	Trade from *Sapphire*
SAPPHIRE	Rarity: **Common**	Route 102, Route 114
FIRERED	Rarity: **None**	Trade from *Sapphire*
LEAFGREEN	Rarity: **None**	Trade from *Sapphire*
COLOSSEUM	Rarity: **None**	Trade from *Sapphire*
EMERALD	Rarity: **Common**	Route 102, Route 114
XD	Rarity: **None**	Trade from *Sapphire/Emerald*

MOVES

Level	Attack	Type	Power	ACC	PP
—	Astonish	Ghost	30	100	15
3	Growl	Normal	—	100	40
7	Absorb	Grass	20	100	20

Level	Attack	Type	Power	ACC	PP
13	Nature Power	Normal	—	95	20
21	Mist	Ice	—	—	30
31	Rain Dance	Water	—	—	5
43	Mega Drain	Grass	40	100	10

TM/HM

TM/HM#	Name	Type	Power	ACC	PP
TM03	Water Pulse	Water	60	100	20
TM06	Toxic	Poison	—	85	10
TM07	Hail	Ice	—	—	10
TM09	Bullet Seed	Grass	10	100	30
TM10	Hidden Power	Normal	—	100	15
TM11	Sunny Day	Fire	—	—	5
TM13	Ice Beam	Ice	95	100	10
TM14	Blizzard	Ice	120	70	5
TM17	Protect	Normal	—	—	10
TM18	Rain Dance	Water	—	—	5
TM19	Giga Drain	Grass	60	100	5

TM/HM#	Name	Type	Power	ACC	PP
TM21	Frustration	Normal	—	100	20
TM22	Solarbeam	Grass	120	100	10
TM27	Return	Normal	—	100	20
TM32	Double Team	Normal	—	—	15
TM42	Facade	Normal	70	100	20
TM43	Secret Power	Normal	70	100	20
TM44	Rest	Psychic	—	—	10
TM45	Attract	Normal	—	100	15
TM46	Thief	Dark	40	100	10
HM03	Surf	Water	95	100	15
HM05	Flash	Normal	—	70	20

EGG MOVES*

Name	Type	Power	ACC	PP
Synthesis	Grass	—	—	5
Razor Leaf	Grass	55	95	25
Sweet Scent	Normal	—	100	20
Leech Seed	Grass	—	90	10
Flail	Normal	—	100	15
Water Gun	Water	40	100	25

*Learned Via Breeding

MOVE TUTOR

FireRed/LeafGreen and Emerald Only

Body Slam*	Mimic	Swords Dance*
Double-Edge	Substitute	

Emerald Only

Endure*	Sleep Talk	Swagger
Icy Wind*	Snore*	

*Battle Frontier tutor move (*Emerald*)

271 Lombre™

WATER | GRASS

GENERAL INFO

SPECIES: Jolly Pokémon
HEIGHT: 3'11"
WEIGHT: 72 lbs.
ABILITY 1: Swift Swim
Doubles Lombre's Speed when it is raining.
ABILITY 2: Rain Dish
Restores a few HPs every turn that it is raining.

STATS

HP · ATK · DEF · SP ATK · SP DEF · SPEED

EVOLUTIONS

LV14 · WATER STONE

LOCATION[s]:

RUBY	Rarity: **None**	Trade from *Sapphire*
SAPPHIRE	Rarity: **Rare**	Route 114
FIRERED	Rarity: **None**	Trade from *Sapphire*
LEAFGREEN	Rarity: **None**	Trade from *Sapphire*
COLOSSEUM	Rarity: **None**	Trade from *Sapphire*
EMERALD	Rarity: **Rare**	Evolve Lotad, Route 114
XD	Rarity: **None**	Trade from *Sapphire/Emerald*

MOVES

Level	Attack	Type	Power	ACC	PP		Level	Attack	Type	Power	ACC	PP
—	Astonish	Ghost	30	100	15		25	Fury Swipes	Normal	18	80	15
3	Growl	Normal	—	100	40		31	Water Sport	Water	—	100	15
7	Absorb	Grass	20	100	20		37	Thief	Dark	40	100	10
13	Nature Power	Normal	—	95	20		43	Uproar	Normal	50	100	10
19	Fake Out	Normal	40	100	10		49	Hydro Pump	Water	120	80	5

TM/HM

TM/HM#	Name	Type	Power	ACC	PP		TM/HM#	Name	Type	Power	ACC	PP
TM03	Water Pulse	Water	60	100	20		TM31	Brick Break	Fighting	75	100	15
TM06	Toxic	Poison	—	85	10		TM32	Double Team	Normal	—	—	15
TM07	Hail	Ice	—	—	10		TM42	Facade	Normal	70	100	20
TM09	Bullet Seed	Grass	10	100	30		TM43	Secret Power	Normal	70	100	20
TM10	Hidden Power	Normal	—	100	15		TM44	Rest	Psychic	—	—	10
TM11	Sunny Day	Fire	—	—	5		TM45	Attract	Normal	—	100	15
TM13	Ice Beam	Ice	95	100	10		TM46	Thief	Dark	40	100	10
TM14	Blizzard	Ice	120	70	5		HM03	Surf	Water	95	100	15
TM17	Protect	Normal	—	—	10		HM04	Strength	Normal	80	100	15
TM18	Rain Dance	Water	—	—	5		HM05	Flash	Normal	—	70	20
TM19	Giga Drain	Grass	60	100	5		HM06	Rock Smash	Fighting	20	100	15
TM21	Frustration	Normal	—	100	20		HM07	Waterfall	Water	80	100	15
TM22	Solarbeam	Grass	120	100	10		HM08	Dive	Water	60	100	10
TM27	Return	Normal	—	100	20							

MOVE TUTOR

FireRed/LeafGreen and Emerald Only

Body Slam*	Mimic	Swords Dance*
Double-Edge	Substitute	

Emerald Only

Dynamicpunch*	Icy Wind*	Swagger
Endure*	Mud-Slap*	Thunderpunch*
Fire Punch*	Sleep Talk	
Ice Punch*	Snore*	

*Battle Frontier tutor move (*Emerald*)

272 Ludicolo™

WATER · GRASS

GENERAL INFO

SPECIES: Carefree Pokémon
HEIGHT: 4'11"
WEIGHT: 121 lbs.
ABILITY 1: Swift Swim
Doubles Ludicolo's Speed when it is raining.
ABILITY 2: Rain Dish
Restores a few HPs every turn that it is raining.

STATS

EVOLUTIONS

LV14 · WATER STONE

LOCATION(S):

RUBY	Rarity: **None**	Trade from *Sapphire*
SAPPHIRE	Rarity: **Evolve**	Evolve Lombre
FIRERED	Rarity: **None**	Trade from *Sapphire*
LEAFGREEN	Rarity: **None**	Trade from *Sapphire*
COLOSSEUM	Rarity: **None**	Trade from *Sapphire*
EMERALD	Rarity: **Evolve**	Evolve Lombre
XD	Rarity: **None**	Trade from *Sapphire/Emerald*

MOVES

Level	Attack	Type	Power	ACC	PP
—	Astonish	Ghost	30	100	15
—	Growl	Normal	—	100	40
—	Absorb	Grass	20	100	20
—	Nature Power	Normal	—	95	20

TM/HM

TM/HM#	Name	Type	Power	ACC	PP
TM01	Focus Punch	Fighting	150	100	20
TM03	Water Pulse	Water	60	100	20
TM06	Toxic	Poison	—	85	10
TM07	Hail	Ice	—	—	10
TM09	Bullet Seed	Grass	10	100	30
TM10	Hidden Power	Normal	—	100	15
TM11	Sunny Day	Fire	—	—	5
TM13	Ice Beam	Ice	95	100	10
TM14	Blizzard	Ice	120	70	5
TM15	Hyper Beam	Normal	150	90	5
TM17	Protect	Normal	—	—	10
TM18	Rain Dance	Water	—	—	5
TM19	Giga Drain	Grass	60	100	5
TM21	Frustration	Normal	—	100	20
TM22	Solarbeam	Grass	120	100	10
TM27	Return	Normal	—	100	20
TM31	Brick Break	Fighting	75	100	15
TM32	Double Team	Normal	—	—	15
TM42	Facade	Normal	70	100	20
TM43	Secret Power	Normal	70	100	20
TM44	Rest	Psychic	—	—	10
TM45	Attract	Normal	—	100	15
TM46	Thief	Dark	40	100	10
HM03	Surf	Water	95	100	15
HM04	Strength	Normal	80	100	15
HM05	Flash	Normal	—	70	20
HM06	Rock Smash	Fighting	20	100	15
HM07	Waterfall	Water	80	100	15
HM08	Dive	Water	60	100	10

MOVE TUTOR

FireRed/LeafGreen and Emerald Only
Body Slam* · Mimic · Counter* · Double-Edge · Substitute · Seismic Toss* · Mega Punch* · Metronome · Swords Dance* · Mega Kick*

Emerald Only
Dynamicpunch · Icy Wind* · Snore* · Endure* · Metronome · Swagger · Fire Punch* · Mud-Slap* · Thunderpunch* · Ice Punch* · Sleep Talk

*Battle Frontier tutor move (*Emerald*)

PRIMA OFFICIAL GAME GUIDE

273 Seedot™

GRASS

GENERAL INFO

SPECIES: Acorn Pokémon
HEIGHT: 1'08"
WEIGHT: 9 lbs.
ABILITY 1: Chlorophyll
Doubles Seedot's Speed when the sunlight is strong.
ABILITY 2: Early Bird
Seedot recovers from Sleep earlier.

STATS

HP, ATK, DEF, SP ATK, SP DEF, SPEED

EVOLUTIONS

  LV14   LEAF STONE

LOCATION[s]:

RUBY	Rarity:	Common	Route 102, Route 114
SAPPHIRE	Rarity:	None	Trade from *Ruby*
FIRERED	Rarity:	None	Trade from *Ruby*
LEAFGREEN	Rarity:	None	Trade from *Ruby*
COLOSSEUM	Rarity:	None	Trade from *Ruby*
EMERALD	Rarity:	Rare	Routes 102, 117, 120, Rustboro City
XD	Rarity:	Only One	Cipher Lab (Capture from Cipher Peon Greesix)

MOVES

Level	Attack	Type	Power	ACC	PP
—	Bide	Normal	—	100	10
—	Pound*	Normal	40	100	35
3	Harden	Normal	—	—	30
7	Growth	Normal	—	—	40

Level	Attack	Type	Power	ACC	PP
13	Nature Power	Normal	—	95	20
21	Synthesis	Grass	—	—	5
31	Sunny Day	Fire	—	—	5
43	Explosion	Normal	250	100	5

* Emerald Only

TM/HM

TM/HM#	Name	Type	Power	ACC	PP
TM06	Toxic	Poison	—	85	10
TM09	Bullet Seed	Grass	10	100	30
TM10	Hidden Power	Normal	—	100	15
TM11	Sunny Day	Fire	—	—	5
TM17	Protect	Normal	—	—	10
TM19	Giga Drain	Grass	60	100	5
TM21	Frustration	Normal	—	100	20
TM22	Solarbeam	Grass	120	100	10
TM27	Return	Normal	—	100	20

TM/HM#	Name	Type	Power	ACC	PP
TM28	Dig	Ground	60	100	10
TM30	Shadow Ball	Ghost	60	—	20
TM32	Double Team	Normal	—	—	15
TM42	Facade	Normal	70	100	20
TM43	Secret Power	Normal	70	100	20
TM44	Rest	Psychic	—	—	10
TM45	Attract	Normal	—	100	15
HM05	Flash	Normal	—	70	20
HM06	Rock Smash	Fighting	20	100	15

EGG MOVES*

Name	Type	Power	ACC	PP
Leech Seed	Grass	—	90	10
Amnesia	Psychic	—	—	20
Quick Attack	Normal	40	100	30
Razor Wind	Normal	80	100	10
Take Down	Normal	90	85	20
False Swipe	Normal	40	100	40

*Learned Via Breeding

MOVE TUTOR

FireRed/LeafGreen and Emerald Only

Body Slam*	Mimic	Explosion
Double-Edge	Substitute	Swords Dance*

Emerald Only

Defense Curl*	Rollout	Snore*
Endure*	Sleep Talk	Swagger

*Battle Frontier tutor move (Emerald)

274 Nuzleaf™

GRASS | DARK

GENERAL INFO

SPECIES: Wily Pokémon
HEIGHT: 3'03"
WEIGHT: 62 lbs.
ABILITY 1: Chlorophyll
Doubles Nuzleaf's Speed when the sunlight is strong.
ABILITY 2: Early Bird
Nuzleaf recovers from Sleep earlier.

STATS

EVOLUTIONS

LV14 — LEAF STONE

LOCATION(S):

RUBY	Rarity: **Rare**	Route 114
SAPPHIRE	Rarity: **None**	Trade from *Ruby*
FIRERED	Rarity: **None**	Trade from *Ruby*
LEAFGREEN	Rarity: **None**	Trade from *Ruby*
COLOSSEUM	Rarity: **None**	Trade from *Ruby*
EMERALD	Rarity: **Rare**	Evolve Seedot, Route 114
XD	Rarity: **Evolve**	Evolve Seedot

MOVES

Level	Attack	Type	Power	ACC	PP
—	Bide*	Normal	—	100	10
—	Pound	Normal	40	100	35
—/3	Harden	Normal	—	—	30
—/7	Growth	Normal	—	—	40
—/13	Nature Power	Normal	—	95	20
19	Fake Out	Normal	40	100	10
25	Torment	Dark	—	100	15
31	Faint Attack	Dark	60	—	20
37	Razor Wind	Normal	80	100	10
43	Swagger	Normal	—	90	15
49	Extrasensory	Psychic	80	100	30

= *Emerald* Only   * Not Available in *Emerald*

TM/HM

TM/HM#	Name	Type	Power	ACC	PP
TM06	Toxic	Poison	—	85	10
TM09	Bullet Seed	Grass	10	100	30
TM10	Hidden Power	Normal	—	100	15
TM11	Sunny Day	Fire	—	—	5
TM15	Hyper Beam	Normal	150	90	5
TM17	Protect	Normal	—	—	10
TM19	Giga Drain	Grass	60	100	5
TM21	Frustration	Normal	—	100	20
TM22	Solarbeam	Grass	120	100	10
TM27	Return	Normal	—	100	20
TM28	Dig	Ground	60	100	10
TM30	Shadow Punch	Ghost	60	—	20
TM31	Brick Break	Fighting	75	100	15
TM32	Double Team	Normal	—	—	15
TM39	Rock Tomb	Rock	50	80	10
TM41	Torment	Dark	—	100	15
TM42	Facade	Normal	70	100	20
TM43	Secret Power	Normal	70	100	20
TM44	Rest	Psychic	—	—	10
TM45	Attract	Normal	—	100	15
TM46	Thief	Dark	40	100	10
HM01	Cut	Normal	50	95	30
HM04	Strength	Normal	80	100	15
HM05	Flash	Normal	—	70	20
HM06	Rock Smash	Fighting	20	100	15

MOVE TUTOR

FireRed/LeafGreen and Emerald Only

Body Slam* | Substitute | Swords Dance*
Double-Edge | Explosion | Mega Kick*
Mimic

Emerald Only

Defense Curl* | Psych Up* | Snore*
Endure* | Rollout | Swagger
Fury Cutter | Sleep Talk | Swift*
Mud-Slap*

*Battle Frontier tutor move (*Emerald*)

PRIMA OFFICIAL GAME GUIDE

275 Shiftry™

GRASS DARK

GENERAL INFO
SPECIES: Wicked Pokémon
HEIGHT: 4'03"
WEIGHT: 131 lbs.
ABILITY 1: Chlorophyll
Doubles Shiftry's Speed when the sunlight is strong.
ABILITY 2: Early Bird
Shiftry recovers from Sleep earlier.

STATS

EVOLUTIONS

LV14   LEAF STONE

LOCATION[s]:

RUBY	Rarity:	Evolve	Evolve Nuzleaf
SAPPHIRE	Rarity:	None	Trade from *Ruby*
FIRERED	Rarity:	None	Trade from *Ruby*
LEAFGREEN	Rarity:	None	Trade from *Ruby*
COLOSSEUM	Rarity:	None	Trade from *Ruby*
EMERALD	Rarity:	Evolve	Evolve Nuzleaf
XD	Rarity:	Evolve	Evolve Nuzleaf

MOVES

Level	Attack	Type	Power	ACC	PP	Level	Attack	Type	Power	ACC	PP
—	Pound	Normal	40	100	35	—	Growth	Normal	—	—	40
—	Harden	Normal	—	—	30	—	Nature Power	Normal	—	95	20

TM/HM

TM/HM#	Name	Type	Power	ACC	PP	TM/HM#	Name	Type	Power	ACC	PP
TM06	Toxic	Poison	—	85	10	TM32	Double Team	Normal	—	—	15
TM09	Bullet Seed	Grass	10	100	30	TM39	Rock Tomb	Rock	50	80	10
TM10	Hidden Power	Normal	—	100	15	TM40	Aerial Ace	Flying	60	—	20
TM11	Sunny Day	Fire	—	—	5	TM41	Torment	Dark	—	100	15
TM15	Hyper Beam	Normal	150	90	5	TM42	Facade	Normal	70	100	20
TM17	Protect	Normal	—	—	10	TM43	Secret Power	Normal	70	100	20
TM19	Giga Drain	Grass	60	100	5	TM44	Rest	Psychic	—	—	10
TM21	Frustration	Normal	—	100	20	TM45	Attract	Normal	—	100	15
TM22	Solarbeam	Grass	120	100	10	TM46	Thief	Dark	40	100	10
TM27	Return	Normal	—	100	20	HM01	Cut	Normal	50	95	30
TM28	Dig	Ground	60	100	10	HM04	Strength	Normal	80	100	15
TM30	Shadow Ball	Ghost	60	—	20	HM05	Flash	Normal	—	70	20
TM31	Brick Break	Fighting	75	100	15	HM06	Rock Smash	Fighting	20	100	15

MOVE TUTOR

FireRed/LeafGreen and Emerald Only

Body Slam*	Substitute	Swords Dance*
Double-Edge	Explosion	Mega Kick*
Mimic		

Emerald Only

Defense Curl*	Psych Up*	Snore*
Endure*	Rollout	Swagger
Fury Cutter	Sleep Talk	Swift*
Mud-Slap*		

*Battle Frontier tutor move (*Emerald*)

276 Taillow™

NORMAL | FLYING

GENERAL INFO

SPECIES: Tinyswallow Pokémon
HEIGHT: 1'00"
WEIGHT: 5 lbs.
ABILITY: Guts

Taillow's attack power increases 1.5 times when inflicted with a status condition.

STATS

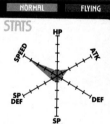

EVOLUTIONS

LV22

LOCATION[S]:

	Rarity	
RUBY	**Common**	Route 104, Route 115, Route 116, Petalburg Woods
SAPPHIRE	**Common**	Route 104, Route 115, Route 116, Petalburg Woods
FIRERED	**None**	Trade from *Ruby/Sapphire/Emerald*
LEAFGREEN	**None**	Trade from *Ruby/Sapphire/Emerald*
COLOSSEUM	**None**	Trade from *Ruby/Sapphire/Emerald*
EMERALD	**Common**	Route 104, Route 115, Route 116, Petalburg Woods
XD	**None**	Trade from *Ruby/Sapphire/Emerald*

MOVES

Level	Attack	Type	Power	ACC	PP
—	Peck	Flying	35	100	35
—	Growl	Normal	—	100	40
4	Focus Energy	Normal	—	—	30
8	Quick Attack	Normal	40	100	30
13	Wing Attack	Flying	60	100	35
19	Double Team	Normal	—	—	15
26	Endeavor	Normal	—	100	5
34	Aerial Ace	Flying	60	—	20
43	Agility	Psychic	—	—	30

TM/HM

TM/HM#	Name	Type	Power	ACC	PP
TM06	Toxic	Poison	—	85	10
TM10	Hidden Power	Normal	—	100	15
TM11	Sunny Day	Fire	—	—	5
TM17	Protect	Normal	—	—	10
TM18	Rain Dance	Water	—	—	5
TM21	Frustration	Normal	—	100	20
TM27	Return	Normal	—	100	20
TM32	Double Team	Normal	—	—	15
TM40	Aerial Ace	Flying	60	—	20
TM42	Facade	Normal	70	100	20
TM43	Secret Power	Normal	70	100	20
TM44	Rest	Psychic	—	—	10
TM45	Attract	Normal	—	100	15
TM46	Thief	Dark	40	100	10
TM47	Steel Wing	Steel	70	90	25
HM02	Fly	Flying	70	95	15

EGG MOVES*

Name	Type	Power	ACC	PP
Pursuit	Dark	40	100	20
Supersonic	Normal	—	55	20
Refresh	Normal	—	100	20
Mirror Move	Flying	—	—	20
Rage	Normal	20	100	20
Sky Attack	Flying	140	90	5

*Learned Via Breeding

MOVE TUTOR

FireRed/LeafGreen and Emerald Only

Double-Edge	Substitute	Counter*
Mimic		

Emerald Only

Endure*	Sleep Talk	Swagger
Mud-Slap*	Snore*	Swift*

*Battle Frontier tutor move (*Emerald*)

277 Swellow™

NORMAL   FLYING

GENERAL INFO

SPECIES: Swallow Pokémon
HEIGHT: 2'04"
WEIGHT: 44 lbs.
ABILITY: Guts

Swellow's attack power increases 1.5 times when inflicted with a status condition.

STATS

EVOLUTIONS

LV22

LOCATION[s]:

RUBY	Rarity: **Rare**		Evolve Taillow, Route 115
SAPPHIRE	Rarity: **Rare**		Evolve Taillow, Route 115
FIRERED	Rarity: **None**		Trade from *Ruby/Sapphire/Emerald*
LEAFGREEN	Rarity: **None**		Trade from *Ruby/Sapphire/Emerald*
COLOSSEUM	Rarity: **None**		Trade from *Ruby/Sapphire/Emerald*
EMERALD	Rarity: **Rare**		Evolve Taillow, Route 115
XD	Rarity: **Only One**		Citadark Island (Capture from Cipher Admin Ardos)

MOVES

Level	Attack	Type	Power	ACC	PP	Level	Attack	Type	Power	ACC	PP
—	Peck	Flying	35	100	35	19	Double Team	Normal	—	—	15
—	Growl	Normal	—	100	40	28	Endeavor	Normal	—	100	5
—/4	Focus Energy	Normal	—	—	30	38	Aerial Ace	Flying	60	—	20
—/8	Quick Attack	Normal	40	100	30	49	Agility	Psychic	—	—	30
13	Wing Attack	Flying	60	100	35						

= Emerald Only

TM/HM

TM/HM#	Name	Type	Power	ACC	PP	TM/HM#	Name	Type	Power	ACC	PP
TM06	Toxic	Poison	—	85	10	TM40	Aerial Ace	Flying	60	—	20
TM10	Hidden Power	Normal	—	100	15	TM42	Facade	Normal	70	100	20
TM11	Sunny Day	Fire	—	—	5	TM43	Secret Power	Normal	70	100	20
TM15	Hyper Beam	Normal	150	90	5	TM44	Rest	Psychic	—	—	10
TM17	Protect	Normal	—	—	10	TM45	Attract	Normal	—	100	15
TM18	Rain Dance	Water	—	—	5	TM46	Thief	Dark	40	100	10
TM21	Frustration	Normal	—	100	20	TM47	Steel Wing	Steel	70	90	25
TM27	Return	Normal	—	100	20	HM02	Fly	Flying	70	95	15
TM32	Double Team	Normal	—	—	15						

MOVE TUTOR

FireRed/LeafGreen and Emerald Only

Double-Edge	Substitute	Counter*
Mimic		

Emerald Only

Endure*	Sleep Talk	Swagger
Mud-Slap*	Snore*	Swift*

*Battle Frontier tutor move (*Emerald*)

Wingull™

WATER | FLYING

GENERAL INFO

SPECIES: Seagull Pokémon
HEIGHT: 2'00"
WEIGHT: 21 lbs.
ABILITY: Keen Eye
Wingull's Accuracy cannot be lowered.

STATS

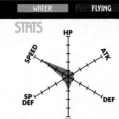

EVOLUTIONS

LV25

LOCATION[s]:

RUBY	Rarity: **Common**	Route 103, Route 104, Route 115, All Water Routes
SAPPHIRE	Rarity: **Common**	Route 103, Route 104, Route 115, All Water Routes
FIRERED	Rarity: **None**	Trade from *Ruby/Sapphire/Emerald*
LEAFGREEN	Rarity: **None**	Trade from *Ruby/Sapphire/Emerald*
COLOSSEUM	Rarity: **None**	Trade from *Ruby/Sapphire/Emerald*
EMERALD	Rarity: **Common**	Routes 103–110, 115, 118, 119, 121–134, Dewford Town, Ever Grande City, Lilycove City, Mossdeep City, Mt. Pyre, Pacifidlog Town, Slateport City
XD	Rarity: **None**	Trade from *Ruby/Sapphire/Emerald*

MOVES

Level	Attack	Type	Power	ACC	PP		Level	Attack	Type	Power	ACC	PP
—	Growl	Normal	—	100	40		21	Mist	Ice	—	—	30
—	Water Gun	Water	40	100	25		31	Quick Attack	Normal	40	100	30
7	Supersonic	Normal	—	55	20		43	Pursuit	Dark	40	100	20
13	Wing Attack	Flying	60	100	35		55	Agility	Psychic	—	—	30

TM/HM

TM/HM#	Name	Type	Power	ACC	PP		TM/HM#	Name	Type	Power	ACC	PP
TM03	Water Pulse	Water	60	100	20		TM32	Double Team	Normal	—	—	15
TM06	Toxic	Poison	—	85	10		TM34	Shock Wave	Electric	60	—	20
TM07	Hail	Ice	—	—	10		TM40	Aerial Ace	Flying	60	—	20
TM10	Hidden Power	Normal	—	100	15		TM42	Facade	Normal	70	100	20
TM13	Ice Beam	Ice	95	100	10		TM43	Secret Power	Normal	70	100	20
TM14	Blizzard	Ice	120	70	5		TM44	Rest	Psychic	—	—	10
TM17	Protect	Normal	—	—	10		TM45	Attract	Normal	—	100	15
TM18	Rain Dance	Water	—	—	5		TM46	Thief	Dark	40	100	10
TM21	Frustration	Normal	—	100	20		TM47	Steel Wing	Steel	70	90	25
TM27	Return	Normal	—	100	20		HM02	Fly	Flying	70	95	15

EGG MOVES*

Name	Type	Power	ACC	PP
Twister	Dragon	40	100	20
Water Sport	Water	—	100	15
Mist	Ice	—	—	30
Agility	Psychic	—	—	30
Whirlwind	Normal	—	100	20

*Learned Via Breeding

MOVE TUTOR

FireRed/LeafGreen and Emerald Only

Double-Edge	Mimic	Substitute

Emerald Only

Endure*	Sleep Talk	Swagger
Icy Wind*	Snore*	Swift*
Mud-Slap*		

*Battle Frontier tutor move (*Emerald*)

PRIMA OFFICIAL GAME GUIDE

279 Pelipper™

WATER | FLYING

GENERAL INFO

SPECIES: Water Bird Pokémon
HEIGHT: 3'11"
WEIGHT: 62 lbs.
ABILITY: Keen Eye

Wingull's Accuracy cannot be lowered.

STATS

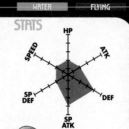

EVOLUTIONS

LV25

LOCATION[s]:

RUBY	Rarity: **Rare**	Evolve Wingull, Route 103, Route 104, Route 115, All Water Routes
SAPPHIRE	Rarity: **Rare**	Evolve Wingull, Route 103, Route 104, Route 115, All Water Routes
FIRERED	Rarity: **None**	Trade from *Ruby/Sapphire/Emerald*
LEAFGREEN	Rarity: **None**	Trade from *Ruby/Sapphire/Emerald*
COLOSSEUM	Rarity: **None**	Trade from *Ruby/Sapphire/Emerald*
EMERALD	Rarity: **Common**	Evolve Wingull, Routes 103–110, 115, 118, 119, 121–134, Dewford Town, Ever Grande City, Lilycove City, Mossdeep City, Mt. Pyre, Pacifidlog Town, Slateport City
XD	Rarity: **None**	Trade from *Ruby/Sapphire/Emerald*

MOVES

Level	Attack	Type	Power	ACC	PP	Level	Attack	Type	Power	ACC	PP
—	Growl	Normal	—	100	40	21	Mist	Ice	—	—	30
—/3	Water Gun	Water	40	100	25	25	Protect	Normal	—	—	10
—	Water Spout	Water	150	100	5	33	Stockpile	Normal	—	—	10
—	Water Sport*	Water	—	100	5	33	Swallow	Normal	—	—	10
—/1	Supersonic	Normal	—	55	20	47	Spit Up	Normal	100	100	10
—/13	Wing Attack	Flying	60	100	35	61	Hydro Pump	Water	120	80	5

*# = Emerald Only   * Emerald Only*

TM/HM

TM/HM#	Name	Type	Power	ACC	PP	TM/HM#	Name	Type	Power	ACC	PP
TM03	Water Pulse	Water	60	100	20	TM32	Double Team	Normal	—	—	15
TM06	Toxic	Poison	—	85	10	TM34	Shock Wave	Electric	60	—	20
TM07	Hail	Ice	—	—	10	TM40	Aerial Ace	Flying	60	—	20
TM10	Hidden Power	Normal	—	100	15	TM42	Facade	Normal	70	100	20
TM13	Ice Beam	Ice	95	100	10	TM43	Secret Power	Normal	70	100	20
TM14	Blizzard	Ice	120	70	5	TM44	Rest	Psychic	—	—	10
TM15	Hyper Beam	Normal	150	90	5	TM45	Attract	Normal	—	100	15
TM17	Protect	Normal	—	—	10	TM46	Thief	Dark	40	100	10
TM18	Rain Dance	Water	—	—	5	TM47	Steel Wing	Steel	70	90	25
TM21	Frustration	Normal	—	100	20	HM02	Fly	Flying	70	95	15
TM27	Return	Normal	—	100	20	HM03	Surf	Water	95	100	15

MOVE TUTOR

FireRed/LeafGreen and Emerald Only

Double-Edge	Mimic	Substitute

Emerald Only

Endure*	Sleep Talk	Swagger
Icy Wind*	Snore*	Swift*
Mud-Slap*		

*Battle Frontier tutor move (Emerald)

290

280 Ralts™

PSYCHIC

GENERAL INFO

SPECIES: Feeling Pokémon
HEIGHT: 1'04"
WEIGHT: 15 lbs.
ABILITY 1: Synchronize
Shares Ralts's Poison, Paralyze, or Burn condition with the opponent Pokémon.
ABILITY 2: Trace
Ralts's ability becomes the same as the opponent's.

STATS

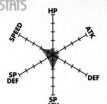

EVOLUTIONS

  LV20 LV30

LOCATION[s]:

RUBY	Rarity: **Rare**	Route 102	
SAPPHIRE	Rarity: **Rare**	Route 102	
FIRERED	Rarity: **None**	Trade from *Ruby/Sapphire/Emerald*	
LEAFGREEN	Rarity: **None**	Trade from *Ruby/Sapphire/Emerald*	
COLOSSEUM	Rarity: **None**	Trade from *Ruby/Sapphire/Emerald*	
EMERALD	Rarity: **Rare**	Route 102	
XD	Rarity: **Only One**	Pyrite Town (Capture from Cipher Peon Feldas)	

MOVES

Level	Attack	Type	Power	ACC	PP	Level	Attack	Type	Power	ACC	PP
—	Growl	Normal	—	100	40	26	Psychic	Psychic	90	100	10
6	Confusion	Psychic	50	100	25	31	Imprison	Psychic	—	100	15
11	Double Team	Normal	—	—	15	36	Future Sight	Psychic	80	90	15
16	Teleport	Psychic	—	—	20	41	Hypnosis	Psychic	—	60	20
21	Calm Mind	Psychic	—	—	20	46	Dream Eater	Psychic	100	100	15

TM/HM

TM/HM#	Name	Type	Power	ACC	PP	TM/HM#	Name	Type	Power	ACC	PP
TM04	Calm Mind	Psychic	—	—	20	TM30	Shadow Ball	Ghost	60	—	20
TM06	Toxic	Poison	—	85	10	TM32	Double Team	Normal	—	—	15
TM10	Hidden Power	Normal	—	100	15	TM33	Reflect	Psychic	—	—	20
TM11	Sunny Day	Fire	—	—	5	TM34	Shock Wave	Electric	60	—	20
TM12	Taunt	Dark	—	100	20	TM41	Torment	Dark	—	100	15
TM16	Light Screen	Psychic	—	—	30	TM42	Facade	Normal	70	100	20
TM17	Protect	Normal	—	—	10	TM43	Secret Power	Normal	70	100	20
TM18	Rain Dance	Water	—	—	5	TM44	Rest	Psychic	—	—	10
TM20	Safeguard	Normal	—	—	25	TM45	Attract	Normal	—	100	15
TM21	Frustration	Normal	—	100	20	TM46	Thief	Dark	40	100	10
TM24	Thunderbolt	Electric	95	100	15	TM48	Skill Swap	Psychic	—	100	10
TM27	Return	Normal	—	100	20	TM49	Snatch	Dark	—	100	10
TM29	Psychic	Psychic	90	100	10	HM05	Flash	Normal	—	70	20

EGG MOVES*

Name	Type	Power	ACC	PP
Disable	Normal	—	55	20
Will-O-Wisp	Fire	—	75	15
Mean Look	Normal	—	100	5
Memento	Dark	—	100	10
Destiny Bond	Ghost	—	—	5

*Learned Via Breeding

MOVE TUTOR

FireRed/LeafGreen and Emerald Only

Body Slam*	Mimic	Thunder Wave*
Double-Edge	Substitute	Dream Eater*

Emerald Only

Defense Curl*	Icy Wind*	Snore*
Endure*	Mud-Slap*	Swagger
Fire Punch*	Psych Up*	Thunderpunch*
Ice Punch*	Sleep Talk	

*Battle Frontier tutor move (*Emerald*)

281 Kirlia™

PSYCHIC

GENERAL INFO

SPECIES: Emotion Pokémon
HEIGHT: 2'07"
WEIGHT: 45 lbs.
ABILITY 1: Synchronize
Shares Kirlia's Poison, Paralyze, or Burn condition with the opponent Pokémon.
ABILITY 2: Trace
Kirlia's ability becomes the same as the opponent's.

STATS

EVOLUTIONS

LV20   LV30

LOCATION(s):

RUBY	Rarity: **Evolve**	Evolve Ralts
SAPPHIRE	Rarity: **Evolve**	Evolve Ralts
FIRERED	Rarity: **None**	Trade from *Ruby/Sapphire/Emerald*
LEAFGREEN	Rarity: **None**	Trade from *Ruby/Sapphire/Emerald*
COLOSSEUM	Rarity: **None**	Trade from *Ruby/Sapphire/Emerald*
EMERALD	Rarity: **Evolve**	Evolve Ralts
XD	Rarity: **Evolve**	Evolve Ralts

MOVES

Level	Attack	Type	Power	ACC	PP	Level	Attack	Type	Power	ACC	PP
—	Growl	Normal	—	100	40	26	Psychic	Psychic	90	100	10
6	Confusion*	Psychic	50	100	25	33	Imprison	Psychic	—	100	15
11	Double Team*	Normal	—	—	15	40	Future Sight	Psychic	80	90	15
16	Teleport*	Psychic	—	—	20	47	Hypnosis	Psychic	—	60	20
—	Magical Leaf	Grass	60	—	20	54	Dream Eater	Psychic	100	100	15
21	Calm Mind	Psychic	—	—	20	*Emerald Only					

TM/HM

TM/HM#	Name	Type	Power	ACC	PP	TM/HM#	Name	Type	Power	ACC	PP
TM04	Calm Mind	Psychic	—	—	20	TM30	Shadow Ball	Ghost	60	—	20
TM06	Toxic	Poison	—	85	10	TM32	Double Team	Normal	—	—	15
TM10	Hidden Power	Normal	—	100	15	TM33	Reflect	Psychic	—	—	20
TM11	Sunny Day	Fire	—	—	5	TM34	Shock Wave	Electric	60	—	20
TM12	Taunt	Dark	—	100	20	TM41	Torment	Dark	—	100	15
TM16	Light Screen	Psychic	—	—	30	TM42	Facade	Normal	70	100	20
TM17	Protect	Normal	—	—	10	TM43	Secret Power	Normal	70	100	20
TM18	Rain Dance	Water	—	—	5	TM44	Rest	Psychic	—	—	10
TM20	Safeguard	Normal	—	—	25	TM45	Attract	Normal	—	100	15
TM21	Frustration	Normal	—	100	20	TM46	Thief	Dark	40	100	10
TM24	Thunderbolt	Electric	95	100	15	TM48	Skill Swap	Psychic	—	100	10
TM27	Return	Normal	—	100	20	TM49	Snatch	Dark	—	100	10
TM29	Psychic	Psychic	90	100	10	HM05	Flash	Normal	—	70	20

MOVE TUTOR

FireRed/LeafGreen and Emerald Only

Body Slam*	Mimic	Thunder Wave*
Double-Edge	Substitute	Dream Eater*

Emerald Only

Defense Curl*	Icy Wind*	Snore*
Endure*	Mud-Slap*	Swagger
Fire Punch*	Psych Up*	Thunderpunch*
Ice Punch*	Sleep Talk	

*Battle Frontier tutor move (*Emerald*)

282 Gardevoir™

GENERAL INFO

SPECIES: Embrace Pokémon
HEIGHT: 5'03"
WEIGHT: 107 lbs.
ABILITY 1: Synchronize
Shares Gardevoir's Poison, Paralyze, or Burn condition with the opponent Pokémon.
ABILITY 2: Trace
Gardevoir's ability becomes the same as the opponent's.

STATS

EVOLUTIONS

 ▶ LV20 ▶ LV30

LOCATION[S]:

RUBY	Rarity: **Evolve**	Evolve Kirlia
SAPPHIRE	Rarity: **Evolve**	Evolve Kirlia
FIRERED	Rarity: **None**	Trade from *Ruby/Sapphire/Emerald*
LEAFGREEN	Rarity: **None**	Trade from *Ruby/Sapphire/Emerald*
COLOSSEUM	Rarity: **None**	Trade from *Ruby/Sapphire/Emerald*
EMERALD	Rarity: **Evolve**	Evolve Kirlia
XD	Rarity: **Evolve**	Evolve Kirlia

MOVES

Level	Attack	Type	Power	ACC	PP	Level	Attack	Type	Power	ACC	PP
—	Growl	Normal	—	100	40	26	Psychic	Psychic	90	100	10
6	Confusion*	Psychic	50	100	25	33	Imprison	Psychic	—	100	15
11	Double Team*	Normal	—	—	15	42	Future Sight	Psychic	80	90	15
16	Teleport*	Psychic	—	—	20	51	Hypnosis	Psychic	—	60	20
21	Calm Mind	Psychic	—	—	20	60	Dream Eater	Psychic	100	100	15

* Emerald Only

TM/HM

TM/HM#	Name	Type	Power	ACC	PP	TM/HM#	Name	Type	Power	ACC	PP
TM04	Calm Mind	Psychic	—	—	20	TM30	Shadow Ball	Ghost	60	—	20
TM06	Toxic	Poison	—	85	10	TM32	Double Team	Normal	—	—	15
TM10	Hidden Power	Normal	—	100	15	TM33	Reflect	Psychic	—	—	20
TM11	Sunny Day	Fire	—	—	5	TM34	Shock Wave	Electric	60	—	20
TM12	Taunt	Dark	—	100	20	TM41	Torment	Dark	—	100	15
TM15	Hyper Beam	Normal	150	90	5	TM42	Facade	Normal	70	100	20
TM16	Light Screen	Psychic	—	—	30	TM43	Secret Power	Normal	70	100	20
TM17	Protect	Normal	—	—	10	TM44	Rest	Psychic	—	—	10
TM18	Rain Dance	Water	—	—	5	TM45	Attract	Normal	—	100	15
TM20	Safeguard	Normal	—	25		TM46	Thief	Dark	40	100	10
TM21	Frustration	Normal	—	100	20	TM48	Skill Swap	Psychic	—	100	10
TM24	Thunderbolt	Electric	95	100	15	TM49	Snatch	Dark	—	100	10
TM27	Return	Normal	—	100	20	HM05	Flash	Normal	—	70	20
TM29	Psychic	Psychic	90	100	10						

MOVE TUTOR

FireRed/LeafGreen and Emerald Only

Body Slam*	Mimic	Thunder Wave*	
Double-Edge	Substitute	Dream Eater*	

Emerald Only

Defense Curl*	Icy Wind*	Snore*
Endure*	Mud-Slap*	Swagger
Fire Punch*	Psych Up*	Thunderpunch*
Ice Punch*	Sleep Talk	

*Battle Frontier tutor move (Emerald)

283 Surskit™

BUG   WATER

GENERAL INFO
SPECIES: Pond Skater Pokémon
HEIGHT: 1'08"
WEIGHT: 4 lbs.
ABILITY: Swift Swim
Doubles Surskit's Speed when it is raining.

STATS

EVOLUTIONS

LV22

LOCATION[s]:

RUBY	Rarity: **Rare**	Routes 102, 111, 114, 117, 120
SAPPHIRE	Rarity: **Rare**	Routes 102, 111, 114, 117, 120
FIRERED	Rarity: **None**	Trade from *Ruby/Sapphire*
LEAFGREEN	Rarity: **None**	Trade from *Ruby/Sapphire*
COLOSSEUM	Rarity: **None**	Trade from *Ruby/Sapphire*
EMERALD	Rarity: **None**	Trade from *Ruby/Sapphire*
XD	Rarity: **Rare**	Oasis Poké Spot

MOVES

Level	Attack	Type	Power	ACC	PP	Level	Attack	Type	Power	ACC	PP
—	Bubble	Water	20	100	30	25	Bubblebeam	Water	65	100	20
7	Quick Attack	Normal	40	100	30	31	Agility	Psychic	—	—	30
13	Sweet Scent	Normal	—	100	20	37	Mist	Ice	—	—	30
19	Water Sport	Water	—	100	15	37	Haze	Ice	—	—	30

TM/HM

TM/HM#	Name	Type	Power	ACC	PP	TM/HM#	Name	Type	Power	ACC	PP
TM03	Water Pulse	Water	60	100	20	TM22	Solarbeam	Grass	120	100	10
TM06	Toxic	Poison	—	85	10	TM27	Return	Normal	—	100	20
TM10	Hidden Power	Normal	—	100	15	TM30	Shadow Ball	Ghost	60	—	20
TM11	Sunny Day	Fire	—	—	5	TM32	Double Team	Normal	—	—	15
TM13	Ice Beam	Ice	95	100	10	TM42	Facade	Normal	70	100	20
TM14	Blizzard	Ice	120	70	5	TM43	Secret Power	Normal	70	100	20
TM17	Protect	Normal	—	—	10	TM44	Rest	Psychic	—	—	10
TM18	Rain Dance	Water	—	—	5	TM45	Attract	Normal	—	100	15
TM19	Giga Drain	Grass	60	100	5	TM46	Thief	Dark	40	100	10
TM21	Frustration	Normal	—	100	20	HM05	Flash	Normal	—	70	20

EGG MOVES*

Name	Type	Power	ACC	PP
Foresight	Normal	—	100	40
Mud Shot	Ground	55	95	15
Psybeam	Psychic	65	100	20
Hydro Pump	Water	120	80	5
Mind Reader	Normal	—	100	5

*Learned Via Breeding

MOVE TUTOR

FireRed/LeafGreen and Emerald Only

Double-Edge	Mimic	Substitute

Emerald Only

Endure*	Sleep Talk	Swagger
Icy Wind*	Snore*	Swift*
Psych Up*		

*Battle Frontier tutor move (*Emerald*)

284 Masquerain ™

BUG   FLYING

GENERAL INFO
SPECIES: Eyeball Pokémon
HEIGHT: 2'07"
WEIGHT: 8 lbs.
ABILITY: Intimidate
Lowers the opponent's Attack by one point at the start of a battle.

STATS

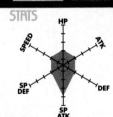

EVOLUTIONS

LV22

LOCATION(S):

RUBY	Rarity: **Evolve**	Evolve Surskit
SAPPHIRE	Rarity: **Evolve**	Evolve Surskit
FIRERED	Rarity: **None**	Trade from *Ruby/Sapphire*
LEAFGREEN	Rarity: **None**	Trade from *Ruby/Sapphire*
COLOSSEUM	Rarity: **None**	Trade from *Ruby/Sapphire*
EMERALD	Rarity: **None**	Trade from *Ruby/Sapphire*
XD	Rarity: **Evolve**	Evolve Surskit

MOVES

Level	Attack	Type	Power	ACC	PP	Level	Attack	Type	Power	ACC	PP
—	Bubble	Water	20	100	30	33	Scary Face	Normal	—	90	10
—/7	Quick Attack	Normal	40	100	30	40	Stun Spore	Grass	—	75	30
—/13	Sweet Scent	Normal	—	100	20	47	Silver Wind	Bug	60	100	5
—/19	Water Sport	Water	—	100	15	53	Whirlwind	Normal	—	100	20
26	Gust	Flying	40	100	35	# = *Emerald* Only					

TM/HM

TM/HM#	Name	Type	Power	ACC	PP	TM/HM#	Name	Type	Power	ACC	PP
TM03	Water Pulse	Water	60	100	20	TM22	Solarbeam	Grass	120	100	10
TM06	Toxic	Poison	—	85	10	TM27	Return	Normal	—	100	20
TM10	Hidden Power	Normal	—	100	15	TM30	Shadow Ball	Ghost	60	—	20
TM11	Sunny Day	Fire	—	—	5	TM32	Double Team	Normal	—	—	15
TM13	Ice Beam	Ice	95	100	10	TM40	Aerial Ace	Flying	60	—	20
TM14	Blizzard	Ice	120	70	5	TM42	Facade	Normal	70	100	20
TM15	Hyper Beam	Normal	150	90	5	TM43	Secret Power	Normal	70	100	20
TM17	Protect	Normal	—	—	10	TM44	Rest	Psychic	—	—	10
TM18	Rain Dance	Water	—	—	5	TM45	Attract	Normal	—	100	15
TM19	Giga Drain	Grass	60	100	5	TM46	Thief	Dark	40	100	10
TM21	Frustration	Normal	—	100	20	HM05	Flash	Normal	—	70	20

MOVE TUTOR

FireRed/LeafGreen and Emerald Only

Double-Edge	Mimic	Substitute

Emerald Only

Endure*	Sleep Talk	Swagger
Icy Wind*	Snore*	Swift*
Psych Up*		

*Battle Frontier tutor move (*Emerald*)

285 Shroomish™

GRASS

GENERAL INFO
SPECIES: Mushroom Pokémon
HEIGHT: 1'04"
WEIGHT: 10 lbs.
ABILITY: Effect Spore
If physically attacked, Shroomish has a 10% chance of inflicting Paralysis, Poison, or Sleep on its opponent.

STATS

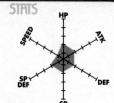

EVOLUTIONS

LV23

LOCATION(s):

RUBY	Rarity: **Rare**		Petalburg Woods
SAPPHIRE	Rarity: **Rare**		Petalburg Woods
FIRERED	Rarity: **None**		Trade from *Ruby/Sapphire*
LEAFGREEN	Rarity: **None**		Trade from *Ruby/Sapphire*
COLOSSEUM	Rarity: **None**		Trade from *Ruby/Sapphire*
EMERALD	Rarity: **Common**		Petalburg Woods
XD	Rarity: **Only One**		Cipher Lab (Capture from Cipher R&D Klots)

MOVES

Level	Attack	Type	Power	ACC	PP	Level	Attack	Type	Power	ACC	PP
—	Absorb	Grass	20	100	20	22	Headbutt	Normal	70	100	15
4	Tackle	Normal	35	95	35	28	Poisonpowder	Poison	—	75	35
7	Stun Spore	Grass	—	75	30	36	Growth	Normal	—	—	40
10	Leech Seed	Grass	—	90	10	45	Giga Drain	Grass	60	100	5
16	Mega Drain	Grass	40	100	10	54	Spore	Grass	—	100	15

TM/HM

TM/HM#	Name	Type	Power	ACC	PP	TM/HM#	Name	Type	Power	ACC	PP
TM06	Toxic	Poison	—	85	10	TM27	Return	Normal	—	100	20
TM09	Bullet Seed	Grass	10	100	30	TM32	Double Team	Normal	—	—	15
TM10	Hidden Power	Normal	—	100	15	TM36	Sludge Bomb	Poison	90	100	10
TM11	Sunny Day	Fire	—	—	5	TM42	Facade	Normal	70	100	20
TM17	Protect	Normal	—	—	10	TM43	Secret Power	Normal	70	100	20
TM19	Giga Drain	Grass	60	100	5	TM44	Rest	Psychic	—	—	10
TM20	Safeguard	Normal	—	—	25	TM45	Attract	Normal	—	100	15
TM21	Frustration	Normal	—	100	20	TM49	Snatch	Dark	—	100	10
TM22	Solarbeam	Grass	120	100	10	HM05	Flash	Normal	—	70	20

EGG MOVES*

Name	Type	Power	ACC	PP
Fake Tears	Dark	—	100	20
Swagger	Normal	—	90	15
Charm	Normal	—	100	20
False Swipe	Normal	40	100	40
Helping Hand	Normal	—	100	20

*Learned Via Breeding

MOVE TUTOR

FireRed/LeafGreen and Emerald Only

Body Slam*	Mimic	Swords Dance*
Double-Edge	Substitute	

Emerald Only

Endure*	Snore*	Swagger
Sleep Talk		

*Battle Frontier tutor move (*Emerald*)

286 Breloom ™

GRASS | FIGHTING

GENERAL INFO

SPECIES: Mushroom Pokémon
HEIGHT: 3'11"
WEIGHT: 86 lbs.
ABILITY: Effect Spore

If physically attacked, Breloom has a 10% chance of inflicting Paralysis, Poison, or Sleep on its opponent.

STATS

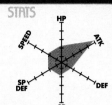

EVOLUTIONS

LV23

LOCATION[s]:

RUBY	Rarity: **Evolve**	Evolve Shroomish
SAPPHIRE	Rarity: **Evolve**	Evolve Shroomish
FIRERED	Rarity: **None**	Trade from *Ruby/Sapphire*
LEAFGREEN	Rarity: **None**	Trade from *Ruby/Sapphire*
COLOSSEUM	Rarity: **None**	Trade from *Ruby/Sapphire*
EMERALD	Rarity: **Evolve**	Evolve Shroomish
XD	Rarity: **Evolve**	Evolve Shroomish

MOVES

Level	Attack	Type	Power	ACC	PP	Level	Attack	Type	Power	ACC	PP
—	Absorb	Grass	20	100	20	23	Mach Punch	Fighting	40	100	30
—/4	Tackle	Normal	35	95	35	28	Counter	Fighting	—	100	20
—/7	Stun Spore	Grass	—	75	30	36	Sky Uppercut	Fighting	85	90	15
—/10	Leech Seed	Grass	—	90	10	45	Mind Reader	Normal	—	100	5
16	Mega Drain	Grass	40	100	10	54	Dynamicpunch	Fighting	100	50	5
22	Headbutt	Normal	70	100	15		# = *Emerald Only*				

TM/HM

TM/HM#	Name	Type	Power	ACC	PP	TM/HM#	Name	Type	Power	ACC	PP
TM01	Focus Punch	Fighting	150	100	20	TM27	Return	Normal	—	100	20
TM06	Toxic	Poison	—	85	10	TM31	Brick Break	Fighting	75	100	15
TM08	Bulk Up	Fighting	—	—	20	TM32	Double Team	Normal	—	—	15
TM09	Bullet Seed	Grass	10	100	30	TM36	Sludge Bomb	Poison	90	100	10
TM10	Hidden Power	Normal	—	100	15	TM42	Facade	Normal	70	100	20
TM11	Sunny Day	Fire	—	—	5	TM43	Secret Power	Normal	70	100	20
TM15	Hyper Beam	Normal	150	90	5	TM44	Rest	Psychic	—	—	10
TM17	Protect	Normal	—	—	10	TM45	Attract	Normal	—	100	15
TM19	Giga Drain	Grass	60	100	10	TM49	Snatch	Dark	—	100	10
TM20	Safeguard	Normal	—	—	25	HM01	Cut	Normal	50	95	30
TM21	Frustration	Normal	—	100	20	HM04	Strength	Normal	80	100	15
TM22	Solarbeam	Grass	120	100	10	HM05	Flash	Normal	—	70	20
TM23	Iron Tail	Steel	100	75	15	HM06	Rock Smash	Fighting	20	100	15

MOVE TUTOR

FireRed/LeafGreen and Emerald Only

Body Slam*	Mega Kick*	Swords Dance*
Double-Edge	Mimic	Counter*
Mega Punch*	Substitute	Seismic Toss*

Emerald Only

Dynamicpunch	Mud-Slap*	Swagger
Endure*	Sleep Talk	Thunderpunch*
Fury Cutter	Snore*	

*Battle Frontier tutor move (*Emerald*)

287 Slakoth™

NORMAL

GENERAL INFO
SPECIES: Slacker Pokémon
HEIGHT: 2'07"
WEIGHT: 53 lbs.
ABILITY: Truant
Can only attack every other turn.

STATS

EVOLUTIONS

LV18   LV36

LOCATION[s]:

RUBY	Rarity: **Rare**	Petalburg Woods
SAPPHIRE	Rarity: **Rare**	Petalburg Woods
FIRERED	Rarity: **None**	Trade from *Ruby/Sapphire/Emerald*
LEAFGREEN	Rarity: **None**	Trade from *Ruby/Sapphire/Emerald*
COLOSSEUM	Rarity: **None**	Trade from *Ruby/Sapphire/Emerald*
EMERALD	Rarity: **Rare**	Petalburg Woods
XD	Rarity: **None**	Trade from *Ruby/Sapphire/Emerald*

MOVES

Level	Attack	Type	Power	ACC	PP	Level	Attack	Type	Power	ACC	PP
—	Scratch	Normal	40	100	35	19	Faint Attack	Dark	60	—	20
—	Yawn	Normal	—	100	10	25	Amnesia	Psychic	—	—	20
7	Encore	Normal	—	100	5	31	Covet	Normal	40	100	40
13	Slack Off	Normal	—	100	10	37	Counter	Fighting	—	100	20
						43	Flail	Normal	—	100	15

TM/HM

TM/HM#	Name	Type	Power	ACC	PP	TM/HM#	Name	Type	Power	ACC	PP
TM01	Focus Punch	Fighting	150	100	20	TM30	Shadow Ball	Ghost	60	—	20
TM03	Water Pulse	Water	60	100	20	TM31	Brick Break	Fighting	75	100	15
TM06	Toxic	Poison	—	85	10	TM32	Double Team	Normal	—	—	15
TM08	Bulk Up	Fighting	—	—	20	TM34	Shock Wave	Electric	60	—	20
TM10	Hidden Power	Normal	—	100	15	TM35	Flamethrower	Fire	95	100	15
TM11	Sunny Day	Fire	—	—	5	TM38	Fire Blast	Fire	120	85	5
TM13	Ice Beam	Ice	95	100	10	TM40	Aerial Ace	Flying	60	—	20
TM14	Blizzard	Ice	120	70	5	TM42	Facade	Normal	70	100	20
TM17	Protect	Normal	—	—	10	TM43	Secret Power	Normal	70	100	20
TM18	Rain Dance	Water	—	—	5	TM44	Rest	Psychic	—	—	10
TM21	Frustration	Normal	—	100	20	TM45	Attract	Normal	—	100	15
TM22	Solarbeam	Grass	120	100	10	HM01	Cut	Normal	50	95	30
TM24	Thunderbolt	Electric	95	100	15	HM04	Strength	Normal	80	100	15
TM25	Thunder	Electric	120	70	10	HM06	Rock Smash	Fighting	20	100	15
TM27	Return	Normal	—	100	20						

EGG MOVES*

Name	Type	Power	ACC	PP
Pursuit	Dark	40	100	20
Slash	Normal	70	100	20
Body Slam	Normal	85	100	15
Snore	Normal	40	100	15
Crush Claw	Normal	75	95	10
Curse	—	—	—	10
Sleep Talk	Normal	—	—	10

*Learned Via Breeding

MOVE TUTOR

FireRed/LeafGreen and Emerald Only

Body Slam*	Mega Kick*	Counter*
Double-Edge	Mimic	Seismic Toss*
Mega Punch*	Substitute	Rock Slide*

Emerald Only

Dynamicpunch*	Ice Punch*	Snore*
Endure*	Icy Wind*	Swagger
Fire Punch*	Mud-Slap*	Thunderpunch*
Fury Cutter	Sleep Talk	

*Battle Frontier tutor move (*Emerald*)

288 Vigoroth

NORMAL

GENERAL INFO

SPECIES: Wild Monkey Pokémon
HEIGHT: 4'07"
WEIGHT: 103 lbs.
ABILITY: Vital Spirit
Vigoroth cannot be put to Sleep.

STATS

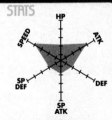

EVOLUTIONS

LV18   LV36

LOCATION(s):

RUBY	Rarity: **Evolve**	Evolve Slakoth
SAPPHIRE	Rarity: **Evolve**	Evolve Slakoth
FIRERED	Rarity: **None**	Trade from *Ruby/Sapphire/Emerald*
LEAFGREEN	Rarity: **None**	Trade from *Ruby/Sapphire/Emerald*
COLOSSEUM	Rarity: **None**	Trade from *Ruby/Sapphire/Emerald*
EMERALD	Rarity: **Evolve**	Evolve Slakoth
XD	Rarity: **None**	Trade from *Ruby/Sapphire/Emerald*

MOVES

Level	Attack	Type	Power	ACC	PP
—	Scratch	Normal	40	100	35
—	Focus Energy	Normal	—	—	30
—/1	Encore	Normal	—	100	5
—/3	Uproar	Normal	50	100	10
19	Fury Swipes	Normal	18	80	15
25	Endure	Normal	—	—	10
31	Slash	Normal	70	100	20
37	Counter	Fighting	—	100	20
43	Focus Punch	Fighting	150	100	20
49	Reversal	Fighting	—	100	15

= *Emerald Only*

TM/HM

TM/HM#	Name	Type	Power	ACC	PP
TM01	Focus Punch	Fighting	150	100	20
TM03	Water Pulse	Water	60	100	20
TM05	Roar	Normal	—	100	20
TM06	Toxic	Poison	—	85	10
TM08	Bulk Up	Fighting	—	—	20
TM10	Hidden Power	Normal	—	100	15
TM11	Sunny Day	Fire	—	—	5
TM12	Taunt	Dark	—	100	20
TM13	Ice Beam	Ice	95	100	10
TM14	Blizzard	Ice	120	70	5
TM17	Protect	Normal	—	—	10
TM18	Rain Dance	Water	—	—	5
TM21	Frustration	Normal	—	100	20
TM22	Solarbeam	Grass	120	100	10
TM24	Thunderbolt	Electric	95	100	15
TM25	Thunder	Electric	120	70	10
TM26	Earthquake	Ground	100	100	10
TM27	Return	Normal	—	100	20
TM30	Shadow Punch	Ghost	60	—	20
TM31	Brick Break	Fighting	75	100	15
TM32	Double Team	Normal	—	—	15
TM34	Shock Wave	Electric	60	—	20
TM35	Flamethrower	Fire	95	100	15
TM38	Fire Blast	Fire	120	85	5
TM40	Aerial Ace	Flying	60	—	20
TM42	Facade	Normal	70	100	20
TM43	Secret Power	Normal	70	100	20
TM44	Rest	Psychic	—	—	10
TM45	Attract	Normal	—	100	15
HM01	Cut	Normal	50	95	30
HM04	Strength	Normal	80	100	15
HM06	Rock Smash	Fighting	20	100	15

MOVE TUTOR

FireRed/LeafGreen and Emerald Only
Body Slam* | Mega Kick* | Counter* | Seismic Toss* | Rock Slide*
Double-Edge | Mimic |
Mega Punch* | Substitute

Emerald Only
Dynamicpunch | Ice Punch* | Snore*
Endure* | Icy Wind* | Swagger
Fire Punch* | Mud-Slap* | Thunderpunch*
Fury Cutter | Sleep Talk

*Battle Frontier tutor move (*Emerald*)

PRIMA OFFICIAL GAME GUIDE

289 Slaking™

NORMAL

GENERAL INFO
SPECIES: Lazy Pokémon
HEIGHT: 6'07"
WEIGHT: 288 lbs.
ABILITY: Truant
Slaking can only attack every other turn.

STATS

HP · SPEED · ATK · DEF · SP ATK · SP DEF

EVOLUTIONS

LV18 · LV36

LOCATION[s]:

RUBY	**Rarity: Evolve**	Evolve Vigoroth
SAPPHIRE	**Rarity: Evolve**	Evolve Vigoroth
FIRERED	**Rarity: None**	Trade from *Ruby/Sapphire/Emerald*
LEAFGREEN	**Rarity: None**	Trade from *Ruby/Sapphire/Emerald*
COLOSSEUM	**Rarity: None**	Trade from *Ruby/Sapphire/Emerald*
EMERALD	**Rarity: Evolve**	Evolve Vigoroth
XD	**Rarity: None**	Trade from *Ruby/Sapphire/Emerald*

MOVES

Level	Attack	Type	Power	ACC	PP		Level	Attack	Type	Power	ACC	PP
—	Scratch	Normal	40	100	35		25	Amnesia	Psychic	—	—	20
—	Yawn	Normal	—	100	10		31	Covet	Normal	40	100	40
—/1	Encore	Normal	—	100	5		36	Swagger	Normal	—	90	15
—/13	Slack Off	Normal	—	100	10		37	Counter	Fighting	—	100	20
19	Faint Attack	Dark	60	—	20		43	Flail	Normal	—	100	15

= *Emerald* Only

TM/HM

TM/HM#	Name	Type	Power	ACC	PP		TM/HM#	Name	Type	Power	ACC	PP
TM01	Focus Punch	Fighting	150	100	20		TM26	Earthquake	Ground	100	100	10
TM03	Water Pulse	Water	60	100	20		TM27	Return	Normal	—	100	20
TM05	Roar	Normal	—	100	20		TM30	Shadow Ball	Ghost	60	100	20
TM06	Toxic	Poison	—	85	10		TM31	Brick Break	Fighting	75	100	15
TM08	Bulk Up	Fighting	—	—	20		TM32	Double Team	Normal	—	—	15
TM10	Hidden Power	Normal	—	100	15		TM34	Shock Wave	Electric	60	—	20
TM11	Sunny Day	Fire	—	—	5		TM35	Flamethrower	Fire	95	100	15
TM12	Taunt	Dark	—	100	20		TM38	Fire Blast	Fire	120	85	5
TM13	Ice Beam	Ice	95	100	10		TM40	Aerial Ace	Flying	60	—	20
TM14	Blizzard	Ice	120	70	5		TM42	Facade	Normal	70	100	20
TM15	Hyper Beam	Normal	150	90	5		TM43	Secret Power	Normal	70	100	20
TM17	Protect	Normal	—	—	10		TM44	Rest	Psychic	—	—	10
TM18	Rain Dance	Water	—	—	5		TM45	Attract	Normal	—	100	15
TM21	Frustration	Normal	—	100	20		HM01	Cut	Normal	50	95	30
TM22	Solarbeam	Grass	120	100	10		HM04	Strength	Normal	80	100	15
TM24	Thunderbolt	Electric	95	100	15		HM06	Rock Smash	Fighting	20	100	15
TM25	Thunder	Electric	120	70	10							

MOVE TUTOR

FireRed/LeafGreen and Emerald Only

Body Slam*	Mega Kick*	Counter*
Double-Edge	Mimic	Seismic Toss*
Mega Punch*	Substitute	Rock Slide*

Emerald Only

Dynamicpunch	Ice Punch*	Snore*
Endure*	Icy Wind*	Swagger
Fire Punch*	Mud-Slap*	Thunderpunch*
Fury Cutter	Sleep Talk	

*Battle Frontier tutor move (*Emerald*)

290 Nincada™

BUG | GROUND

GENERAL INFO

SPECIES: Trainee Pokémon
HEIGHT: 1'08"
WEIGHT: 12 lbs.
ABILITY: Compoundeyes
Raises Nincada's Accuracy 30% in battle.

STATS

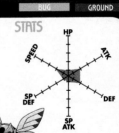

EVOLUTIONS

LV20

LV20
(WHEN SPARE SLOT IN TEAM WITH AN EMPTY POKÉ BALL AVAILABLE)

LOCATION[s]:

RUBY	Rarity: **Rare**	Route 116
SAPPHIRE	Rarity: **Rare**	Route 116
FIRERED	Rarity: **None**	Trade from *Ruby/Sapphire/Emerald*
LEAFGREEN	Rarity: **None**	Trade from *Ruby/Sapphire/Emerald*
COLOSSEUM	Rarity: **None**	Trade from *Ruby/Sapphire/Emerald*
EMERALD	Rarity: **Rare**	Route 116
XD	Rarity: **None**	Trade from *Ruby/Sapphire/Emerald*

MOVES

Level	Attack	Type	Power	ACC	PP	Level	Attack	Type	Power	ACC	PP
—	Scratch	Normal	40	100	35	19	Mind Reader	Normal	—	100	5
—	Harden	Normal	—	—	30	25	False Swipe	Normal	40	100	40
5	Leech Life	Bug	20	100	15	31	Mud-Slap	Ground	20	100	10
9	Sand-Attack	Ground	—	100	15	38	Metal-Claw	Steel	50	95	35
14	Fury Swipes	Normal	18	80	15	45	Dig	Ground	60	100	10

TM/HM

TM/HM#	Name	Type	Power	ACC	PP	TM/HM#	Name	Type	Power	ACC	PP
TM06	Toxic	Poison	—	85	10	TM30	Shadow Ball	Ghost	60	—	20
TM10	Hidden Power	Normal	—	100	15	TM32	Double Team	Normal	—	—	15
TM11	Sunny Day	Fire	—	—	5	TM37	Sandstorm	Rock	—	—	10
TM17	Protect	Normal	—	—	10	TM40	Aerial Ace	Flying	60	—	20
TM19	Giga Drain	Grass	60	100	5	TM42	Facade	Normal	70	100	20
TM21	Frustration	Normal	—	100	20	TM43	Secret Power	Normal	70	100	20
TM22	Solarbeam	Grass	120	100	10	TM44	Rest	Psychic	—	—	10
TM27	Return	Normal	—	100	20	HM01	Cut	Normal	50	95	30
TM28	Dig	Ground	60	100	10	HM05	Flash	Normal	—	70	20

EGG MOVES*

Name	Type	Power	ACC	PP
Endure	Normal	—	—	10
Faint Attack	Dark	60	—	20
Silver Wind	Bug	60	100	5
Whirlwind	Normal	—	100	20

*Learned Via Breeding

MOVE TUTOR

FireRed/LeafGreen and Emerald Only

Double-Edge	Mimic	Substitute

Emerald Only

Endure*	Mud-Slap*	Snore*
Fury Cutter	Sleep Talk	Swagger

*Battle Frontier tutor move (*Emerald*)

PRIMA OFFICIAL GAME GUIDE

291 Ninjask™

BUG | FLYING

GENERAL INFO
SPECIES: Ninja Pokémon
HEIGHT: 2'07"
WEIGHT: 26 lbs.
ABILITY: Speed Boost
Increases Ninjask's Speed by one point each turn.

STATS

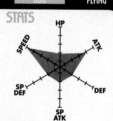

EVOLUTIONS

LV20

LOCATION[s]:

RUBY	Rarity: **Evolve**	Evolve Nincada
SAPPHIRE	Rarity: **Evolve**	Evolve Nincada
FIRERED	Rarity: **None**	Trade from *Ruby/Sapphire/Emerald*
LEAFGREEN	Rarity: **None**	Trade from *Ruby/Sapphire/Emerald*
COLOSSEUM	Rarity: **None**	Trade from *Ruby/Sapphire/Emerald*
EMERALD	Rarity: **Evolve**	Evolve Nincada
XD	Rarity: **None**	Trade from *Ruby/Sapphire/Emerald*

MOVES

Level	Attack	Type	Power	ACC	PP
—	Scratch	Normal	40	100	35
—	Harden	Normal	—	—	30
—/5	Leech Life	Bug	20	100	15
—/9	Sand-Attack	Ground	—	100	15
14	Fury Swipes	Normal	18	80	15
19	Mind Reader	Normal	—	100	5
20	Double Team	Normal	—	—	15

Level	Attack	Type	Power	ACC	PP
20	Fury Cutter	Bug	10	95	20
20	Screech	Normal	—	85	40
25	Swords Dance	Normal	—	—	30
31	Slash	Normal	70	100	20
38	Agility	Psychic	—	—	30
45	Baton Pass	Normal	—	—	40

 # = Emerald Only

TM/HM

TM/HM#	Name	Type	Power	ACC	PP
TM06	Toxic	Poison	—	85	10
TM10	Hidden Power	Normal	—	100	15
TM11	Sunny Day	Fire	—	—	5
TM15	Hyper Beam	Normal	150	90	5
TM17	Protect	Normal	—	—	10
TM19	Giga Drain	Grass	60	100	5
TM21	Frustration	Normal	—	100	20
TM22	Solarbeam	Grass	120	100	10
TM27	Return	Normal	—	100	20
TM28	Dig	Ground	60	100	10
TM30	Shadow Ball	Ghost	60	—	20

TM/HM#	Name	Type	Power	ACC	PP
TM32	Double Team	Normal	—	—	15
TM37	Sandstorm	Rock	—	—	10
TM40	Aerial Ace	Flying	60	—	20
TM42	Facade	Normal	70	100	20
TM43	Secret Power	Normal	70	100	20
TM44	Rest	Psychic	—	—	10
TM45	Attract	Normal	—	100	15
TM46	Thief	Dark	40	100	10
HM01	Cut	Normal	50	95	30
HM05	Flash	Normal	—	70	20

MOVE TUTOR

FireRed/LeafGreen and Emerald Only

Double-Edge	Substitute	Swords Dance*
Mimic		

Emerald Only

Endure*	Sleep Talk	Swagger
Fury Cutter	Snore*	Swift*
Mud-Slap*		

*Battle Frontier tutor move (*Emerald*)

292 Shedinja™

BUG | GHOST

GENERAL INFO
SPECIES: Shed Pokémon
HEIGHT: 2'07"
WEIGHT: 3 lbs.
ABILITY: Wonder Guard
Shedinja is only harmed by moves that cause "Super Effective" damage.

STATS
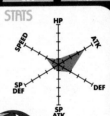

EVOLUTIONS

LV20
(WHEN SPARE SLOT IN TEAM WITH AN EMPTY POKÉ BALL AVAILABLE)

LOCATION[s]:

RUBY	Rarity: **Evolve**	Evolve Nincada
SAPPHIRE	Rarity: **Evolve**	Evolve Nincada
FIRERED	Rarity: **None**	Trade from *Ruby/Sapphire/Emerald*
LEAFGREEN	Rarity: **None**	Trade from *Ruby/Sapphire/Emerald*
COLOSSEUM	Rarity: **None**	Trade from *Ruby/Sapphire/Emerald*
EMERALD	Rarity: **Evolve**	Evolve Nincada
XD	Rarity: **None**	Trade from *Ruby/Sapphire/Emerald*

MOVES

Level	Attack	Type	Power	ACC	PP	Level	Attack	Type	Power	ACC	PP
—	Scratch	Normal	40	100	35	19	Mind Reader	Normal	—	100	5
—	Harden	Normal	—	—	30	25	Spite	Ghost	—	100	10
5	Leech Life	Bug	20	100	15	31	Confuse Ray	Ghost	—	100	10
9	Sand Attack	Ground	—	100	15	38	Shadow Ball	Ghost	80	100	15
14	Fury Swipes	Normal	18	80	15	45	Grudge	Ghost	—	100	5

TM/HM

TM/HM#	Name	Type	Power	ACC	PP	TM/HM#	Name	Type	Power	ACC	PP
TM06	Toxic	Poison	—	85	10	TM30	Shadow Ball	Ghost	60	—	20
TM10	Hidden Power	Normal	—	100	15	TM32	Double Team	Normal	—	—	15
TM11	Sunny Day	Fire	—	—	5	TM37	Sandstorm	Rock	—	—	10
TM15	Hyper Beam	Normal	150	90	5	TM40	Aerial Ace	Flying	60	—	20
TM17	Protect	Normal	—	—	10	TM42	Facade	Normal	70	100	20
TM19	Giga Drain	Grass	60	100	5	TM43	Secret Power	Normal	70	100	20
TM21	Frustration	Normal	—	100	20	TM44	Rest	Psychic	—	—	10
TM22	Solarbeam	Grass	120	100	10	TM46	Thief	Dark	40	100	10
TM27	Return	Normal	—	100	20	HM01	Cut	Normal	50	95	30
TM28	Dig	Ground	60	100	10	HM05	Flash	Normal	—	70	20

MOVE TUTOR
FireRed/LeafGreen and Emerald Only
Double-Edge | Substitute | Dream Eater*
Mimic

Emerald Only
Endure* | Sleep Talk | Swagger
Fury Cutter | Snore* | Swift*
Mud-Slap*

*Battle Frontier tutor move (*Emerald*)

293 Whismur™

NORMAL

GENERAL INFO

SPECIES: Whisper Pokémon
HEIGHT: 2'00"
WEIGHT: 36 lbs.
ABILITY: Soundproof

Prevents Whismur from being hit by Grasswhistle, Growl, Heal Bell, Hyper Voice, Metal Sound, Perish Song, Roar, Screech, Sing, Snore, Supersonic, and Uproar.

STATS

HP / ATK / DEF / SP ATK / SP DEF / SPEED

EVOLUTIONS

LV20   LV40

LOCATION(s):

RUBY	Rarity: **Common**	Route 116, Victory Road
SAPPHIRE	Rarity: **Common**	Route 116, Victory Road
FIRERED	Rarity: **None**	Trade from *Ruby/Sapphire/Emerald*
LEAFGREEN	Rarity: **None**	Trade from *Ruby/Sapphire/Emerald*
COLOSSEUM	Rarity: **None**	Trade from *Ruby/Sapphire/Emerald*
EMERALD	Rarity: **Common**	Route 116, Desert Pass, Rusturf Tunnel, Victory Road
XD	Rarity: **None**	Trade from *Ruby/Sapphire/Emerald*

MOVES

Level	Attack	Type	Power	ACC	PP
—	Pound	Normal	40	100	35
5	Uproar	Normal	50	100	10
11	Astonish	Ghost	30	100	15
15	Howl	Normal	—	—	40
21	Supersonic	Normal	—	55	20

Level	Attack	Type	Power	ACC	PP
25	Stomp	Normal	65	100	20
31	Screech	Normal	—	85	40
35	Roar	Normal	—	100	20
41	Rest	Psychic	—	—	10
41	Sleep Talk	Normal	—	—	10
45	Hyper Voice	Normal	90	100	10

TM/HM

TM/HM#	Name	Type	Power	ACC	PP
TM03	Water Pulse	Water	60	100	20
TM05	Roar	Normal	—	100	20
TM06	Toxic	Poison	—	85	10
TM10	Hidden Power	Normal	—	100	15
TM11	Sunny Day	Fire	—	—	5
TM13	Ice Beam	Ice	95	100	10
TM14	Blizzard	Ice	120	70	5
TM17	Protect	Normal	—	—	10
TM18	Rain Dance	Water	—	—	5
TM21	Frustration	Normal	—	100	20
TM22	Solarbeam	Grass	120	100	10

TM/HM#	Name	Type	Power	ACC	PP
TM27	Return	Normal	—	100	20
TM30	Shadow Ball	Ghost	60	—	20
TM32	Double Team	Normal	—	—	15
TM34	Shock Wave	Electric	60	—	20
TM35	Flamethrower	Fire	95	100	15
TM38	Fire Blast	Fire	120	85	5
TM42	Facade	Normal	70	100	20
TM43	Secret Power	Normal	70	100	20
TM44	Rest	Psychic	—	—	10
TM45	Attract	Normal	—	100	15

EGG MOVES*

Name	Type	Power	ACC	PP
Take Down	Normal	90	85	20
Snore	Normal	40	100	15
Swagger	Normal	—	90	15
Extrasensory	Psychic	80	100	30
Smellingsalt	Normal	60	100	10

*Learned Via Breeding

MOVE TUTOR

FireRed/LeafGreen and Emerald Only

Body Slam*	Mega Kick*	Counter*
Double-Edge*	Mimic	Seismic Toss*
Mega Punch*	Substitute	

Emerald Only

Dynamicpunch*	Icy Wind*	Sleep Talk
Endure*	Mud-Slap*	Snore*
Fire Punch*	Psych Up*	Swagger
Ice Punch*	Rollout	Thunderpunch*

*Battle Frontier tutor move (*Emerald*)

294 Loudred™

NORMAL

GENERAL INFO

SPECIES: Big Voice Pokémon
HEIGHT: 3'03"
WEIGHT: 89 lbs.
ABILITY: Soundproof

Prevents Loudred from being hit by Grasswhistle, Growl, Heal Bell, Hyper Voice, Metal Sound, Perish Song, Roar, Screech, Sing, Snore, Supersonic, and Uproar.

STATS

EVOLUTIONS

LV20   LV40

LOCATION[s]:

RUBY	Rarity: **Rare**	Victory Road
SAPPHIRE	Rarity: **Rare**	Victory Road
FIRERED	Rarity: **None**	Trade from *Ruby/Sapphire/Emerald*
LEAFGREEN	Rarity: **None**	Trade from *Ruby/Sapphire/Emerald*
COLOSSEUM	Rarity: **None**	Trade from *Ruby/Sapphire/Emerald*
EMERALD	Rarity: **Rare**	Desert Pass, Victory Road
XD	Rarity: **None**	Trade from *Ruby/Sapphire/Emerald*

MOVES

Level	Attack	Type	Power	ACC	PP	Level	Attack	Type	Power	ACC	PP
—	Pound	Normal	40	100	35	37	Screech	Normal	—	85	40
—/5	Uproar	Normal	50	100	10	43	Roar	Normal	—	100	20
—/11	Astonish	Ghost	30	100	15	51	Rest	Psychic	—	—	10
—/15	Howl	Normal	—	—	40	51	Sleep Talk	Normal	—	—	10
23	Supersonic	Normal	—	55	20	57	Hyper Voice	Normal	90	100	10
29	Stomp	Normal	65	100	20		# = Emerald Only				

TM/HM

TM/HM#	Name	Type	Power	ACC	PP	TM/HM#	Name	Type	Power	ACC	PP
TM03	Water Pulse	Water	60	100	20	TM30	Shadow Ball	Ghost	60	—	20
TM05	Roar	Normal	—	100	20	TM31	Brick Break	Fighting	75	100	15
TM06	Toxic	Poison	—	85	10	TM32	Double Team	Normal	—	—	15
TM10	Hidden Power	Normal	—	100	15	TM34	Shock Wave	Electric	60	—	20
TM11	Sunny Day	Fire	—	—	5	TM35	Flamethrower	Fire	95	100	15
TM12	Taunt	Dark	—	100	20	TM38	Fire Blast	Fire	120	85	5
TM13	Ice Beam	Ice	95	100	10	TM41	Torment	Dark	—	100	15
TM14	Blizzard	Ice	120	70	5	TM42	Facade	Normal	70	100	20
TM17	Protect	Normal	—	—	10	TM43	Secret Power	Normal	70	100	20
TM18	Rain Dance	Water	—	—	5	TM44	Rest	Psychic	—	—	10
TM21	Frustration	Normal	—	100	20	TM45	Attract	Normal	—	100	15
TM22	Solarbeam	Grass	120	100	10	TM50	Overheat	Fire	140	90	5
TM26	Earthquake	Ground	100	100	10	HM04	Strength	Normal	80	100	15
TM27	Return	Normal	—	100	20	HM06	Rock Smash	Fighting	20	100	15

MOVE TUTOR

FireRed/LeafGreen and Emerald Only

Body Slam*	Mega Kick*	Counter*
Double-Edge	Mimic	Seismic Toss*
Mega Punch*	Substitute	

Emerald Only

Dynamicpunch*	Icy Wind*	Sleep Talk
Endure*	Mud-Slap*	Snore*
Fire Punch*	Psych Up*	Swagger
Ice Punch*	Rollout	Thunderpunch*

*Battle Frontier tutor move (*Emerald*)

295 Exploud™

NORMAL

GENERAL INFO

SPECIES: Loud Noise Pokémon
HEIGHT: 4'11"
WEIGHT: 185 lbs.
ABILITY: Soundproof

Prevents Exploud from being hit by Grasswhistle, Growl, Heal Bell, Hyper Voice, Metal Sound, Perish Song, Roar, Screech, Sing, Snore, Supersonic, and Uproar.

STATS

(radar chart with axes: HP, ATK, DEF, SP ATK, SP DEF, SPEED)

EVOLUTIONS

  ▶   LV20 ▶ LV40

LOCATION(s):

RUBY	Rarity: **Evolve**	Evolve Loudred	
SAPPHIRE	Rarity: **Evolve**	Evolve Loudred	
FIRERED	Rarity: **None**	Trade from *Ruby/Sapphire/Emerald*	
LEAFGREEN	Rarity: **None**	Trade from *Ruby/Sapphire/Emerald*	
COLOSSEUM	Rarity: **None**	Trade from *Ruby/Sapphire/Emerald*	
EMERALD	Rarity: **Evolve**	Evolve Loudred	
XD	Rarity: **None**	Trade from *Ruby/Sapphire/Emerald*	

MOVES

Level	Attack	Type	Power	ACC	PP	Level	Attack	Type	Power	ACC	PP
—	Pound	Normal	40	100	35	37	Screech	Normal	—	85	40
—/5	Uproar	Normal	50	100	10	40	Hyper Beam	Normal	150	90	5
—/11	Astonish	Ghost	30	100	15	45	Roar	Normal	—	100	20
—/15	Howl	Normal	—	—	40	55	Rest	Psychic	—	—	10
23	Supersonic	Normal	—	55	20	55	Sleep Talk	Normal	—	—	10
29	Stomp	Normal	65	100	20	63	Hyper Voice	Normal	90	100	10

= Emerald Only

TM/HM

TM/HM#	Name	Type	Power	ACC	PP	TM/HM#	Name	Type	Power	ACC	PP
TM03	Water Pulse	Water	60	100	20	TM30	Shadow Ball	Ghost	60	—	20
TM05	Roar	Normal	—	100	20	TM31	Brick Break	Fighting	75	100	15
TM06	Toxic	Poison	—	85	10	TM32	Double Team	Normal	—	—	15
TM10	Hidden Power	Normal	—	100	15	TM34	Shock Wave	Electric	60	—	20
TM11	Sunny Day	Fire	—	—	5	TM35	Flamethrower	Fire	95	100	15
TM12	Taunt	Dark	—	100	20	TM38	Fire Blast	Fire	120	85	5
TM13	Ice Beam	Ice	95	100	10	TM41	Torment	Dark	—	100	15
TM14	Blizzard	Ice	120	70	5	TM42	Facade	Normal	70	100	20
TM15	Hyper Beam	Normal	150	90	5	TM43	Secret Power	Normal	70	100	20
TM17	Protect	Normal	—	—	10	TM44	Rest	Psychic	—	—	10
TM18	Rain Dance	Water	—	—	5	TM45	Attract	Normal	—	100	15
TM21	Frustration	Normal	—	100	20	TM50	Overheat	Fire	140	90	5
TM22	Solarbeam	Grass	120	100	10	HM04	Strength	Normal	80	100	15
TM26	Earthquake	Ground	100	100	10	HM06	Rock Smash	Fighting	20	100	15
TM27	Return	Normal	—	100	20						

MOVE TUTOR

FireRed/LeafGreen and Emerald Only

Body Slam*	Mega Kick*	Counter*
Double-Edge	Mimic	Seismic Toss*
Mega Punch*	Substitute	

Emerald Only

Dynamicpunch*	Icy Wind*	Sleep Talk
Endure*	Mud-Slap*	Snore*
Fire Punch*	Psych Up*	Swagger
Ice Punch*	Rollout	Thunderpunch*

*Battle Frontier tutor move (*Emerald*)

296 Makuhita ™

FIGHTING

GENERAL INFO

SPECIES: Guts Pokémon
HEIGHT: 3'03"
WEIGHT: 191 lbs.
ABILITY 1: Thick Fat
Fire- and Ice-type moves inflict only 50% damage.
ABILITY 2: Guts
Makuhita's attack power increases 1.5 times when inflicted with a status condition.

STATS

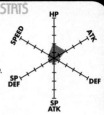

EVOLUTIONS

LV24

LOCATION[s]:

RUBY	Rarity: **Common**	Granite Cave, Victory Road
SAPPHIRE	Rarity: **Common**	Granite Cave, Victory Road
FIRERED	Rarity: **None**	Trade from *Ruby/Sapphire/Emerald/Colosseum*
LEAFGREEN	Rarity: **None**	Trade from *Ruby/Sapphire/Emerald/Colosseum*
COLOSSEUM	Rarity: **Only One**	Phenac City
EMERALD	Rarity: **Common**	Granite Cave, Victory Road
XD	Rarity: **Only One**	Pyrite Town (Capture from Cipher Peon Torkin)

MOVES

Level	Attack	Type	Power	ACC	PP	Level	Attack	Type	Power	ACC	PP
—	Tackle	Normal	35	95	35	22	Whirlwind	Normal	—	100	20
—	Focus Energy	Normal	—	—	30	28	Knock Off	Dark	20	100	20
4	Sand Attack	Ground	—	100	15	31	Smellingsalt	Normal	60	100	10
10	Arm Thrust	Fighting	15	100	20	37	Belly Drum	Normal	—	—	10
13	Vital Throw	Fighting	70	100	10	40	Endure	Normal	—	—	10
19	Fake Out	Normal	40	100	10	46	Seismic Toss	Fighting	—	100	20
						49	Reversal	Fighting	—	100	15

TM/HM

TM/HM#	Name	Type	Power	ACC	PP	TM/HM#	Name	Type	Power	ACC	PP
TM01	Focus Punch	Fighting	150	100	20	TM31	Brick Break	Fighting	75	100	15
TM06	Toxic	Poison	—	85	10	TM32	Double Team	Normal	—	—	15
TM08	Bulk Up	Fighting	—	—	20	TM39	Rock Tomb	Rock	50	80	10
TM10	Hidden Power	Normal	—	100	15	TM42	Facade	Normal	70	100	20
TM11	Sunny Day	Fire	—	—	5	TM43	Secret Power	Normal	70	100	20
TM17	Protect	Normal	—	—	10	TM44	Rest	Psychic	—	—	10
TM18	Rain Dance	Water	—	—	5	TM45	Attract	Normal	—	100	15
TM21	Frustration	Normal	—	100	20	HM03	Surf	Water	95	100	15
TM26	Earthquake	Ground	100	100	10	HM04	Strength	Normal	80	100	15
TM27	Return	Normal	—	100	20	HM06	Rock Smash	Fighting	20	100	15
TM28	Dig	Ground	60	100	10						

EGG MOVES*

Name	Type	Power	ACC	PP
Faint Attack	Dark	60	—	20
Detect	Fighting	—	—	5
Foresight	Normal	—	100	40
Helping Hand	Normal	—	100	20
Cross Chop	Fighting	100	80	5
Revenge	Fighting	60	100	10
Dynamicpunch	Fighting	100	50	5
Counter	Fighting	—	100	20

*Learned Via Breeding

MOVE TUTOR

FireRed/LeafGreen and Emerald Only

Body Slam*	Mega Kick*	Counter*
Double-Edge	Mimic	Seismic Toss*
Mega Punch*	Substitute	Rock Slide*

Emerald Only

Dynamicpunch	Metronome	Swagger
Endure*	Mud-Slap*	Thunderpunch*
Fire Punch*	Sleep Talk	
Ice Punch*	Snore*	

*Battle Frontier tutor move (*Emerald*)

297 / Hariyama™

FIGHTING

GENERAL INFO

SPECIES: Arm Thrust Pokémon
HEIGHT: 7'07"
WEIGHT: 560 lbs.
ABILITY 1: Thick Fat
Fire- and Ice-type moves inflict only 50% damage.

ABILITY 2: Guts
Hariyama's attack power increases 1.5 times when inflicted with a status condition.

STATS

EVOLUTIONS

LV24

LOCATION[S]:

RUBY	Rarity: **Rare**	Evolve Makuhita, Victory Road
SAPPHIRE	Rarity: **Rare**	Evolve Makuhita, Victory Road
FIRERED	Rarity: **None**	Trade from *Ruby/Sapphire/Emerald/Colosseum*
LEAFGREEN	Rarity: **None**	Trade from *Ruby/Sapphire/Emerald/Colosseum*
COLOSSEUM	Rarity: **Evolve**	Evolve Makuhita
EMERALD	Rarity: **Common**	Evolve Makuhita, Victory Road
XD	Rarity: **Evolve**	Evolve Makuhita

MOVES

Level	Attack	Type	Power	ACC	PP	Level	Attack	Type	Power	ACC	PP
—	Tackle	Normal	35	95	35	29	Knock Off	Dark	20	100	20
—	Focus Energy	Normal	—	—	30	33	Smellingsalt	Normal	60	100	10
—/4	Sand-Attack	Ground	—	100	15	40	Belly Drum	Normal	—	—	10
—/10	Arm Thrust	Fighting	15	100	20	44	Endure	Normal	—	—	10
13	Vital Throw	Fighting	70	100	10	51	Seismic Toss	Fighting	—	100	20
19	Fake Out	Normal	40	100	10	55	Reversal	Fighting	—	100	15
22	Whirlwind	Normal	—	100	20		# = *Emerald* Only				

TM/HM

TM/HM#	Name	Type	Power	ACC	PP	TM/HM#	Name	Type	Power	ACC	PP
TM01	Focus Punch	Fighting	150	100	20	TM28	Dig	Ground	60	100	10
TM06	Toxic	Poison	—	85	10	TM31	Brick Break	Fighting	75	100	15
TM08	Bulk Up	Fighting	—	—	20	TM32	Double Team	Normal	—	—	15
TM10	Hidden Power	Normal	—	100	15	TM39	Rock Tomb	Rock	50	80	10
TM11	Sunny Day	Fire	—	—	5	TM42	Facade	Normal	70	100	20
TM15	Hyper Beam	Normal	150	90	5	TM43	Secret Power	Normal	70	100	20
TM17	Protect	Normal	—	—	10	TM44	Rest	Psychic	—	—	10
TM18	Rain Dance	Water	—	—	5	TM45	Attract	Normal	—	100	15
TM21	Frustration	Normal	—	100	20	HM03	Surf	Water	95	100	15
TM26	Earthquake	Ground	100	100	10	HM04	Strength	Normal	80	100	15
TM27	Return	Normal	—	100	20	HM06	Rock Smash	Fighting	20	100	15

MOVE TUTOR

FireRed/LeafGreen and Emerald Only

Body Slam*	Mega Kick*	Counter*
Double-Edge	Mimic	Seismic Toss*
Mega Punch*	Substitute	Rock Slide*

Emerald Only

Dynamicpunch	Metronome	Swagger
Endure*	Mud-Slap*	Thunderpunch*
Fire Punch*	Sleep Talk	
Ice Punch*	Snore*	

*Battle Frontier tutor move (*Emerald*)

298 Azurill™

NORMAL

GENERAL INFO

SPECIES: Polka Dot Pokémon
HEIGHT: 0'08"
WEIGHT: 4 lbs.
ABILITY 1: Thick Fat
Fire- and Ice-type moves inflict only 50% damage.

ABILITY 2: Huge Power
Azurill's attack power is increased in battle.

STATS

(radar chart: HP, ATK, DEF, SP ATK, SP DEF, SPEED)

EVOLUTIONS

FRIENDSHIP   LV18

LOCATION(s):

RUBY	Rarity: **Breed**	Breed a female Marill or Azumarill with Sea Incense attached
SAPPHIRE	Rarity: **Breed**	Breed a female Marill or Azumarill with Sea Incense attached
FIRERED	Rarity: **None**	Trade from *Ruby/Sapphire/LeafGreen/Emerald*
LEAFGREEN	Rarity: **Breed**	Breed a female Marill or Azumarill with Sea Incense attached
COLOSSEUM	Rarity: **None**	Trade from *Ruby/Sapphire/LeafGreen/Emerald*
EMERALD	Rarity: **Breed**	Breed a female Marill or Azumarill with Sea Incense attached
XD	Rarity: **None**	Trade from *Ruby/Sapphire/LeafGreen/Emerald*

MOVES

Level	Attack	Type	Power	ACC	PP	Level	Attack	Type	Power	ACC	PP
—	Splash	Normal	—	—	40	10	Bubble	Water	20	100	30
3	Charm	Normal	—	100	20	15	Slam	Normal	80	75	20
6	Tail Whip	Normal	—	100	30	21	Water Gun	Water	40	100	25

TM/HM

TM/HM#	Name	Type	Power	ACC	PP	TM/HM#	Name	Type	Power	ACC	PP
TM03	Water Pulse	Water	60	100	20	TM23	Iron Tail	Steel	100	75	15
TM06	Toxic	Poison	—	85	10	TM27	Return	Normal	—	100	20
TM07	Hail	Ice	—	—	10	TM32	Double Team	Normal	—	—	15
TM10	Hidden Power	Normal	—	100	15	TM42	Facade	Normal	70	100	20
TM13	Ice Beam	Ice	95	100	10	TM43	Secret Power	Normal	70	100	20
TM14	Blizzard	Ice	120	70	5	TM44	Rest	Psychic	—	—	10
TM17	Protect	Normal	—	—	10	TM45	Attract	Normal	—	100	15
TM18	Rain Dance	Water	—	—	5	HM03	Surf	Water	95	100	15
TM21	Frustration	Normal	—	100	20	HM07	Waterfall	Water	80	100	15

EGG MOVES*

Name	Type	Power	ACC	PP
Encore	Normal	—	100	5
Sing	Normal	—	55	15
Refresh	Normal	—	100	20
Tickle	Normal	—	100	20
Slam	Normal	80	75	30

*Learned Via Breeding

MOVE TUTOR

FireRed/LeafGreen and Emerald Only

Body Slam*	Mimic	Substitute
Double-Edge		

Emerald Only

Defense Curl*	Mud-Slap*	Snore*
Endure*	Rollout	Swagger
Icy Wind*	Sleep Talk	Swift*

*Battle Frontier tutor move (*Emerald*)

299 Nosepass™

ROCK

GENERAL INFO

SPECIES: Compass Pokémon
HEIGHT: 3'03"
WEIGHT: 214 lbs.
ABILITY 1: Sturdy
One hit KO moves have no effect.
ABILITY 2: Magnet Pull
Prevents Steel-type Pokémon from fleeing in battle.

STATS

EVOLUTIONS

DOES NOT EVOLVE

LOCATION(s):

RUBY	Rarity: **Rare**	Granite Cave
SAPPHIRE	Rarity: **Rare**	Granite Cave
FIRERED	Rarity: **None**	Trade from *Ruby/Sapphire/Emerald*
LEAFGREEN	Rarity: **None**	Trade from *Ruby/Sapphire/Emerald*
COLOSSEUM	Rarity: **None**	Trade from *Ruby/Sapphire/Emerald*
EMERALD	Rarity: **Rare**	Granite Cave
XD	Rarity: **Only One**	Capture from Wanderer Miror B. at the Outskirt Stand

MOVES

Level	Attack	Type	Power	ACC	PP		Level	Attack	Type	Power	ACC	PP
—	Tackle	Normal	35	95	35		28	Rock Slide	Rock	75	90	10
7	Harden	Normal	—	—	30		31	Sandstorm	Rock	—	—	10
13	Rock Throw	Rock	50	90	15		37	Rest	Psychic	—	—	10
16	Block	Normal	—	100	5		43	Zap Cannon	Electric	100	50	5
22	Thunder Wave	Electric	—	100	20		46	Lock-on	Normal	—	100	5

TM/HM

TM/HM#	Name	Type	Power	ACC	PP		TM/HM#	Name	Type	Power	ACC	PP
TM06	Toxic	Poison	—	85	10		TM34	Shock Wave	Electric	60	—	20
TM10	Hidden Power	Normal	—	100	15		TM37	Sandstorm	Rock	—	—	10
TM11	Sunny Day	Fire	—	—	5		TM39	Rock Tomb	Rock	50	80	10
TM12	Taunt	Dark	—	100	20		TM41	Torment	Dark	—	100	15
TM17	Protect	Normal	—	—	10		TM42	Facade	Normal	70	100	20
TM21	Frustration	Normal	—	100	20		TM43	Secret Power	Normal	70	100	20
TM24	Thunderbolt	Electric	95	100	15		TM44	Rest	Psychic	—	—	10
TM25	Thunder	Electric	120	70	10		TM45	Attract	Normal	—	100	15
TM26	Earthquake	Ground	100	100	10		HM04	Strength	Normal	80	100	15
TM27	Return	Normal	—	100	20		HM06	Rock Smash	Fighting	20	100	15
TM32	Double Team	Normal	—	—	15							

EGG MOVES*

Name	Type	Power	ACC	PP
Magnitude	Ground	—	100	30
Rollout	Rock	30	90	20
Explosion	Normal	250	100	5

*Learned Via Breeding

MOVE TUTOR

FireRed/LeafGreen and Emerald Only

Body Slam*	Substitute	Rock Slide*
Double-Edge	Thunder Wave*	Explosion*
Mimic		

Emerald Only

Defense Curl*	Ice Punch*	Snore*
Dynamicpunch	Mud-Slap*	Thunderpunch*
Endure*	Rollout	
Fire Punch*	Sleep Talk	

*Battle Frontier tutor move (*Emerald*)

300 Skitty™

NORMAL

GENERAL INFO

SPECIES: Kitten Pokémon
HEIGHT: 2'00"
WEIGHT: 24 lbs.
ABILITY: Cute Charm

If an opponent physically strikes Skitty, it has a 30% chance of becoming attracted to it.

STATS

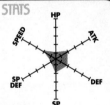

EVOLUTIONS

MOONSTONE

LOCATION[s]:

RUBY	Rarity: **Rare**	Route 116
SAPPHIRE	Rarity: **Rare**	Route 116
FIRERED	Rarity: **None**	Trade from *Ruby/Sapphire/Emerald*
LEAFGREEN	Rarity: **None**	Trade from *Ruby/Sapphire/Emerald*
COLOSSEUM	Rarity: **None**	Trade from *Ruby/Sapphire/Emerald*
EMERALD	Rarity: **Rare**	Route 116
XD	Rarity: **None**	Trade from *Ruby/Sapphire/Emerald*

MOVES

Level	Attack	Type	Power	ACC	PP
—	Growl	Normal	—	100	40
—	Tackle	Normal	35	95	35
3	Tail Whip	Normal	—	100	30
7	Attract	Normal	—	100	15
13	Sing	Normal	—	55	15
15	Doubleslap	Normal	15	85	10
19	Assist	Normal	—	100	20
25	Charm	Normal	—	100	20
27	Faint Attack	Dark	60	—	20
31	Covet	Normal	40	100	40
37	Heal Bell	Normal	—	—	5
39	Double-Edge	Normal	120	100	15

TM/HM

TM/HM#	Name	Type	Power	ACC	PP
TM03	Water Pulse	Water	60	100	20
TM04	Calm Mind	Psychic	—	—	20
TM06	Toxic	Poison	—	85	10
TM10	Hidden Power	Normal	—	100	15
TM11	Sunny Day	Fire	—	—	5
TM13	Ice Beam	Ice	95	100	10
TM14	Blizzard	Ice	120	70	5
TM17	Protect	Normal	—	—	10
TM18	Rain Dance	Water	—	—	5
TM20	Safeguard	Normal	—	—	25
TM21	Frustration	Normal	—	100	20
TM22	Solarbeam	Grass	120	100	10
TM23	Iron Tail	Steel	100	75	15
TM24	Thunderbolt	Electric	95	100	15
TM25	Thunder	Electric	120	70	10
TM27	Return	Normal	—	100	20
TM28	Dig	Ground	60	100	10
TM30	Shadow Ball	Ghost	60	—	20
TM32	Double Team	Normal	—	—	15
TM34	Shock Wave	Electric	60	—	20
TM42	Facade	Normal	70	100	20
TM43	Secret Power	Normal	70	100	20
TM44	Rest	Psychic	—	—	10
TM45	Attract	Normal	—	100	15
HM05	Flash	Normal	—	70	20

EGG MOVES*

Name	Type	Power	ACC	PP
Helping Hand	Normal	—	100	20
Psych Up	Normal	—	—	10
Uproar	Normal	50	100	10
Fake Tears	Dark	—	100	20
Baton Pass	Normal	—	—	40
Substitute	Normal	—	—	10
Tickle	Normal	—	100	20
Wish	Normal	—	100	10

*Learned Via Breeding

MOVE TUTOR

FireRed/LeafGreen and Emerald Only

Body Slam*	Mimic	Thunder Wave*
Double-Edge	Substitute	Dream Eater*

Emerald Only

Defense Curl*	Psych Up*	Swagger
Endure*	Rollout	Swift*
Icy Wind*	Sleep Talk	
Mud-Slap*	Snore*	

*Battle Frontier tutor move (*Emerald*)

301 Delcatty™

NORMAL

GENERAL INFO

SPECIES: Prim Pokémon
HEIGHT: 3'07"
WEIGHT: 72 lbs.
ABILITY: Cute Charm

If an opponent physically strikes Delcatty, it has a 30% chance of becoming attracted to it.

STATS

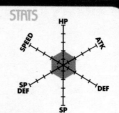

EVOLUTIONS

MOONSTONE

LOCATION(s):

RUBY	Rarity: **Evolve**	Evolve Skitty
SAPPHIRE	Rarity: **Evolve**	Evolve Skitty
FIRERED	Rarity: **None**	Trade from *Ruby/Sapphire/Emerald*
LEAFGREEN	Rarity: **None**	Trade from *Ruby/Sapphire/Emerald*
COLOSSEUM	Rarity: **None**	Trade from *Ruby/Sapphire/Emerald*
EMERALD	Rarity: **Evolve**	Evolve Skitty
XD	Rarity: **Only One**	Cipher Lab (Capture from Cipher Admin Lovrina)

MOVES

Level	Attack	Type	Power	ACC	PP	Level	Attack	Type	Power	ACC	PP
—	Growl	Normal	—	100	40	—	Sing	Normal	—	55	15
—	Attract	Normal	—	100	15	—	Doubleslap	Normal	15	85	10

TM/HM

TM/HM#	Name	Type	Power	ACC	PP	TM/HM#	Name	Type	Power	ACC	PP
TM03	Water Pulse	Water	60	100	20	TM24	Thunderbolt	Electric	95	100	15
TM04	Calm Mind	Psychic	—	—	20	TM25	Thunder	Electric	120	70	10
TM06	Toxic	Poison	—	85	10	TM27	Return	Normal	—	100	20
TM10	Hidden Power	Normal	—	100	15	TM28	Dig	Ground	60	100	10
TM11	Sunny Day	Fire	—	—	5	TM30	Shadow Ball	Ghost	60	—	20
TM13	Ice Beam	Ice	95	100	10	TM32	Double Team	Normal	—	—	15
TM14	Blizzard	Ice	120	70	5	TM34	Shock Wave	Electric	60	—	20
TM15	Hyper Beam	Normal	150	90	5	TM42	Facade	Normal	70	100	20
TM17	Protect	Normal	—	—	10	TM43	Secret Power	Normal	70	100	20
TM18	Rain Dance	Water	—	—	5	TM44	Rest	Psychic	—	—	10
TM20	Safeguard	Normal	—	—	25	TM45	Attract	Normal	—	100	15
TM21	Frustration	Normal	—	100	20	HM04	Strength	Normal	80	100	15
TM22	Solarbeam	Grass	120	100	10	HM05	Flash	Normal	—	70	20
TM23	Iron Tail	Steel	100	75	15	HM06	Rock Smash	Fighting	20	100	15

MOVE TUTOR

FireRed/LeafGreen and Emerald Only

Body Slam*	Mimic	Thunder Wave*
Double-Edge	Substitute	Dream Eater*

Emerald Only

Defense Curl*	Psych Up*	Swagger
Endure*	Rollout	Swift*
Icy Wind*	Sleep Talk	
Mud-Slap*	Snore*	

*Battle Frontier tutor move (*Emerald*)

302 Sableye™

DARK | GHOST

GENERAL INFO

SPECIES: Darkness Pokémon
HEIGHT: 1'08"
WEIGHT: 24 lbs.
ABILITY: Keen Eye
Sableye's Accuracy cannot be lowered.

STATS

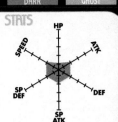

EVOLUTIONS

DOES NOT EVOLVE

LOCATION(s):

RUBY	Rarity: **None**	Trade from *Sapphire/Emerald*
SAPPHIRE	Rarity: **Rare**	Cave of Origin, Granite Cave, Victory Road
FIRERED	Rarity: **None**	Trade from *Sapphire/Emerald*
LEAFGREEN	Rarity: **None**	Trade from *Sapphire/Emerald*
COLOSSEUM	Rarity: **None**	Trade from *Sapphire/Emerald*
EMERALD	Rarity: **Common**	Cave of Origin, Granite Cave, Sky Pillar, Victory Road
XD	Rarity: **Only One**	Citadark Island (Capture from Navigator Abson)

MOVES

Level	Attack	Type	Power	ACC	PP
—	Leer	Normal	—	100	30
—	Scratch	Normal	40	100	35
5	Foresight	Normal	—	100	40
9	Night Shade	Ghost	—	100	15
13	Astonish	Ghost	30	100	15
17	Fury Swipes	Normal	18	80	15

Level	Attack	Type	Power	ACC	PP
21	Fake Out	Normal	40	100	10
25	Detect	Fighting	—	—	5
29	Faint Attack	Dark	60	—	20
33	Knock Off	Dark	20	100	20
37	Confuse Ray	Ghost	—	100	10
41	Shadow Ball	Ghost	80	100	15
45	Mean Look	Normal	—	100	5

TM/HM

TM/HM#	Name	Type	Power	ACC	PP
TM01	Focus Punch	Fighting	150	100	20
TM03	Water Pulse	Water	60	100	20
TM04	Calm Mind	Psychic	—	—	20
TM06	Toxic	Poison	—	85	10
TM10	Hidden Power	Normal	—	100	15
TM11	Sunny Day	Fire	—	—	5
TM12	Taunt	Dark	—	100	20
TM17	Protect	Normal	—	—	10
TM18	Rain Dance	Water	—	—	5
TM21	Frustration	Normal	—	100	20
TM27	Return	Normal	—	100	20
TM28	Dig	Ground	60	100	10
TM29	Psychic	Psychic	90	100	10
TM30	Shadow Ball	Ghost	60	—	20
TM31	Brick Break	Fighting	75	100	15

TM/HM#	Name	Type	Power	ACC	PP
TM32	Double Team	Normal	—	—	15
TM34	Shock Wave	Electric	60	—	20
TM39	Rock Tomb	Rock	50	80	10
TM40	Aerial Ace	Flying	60	—	20
TM41	Torment	Dark	—	100	15
TM42	Facade	Normal	70	100	20
TM43	Secret Power	Normal	70	100	20
TM44	Rest	Psychic	—	—	10
TM45	Attract	Normal	—	100	15
TM46	Thief	Dark	40	100	10
TM49	Snatch	Dark	—	100	10
HM01	Cut	Normal	50	95	30
HM05	Flash	Normal	—	70	20
HM06	Rock Smash	Fighting	20	100	15

EGG MOVES*

Name	Type	Power	ACC	PP
Psych Up	Normal	—	—	10
Recover	Normal	—	—	20
Moonlight	Normal	—	—	5

*Learned Via Breeding

MOVE TUTOR

FireRed/LeafGreen and Emerald Only

Body Slam*	Mega Kick*	Counter*
Double-Edge	Mimic	Seismic Toss*
Mega Punch*	Substitute	Dream Eater*

Emerald Only

Dynamicpunch*	Metronome	Snore*
Endure*	Mud-Slap*	Swagger
Fire Punch*	Psych Up*	Thunderpunch*
Ice Punch*	Sleep Talk	

*Battle Frontier tutor move (*Emerald*)

303 Mawile™

STEEL

GENERAL INFO
SPECIES: Deceiver Pokémon
HEIGHT: 2'00"
WEIGHT: 25 lbs.
ABILITY 1: Hyper Cutter
Mawile's attack power cannot be lowered.
ABILITY 2: Intimidate
Lowers the opponent's attack by one at a battle's start.

STATS

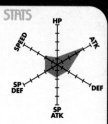

EVOLUTIONS

DOES NOT EVOLVE

LOCATION[s]:

	Rarity	
RUBY	**Rare**	Cave of Origin, Granite Cave, Victory Road
SAPPHIRE	**None**	Trade from *Ruby/Emerald*
FIRERED	**None**	Trade from *Ruby/Emerald*
LEAFGREEN	**None**	Trade from *Ruby/Emerald*
COLOSSEUM	**None**	Trade from *Ruby/Emerald*
EMERALD	**Rare**	Victory Road
XD	**Only One**	Pyrite Town (Capture from Cipher Peon Exol)

MOVES

Level	Attack	Type	Power	ACC	PP	Level	Attack	Type	Power	ACC	PP
—	Astonish	Ghost	30	100	15	31	Baton Pass	Normal	—	—	40
6	Fake Tears	Dark	—	100	20	36	Crunch	Dark	80	100	15
11	Bite	Dark	60	100	25	41	Iron Defense	Steel	—	—	15
16	Sweet Scent	Normal	—	100	20	46	Stockpile	Normal	—	—	10
21	Vicegrip	Normal	55	100	30	46	Swallow	Normal	—	—	10
26	Faint Attack	Dark	60	—	20	46	Spit Up	Normal	100	100	10

TM/HM

TM/HM#	Name	Type	Power	ACC	PP	TM/HM#	Name	Type	Power	ACC	PP
TM01	Focus Punch	Fighting	150	100	20	TM32	Double Team	Normal	—	—	15
TM06	Toxic	Poison	—	85	10	TM35	Flamethrower	Fire	95	100	15
TM10	Hidden Power	Normal	—	100	15	TM36	Sludge Bomb	Poison	90	100	10
TM11	Sunny Day	Fire	—	—	5	TM37	Sandstorm	Rock	—	—	10
TM12	Taunt	Dark	—	100	20	TM38	Fire Blast	Fire	120	85	5
TM13	Ice Beam	Ice	95	100	10	TM39	Rock Tomb	Rock	50	80	10
TM15	Hyper Beam	Normal	150	90	5	TM41	Torment	Dark	—	100	15
TM17	Protect	Normal	—	—	10	TM42	Facade	Normal	70	100	20
TM18	Rain Dance	Water	—	—	5	TM43	Secret Power	Normal	70	100	20
TM21	Frustration	Normal	—	100	20	TM44	Rest	Psychic	—	—	10
TM22	Solarbeam	Grass	120	100	10	TM45	Attract	Normal	—	100	15
TM27	Return	Normal	—	100	20	HM04	Strength	Normal	80	100	15
TM31	Brick Break	Fighting	75	100	15	HM06	Rock Smash	Fighting	20	100	15

EGG MOVES*

Name	Type	Power	ACC	PP
Swords Dance	Normal	—	—	30
False Swipe	Normal	40	100	40
Poison Fang	Poison	50	100	15
Psych Up	Normal	—	—	10
Ancientpower	Rock	60	100	5
Tickle	Normal	—	100	20

*Learned Via Breeding

MOVE TUTOR

FireRed/LeafGreen and Emerald Only

Body Slam*	Mimic	Seismic Toss*
Double-Edge	Substitute	Rock Slide*
Mega Punch*	Swords Dance*	
Mega Kick*	Counter*	

Emerald Only

Dynamicpunch*	Mud-Slap*	Swagger
Endure*	Psych Up*	Thunderpunch*
Ice Punch*	Sleep Talk*	
Icy Wind*	Snore*	

*Battle Frontier tutor move (*Emerald*)

304 Aron™

`STEEL` `ROCK`

GENERAL INFO

SPECIES: Iron Armor Pokémon
HEIGHT: 1'04"
WEIGHT: 132 lbs.
ABILITY 1: Sturdy
One hit KO moves have no effect.
ABILITY 2: Rock Head
Aron does not receive recoil damage from moves such as Double-Edge.

STATS

HP · SPEED · ATK · DEF · SP DEF · SP ATK

EVOLUTIONS

LV32   LV42

LOCATION[S]:

RUBY	Rarity: **Common**	Granite Cave, Victory Road
SAPPHIRE	Rarity: **Common**	Granite Cave, Victory Road
FIRERED	Rarity: **None**	Trade from Ruby/Sapphire/Emerald
LEAFGREEN	Rarity: **None**	Trade from Ruby/Sapphire/Emerald
COLOSSEUM	Rarity: **None**	Trade from Ruby/Sapphire/Emerald
EMERALD	Rarity: **Common**	Granite Cave, Victory Road
XD	Rarity: **Rare**	Cave Poké Spot

MOVES

Level	Attack	Type	Power	ACC	PP	Level	Attack	Type	Power	ACC	PP
—	Tackle	Normal	35	95	35	21	Roar	Normal	—	100	20
4	Harden	Normal	—	—	30	25	Take Down	Normal	90	85	20
7	Mud-Slap	Ground	20	100	10	29	Iron Tail	Steel	100	75	15
10	Headbutt	Normal	70	100	15	34	Protect	Normal	—	—	10
13	Metal Claw	Steel	50	95	35	39	Metal Sound	Steel	—	85	40
17	Iron Defense	Steel	—	—	15	44	Double-Edge	Normal	120	100	15

TM/HM

TM/HM#	Name	Type	Power	ACC	PP	TM/HM#	Name	Type	Power	ACC	PP
TM03	Water Pulse	Water	60	100	20	TM32	Double Team	Normal	—	—	15
TM05	Roar	Normal	—	100	20	TM34	Shock Wave	Electric	60	—	20
TM06	Toxic	Poison	—	85	10	TM37	Sandstorm	Rock	—	—	10
TM10	Hidden Power	Normal	—	100	15	TM39	Rock Tomb	Rock	50	80	10
TM11	Sunny Day	Fire	—	—	5	TM40	Aerial Ace	Flying	60	—	20
TM17	Protect	Normal	—	—	10	TM42	Facade	Normal	70	100	20
TM18	Rain Dance	Water	—	—	5	TM43	Secret Power	Normal	70	100	20
TM21	Frustration	Normal	—	100	20	TM44	Rest	Psychic	—	—	10
TM23	Iron Tail	Steel	100	75	15	TM45	Attract	Normal	—	100	15
TM26	Earthquake	Ground	100	100	10	HM01	Cut	Normal	50	95	30
TM27	Return	Normal	—	100	20	HM04	Strength	Normal	80	100	15
TM28	Dig	Ground	60	100	10	HM06	Rock Smash	Fighting	20	100	15

EGG MOVES*

Name	Type	Power	ACC	PP
Endeavor	Normal	—	100	5
Body Slam	Normal	85	100	15
Stomp	Normal	65	100	20
Smellingsalt	Normal	60	100	10

*Learned Via Breeding

MOVE TUTOR

FireRed/LeafGreen and Emerald Only

Body Slam*	Mimic	Substitute
Double-Edge	Rock Slide*	

Emerald Only

Defense Curl*	Mud-Slap*	Snore*
Endure*	Rollout	Swagger
Fury Cutter	Sleep Talk	

*Battle Frontier tutor move (Emerald)

PRIMA OFFICIAL GAME GUIDE

305 Lairon™

STEEL ROCK

GENERAL INFO
SPECIES: Iron Armor Pokémon
HEIGHT: 2'11"
WEIGHT: 265 lbs.
ABILITY 1: Sturdy
One hit KO moves have no effect.
ABILITY 2: Rock Head
Lairon does not receive recoil damage
from moves such as Double-Edge.

STATS

HP
SPEED ATK
SP DEF DEF
SP ATK

EVOLUTIONS

LV32 LV42

LOCATION[s]:

RUBY	Rarity: **Rare**	Victory Road
SAPPHIRE	Rarity: **Rare**	Victory Road
FIRERED	Rarity: **None**	Trade from *Ruby/Sapphire/Emerald*
LEAFGREEN	Rarity: **None**	Trade from *Ruby/Sapphire/Emerald*
COLOSSEUM	Rarity: **None**	Trade from *Ruby/Sapphire/Emerald*
EMERALD	Rarity: **Rare**	Victory Road
XD	Rarity: **Evolve**	Evolve Aron

MOVES

Level	Attack	Type	Power	ACC	PP
—	Tackle	Normal	35	95	35
—/4	Harden	Normal	—	—	30
—/7	Mud-Slap	Ground	20	100	10
—/10	Headbutt	Normal	70	100	15
13	Metal Claw	Steel	50	95	35
17	Iron Defense	Steel	—	—	15

Level	Attack	Type	Power	ACC	PP
21	Roar	Normal	—	100	20
25	Take Down	Normal	90	85	20
29	Iron Tail	Steel	100	75	15
37	Protect	Normal	—	—	10
45	Metal Sound	Steel	—	85	40
53	Double-Edge	Normal	120	100	15

= Emerald Only

TM/HM

TM/HM#	Name	Type	Power	ACC	PP
TM03	Water Pulse	Water	60	100	20
TM05	Roar	Normal	—	100	20
TM06	Toxic	Poison	—	85	10
TM10	Hidden Power	Normal	—	100	15
TM11	Sunny Day	Fire	—	—	5
TM17	Protect	Normal	—	—	10
TM18	Rain Dance	Water	—	—	5
TM21	Frustration	Normal	—	100	20
TM23	Iron Tail	Steel	100	75	15
TM26	Earthquake	Ground	100	100	10
TM27	Return	Normal	—	100	20
TM28	Dig	Ground	60	100	10

TM/HM#	Name	Type	Power	ACC	PP
TM32	Double Team	Normal	—	—	15
TM34	Shock Wave	Electric	60	—	20
TM37	Sandstorm	Rock	—	—	10
TM39	Rock Tomb	Rock	50	80	10
TM40	Aerial Ace	Flying	60	—	20
TM42	Facade	Normal	70	100	20
TM43	Secret Power	Normal	70	100	20
TM44	Rest	Psychic	—	—	10
TM45	Attract	Normal	—	100	15
HM01	Cut	Normal	50	95	30
HM04	Strength	Normal	80	100	15
HM06	Rock Smash	Fighting	20	100	15

MOVE TUTOR
FireRed/LeafGreen and Emerald Only
Body Slam*	Mimic	Substitute
Double-Edge	Rock Slide*	

Emerald Only
Defense Curl*	Mud-Slap*	Snore*
Endure*	Rollout	Swagger
Fury Cutter	Sleep Talk	

*Battle Frontier tutor move (*Emerald*)

306 Aggron™

STEEL ROCK

GENERAL INFO
SPECIES: Iron Armor Pokémon
HEIGHT: 6'11"
WEIGHT: 794 lbs.
ABILITY 1: Sturdy
One hit KO moves have no effect.
ABILITY 2: Rock Head
Aggron does not receive recoil damage from moves such as Double-Edge.

STATS

HP
SPEED
ATK
SP DEF
DEF
SP ATK

EVOLUTIONS

LV32 LV42

LOCATION(s):

RUBY	Rarity: **Evolve**	Evolve Lairon
SAPPHIRE	Rarity: **Evolve**	Evolve Lairon
FIRERED	Rarity: **None**	Trade from *Ruby/Sapphire/Emerald*
LEAFGREEN	Rarity: **None**	Trade from *Ruby/Sapphire/Emerald*
COLOSSEUM	Rarity: **None**	Trade from *Ruby/Sapphire/Emerald*
EMERALD	Rarity: **Evolve**	Evolve Lairon
XD	Rarity: **Evolve**	Evolve Lairon

MOVES

Level	Attack	Type	Power	ACC	PP
—	Tackle	Normal	35	95	35
—/4	Harden	Normal	—	—	30
—/7	Mud-Slap	Ground	20	100	10
—/10	Headbutt	Normal	70	100	15
13	Metal Claw	Steel	50	95	35
17	Iron Defense	Steel	—	—	15

Level	Attack	Type	Power	ACC	PP
21	Roar	Normal	—	100	20
25	Take Down	Normal	90	85	20
29	Iron Tail	Steel	100	75	15
37	Protect	Normal	—	—	10
50	Metal Sound	Steel	—	85	40
63	Double-Edge	Normal	120	100	15

\# = *Emerald* Only

TM/HM

TM/HM#	Name	Type	Power	ACC	PP
TM01	Focus Punch	Fighting	150	100	20
TM02	Dragon Claw	Dragon	80	100	15
TM03	Water Pulse	Water	60	100	20
TM05	Roar	Normal	—	100	20
TM06	Toxic	Poison	—	85	10
TM10	Hidden Power	Normal	—	100	15
TM11	Sunny Day	Fire	—	—	5
TM12	Taunt	Dark	—	100	20
TM13	Ice Beam	Ice	95	100	10
TM14	Blizzard	Ice	120	70	5
TM15	Hyper Beam	Normal	150	90	5
TM17	Protect	Normal	—	—	10
TM18	Rain Dance	Water	—	—	5
TM21	Frustration	Normal	—	100	20
TM22	Solarbeam	Grass	120	100	10
TM23	Iron Tail	Steel	100	75	15
TM24	Thunderbolt	Electric	95	100	15
TM25	Thunder	Electric	120	70	10
TM26	Earthquake	Ground	100	100	10

TM/HM#	Name	Type	Power	ACC	PP
TM27	Return	Normal	—	100	20
TM28	Dig	Ground	60	100	10
TM31	Brick Break	Fighting	75	100	15
TM32	Double Team	Normal	—	—	15
TM34	Shock Wave	Electric	60	—	20
TM35	Flamethrower	Fire	95	100	15
TM37	Sandstorm	Rock	—	—	10
TM38	Fire Blast	Fire	120	85	5
TM39	Rock Tomb	Rock	50	80	10
TM40	Aerial Ace	Flying	60	—	20
TM42	Facade	Normal	70	100	20
TM43	Secret Power	Normal	70	100	20
TM44	Rest	Psychic	—	—	10
TM45	Attract	Normal	—	100	15
HM01	Cut	Normal	50	95	30
HM03	Surf	Water	95	100	15
HM04	Strength	Normal	80	100	15
HM06	Rock Smash	Fighting	20	100	15

MOVE TUTOR

FireRed/LeafGreen and Emerald Only
- Body Slam*
- Double-Edge*
- Mega Punch*
- Mega Kick*
- Mimic
- Substitute
- Counter*
- Seismic Toss*
- Rock Slide*
- Thunder Wave*

Emerald Only
- Dynamicpunch*
- Endure*
- Fire Punch*
- Fury Cutter
- Ice Punch*
- Icy Wind*
- Mud-Slap*
- Rollout
- Sleep Talk
- Snore*
- Swagger
- Thunderpunch*

*Battle Frontier tutor move (*Emerald*)

307 Meditite™

FIGHTING · PSYCHIC

GENERAL INFO

SPECIES: Meditate Pokémon
HEIGHT: 2'00"
WEIGHT: 25 lbs.
ABILITY: Pure Power
Raises attack power, but effect is lessened by half when ability is changed.

STATS

(Stat hexagon: HP, ATK, DEF, SP ATK, SP DEF, SPEED)

EVOLUTIONS

LV37

LOCATION[s]:

RUBY	**Rarity: Rare**	Mt. Pyre, Victory Road
SAPPHIRE	**Rarity: Rare**	Mt. Pyre, Victory Road
FIRERED	**Rarity: None**	Trade from *Ruby/Sapphire/Colosseum*
LEAFGREEN	**Rarity: None**	Trade from *Ruby/Sapphire/Colosseum*
COLOSSEUM	**Rarity: Only One**	Pyrite Cave
EMERALD	**Rarity: None**	Trade from *Ruby/Sapphire/Colosseum*
XD	**Rarity: Only One**	Trade with Duking

MOVES

Level	Attack	Type	Power	ACC	PP
—	Bide	Normal	—	100	10
4	Meditate	Psychic	—	—	40
9	Confusion	Psychic	50	100	25
12	Detect	Fighting	—	—	5
17/18	Hidden Power	Normal	—	100	15
20	Swagger*	Normal	—	90	15

Level	Attack	Type	Power	ACC	PP
25	Mind Reader	Normal	—	100	5
28	Calm Mind	Psychic	—	—	20
33	Hi Jump Kick	Fighting	85	90	20
36	Psych Up	Normal	—	—	10
41	Reversal	Fighting	—	100	15
49/44	Recover	Normal	—	—	20

= *Emerald* Only   * Not Available in *Emerald*

TM/HM

TM/HM#	Name	Type	Power	ACC	PP
TM01	Focus Punch	Fighting	150	100	20
TM04	Calm Mind	Psychic	—	—	20
TM06	Toxic	Poison	—	85	10
TM08	Bulk Up	Fighting	—	—	20
TM10	Hidden Power	Normal	—	100	15
TM11	Sunny Day	Fire	—	—	5
TM16	Light Screen	Psychic	—	—	30
TM17	Protect	Normal	—	—	10
TM18	Rain Dance	Water	—	—	5
TM21	Frustration	Normal	—	100	20
TM27	Return	Normal	—	100	20
TM29	Psychic	Psychic	90	100	10

TM/HM#	Name	Type	Power	ACC	PP
TM30	Shadow Ball	Ghost	60	—	20
TM31	Brick Break	Fighting	75	100	15
TM32	Double Team	Normal	—	—	15
TM33	Reflect	Psychic	—	—	20
TM39	Rock Tomb	Rock	50	80	10
TM42	Facade	Normal	70	100	20
TM43	Secret Power	Normal	70	100	20
TM44	Rest	Psychic	—	—	10
TM45	Attract	Normal	—	100	15
HM04	Strength	Normal	80	100	15
HM05	Flash	Normal	—	70	20
HM06	Rock Smash	Fighting	20	100	15

EGG MOVES*

Name	Type	Power	ACC	PP
Fire Punch	Fire	75	100	15
Thunderpunch	Electric	75	100	15
Ice Punch	Ice	75	100	15
Foresight	Normal	—	100	40
Fake Out	Normal	40	100	10
Baton Pass	Normal	—	—	40
Dynamicpunch	Fighting	100	50	5

*Learned Via Breeding

MOVE TUTOR

FireRed/LeafGreen and Emerald Only

Body Slam*	Mega Kick*	Counter*
Double-Edge	Mimic	Seismic Toss*
Mega Punch*	Substitute	Dream Eater*

Emerald Only

Dynamicpunch	Metronome	Snore*
Endure*	Mud-Slap*	Swagger
Fire Punch*	Psych Up*	Swift*
Ice Punch*	Sleep Talk	Thunderpunch*

*Battle Frontier tutor move (*Emerald*)

308 Medicham™

FIGHTING PSYCHIC

GENERAL INFO

SPECIES: Meditate Pokémon
HEIGHT: 4'03"
WEIGHT: 69 lbs.
ABILITY: Pure Power
Raises attack power, but effect is lessened by half when ability is changed.

STATS

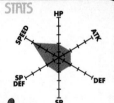

EVOLUTIONS

LV37

LOCATION[S]:

RUBY	Rarity: **Rare**	Evolve Meditite, Victory Road
SAPPHIRE	Rarity: **Rare**	Evolve Meditite, Victory Road
FIRERED	Rarity: **None**	Trade from *Ruby/Sapphire/Colosseum*
LEAFGREEN	Rarity: **None**	Trade from *Ruby/Sapphire/Colosseum*
COLOSSEUM	Rarity: **Evolve**	Evolve Meditite
EMERALD	Rarity: **None**	Trade from *Ruby/Sapphire/Colosseum*
XD	Rarity: **Only One**	Trade with Duking

MOVES

Level	Attack	Type	Power	ACC	PP
—	Fire Punch	Fire	75	100	15
—	Thunderpunch	Electric	75	100	15
—	Ice Punch	Ice	75	100	15
—	Bide	Normal	—	100	10
4	Meditate*	Psychic	—	—	40
9	Confusion*	Psychic	50	100	25
12	Detect*	Fighting	—	—	5
17	Hidden Power	Normal	—	100	15

Level	Attack	Type	Power	ACC	PP
20	Swagger	Normal	—	20	15
25	Mind Reader	Normal	—	100	5
28	Calm Mind	Psychic	—	—	20
33	Hi Jump Kick	Fighting	85	90	20
36	Psych Up	Normal	—	—	10
47/44	Reversal	Fighting	—	100	15
56	Recover	Normal	—	—	20

= Emerald Only   *Emerald Only

TM/HM

TM/HM#	Name	Type	Power	ACC	PP
TM01	Focus Punch	Fighting	150	100	20
TM04	Calm Mind	Psychic	—	—	20
TM06	Toxic	Poison	—	85	10
TM08	Bulk Up	Fighting	—	—	20
TM10	Hidden Power	Normal	—	100	15
TM11	Sunny Day	Fire	—	—	5
TM15	Hyper Beam	Normal	150	90	5
TM16	Light Screen	Psychic	—	—	30
TM17	Protect	Normal	—	—	10
TM18	Rain Dance	Water	—	—	5
TM21	Frustration	Normal	—	100	20
TM27	Return	Normal	—	100	20
TM29	Psychic	Psychic	90	100	10

TM/HM#	Name	Type	Power	ACC	PP
TM30	Shadow Ball	Ghost	60	—	20
TM31	Brick Break	Fighting	75	100	15
TM32	Double Team	Normal	—	—	15
TM33	Reflect	Psychic	—	—	20
TM39	Rock Tomb	Rock	50	80	10
TM42	Facade	Normal	70	100	20
TM43	Secret Power	Normal	70	100	20
TM44	Rest	Psychic	—	—	10
TM45	Attract	Normal	—	100	15
HM04	Strength	Normal	80	100	15
HM05	Flash	Normal	—	70	20
HM06	Rock Smash	Fighting	20	100	15

EGG MOVES*

Name	Type	Power	ACC	PP
Fire Punch	Fire	75	100	15
Thunderpunch	Electric	75	100	15
Ice Punch	Ice	75	100	15
Foresight	Normal	—	100	40
Fake Out	Normal	40	100	10
Baton Pass	Normal	—	—	40
Dynamicpunch	Fighting	100	50	5

*Learned Via Breeding

MOVE TUTOR

FireRed/LeafGreen and Emerald Only

Body Slam*	Mimic	Dream Eater*
Double-Edge	Substitute	Rock Slide*
Mega Punch*	Counter*	Thunder Wave*
Mega Kick*	Seismic Toss*	

Emerald Only

Dynamicpunch*	Metronome	Snore*
Endure*	Mud-Slap*	Swagger
Fire Punch*	Psych Up*	Swift*
Ice Punch*	Sleep Talk*	Thunderpunch*

*Battle Frontier tutor move (Emerald)

309 Electrike™

ELECTRIC

GENERAL INFO

SPECIES: Lightning Pokémon
HEIGHT: 2'00"
WEIGHT: 34 lbs.
ABILITY 1: Static
An opponent has a 30% chance of being paralyzed if it strikes Elecktrike.

ABILITY 2: Lightningrod
Draws Electric-type moves to itself.

STATS

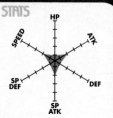

EVOLUTIONS

 ▶

LV26

LOCATION[s]:

RUBY	Rarity: **Common**	Route 110, Route 118
SAPPHIRE	Rarity: **Common**	Route 110, Route 118
FIRERED	Rarity: **None**	Trade from *Ruby/Sapphire/Emerald*
LEAFGREEN	Rarity: **None**	Trade from *Ruby/Sapphire/Emerald*
COLOSSEUM	Rarity: **None**	Trade from *Ruby/Sapphire/Emerald*
EMERALD	Rarity: **Common**	Route 110, Route 118
XD	Rarity: **None**	Trade from *Ruby/Sapphire/Emerald*

MOVES

Level	Attack	Type	Power	ACC	PP	Level	Attack	Type	Power	ACC	PP
—	Tackle	Normal	35	95	35	20	Spark	Electric	65	100	20
4	Thunder Wave	Electric	—	100	20	25	Odor Sleuth	Normal	—	100	40
9	Leer	Normal	—	100	30	28	Roar	Normal	—	100	20
12	Howl	Normal	—	—	40	33	Bite	Dark	60	100	25
17	Quick Attack	Normal	40	100	30	36	Thunder	Electric	120	70	10
						41	Charge	Electric	—	100	20

TM/HM

TM/HM#	Name	Type	Power	ACC	PP	TM/HM#	Name	Type	Power	ACC	PP
TM05	Roar	Normal	—	100	20	TM27	Return	Normal	—	100	20
TM06	Toxic	Poison	—	85	10	TM32	Double Team	Normal	—	—	15
TM10	Hidden Power	Normal	—	100	15	TM34	Shock Wave	Electric	60	—	20
TM17	Protect	Normal	—	—	10	TM42	Facade	Normal	70	100	20
TM18	Rain Dance	Water	—	—	5	TM43	Secret Power	Normal	70	100	20
TM21	Frustration	Normal	—	100	20	TM44	Rest	Psychic	—	—	10
TM23	Iron Tail	Steel	100	75	15	TM45	Attract	Normal	—	100	15
TM24	Thunderbolt	Electric	95	100	15	TM46	Thief	Dark	40	100	10
TM25	Thunder	Electric	120	70	10	HM04	Strength	Normal	80	100	15
						HM05	Flash	Normal	—	70	20

EGG MOVES*

Name	Type	Power	ACC	PP
Crunch	Dark	80	100	15
Uproar	Normal	50	100	10
Headbutt	Normal	70	100	15
Curse	—	—	—	10
Swift	Normal	60	—	20

*Learned Via Breeding

MOVE TUTOR

FireRed/LeafGreen and Emerald Only

Body Slam*	Mimic	Thunder Wave*
Double-Edge	Substitute	

Emerald Only

Endure*	Sleep Talk	Swagger
Mud-Slap*	Snore*	Swift*

*Battle Frontier tutor move (*Emerald*)

Magnectric™

ELECTRIC

GENERAL INFO

SPECIES: Discharge Pokémon
HEIGHT: 4'11"
WEIGHT: 89 lbs.
ABILITY 1: Static
An opponent has a 30% chance of being paralyzed if it strikes Magnectric.
ABILITY 2: Lightningrod
Draws Electric-type moves to itself.

STATS

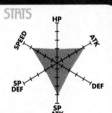

EVOLUTIONS

LV26

LOCATION[s]:

RUBY	Rarity: **Rare**	Route 118
SAPPHIRE	Rarity: **Rare**	Route 118
FIRERED	Rarity: **None**	Trade from *Ruby/Sapphire/Emerald*
LEAFGREEN	Rarity: **None**	Trade from *Ruby/Sapphire/Emerald*
COLOSSEUM	Rarity: **None**	Trade from *Ruby/Sapphire/Emerald*
EMERALD	Rarity: **Rare**	Evolve Electrike, Route 118
XD	Rarity: **Only One**	Citadark Island (Capture from Cipher Admin Eldes)

MOVES

Level	Attack	Type	Power	ACC	PP	Level	Attack	Type	Power	ACC	PP
—	Tackle	Normal	35	95	35	25	Odor Sleuth	Normal	—	100	40
—/4	Thunder Wave	Electric	—	100	20	31	Roar	Normal	—	100	20
—/9	Leer	Normal	—	100	30	39	Bite	Dark	60	100	25
—/12	Howl	Normal	—	—	40	45	Thunder	Electric	120	70	10
17	Quick Attack	Normal	40	100	30	53	Charge	Electric	—	100	20
20	Spark	Electric	65	100	20	# = *Emerald* Only					

TM/HM

TM/HM#	Name	Type	Power	ACC	PP	TM/HM#	Name	Type	Power	ACC	PP
TM05	Roar	Normal	—	100	20	TM27	Return	Normal	—	100	20
TM06	Toxic	Poison	—	85	10	TM32	Double Team	Normal	—	—	15
TM10	Hidden Power	Normal	—	100	15	TM34	Shock Wave	Electric	60	—	20
TM15	Hyper Beam	Normal	150	90	5	TM42	Facade	Normal	70	100	20
TM17	Protect	Normal	—	—	10	TM43	Secret Power	Normal	70	100	20
TM18	Rain Dance	Water	—	—	5	TM44	Rest	Psychic	—	—	10
TM21	Frustration	Normal	—	100	20	TM45	Attract	Normal	—	100	15
TM23	Iron Tail	Steel	100	75	15	TM46	Thief	Dark	40	100	10
TM24	Thunderbolt	Electric	95	100	15	HM04	Strength	Normal	80	100	15
TM25	Thunder	Electric	120	70	10	HM05	Flash	Normal	—	70	20

MOVE TUTOR

FireRed/LeafGreen and Emerald Only

Body Slam*	Mimic	Thunder Wave*
Double-Edge	Substitute	

Emerald Only

Endure*	Sleep Talk	Swagger
Mud-Slap*	Snore*	Swift*

*Battle Frontier tutor move (*Emerald*)

311 Plusle™

ELECTRIC

GENERAL INFO

SPECIES: Cheering Pokémon
HEIGHT: 1'04"
WEIGHT: 9 lbs.
ABILITY: Plus

Increases Special Attack 1.5 times when faced with a Pokémon with the Minus Ability.

STATS

EVOLUTIONS

DOES NOT EVOLVE

LOCATION(s):

RUBY	Rarity: **Rare**	Route 110
SAPPHIRE	Rarity: **Common**	Route 110
FIRERED	Rarity: **None**	Trade from *Ruby/Sapphire/Colosseum/Emerald*
LEAFGREEN	Rarity: **None**	Trade from *Ruby/Sapphire/Colosseum/Emerald*
COLOSSEUM	Rarity: **Only One**	Pyrite Town
EMERALD	Rarity: **Rare**	Route 110, Fortree City
XD	Rarity: **None**	Trade from *Ruby/Sapphire/Colosseum/Emerald*

MOVES

Level	Attack	Type	Power	ACC	PP	Level	Attack	Type	Power	ACC	PP
—	Growl	Normal	—	100	40	22	Encore	Normal	—	100	5
4	Thunder Wave	Electric	—	100	20	28	Fake Tears	Dark	—	100	20
10	Quick Attack	Normal	40	100	30	31	Charge	Electric	—	100	20
13	Helping Hand	Normal	—	100	20	37	Thunder	Electric	120	70	10
19	Spark	Electric	65	100	20	40	Baton Pass	Normal	—	—	40
						47	Agility	Psychic	—	—	30

TM/HM

TM/HM#	Name	Type	Power	ACC	PP	TM/HM#	Name	Type	Power	ACC	PP
TM06	Toxic	Poison	—	85	10	TM27	Return	Normal	—	100	20
TM10	Hidden Power	Normal	—	100	15	TM32	Double Team	Normal	—	—	15
TM16	Light Screen	Psychic	—	—	30	TM34	Shock Wave	Electric	60	—	20
TM17	Protect	Normal	—	—	10	TM42	Facade	Normal	70	100	20
TM18	Rain Dance	Water	—	—	5	TM43	Secret Power	Normal	70	100	20
TM21	Frustration	Normal	—	100	20	TM44	Rest	Psychic	—	—	10
TM23	Iron Tail	Steel	100	75	15	TM45	Attract	Normal	—	100	15
TM24	Thunderbolt	Electric	95	100	15	HM05	Flash	Normal	—	70	20
TM25	Thunder	Electric	120	70	10						

EGG MOVES*

Name	Type	Power	ACC	PP
Substitute	Normal	—	—	10
Wish	Normal	—	100	10

*Learned Via Breeding

MOVE TUTOR

FireRed/LeafGreen and Emerald Only

Body Slam*	Mega Kick*	Counter*
Double-Edge	Mimic	Seismic Toss*
Mega Punch*	Substitute	Thunder Wave*

Emerald Only

Defense Curl*	Mud-Slap*	Swagger
Dynamicpunch*	Rollout	Swift*
Endure*	Sleep Talk	Thunderpunch*
Metronome	Snore*	

*Battle Frontier tutor move (*Emerald*)

312 Minun™

GENERAL INFO
SPECIES: Cheering Pokémon
HEIGHT: 1'04"
WEIGHT: 9 lbs.
ABILITY: Minus
Increases Special Attack 1.5 times when faced with a Pokémon with the Plus Ability.

STATS
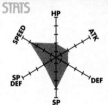

EVOLUTIONS

DOES NOT EVOLVE

LOCATION[s]:

RUBY	Rarity: **Common**	Route 110
SAPPHIRE	Rarity: **Rare**	Route 110
FIRERED	Rarity: **None**	Trade from *Ruby/Sapphire/Emerald*
LEAFGREEN	Rarity: **None**	Trade from *Ruby/Sapphire/Emerald*
COLOSSEUM	Rarity: **None**	Trade from *Ruby/Sapphire/Emerald*
EMERALD	Rarity: **Rare**	Route 110
XD	Rarity: **None**	Trade from *Ruby/Sapphire/Emerald*

MOVES

Level	Attack	Type	Power	ACC	PP
—	Growl	Normal	—	100	40
4	Thunder Wave	Electric	—	100	20
10	Quick Attack	Normal	40	100	30
13	Helping Hand	Normal	—	100	20
19	Spark	Electric	65	100	20
22	Encore	Normal	—	100	5
28	Charm	Normal	—	100	20
31	Charge	Electric	—	100	20
37	Thunder	Electric	120	70	10
40	Baton Pass	Normal	—	—	40
47	Agility	Psychic	—	—	30

TM/HM

TM/HM#	Name	Type	Power	ACC	PP
TM06	Toxic	Poison	—	85	10
TM10	Hidden Power	Normal	—	100	15
TM16	Light Screen	Psychic	—	—	30
TM17	Protect	Normal	—	—	10
TM18	Rain Dance	Water	—	—	5
TM21	Frustration	Normal	—	100	20
TM23	Iron Tail	Steel	100	75	15
TM24	Thunderbolt	Electric	95	100	15
TM25	Thunder	Electric	120	70	10
TM27	Return	Normal	—	100	20
TM32	Double Team	Normal	—	—	15
TM34	Shock Wave	Electric	60	—	20
TM42	Facade	Normal	70	100	20
TM43	Secret Power	Normal	70	100	20
TM44	Rest	Psychic	—	—	10
TM45	Attract	Normal	—	100	15
HM05	Flash	Normal	—	70	20

EGG MOVES*

Name	Type	Power	ACC	PP
Substitute	Normal	—	—	10
Wish	Normal	—	100	10

*Learned Via Breeding

MOVE TUTOR
FireRed/LeafGreen and Emerald Only

Body Slam* · Mega Kick* · Counter*
Double-Edge · Mimic · Seismic Toss*
Mega Punch* · Substitute · Thunder Wave*

Emerald Only

Defense Curl* · Mud-Slap* · Swagger
Dynamicpunch · Rollout · Swift*
Endure* · Sleep Talk · Thunderpunch*
Metronome · Snore*

*Battle Frontier tutor move (*Emerald*)

PRIMA OFFICIAL GAME GUIDE

313 Volbeat™

BUG

GENERAL INFO

SPECIES: **Firefly Pokémon**
HEIGHT: **2'04"**
WEIGHT: **39 lbs.**
ABILITY 1: **Illuminate**
Increases the chance of encountering wild Pokémon.
ABILITY 2: **Swarm**
When Volbeat's HPs fall below 1/3, the power of Bug-type moves increases 1.5 times.

STATS

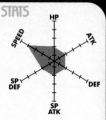

EVOLUTIONS

DOES NOT EVOLVE

LOCATION[s]:

RUBY	Rarity: **Rare**	Route 117
SAPPHIRE	Rarity: **Rare**	Route 117
FIRERED	Rarity: **None**	Trade from *Ruby/Sapphire/Emerald*
LEAFGREEN	Rarity: **None**	Trade from *Ruby/Sapphire/Emerald*
COLOSSEUM	Rarity: **None**	Trade from *Ruby/Sapphire/Emerald*
EMERALD	Rarity: **Rare**	Route 117
XD	Rarity: **None**	Trade from *Ruby/Sapphire/Emerald*

MOVES

Level	Attack	Type	Power	ACC	PP	Level	Attack	Type	Power	ACC	PP
—	Tackle	Normal	35	95	35	21	Tail Glow	Bug	—	100	20
5	Confuse Ray	Ghost	—	100	10	25	Signal Beam	Bug	75	100	15
9	Double Team	Normal	—	—	15	29	Protect	Normal	—	—	10
13	Moonlight	Normal	—	—	5	33	Helping Hand	Normal	—	100	20
17	Quick Attack	Normal	40	100	30	37	Double-Edge	Normal	120	100	15

TM/HM

TM/HM#	Name	Type	Power	ACC	PP	TM/HM#	Name	Type	Power	ACC	PP
TM01	Focus Punch	Fighting	150	100	20	TM27	Return	Normal	—	100	20
TM03	Water Pulse	Water	60	100	20	TM30	Shadow Ball	Ghost	60	—	20
TM06	Toxic	Poison	—	85	10	TM31	Brick Break	Fighting	75	100	15
TM10	Hidden Power	Normal	—	100	15	TM32	Double Team	Normal	—	—	15
TM11	Sunny Day	Fire	—	—	5	TM34	Shock Wave	Electric	60	—	20
TM16	Light Screen	Psychic	—	—	30	TM40	Aerial Ace	Flying	60	—	20
TM17	Protect	Normal	—	—	10	TM42	Facade	Normal	70	100	20
TM18	Rain Dance	Water	—	—	5	TM43	Secret Power	Normal	70	100	20
TM19	Giga Drain	Grass	60	100	5	TM44	Rest	Psychic	—	—	10
TM21	Frustration	Normal	—	100	20	TM45	Attract	Normal	—	100	15
TM22	Solarbeam	Grass	120	100	10	TM46	Thief	Dark	40	100	10
TM24	Thunderbolt	Electric	95	100	15	HM05	Flash	Normal	—	70	20
TM25	Thunder	Electric	120	70	10						

EGG MOVES*

Name	Type	Power	ACC	PP
Baton Pass	Normal	—	—	40
Silver Wind	Bug	60	100	5
Trick	Psychic	—	100	10

*Learned Via Breeding

MOVE TUTOR

FireRed/LeafGreen and Emerald Only

Body Slam*	Mega Kick*	Counter*
Double-Edge	Mimic	Seismic Toss*
Mega Punch*	Substitute	Thunder Wave*

Emerald Only

Dynamicpunch*	Mud-Slap*	Swagger
Endure*	Psych Up*	Swift*
Ice Punch*	Sleep Talk	Thunderpunch*
Metronome	Snore*	

*Battle Frontier tutor move (*Emerald*)

324

314 Illumise™

BUG

GENERAL INFO
SPECIES: Firefly Pokémon
HEIGHT: 2'00"
WEIGHT: 39 lbs.
ABILITY: Oblivious
Illumise is not affected by the Attract condition.

STATS

(Radar chart with axes: HP, ATK, DEF, SP ATK, SP DEF, SPEED)

EVOLUTIONS

DOES NOT EVOLVE

LOCATION[s]:

RUBY	Rarity: **Rare**	Route 117
SAPPHIRE	Rarity: **Rare**	Route 117
FIRERED	Rarity: **None**	Trade from *Ruby/Sapphire/Emerald*
LEAFGREEN	Rarity: **None**	Trade from *Ruby/Sapphire/Emerald*
COLOSSEUM	Rarity: **None**	Trade from *Ruby/Sapphire/Emerald*
EMERALD	Rarity: **Rare**	Route 117
XD	Rarity: **None**	Trade from *Ruby/Sapphire/Emerald*

MOVES

Level	Attack	Type	Power	ACC	PP
—	Tackle	Normal	35	95	35
5	Sweet Scent	Normal	—	100	20
9	Charm	Normal	—	100	20
13	Moonlight	Normal	—	—	5
17	Quick Attack	Normal	40	100	30

Level	Attack	Type	Power	ACC	PP
21	Wish	Normal	—	100	10
25	Encore	Normal	—	100	5
29	Flatter	Dark	—	100	15
33	Helping Hand	Normal	—	100	20
37	Covet	Normal	40	100	40

TM/HM

TM/HM#	Name	Type	Power	ACC	PP
TM01	Focus Punch	Fighting	150	100	20
TM03	Water Pulse	Water	60	100	20
TM06	Toxic	Poison	—	85	10
TM10	Hidden Power	Normal	—	100	15
TM11	Sunny Day	Fire	—	—	5
TM16	Light Screen	Psychic	—	—	30
TM17	Protect	Normal	—	—	10
TM18	Rain Dance	Water	—	—	5
TM19	Giga Drain	Grass	60	100	5
TM21	Frustration	Normal	—	100	20
TM22	Solarbeam	Grass	120	100	10
TM24	Thunderbolt	Electric	95	100	15
TM25	Thunder	Electric	120	70	10

TM/HM#	Name	Type	Power	ACC	PP
TM27	Return	Normal	—	100	20
TM30	Shadow Ball	Ghost	60	—	20
TM31	Brick Break	Fighting	75	100	15
TM32	Double Team	Normal	—	—	15
TM34	Shock Wave	Electric	60	—	20
TM40	Aerial Ace	Flying	60	—	20
TM42	Facade	Normal	70	100	20
TM43	Secret Power	Normal	70	100	20
TM44	Rest	Psychic	—	—	10
TM45	Attract	Normal	—	100	15
TM46	Thief	Dark	40	100	10
HM05	Flash	Normal	—	70	20

EGG MOVES*

Name	Type	Power	ACC	PP
Baton Pass	Normal	—	—	40
Silver Wind	Bug	60	100	5
Growth	Normal	—	—	40

*Learned Via Breeding

MOVE TUTOR
FireRed/LeafGreen and Emerald Only

Body Slam*	Mega Kick*	Counter*
Double-Edge	Mimic	Seismic Toss*
Mega Punch*	Substitute	Thunder Wave*

Emerald Only

Dynamicpunch	Mud-Slap*	Swagger
Endure*	Psych Up*	Swift*
Ice Punch*	Sleep Talk	Thunderpunch*
Metronome	Snore*	

*Battle Frontier tutor move (*Emerald*)

315 Roselia™

GRASS · POISON

GENERAL INFO

SPECIES: Thorn Pokémon
HEIGHT: 1'00"
WEIGHT: 4 lbs.
ABILITY 1: Natural Cure
Any negative status conditions are automatically healed when you remove Roselia from battle.

ABILITY 2: Poison Point
If an opponent is striking Roselia, it has a 30% chance of being poisoned.

STATS

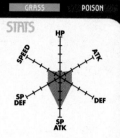

HP · ATK · DEF · SP ATK · SP DEF · SPEED

EVOLUTIONS

DOES NOT EVOLVE

LOCATION[s]:

RUBY	Rarity: **Common**	Route 117
SAPPHIRE	Rarity: **Common**	Route 117
FIRERED	Rarity: **None**	Trade from *Ruby/Sapphire*
LEAFGREEN	Rarity: **None**	Trade from *Ruby/Sapphire*
COLOSSEUM	Rarity: **None**	Trade from *Ruby/Sapphire*
EMERALD	Rarity: **None**	Trade from *Ruby/Sapphire*
XD	Rarity: **Only One**	Phenac City (Capture from Cipher Peon Fasin)

MOVES

Level	Attack	Type	Power	ACC	PP
—	Absorb	Grass	20	100	20
5	Growth	Normal	—	—	40
9	Poison Sting	Poison	15	100	35
13	Stun Spore	Grass	—	75	30
17	Mega Drain	Grass	40	100	10
21	Leech Seed	Grass	—	90	10
25	Magical Leaf	Grass	60	—	20

Level	Attack	Type	Power	ACC	PP
29	Grasswhistle	Grass	—	55	15
33	Giga Drain	Grass	60	100	5
37	Sweet Scent	Normal	—	100	20
41	Ingrain	Grass	—	100	20
45	Toxic	Poison	—	85	10
49	Petal Dance	Grass	70	100	20
53	Aromatherapy	Grass	—	—	5
57	Synthesis	Grass	—	—	5

TM/HM

TM/HM#	Name	Type	Power	ACC	PP
TM06	Toxic	Poison	—	85	10
TM09	Bullet Seed	Grass	10	100	30
TM10	Hidden Power	Normal	—	100	15
TM11	Sunny Day	Fire	—	—	5
TM17	Protect	Normal	—	—	10
TM19	Giga Drain	Grass	60	100	5
TM21	Frustration	Normal	—	100	20
TM22	Solarbeam	Grass	120	100	10
TM27	Return	Normal	—	100	20

TM/HM#	Name	Type	Power	ACC	PP
TM30	Shadow Ball	Ghost	60	—	20
TM32	Double Team	Normal	—	—	15
TM36	Sludge Bomb	Poison	90	100	10
TM42	Facade	Normal	70	100	20
TM43	Secret Power	Normal	70	100	20
TM44	Rest	Psychic	—	—	10
TM45	Attract	Normal	—	100	15
HM01	Cut	Normal	50	95	30
HM05	Flash	Normal	—	70	20

EGG MOVES*

Name	Type	Power	ACC	PP
Spikes	Ground	—	—	20
Pin Missile	Bug	14	85	20
Cotton Spore	Grass	—	85	40
Synthesis	Grass	—	—	5

*Learned Via Breeding

MOVE TUTOR

FireRed/LeafGreen and Emerald Only

Body Slam*	Mimic	Swords Dance*
Double-Edge	Substitute	

Emerald Only

Endure*	Sleep Talk	Swagger
Mud-Slap*	Snore*	Swift*
Psych Up*		

*Battle Frontier tutor move (*Emerald*)

316 Gulpin™

POISON

GENERAL INFO

SPECIES: Stomach Pokémon
HEIGHT: 1'04"
WEIGHT: 23 lbs.
ABILITY 1: Liquid Ooze
Gulpin inflicts damage on an opponent who uses HP-absorbing moves.
ABILITY 2: Sticky Hold
Protects Gulpin's Held Item from an opponent using Thief.

STATS

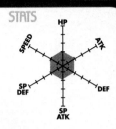

EVOLUTIONS

LV26

LOCATION[s]:

RUBY	Rarity: **Common**	Route 110
SAPPHIRE	Rarity: **Common**	Route 110
FIRERED	Rarity: **None**	Trade from *Ruby/Sapphire/Emerald*
LEAFGREEN	Rarity: **None**	Trade from *Ruby/Sapphire/Emerald*
COLOSSEUM	Rarity: **None**	Trade from *Ruby/Sapphire/Emerald*
EMERALD	Rarity: **Rare**	Route 110
XD	Rarity: **Only One**	Cipher Lab (Capture from Cipher Peon Purpsix)

MOVES

Level	Attack	Type	Power	ACC	PP
—	Pound	Normal	40	100	35
6	Yawn	Normal	—	100	10
9	Poison Gas	Poison	—	55	40
14	Sludge	Poison	65	100	20
17	Amnesia	Psychic	—	—	20

Level	Attack	Type	Power	ACC	PP
23	Encore	Normal	—	100	5
28	Toxic	Poison	—	85	10
34	Stockpile	Normal	—	—	10
34	Spit Up	Normal	100	100	10
34	Swallow	Normal	—	—	10
39	Sludge Bomb	Poison	90	100	10

TM/HM

TM/HM#	Name	Type	Power	ACC	PP
TM03	Water Pulse	Water	60	100	20
TM06	Toxic	Poison	—	85	10
TM09	Bullet Seed	Grass	10	100	30
TM10	Hidden Power	Normal	—	100	15
TM11	Sunny Day	Fire	—	—	5
TM13	Ice Beam	Ice	95	100	10
TM17	Protect	Normal	—	—	10
TM18	Rain Dance	Water	—	—	5
TM19	Giga Drain	Grass	60	100	5
TM21	Frustration	Normal	—	100	20
TM22	Solarbeam	Grass	120	100	10
TM27	Return	Normal	—	100	20

TM/HM#	Name	Type	Power	ACC	PP
TM30	Shadow Ball	Ghost	60	—	20
TM32	Double Team	Normal	—	—	15
TM34	Shock Wave	Electric	60	—	20
TM36	Sludge Bomb	Poison	90	100	10
TM42	Facade	Normal	70	100	20
TM43	Secret Power	Normal	70	100	20
TM44	Rest	Psychic	—	—	10
TM45	Attract	Normal	—	100	15
TM49	Snatch	Dark	—	100	10
HM04	Strength	Normal	80	100	15
HM06	Rock Smash	Fighting	20	100	15

EGG MOVES*

Name	Type	Power	ACC	PP
Dream Eater	Psychic	100	100	15
Acid Armor	Poison	—	—	40
Smog	Poison	20	70	20
Pain Split	Normal	—	100	20

*Learned Via Breeding

MOVE TUTOR

FireRed/LeafGreen and Emerald Only

Body Slam*	Substitute	Dream Eater*
Double-Edge	Counter*	Explosion
Mimic		

Emerald Only

Defense Curl*	Mud-Slap*	Swagger
Dynamicpunch	Rollout	Thunderpunch*
Endure*	Sleep Talk	
Fire Punch*	Snore*	

*Battle Frontier tutor move (Emerald)

317 Swalot™

POISON

GENERAL INFO

SPECIES: Poison Bag Pokémon
HEIGHT: 5'07"
WEIGHT: 176 lbs.
ABILITY 1: Liquid Ooze
Swalot inflicts damage on an opponent who uses HP-absorbing moves.
ABILITY 2: Sticky Hold
Protects Swalot's Held Item from an opponent using Thief.

STATS

EVOLUTIONS

LV26

LOCATION[s]:

RUBY	Rarity: **Evolve**	Evolve Gulpin
SAPPHIRE	Rarity: **Evolve**	Evolve Gulpin
FIRERED	Rarity: **None**	Trade from Ruby/Sapphire/Emerald
LEAFGREEN	Rarity: **None**	Trade from Ruby/Sapphire/Emerald
COLOSSEUM	Rarity: **None**	Trade from Ruby/Sapphire/Emerald
EMERALD	Rarity: **Evolve**	Evolve Gulpin
XD	Rarity: **Evolve**	Evolve Gulpin

MOVES

Level	Attack	Type	Power	ACC	PP	Level	Attack	Type	Power	ACC	PP
—	Pound	Normal	40	100	35	26	Body Slam	Normal	85	100	15
—	Yawn	Normal	—	100	10	31	Toxic	Poison	—	85	10
—	Poison Gas	Poison	—	55	40	40	Stockpile	Normal	—	—	10
—	Sludge	Poison	65	100	20	40	Spit Up	Normal	100	100	10
17	Amnesia	Psychic	—	—	20	40	Swallow	Normal	—	—	10
23	Encore	Normal	—	100	5	48	Sludge Bomb	Poison	90	100	10

TM/HM

TM/HM#	Name	Type	Power	ACC	PP	TM/HM#	Name	Type	Power	ACC	PP
TM03	Water Pulse	Water	60	100	20	TM27	Return	Normal	—	100	20
TM06	Toxic	Poison	—	85	10	TM30	Shadow Ball	Ghost	60	—	20
TM09	Bullet Seed	Grass	10	100	30	TM32	Double Team	Normal	—	—	15
TM10	Hidden Power	Normal	—	100	15	TM34	Shock Wave	Electric	60	—	20
TM11	Sunny Day	Fire	—	—	5	TM36	Sludge Bomb	Poison	90	100	10
TM13	Ice Beam	Ice	95	100	5	TM42	Facade	Normal	70	100	20
TM15	Hyper Beam	Normal	150	90	5	TM43	Secret Power	Normal	70	100	20
TM17	Protect	Normal	—	—	10	TM44	Rest	Psychic	—	—	10
TM18	Rain Dance	Water	—	—	5	TM45	Attract	Normal	—	100	15
TM19	Giga Drain	Grass	60	100	5	TM49	Snatch	Dark	—	100	10
TM21	Frustration	Normal	—	100	20	HM04	Strength	Normal	80	100	15
TM22	Solarbeam	Grass	120	100	10	HM06	Rock Smash	Fighting	20	100	15

MOVE TUTOR

FireRed/LeafGreen and Emerald Only

Body Slam*	Substitute	Dream Eater*
Double-Edge	Counter*	Explosion
Mimic		

Emerald Only

Defense Curl*	Mud-Slap*	Swagger
Dynamicpunch	Rollout	Thunderpunch*
Endure*	Sleep Talk	
Fire Punch*	Snore*	

*Battle Frontier tutor move (Emerald)

318 Carvanha™

GENERAL INFO

SPECIES: Savage Pokémon
HEIGHT: 2'07"
WEIGHT: 46 lbs.
ABILITY: Rough Skin

Recoil hurts the opponent Pokémon when it uses a physical attack.

STATS

EVOLUTIONS

LV30

LOCATION[s]:

Game	Rarity	Location
RUBY	**Common**	Route 118, Route 119
SAPPHIRE	**Common**	Route 118, Route 119
FIRERED	**None**	Trade from *Ruby/Sapphire/Emerald*
LEAFGREEN	**None**	Trade from *Ruby/Sapphire/Emerald*
COLOSSEUM	**None**	Trade from *Ruby/Sapphire/Emerald*
EMERALD	**Common**	Route 118, Route 119
XD	**Only One**	Cipher Lab (Capture from Cipher Peon Cabol)

MOVES

Level	Attack	Type	Power	ACC	PP	Level	Attack	Type	Power	ACC	PP
—	Leer	Normal	—	100	30	22	Crunch	Dark	80	100	15
—	Bite	Dark	60	100	25	28	Screech	Normal	—	85	40
7	Rage	Normal	20	100	20	31	Take Down	Normal	90	85	20
13	Focus Energy	Normal	—	—	30	37	Swagger	Normal	—	90	15
16	Scary Face	Normal	—	90	10	43	Agility	Psychic	—	—	30

TM/HM

TM/HM#	Name	Type	Power	ACC	PP	TM/HM#	Name	Type	Power	ACC	PP
TM03	Water Pulse	Water	60	100	20	TM32	Double Team	Normal	—	—	15
TM06	Toxic	Poison	—	85	10	TM41	Torment	Dark	—	100	15
TM07	Hail	Ice	—	—	10	TM42	Facade	Normal	70	100	20
TM10	Hidden Power	Normal	—	100	15	TM43	Secret Power	Normal	70	100	20
TM12	Taunt	Dark	—	100	20	TM44	Rest	Psychic	—	—	10
TM13	Ice Beam	Ice	95	100	10	TM45	Attract	Normal	—	100	15
TM14	Blizzard	Ice	120	70	5	TM46	Thief	Dark	40	100	10
TM17	Protect	Normal	—	—	10	HM03	Surf	Water	95	100	15
TM18	Rain Dance	Water	—	—	5	HM07	Waterfall	Water	80	100	15
TM21	Frustration	Normal	—	100	20	HM08	Dive	Water	60	100	10
TM27	Return	Normal	—	100	20						

EGG MOVES*

Name	Type	Power	ACC	PP
Hydro Pump	Water	120	80	5
Double-Edge	Normal	120	100	15
Thrash	Normal	90	100	20

*Learned Via Breeding

MOVE TUTOR

FireRed/LeafGreen and Emerald Only

Double-Edge	Mimic	Substitute

Emerald Only

Endure*	Mud-Slap*	Swagger
Fury Cutter	Sleep Talk	Swift*
Icy Wind*	Snore*	

*Battle Frontier tutor move (*Emerald*)

319 Sharpedo™

WATER DARK

GENERAL INFO
SPECIES: Brutal Pokémon
HEIGHT: 5'11"
WEIGHT: 196 lbs.
ABILITY: Rough Skin
The opponent Pokémon is hurt when it uses a physical attack against Sharpedo.

STATS

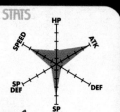

EVOLUTIONS

LV30

LOCATION[s]:

RUBY	Rarity: **Rare**	Route 103, Route 118, Route 122
SAPPHIRE	Rarity: **Rare**	Route 103, Route 118, Route 122
FIRERED	Rarity: **None**	Trade from *Ruby/Sapphire/Emerald*
LEAFGREEN	Rarity: **None**	Trade from *Ruby/Sapphire/Emerald*
COLOSSEUM	Rarity: **None**	Trade from *Ruby/Sapphire/Emerald*
EMERALD	Rarity: **Common**	Routes 103, 118, 122, 124–127, 129–134, Mossdeep City, Pacifidlog Town
XD	Rarity: **Evolve**	Evolve Carvanha

MOVES

Level	Attack	Type	Power	ACC	PP	Level	Attack	Type	Power	ACC	PP
—	Leer	Normal	—	100	30	28	Screech	Normal	—	85	40
—	Bite	Dark	60	100	25	33	Slash	Normal	70	100	20
—	Rage	Normal	20	100	20	38	Taunt	Dark	—	100	20
—	Focus Energy	Normal	—	—	30	43	Swagger	Normal	—	90	15
16	Scary Face	Normal	—	90	10	48	Skull Bash	Normal	100	100	15
22	Crunch	Dark	80	100	15	53	Agility	Psychic	—	—	30

TM/HM

TM/HM#	Name	Type	Power	ACC	PP	TM/HM#	Name	Type	Power	ACC	PP
TM03	Water Pulse	Water	60	100	20	TM32	Double Team	Normal	—	—	15
TM05	Roar	Normal	—	100	20	TM39	Rock Tomb	Rock	50	80	10
TM06	Toxic	Poison	—	85	10	TM41	Torment	Dark	—	100	15
TM07	Hail	Ice	—	—	10	TM42	Facade	Normal	70	100	20
TM10	Hidden Power	Normal	—	100	15	TM43	Secret Power	Normal	70	100	20
TM12	Taunt	Dark	—	100	20	TM44	Rest	Psychic	—	—	10
TM13	Ice Beam	Ice	95	100	10	TM45	Attract	Normal	—	100	15
TM14	Blizzard	Ice	120	70	5	TM46	Thief	Dark	40	100	10
TM15	Hyper Beam	Normal	150	90	5	HM03	Surf	Water	95	100	15
TM17	Protect	Normal	—	—	10	HM04	Strength	Normal	80	100	15
TM18	Rain Dance	Water	—	—	5	HM06	Rock Smash	Fighting	20	100	15
TM21	Frustration	Normal	—	100	20	HM07	Waterfall	Water	80	100	15
TM26	Earthquake	Ground	100	100	10	HM08	Dive	Water	60	100	10
TM27	Return	Normal	—	100	20						

MOVE TUTOR

FireRed/LeafGreen and Emerald Only

Double-Edge	Mimic	Substitute

Emerald Only

Endure*	Mud-Slap*	Swagger
Fury Cutter	Sleep Talk	Swift*
Icy Wind*	Snore*	

*Battle Frontier tutor move (*Emerald*)

320 Wailmer™

WATER

GENERAL INFO

SPECIES: Ball Whale Pokémon
HEIGHT: 6'07"
WEIGHT: 287 lbs.
ABILITY 1: Water Veil
Wailmer cannot be burned.
ABILITY 2: Oblivious
The Attract condition does not affect Wailmer.

STATS

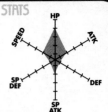

EVOLUTIONS

LV40

LOCATION[s]:

RUBY	Rarity: **Rare**	Fish in most waters, Route 103, Route 110
SAPPHIRE	Rarity: **Rare**	Fish in most waters, Route 103, Route 110
FIRERED	Rarity: **None**	Trade from *Ruby/Sapphire/Emerald*
LEAFGREEN	Rarity: **None**	Trade from *Ruby/Sapphire/Emerald*
COLOSSEUM	Rarity: **None**	Trade from *Ruby/Sapphire/Emerald*
EMERALD	Rarity: **Common**	Routes 103, 105–110, 115, 121–134, Ever Grande City, Lilycove City, Mossdeep City, Pacifidlog Town, Seafloor Cavern, Shoal Cave
XD	Rarity: **None**	Trade from *Ruby/Sapphire/Emerald*

MOVES

Level	Attack	Type	Power	ACC	PP	Level	Attack	Type	Power	ACC	PP
—	Scratch	Normal	40	100	35	28	Water Pulse	Water	60	100	20
5	Growl	Normal	—	100	40	32	Mist	Ice	—	—	30
10	Water Gun	Water	40	100	25	37	Rest	Psychic	—	—	10
14	Rollout	Rock	30	90	20	41	Water Spout	Water	150	100	5
19	Whirlpool	Water	15	70	15	46	Amnesia	Psychic	—	—	20
23	Astonish	Ghost	30	100	15	50	Hydro Pump	Water	120	80	5

TM/HM

TM/HM#	Name	Type	Power	ACC	PP	TM/HM#	Name	Type	Power	ACC	PP
TM03	Water Pulse	Water	60	100	20	TM32	Double Team	Normal	—	—	15
TM05	Roar	Normal	—	100	20	TM39	Rock Tomb	Rock	50	80	10
TM06	Toxic	Poison	—	85	10	TM42	Facade	Normal	70	100	20
TM07	Hail	Ice	—	—	10	TM43	Secret Power	Normal	70	100	20
TM10	Hidden Power	Normal	—	100	15	TM44	Rest	Psychic	—	—	10
TM13	Ice Beam	Ice	95	100	10	TM45	Attract	Normal	—	100	15
TM14	Blizzard	Ice	120	70	5	HM03	Surf	Water	95	100	15
TM17	Protect	Normal	—	—	10	HM04	Strength	Normal	80	100	15
TM18	Rain Dance	Water	—	—	5	HM06	Rock Smash	Fighting	20	100	15
TM21	Frustration	Normal	—	100	20	HM07	Waterfall	Water	80	100	15
TM26	Earthquake	Ground	100	100	10	HM08	Dive	Water	60	100	10
TM27	Return	Normal	—	100	20						

EGG MOVES*

Name	Type	Power	ACC	PP
Double-Edge	Normal	120	100	15
Thrash	Normal	90	100	20
Swagger	Normal	—	90	15
Snore	Normal	40	100	15
Sleep Talk	Normal	—	—	10
Curse	—	—	—	10
Fissure	Ground	—	30	5
Tickle	Normal	—	100	20

*Learned Via Breeding

MOVE TUTOR

FireRed/LeafGreen and Emerald Only

Body Slam*	Mimic	Substitute
Double-Edge		

Emerald Only

Defense Curl*	Icy Wind*	Snore*
Dynamicpunch	Rollout	Swagger
Endure*	Sleep Talk	

*Battle Frontier tutor move (*Emerald*)

321 Wailord™

WATER

GENERAL INFO

SPECIES: Float Whale Pokémon
HEIGHT: 47'07"
WEIGHT: 878 lbs.
ABILITY 1: Water Veil
Wailord cannot be burned.
ABILITY 2: Oblivious
The Attract condition does not affect Wailord.

STATS

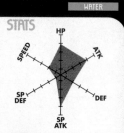

EVOLUTIONS

LV40

LOCATION[s]:

RUBY	**Rarity: Rare**	Route 129
SAPPHIRE	**Rarity: Rare**	Route 129
FIRERED	**Rarity: None**	Trade from *Ruby/Sapphire/Emerald*
LEAFGREEN	**Rarity: None**	Trade from *Ruby/Sapphire/Emerald*
COLOSSEUM	**Rarity: None**	Trade from *Ruby/Sapphire/Emerald*
EMERALD	**Rarity: Rare**	Route 129
XD	**Rarity: None**	Trade from *Ruby/Sapphire/Emerald*

MOVES

Level	Attack	Type	Power	ACC	PP	Level	Attack	Type	Power	ACC	PP
—	Splash	Normal	—	—	40	28	Water Pulse	Water	60	100	20
—	Growl	Normal	—	100	40	32	Mist	Ice	—	—	30
—	Water Gun	Water	40	100	25	37	Rest	Psychic	—	—	10
—	Rollout	Rock	30	90	20	44	Water Spout	Water	150	100	5
19	Whirlpool	Water	15	70	15	52	Amnesia	Psychic	—	—	20
23	Astonish	Ghost	30	100	15	59	Hydro Pump	Water	120	80	5

TM/HM

TM/HM#	Name	Type	Power	ACC	PP	TM/HM#	Name	Type	Power	ACC	PP
TM03	Water Pulse	Water	60	100	20	TM27	Return	Normal	—	100	20
TM05	Roar	Normal	—	100	20	TM32	Double Team	Normal	—	—	15
TM06	Toxic	Poison	—	85	10	TM39	Rock Tomb	Rock	50	80	10
TM07	Hail	Ice	—	—	10	TM42	Facade	Normal	70	100	20
TM10	Hidden Power	Normal	—	100	15	TM43	Secret Power	Normal	70	100	20
TM13	Ice Beam	Ice	95	100	10	TM44	Rest	Psychic	—	—	10
TM14	Blizzard	Ice	120	70	5	TM45	Attract	Normal	—	100	15
TM15	Hyper Beam	Normal	150	90	5	HM03	Surf	Water	95	100	15
TM17	Protect	Normal	—	—	10	HM04	Strength	Normal	80	100	15
TM18	Rain Dance	Water	—	—	5	HM06	Rock Smash	Fighting	20	100	15
TM21	Frustration	Normal	—	100	20	HM07	Waterfall	Water	80	100	15
TM26	Earthquake	Ground	100	100	10	HM08	Dive	Water	60	100	10

MOVE TUTOR
FireRed/LeafGreen and Emerald Only

Body Slam*	Mimic	Substitute
Double-Edge		

Emerald Only

Defense Curl*	Icy Wind*	Snore*
Dynamicpunch	Rollout	Swagger
Endure*	Sleep Talk	

*Battle Frontier tutor move (*Emerald*)

322 Numel™

FIRE | GROUND

GENERAL INFO
SPECIES: Numb Pokémon
HEIGHT: 2'04"
WEIGHT: 53 lbs.
ABILITY: Oblivious
Numel is not affected by the Attract condition.

STATS

EVOLUTIONS

LV33

LOCATION[s]:

RUBY	Rarity: **Common**	Route 112
SAPPHIRE	Rarity: **Common**	Route 112
FIRERED	Rarity: **None**	Trade from *Ruby/Sapphire/Emerald*
LEAFGREEN	Rarity: **None**	Trade from *Ruby/Sapphire/Emerald*
COLOSSEUM	Rarity: **None**	Trade from *Ruby/Sapphire/Emerald*
EMERALD	Rarity: **Common**	Route 112, Fiery Path, Jagged Pass
XD	Rarity: **Only One**	Cipher Lab (Capture from Cipher Peon Solox)

MOVES

Level	Attack	Type	Power	ACC	PP	Level	Attack	Type	Power	ACC	PP
—	Growl	Normal	—	100	40	29	Take Down	Normal	90	85	20
—	Tackle	Normal	35	95	35	31	Amnesia	Psychic	—	—	20
11	Ember	Fire	40	100	25	35	Earthquake	Ground	100	100	10
19	Magnitude	Ground	—	100	30	41	Flamethrower	Fire	95	100	15
25	Focus Energy	Normal	—	—	30	49	Double-Edge	Normal	120	100	15

TM/HM

TM/HM#	Name	Type	Power	ACC	PP	TM/HM#	Name	Type	Power	ACC	PP
TM06	Toxic	Poison	—	85	10	TM37	Sandstorm	Rock	—	—	10
TM10	Hidden Power	Normal	—	100	15	TM38	Fire Blast	Fire	120	85	5
TM11	Sunny Day	Fire	—	—	5	TM39	Rock Tomb	Rock	50	80	10
TM17	Protect	Normal	—	—	10	TM42	Facade	Normal	70	100	20
TM21	Frustration	Normal	—	100	20	TM43	Secret Power	Normal	70	100	20
TM26	Earthquake	Ground	100	100	10	TM44	Rest	Psychic	—	—	10
TM27	Return	Normal	—	100	20	TM45	Attract	Normal	—	100	15
TM28	Dig	Ground	60	100	10	TM50	Overheat	Fire	140	90	5
TM32	Double Team	Normal	—	—	15	HM04	Strength	Normal	80	100	15
TM35	Flamethrower	Fire	95	100	15	HM06	Rock Smash	Fighting	20	100	15

EGG MOVES*

Name	Type	Power	ACC	PP
Howl	Normal	—	—	40
Scary Face	Normal	—	90	10
Body Slam	Normal	85	100	15
Rollout	Rock	30	90	20
Defense Curl	Normal	—	—	40
Stomp	Normal	65	100	20

*Learned Via Breeding

MOVE TUTOR
FireRed/LeafGreen and Emerald Only

Body Slam*	Mimic	Rock Slide*
Double-Edge	Substitute	

Emerald Only

Defense Curl*	Rollout	Swagger
Endure*	Sleep Talk	
Mud-Slap*	Snore*	

*Battle Frontier tutor move (*Emerald*)

323 Camerupt™

FIRE | GROUND

GENERAL INFO
SPECIES: Eruption Pokémon
HEIGHT: 6'03"
WEIGHT: 485 lbs.
ABILITY: Magma Armor
Camerupt is unaffected by the Freeze condition.

STATS

(Stat chart: HP, ATK, DEF, SP ATK, SP DEF, SPEED)

EVOLUTIONS

LV33

LOCATION[S]:

Game	Rarity	Location
RUBY	Rarity: **Evolve**	Evolve Numel
SAPPHIRE	Rarity: **Evolve**	Evolve Numel
FIRERED	Rarity: **None**	Trade from *Ruby/Sapphire/Emerald*
LEAFGREEN	Rarity: **None**	Trade from *Ruby/Sapphire/Emerald*
COLOSSEUM	Rarity: **None**	Trade from *Ruby/Sapphire/Emerald*
EMERALD	Rarity: **Evolve**	Evolve Numel
XD	Rarity: **Evolve**	Evolve Numel

MOVES

Level	Attack	Type	Power	ACC	PP	Level	Attack	Type	Power	ACC	PP
—	Growl	Normal	—	100	40	29	Take Down	Normal	90	85	20
—	Tackle	Normal	35	95	35	31	Amnesia	Psychic	—	—	20
—	Ember	Fire	40	100	25	33	Rock Slide	Rock	75	90	10
—	Magnitude	Ground	—	100	30	37	Earthquake	Ground	100	100	10
25	Focus Energy	Normal	—	—	30	45	Eruption	Fire	150	100	5
						55	Fissure	Ground	—	30	5

TM/HM

TM/HM#	Name	Type	Power	ACC	PP	TM/HM#	Name	Type	Power	ACC	PP
TM05	Roar	Normal	—	100	20	TM35	Flamethrower	Fire	—	95	100	15
TM06	Toxic	Poison	—	85	10	TM37	Sandstorm	Rock	—	—	10
TM10	Hidden Power	Normal	—	100	15	TM38	Fire Blast	Fire	120	85	5
TM11	Sunny Day	Fire	—	—	5	TM39	Rock Tomb	Rock	50	80	10
TM15	Hyper Beam	Normal	150	90	5	TM42	Facade	Normal	70	100	20
TM17	Protect	Normal	—	—	10	TM43	Secret Power	Normal	70	100	20
TM21	Frustration	Normal	—	100	20	TM44	Rest	Psychic	—	—	10
TM22	Solarbeam	Grass	120	100	10	TM45	Attract	Normal	—	100	15
TM26	Earthquake	Ground	100	100	10	TM50	Overheat	Fire	140	90	5
TM27	Return	Normal	—	100	20	HM04	Strength	Normal	80	100	15
TM28	Dig	Ground	60	100	10	HM06	Rock Smash	Fighting	20	100	15
TM32	Double Team	Normal	—	—	15						

MOVE TUTOR*

Move	Type	Power	ACC	PP
Body Slam	Normal	85	100	15
Double-Edge	Normal	120	100	15
Mimic	Normal	—	100	10
Substitute	Normal	—	—	10
Rock Slide	Rock	75	90	10
Explosion	Normal	250	100	5

*FireRed/LeafGreen Only

MOVE TUTOR
FireRed/LeafGreen and Emerald Only

Body Slam*	Explosion	Substitute
Double-Edge	Mimic	Rock Slide*

Emerald Only

Defense Curl*	Rollout	Swagger
Endure*	Sleep Talk	
Mud-Slap*	Snore*	

*Battle Frontier tutor move (*Emerald*)

324 Torkoal™

FIRE

GENERAL INFO
SPECIES: Coal Pokémon
HEIGHT: 1'08"
WEIGHT: 177 lbs.
ABILITY: White Smoke
Torkoal is not affected by moves that lower stats.

STATS

(Radar chart with axes: HP, ATK, DEF, SP ATK, SP DEF, SPEED)

EVOLUTIONS

DOES NOT EVOLVE

LOCATION[s]:

RUBY	Rarity: **Rare**	Fiery Path
SAPPHIRE	Rarity: **Rare**	Fiery Path
FIRERED	Rarity: **None**	Trade from *Ruby/Sapphire/Emerald*
LEAFGREEN	Rarity: **None**	Trade from *Ruby/Sapphire/Emerald*
COLOSSEUM	Rarity: **None**	Trade from *Ruby/Sapphire/Emerald*
EMERALD	Rarity: **Rare**	Fiery Path, Magma Hideout
XD	Rarity: **None**	Trade from *Ruby/Sapphire/Emerald*

MOVES

Level	Attack	Type	Power	ACC	PP
—	Ember	Fire	40	100	25
4	Smog	Poison	20	70	20
7	Curse	—	—	—	10
14	Smokescreen	Normal	—	100	20
17	Fire Spin	Fire	15	70	15
20	Body Slam	Normal	85	100	15

Level	Attack	Type	Power	ACC	PP
27	Protect	Normal	—	—	10
30	Flamethrower	Fire	95	100	15
33	Iron Defense	Steel	—	—	15
40	Amnesia	Psychic	—	—	20
43	Flail	Normal	—	100	15
46	Heat Wave	Fire	100	90	10

TM/HM

TM/HM#	Name	Type	Power	ACC	PP
TM06	Toxic	Poison	—	85	10
TM10	Hidden Power	Normal	—	100	15
TM11	Sunny Day	Fire	—	—	5
TM17	Protect	Normal	—	—	10
TM21	Frustration	Normal	—	100	20
TM23	Iron Tail	Steel	100	75	15
TM27	Return	Normal	—	100	20
TM32	Double Team	Normal	—	—	15
TM35	Flamethrower	Fire	95	100	15

TM/HM#	Name	Type	Power	ACC	PP
TM36	Sludge Bomb	Poison	90	100	10
TM38	Fire Blast	Fire	120	85	5
TM42	Facade	Normal	70	100	20
TM43	Secret Power	Normal	70	100	20
TM44	Rest	Psychic	—	—	10
TM45	Attract	Normal	—	100	15
TM50	Overheat	Fire	140	90	5
HM04	Strength	Normal	80	100	15
HM06	Rock Smash	Fighting	20	100	15

EGG MOVES*

Name	Type	Power	ACC	PP
Eruption	Fire	150	100	5
Endure	Normal	—	—	10
Sleep Talk	Normal	—	—	10
Yawn	Normal	—	100	10

*Learned Via Breeding

MOVE TUTOR
FireRed/LeafGreen and Emerald Only

Body Slam*	Explosion	Substitute
Double-Edge	Mimic	Rock Slide*

Emerald Only

Endure*	Sleep Talk	Swagger
Mud-Slap*	Snore*	

*Battle Frontier tutor move (*Emerald*)

325 Spoink™

PSYCHIC

GENERAL INFO
SPECIES: Bounce Pokémon
HEIGHT: 2'04"
WEIGHT: 67 lbs.
ABILITY 1: Thick Fat
Fire- and Ice-type moves inflict only 50% of the damage.
ABILITY 2: Own Tempo
Spoink cannot become confused.

STATS

EVOLUTIONS

LV32

LOCATION[s]:

RUBY	Rarity: **Rare**	Jagged Pass	
SAPPHIRE	Rarity: **Rare**	Jagged Pass	
FIRERED	Rarity: **None**	Trade from *Ruby/Sapphire/Emerald*	
LEAFGREEN	Rarity: **None**	Trade from *Ruby/Sapphire/Emerald*	
COLOSSEUM	Rarity: **None**	Trade from *Ruby/Sapphire/Emerald*	
EMERALD	Rarity: **Rare**	Jagged Pass	
XD	Rarity: **None**	Trade from *Ruby/Sapphire/Emerald*	

MOVES

Level	Attack	Type	Power	ACC	PP	Level	Attack	Type	Power	ACC	PP
—	Splash	Normal	—	—	40	25	Confuse Ray	Ghost	—	100	10
7	Psywave	Psychic	—	80	15	28	Magic Coat	Psychic	—	100	15
10	Odor Sleuth	Normal	—	100	40	34	Psychic	Psychic	90	100	10
16	Psybeam	Psychic	65	100	20	37	Rest	Psychic	—	—	10
19	Psych Up	Normal	—	—	10	37	Snore	Normal	40	100	15
						43	Bounce	Flying	85	85	5

TM/HM

TM/HM#	Name	Type	Power	ACC	PP	TM/HM#	Name	Type	Power	ACC	PP
TM04	Calm Mind	Psychic	—	—	20	TM32	Double Team	Normal	—	—	15
TM06	Toxic	Poison	—	85	10	TM33	Reflect	Psychic	—	—	20
TM10	Hidden Power	Normal	—	100	15	TM34	Shock Wave	Electric	60	—	20
TM11	Sunny Day	Fire	—	—	5	TM41	Torment	Dark	—	100	15
TM12	Taunt	Dark	—	100	20	TM42	Facade	Normal	70	100	20
TM16	Light Screen	Psychic	—	—	30	TM43	Secret Power	Normal	70	100	20
TM17	Protect	Normal	—	—	10	TM44	Rest	Psychic	—	—	10
TM18	Rain Dance	Water	—	—	5	TM45	Attract	Normal	—	100	15
TM21	Frustration	Normal	—	100	20	TM46	Thief	Dark	40	100	10
TM23	Iron Tail	Steel	100	75	15	TM48	Skill Swap	Psychic	—	100	10
TM27	Return	Normal	—	100	20	TM49	Snatch	Dark	—	100	10
TM29	Psychic	Psychic	90	100	10	HM05	Flash	Normal	—	70	20
TM30	Shadow Ball	Ghost	60	—	20						

EGG MOVES*

Name	Type	Power	ACC	PP
Future Sight	Psychic	80	90	15
Extrasensory	Psychic	80	100	30
Substitute	Normal	—	—	10
Trick	Psychic	—	100	10

*Learned Via Breeding

MOVE TUTOR
FireRed/LeafGreen and Emerald Only

Body Slam*	Mimic	Dream Eater*
Double-Edge	Substitute	

Emerald Only

Endure*	Sleep Talk	Swift*
Icy Wind*	Snore*	
Psych Up*	Swagger	

*Battle Frontier tutor move (Emerald)

326 Grumpig™

PSYCHIC

GENERAL INFO

SPECIES: Manipulate Pokémon
HEIGHT: 2'11"
WEIGHT: 158 lbs.
ABILITY 1: Thick Fat
Fire- and Ice-type moves inflict only 50% of the damage.
ABILITY 2: Own Tempo
Grumpig cannot become confused.

STATS

HP, ATK, DEF, SP ATK, SP DEF, SPEED

EVOLUTIONS

LV32

LOCATION[s]:

RUBY	Rarity: **Evolve**	Evolve Spoink
SAPPHIRE	Rarity: **Evolve**	Evolve Spoink
FIRERED	Rarity: **None**	Trade from *Ruby/Sapphire/Emerald*
LEAFGREEN	Rarity: **None**	Trade from *Ruby/Sapphire/Emerald*
COLOSSEUM	Rarity: **None**	Trade from *Ruby/Sapphire/Emerald*
EMERALD	Rarity: **Evolve**	Evolve Spoink
XD	Rarity: **None**	Trade from *Ruby/Sapphire/Emerald*

MOVES

Level	Attack	Type	Power	ACC	PP	Level	Attack	Type	Power	ACC	PP
—	Splash	Normal	—	—	40	25	Confuse Ray	Ghost	—	100	10
—	Psywave	Psychic	—	80	15	28	Magic Coat	Psychic	—	100	15
—	Odor Sleuth	Normal	—	100	40	37	Psychic	Psychic	90	100	10
—	Psybeam	Psychic	65	100	20	43	Rest	Psychic	—	—	10
19	Psych Up	Normal	—	—	10	43	Snore	Normal	40	100	15
						55	Bounce	Flying	85	85	5

TM/HM

TM/HM#	Name	Type	Power	ACC	PP	TM/HM#	Name	Type	Power	ACC	PP
TM01	Focus Punch	Fighting	150	100	20	TM30	Shadow Ball	Ghost	60	—	20
TM04	Calm Mind	Psychic	—	—	20	TM32	Double Team	Normal	—	—	15
TM06	Toxic	Poison	—	85	10	TM33	Reflect	Psychic	—	—	20
TM10	Hidden Power	Normal	—	100	15	TM34	Shock Wave	Electric	60	—	20
TM11	Sunny Day	Fire	—	—	5	TM41	Torment	Dark	—	100	15
TM12	Taunt	Dark	—	100	20	TM42	Facade	Normal	70	100	20
TM15	Hyper Beam	Normal	150	90	5	TM43	Secret Power	Normal	70	100	20
TM16	Light Screen	Psychic	—	—	30	TM44	Rest	Psychic	—	—	10
TM17	Protect	Normal	—	—	10	TM45	Attract	Normal	—	100	15
TM18	Rain Dance	Water	—	—	5	TM46	Thief	Dark	40	100	10
TM21	Frustration	Normal	—	100	20	TM48	Skill Swap	Psychic	—	100	10
TM23	Iron Tail	Steel	100	75	15	TM49	Snatch	Dark	—	100	10
TM27	Return	Normal	—	100	20	HM05	Flash	Normal	—	70	20
TM29	Psychic	Psychic	90	100	10						

MOVE TUTOR

FireRed/LeafGreen and Emerald Only

Body Slam*	Mega Kick*	Counter*
Double-Edge*	Mimic	Seismic Toss*
Mega Punch*	Substitute	Dream Eater*

Emerald Only

Dynamicpunch	Metronome	Swagger
Endure*	Mud-Slap*	Swift*
Fire Punch*	Psych Up*	Thunderpunch*
Ice Punch*	Sleep Talk	
Icy Wind*	Snore*	

*Battle Frontier tutor move (*Emerald*)

PRIMA OFFICIAL GAME GUIDE

327 Spinda™

NORMAL

GENERAL INFO
SPECIES: Spot Panda Pokémon
HEIGHT: 3'07"
WEIGHT: 11 lbs.
ABILITY: Own Tempo
Spinda cannot become confused.

STATS

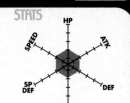

EVOLUTIONS

DOES NOT EVOLVE

LOCATION[s]:

RUBY	Rarity: **Rare**	Route 113
SAPPHIRE	Rarity: **Rare**	Route 113
FIRERED	Rarity: **None**	Trade from *Ruby/Sapphire/Emerald*
LEAFGREEN	Rarity: **None**	Trade from *Ruby/Sapphire/Emerald*
COLOSSEUM	Rarity: **None**	Trade from *Ruby/Sapphire/Emerald*
EMERALD	Rarity: **Common**	Route 113
XD	Rarity: **None**	Trade from *Ruby/Sapphire/Emerald*

MOVES

Level	Attack	Type	Power	ACC	PP	Level	Attack	Type	Power	ACC	PP
—	Tackle	Normal	35	95	35	27	Dizzy Punch	Normal	70	100	10
5	Uproar	Normal	50	100	10	34	Teeter Dance	Normal	—	100	20
12	Faint Attack	Dark	60	—	20	38	Psych Up	Normal	—	—	10
16	Psybeam	Psychic	65	100	20	45	Double-Edge	Normal	120	100	15
23	Hypnosis	Psychic	—	60	20	49	Flail	Normal	—	100	15
						56	Thrash	Normal	90	100	20

TM/HM

TM/HM#	Name	Type	Power	ACC	PP	TM/HM#	Name	Type	Power	ACC	PP
TM01	Focus Punch	Fighting	150	100	20	TM31	Brick Break	Fighting	75	100	15
TM03	Water Pulse	Water	60	100	20	TM32	Double Team	Normal	—	—	15
TM04	Calm Mind	Psychic	—	—	20	TM34	Shock Wave	Electric	60	—	20
TM06	Toxic	Poison	—	85	10	TM39	Rock Tomb	Rock	50	80	10
TM10	Hidden Power	Normal	—	100	15	TM42	Facade	Normal	70	100	20
TM11	Sunny Day	Fire	—	—	5	TM43	Secret Power	Normal	70	100	20
TM17	Protect	Normal	—	—	10	TM44	Rest	Psychic	—	—	10
TM18	Rain Dance	Water	—	—	5	TM45	Attract	Normal	—	100	15
TM20	Safeguard	Normal	—	—	25	TM46	Thief	Dark	40	100	10
TM21	Frustration	Normal	—	100	20	TM48	Skill Swap	Psychic	—	100	10
TM27	Return	Normal	—	100	20	TM49	Snatch	Dark	—	100	10
TM28	Dig	Ground	60	100	10	HM04	Strength	Normal	80	100	15
TM29	Psychic	Psychic	90	100	10	HM05	Flash	Normal	—	70	20
TM30	Shadow Ball	Ghost	60	—	20	HM06	Rock Smash	Fighting	20	100	15

EGG MOVES*

Name	Type	Power	ACC	PP
Encore	Normal	—	100	5
Rock Slide	Rock	75	90	10
Assist	Normal	—	100	20
Disable	Normal	—	55	20
Baton Pass	Normal	—	—	40
Trick	Psychic	—	100	10
Smellingsalt	Normal	60	100	10
Wish	Normal	—	100	10

*Learned Via Breeding

MOVE TUTOR
FireRed/LeafGreen and Emerald Only

Body Slam*	Mimic	Seismic Toss*
Double-Edge	Substitute	Dream Eater*
Mega Punch*	Metronome	Rock Slide*
Mega Kick*	Counter*	

Emerald Only

Defense Curl*	Icy Wind*	Sleep Talk
Dynamicpunch*	Metronome	Snore*
Endure*	Mud-Slap*	Swagger
Fire Punch*	Psych Up*	Swift*
Ice Punch*	Rollout	Thunderpunch*

*Battle Frontier tutor move (*Emerald*)

328 Trapinch™

GENERAL INFO

SPECIES: Ant Pit Pokémon
HEIGHT: 2'04"
WEIGHT: 33 lbs.
ABILITY 1: Hyper Cutter
Trapinch's attack power cannot be lowered.

ABILITY 2: Arena Trap
Prevents the opponent Pokémon from fleeing or switching out of battle. Does not affect Flying-type Pokémon or Pokémon with the Levitate Ability.

STATS

EVOLUTIONS

LV35   LV45

LOCATION(s):

RUBY	Rarity: **Rare**	Route 111
SAPPHIRE	Rarity: **Rare**	Route 111
FIRERED	Rarity: **None**	Trade from *Ruby/Sapphire*
LEAFGREEN	Rarity: **None**	Trade from *Ruby/Sapphire*
COLOSSEUM	Rarity: **None**	Trade from *Ruby/Sapphire*
EMERALD	Rarity: **Common**	Route 111, Mirage Tower
XD	Rarity: **Rare**	Rock Poké Spot

MOVES

Level	Attack	Type	Power	ACC	PP	Level	Attack	Type	Power	ACC	PP
—	Bite	Dark	60	100	25	33	Crunch	Dark	80	100	15
9	Sand-Attack	Ground	—	100	15	41	Dig	Ground	60	100	10
17	Faint Attack	Dark	60	—	20	49	Sandstorm	Rock	—	—	10
25	Sand Tomb	Ground	15	70	15	57	Hyper Beam	Normal	150	90	5

TM/HM

TM/HM#	Name	Type	Power	ACC	PP	TM/HM#	Name	Type	Power	ACC	PP
TM06	Toxic	Poison	—	85	10	TM28	Dig	Ground	60	100	10
TM10	Hidden Power	Normal	—	100	15	TM32	Double Team	Normal	—	—	15
TM11	Sunny Day	Fire	—	—	5	TM37	Sandstorm	Rock	—	—	10
TM15	Hyper Beam	Normal	150	90	5	TM39	Rock Tomb	Rock	50	80	10
TM17	Protect	Normal	—	—	10	TM42	Facade	Normal	70	100	20
TM19	Giga Drain	Grass	60	100	5	TM43	Secret Power	Normal	70	100	20
TM21	Frustration	Normal	—	100	20	TM44	Rest	Psychic	—	—	10
TM22	Solarbeam	Grass	120	100	10	TM45	Attract	Normal	—	100	15
TM26	Earthquake	Ground	100	100	10	HM04	Strength	Normal	80	100	15
TM27	Return	Normal	—	100	20	HM06	Rock Smash	Fighting	20	100	15

EGG MOVES*

Name	Type	Power	ACC	PP
Focus Energy	Normal	—	—	30
Quick Attack	Normal	40	100	30
Whirlwind	Normal	—	100	20

*Learned Via Breeding

MOVE TUTOR
FireRed/LeafGreen and Emerald Only
Body Slam*   Mimic   Rock Slide*
Double-Edge   Substitute

Emerald Only
Endure*   Sleep Talk   Swagger
Mud-Slap*   Snore*

*Battle Frontier tutor move (*Emerald*)

PRIMA OFFICIAL GAME GUIDE

329 Vibrava™

GROUND · DRAGON

GENERAL INFO

SPECIES: Vibration Pokémon
HEIGHT: 3'07"
WEIGHT: 34 lbs.
ABILITY: Levitate
Vibrava is not affected by Ground-type moves.

STATS

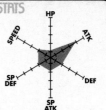

EVOLUTIONS

  LV35 LV45

LOCATION[s]:

RUBY	Rarity: **Evolve**	Evolve Trapinch	
SAPPHIRE	Rarity: **Evolve**	Evolve Trapinch	
FIRERED	Rarity: **None**	Trade from *Ruby/Sapphire/Emerald/Colosseum*	
LEAFGREEN	Rarity: **None**	Trade from *Ruby/Sapphire/Emerald/Colosseum*	
COLOSSEUM	Rarity: **Only One**	Shadow Pokémon Lab	
EMERALD	Rarity: **Evolve**	Evolve Trapinch	
XD	Rarity: **Evolve**	Evolve Trapinch	

MOVES

Level	Attack	Type	Power	ACC	PP	Level	Attack	Type	Power	ACC	PP
—	Bite	Dark	60	100	25	33	Crunch	Dark	80	100	15
—	Sand-Attack	Ground	—	100	15	35	Dragonbreath	Dragon	60	100	20
—	Faint Attack	Dark	60	—	20	41	Screech	Normal	—	85	40
—	Sand Tomb	Ground	15	70	15	49	Sandstorm	Rock	—	—	10
						57	Hyper Beam	Normal	150	90	5

TM/HM

TM/HM#	Name	Type	Power	ACC	PP	TM/HM#	Name	Type	Power	ACC	PP
TM06	Toxic	Poison	—	85	10	TM32	Double Team	Normal	—	—	15
TM10	Hidden Power	Normal	—	100	15	TM37	Sandstorm	Rock	—	—	10
TM11	Sunny Day	Fire	—	—	5	TM39	Rock Tomb	Rock	50	80	10
TM15	Hyper Beam	Normal	150	90	5	TM42	Facade	Normal	70	100	20
TM17	Protect	Normal	—	—	10	TM43	Secret Power	Normal	70	100	20
TM19	Giga Drain	Grass	60	100	5	TM44	Rest	Psychic	—	—	10
TM21	Frustration	Normal	—	100	20	TM45	Attract	Normal	—	100	15
TM22	Solarbeam	Grass	120	100	10	TM47	Steel Wing	Steel	70	90	25
TM26	Earthquake	Ground	100	100	10	HM02	Fly	Flying	70	95	15
TM27	Return	Normal	—	100	20	HM04	Strength	Normal	80	100	15
TM28	Dig	Ground	60	100	10	HM06	Rock Smash	Fighting	20	100	15

MOVE TUTOR
FireRed/LeafGreen and Emerald Only

Body Slam*	Mimic	Rock Slide*
Double-Edge	Substitute	

Emerald **Only**

Endure*	Sleep Talk	Swagger
Mud-Slap*	Snore*	Swift*

*Battle Frontier tutor move (*Emerald*)

330 Flygon ™

GROUND   DRAGON

GENERAL INFO

SPECIES: Mystic Pokémon
HEIGHT: 6'07"
WEIGHT: 181 lbs.
ABILITY: Levitate
Flygon is not affected by Ground-type moves.

STATS

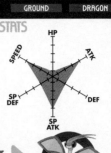

EVOLUTIONS

LV35   LV45

LOCATION[s]:

Game	Rarity	Location
RUBY	**Evolve**	Evolve Vibrava
SAPPHIRE	**Evolve**	Evolve Vibrava
FIRERED	**None**	Trade from *Ruby/Sapphire/Emerald/Colosseum*
LEAFGREEN	**None**	Trade from *Ruby/Sapphire/Emerald/Colosseum*
COLOSSEUM	**Evolve**	Evolve Vibrava
EMERALD	**Evolve**	Evolve Vibrava
XD	**Evolve**	Evolve Vibrava

MOVES

Level	Attack	Type	Power	ACC	PP	Level	Attack	Type	Power	ACC	PP
—	Bite	Dark	60	100	25	33	Crunch	Dark	80	100	15
—	Sand-Attack	Ground	—	100	15	35	Dragonbreath	Dragon	60	100	20
—	Faint Attack	Dark	60	—	20	41	Screech	Normal	—	85	40
—	Sand Tomb	Ground	15	70	15	53	Sandstorm	Rock	—	—	10
						65	Hyper Beam	Normal	150	90	5

TM/HM

TM/HM#	Name	Type	Power	ACC	PP	TM/HM#	Name	Type	Power	ACC	PP
TM02	Dragon Claw	Dragon	80	100	15	TM32	Double Team	Normal	—	—	15
TM06	Toxic	Poison	—	85	10	TM35	Flamethrower	Fire	95	100	15
TM10	Hidden Power	Normal	—	100	15	TM37	Sandstorm	Rock	—	—	10
TM11	Sunny Day	Fire	—	—	5	TM38	Fire Blast	Fire	120	85	5
TM15	Hyper Beam	Normal	150	90	5	TM39	Rock Tomb	Rock	50	80	10
TM17	Protect	Normal	—	—	10	TM42	Facade	Normal	70	100	20
TM19	Giga Drain	Grass	60	100	5	TM43	Secret Power	Normal	70	100	20
TM21	Frustration	Normal	—	100	20	TM44	Rest	Psychic	—	—	10
TM22	Solarbeam	Grass	120	100	10	TM45	Attract	Normal	—	100	15
TM23	Iron Tail	Steel	100	75	15	TM47	Steel Wing	Steel	70	90	25
TM26	Earthquake	Ground	100	100	10	HM02	Fly	Flying	70	95	15
TM27	Return	Normal	—	100	20	HM04	Strength	Normal	80	100	15
TM28	Dig	Ground	60	100	10	HM06	Rock Smash	Fighting	20	100	15

MOVE TUTOR

FireRed/LeafGreen and Emerald Only

Body Slam*	Mimic	Rock Slide*
Double-Edge	Substitute	

Emerald Only

Endure*	Mud-Slap*	Swagger
Fire Punch*	Sleep Talk	Swift*
Fury Cutter	Snore*	

*Battle Frontier tutor move (*Emerald*)

331 Cacnea™

GRASS

GENERAL INFO

SPECIES: Cactus Pokémon
HEIGHT: 1'04"
WEIGHT: 113 lbs.
ABILITY: Sand Veil

Cacnea's evasion stat rises when a sandstorm blows.

STATS

EVOLUTIONS

LV32

LOCATION(s):

RUBY	Rarity: **Rare**	Route 111
SAPPHIRE	Rarity: **Rare**	Route 111
FIRERED	Rarity: **None**	Trade from *Ruby/Sapphire/Emerald*
LEAFGREEN	Rarity: **None**	Trade from *Ruby/Sapphire/Emerald*
COLOSSEUM	Rarity: **None**	Trade from *Ruby/Sapphire/Emerald*
EMERALD	Rarity: **Rare**	Route 111
XD	Rarity: **None**	Trade from *Ruby/Sapphire/Emerald*

MOVES

Level	Attack	Type	Power	ACC	PP	Level	Attack	Type	Power	ACC	PP
—	Poison Sting	Poison	15	100	35	25	Ingrain	Grass	—	100	20
—	Leer	Normal	—	100	30	29	Faint Attack	Dark	60	—	20
5	Absorb	Grass	20	100	25	33	Spikes	Ground	—	—	20
9	Growth	Normal	—	—	40	37	Needle Arm	Grass	60	100	15
13	Leech Seed	Grass	—	90	10	41	Cotton Spore	Grass	—	85	40
17	Sand-Attack	Ground	—	100	15	45	Sandstorm	Rock	—	—	10
21	Pin Missile	Bug	14	85	20	49	Destiny Bond*	Ghost	—	—	5

* Not Available in *Emerald*

TM/HM

TM/HM#	Name	Type	Power	ACC	PP	TM/HM#	Name	Type	Power	ACC	PP
TM01	Focus Punch	Fighting	150	100	20	TM27	Return	Normal	—	100	20
TM06	Toxic	Poison	—	85	10	TM32	Double Team	Normal	—	—	15
TM09	Bullet Seed	Grass	10	100	30	TM37	Sandstorm	Rock	—	—	10
TM10	Hidden Power	Normal	—	100	15	TM42	Facade	Normal	70	100	20
TM11	Sunny Day	Fire	—	—	5	TM43	Secret Power	Normal	70	100	20
TM17	Protect	Normal	—	—	10	TM44	Rest	Psychic	—	—	10
TM19	Giga Drain	Grass	60	100	5	TM45	Attract	Normal	—	100	15
TM21	Frustration	Normal	—	100	20	HM01	Cut	Normal	50	95	30
TM22	Solarbeam	Grass	120	100	10	HM05	Flash	Normal	—	70	20

EGG MOVES*

Name	Type	Power	ACC	PP
Grasswhistle	Grass	—	55	15
Acid	Poison	40	100	30
Teeter Dance	Normal	—	100	20
Dynamicpunch	Fighting	100	50	5
Counter	Fighting	—	100	20

*Learned Via Breeding

MOVE TUTOR

FireRed/LeafGreen and Emerald Only

Body Slam*	Mimic	Counter*
Double-Edge	Substitute	Seismic Toss*
Mega Punch*	Swords Dance*	

Emerald Only

Dynamicpunch	Mud-Slap*	Swagger
Endure*	Sleep Talk	Thunderpunch*
Fury Cutter	Snore*	

*Battle Frontier tutor move (*Emerald*)

332 Cacturne™

GRASS | DARK

GENERAL INFO
SPECIES: Scarecrow Pokémon
HEIGHT: 4'03"
WEIGHT: 171 lbs.
ABILITY: Sand Veil
Cacturne's evasion stat rises when a sandstorm blows.

STATS

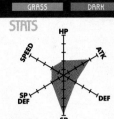

EVOLUTIONS

LV32

LOCATION[S]:

RUBY	**Rarity: Evolve**	Evolve Cacnea
SAPPHIRE	**Rarity: Evolve**	Evolve Cacnea
FIRERED	**Rarity: None**	Trade from *Ruby/Sapphire/Emerald*
LEAFGREEN	**Rarity: None**	Trade from *Ruby/Sapphire/Emerald*
COLOSSEUM	**Rarity: None**	Trade from *Ruby/Sapphire/Emerald*
EMERALD	**Rarity: Evolve**	Evolve Cacnea
XD	**Rarity: None**	Trade from *Ruby/Sapphire/Emerald*

MOVES

Level	Attack	Type	Power	ACC	PP	Level	Attack	Type	Power	ACC	PP
—	Revenge	Fighting	60	100	10	25	Ingrain	Grass	—	100	20
—	Poison Sting	Poison	15	100	35	29	Faint Attack	Dark	60	—	20
—	Leer	Normal	—	100	30	35	Spikes	Ground	—	—	20
—	Absorb	Grass	20	100	20	41	Needle Arm	Grass	60	100	15
—	Growth	Normal	—	—	40	47	Cotton Spore	Grass	—	85	40
13	Leech Seed	Grass	—	90	10	53	Sandstorm	Rock	—	—	10
17	Sand-Attack	Ground	—	100	15	59	Destiny Bond*	Ghost	—	—	5
21	Pin Missile	Bug	14	85	20						

* Not Available in *Emerald*

TM/HM

TM/HM#	Name	Type	Power	ACC	PP	TM/HM#	Name	Type	Power	ACC	PP
TM01	Focus Punch	Fighting	150	100	20	TM27	Return	Normal	—	100	20
TM06	Toxic	Poison	—	85	10	TM32	Double Team	Normal	—	—	15
TM09	Bullet Seed	Grass	10	100	30	TM37	Sandstorm	Rock	—	—	10
TM10	Hidden Power	Normal	—	100	15	TM42	Facade	Normal	70	100	20
TM11	Sunny Day	Fire	—	—	5	TM43	Secret Power	Normal	70	100	20
TM15	Hyper Beam	Normal	150	90	5	TM44	Rest	Psychic	—	—	10
TM17	Protect	Normal	—	—	10	TM45	Attract	Normal	—	100	15
TM19	Giga Drain	Grass	60	100	5	HM01	Cut	Normal	50	95	30
TM21	Frustration	Normal	—	100	20	HM04	Strength	Normal	80	100	15
TM22	Solarbeam	Grass	120	100	10	HM05	Flash	Normal	—	70	20

MOVE TUTOR

FireRed/LeafGreen and Emerald Only

Body Slam*	Mega Kick*	Swords Dance*
Double-Edge	Mimic	Counter*
Mega Punch*	Substitute	Seismic Toss*

Emerald Only

Dynamicpunch*	Mud-Slap*	Swagger
Endure*	Sleep Talk	Thunderpunch*
Fury Cutter	Snore*	

*Battle Frontier tutor move (*Emerald*)

333 Swablu™

`NORMAL` `FLYING`

GENERAL INFO

SPECIES: Cotton Bird Pokémon
HEIGHT: 1'04"
WEIGHT: 3 lbs.
ABILITY: Natural Cure

Any negative status conditions are healed when Swablu is removed from battle.

STATS

EVOLUTIONS

LV35

LOCATION[s]:

	Rarity	
RUBY	**Rare**	Route 114, Route 115
SAPPHIRE	**Rare**	Route 114, Route 115
FIRERED	**None**	Trade from *Ruby/Sapphire/Colosseum/Emerald*
LEAFGREEN	**None**	Trade from *Ruby/Sapphire/Colosseum/Emerald*
COLOSSEUM	**Only One**	Pyrite Cave
EMERALD	**Common**	Route 114, Route 115
XD	**None**	Trade from *Ruby/Sapphire/Colosseum/Emerald*

MOVES

Level	Attack	Type	Power	ACC	PP	Level	Attack	Type	Power	ACC	PP
—	Peck	Flying	35	100	35	21	Safeguard	Normal	—	—	25
—	Growl	Normal	—	100	40	28	Mist	Ice	—	—	30
8	Astonish	Ghost	30	100	15	31	Take Down	Normal	90	85	20
11	Sing	Normal	—	55	15	38	Mirror Move	Flying	—	—	20
18	Fury Attack	Normal	15	85	20	41	Refresh	Normal	—	100	20
						48	Perish Song	Normal	—	—	5

TM/HM

TM/HM#	Name	Type	Power	ACC	PP	TM/HM#	Name	Type	Power	ACC	PP
TM06	Toxic	Poison	—	85	10	TM32	Double Team	Normal	—	—	15
TM10	Hidden Power	Normal	—	100	15	TM40	Aerial Ace	Flying	60	—	20
TM11	Sunny Day	Fire	—	—	5	TM42	Facade	Normal	70	100	20
TM13	Ice Beam	Ice	95	100	10	TM43	Secret Power	Normal	70	100	20
TM17	Protect	Normal	—	—	10	TM44	Rest	Psychic	—	—	10
TM18	Rain Dance	Water	—	—	5	TM45	Attract	Normal	—	100	15
TM20	Safeguard	Normal	—	—	25	TM46	Thief	Dark	40	100	10
TM21	Frustration	Normal	—	100	20	TM47	Steel Wing	Steel	70	90	25
TM22	Solarbeam	Grass	120	100	10	HM02	Fly	Flying	70	95	15
TM27	Return	Normal	—	100	20						

EGG MOVES*

Name	Type	Power	ACC	PP
Agility	Psychic	—	—	30
Haze	Ice	—	—	30
Pursuit	Dark	40	100	20
Rage	Normal	20	100	20

*Learned Via Breeding

MOVE TUTOR
FireRed/LeafGreen and Emerald Only

Body Slam*	Mimic	Dream Eater*
Double-Edge	Substitute	

Emerald Only

Endure*	Sleep Talk	Swagger
Mud-Slap*	Snore*	Swift*
Psych Up*		

*Battle Frontier tutor move (*Emerald*)

334 Altaria™

DRAGON　FLYING

GENERAL INFO

SPECIES: Humming Pokémon
HEIGHT: 3'07"
WEIGHT: 45 lbs.
ABILITY: Natural Cure

Any negative status conditions are healed when Altaria is removed from battle.

STATS

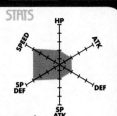

HP, ATK, DEF, SP ATK, SP DEF, SPEED

EVOLUTIONS

 ▶

LV35

LOCATION(s):

RUBY	Rarity: **Rare**	Sky Pillar
SAPPHIRE	Rarity: **Rare**	Sky Pillar
FIRERED	Rarity: **None**	Trade from *Ruby/Sapphire/Colosseum/Emerald*
LEAFGREEN	Rarity: **None**	Trade from *Ruby/Sapphire/Colosseum/Emerald*
COLOSSEUM	Rarity: **Evolve**	Evolve Swablu
EMERALD	Rarity: **Rare**	Evolve Swablu, Sky Pillar
XD	Rarity: **Only One**	Citadark Island (Capture from Admin Lovrina)

MOVES

Level	Attack	Type	Power	ACC	PP	Level	Attack	Type	Power	ACC	PP
—	Peck	Flying	35	100	35	28	Mist	Ice	—	—	30
—	Growl	Normal	—	100	40	31	Take Down	Normal	90	85	20
—	Sing	Normal	—	55	15	35	Dragonbreath	Dragon	60	100	20
—	Astonish	Ghost	30	100	15	40	Dragon Dance	Dragon	—	—	20
18	Fury Attack	Normal	15	85	20	45	Refresh	Normal	—	100	20
21	Safeguard	Normal	—	—	25	54	Perish Song	Normal	—	—	5
						59	Sky Attack	Flying	140	90	5

TM/HM

TM/HM#	Name	Type	Power	ACC	PP	TM/HM#	Name	Type	Power	ACC	PP
TM02	Dragon Claw	Dragon	80	100	15	TM27	Return	Normal	—	100	20
TM05	Roar	Normal	—	100	20	TM32	Double Team	Normal	—	—	15
TM06	Toxic	Poison	—	85	10	TM35	Flamethrower	Fire	95	100	15
TM10	Hidden Power	Normal	—	100	15	TM38	Fire Blast	Fire	120	85	5
TM11	Sunny Day	Fire	—	—	5	TM40	Aerial Ace	Flying	60	—	20
TM13	Ice Beam	Ice	95	100	10	TM42	Facade	Normal	70	100	20
TM15	Hyper Beam	Normal	150	90	5	TM43	Secret Power	Normal	70	100	20
TM17	Protect	Normal	—	—	10	TM44	Rest	Psychic	—	—	10
TM18	Rain Dance	Water	—	—	5	TM45	Attract	Normal	—	100	15
TM20	Safeguard	Normal	—	—	25	TM46	Thief	Dark	40	100	10
TM21	Frustration	Normal	—	100	20	TM47	Steel Wing	Steel	70	90	25
TM22	Solarbeam	Grass	120	100	10	HM02	Fly	Flying	70	95	15
TM23	Iron Tail	Steel	100	75	15	HM06	Rock Smash	Fighting	20	100	15
TM26	Earthquake	Ground	100	100	10						

MOVE TUTOR

FireRed/LeafGreen and Emerald Only

Body Slam*	Mimic	Dream Eater*
Double-Edge	Substitute	

*Battle Frontier tutor move (*Emerald*)

Emerald Only

Endure*	Sleep Talk	Swagger
Mud-Slap*	Snore*	Swift*
Psych Up*		

335 Zangoose™

NORMAL

GENERAL INFO
SPECIES: Cat Ferret Pokémon
HEIGHT: 4'03"
WEIGHT: 89 lbs.
ABILITY: Immunity
Zangoose cannot be poisoned.

STATS

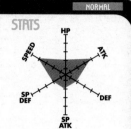

EVOLUTIONS

DOES NOT EVOLVE

LOCATION[s]:

RUBY	Rarity: **Rare**	Route 114
SAPPHIRE	Rarity: **None**	Trade from *Ruby*
FIRERED	Rarity: **None**	Trade from *Ruby*
LEAFGREEN	Rarity: **None**	Trade from *Ruby*
COLOSSEUM	Rarity: **None**	Trade from *Ruby*
EMERALD	Rarity: **None**	Trade from *Ruby*
XD	Rarity: **Only One**	Cipher Key Lair (Capture from Bodybuilder Zook)

MOVES

Level	Attack	Type	Power	ACC	PP
—	Scratch	Normal	40	100	35
4	Leer	Normal	—	100	30
7	Quick Attack	Normal	40	100	30
10	Swords Dance	Normal	—	—	30
13	Fury Cutter	Bug	10	95	20

Level	Attack	Type	Power	ACC	PP
19	Slash	Normal	70	100	20
25	Pursuit	Dark	40	100	20
31	Crush Claw	Normal	75	95	10
37	Taunt	Dark	—	100	20
46	Detect	Fighting	—	—	5
55	False Swipe	Normal	40	100	40

TM/HM

TM/HM#	Name	Type	Power	ACC	PP
TM01	Focus Punch	Fighting	150	100	20
TM03	Water Pulse	Water	60	100	20
TM05	Roar	Normal	—	100	20
TM06	Toxic	Poison	—	85	10
TM10	Hidden Power	Normal	—	100	15
TM11	Sunny Day	Fire	—	—	5
TM12	Taunt	Dark	—	100	20
TM13	Ice Beam	Ice	95	100	10
TM14	Blizzard	Ice	120	70	5
TM17	Protect	Normal	—	—	10
TM18	Rain Dance	Water	—	—	5
TM19	Giga Drain	Grass	60	100	5
TM21	Frustration	Normal	—	100	20
TM22	Solarbeam	Grass	120	100	10
TM23	Iron Tail	Steel	100	75	15
TM24	Thunderbolt	Electric	95	100	15
TM25	Thunder	Electric	120	70	10

TM/HM#	Name	Type	Power	ACC	PP
TM27	Return	Normal	—	100	20
TM28	Dig	Ground	60	100	10
TM30	Shadow Ball	Ghost	80	—	20
TM31	Brick Break	Fighting	75	100	15
TM32	Double Team	Normal	—	—	15
TM34	Shock Wave	Electric	60	—	20
TM35	Flamethrower	Fire	95	100	15
TM38	Fire Blast	Fire	120	85	5
TM40	Aerial Ace	Flying	60	—	20
TM42	Facade	Normal	70	100	20
TM43	Secret Power	Normal	70	100	20
TM44	Rest	Psychic	—	—	10
TM45	Attract	Normal	—	100	15
TM46	Thief	Dark	40	100	10
HM04	Strength	Normal	80	100	15
HM06	Rock Smash	Fighting	20	100	15

EGG MOVES*

Name	Type	Power	ACC	PP
Flail	Normal	—	100	15
Double Kick	Fighting	30	100	30
Razor Wind	Normal	80	100	10
Counter	Fighting	—	100	20
Roar	Normal	—	100	20
Curse	—	—	—	10

*Learned Via Breeding

MOVE TUTOR
FireRed/LeafGreen and Emerald Only

Body Slam*	Mimic	Thunder Wave*
Double-Edge	Substitute	Rock Slide*
Mega Punch*	Counter*	Swords Dance*
Mega Kick*	Seismic Toss*	

Emerald Only

Defense Curl*	Ice Punch*	Snore*
Dynamicpunch*	Icy Wind*	Swagger
Endure*	Mud-Slap*	Swift*
Fire Punch*	Rollout	Thunderpunch*
Fury Cutter	Sleep Talk	

*Battle Frontier tutor move (*Emerald*)

336 Seviper™

GENERAL INFO
SPECIES: Fang Snake Pokémon
HEIGHT: 8'10"
WEIGHT: 116 lbs.
ABILITY: Shed Skin
Every turn, Seviper has a 1/3 chance of recovering from a status condition.

STATS

EVOLUTIONS

DOES NOT EVOLVE

LOCATION(s):

RUBY	Rarity: **None**	Trade from *Sapphire/Emerald*
SAPPHIRE	Rarity: **Rare**	Route 114
FIRERED	Rarity: **None**	Trade from *Sapphire/Emerald*
LEAFGREEN	Rarity: **None**	Trade from *Sapphire/Emerald*
COLOSSEUM	Rarity: **None**	Trade from *Sapphire/Emerald*
EMERALD	Rarity: **Rare**	Route 114
XD	Rarity: **None**	Trade from *Sapphire/Emerald*

MOVES

Level	Attack	Type	Power	ACC	PP	Level	Attack	Type	Power	ACC	PP
—	Wrap	Normal	15	85	20	25	Glare	Normal	—	75	30
7	Lick	Ghost	20	100	30	28	Crunch	Dark	80	100	15
10	Bite	Dark	60	100	25	34	Poison Fang	Poison	50	100	15
16	Poison Tail	Poison	50	100	25	37	Swagger	Normal	—	90	15
19	Screech	Normal	—	85	40	43	Haze	Ice	—	—	30

TM/HM

TM/HM#	Name	Type	Power	ACC	PP	TM/HM#	Name	Type	Power	ACC	PP
TM06	Toxic	Poison	—	85	10	TM32	Double Team	Normal	—	—	15
TM10	Hidden Power	Normal	—	100	15	TM35	Flamethrower	Fire	95	100	15
TM11	Sunny Day	Fire	—	—	5	TM36	Sludge Bomb	Poison	90	100	10
TM12	Taunt	Dark	—	100	20	TM42	Facade	Normal	70	100	20
TM17	Protect	Normal	—	—	10	TM43	Secret Power	Normal	70	100	20
TM18	Rain Dance	Water	—	—	5	TM44	Rest	Psychic	—	—	10
TM19	Giga Drain	Grass	60	100	5	TM45	Attract	Normal	—	100	15
TM21	Frustration	Normal	—	100	20	TM46	Thief	Dark	40	100	10
TM23	Iron Tail	Steel	100	75	15	TM49	Snatch	Dark	—	100	10
TM26	Earthquake	Ground	100	100	10	HM04	Strength	Normal	80	100	15
TM27	Return	Normal	—	100	20	HM06	Rock Smash	Fighting	20	100	15
TM28	Dig	Ground	60	100	10						

EGG MOVES*

Name	Type	Power	ACC	PP
Stockpile	Normal	—	—	10
Swallow	Normal	—	—	10
Spit Up	Normal	100	100	10
Body Slam	Normal	85	100	15

*Learned Via Breeding

MOVE TUTOR
FireRed/LeafGreen and Emerald Only

Body Slam*	Mimic	Substitute
Double-Edge		

Emerald Only

Endure*	Sleep Talk	Swagger
Fury Cutter	Snore*	Swift*
Mud-Slap*		

*Battle Frontier tutor move (*Emerald*)

337 Lunatone™

ROCK   PSYCHIC

GENERAL INFO
SPECIES: Meteorite Pokémon
HEIGHT: 3'03"
WEIGHT: 370 lbs.
ABILITY: Levitate

Lunatone is not affected by Ground-type moves.

STATS

HP, ATK, DEF, SP ATK, SP DEF, SPEED

EVOLUTIONS

DOES NOT EVOLVE

LOCATION[s]:

RUBY	Rarity: **None**	Trade from *Sapphire*	
SAPPHIRE	Rarity: **Common**	Meteor Falls	
FIRERED	Rarity: **None**	Trade from *Sapphire*	
LEAFGREEN	Rarity: **None**	Trade from *Sapphire*	
COLOSSEUM	Rarity: **None**	Trade from *Sapphire*	
EMERALD	Rarity: **None**	Trade from *Sapphire*	
XD	Rarity: **Only One**	Phenac City (Capture from Cipher Admin Snattle)	

MOVES

Level	Attack	Type	Power	ACC	PP	Level	Attack	Type	Power	ACC	PP
—	Tackle	Normal	35	95	35	25	Psywave	Psychic	—	80	15
—	Harden	Normal	—	—	30	31	Cosmic Power	Normal	—	—	20
7	Confusion	Psychic	50	100	25	37	Psychic	Psychic	90	100	10
13	Rock Throw	Rock	50	90	15	43	Future Sight	Psychic	80	90	15
19	Hypnosis	Psychic	—	60	20	49	Explosion	Normal	250	100	5

TM/HM

TM/HM#	Name	Type	Power	ACC	PP	TM/HM#	Name	Type	Power	ACC	PP
TM04	Calm Mind	Psychic	—	—	20	TM29	Psychic	Psychic	90	100	10
TM06	Toxic	Poison	—	85	10	TM30	Shadow Ball	Ghost	60	—	20
TM10	Hidden Power	Normal	—	100	15	TM32	Double Team	Normal	—	—	15
TM13	Ice Beam	Ice	95	100	10	TM33	Reflect	Psychic	—	—	20
TM15	Hyper Beam	Normal	150	90	5	TM37	Sandstorm	Rock	—	—	10
TM16	Light Screen	Psychic	—	—	30	TM39	Rock Tomb	Rock	50	80	10
TM17	Protect	Normal	—	—	10	TM42	Facade	Normal	70	100	20
TM18	Rain Dance	Water	—	—	5	TM43	Secret Power	Normal	70	100	20
TM20	Safeguard	Normal	—	—	25	TM44	Rest	Psychic	—	—	10
TM21	Frustration	Normal	—	100	20	TM48	Skill Swap	Psychic	—	100	10
TM26	Earthquake	Ground	100	100	10	HM05	Flash	Normal	—	70	20
TM27	Return	Normal	—	100	20						

EGG MOVES*

Name	Type	Power	ACC	PP
None				

*Learned Via Breeding

MOVE TUTOR

FireRed/LeafGreen and Emerald Only

Body Slam*	Substitute	Explosion
Double-Edge	Rock Slide*	Dream Eater*
Mimic		

Emerald Only

Defense Curl*	Rollout	Swagger
Endure*	Sleep Talk	Swift*
Psych Up*	Snore*	

*Battle Frontier tutor move (*Emerald*)

338 Solrock ™

ROCK | PSYCHIC

GENERAL INFO

SPECIES: Meteorite Pokémon
HEIGHT: 3'11"
WEIGHT: 340 lbs.
ABILITY: Levitate
Solrock is not affected by Ground-type moves.

STATS

EVOLUTIONS

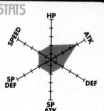

DOES NOT EVOLVE

LOCATION[s]:

RUBY	Rarity: **Common**	Meteor Falls
SAPPHIRE	Rarity: **None**	Trade from *Ruby/Emerald*
FIRERED	Rarity: **None**	Trade from *Ruby/Emerald*
LEAFGREEN	Rarity: **None**	Trade from *Ruby/Emerald*
COLOSSEUM	Rarity: **None**	Trade from *Ruby/Emerald*
EMERALD	Rarity: **Common**	Meteor Falls
XD	Rarity: **Only One**	Citadark Island (Capture from Cipher Admin Snattle)

MOVES

Level	Attack	Type	Power	ACC	PP
—	Harden	Normal	—	—	30
—	Tackle	Normal	35	95	35
7	Confusion	Psychic	50	100	25
13	Rock Throw	Rock	50	90	15
19	Fire Spin	Fire	15	70	15

Level	Attack	Type	Power	ACC	PP
25	Psywave	Psychic	—	80	15
31	Cosmic Power	Normal	—	—	20
37	Rock Slide	Rock	75	90	10
43	Solarbeam	Grass	120	100	10
49	Explosion	Normal	250	100	5

TM/HM

TM/HM#	Name	Type	Power	ACC	PP
TM04	Calm Mind	Psychic	—	—	20
TM06	Toxic	Poison	—	85	10
TM10	Hidden Power	Normal	—	100	15
TM11	Sunny Day	Normal	—	—	30
TM15	Hyper Beam	Normal	150	90	5
TM16	Light Screen	Psychic	—	—	30
TM17	Protect	Normal	—	—	10
TM20	Safeguard	Normal	—	—	25
TM21	Frustration	Normal	—	100	20
TM22	Solarbeam	Grass	120	100	10
TM26	Earthquake	Ground	100	100	10
TM27	Return	Normal	—	100	20
TM29	Psychic	Psychic	90	100	10

TM/HM#	Name	Type	Power	ACC	PP
TM30	Shadow Ball	Ghost	60	—	20
TM32	Double Team	Normal	—	—	15
TM33	Reflect	Psychic	—	—	20
TM35	Flamethrower	Fire	95	100	15
TM37	Sandstorm	Rock	—	—	10
TM38	Fire Blast	Fire	120	85	5
TM39	Rock Tomb	Rock	50	80	10
TM42	Facade	Normal	70	100	20
TM43	Secret Power	Normal	70	100	20
TM44	Rest	Psychic	—	—	10
TM48	Skill Swap	Psychic	—	100	10
TM50	Overheat	Fire	140	90	5
HM05	Flash	Normal	—	70	20

EGG MOVES*

Name	Type	Power	ACC	PP
None				

*Learned Via Breeding

MOVE TUTOR

FireRed/LeafGreen and Emerald Only

Body Slam*	Substitute	Explosion
Double-Edge	Rock Slide*	Dream Eater*
Mimic		

Emerald Only

Defense Curl*	Rollout	Swagger
Endure*	Sleep Talk	Swift*
Psych Up*	Snore*	

*Battle Frontier tutor move (*Emerald*)

339 Barboach™

| WATER | GROUND |

GENERAL INFO
SPECIES: Whiskers Pokémon
HEIGHT: 1'04"
WEIGHT: 4 lbs.
ABILITY: Oblivious
Barboach is not affected by the Attract condition.

STATS

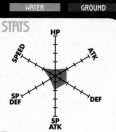

EVOLUTIONS

LV30

LOCATION[s]:

RUBY	Rarity: **Rare**	Victory Road, Routes 111, 114, 120
SAPPHIRE	Rarity: **Rare**	Victory Road, Routes 111, 114, 120
FIRERED	Rarity: **None**	Trade from *Ruby/Sapphire/Emerald*
LEAFGREEN	Rarity: **None**	Trade from *Ruby/Sapphire/Emerald*
COLOSSEUM	Rarity: **None**	Trade from *Ruby/Sapphire/Emerald*
EMERALD	Rarity: **Common**	Routes 111, 114, 120, Meteor Falls, Victory Road
XD	Rarity: **None**	Trade from *Ruby/Sapphire/Emerald*

MOVES

Level	Attack	Type	Power	ACC	PP	Level	Attack	Type	Power	ACC	PP
—	Mud-Slap	Ground	20	100	10	21	Amnesia	Psychic	—	—	20
6	Mud Sport	Ground	—	100	15	26	Rest	Psychic	—	—	10
6	Water Sport	Water	—	100	15	26	Snore	Normal	40	100	15
11	Water Gun	Water	40	100	25	31	Earthquake	Ground	100	100	10
16	Magnitude	Ground	—	100	30	36	Future Sight	Psychic	80	90	15
						41	Fissure	Ground	—	30	5

TM/HM

TM/HM#	Name	Type	Power	ACC	PP	TM/HM#	Name	Type	Power	ACC	PP
TM03	Water Pulse	Water	60	100	20	TM32	Double Team	Normal	—	—	15
TM06	Toxic	Poison	—	85	10	TM37	Sandstorm	Rock	—	—	10
TM07	Hail	Ice	—	—	10	TM39	Rock Tomb	Rock	50	80	10
TM10	Hidden Power	Normal	—	100	15	TM42	Facade	Normal	70	100	20
TM13	Ice Beam	Ice	95	100	10	TM43	Secret Power	Normal	70	100	20
TM14	Blizzard	Ice	120	70	5	TM44	Rest	Psychic	—	—	10
TM17	Protect	Normal	—	—	10	TM45	Attract	Normal	—	100	15
TM18	Rain Dance	Water	—	—	5	HM03	Surf	Water	95	100	15
TM21	Frustration	Normal	—	100	20	HM07	Waterfall	Water	80	100	15
TM26	Earthquake	Ground	100	100	10	HM08	Dive	Water	60	100	10
TM27	Return	Normal	—	100	20						

EGG MOVES*

Name	Type	Power	ACC	PP
Thrash	Normal	90	100	20
Whirlpool	Water	15	70	15
Spark	Electric	65	100	20

*Learned Via Breeding

MOVE TUTOR
FireRed/LeafGreen and Emerald Only

Double-Edge	Mimic	Substitute

Emerald Only

Endure*	Mud-Slap*	Snore*
Icy Wind*	Sleep Talk	Swagger

*Battle Frontier tutor move (*Emerald*)

Whiscash™

WATER | GROUND

GENERAL INFO

SPECIES: Whiskers Pokémon
HEIGHT: 2'11"
WEIGHT: 52 lbs.
ABILITY: Oblivious

Whiscash is not affected by the Attract condition.

STATS

EVOLUTIONS

LV30

LOCATION(S):

RUBY	Rarity: **Rare**	Victory Road, Meteor Falls
SAPPHIRE	Rarity: **Rare**	Victory Road, Meteor Falls
FIRERED	Rarity: **None**	Trade from *Ruby/Sapphire/Emerald*
LEAFGREEN	Rarity: **None**	Trade from *Ruby/Sapphire/Emerald*
COLOSSEUM	Rarity: **None**	Trade from *Ruby/Sapphire/Emerald*
EMERALD	Rarity: **Common**	Evolve Barboach, Meteor Falls, Victory Road
XD	Rarity: **None**	Trade from *Ruby/Sapphire*

MOVES

Level	Attack	Type	Power	ACC	PP	Level	Attack	Type	Power	ACC	PP
—	Tickle	Normal	—	100	20	21	Amnesia	Psychic	—	—	20
—	Mud-Slap	Ground	20	100	10	26	Rest	Psychic	—	—	10
—	Mud Sport	Ground	—	100	15	26	Snore	Normal	40	100	15
—	Water Sport	Water	—	100	15	36	Earthquake	Ground	100	100	10
11	Water Gun	Water	40	100	25	46	Future Sight	Psychic	80	90	15
16	Magnitude	Ground	—	100	30	56	Fissure	Ground	—	30	5

TM/HM

TM/HM#	Name	Type	Power	ACC	PP	TM/HM#	Name	Type	Power	ACC	PP
TM03	Water Pulse	Water	60	100	20	TM32	Double Team	Normal	—	—	15
TM06	Toxic	Poison	—	85	10	TM37	Sandstorm	Rock	—	—	10
TM07	Hail	Ice	—	—	10	TM39	Rock Tomb	Rock	50	80	10
TM10	Hidden Power	Normal	—	100	15	TM42	Facade	Normal	70	100	20
TM13	Ice Beam	Ice	95	100	10	TM43	Secret Power	Normal	70	100	20
TM14	Blizzard	Ice	120	70	5	TM44	Rest	Psychic	—	—	10
TM15	Hyper Beam	Normal	150	90	5	TM45	Attract	Normal	—	100	15
TM17	Protect	Normal	—	—	10	HM03	Surf	Water	95	100	15
TM18	Rain Dance	Water	—	—	5	HM04	Strength	Normal	80	100	15
TM21	Frustration	Normal	—	100	20	HM06	Rock Smash	Fighting	20	100	15
TM26	Earthquake	Ground	100	100	10	HM07	Waterfall	Water	80	100	15
TM27	Return	Normal	—	100	20	HM08	Dive	Water	60	100	10

MOVE TUTOR

FireRed/LeafGreen and Emerald Only

Double-Edge	Substitute	Rock Slide*
Mimic		

Emerald Only

Endure*	Mud-Slap*	Snore*
Icy Wind*	Sleep Talk	Swagger

*Battle Frontier tutor move (*Emerald*)

341 Corphish™

WATER

GENERAL INFO

SPECIES: Ruffian Pokémon
HEIGHT: 2'00"
WEIGHT: 25 lbs.
ABILITY 1: Shell Armor
Prevents the opponent Pokémon from scoring a critical hit.
ABILITY 2: Hyper Cutter
Corphish's attack power cannot be lowered.

STATS

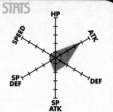

EVOLUTIONS

LV30

LOCATION[s]:

RUBY	Rarity: **Common**	Route 102, Route 117, Petalburg City
SAPPHIRE	Rarity: **Common**	Route 102, Route 117, Petalburg City
FIRERED	Rarity: **None**	Trade from *Ruby/Sapphire/Emerald*
LEAFGREEN	Rarity: **None**	Trade from *Ruby/Sapphire/Emerald*
COLOSSEUM	Rarity: **None**	Trade from *Ruby/Sapphire/Emerald*
EMERALD	Rarity: **Common**	Route 102, Route 117
XD	Rarity: **None**	Trade from *Ruby/Sapphire/Emerald*

MOVES

Level	Attack	Type	Power	ACC	PP
—	Bubble	Water	20	100	30
7	Harden	Normal	—	—	30
10	Vicegrip	Normal	55	100	30
13	Leer	Normal	—	100	30
19	Bubblebeam	Water	65	100	20
22	Protect	Normal	—	—	10

Level	Attack	Type	Power	ACC	PP
25	Knock Off	Dark	20	100	20
31	Taunt	Dark	—	100	20
34	Crabhammer	Water	90	85	10
37	Swords Dance	Normal	—	—	30
43	Crunch*	Dark	80	100	15
46	Guillotine	Normal	—	30	5

* Not Available in *Emerald*

TM/HM

TM/HM#	Name	Type	Power	ACC	PP
TM03	Water Pulse	Water	60	100	20
TM06	Toxic	Poison	—	85	10
TM07	Hail	Ice	—	—	10
TM10	Hidden Power	Normal	—	100	15
TM12	Taunt	Dark	—	100	20
TM13	Ice Beam	Ice	95	100	10
TM14	Blizzard	Ice	120	70	5
TM17	Protect	Normal	—	—	10
TM18	Rain Dance	Water	—	—	5
TM21	Frustration	Normal	—	100	20
TM27	Return	Normal	—	100	20
TM28	Dig	Ground	60	100	10
TM31	Brick Break	Fighting	75	100	15

TM/HM#	Name	Type	Power	ACC	PP
TM32	Double Team	Normal	—	—	15
TM36	Sludge Bomb	Poison	90	100	10
TM39	Rock Tomb	Rock	50	80	10
TM40	Aerial Ace	Flying	60	—	20
TM42	Facade	Normal	70	100	20
TM43	Secret Power	Normal	70	100	20
TM44	Rest	Psychic	—	—	10
TM45	Attract	Normal	—	100	15
HM01	Cut	Normal	50	95	30
HM03	Surf	Water	95	100	15
HM04	Strength	Normal	80	100	15
HM06	Rock Smash	Fighting	20	100	15
HM07	Waterfall	Water	80	100	15

EGG MOVES*

Name	Type	Power	ACC	PP
Mud Sport	Ground	—	100	15
Endeavor	Normal	—	100	5
Body Slam	Normal	85	100	15
Ancientpower	Rock	60	100	5

*Learned Via Breeding

MOVE TUTOR

FireRed/LeafGreen and Emerald Only

Body Slam*	Mimic	Counter*
Double-Edge	Substitute	Swords Dance*

Emerald Only

Endure*	Mud-Slap*	Snore*
Fury Cutter	Sleep Talk	Swagger
Icy Wind*		

*Battle Frontier tutor move (*Emerald*)

342 Crawdaunt™

WATER | DARK

GENERAL INFO
SPECIES: Rogue Pokémon
HEIGHT: 3'07"
WEIGHT: 72 lbs.
ABILITY 1: Shell Armor
Prevents the opponent Pokémon from scoring a critical hit.
ABILITY 2: Hyper Cutter
Crawdaunt's attack power cannot be lowered.

STATS

HP / SPEED / ATK / SP DEF / DEF / SP ATK

EVOLUTIONS

LV30

LOCATION(S):

RUBY	Rarity: **Evolve**	Evolve Corphish
SAPPHIRE	Rarity: **Evolve**	Evolve Corphish
FIRERED	Rarity: **None**	Trade from *Ruby/Sapphire/Emerald*
LEAFGREEN	Rarity: **None**	Trade from *Ruby/Sapphire/Emerald*
COLOSSEUM	Rarity: **None**	Trade from *Ruby/Sapphire/Emerald*
EMERALD	Rarity: **Evolve**	Evolve Corphish
XD	Rarity: **None**	Trade from *Ruby/Sapphire/Emerald*

MOVES

Level	Attack	Type	Power	ACC	PP	Level	Attack	Type	Power	ACC	PP
—	Bubble	Water	20	100	30	25	Knock Off	Dark	20	100	20
—	Harden	Normal	—	—	30	33	Taunt	Dark	—	100	20
—	Vicegrip	Normal	55	100	30	38	Crabhammer	Water	90	85	10
—	Leer	Normal	—	100	30	43	Swords Dance	Normal	—	—	30
19	Bubblebeam	Water	65	100	20	51	Crunch	Dark	80	100	15
22	Protect	Normal	—	—	10	56	Guillotine	Normal	—	30	5

TM/HM

TM/HM#	Name	Type	Power	ACC	PP	TM/HM#	Name	Type	Power	ACC	PP
TM03	Water Pulse	Water	60	100	20	TM32	Double Team	Normal	—	—	15
TM06	Toxic	Poison	—	85	10	TM36	Sludge Bomb	Poison	90	100	10
TM07	Hail	Ice	—	—	10	TM39	Rock Tomb	Rock	50	80	10
TM10	Hidden Power	Normal	—	100	15	TM40	Aerial Ace	Flying	60	—	20
TM12	Taunt	Dark	—	100	20	TM42	Facade	Normal	70	100	20
TM13	Ice Beam	Ice	95	100	10	TM43	Secret Power	Normal	70	100	20
TM14	Blizzard	Ice	120	70	5	TM44	Rest	Psychic	—	—	10
TM15	Hyper Beam	Normal	150	90	5	TM45	Attract	Normal	—	100	15
TM17	Protect	Normal	—	—	10	HM01	Cut	Normal	50	95	30
TM18	Rain Dance	Water	—	—	5	HM03	Surf	Water	95	100	15
TM21	Frustration	Normal	—	100	20	HM04	Strength	Normal	80	100	15
TM27	Return	Normal	—	100	20	HM06	Rock Smash	Fighting	20	100	15
TM28	Dig	Ground	60	100	10	HM07	Waterfall	Water	80	100	15
TM31	Brick Break	Fighting	75	100	15	HM08	Dive	Water	60	100	10

MOVE TUTOR

FireRed/LeafGreen and Emerald Only

Body Slam*	Mimic	Counter*	
Double-Edge	Substitute	Swords Dance*	

*Battle Frontier tutor move (*Emerald*)

Emerald Only

Endure*	Mud-Slap*	Swagger
Fury Cutter	Sleep Talk	Swift*
Icy Wind*	Snore*	

343 Baltoy™

GROUND   PSYCHIC

GENERAL INFO
SPECIES: Clay Doll Pokémon
HEIGHT: 1'08"
WEIGHT: 47 lbs.
ABILITY: Levitate
Baltoy is not affected by Ground-type moves.

STATS

EVOLUTIONS

LV36

LOCATION(s):

RUBY	Rarity: **Rare**	Route 111
SAPPHIRE	Rarity: **Rare**	Route 111
FIRERED	Rarity: **None**	Trade from *Ruby/Sapphire/Emerald*
LEAFGREEN	Rarity: **None**	Trade from *Ruby/Sapphire/Emerald*
COLOSSEUM	Rarity: **None**	Trade from *Ruby/Sapphire/Emerald*
EMERALD	Rarity: **Rare**	Route 111
XD	Rarity: **Only One**	Cipher Lab (Capture from Cipher Peon Browsix)

MOVES

Level	Attack	Type	Power	ACC	PP	Level	Attack	Type	Power	ACC	PP
—	Confusion	Psychic	50	100	25	15	Rock Tomb	Rock	50	80	10
3	Harden	Normal	—	—	30	19	Selfdestruct	Normal	200	100	5
5	Rapid Spin	Normal	20	100	40	25	Ancientpower	Rock	60	100	5
7	Mud-Slap	Ground	20	100	10	31	Sandstorm	Rock	—	—	10
11	Psybeam	Psychic	65	100	20	37	Cosmic Power	Normal	—	—	20
						45	Explosion	Normal	250	100	5

TM/HM

TM/HM#	Name	Type	Power	ACC	PP	TM/HM#	Name	Type	Power	ACC	PP
TM06	Toxic	Poison	—	85	10	TM29	Psychic	Psychic	90	100	10
TM10	Hidden Power	Normal	—	100	15	TM30	Shadow Ball	Ghost	60	—	20
TM11	Sunny Day	Fire	—	—	5	TM32	Double Team	Normal	—	—	15
TM13	Ice Beam	Ice	95	100	10	TM33	Reflect	Psychic	—	—	20
TM16	Light Screen	Psychic	—	—	30	TM37	Sandstorm	Rock	—	—	10
TM17	Protect	Normal	—	—	10	TM39	Rock Tomb	Rock	50	80	10
TM18	Rain Dance	Water	—	—	5	TM42	Facade	Normal	70	100	20
TM21	Frustration	Normal	—	100	20	TM43	Secret Power	Normal	70	100	20
TM22	Solarbeam	Grass	120	100	10	TM44	Rest	Psychic	—	—	10
TM26	Earthquake	Ground	100	100	10	TM48	Skill Swap	Psychic	—	100	10
TM27	Return	Normal	—	100	20	HM05	Flash	Normal	—	70	20
TM28	Dig	Ground	60	100	10						

EGG MOVES*

Name	Type	Power	ACC	PP
None				

*Learned Via Breeding

MOVE TUTOR
FireRed/LeafGreen and Emerald Only

Emerald Only

Double-Edge	Substitute	Rock Slide*		Endure*	Psych Up*	Snore*
Mimic	Dream Eater*	Explosion		Mud-Slap*	Sleep Talk	Swagger

*Battle Frontier tutor move (*Emerald*)

344 Claydol™

GROUND　PSYCHIC

GENERAL INFO

SPECIES: Clay Doll Pokémon
HEIGHT: 4'11"
WEIGHT: 238 lbs.
ABILITY: Levitate

Claydol is not affected by Ground-type moves.

STATS

EVOLUTIONS

LV36

LOCATION[s]:

Game	Rarity	Location
RUBY	**Common**	Evolve Baltoy, Sky Pillar
SAPPHIRE	**Common**	Evolve Baltoy, Sky Pillar
FIRERED	**None**	Trade from *Ruby/Sapphire/Emerald*
LEAFGREEN	**None**	Trade from *Ruby/Sapphire/Emerald*
COLOSSEUM	**None**	Trade from *Ruby/Sapphire/Emerald*
EMERALD	**Rare**	Evolve Baltoy, Sky Pillar
XD	**Evolve**	Evolve Baltoy

MOVES

Level	Attack	Type	Power	ACC	PP
—	Teleport	Psychic	—	—	20
—	Confusion	Psychic	50	100	25
—	Harden	Normal	—	—	30
—	Rapid Spin	Normal	20	100	40
7	Mud-Slap	Ground	20	100	10
11	Psybeam	Psychic	65	100	20
15	Rock Tomb	Rock	50	80	10
19	Selfdestruct	Normal	200	100	5
25	Ancientpower	Rock	60	100	5
31	Sandstorm	Rock	—	—	10
36	Hyper Beam	Normal	150	90	5
42	Cosmic Power	Normal	—	—	20
55	Explosion	Normal	250	100	5

TM/HM

TM/HM#	Name	Type	Power	ACC	PP
TM06	Toxic	Poison	—	85	10
TM10	Hidden Power	Normal	—	100	15
TM11	Sunny Day	Fire	—	—	5
TM13	Ice Beam	Ice	95	100	10
TM15	Hyper Beam	Normal	150	90	5
TM16	Light Screen	Psychic	—	—	30
TM17	Protect	Normal	—	—	10
TM18	Rain Dance	Water	—	—	5
TM21	Frustration	Normal	—	100	20
TM22	Solarbeam	Grass	120	100	10
TM26	Earthquake	Ground	100	100	10
TM27	Return	Normal	—	100	20
TM28	Dig	Ground	60	100	10
TM29	Psychic	Psychic	90	100	10
TM30	Shadow Ball	Ghost	60	—	20
TM32	Double Team	Normal	—	—	15
TM33	Reflect	Psychic	—	—	20
TM37	Sandstorm	Rock	—	—	10
TM39	Rock Tomb	Rock	50	80	10
TM42	Facade	Normal	70	100	20
TM43	Secret Power	Normal	70	100	20
TM44	Rest	Psychic	—	—	10
TM48	Skill Swap	Psychic	—	100	10
HM04	Strength	Normal	80	100	15
HM05	Flash	Normal	—	70	20
HM06	Rock Smash	Fighting	20	100	15

MOVE TUTOR

FireRed/LeafGreen and Emerald Only

Double-Edge	Substitute	Rock Slide*
Mimic	Dream Eater*	Explosion

Emerald Only

Endure*	Psych Up*	Snore*
Mud-Slap*	Sleep Talk	Swagger

*Battle Frontier tutor move (*Emerald*)

345 Lileep™

ROCK   GRASS

GENERAL INFO

SPECIES: Sea Lily Pokémon
HEIGHT: 3'03"
WEIGHT: 52 lbs.
ABILITY: Suction Cups
Lileep cannot be switched out of the battle by the Roar or Whirlwind moves.

STATS

EVOLUTIONS

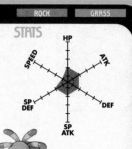

LV40

LOCATION[s]:

RUBY	Rarity: **Only One**	Obtained on Route 111
SAPPHIRE	Rarity: **Only One**	Obtained on Route 111
FIRERED	Rarity: **None**	Trade from *Ruby/Sapphire/Emerald*
LEAFGREEN	Rarity: **None**	Trade from *Ruby/Sapphire/Emerald*
COLOSSEUM	Rarity: **None**	Trade from *Ruby/Sapphire/Emerald*
EMERALD	Rarity: **Only One**	Route 111 (Root Fossil—bring to Devon Corp. in Rustboro)
XD	Rarity: **None**	Trade from *Ruby/Sapphire/Emerald*

MOVES

Level	Attack	Type	Power	ACC	PP	Level	Attack	Type	Power	ACC	PP
—	Astonish	Ghost	30	100	15	36	Amnesia	Psychic	—	—	20
8	Constrict	Normal	10	100	35	43	Ancientpower	Rock	60	100	5
15	Acid	Poison	40	100	30	50	Stockpile	Normal	—	—	10
22	Ingrain	Grass	—	100	20	50	Spit Up	Normal	100	100	10
29	Confuse Ray	Ghost	—	100	10	50	Swallow	Normal	—	—	10

TM/HM

TM/HM#	Name	Type	Power	ACC	PP	TM/HM#	Name	Type	Power	ACC	PP
TM06	Toxic	Poison	—	85	10	TM27	Return	Normal	—	100	20
TM09	Bullet Seed	Grass	10	100	30	TM32	Double Team	Normal	—	—	15
TM10	Hidden Power	Normal	—	100	15	TM36	Sludge Bomb	Poison	90	100	10
TM11	Sunny Day	Fire	—	—	5	TM37	Sandstorm	Rock	—	—	10
TM17	Protect	Normal	—	—	10	TM42	Facade	Normal	70	100	20
TM19	Giga Drain	Grass	60	100	5	TM43	Secret Power	Normal	70	100	20
TM21	Frustration	Normal	—	100	20	TM44	Rest	Psychic	—	—	10
TM22	Solarbeam	Grass	120	100	10	TM45	Attract	Normal	—	100	15

EGG MOVES*

Name	Type	Power	ACC	PP
Barrier	Psychic	—	—	30
Recover	Normal	—	—	20
Mirror Coat	Psychic	—	100	20
Rock Slide	Rock	75	90	10

*Learned Via Breeding

MOVE TUTOR

FireRed/LeafGreen and Emerald Only

Body Slam*	Mimic	Rock Slide*
Double-Edge	Substitute	

Emerald Only

Endure*	Psych Up*	Snore*
Mud-Slap*	Sleep Talk	Swagger

*Battle Frontier tutor move (*Emerald*)

346 Cradily™

ROCK | GRASS

GENERAL INFO

SPECIES: Barnacle Pokémon
HEIGHT: 4'11"
WEIGHT: 133 lbs.
ABILITY: Suction Cups

Cradily cannot be switched out of the battle by the Roar or Whirlwind moves.

STATS

EVOLUTIONS

LV40

LOCATION(s):

RUBY	Rarity: **None**	Evolve Lileep
SAPPHIRE	Rarity: **None**	Evolve Lileep
FIRERED	Rarity: **None**	Trade from *Ruby/Sapphire/Emerald*
LEAFGREEN	Rarity: **None**	Trade from *Ruby/Sapphire/Emerald*
COLOSSEUM	Rarity: **None**	Trade from *Ruby/Sapphire/Emerald*
EMERALD	Rarity: **Evolve**	Evolve Lileep
XD	Rarity: **None**	Trade from *Ruby/Sapphire/Emerald*

MOVES

Level	Attack	Type	Power	ACC	PP	Level	Attack	Type	Power	ACC	PP
—	Astonish	Ghost	30	100	15	36	Amnesia	Psychic	—	—	20
—	Constrict	Normal	10	100	35	48	Ancientpower	Rock	60	100	5
—	Acid	Poison	40	100	30	60	Stockpile	Normal	—	—	10
—	Ingrain	Grass	—	100	20	60	Spit Up	Normal	100	100	10
29	Confuse Ray	Ghost	—	100	10	60	Swallow	Normal	—	—	10

TM/HM

TM/HM#	Name	Type	Power	ACC	PP	TM/HM#	Name	Type	Power	ACC	PP
TM06	Toxic	Poison	—	85	10	TM32	Double Team	Normal	—	—	15
TM09	Bullet Seed	Grass	10	100	30	TM36	Sludge Bomb	Poison	90	100	10
TM10	Hidden Power	Normal	—	100	15	TM37	Sandstorm	Rock	—	—	10
TM11	Sunny Day	Fire	—	—	5	TM39	Rock Tomb	Rock	50	80	10
TM15	Hyper Beam	Normal	150	90	5	TM42	Facade	Normal	70	100	20
TM17	Protect	Normal	—	—	10	TM43	Secret Power	Normal	70	100	20
TM19	Giga Drain	Grass	60	100	5	TM44	Rest	Psychic	—	—	10
TM21	Frustration	Normal	—	100	20	TM45	Attract	Normal	—	100	15
TM22	Solarbeam	Grass	120	100	10	HM04	Strength	Normal	80	100	15
TM26	Earthquake	Ground	100	100	10	HM06	Rock Smash	Fighting	20	100	15
TM27	Return	Normal	—	100	20						

MOVE TUTOR
FireRed/LeafGreen and Emerald Only

Body Slam*	Mimic	Rock Slide*
Double-Edge	Substitute	

Emerald Only

Endure*	Psych Up*	Snore*
Mud-Slap*	Sleep Talk	Swagger

*Battle Frontier tutor move (*Emerald*)

347 Anorith™

ROCK | BUG

GENERAL INFO

SPECIES: Old Shrimp Pokémon
HEIGHT: 2'04"
WEIGHT: 28 lbs.
ABILITY: Battle Armor
Prevents the opponent Pokémon from scoring a critical hit.

STATS

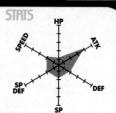

EVOLUTIONS

LV40

LOCATION(s):

RUBY	Rarity: **Only One**	Route 111 (Claw Fossil—bring to Devon Corp. in Rustboro)
SAPPHIRE	Rarity: **Only One**	Route 111 (Claw Fossil—bring to Devon Corp. in Rustboro)
FIRERED	Rarity: **None**	Trade from *Ruby/Sapphire/Emerald*
LEAFGREEN	Rarity: **None**	Trade from *Ruby/Sapphire/Emerald*
COLOSSEUM	Rarity: **None**	Trade from *Ruby/Sapphire/Emerald*
EMERALD	Rarity: **Only One**	Route 111 (Claw Fossil—bring to Devon Corp. in Rustboro)
XD	Rarity: **None**	Trade from *Ruby/Sapphire/Emerald*

MOVES

Level	Attack	Type	Power	ACC	PP	Level	Attack	Type	Power	ACC	PP
—	Scratch	Normal	40	100	35	31	Protect	Normal	—	—	10
7	Harden	Normal	—	—	30	37	Ancientpower	Rock	60	100	5
13	Mud Sport	Ground	—	100	15	43	Fury Cutter	Bug	10	95	20
19	Water Gun	Water	40	100	25	49	Slash	Normal	70	100	20
25	Metal Claw	Steel	50	95	35	55	Rock Blast	Rock	25	80	10

TM/HM

TM/HM#	Name	Type	Power	ACC	PP	TM/HM#	Name	Type	Power	ACC	PP
TM03	Water Pulse	Water	60	100	20	TM37	Sandstorm	Rock	—	—	10
TM06	Toxic	Poison	—	85	10	TM39	Rock Tomb	Rock	50	80	10
TM10	Hidden Power	Normal	—	100	15	TM40	Aerial Ace	Flying	60	—	20
TM11	Sunny Day	Fire	—	—	5	TM42	Facade	Normal	70	100	20
TM17	Protect	Normal	—	—	10	TM43	Secret Power	Normal	70	100	20
TM21	Frustration	Normal	—	100	20	TM44	Rest	Psychic	—	—	10
TM27	Return	Normal	—	100	20	TM45	Attract	Normal	—	100	15
TM28	Dig	Ground	60	100	10	HM01	Cut	Normal	50	95	30
TM31	Brick Break	Fighting	75	100	15	HM06	Rock Smash	Fighting	20	100	15
TM32	Double Team	Normal	—	—	15						

EGG MOVES*

Name	Type	Power	ACC	PP
Knock Off	Dark	20	100	20
Rock Slide	Rock	75	90	10
Rapid Spin	Normal	20	100	40
Swords Dance	Normal	—	—	30

*Learned Via Breeding

MOVE TUTOR
FireRed/LeafGreen and Emerald Only

Body Slam*	Mimic	Rock Slide*
Double-Edge	Substitute	Swords Dance*

Emerald Only

Endure*	Mud-Slap*	Snore*
Fury Cutter	Sleep Talk	Swagger

*Battle Frontier tutor move (*Emerald*)

348 Armaldo™

ROCK | BUG

GENERAL INFO
SPECIES: Plate Pokémon
HEIGHT: 4'11"
WEIGHT: 150 lbs.
ABILITY: Battle Armor
Prevents the opponent Pokémon from scoring a critical hit.

STATS

EVOLUTIONS

LV40

LOCATION[s]:

RUBY	Rarity: Evolve	Evolve Anorith
SAPPHIRE	Rarity: Evolve	Evolve Anorith
FIRERED	Rarity: None	Trade from *Ruby/Sapphire/Emerald*
LEAFGREEN	Rarity: None	Trade from *Ruby/Sapphire/Emerald*
COLOSSEUM	Rarity: None	Trade from *Ruby/Sapphire/Emerald*
EMERALD	Rarity: Evolve	Evolve Anorith
XD	Rarity: None	Trade from *Ruby/Sapphire/Emerald*

MOVES

Level	Attack	Type	Power	ACC	PP		Level	Attack	Type	Power	ACC	PP
—	Scratch	Normal	40	100	35		31	Protect	Normal	—	—	10
—	Harden	Normal	—	—	30		37	Ancientpower	Rock	60	100	5
—	Mud Sport	Ground	—	100	15		46	Fury Cutter	Bug	10	95	20
—	Water Gun	Water	40	100	25		55	Slash	Normal	70	100	20
25	Metal Claw	Steel	50	95	35		64	Rock Blast	Rock	25	80	10

TM/HM

TM/HM#	Name	Type	Power	ACC	PP		TM/HM#	Name	Type	Power	ACC	PP
TM03	Water Pulse	Water	60	100	20		TM32	Double Team	Normal	—	—	15
TM06	Toxic	Poison	—	85	10		TM37	Sandstorm	Rock	—	—	10
TM10	Hidden Power	Normal	—	100	15		TM39	Rock Tomb	Rock	50	80	10
TM11	Sunny Day	Fire	—	—	5		TM40	Aerial Ace	Flying	60	—	20
TM15	Hyper Beam	Normal	150	90	5		TM42	Facade	Normal	70	100	20
TM17	Protect	Normal	—	—	10		TM43	Secret Power	Normal	70	100	20
TM21	Frustration	Normal	—	100	20		TM44	Rest	Psychic	—	—	10
TM23	Iron Tail	Steel	100	75	15		TM45	Attract	Normal	—	100	15
TM26	Earthquake	Ground	100	100	10		HM01	Cut	Normal	50	95	30
TM27	Return	Normal	—	100	20		HM04	Strength	Normal	80	100	15
TM28	Dig	Ground	60	100	10		HM06	Rock Smash	Fighting	20	100	15
TM31	Brick Break	Fighting	75	100	15							

MOVE TUTOR
FireRed/LeafGreen and Emerald Only

Body Slam*	Substitute	Swords Dance*
Double-Edge	Rock Slide*	Seismic Toss*
Mimic		

Emerald Only

| Endure* | Mud-Slap* | Snore* |
| Fury Cutter | Sleep Talk | Swagger |

*Battle Frontier tutor move (*Emerald*)

349 Feebas™

WATER

GENERAL INFO

SPECIES: Fish Pokémon
HEIGHT: 2'00"
WEIGHT: 16 lbs.
ABILITY: Swift Swim
Doubles Feebas's Speed when it's raining.

STATS

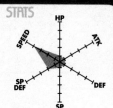

EVOLUTIONS

MAX BEAUTY

LOCATION(s):

RUBY	Rarity: **Rare**	Route 119 (Six random spots to fish from, depending on the current Trendy Phrase in Dewford Town)
SAPPHIRE	Rarity: **Rare**	Route 119 (Six random spots to fish from, depending on the current Trendy Phrase in Dewford Town)
FIRERED	Rarity: **None**	Trade from *Ruby/Sapphire/Emerald*
LEAFGREEN	Rarity: **None**	Trade from *Ruby/Sapphire/Emerald*
COLOSSEUM	Rarity: **None**	Trade from *Ruby/Sapphire/Emerald*
EMERALD	Rarity: **Rare**	Route 119 (Six random spots to fish from, depending on the current Trendy Phrase in Dewford Town)
XD	Rarity: **None**	Trade from *Ruby/Sapphire/Emerald*

MOVES

Level	Attack	Type	Power	ACC	PP
—	Splash	Normal	—	—	40
15	Tackle	Normal	35	95	35
30	Flail	Normal	—	100	15

TM/HM

TM/HM#	Name	Type	Power	ACC	PP
TM03	Water Pulse	Water	60	100	20
TM06	Toxic	Poison	—	85	10
TM07	Hail	Ice	—	—	10
TM10	Hidden Power	Normal	—	100	15
TM13	Ice Beam	Ice	95	100	10
TM14	Blizzard	Ice	120	70	5
TM17	Protect	Normal	—	—	10
TM18	Rain Dance	Water	—	—	5
TM21	Frustration	Normal	—	100	20

TM/HM#	Name	Type	Power	ACC	PP
TM27	Return	Normal	—	100	20
TM32	Double Team	Normal	—	—	15
TM42	Facade	Normal	70	100	20
TM43	Secret Power	Normal	70	100	20
TM44	Rest	Psychic	—	—	10
TM45	Attract	Normal	—	100	15
HM03	Surf	Water	95	100	15
HM07	Waterfall	Water	80	100	15
HM08	Dive	Water	60	100	10

EGG MOVES*

Name	Type	Power	ACC	PP
Mirror Coat	Psychic	—	100	20
Dragonbreath	Dragon	60	100	20
Mud Sport	Ground	—	100	15
Hypnosis	Psychic	—	60	20
Light Screen	Psychic	—	—	30
Confuse Ray	Ghost	—	100	10

*Learned Via Breeding

MOVE TUTOR
FireRed/LeafGreen and Emerald Only

Body Slam*	Mimic	Substitute
Double-Edge		

Emerald Only

Endure*	Sleep Talk	Swagger
Icy Wind*	Snore*	Swift*
Mud-Slap*		

*Battle Frontier tutor move (*Emerald*)

350 Milotic™

WATER

GENERAL INFO
SPECIES: Tender Pokémon
HEIGHT: 20'04"
WEIGHT: 357 lbs.
ABILITY: Marvel Scale
Marvel Scale multiplies Defense by 1.5 when Milotic has a status condition.

STATS

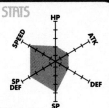

EVOLUTIONS

MAX BEAUTY

LOCATION[s]:

RUBY	Rarity: **Evolve**	Evolve Feebas
SAPPHIRE	Rarity: **Evolve**	Evolve Feebas
FIRERED	Rarity: **None**	Trade from *Ruby/Sapphire/Emerald*
LEAFGREEN	Rarity: **None**	Trade from *Ruby/Sapphire/Emerald*
COLOSSEUM	Rarity: **None**	Trade from *Ruby/Sapphire/Emerald*
EMERALD	Rarity: **Evolve**	Evolve Feebas
XD	Rarity: **None**	Trade from *Ruby/Sapphire/Emerald*

MOVES

Level	Attack	Type	Power	ACC	PP	Level	Attack	Type	Power	ACC	PP
—	Water Gun	Water	40	100	25	25	Twister	Dragon	40	100	20
5	Wrap	Normal	15	85	20	30	Recover	Normal	—	—	20
10	Water Sport	Water	—	100	15	35	Rain Dance	Water	—	—	5
15	Refresh	Normal	—	100	20	40	Hydro Pump	Water	120	80	5
20	Water Pulse	Water	60	100	20	45	Attract	Normal	—	100	15
						50	Safeguard	Normal	—	—	25

TM/HM

TM/HM#	Name	Type	Power	ACC	PP	TM/HM#	Name	Type	Power	ACC	PP
TM03	Water Pulse	Water	60	100	20	TM23	Iron Tail	Steel	100	75	15
TM06	Toxic	Poison	—	85	10	TM27	Return	Normal	—	100	20
TM07	Hail	Ice	—	—	10	TM32	Double Team	Normal	—	—	15
TM10	Hidden Power	Normal	—	100	15	TM42	Facade	Normal	70	100	20
TM13	Ice Beam	Ice	95	100	10	TM43	Secret Power	Normal	70	100	20
TM14	Blizzard	Ice	120	70	5	TM44	Rest	Psychic	—	—	10
TM15	Hyper Beam	Normal	150	90	5	TM45	Attract	Normal	—	100	15
TM17	Protect	Normal	—	—	10	HM03	Surf	Water	95	100	15
TM18	Rain Dance	Water	—	—	5	HM07	Waterfall	Water	80	100	15
TM20	Safeguard	Normal	—	—	25	HM08	Dive	Water	60	100	10
TM21	Frustration	Normal	—	100	20						

MOVE TUTOR
FireRed/LeafGreen and Emerald Only

Body Slam*	Mimic	Substitute
Double-Edge		

*Battle Frontier tutor move (*Emerald*)

Emerald Only

Endure*	Psych Up*	Swagger
Icy Wind*	Sleep Talk	Swift*
Mud-Slap*	Snore*	

351 Castform™

NORMAL

GENERAL INFO

SPECIES: Weather Pokémon
HEIGHT: 1'00"
WEIGHT: 2 lbs.
ABILITY: Forecast
Changes Castform's type and shape depending upon the weather.

STATS

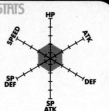

EVOLUTIONS

DOES NOT EVOLVE

LOCATION[s]:

RUBY	Rarity: **Only One**	Route 119 (Weather Institute)
SAPPHIRE	Rarity: **Only One**	Route 119 (Weather Institute)
FIRERED	Rarity: **None**	Trade from *Ruby/Sapphire/Emerald*
LEAFGREEN	Rarity: **None**	Trade from *Ruby/Sapphire/Emerald*
COLOSSEUM	Rarity: **None**	Trade from *Ruby/Sapphire/Emerald*
EMERALD	Rarity: **Only One**	Route 119 (Weather Institute)
XD	Rarity: **None**	Trade from *Ruby/Sapphire/Emerald*

MOVES

Level	Attack	Type	Power	ACC	PP	Level	Attack	Type	Power	ACC	PP
—	Tackle	Normal	35	95	35	20	Rain Dance	Water	—	—	5
10	Water Gun	Water	40	100	25	20	Sunny Day	Fire	—	—	5
10	Ember	Fire	40	100	25	20	Hail	Ice	—	—	10
10	Powder Snow	Ice	40	100	25	30	Weather Ball	Normal	50	100	10

TM/HM

TM/HM#	Name	Type	Power	ACC	PP	TM/HM#	Name	Type	Power	ACC	PP
TM03	Water Pulse	Water	60	100	20	TM27	Return	Normal	—	100	20
TM06	Toxic	Poison	—	85	10	TM30	Shadow Ball	Ghost	60	—	20
TM07	Hail	Ice	—	—	10	TM32	Double Team	Normal	—	—	15
TM10	Hidden Power	Normal	—	100	15	TM34	Shock Wave	Electric	60	—	20
TM11	Sunny Day	Fire	—	—	5	TM35	Flamethrower	Fire	95	100	15
TM13	Ice Beam	Ice	95	100	10	TM37	Sandstorm	Rock	—	—	10
TM14	Blizzard	Ice	120	70	5	TM38	Fire Blast	Fire	120	85	5
TM17	Protect	Normal	—	—	10	TM42	Facade	Normal	70	100	20
TM18	Rain Dance	Water	—	—	5	TM43	Secret Power	Normal	70	100	20
TM21	Frustration	Normal	—	100	20	TM44	Rest	Psychic	—	—	10
TM22	Solarbeam	Grass	120	100	10	TM45	Attract	Normal	—	100	15
TM24	Thunderbolt	Electric	95	100	15	TM46	Thief	Dark	40	100	10
TM25	Thunder	Electric	120	70	10	HM05	Flash	Normal	—	70	20

EGG MOVES*

Name	Type	Power	ACC	PP
Future Sight	Psychic	80	90	15
Psych Up	Normal	—	—	10

*Learned Via Breeding

MOVE TUTOR

FireRed/LeafGreen and Emerald Only

Body Slam*	Mimic	Thunder Wave*
Double-Edge	Substitute	

Emerald Only

Defense Curl*	Psych Up*	Swagger
Endure*	Sleep Talk*	Swift*
Icy Wind*	Snore*	

*Battle Frontier tutor move (*Emerald*)

352 Kecleon™

NORMAL

GENERAL INFO
SPECIES: Color Swap Pokémon
HEIGHT: 3'03"
WEIGHT: 49 lbs.
ABILITY: Change Color
Changes Kecleon's type to the type of move that hits it.

STATS

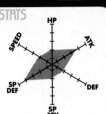

EVOLUTIONS

DOES NOT EVOLVE

LOCATION(s):

RUBY	Rarity: **Rare**	Routes 118, 119, 120, 121, 123 (Devon Scope)
SAPPHIRE	Rarity: **Rare**	Routes 118, 119, 120, 121, 123 (Devon Scope)
FIRERED	Rarity: **None**	Trade from *Ruby/Sapphire/Emerald*
LEAFGREEN	Rarity: **None**	Trade from *Ruby/Sapphire/Emerald*
COLOSSEUM	Rarity: **None**	Trade from *Ruby/Sapphire/Emerald*
EMERALD	Rarity: **Rare**	Routes 118, 119, 120, 121, 123 (Devon Scope)
XD	Rarity: **None**	Trade from *Ruby/Sapphire/Emerald*

MOVES

Level	Attack	Type	Power	ACC	PP
—	Thief	Dark	40	100	10
—	Tail Whip	Normal	—	100	30
—	Astonish	Ghost	30	100	15
—	Lick	Ghost	20	100	30
—	Scratch	Normal	40	100	35
4	Bind	Normal	15	75	20

Level	Attack	Type	Power	ACC	PP
7	Faint Attack	Dark	60	—	20
12	Fury Swipes	Normal	18	80	15
17	Psybeam	Psychic	65	100	20
24	Screech	Normal	—	85	40
31	Slash	Normal	70	100	20
40	Substitute	Normal	—	—	10
49	Ancientpower	Rock	60	100	5

TM/HM

TM/HM#	Name	Type	Power	ACC	PP
TM01	Focus Punch	Fighting	150	100	20
TM03	Water Pulse	Water	60	100	20
TM06	Toxic	Poison	—	85	10
TM10	Hidden Power	Normal	—	100	15
TM11	Sunny Day	Fire	—	—	5
TM13	Ice Beam	Ice	95	100	10
TM14	Blizzard	Ice	120	70	5
TM17	Protect	Normal	—	—	10
TM18	Rain Dance	Water	—	—	5
TM21	Frustration	Normal	—	100	20
TM22	Solarbeam	Grass	120	100	10
TM23	Iron Tail	Steel	100	75	15
TM24	Thunderbolt	Electric	95	100	15
TM25	Thunder	Electric	120	70	10
TM27	Return	Normal	—	100	20
TM28	Dig	Ground	60	100	10
TM30	Shadow Ball	Ghost	80	—	20
TM31	Brick Break	Fighting	75	100	15

TM/HM#	Name	Type	Power	ACC	PP
TM32	Double Team	Normal	—	—	15
TM34	Shock Wave	Electric	60	—	20
TM35	Flamethrower	Fire	95	100	15
TM38	Fire Blast	Fire	120	85	5
TM39	Rock Tomb	Rock	50	80	10
TM40	Aerial Ace	Flying	60	—	20
TM42	Facade	Normal	70	100	20
TM43	Secret Power	Normal	70	100	20
TM44	Rest	Psychic	—	—	10
TM45	Attract	Normal	—	100	15
TM46	Thief	Dark	40	100	10
TM48	Skill Swap	Psychic	—	100	10
TM49	Snatch	Dark	—	100	10
HM01	Cut	Normal	50	95	30
HM04	Strength	Normal	80	100	15
HM05	Flash	Normal	—	70	20
HM06	Rock Smash	Fighting	20	100	15

EGG MOVES*

Name	Type	Power	ACC	PP
Disable	Normal	—	55	20
Magic Coat	Psychic	—	100	15

Name	Type	Power	ACC	PP
Trick	Psychic	—	100	10
*Learned Via Breeding				

MOVE TUTOR
FireRed/LeafGreen and Emerald Only

Body Slam*	Mimic	Rock Slide*
Double-Edge	Substitute	Thunder Wave*
Mega Punch*	Counter*	
Mega Kick*	Seismic Toss*	

*Battle Frontier tutor move (*Emerald*)

Emerald Only

Defense Curl*	Icy Wind*	Snore*
Dynamicpunch*	Metronome	Swagger
Endure*	Mud-Slap*	Swift*
Fire Punch*	Psych Up*	Thunderpunch*
Fury Cutter*	Rollout	
Ice Punch*	Sleep Talk	

353 Shuppet™

GHOST

GENERAL INFO

SPECIES: Puppet Pokémon
HEIGHT: 2'00"
WEIGHT: 5 lbs.
ABILITY: Insomnia
Shuppet cannot be put to sleep.

STATS

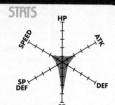

EVOLUTIONS

LV37

LOCATION(s):

RUBY	Rarity: **Common**	Mt. Pyre
SAPPHIRE	Rarity: **Common**	Route 121, Mt. Pyre
FIRERED	Rarity: **None**	Trade from *Ruby/Sapphire/Emerald*
LEAFGREEN	Rarity: **None**	Trade from *Ruby/Sapphire/Emerald*
COLOSSEUM	Rarity: **None**	Trade from *Ruby/Sapphire/Emerald*
EMERALD	Rarity: **Common**	Route 121, Route 123, Mt. Pyre
XD	Rarity: **None**	Trade from *Ruby/Sapphire/Emerald*

MOVES

Level	Attack	Type	Power	ACC	PP	Level	Attack	Type	Power	ACC	PP
—	Knock Off	Dark	20	100	20	32	Will-O-Wisp	Fire	—	75	15
8	Screech	Normal	—	85	40	37	Faint Attack	Dark	60	—	20
13	Night Shade	Ghost	—	100	15	44	Shadow Ball	Ghost	80	100	15
20	Curse	—	—	—	10	49	Snatch	Dark	—	100	10
25	Spite	Ghost	—	100	10	56	Grudge	Ghost	—	100	5

TM/HM

TM/HM#	Name	Type	Power	ACC	PP	TM/HM#	Name	Type	Power	ACC	PP
TM04	Calm Mind	Psychic	—	—	20	TM30	Shadow Ball	Ghost	60	—	20
TM06	Toxic	Poison	—	85	10	TM32	Double Team	Normal	—	—	15
TM10	Hidden Power	Normal	—	100	15	TM34	Shock Wave	Electric	60	—	20
TM11	Sunny Day	Fire	—	—	5	TM41	Torment	Dark	—	100	15
TM12	Taunt	Dark	—	100	20	TM42	Facade	Normal	70	100	20
TM17	Protect	Normal	—	—	10	TM43	Secret Power	Normal	70	100	20
TM18	Rain Dance	Water	—	—	5	TM44	Rest	Psychic	—	—	10
TM21	Frustration	Normal	—	100	20	TM45	Attract	Normal	—	100	15
TM24	Thunderbolt	Electric	95	100	15	TM46	Thief	Dark	40	100	10
TM25	Thunder	Electric	120	70	10	TM48	Skill Swap	Psychic	—	100	10
TM27	Return	Normal	—	100	20	TM49	Snatch	Dark	—	100	10
TM29	Psychic	Psychic	90	100	10	HM05	Flash	Normal	—	70	20

EGG MOVES*

Name	Type	Power	ACC	PP
Disable	Normal	—	55	20
Destiny Bond	Ghost	—	—	5
Foresight	Normal	—	100	40
Astonish	Ghost	30	100	15
Imprison	Psychic	—	100	15

*Learned Via Breeding

MOVE TUTOR
FireRed/LeafGreen and Emerald Only

Body Slam*	Mimic	Thunder Wave*
Double-Edge	Substitute	Dream Eater*

Emerald Only

Endure*	Mud-Slap*	Snore*
Icy Wind*	Sleep Talk	Swagger

*Battle Frontier tutor move (*Emerald*)

354 Banette™

GHOST

GENERAL INFO
SPECIES: Marionette Pokémon
HEIGHT: 3'07"
WEIGHT: 28 lbs.
ABILITY: Insomnia
Banette cannot be put to sleep.

STATS
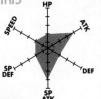

EVOLUTIONS

LV37

LOCATION[s]:

	Rarity	
RUBY	**Evolve**	Evolve Shuppet
SAPPHIRE	**Common**	Sky Pillar
FIRERED	**None**	Trade from *Ruby/Sapphire/Emerald*
LEAFGREEN	**None**	Trade from *Ruby/Sapphire/Emerald*
COLOSSEUM	**None**	Trade from *Ruby/Sapphire/Emerald*
EMERALD	**Rare**	Evolve Shuppet, Sky Pillar
XD	**Only One**	Citadark Island (Capture from Cipher Peon Litnar)

MOVES

Level	Attack	Type	Power	ACC	PP
—	Knock Off	Dark	20	100	20
—	Screech	Normal	—	85	40
—	Night Shade	Ghost	—	100	15
—	Curse	—	—	—	10
25	Spite	Ghost	—	100	10

Level	Attack	Type	Power	ACC	PP
32	Will-O-Wisp	Fire	—	75	15
39	Faint Attack	Dark	60	—	20
48	Shadow Ball	Ghost	80	100	15
55	Snatch	Dark	—	100	10
64	Grudge	Ghost	—	100	5

TM/HM

TM/HM#	Name	Type	Power	ACC	PP
TM04	Calm Mind	Psychic	—	—	20
TM06	Toxic	Poison	—	85	10
TM10	Hidden Power	Normal	—	100	15
TM11	Sunny Day	Fire	—	—	5
TM12	Taunt	Dark	—	100	20
TM15	Hyper Beam	Normal	150	90	5
TM17	Protect	Normal	—	—	10
TM18	Rain Dance	Water	—	—	5
TM21	Frustration	Normal	—	100	20
TM24	Thunderbolt	Electric	95	100	15
TM25	Thunder	Electric	120	70	10
TM27	Return	Normal	—	100	20
TM29	Psychic	Psychic	90	100	10

TM/HM#	Name	Type	Power	ACC	PP
TM30	Shadow Ball	Ghost	60	—	20
TM32	Double Team	Normal	—	—	15
TM34	Shock Wave	Electric	60	—	20
TM41	Torment	Dark	—	100	15
TM42	Facade	Normal	70	100	20
TM43	Secret Power	Normal	70	100	20
TM44	Rest	Psychic	—	—	10
TM45	Attract	Normal	—	100	15
TM46	Thief	Dark	40	100	10
TM48	Skill Swap	Psychic	—	100	10
TM49	Snatch	Dark	—	100	10
HM05	Flash	Normal	—	70	20

MOVE TUTOR
FireRed/LeafGreen and Emerald Only
Body Slam* | Substitute | Dream Eater*
Double-Edge | Thunder Wave* | Metronome
Mimic

Emerald Only
Endure* | Psych Up* | Snore*
Icy Wind* | Sleep Talk | Swagger
Mud-Slap*

*Battle Frontier tutor move (*Emerald*)

355 Duskull™

GHOST

GENERAL INFO
SPECIES: Requiem Pokémon
HEIGHT: 2'07"
WEIGHT: 33 lbs.
ABILITY: Levitate
Duskull is not affected by Ground-type moves.

STATS

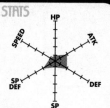

EVOLUTIONS

 ▶

LV37

LOCATION(s):

RUBY	Rarity: **Common**	Route 121, Mt. Pyre
SAPPHIRE	Rarity: **Common**	Mt. Pyre
FIRERED	Rarity: **None**	Trade from *Ruby/Sapphire/Emerald*
LEAFGREEN	Rarity: **None**	Trade from *Ruby/Sapphire/Emerald*
COLOSSEUM	Rarity: **None**	Trade from *Ruby/Sapphire/Emerald*
EMERALD	Rarity: **Common**	Mt. Pyre
XD	Rarity: **Only One**	Pyrite Town (Capture from Cipher Peon Lobar)

MOVES

Level	Attack	Type	Power	ACC	PP	Level	Attack	Type	Power	ACC	PP
—	Leer	Normal	—	100	30	23	Confuse Ray	Ghost	—	100	10
—	Night Shade	Ghost	—	100	15	27	Pursuit	Dark	40	100	20
5	Disable	Normal	—	55	20	34	Curse	—	—	—	10
12	Foresight	Normal	—	100	40	38	Will-O-Wisp	Fire	—	75	15
16	Astonish	Ghost	30	100	15	45	Mean Look	Normal	—	100	5
						49	Future Sight	Psychic	80	90	15

TM/HM

TM/HM#	Name	Type	Power	ACC	PP	TM/HM#	Name	Type	Power	ACC	PP
TM04	Calm Mind	Psychic	—	—	20	TM30	Shadow Ball	Ghost	60	—	20
TM06	Toxic	Poison	—	85	10	TM32	Double Team	Normal	—	—	15
TM10	Hidden Power	Normal	—	100	15	TM41	Torment	Dark	—	100	15
TM11	Sunny Day	Fire	—	—	5	TM42	Facade	Normal	70	100	20
TM12	Taunt	Dark	—	100	20	TM43	Secret Power	Normal	70	100	20
TM13	Ice Beam	Ice	95	100	10	TM44	Rest	Psychic	—	—	10
TM14	Blizzard	Ice	120	70	5	TM45	Attract	Normal	—	100	15
TM17	Protect	Normal	—	—	10	TM46	Thief	Dark	40	100	10
TM18	Rain Dance	Water	—	—	5	TM48	Skill Swap	Psychic	—	—	10
TM21	Frustration	Normal	—	100	20	TM49	Snatch	Dark	—	100	10
TM27	Return	Normal	—	100	20	HM05	Flash	Normal	—	70	20
TM29	Psychic	Psychic	90	100	10						

EGG MOVES*

Name	Type	Power	ACC	PP
Imprison	Psychic	—	100	15
Destiny Bond	Ghost	—	—	5
Grudge	Ghost	—	100	5
Memento	Dark	—	100	10
Faint Attack	Dark	60	—	20
Pain Split	Normal	—	100	10

*Learned Via Breeding

MOVE TUTOR
FireRed/LeafGreen and Emerald Only

Body Slam*	Mimic	Dream Eater*
Double-Edge	Substitute	

Emerald Only

Endure*	Psych Up*	Snore*
Icy Wind*	Sleep Talk	Swagger

*Battle Frontier tutor move (*Emerald*)

356 Dusclops™

GHOST

GENERAL INFO

SPECIES: Beckon Pokémon
HEIGHT: 5'03"
WEIGHT: 67 lbs.
ABILITY: Pressure
The opponent spends 2 PP for damage inflicted against Dusclops.

STATS

EVOLUTIONS

LV37

LOCATION[S]:

RUBY	Rarity: **Common**	Sky Pillar
SAPPHIRE	Rarity: **Evolve**	Evolve Duskull
FIRERED	Rarity: **None**	Trade from *Ruby/Sapphire/Emerald*
LEAFGREEN	Rarity: **None**	Trade from *Ruby/Sapphire/Emerald*
COLOSSEUM	Rarity: **None**	Trade from *Ruby/Sapphire/Emerald*
EMERALD	Rarity: **Evolve**	Evolve Duskull
XD	Rarity: **Evolve**	Evolve Duskull

MOVES

Level	Attack	Type	Power	ACC	PP		Level	Attack	Type	Power	ACC	PP
—	Bind	Normal	15	75	20		23	Confuse Ray	Ghost	—	100	10
—	Leer	Normal	—	100	30		27	Pursuit	Dark	40	100	20
—	Night Shade	Ghost	—	100	15		34	Curse	—	—	—	10
—	Disable	Normal	—	55	20		37	Shadow Punch	Ghost	60	—	20
12	Foresight	Normal	—	100	40		41	Will-O-Wisp	Fire	—	75	15
16	Astonish	Ghost	30	100	15		51	Mean Look	Normal	—	100	5
							58	Future Sight	Psychic	80	90	15

TM/HM

TM/HM#	Name	Type	Power	ACC	PP		TM/HM#	Name	Type	Power	ACC	PP
TM01	Focus Punch	Fighting	150	100	20		TM30	Shadow Ball	Ghost	60	—	20
TM04	Calm Mind	Psychic	—	—	20		TM32	Double Team	Normal	—	—	15
TM06	Toxic	Poison	—	85	10		TM39	Rock Tomb	Rock	50	80	10
TM10	Hidden Power	Normal	—	100	15		TM41	Torment	Dark	—	100	15
TM11	Sunny Day	Fire	—	—	5		TM42	Facade	Normal	70	100	20
TM12	Taunt	Dark	—	100	20		TM43	Secret Power	Normal	70	100	20
TM13	Ice Beam	Ice	95	100	10		TM44	Rest	Psychic	—	—	10
TM14	Blizzard	Ice	120	70	5		TM45	Attract	Normal	—	100	15
TM15	Hyper Beam	Normal	150	90	5		TM46	Thief	Dark	40	100	10
TM17	Protect	Normal	—	—	10		TM48	Skill Swap	Psychic	—	100	10
TM18	Rain Dance	Water	—	—	5		TM49	Snatch	Dark	—	100	10
TM21	Frustration	Normal	—	100	20		HM04	Strength	Normal	80	100	15
TM26	Earthquake	Ground	100	100	10		HM05	Flash	Normal	—	70	20
TM27	Return	Normal	—	100	20		HM06	Rock Smash	Fighting	20	100	15
TM29	Psychic	Psychic	90	100	10							

MOVE TUTOR

FireRed/LeafGreen and Emerald Only

Body Slam*	Mimic	Seismic Toss*
Double-Edge*	Substitute	Dream Eater*
Mega Punch*	Metronome	Rock Slide*
Mega Kick*	Counter*	

Emerald Only

Dynamicpunch*	Icy Wind*	Snore*
Endure*	Mud-Slap*	Swagger
Fire Punch*	Psych Up*	Thunderpunch*
Ice Punch*	Sleep Talk	

*Battle Frontier tutor move (*Emerald*)

PRIMA OFFICIAL GAME GUIDE

357 Tropius™

GRASS   FLYING

GENERAL INFO
SPECIES: **Fruit Pokémon**
HEIGHT: **6'07"**
WEIGHT: **221 lbs.**
ABILITY: **Chlorophyll**
Doubles Tropius's Speed when the sunlight is strong.

STATS

EVOLUTIONS
DOES NOT EVOLVE

LOCATION[s]:

RUBY	Rarity: **Rare**	Route 119
SAPPHIRE	Rarity: **Rare**	Route 119
FIRERED	Rarity: **None**	Trade from *Ruby/Sapphire/Colosseum/Emerald*
LEAFGREEN	Rarity: **None**	Trade from *Ruby/Sapphire/Colosseum/Emerald*
COLOSSEUM	Rarity: **Only One**	Realgam Tower
EMERALD	Rarity: **Rare**	Route 119
XD	Rarity: **None**	Trade from *Ruby/Sapphire/Colosseum/Emerald*

MOVES

Level	Attack	Type	Power	ACC	PP		Level	Attack	Type	Power	ACC	PP
—	Leer	Normal	—	100	30		21	Sweet Scent	Normal	—	100	20
—	Gust	Flying	40	100	35		27	Whirlwind	Normal	—	100s	20
7	Growth	Normal	—	—	40		31	Magical Leaf	Grass	60	—	20
11	Razor Leaf	Grass	55	95	25		37	Body Slam	Normal	85	100	15
17	Stomp	Normal	65	100	20		41	Solarbeam	Grass	120	100	10
							47	Synthesis	Grass	—	—	5

TM/HM

TM/HM#	Name	Type	Power	ACC	PP		TM/HM#	Name	Type	Power	ACC	PP
TM05	Roar	Normal	—	100	20		TM32	Double Team	Normal	—	—	15
TM06	Toxic	Poison	—	85	10		TM40	Aerial Ace	Flying	60	—	20
TM09	Bullet Seed	Grass	10	100	30		TM42	Facade	Normal	70	100	20
TM10	Hidden Power	Normal	—	100	15		TM43	Secret Power	Normal	70	100	20
TM11	Sunny Day	Fire	—	—	5		TM44	Rest	Psychic	—	—	10
TM15	Hyper Beam	Normal	150	90	5		TM45	Attract	Normal	—	100	15
TM17	Protect	Normal	—	—	10		TM47	Steel Wing	Steel	70	90	25
TM19	Giga Drain	Grass	60	100	5		HM01	Cut	Normal	50	95	30
TM20	Safeguard	Normal	—	—	25		HM02	Fly	Flying	70	95	15
TM21	Frustration	Normal	—	100	20		HM04	Strength	Normal	80	100	15
TM22	Solarbeam	Grass	120	100	10		HM05	Flash	Normal	—	70	20
TM26	Earthquake	Ground	100	100	10		HM06	Rock Smash	Fighting	20	100	15
TM27	Return	Normal	—	100	20							

EGG MOVES*

Name	Type	Power	ACC	PP
Headbutt	Normal	70	100	15
Slam	Normal	80	75	20
Razor Wind	Normal	80	100	10
Leech Seed	Grass	—	90	10
Nature Power	Normal	—	95	20

*Learned Via Breeding

MOVE TUTOR
FireRed/LeafGreen and Emerald Only

Body Slam*	Mimic	Swords Dance*
Double-Edge	Substitute	

Emerald Only

Endure*	Mud-Slap*	Snore*
Fury Cutter	Sleep Talk	Swagger

*Battle Frontier tutor move (*Emerald*)

358 Chimecho™

GENERAL INFO
SPECIES: Wind Chime Pokémon
HEIGHT: 2'00"
WEIGHT: 2 lbs.
ABILITY: Levitate
Chimecho is not affected by Ground-type moves.

STATS

EVOLUTIONS

DOES NOT EVOLVE

LOCATION[s]:

RUBY	Rarity: **Rare**	Mt. Pyre
SAPPHIRE	Rarity: **Rare**	Mt. Pyre
FIRERED	Rarity: **None**	Trade from *Ruby/Sapphire/Emerald*
LEAFGREEN	Rarity: **None**	Trade from *Ruby/Sapphire/Emerald*
COLOSSEUM	Rarity: **None**	Trade from *Ruby/Sapphire/Emerald*
EMERALD	Rarity: **Rare**	Mt. Pyre
XD	Rarity: **None**	Trade from *Ruby/Sapphire/Emerald*

MOVES

Level	Attack	Type	Power	ACC	PP	Level	Attack	Type	Power	ACC	PP
—	Wrap	Normal	15	85	20	25	Yawn	Normal	—	100	10
6	Growl	Normal	—	100	40	30	Psywave	Psychic	—	80	15
9	Astonish	Ghost	30	100	15	33	Double-Edge	Normal	120	100	15
14	Confusion	Psychic	50	100	25	38	Heal Bell	Normal	—	—	5
17	Take Down	Normal	90	85	20	41	Safeguard	Normal	—	—	25
22	Uproar	Normal	50	100	10	46	Psychic	Psychic	90	100	10

TM/HM

TM/HM#	Name	Type	Power	ACC	PP	TM/HM#	Name	Type	Power	ACC	PP
TM04	Calm Mind	Psychic	—	—	20	TM30	Shadow Ball	Ghost	60	—	20
TM06	Toxic	Poison	—	85	10	TM32	Double Team	Normal	—	—	15
TM10	Hidden Power	Normal	—	100	15	TM33	Reflect	Psychic	—	—	20
TM11	Sunny Day	Fire	—	—	5	TM34	Shock Wave	Electric	60	—	20
TM12	Taunt	Dark	—	100	20	TM41	Torment	Dark	—	100	15
TM16	Light Screen	Psychic	—	—	30	TM42	Facade	Normal	70	100	20
TM17	Protect	Normal	—	—	10	TM43	Secret Power	Normal	70	100	20
TM18	Rain Dance	Water	—	—	5	TM44	Rest	Psychic	—	—	10
TM20	Safeguard	Normal	—	—	25	TM45	Attract	Normal	—	100	15
TM21	Frustration	Normal	—	100	20	TM48	Skill Swap	Psychic	—	100	10
TM27	Return	Normal	—	100	20	TM49	Snatch	Dark	—	100	10
TM29	Psychic	Psychic	90	100	10	HM05	Flash	Normal	—	70	20

EGG MOVES*

Name	Type	Power	ACC	PP
Disable	Normal	—	55	20
Curse	—	—	—	10
Hypnosis	Psychic	—	60	20
Dream Eater	Psychic	100	100	15

*Learned Via Breeding

MOVE TUTOR
FireRed/LeafGreen and Emerald Only

Double-Edge	Substitute	Dream Eater*
Mimic		

Emerald Only

Defense Curl*	Psych Up*	Snore*
Endure*	Rollout	Swagger
Icy Wind*	Sleep Talk	

*Battle Frontier tutor move (*Emerald*)

359 Absol™

DARK

GENERAL INFO
SPECIES: Disaster Pokémon
HEIGHT: 3'11"
WEIGHT: 104 lbs.
ABILITY: Pressure
When hit by a move, the opponent's Pokémon loses 2 PP.

STATS

(Radar chart with axes: HP, ATK, DEF, SP ATK, SP DEF, SPEED)

EVOLUTIONS

DOES NOT EVOLVE

LOCATION(S):

RUBY	Rarity: **Rare**	Route 120	
SAPPHIRE	Rarity: **Rare**	Route 120	
FIRERED	Rarity: **None**	Trade from *Ruby/Sapphire/Colosseum/Emerald*	
LEAFGREEN	Rarity: **None**	Trade from *Ruby/Sapphire/Colosseum/Emerald*	
COLOSSEUM	Rarity: **Only One**	Realgam Tower	
EMERALD	Rarity: **Rare**	Route 120	
XD	Rarity: **None**	Trade from *Ruby/Sapphire/Colosseum/Emerald*	

MOVES

Level	Attack	Type	Power	ACC	PP
—	Scratch	Normal	40	100	35
5	Leer	Normal	—	100	30
9	Taunt	Dark	—	100	20
13	Quick Attack	Normal	40	100	30
17	Razor Wind	Normal	80	100	10

Level	Attack	Type	Power	ACC	PP
21	Bite	Dark	60	100	25
26	Swords Dance	Normal	—	—	30
31	Double Team	Normal	—	—	15
36	Slash	Normal	70	100	20
41	Future Sight	Psychic	80	90	15
46	Perish Song	Normal	—	—	5

TM/HM

TM/HM#	Name	Type	Power	ACC	PP
TM03	Water Pulse	Water	60	100	20
TM04	Calm Mind	Psychic	—	—	20
TM06	Toxic	Poison	—	85	10
TM07	Hail	Ice	—	—	10
TM10	Hidden Power	Normal	—	100	15
TM11	Sunny Day	Fire	—	—	5
TM12	Taunt	Dark	—	100	20
TM13	Ice Beam	Ice	95	100	10
TM14	Blizzard	Ice	120	70	5
TM15	Hyper Beam	Normal	150	90	5
TM17	Protect	Normal	—	—	10
TM18	Rain Dance	Water	—	—	5
TM21	Frustration	Normal	—	100	20
TM23	Iron Tail	Steel	100	75	15
TM24	Thunderbolt	Electric	95	100	15
TM25	Thunder	Electric	120	70	10
TM27	Return	Normal	—	100	20
TM30	Shadow Ball	Ghost	60	—	20

TM/HM#	Name	Type	Power	ACC	PP
TM32	Double Team	Normal	—	—	15
TM34	Shock Wave	Electric	60	—	20
TM35	Flamethrower	Fire	95	100	15
TM37	Sandstorm	Rock	—	—	10
TM38	Fire Blast	Fire	120	85	5
TM40	Aerial Ace	Flying	60	—	20
TM41	Torment	Dark	—	100	15
TM42	Facade	Normal	70	100	20
TM43	Secret Power	Normal	70	100	20
TM44	Rest	Psychic	—	—	10
TM45	Attract	Normal	—	100	15
TM46	Thief	Dark	40	100	10
TM49	Snatch	Dark	—	100	10
HM01	Cut	Normal	50	95	30
HM04	Strength	Normal	80	100	15
HM05	Flash	Normal	—	70	20
HM06	Rock Smash	Fighting	20	100	15

EGG MOVES*

Name	Type	Power	ACC	PP
Baton Pass	Normal	—	—	40
Faint Attack	Dark	60	—	20
Double-Edge	Normal	120	100	15
Magic Coat	Psychic	—	100	15
Curse	—	—	—	10
Substitute	Normal	—	—	10

*Learned Via Breeding

MOVE TUTOR
FireRed/LeafGreen and Emerald Only

Body Slam*	Substitute	Dream Eater*
Double-Edge	Counter*	Rock Slide*
Mimic	Thunder Wave*	Swords Dance*

Emerald Only

Endure*	Sleep Talk	Swagger
Mud-Slap*	Snore*	Swift*

*Battle Frontier tutor move (*Emerald*)

360 Wynaut™

GENERAL INFO

SPECIES: Bright Pokémon
HEIGHT: 2'00"
WEIGHT: 31 lbs.
ABILITY: Shadow Tag

The opponent Pokémon cannot run or switch out from the battle.

STATS

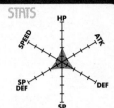

EVOLUTIONS

LV15

LOCATION(s):

RUBY	Rarity: **Common**	Lavaridge Town (Receive Egg)
SAPPHIRE	Rarity: **Common**	Lavaridge Town (Receive Egg)
FIRERED	Rarity: **Breed**	Must Breed two Wobbuffet; one needs Lax Incense attached
LEAFGREEN	Rarity: **Breed**	Must Breed two Wobbuffet; one needs Lax Incense attached
COLOSSEUM	Rarity: **None**	Trade from *Ruby/Sapphire/Emerald*
EMERALD	Rarity: **Common**	Lavaridge Town (Receive Egg), Mirage Island
XD	Rarity: **None**	Trade from *Ruby/Sapphire/Emerald*

MOVES

Level	Attack	Type	Power	ACC	PP
—	Splash	Normal	—	—	40
—	Charm	Normal	—	100	20
—	Encore	Normal	—	100	5

Level	Attack	Type	Power	ACC	PP
15	Counter	Fighting	—	100	20
15	Mirror Coat	Psychic	—	100	20
15	Safeguard	Normal	—	—	25
15	Destiny Bond	Ghost	—	—	5

TM/HM

TM/HM#	Name	Type	Power	ACC	PP
None					

EGG MOVES*

Name	Type	Power	ACC	PP
None				

*Learned Via Breeding

MOVE TUTOR*

FireRed/LeafGreen and Emerald Only

None

361 Snorunt™

ICE

GENERAL INFO

SPECIES: Snow Hat Pokémon
HEIGHT: 2'04"
WEIGHT: 37 lbs.
ABILITY: Inner Focus
Prevents Snorunt from flinching.

STATS

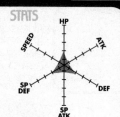

EVOLUTIONS

LV42

LOCATION[s]:

RUBY	Rarity: **Common**	Shoal Cave	
SAPPHIRE	Rarity: **Common**	Shoal Cave	
FIRERED	Rarity: **None**	Trade from *Ruby/Sapphire/Emerald*	
LEAFGREEN	Rarity: **None**	Trade from *Ruby/Sapphire/Emerald*	
COLOSSEUM	Rarity: **None**	Trade from *Ruby/Sapphire/Emerald*	
EMERALD	Rarity: **Common**	Shoal Cave	
XD	Rarity: **Only One**	Phenac City (Capture from Cipher Peon Exinn)	

MOVES

Level	Attack	Type	Power	ACC	PP	Level	Attack	Type	Power	ACC	PP
—	Powder Snow	Ice	40	100	25	19	Headbutt	Normal	70	100	15
—	Leer	Normal	—	100	30	25	Protect	Normal	—	—	10
7	Double Team	Normal	—	—	15	28	Crunch	Dark	80	100	15
10	Bite	Dark	60	100	25	34	Ice Beam	Ice	95	100	10
16	Icy Wind	Ice	55	95	15	37	Hail	Ice	—	—	10
						43	Blizzard	Ice	120	70	5

TM/HM

TM/HM#	Name	Type	Power	ACC	PP	TM/HM#	Name	Type	Power	ACC	PP
TM03	Water Pulse	Water	60	100	20	TM21	Frustration	Normal	—	100	20
TM06	Toxic	Poison	—	85	10	TM27	Return	Normal	—	100	20
TM07	Hail	Ice	—	—	10	TM30	Shadow Ball	Ghost	60	—	20
TM10	Hidden Power	Normal	—	100	15	TM32	Double Team	Normal	—	—	15
TM13	Ice Beam	Ice	95	100	10	TM42	Facade	Normal	70	100	20
TM14	Blizzard	Ice	120	70	5	TM43	Secret Power	Normal	70	100	20
TM16	Light Screen	Psychic	—	—	30	TM44	Rest	Psychic	—	—	10
TM17	Protect	Normal	—	—	10	TM45	Attract	Normal	—	100	15
TM18	Rain Dance	Water	—	—	5	HM05	Flash	Normal	—	70	20
TM20	Safeguard	Normal	—	—	25						

EGG MOVES*

Name	Type	Power	ACC	PP
Block	Normal	—	100	5
Spikes	Ground	—	—	20

*Learned Via Breeding

MOVE TUTOR

FireRed/LeafGreen and Emerald Only

Body Slam*	Mimic	Substitute
Double-Edge		

Emerald Only

Endure*	Sleep Talk	Swagger
Icy Wind*	Snore*	

*Battle Frontier tutor move (*Emerald*)

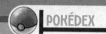

362 Glalie™

ICE

GENERAL INFO

SPECIES: Face Pokémon
HEIGHT: 4'11"
WEIGHT: 566 lbs.
ABILITY: Inner Focus
Prevents Glalie from flinching.

STATS

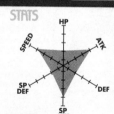

EVOLUTIONS

 ▶

LV42

LOCATION[s]:

Game	Rarity	Location
RUBY	Rarity: **Evolve**	Evolve Snorunt
SAPPHIRE	Rarity: **Evolve**	Evolve Snorunt
FIRERED	Rarity: **None**	Trade from *Ruby/Sapphire/Emerald*
LEAFGREEN	Rarity: **None**	Trade from *Ruby/Sapphire/Emerald*
COLOSSEUM	Rarity: **None**	Trade from *Ruby/Sapphire/Emerald*
EMERALD	Rarity: **Evolve**	Evolve Snorunt
XD	Rarity: **Evolve**	Evolve Snorunt

MOVES

Level	Attack	Type	Power	ACC	PP
—	Powder Snow	Ice	40	100	25
—	Leer	Normal	—	100	30
—	Double Team	Normal	—	—	15
—	Bite	Dark	60	100	25
16	Icy Wind	Ice	55	95	15
19	Headbutt	Normal	70	100	15

Level	Attack	Type	Power	ACC	PP
25	Protect	Normal	—	—	10
28	Crunch	Dark	80	100	15
34	Ice Beam	Ice	95	100	10
42	Hail	Ice	—	—	10
53	Blizzard	Ice	120	70	5
61	Sheer Cold	Ice	—	30	5

TM/HM

TM/HM#	Name	Type	Power	ACC	PP
TM03	Water Pulse	Water	60	100	20
TM06	Toxic	Poison	—	85	10
TM07	Hail	Ice	—	—	10
TM10	Hidden Power	Normal	—	100	15
TM12	Taunt	Dark	—	100	20
TM13	Ice Beam	Ice	95	100	10
TM14	Blizzard	Ice	120	70	5
TM15	Hyper Beam	Normal	150	90	5
TM16	Light Screen	Psychic	—	—	30
TM17	Protect	Normal	—	—	10
TM18	Rain Dance	Water	—	—	5
TM20	Safeguard	Normal	—	—	25

TM/HM#	Name	Type	Power	ACC	PP
TM21	Frustration	Normal	—	100	20
TM26	Earthquake	Ground	100	100	10
TM27	Return	Normal	—	100	20
TM30	Shadow Ball	Ghost	60	—	20
TM32	Double Team	Normal	—	—	15
TM41	Torment	Dark	—	100	15
TM42	Facade	Normal	70	100	20
TM43	Secret Power	Normal	70	100	20
TM44	Rest	Psychic	—	—	10
TM45	Attract	Normal	—	100	15
HM05	Flash	Normal	—	70	20

MOVE TUTOR

FireRed/LeafGreen and Emerald Only

Body Slam* Mimic Explosion
Double-Edge Substitute

Emerald Only

Defense Curl* Rollout Thunderpunch*
Endure* Sleep Talk
Icy Wind* Snore*

*Battle Frontier tutor move (*Emerald*)

PRIMA OFFICIAL GAME GUIDE

363 Spheal™

ICE   WATER

GENERAL INFO
SPECIES: Clap Pokémon
HEIGHT: 2'07"
WEIGHT: 87 lbs.
ABILITY: Thick Fat
Fire- and Ice-type moves inflict only 50% of the damage.

STATS

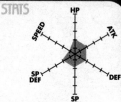

EVOLUTIONS

LV32   LV44

LOCATION[s]:

RUBY	Rarity: **Common**	Shoal Cave
SAPPHIRE	Rarity: **Common**	Shoal Cave
FIRERED	Rarity: **None**	Trade from *Ruby/Sapphire/Emerald*
LEAFGREEN	Rarity: **None**	Trade from *Ruby/Sapphire/Emerald*
COLOSSEUM	Rarity: **None**	Trade from *Ruby/Sapphire/Emerald*
EMERALD	Rarity: **Common**	Shoal Cave
XD	Rarity: **Only One**	Cipher Lab (Capture from Cipher Peon Blusix)

MOVES

Level	Attack	Type	Power	ACC	PP	Level	Attack	Type	Power	ACC	PP
—	Powder Snow	Ice	40	100	25	19	Body Slam	Normal	85	100	15
—	Growl	Normal	—	100	40	25	Aurora Beam	Ice	65	100	20
—	Defense Curl	Normal	—	—	40	31	Hail	Ice	—	—	10
—	Water Gun	Water	40	100	25	37	Rest	Psychic	—	—	10
7	Encore	Normal	—	100	5	37	Snore	Normal	40	100	15
13	Ice Ball	Ice	30	90	20	43	Blizzard	Ice	120	70	5
						49	Sheer Cold	Ice	—	30	5

TM/HM

TM/HM#	Name	Type	Power	ACC	PP	TM/HM#	Name	Type	Power	ACC	PP
TM03	Water Pulse	Water	60	100	20	TM32	Double Team	Normal	—	—	15
TM06	Toxic	Poison	—	85	10	TM39	Rock Tomb	Rock	50	80	10
TM07	Hail	Ice	—	—	10	TM42	Facade	Normal	70	100	20
TM10	Hidden Power	Normal	—	100	15	TM43	Secret Power	Normal	70	100	20
TM13	Ice Beam	Ice	95	100	10	TM44	Rest	Psychic	—	—	10
TM14	Blizzard	Ice	120	70	5	TM45	Attract	Normal	—	100	15
TM17	Protect	Normal	—	—	10	HM03	Surf	Water	95	100	15
TM18	Rain Dance	Water	—	—	5	HM04	Strength	Normal	80	100	15
TM21	Frustration	Normal	—	100	20	HM06	Rock Smash	Fighting	20	100	15
TM23	Iron Tail	Steel	100	75	15	HM07	Waterfall	Water	80	100	15
TM26	Earthquake	Ground	100	100	10	HM08	Dive	Water	60	100	10
TM27	Return	Normal	—	100	20						

EGG MOVES*

Name	Type	Power	ACC	PP
Water Sport	Water	—	100	15
Stockpile	Normal	—	—	10
Swallow	Normal	—	—	10
Spit Up	Normal	100	100	10
Yawn	Normal	—	100	10
Rock Slide	Rock	75	90	10
Curse	—	—	—	10
Fissure	Ground	—	30	5

*Learned Via Breeding

MOVE TUTOR
FireRed/LeafGreen and Emerald Only

Body Slam*	Mimic	Rock Slide*
Double-Edge	Substitute	

Emerald Only

Defense Curl*	Mud-Slap*	Snore*
Endure*	Rollout	Swagger
Icy Wind*	Sleep Talk	

*Battle Frontier tutor move (*Emerald*)

364 Sealeo™

ICE | WATER

GENERAL INFO

SPECIES: Ball Roll Pokémon
HEIGHT: 3'07"
WEIGHT: 193 lbs.
ABILITY: Thick Fat
Fire- and Ice-type moves inflict only 50% of the damage.

STATS

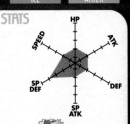

EVOLUTIONS

  LV32  LV44

LOCATION[s]:

RUBY	Rarity: **Evolve**	Evolve Spheal
SAPPHIRE	Rarity: **Evolve**	Evolve Spheal
FIRERED	Rarity: **None**	Trade from *Ruby/Sapphire/Emerald*
LEAFGREEN	Rarity: **None**	Trade from *Ruby/Sapphire/Emerald*
COLOSSEUM	Rarity: **None**	Trade from *Ruby/Sapphire/Emerald*
EMERALD	Rarity: **Evolve**	Evolve Spheal
XD	Rarity: **Evolve**	Evolve Spheal

MOVES

Level	Attack	Type	Power	ACC	PP	Level	Attack	Type	Power	ACC	PP
—	Defense Curl	Normal	—	—	80	25	Aurora Beam	Ice	65	100	20
—	Powder Snow	Ice	40	100	25	31	Hail	Ice	—	—	10
—	Growl	Normal	—	100	40	39	Rest	Psychic	—	—	10
—	Water Gun	Water	40	100	25	39	Snore	Normal	40	100	15
7	Encore	Normal	—	100	5	47	Blizzard	Ice	120	70	5
13	Ice Ball	Ice	30	90	20	55	Sheer Cold	Ice	—	30	5
19	Body Slam	Normal	85	100	15						

TM/HM

TM/HM#	Name	Type	Power	ACC	PP	TM/HM#	Name	Type	Power	ACC	PP
TM03	Water Pulse	Water	60	100	20	TM27	Return	Normal	—	100	20
TM05	Roar	Normal	—	100	20	TM32	Double Team	Normal	—	—	15
TM06	Toxic	Poison	—	85	10	TM39	Rock Tomb	Rock	50	80	10
TM07	Hail	Ice	—	—	10	TM42	Facade	Normal	70	100	20
TM10	Hidden Power	Normal	—	100	15	TM43	Secret Power	Normal	70	100	20
TM13	Ice Beam	Ice	95	100	10	TM44	Rest	Psychic	—	—	10
TM14	Blizzard	Ice	120	70	5	TM45	Attract	Normal	—	100	15
TM17	Protect	Normal	—	—	10	HM03	Surf	Water	95	100	15
TM18	Rain Dance	Water	—	—	5	HM04	Strength	Normal	80	100	15
TM21	Frustration	Normal	—	100	20	HM06	Rock Smash	Fighting	20	100	15
TM23	Iron Tail	Steel	100	75	15	HM07	Waterfall	Water	80	100	15
TM26	Earthquake	Ground	100	100	10	HM08	Dive	Water	60	100	10

MOVE TUTOR

FireRed/LeafGreen and Emerald Only

Body Slam*	Mimic	Rock Slide*
Double-Edge	Substitute	

*Battle Frontier tutor move (*Emerald*)

Emerald Only

Defense Curl*	Mud-Slap*	Snore*
Endure*	Rollout	Swagger
Icy Wind*	Sleep Talk	

PRIMA OFFICIAL GAME GUIDE

365 Walrein™

ICE   WATER

GENERAL INFO

SPECIES: Ice Break Pokémon
HEIGHT: 4'07"
WEIGHT: 332 lbs.
ABILITY: Thick Fat
Fire- and Ice-type moves inflict only 50% of the damage.

STATS

EVOLUTIONS

LV32   LV44

LOCATION[s]:

RUBY	Rarity: **Evolve**	Evolve Sealeo
SAPPHIRE	Rarity: **Evolve**	Evolve Sealeo
FIRERED	Rarity: **None**	Trade from *Ruby/Sapphire/Emerald*
LEAFGREEN	Rarity: **None**	Trade from *Ruby/Sapphire/Emerald*
COLOSSEUM	Rarity: **None**	Trade from *Ruby/Sapphire/Emerald*
EMERALD	Rarity: **Evolve**	Evolve Sealeo
XD	Rarity: **Evolve**	Evolve Sealeo

MOVES

Level	Attack	Type	Power	ACC	PP		Level	Attack	Type	Power	ACC	PP
—	Powder Snow	Ice	40	100	25		25	Aurora Beam	Ice	65	100	20
—	Growl	Normal	—	100	40		31	Hail	Ice	—	—	10
—	Defense Curl	Normal	—	—	40		39	Rest	Psychic	—	—	10
—	Water Gun	Water	40	100	25		39	Snore	Normal	40	100	15
7	Encore	Normal	—	100	5		50	Blizzard	Ice	120	70	5
13	Ice Ball	Ice	30	90	20		61	Sheer Cold	Ice	—	30	5
19	Body Slam	Normal	85	100	15							

TM/HM

TM/HM#	Name	Type	Power	ACC	PP		TM/HM#	Name	Type	Power	ACC	PP
TM03	Water Pulse	Water	60	100	20		TM27	Return	Normal	—	100	20
TM05	Roar	Normal	—	100	20		TM32	Double Team	Normal	—	—	15
TM06	Toxic	Poison	—	85	10		TM39	Rock Tomb	Rock	50	80	10
TM07	Hail	Ice	—	—	10		TM42	Facade	Normal	70	100	20
TM10	Hidden Power	Normal	—	100	15		TM43	Secret Power	Normal	70	100	20
TM13	Ice Beam	Ice	95	100	10		TM44	Rest	Psychic	—	—	10
TM14	Blizzard	Ice	120	70	5		TM45	Attract	Normal	—	100	15
TM15	Hyper Beam	Normal	150	90	5		HM03	Surf	Water	95	100	15
TM17	Protect	Normal	—	—	10		HM04	Strength	Normal	80	100	15
TM18	Rain Dance	Water	—	—	5		HM06	Rock Smash	Fighting	20	100	15
TM21	Frustration	Normal	—	100	20		HM07	Waterfall	Water	80	100	15
TM23	Iron Tail	Steel	100	75	15		HM08	Dive	Water	60	100	10
TM26	Earthquake	Ground	100	100	10							

MOVE TUTOR

FireRed/LeafGreen and Emerald Only

Body Slam*	Mimic	Rock Slide*
Double-Edge	Substitute	

Emerald Only

Defense Curl*	Mud-Slap*	Snore*
Endure*	Rollouot	Swagger
Icy Wind*	Sleep Talk	

*Battle Frontier tutor move (*Emerald*)

366 Clamperl™

GENERAL INFO

SPECIES: Bivalve Pokémon
HEIGHT: 1'04"
WEIGHT: 116 lbs.
ABILITY: Shell Armor

Prevents the opponent Pokémon from scoring a critical hit.

STATS

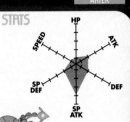

EVOLUTIONS

TRADE WITH DEEPSEATOOTH

TRADE WITH DEEPSEASCALE

LOCATION[s]:

Game	Rarity	Location
RUBY	Rarity: **Common**	Underwater Route 124, Underwater Route 126
SAPPHIRE	Rarity: **Common**	Underwater Route 124, Underwater Route 126
FIRERED	Rarity: **None**	Trade from *Ruby/Sapphire/Emerald*
LEAFGREEN	Rarity: **None**	Trade from *Ruby/Sapphire/Emerald*
COLOSSEUM	Rarity: **None**	Trade from *Ruby/Sapphire/Emerald*
EMERALD	Rarity: **Common**	Underwater Route 124, Underwater Route 126
XD	Rarity: **None**	Trade from *Ruby/Sapphire/Emerald*

MOVES

Level	Attack	Type	Power	ACC	PP	Level	Attack	Type	Power	ACC	PP
—	Clamp	Water	35	75	10	—	Whirlpool	Water	15	70	15
—	Water Gun	Water	40	100	25	—	Iron Defense	Steel	—	—	15

TM/HM

TM/HM#	Name	Type	Power	ACC	PP	TM/HM#	Name	Type	Power	ACC	PP
TM03	Water Pulse	Water	60	100	20	TM27	Return	Normal	—	100	20
TM06	Toxic	Poison	—	85	10	TM32	Double Team	Normal	—	—	15
TM07	Hail	Ice	—	—	10	TM42	Facade	Normal	70	100	20
TM10	Hidden Power	Normal	—	100	15	TM43	Secret Power	Normal	70	100	20
TM13	Ice Beam	Ice	95	100	10	TM44	Rest	Psychic	—	—	10
TM14	Blizzard	Ice	120	70	5	TM45	Attract	Normal	—	100	15
TM17	Protect	Normal	—	—	10	HM03	Surf	Water	95	100	15
TM18	Rain Dance	Normal	—	—	5	HM07	Waterfall	Water	80	100	15
TM21	Frustration	Normal	—	100	20	HM08	Dive	Water	60	100	10

EGG MOVES*

Name	Type	Power	ACC	PP
Refresh	Normal	—	100	20
Mud Sport	Ground	—	100	15
Body Slam	Normal	85	100	15
Supersonic	Normal	—	55	20
Barrier	Psychic	—	—	30
Confuse Ray	Ghost	—	100	10

*Learned Via Breeding

MOVE TUTOR

FireRed/LeafGreen and Emerald Only

Body Slam*	Mimic	Substitute
Double-Edge		

Emerald Only

Endure*	Sleep Talk	Swagger
Icy Wind*	Snore*	

*Battle Frontier tutor move (*Emerald*)

PRIMA OFFICIAL GAME GUIDE

367 Huntail™

WATER

GENERAL INFO
SPECIES: Deep Sea Pokémon
HEIGHT: 5'07"
WEIGHT: 60 lbs.
ABILITY: Swift Swim
Doubles Huntail's Speed when it's raining.

STATS

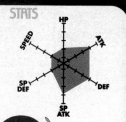

EVOLUTIONS

TRADE WITH DEEPSEATOOTH

LOCATION[s]:

	Rarity	
RUBY	**None**	Trade Clamperl (Deepseatooth)
SAPPHIRE	**None**	Trade Clamperl (Deepseatooth)
FIRERED	**None**	Trade from *Ruby/Sapphire/Emerald*
LEAFGREEN	**None**	Trade from *Ruby/Sapphire/Emerald*
COLOSSEUM	**None**	Trade from *Ruby/Sapphire/Emerald*
EMERALD	**Evolve**	Trade Clamperl (Deepseatooth)
XD	**None**	Trade from *Ruby/Sapphire/Emerald*

MOVES

Level	Attack	Type	Power	ACC	PP	Level	Attack	Type	Power	ACC	PP
—	Whirlpool	Water	15	70	15	29	Scary Face	Normal	—	90	10
8	Bite	Dark	60	100	25	36	Crunch	Dark	80	100	15
15	Screech	Normal	—	85	40	43	Baton Pass	Normal	—	—	40
22	Water Pulse	Water	60	100	20	50	Hydro Pump	Water	120	80	5

TM/HM

TM/HM#	Name	Type	Power	ACC	PP	TM/HM#	Name	Type	Power	ACC	PP
TM03	Water Pulse	Water	60	100	20	TM32	Double Team	Normal	—	—	15
TM06	Toxic	Poison	—	85	10	TM39	Rock Tomb	Rock	50	80	10
TM07	Hail	Ice	—	—	10	TM42	Facade	Normal	70	100	20
TM10	Hidden Power	Normal	—	100	15	TM43	Secret Power	Normal	70	100	20
TM13	Ice Beam	Ice	95	100	10	TM44	Rest	Psychic	—	—	10
TM14	Blizzard	Ice	120	70	5	TM45	Attract	Normal	—	100	15
TM15	Hyper Beam	Normal	150	90	5	TM49	Snatch	Dark	—	100	10
TM17	Protect	Normal	—	—	10	HM03	Surf	Water	95	100	15
TM18	Rain Dance	Water	—	—	5	HM07	Waterfall	Water	80	100	15
TM21	Frustration	Normal	—	100	20	HM08	Dive	Water	60	100	10
TM27	Return	Normal	—	100	20						

MOVE TUTOR

FireRed/LeafGreen and Emerald Only

Body Slam*	Mimic	Substitute
Double-Edge		

Emerald Only

Endure*	Sleep Talk	Swift*
Icy Wind*	Snore*	
Mud-Slap*	Swagger	

*Battle Frontier tutor move (*Emerald*)

368 Gorebyss ™

WATER

GENERAL INFO

SPECIES: South Sea Pokémon
HEIGHT: 5'11"
WEIGHT: 50 lbs.
ABILITY: Swift Swim

Doubles Gorebyss's Speed when it's raining.

STATS

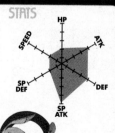

EVOLUTIONS

TRADE WITH DEEPSEASCALE

LOCATION[S]:

RUBY	Rarity: **None**	Trade Clamperl (Deepseascale)
SAPPHIRE	Rarity: **None**	Trade Clamperl (Deepseascale)
FIRERED	Rarity: **None**	Trade from *Ruby/Sapphire/Emerald*
LEAFGREEN	Rarity: **None**	Trade from *Ruby/Sapphire/Emerald*
COLOSSEUM	Rarity: **None**	Trade from *Ruby/Sapphire/Emerald*
EMERALD	Rarity: **Evolve**	Trade Clamperl (Deepseascale)
XD	Rarity: **None**	Trade from *Ruby/Sapphire/Emerald*

MOVES

Level	Attack	Type	Power	ACC	PP	Level	Attack	Type	Power	ACC	PP
—	Whirlpool	Water	15	70	15	29	Amnesia	Psychic	—	—	20
8	Confusion	Psychic	50	100	25	36	Psychic	Psychic	90	100	10
15	Agility	Psychic	—	—	30	43	Baton Pass	Normal	—	—	40
22	Water Pulse	Water	60	100	20	50	Hydro Pump	Water	120	80	5

TM/HM

TM/HM#	Name	Type	Power	ACC	PP	TM/HM#	Name	Type	Power	ACC	PP
TM03	Water Pulse	Water	60	100	20	TM27	Return	Normal	—	100	20
TM06	Toxic	Poison	—	85	10	TM29	Psychic	Psychic	90	100	10
TM07	Hail	Ice	—	—	10	TM30	Shadow Ball	Ghost	60	—	20
TM10	Hidden Power	Normal	—	100	15	TM32	Double Team	Normal	—	—	15
TM13	Ice Beam	Ice	95	100	10	TM42	Facade	Normal	70	100	20
TM14	Blizzard	Ice	120	70	5	TM43	Secret Power	Normal	70	100	20
TM15	Hyper Beam	Normal	150	90	5	TM44	Rest	Psychic	—	—	10
TM17	Protect	Normal	—	—	10	TM45	Attract	Normal	—	100	15
TM18	Rain Dance	Water	—	—	5	HM03	Surf	Water	95	100	15
TM20	Safeguard	Normal	—	—	25	HM07	Waterfall	Water	80	100	15
TM21	Frustration	Normal	—	100	20	HM08	Dive	Water	60	100	10

MOVE TUTOR

FireRed/LeafGreen and Emerald Only

Body Slam*	Mimic	Substitute
Double-Edge		

Emerald Only

Endure*	Sleep Talk	Swift*
Icy Wind*	Snore*	
Mud-Slap*	Swagger	

*Battle Frontier tutor move (*Emerald*)

369 Relicanth™

WATER | ROCK

GENERAL INFO

SPECIES: Longevity Pokémon
HEIGHT: 3'03"
WEIGHT: 52 lbs.
ABILITY 1: Swift Swim
Doubles Relicanth's Speed when it's raining.

ABILITY 2: Rock Head
Relicanth does not receive recoil damage from moves such as Double-Edge.

STATS

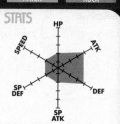

EVOLUTIONS

DOES NOT EVOLVE

LOCATION(s):

RUBY	Rarity: **Rare**		Underwater Route 124, Underwater Route 126
SAPPHIRE	Rarity: **Rare**		Underwater Route 124, Underwater Route 126
FIRERED	Rarity: **None**		Trade from *Ruby/Sapphire/Emerald*
LEAFGREEN	Rarity: **None**		Trade from *Ruby/Sapphire/Emerald*
COLOSSEUM	Rarity: **None**		Trade from *Ruby/Sapphire/Emerald*
EMERALD	Rarity: **Rare**		Underwater Routes 124–126
XD	Rarity: **None**		Trade from *Ruby/Sapphire/Emerald*

MOVES

Level	Attack	Type	Power	ACC	PP	Level	Attack	Type	Power	ACC	PP
—	Tackle	Normal	35	95	35	29	Take Down	Normal	90	85	20
—	Harden	Normal	—	—	30	36	Mud Sport	Ground	—	100	15
8	Water Gun	Water	40	100	25	43	Ancientpower	Rock	60	100	5
15	Rock Tomb	Rock	50	80	10	50	Rest	Psychic	—	—	10
22	Yawn	Normal	—	100	10	57	Double-Edge	Normal	120	100	15
						64	Hydro Pump	Water	120	80	5

TM/HM

TM/HM#	Name	Type	Power	ACC	PP	TM/HM#	Name	Type	Power	ACC	PP
TM03	Water Pulse	Water	60	100	20	TM27	Return	Normal	—	100	20
TM04	Calm Mind	Psychic	—	—	20	TM32	Double Team	Normal	—	—	15
TM06	Toxic	Poison	—	85	10	TM37	Sandstorm	Rock	—	—	10
TM07	Hail	Ice	—	—	10	TM39	Rock Tomb	Rock	50	80	10
TM10	Hidden Power	Normal	—	100	15	TM42	Facade	Normal	70	100	20
TM13	Ice Beam	Ice	95	100	10	TM43	Secret Power	Normal	70	100	20
TM14	Blizzard	Ice	120	70	5	TM44	Rest	Psychic	—	—	10
TM15	Hyper Beam	Normal	150	90	5	TM45	Attract	Normal	—	100	15
TM17	Protect	Normal	—	—	10	HM03	Surf	Water	95	100	15
TM18	Rain Dance	Water	—	—	5	HM06	Rock Smash	Fighting	20	100	15
TM20	Safeguard	Normal	—	—	25	HM07	Waterfall	Water	80	100	15
TM21	Frustration	Normal	—	100	20	HM08	Dive	Water	60	100	10
TM26	Earthquake	Ground	100	100	10						

EGG MOVES*

Name	Type	Power	ACC	PP
Magnitude	Ground	—	100	30
Skull Bash	Normal	100	100	15
Water Sport	Water	—	100	15
Amnesia	Psychic	—	—	20
Sleep Talk	Normal	—	—	10
Rock Slide	Rock	75	90	10

*Learned Via Breeding

MOVE TUTOR

FireRed/LeafGreen and Emerald Only

Body Slam*	Mimic	Rock Slide*
Double-Edge	Substitute	

Emerald Only

Endure*	Mud-Slap*	Snore*
Icy Wind*	Psych Up*	Swagger

*Battle Frontier tutor move (*Emerald*)

370 Luvdisc ™

WATER

GENERAL INFO

SPECIES: Rendezvous Pokémon
HEIGHT: 2'00"
WEIGHT: 19 lbs.
ABILITY: Swift Swim
Doubles Luvdisc's Speed when it's raining.

STATS

HP
SPEED
ATK
SP DEF
DEF
SP ATK

EVOLUTIONS

DOES NOT EVOLVE

LOCATION(s):

RUBY	Rarity: **Common**	Ever Grande City, Route 128
SAPPHIRE	Rarity: **Common**	Ever Grande City, Route 128
FIRERED	Rarity: *None*	Trade from *Ruby/Sapphire/Emerald*
LEAFGREEN	Rarity: *None*	Trade from *Ruby/Sapphire/Emerald*
COLOSSEUM	Rarity: *None*	Trade from *Ruby/Sapphire/Emerald*
EMERALD	Rarity: **Common**	Ever Grande City, Route 128
XD	Rarity: *None*	Trade from *Ruby/Sapphire/Emerald*

MOVES

Level	Attack	Type	Power	ACC	PP	Level	Attack	Type	Power	ACC	PP
—	Tackle	Normal	35	95	35	24	Take Down	Normal	90	85	20
4	Charm	Normal	—	100	20	28	Attract	Normal	—	100	15
12	Water Gun	Water	40	100	25	36	Sweet Kiss	Normal	—	75	10
16	Agility	Psychic	—	—	30	40	Flail	Normal	—	100	15
						48	Safeguard	Normal	—	—	25

TM/HM

TM/HM#	Name	Type	Power	ACC	PP	TM/HM#	Name	Type	Power	ACC	PP
TM03	Water Pulse	Water	60	100	20	TM27	Return	Normal	—	100	20
TM06	Toxic	Poison	—	85	10	TM32	Double Team	Normal	—	—	15
TM07	Hail	Ice	—	—	10	TM42	Facade	Normal	70	100	20
TM10	Hidden Power	Normal	—	100	15	TM43	Secret Power	Normal	70	100	20
TM13	Ice Beam	Ice	95	100	10	TM44	Rest	Psychic	—	—	10
TM14	Blizzard	Ice	120	70	5	TM45	Attract	Normal	—	100	15
TM17	Protect	Normal	—	—	10	HM03	Surf	Water	95	100	15
TM18	Rain Dance	Water	—	—	5	HM07	Waterfall	Water	80	100	15
TM20	Safeguard	Normal	—	—	25	HM08	Dive	Water	60	100	10
TM21	Frustration	Normal	—	100	20						

EGG MOVES*

Name	Type	Power	ACC	PP
Supersonic	Normal	—	55	20
Water Sport	Water	—	100	15
Mud Sport	Ground	—	100	15
Bounce	Flying	85	85	5

*Learned Via Breeding

MOVE TUTOR

FireRed/LeafGreen and Emerald Only

Double-Edge	Mimic	Substitute

Emerald Only

Endure*	Sleep Talk	Swagger
Icy Wind*	Snore*	Swift*
Psych Up*		

*Battle Frontier tutor move (*Emerald*)

371 Bagon™

DRAGON

GENERAL INFO
SPECIES: Rock Head Pokémon
HEIGHT: 2'00"
WEIGHT: 93 lbs.
ABILITY: Rock Head

Bagon does not receive recoil damage from moves such as Double-Edge.

STATS

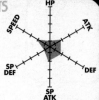

EVOLUTIONS

LV30   LV50

LOCATION[s]:

RUBY	Rarity: **Common**	Meteor Falls
SAPPHIRE	Rarity: **Common**	Meteor Falls
FIRERED	Rarity: **None**	Trade from *Ruby/Sapphire/Emerald*
LEAFGREEN	Rarity: **None**	Trade from *Ruby/Sapphire/Emerald*
COLOSSEUM	Rarity: **None**	Trade from *Ruby/Sapphire/Emerald*
EMERALD	Rarity: **Common**	Meteor Falls
XD	Rarity: **None**	Trade from *Ruby/Sapphire/Emerald*

MOVES

Level	Attack	Type	Power	ACC	PP	Level	Attack	Type	Power	ACC	PP
—	Rage	Normal	20	100	20	25	Ember	Fire	40	100	25
5	Bite	Dark	60	100	25	33	Dragonbreath	Dragon	60	100	20
9	Leer	Normal	—	100	30	37	Scary Face	Normal	—	90	10
17	Headbutt	Normal	70	100	15	41	Crunch	Dark	80	100	15
21	Focus Energy	Normal	—	—	30	49	Dragon Claw	Dragon	80	100	15
						53	Double-Edge	Normal	120	100	15

TM/HM

TM/HM#	Name	Type	Power	ACC	PP	TM/HM#	Name	Type	Power	ACC	PP
TM02	Dragon Claw	Dragon	80	100	15	TM35	Flamethrower	Fire	95	100	15
TM05	Roar	Normal	—	100	20	TM38	Fire Blast	Fire	120	85	5
TM06	Toxic	Poison	—	85	10	TM39	Rock Tomb	Rock	50	80	10
TM10	Hidden Power	Normal	—	100	15	TM40	Aerial Ace	Flying	60	—	20
TM11	Sunny Day	Fire	—	—	5	TM42	Facade	Normal	70	100	20
TM17	Protect	Normal	—	—	10	TM43	Secret Power	Normal	70	100	20
TM18	Rain Dance	Water	—	—	5	TM44	Rest	Psychic	—	—	10
TM21	Frustration	Normal	—	100	20	TM45	Attract	Normal	—	100	15
TM27	Return	Normal	—	100	20	HM01	Cut	Normal	50	95	30
TM31	Brick Break	Fighting	75	100	15	HM04	Strength	Normal	80	100	15
TM32	Double Team	Normal	—	—	15	HM06	Rock Smash	Fighting	20	100	15

EGG MOVES*

Name	Type	Power	ACC	PP
Hydro Pump	Water	120	80	5
Thrash	Normal	90	100	20
Dragon Rage	Dragon	—	100	10
Twister	Dragon	40	100	20
Dragon Dance	Dragon	—	—	20

*Learned Via Breeding

MOVE TUTOR
FireRed/LeafGreen and Emerald Only

Body Slam*	Mimic	Rock Slide*
Double-Edge	Substitute	

Emerald Only

Endure*	Mud-Slap*	Snore*
Fury Cutter	Sleep Talk	Swagger

*Battle Frontier tutor move (*Emerald*)

372 Shelgon™

DRAGON

GENERAL INFO

SPECIES: Endurance Pokémon
HEIGHT: 3'07"
WEIGHT: 244 lbs.
ABILITY: Rock Head

Shelgon does not receive recoil damage from moves such as Double-Edge.

STATS

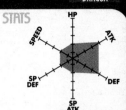

EVOLUTIONS

 ▶ LV30 ▶  LV50

LOCATION[s]:

RUBY	Rarity: **Evolve**	Evolve Bagon	
SAPPHIRE	Rarity: **Evolve**	Evolve Bagon	
FIRERED	Rarity: **None**	Trade from *Ruby/Sapphire/Emerald*	
LEAFGREEN	Rarity: **None**	Trade from *Ruby/Sapphire/Emerald*	
COLOSSEUM	Rarity: **None**	Trade from *Ruby/Sapphire/Emerald*	
EMERALD	Rarity: **Evolve**	Evolve Bagon	
XD	Rarity: **None**	Trade from *Ruby/Sapphire/Emerald*	

MOVES

Level	Attack	Type	Power	ACC	PP		Level	Attack	Type	Power	ACC	PP
—	Rage	Normal	20	100	20		30	Protect	Normal	—	—	10
—	Bite	Dark	60	100	25		38	Dragonbreath	Dragon	60	100	20
—	Leer	Normal	—	100	30		47	Scary Face	Normal	—	90	10
—	Headbutt	Normal	70	100	15		56	Crunch	Dark	80	100	15
21	Focus Energy	Normal	—	—	30		69	Dragon Claw	Dragon	80	100	15
25	Ember	Fire	40	100	25		78	Double-Edge	Normal	120	100	15

TM/HM

TM/HM#	Name	Type	Power	ACC	PP		TM/HM#	Name	Type	Power	ACC	PP
TM02	Dragon Claw	Dragon	80	100	15		TM35	Flamethrower	Fire	95	100	15
TM05	Roar	Normal	—	100	20		TM38	Fire Blast	Fire	120	85	5
TM06	Toxic	Poison	—	85	10		TM39	Rock Tomb	Rock	50	80	10
TM10	Hidden Power	Normal	—	100	15		TM40	Aerial Ace	Flying	60	—	20
TM11	Sunny Day	Fire	—	—	5		TM42	Facade	Normal	70	100	20
TM17	Protect	Normal	—	—	10		TM43	Secret Power	Normal	70	100	20
TM18	Rain Dance	Water	—	—	5		TM44	Rest	Psychic	—	—	10
TM21	Frustration	Normal	—	100	20		TM45	Attract	Normal	—	100	15
TM27	Return	Normal	—	100	20		HM01	Cut	Normal	50	95	30
TM31	Brick Break	Fighting	75	100	15		HM04	Strength	Normal	80	100	15
TM32	Double Team	Normal	—	—	15		HM06	Rock Smash	Fighting	20	100	15

MOVE TUTOR

FireRed/LeafGreen and Emerald Only

Body Slam*	Mimic	Rock Slide*
Double-Edge	Substitute	

Battle Frontier tutor move (Emerald)

Emerald Only

Defense Curl*	Mud-Slap*	Snore*
Endure*	Rollout	Swagger
Fury Cutter	Sleep Talk	

373 Salamence™

 DRAGON FLYING

GENERAL INFO
SPECIES: Dragon Pokémon
HEIGHT: 4'11"
WEIGHT: 226 lbs.
ABILITY: Intimidate
Lowers the opponent's Attack by one at the battle's start.

STATS

EVOLUTIONS

  LV30 LV50

LOCATION[s]:

RUBY	Rarity: **Evolve**	Evolve Shelgon
SAPPHIRE	Rarity: **Evolve**	Evolve Shelgon
FIRERED	Rarity: **None**	Trade from *Ruby/Sapphire/Emerald*
LEAFGREEN	Rarity: **None**	Trade from *Ruby/Sapphire/Emerald*
COLOSSEUM	Rarity: **None**	Trade from *Ruby/Sapphire/Emerald*
EMERALD	Rarity: **Evolve**	Evolve Shelgon
XD	Rarity: **Only One**	Citadark Island (Capture from Cipher Admin Eldes)

MOVES

Level	Attack	Type	Power	ACC	PP	Level	Attack	Type	Power	ACC	PP
—	Rage	Normal	20	100	20	30	Protect	Normal	—	—	10
—	Bite	Dark	60	100	25	38	Dragonbreath	Dragon	60	100	20
—	Leer	Normal	—	100	30	47	Scary Face	Normal	—	90	10
—	Headbutt	Normal	70	100	15	50	Fly	Flying	70	95	15
21	Focus Energy	Normal	—	—	30	61	Crunch	Dark	80	100	15
25	Ember	Fire	40	100	25	79	Dragon Claw	Dragon	80	100	15
						93	Double-Edge	Normal	120	100	15

TM/HM

TM/HM#	Name	Type	Power	ACC	PP	TM/HM#	Name	Type	Power	ACC	PP
TM02	Dragon Claw	Dragon	80	100	15	TM35	Flamethrower	Fire	95	100	15
TM05	Roar	Normal	—	100	20	TM38	Fire Blast	Fire	120	85	5
TM06	Toxic	Poison	—	85	10	TM39	Rock Tomb	Rock	50	80	10
TM10	Hidden Power	Normal	—	100	15	TM40	Aerial Ace	Flying	60	—	20
TM11	Sunny Day	Fire	—	—	5	TM42	Facade	Normal	70	100	20
TM15	Hyper Beam	Normal	150	90	5	TM43	Secret Power	Normal	70	100	20
TM17	Protect	Normal	—	—	10	TM44	Rest	Psychic	—	—	10
TM18	Rain Dance	Water	—	—	5	TM45	Attract	Normal	—	100	15
TM21	Frustration	Normal	—	100	20	TM47	Steel Wing	Steel	70	90	25
TM23	Iron Tail	Steel	100	75	15	HM01	Cut	Normal	50	95	30
TM26	Earthquake	Ground	100	100	10	HM02	Fly	Flying	70	95	15
TM27	Return	Normal	—	100	20	HM04	Strength	Normal	80	100	15
TM31	Brick Break	Fighting	75	100	15	HM06	Rock Smash	Fighting	20	100	15
TM32	Double Team	Normal	—	—	15						

MOVE TUTOR

FireRed/LeafGreen and Emerald Only

Body Slam*	Mimic	Rock Slide*
Double-Edge	Substitute	

Emerald Only

Defense Curl*	Mud-Slap*	Snore*
Endure*	Rollout	Swagger
Fury Cutter	Sleep Talk	Swift*

*Battle Frontier tutor move (*Emerald*)

374 Beldum ™

STEEL | PSYCHIC

GENERAL INFO
SPECIES: Iron Ball Pokémon
HEIGHT: 2'00"
WEIGHT: 210 lbs.
ABILITY: Clear Body
Moves that lower stats don't affect Beldum.

STATS

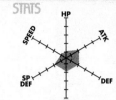

EVOLUTIONS

  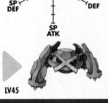

LV20   LV45

LOCATION[s]:

RUBY	Rarity: **Only One**	Mossdeep City (Steven's House after beating Elite Four)
SAPPHIRE	Rarity: **Only One**	Mossdeep City (Steven's House after beating Elite Four)
FIRERED	Rarity: **None**	Trade from *Ruby/Sapphire/Emerald*
LEAFGREEN	Rarity: **None**	Trade from *Ruby/Sapphire/Emerald*
COLOSSEUM	Rarity: **None**	Trade from *Ruby/Sapphire/Emerald*
EMERALD	Rarity: **Only One**	Mossdeep City (Steven's House after beating Elite Four)
XD	Rarity: **None**	Trade from *Ruby/Sapphire/Emerald*

MOVES

Level	Attack	Type	Power	ACC	PP
—	Take Down	Normal	90	85	20

TM/HM

TM/HM#	Name	Type	Power	ACC	PP
None					

MOVE TUTOR*
FireRed/LeafGreen and Emerald Only

None	

PRIMA OFFICIAL GAME GUIDE

375 Metang™

STEEL PSYCHIC

GENERAL INFO

SPECIES: Iron Claw Pokémon
HEIGHT: 3'11"
WEIGHT: 447 lbs.
ABILITY: Clear Body
Moves that lower stats don't affect Metang.

STATS

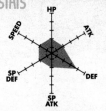

EVOLUTIONS

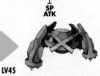

LV20   LV45

LOCATION(s):

RUBY	Rarity: **Evolve**	Evolve Beldum
SAPPHIRE	Rarity: **Evolve**	Evolve Beldum
FIRERED	Rarity: None	Trade from *Ruby/Sapphire/Emerald*
LEAFGREEN	Rarity: None	Trade from *Ruby/Sapphire/Emerald*
COLOSSEUM	Rarity: None	Trade from *Ruby/Sapphire/Emerald*
EMERALD	Rarity: **Evolve**	Evolve Beldum
XD	Rarity: None	Trade from *Ruby/Sapphire/Emerald*

MOVES

Level	Attack	Type	Power	ACC	PP	Level	Attack	Type	Power	ACC	PP
—	Take Down	Normal	90	85	20	38	Psychic	Psychic	90	100	10
20	Confusion	Psychic	50	100	25	44	Iron Defense	Steel	—	—	15
20	Metal Claw	Steel	50	95	35	50	Meteor Mash	Steel	100	85	10
26	Scary Face	Normal	—	90	10	56	Agility	Psychic	—	—	30
32	Pursuit	Dark	40	100	20	62	Hyper Beam	Normal	150	90	5

TM/HM

TM/HM#	Name	Type	Power	ACC	PP	TM/HM#	Name	Type	Power	ACC	PP
TM06	Toxic	Poison	—	85	10	TM32	Double Team	Normal	—	—	15
TM10	Hidden Power	Normal	—	100	15	TM33	Reflect	Psychic	—	—	20
TM11	Sunny Day	Fire	—	—	5	TM36	Sludge Bomb	Poison	90	100	10
TM15	Hyper Beam	Normal	150	90	5	TM37	Sandstorm	Rock	—	—	10
TM16	Light Screen	Psychic	—	—	30	TM39	Rock Tomb	Rock	50	80	10
TM17	Protect	Normal	—	—	10	TM40	Aerial Ace	Flying	60	—	20
TM18	Rain Dance	Water	—	—	5	TM42	Facade	Normal	70	100	20
TM21	Frustration	Normal	—	100	20	TM43	Secret Power	Normal	70	100	20
TM26	Earthquake	Ground	100	100	10	TM44	Rest	Psychic	—	—	10
TM27	Return	Normal	—	100	20	HM01	Cut	Normal	50	95	30
TM29	Psychic	Psychic	90	100	10	HM04	Strength	Normal	80	100	15
TM30	Shadow Ball	Ghost	60	—	20	HM05	Flash	Normal	—	70	20
TM31	Brick Break	Fighting	75	100	15	HM06	Rock Smash	Fighting	20	100	15

MOVE TUTOR

FireRed/LeafGreen and Emerald Only

Body Slam*	Mimic	Rock Slide*
Double-Edge	Substitute	Explosion

Emerald Only

Defense Curl*	Icy Wind*	Snore*
Dynamicpunch	Mud-Slap*	Swagger
Endure*	Psych Up*	Swift*
Fury Cutter	Rollout	Thunderpunch*
Ice Punch*	Sleep Talk	

*Battle Frontier tutor move (*Emerald*)

376 Metagross™

STEEL | PSYCHIC

GENERAL INFO
SPECIES: Iron Leg Pokémon
HEIGHT: 5'03"
WEIGHT: 1,213 lbs.
ABILITY: Clear Body
Moves that lower stats don't affect Metagross.

STATS

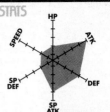

EVOLUTIONS

LV20   LV45

LOCATION[s]:

RUBY	Rarity: Evolve	Evolve Metang
SAPPHIRE	Rarity: Evolve	Evolve Metang
FIRERED	Rarity: None	Trade from *Ruby/Sapphire/Emerald*
LEAFGREEN	Rarity: None	Trade from *Ruby/Sapphire/Emerald*
COLOSSEUM	Rarity: None	Trade from *Ruby/Sapphire/Emerald*
EMERALD	Rarity: Evolve	Evolve Metang
XD	Rarity: None	Trade from *Ruby/Sapphire/Emerald*

MOVES

Level	Attack	Type	Power	ACC	PP
—	Take Down	Normal	90	85	20
—/20	Confusion	Psychic	50	100	25
—/20	Metal Claw	Steel	50	95	35
—/26	Scary Face	Normal	—	90	10
32	Pursuit	Dark	40	100	20

Level	Attack	Type	Power	ACC	PP
38	Psychic	Psychic	90	100	10
44	Iron Defense	Steel	—	—	15
55	Meteor Mash	Steel	100	85	10
66	Agility	Psychic	—	—	30
77	Hyper Beam	Normal	150	90	5

 # = Emerald Only

TM/HM

TM/HM#	Name	Type	Power	ACC	PP
TM06	Toxic	Poison	—	85	10
TM10	Hidden Power	Normal	—	100	15
TM11	Sunny Day	Fire	—	—	5
TM15	Hyper Beam	Normal	150	90	5
TM16	Light Screen	Psychic	—	—	30
TM17	Protect	Normal	—	—	10
TM18	Rain Dance	Water	—	—	5
TM21	Frustration	Normal	—	100	20
TM26	Earthquake	Ground	100	100	10
TM27	Return	Normal	—	100	20
TM29	Psychic	Psychic	90	100	10
TM30	Shadow Ball	Ghost	60	—	20
TM31	Brick Break	Fighting	75	100	15

TM/HM#	Name	Type	Power	ACC	PP
TM32	Double Team	Normal	—	—	15
TM33	Reflect	Psychic	—	—	20
TM36	Sludge Bomb	Poison	90	100	10
TM37	Sandstorm	Rock	—	—	10
TM39	Rock Tomb	Rock	50	80	10
TM40	Aerial Ace	Flying	60	—	20
TM42	Facade	Normal	70	100	20
TM43	Secret Power	Normal	70	100	20
TM44	Rest	Psychic	—	—	10
HM01	Cut	Normal	50	95	30
HM04	Strength	Normal	80	100	15
HM05	Flash	Normal	—	70	20
HM06	Rock Smash	Fighting	20	100	15

MOVE TUTOR
FireRed/LeafGreen and Emerald Only

Body Slam*	Mimic	Rock Slide*
Double-Edge	Substitute	Explosion

Emerald Only

Defense Curl*	Icy Wind*	Snore*
Dynamicpunch*	Mud-Slap*	Swagger
Endure*	Psych Up*	Swift*
Fury Cutter	Rollout	Thunderpunch*
Ice Punch*	Sleep Talk	

*Battle Frontier tutor move (*Emerald*)

377 Regirock™

ROCK

GENERAL INFO

SPECIES: Rock Peak Pokémon
HEIGHT: 5'07"
WEIGHT: 507 lbs.
ABILITY: Clear Body

Moves that lower stats don't affect Regirock.

STATS

EVOLUTIONS

DOES NOT EVOLVE

LOCATION[s]:

RUBY	Rarity: **Only One**	Route 111 (Inside Desert Ruins)
SAPPHIRE	Rarity: **Only One**	Route 111 (Inside Desert Ruins)
FIRERED	Rarity: **None**	Trade from *Ruby/Sapphire/Emerald*
LEAFGREEN	Rarity: **None**	Trade from *Ruby/Sapphire/Emerald*
COLOSSEUM	Rarity: **None**	Trade from *Ruby/Sapphire/Emerald*
EMERALD	Rarity: **Only One**	Route 111 (Inside Desert Ruins)
XD	Rarity: **None**	Trade from *Ruby/Sapphire/Emerald*

MOVES

Level	Attack	Type	Power	ACC	PP
—	Explosion	Normal	250	100	5
9	Rock Throw	Rock	50	90	15
17	Curse	—	—	—	10
25	Superpower	Fighting	120	100	5

Level	Attack	Type	Power	ACC	PP
33	Ancientpower	Rock	60	100	5
41	Iron Defense	Steel	—	—	15
49	Zap Cannon	Electric	100	50	5
57	Lock-on	Normal	—	100	5
65	Hyper Beam	Normal	150	90	5

TM/HM

TM/HM#	Name	Type	Power	ACC	PP
TM01	Focus Punch	Fighting	150	100	20
TM06	Toxic	Poison	—	85	10
TM10	Hidden Power	Normal	—	100	15
TM11	Sunny Day	Fire	—	—	5
TM15	Hyper Beam	Normal	150	90	5
TM17	Protect	Normal	—	—	10
TM20	Safeguard	Normal	—	—	25
TM21	Frustration	Normal	—	100	20
TM24	Thunderbolt	Electric	95	100	15
TM25	Thunder	Electric	120	70	10
TM26	Earthquake	Ground	100	100	10
TM27	Return	Normal	—	100	20

TM/HM#	Name	Type	Power	ACC	PP
TM28	Dig	Ground	60	100	10
TM31	Brick Break	Fighting	75	100	15
TM32	Double Team	Normal	—	—	15
TM34	Shock Wave	Electric	60	—	20
TM37	Sandstorm	Rock	—	—	10
TM39	Rock Tomb	Rock	50	80	10
TM42	Facade	Normal	70	100	20
TM43	Secret Power	Normal	70	100	20
TM44	Rest	Psychic	—	—	10
HM04	Strength	Normal	80	100	15
HM06	Rock Smash	Fighting	20	100	15

MOVE TUTOR

FireRed/LeafGreen and Emerald Only

Body Slam*	Mimic	Thunder Wave*
Double-Edge	Substitute	Rock Slide*
Mega Punch*	Counter*	Explosion
Mega Kick*	Seismic Toss*	

Emerald Only

Defense Curl*	Ice Punch*	Sleep Talk
Dynamicpunch*	Mud-Slap*	Snore*
Endure*	Psych Up*	Swagger
Fire Punch*	Rollout	Thunderpunch*

*Battle Frontier tutor move (*Emerald*)

378 Regice™

ICE

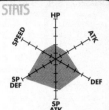

GENERAL INFO
SPECIES: Iceberg Pokémon
HEIGHT: 5'11"
WEIGHT: 386 lbs.
ABILITY: Clear Body
Moves that lower stats don't affect Regice.

STATS

EVOLUTIONS

DOES NOT EVOLVE

LOCATION[s]:

RUBY	Rarity: **Only One**	Route 105 (Inside Island Cave)
SAPPHIRE	Rarity: **Only One**	Route 105 (Inside Island Cave)
FIRERED	Rarity: **None**	Trade from *Ruby/Sapphire/Emerald*
LEAFGREEN	Rarity: **None**	Trade from *Ruby/Sapphire/Emerald*
COLOSSEUM	Rarity: **None**	Trade from *Ruby/Sapphire/Emerald*
EMERALD	Rarity: **Only One**	Route 105 (Inside Island Cave)
XD	Rarity: **None**	Trade from *Ruby/Sapphire/Emerald*

MOVES

Level	Attack	Type	Power	ACC	PP
—	Explosion	Normal	250	100	5
9	Icy Wind	Ice	55	95	15
17	Curse	—	—	—	10
25	Superpower	Fighting	120	100	5

Level	Attack	Type	Power	ACC	PP
33	Ancientpower	Rock	60	100	5
41	Amnesia	Psychic	—	—	20
49	Zap Cannon	Electric	100	50	5
57	Lock-on	Normal	—	100	5
65	Hyper Beam	Normal	150	90	5

TM/HM

TM/HM#	Name	Type	Power	ACC	PP
TM01	Focus Punch	Fighting	150	100	20
TM06	Toxic	Poison	—	85	10
TM07	Hail	Ice	—	—	10
TM10	Hidden Power	Normal	—	100	15
TM13	Ice Beam	Ice	95	100	10
TM14	Blizzard	Ice	120	70	5
TM15	Hyper Beam	Normal	150	90	5
TM17	Protect	Normal	—	—	10
TM18	Rain Dance	Water	—	—	5
TM20	Safeguard	Normal	—	—	25
TM21	Frustration	Normal	—	100	20
TM24	Thunderbolt	Electric	95	100	15

TM/HM#	Name	Type	Power	ACC	PP
TM25	Thunder	Electric	120	70	10
TM26	Earthquake	Ground	100	100	10
TM27	Return	Normal	—	100	20
TM31	Brick Break	Fighting	75	100	15
TM32	Double Team	Normal	—	—	15
TM34	Shock Wave	Electric	60	—	20
TM42	Facade	Normal	70	100	20
TM43	Secret Power	Normal	70	100	20
TM44	Rest	Psychic	—	—	10
HM04	Strength	Normal	80	100	15
HM06	Rock Smash	Fighting	20	100	15

MOVE TUTOR
FireRed/LeafGreen and Emerald Only

Body Slam*	Mimic	Thunder Wave*	
Double-Edge	Substitute	Rock Slide*	
Mega Punch*	Counter*	Explosion	
Mega Kick*	Seismic Toss*		

Emerald Only

Defense Curl*	Ice Punch*	Sleep Talk
Dynamicpunch*	Mud-Slap*	Snore*
Endure*	Psych Up*	Swagger
Fire Punch*	Rollout	Thunderpunch*

*Battle Frontier tutor move (*Emerald*)

379 Registeel™

STEEL

GENERAL INFO

SPECIES: Iron Pokémon
HEIGHT: 6'03"
WEIGHT: 452 lbs.
ABILITY: Clear Body

Moves that lower ability values don't affect Registeel.

STATS

HP · SPEED · ATK · SP DEF · DEF · SP ATK

EVOLUTIONS

DOES NOT EVOLVE

LOCATION(s):

RUBY	Rarity: **Only One**	Route 120 (Inside Ancient Tomb)
SAPPHIRE	Rarity: **Only One**	Route 120 (Inside Ancient Tomb)
FIRERED	Rarity: **None**	Trade from *Ruby/Sapphire/Emerald*
LEAFGREEN	Rarity: **None**	Trade from *Ruby/Sapphire/Emerald*
COLOSSEUM	Rarity: **None**	Trade from *Ruby/Sapphire/Emerald*
EMERALD	Rarity: **Only One**	Route 120 (Inside Ancient Tomb)
XD	Rarity: **None**	Trade from *Ruby/Sapphire/Emerald*

MOVES

Level	Attack	Type	Power	ACC	PP	Level	Attack	Type	Power	ACC	PP
—	Explosion	Normal	250	100	5	41	Iron Defense	Steel	—	—	15
9	Metal Claw	Steel	50	95	35	41	Amnesia	Psychic	—	—	20
17	Curse	—	—	—	10	49	Zap Cannon	Electric	100	50	5
25	Superpower	Fighting	120	100	5	57	Lock-on	Normal	—	100	5
33	Ancientpower	Rock	60	100	5	65	Hyper Beam	Normal	150	90	5

TM/HM

TM/HM#	Name	Type	Power	ACC	PP	TM/HM#	Name	Type	Power	ACC	PP
TM01	Focus Punch	Fighting	150	100	20	TM27	Return	Normal	—	100	20
TM06	Toxic	Poison	—	85	10	TM31	Brick Break	Fighting	75	100	15
TM10	Hidden Power	Normal	—	100	15	TM32	Double Team	Normal	—	—	15
TM11	Sunny Day	Fire	—	—	5	TM34	Shock Wave	Electric	60	—	20
TM15	Hyper Beam	Normal	150	90	5	TM37	Sandstorm	Rock	—	—	10
TM17	Protect	Normal	—	—	10	TM39	Rock Tomb	Rock	50	80	10
TM18	Rain Dance	Water	—	—	5	TM40	Aerial Ace	Flying	60	—	20
TM20	Safeguard	Normal	—	—	25	TM42	Facade	Normal	70	100	20
TM21	Frustration	Normal	—	100	20	TM43	Secret Power	Normal	70	100	20
TM24	Thunderbolt	Electric	95	100	15	TM44	Rest	Psychic	—	—	10
TM25	Thunder	Electric	120	70	10	HM04	Strength	Normal	80	100	15
TM26	Earthquake	Ground	100	100	10	HM06	Rock Smash	Fighting	20	100	15

MOVE TUTOR

FireRed/LeafGreen and Emerald Only

Body Slam*
Double-Edge
Mega Punch*
Mega Kick*

Mimic
Substitute
Counter*
Seismic Toss*

Thunder Wave*
Rock Slide*
Explosion

Emerald Only

Defense Curl*
Dynamicpunch
Endure*
Ice Punch*

Mud-Slap*
Psych Up*
Rollout
Sleep Talk

Snore*
Swagger
Thunderpunch*

*Battle Frontier tutor move (*Emerald*)

380 Latias™

GENERAL INFO
SPECIES: Eon Pokémon
HEIGHT: 4'07"
WEIGHT: 88 lbs.
ABILITY: Levitate
Latias is not affected by Ground-type moves.

STATS

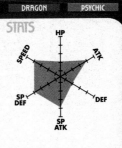

EVOLUTIONS

DOES NOT EVOLVE

LOCATION[s]:

RUBY	Rarity: **None**	Trade from *Sapphire/Emerald*	
SAPPHIRE	Rarity: **Only One**	Random event in Hoenn after beating Elite Four	
FIRERED	Rarity: **None**	Trade from *Sapphire/Emerald*	
LEAFGREEN	Rarity: **None**	Trade from *Sapphire/Emerald*	
COLOSSEUM	Rarity: **None**	Trade from *Sapphire/Emerald*	
EMERALD	Rarity: **Only One**	Random event in Hoenn after beating Elite Four	
XD	Rarity: **None**	Trade from *Sapphire/Emerald*	

MOVES

Level	Attack	Type	Power	ACC	PP
—	Psywave	Psychic	—	80	15
5	Wish	Normal	—	100	10
10	Helping Hand	Normal	—	100	20
15	Safeguard	Normal	—	—	25
20	Dragonbreath	Dragon	60	100	20

Level	Attack	Type	Power	ACC	PP
25	Water Sport	Water	—	100	15
30	Refresh	Normal	—	100	20
35	Mist Ball	Psychic	70	100	5
40	Psychic	Psychic	90	100	10
45	Recover	Normal	—	—	20
50	Charm	Normal	—	100	20

TM/HM

TM/HM#	Name	Type	Power	ACC	PP
TM02	Dragon Claw	Dragon	80	100	15
TM03	Water Pulse	Water	60	100	20
TM04	Calm Mind	Psychic	—	—	20
TM05	Roar	Normal	—	100	20
TM06	Toxic	Poison	—	85	10
TM10	Hidden Power	Normal	—	100	15
TM11	Sunny Day	Fire	—	—	5
TM13	Ice Beam	Ice	95	100	10
TM15	Hyper Beam	Normal	150	90	5
TM16	Light Screen	Psychic	—	—	30
TM17	Protect	Normal	—	—	10
TM18	Rain Dance	Water	—	—	5
TM20	Safeguard	Normal	—	—	25
TM21	Frustration	Normal	—	100	20
TM22	Solarbeam	Grass	120	100	10
TM24	Thunderbolt	Electric	95	100	15
TM25	Thunder	Electric	120	70	10
TM26	Earthquake	Ground	100	100	10
TM27	Return	Normal	—	100	20

TM/HM#	Name	Type	Power	ACC	PP
TM29	Psychic	Psychic	90	100	10
TM30	Shadow Ball	Ghost	60	—	20
TM32	Double Team	Normal	—	—	15
TM33	Reflect	Psychic	—	—	20
TM34	Shock Wave	Electric	60	—	20
TM37	Sandstorm	Rock	—	—	10
TM40	Aerial Ace	Flying	60	—	20
TM42	Facade	Normal	70	100	20
TM43	Secret Power	Normal	70	100	20
TM44	Rest	Psychic	—	—	10
TM45	Attract	Normal	—	100	15
TM47	Steel Wing	Steel	70	90	25
HM01	Cut	Normal	50	95	30
HM02	Fly	Flying	70	95	15
HM03	Surf	Water	95	100	15
HM05	Flash	Normal	—	70	20
HM07	Waterfall	Water	80	100	15
HM08	Dive	Water	60	100	10

MOVE TUTOR
FireRed/LeafGreen and Emerald Only

Body Slam*	Mimic	Thunder Wave*
Double-Edge	Substitute	Dream Eater*

Emerald Only

Endure*	Mud-Slap*	Snore*
Fury Cutter	Psych Up*	Swagger
Icy Wind*	Sleep Talk*	Swift*

*Battle Frontier tutor move (*Emerald*)

381 Latios™

DRAGON | PSYCHIC

GENERAL INFO
SPECIES: Eon Pokémon
HEIGHT: 6'07"
WEIGHT: 132 lbs.
ABILITY: Levitate
Latios is not affected by Ground-type moves.

STATS

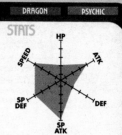

EVOLUTIONS

DOES NOT EVOLVE

LOCATION(s):

RUBY	Rarity:	Only One	Random event in Hoenn after beating Elite Four
SAPPHIRE	Rarity:	None	Trade from *Ruby/Emerald*
FIRERED	Rarity:	None	Trade from *Ruby/Emerald*
LEAFGREEN	Rarity:	None	Trade from *Ruby/Emerald*
COLOSSEUM	Rarity:	None	Trade from *Ruby/Emerald*
EMERALD	Rarity:	Only One	Random event in Hoenn after beating Elite Four
XD	Rarity:	None	Trade from *Ruby/Emerald*

MOVES

Level	Attack	Type	Power	ACC	PP	Level	Attack	Type	Power	ACC	PP
—	Psywave	Psychic	—	80	15	25	Protect	Normal	—	—	10
5	Memento	Dark	—	100	10	30	Refresh	Normal	—	100	20
10	Helping Hand	Normal	—	100	20	35	Luster Purge	Psychic	70	100	5
15	Safeguard	Normal	—	—	25	40	Psychic	Psychic	90	100	10
20	Dragonbreath	Dragon	60	100	20	45	Recover	Normal	—	—	20
						50	Dragon Dance	Dragon	—	—	20

TM/HM

TM/HM#	Name	Type	Power	ACC	PP	TM/HM#	Name	Type	Power	ACC	PP
TM02	Dragon Claw	Dragon	80	100	15	TM29	Psychic	Psychic	90	100	10
TM03	Water Pulse	Water	60	100	20	TM30	Shadow Ball	Ghost	60	—	20
TM04	Calm Mind	Psychic	—	—	20	TM32	Double Team	Normal	—	—	15
TM05	Roar	Normal	—	100	20	TM33	Reflect	Psychic	—	—	20
TM06	Toxic	Poison	—	85	10	TM34	Shock Wave	Electric	60	—	20
TM10	Hidden Power	Normal	—	100	15	TM37	Sandstorm	Rock	—	—	10
TM11	Sunny Day	Fire	—	—	5	TM40	Aerial Ace	Flying	60	—	20
TM13	Ice Beam	Ice	95	100	10	TM42	Facade	Normal	70	100	20
TM15	Hyper Beam	Normal	150	90	5	TM43	Secret Power	Normal	70	100	20
TM16	Light Screen	Psychic	—	—	30	TM44	Rest	Psychic	—	—	10
TM17	Protect	Normal	—	—	10	TM45	Attract	Normal	—	100	15
TM18	Rain Dance	Water	—	—	5	TM47	Steel Wing	Steel	70	90	25
TM20	Safeguard	Normal	—	—	25	HM01	Cut	Normal	50	95	30
TM21	Frustration	Normal	—	100	20	HM02	Fly	Flying	70	95	15
TM22	Solarbeam	Grass	120	100	10	HM03	Surf	Water	95	100	15
TM24	Thunderbolt	Electric	95	100	15	HM05	Flash	Normal	—	70	20
TM25	Thunder	Electric	120	70	10	HM07	Waterfall	Water	80	100	15
TM26	Earthquake	Ground	100	100	10	HM08	Dive	Water	60	100	10
TM27	Return	Normal	—	100	20						

MOVE TUTOR

FireRed/LeafGreen and Emerald Only

Body Slam*	Mimic	Thunder Wave*
Double-Edge	Substitute	Dream Eater*

Emerald Only

Endure*	Mud-Slap*	Snore*
Fury Cutter*	Psych Up*	Swagger
Icy Wind*	Sleep Talk	Swift*

*Battle Frontier tutor move (*Emerald*)

382 Kyogre™

GENERAL INFO
SPECIES: Sea Basin Pokémon
HEIGHT: 14'09"
WEIGHT: 776 lbs.
ABILITY: Drizzle
Rain falls when Kyogre enters battle.

STATS

EVOLUTIONS

DOES NOT EVOLVE

LOCATION(s):

RUBY	Rarity: **None**	Trade from *Sapphire/Emerald*
SAPPHIRE	Rarity: **Only One**	Cave of Origin (After awakening it)
FIRERED	Rarity: **None**	Trade from *Sapphire/Emerald*
LEAFGREEN	Rarity: **None**	Trade from *Sapphire/Emerald*
COLOSSEUM	Rarity: **None**	Trade from *Sapphire/Emerald*
EMERALD	Rarity: **Only One**	Marine Cave
XD	Rarity: **None**	Trade from *Sapphire/Emerald*

MOVES

Level	Attack	Type	Power	ACC	PP	Level	Attack	Type	Power	ACC	PP
—	Water Pulse	Water	60	100	20	35	Ice Beam	Ice	95	100	10
5	Scary Face	Normal	—	90	10	45	Hydro Pump	Water	120	80	5
15	Ancientpower	Rock	60	100	5	50	Rest	Psychic	—	—	10
20	Body Slam	Normal	85	100	15	60	Sheer Cold	Ice	—	30	5
30	Calm Mind	Psychic	—	—	20	65	Double-Edge	Normal	120	100	15
						75	Water Spout	Water	150	100	5

TM/HM

TM/HM#	Name	Type	Power	ACC	PP	TM/HM#	Name	Type	Power	ACC	PP
TM03	Water Pulse	Water	60	100	20	TM25	Thunder	Electric	120	70	10
TM04	Calm Mind	Psychic	—	—	20	TM26	Earthquake	Ground	100	100	10
TM05	Roar	Normal	—	100	20	TM27	Return	Normal	—	100	20
TM06	Toxic	Poison	—	85	10	TM31	Brick Break	Fighting	75	100	15
TM07	Hail	Ice	—	—	10	TM32	Double Team	Normal	—	—	15
TM10	Hidden Power	Normal	—	100	15	TM34	Shock Wave	Electric	60	—	20
TM13	Ice Beam	Ice	95	100	10	TM39	Rock Tomb	Rock	50	80	10
TM14	Blizzard	Ice	120	70	5	TM42	Facade	Normal	70	100	20
TM15	Hyper Beam	Normal	150	90	5	TM43	Secret Power	Normal	70	100	20
TM17	Protect	Normal	—	—	10	TM44	Rest	Psychic	—	—	10
TM18	Rain Dance	Water	—	—	5	HM03	Surf	Water	95	100	15
TM20	Safeguard	Normal	—	—	25	HM04	Strength	Normal	80	100	15
TM21	Frustration	Normal	—	100	20	HM06	Rock Smash	Fighting	20	100	15
TM24	Thunderbolt	Electric	95	100	15	HM07	Waterfall	Water	80	100	15
						HM08	Dive	Water	60	100	10

MOVE TUTOR
FireRed/LeafGreen and Emerald Only

Body Slam*	Mimic
Double-Edge	Substitute

Rock Slide*
Thunder Wave*

Emerald Only

Defense Curl*	Mud-Slap*	Snore*
Endure*	Psych Up*	Swagger
Icy Wind*	Sleep Talk	Swift*

*Battle Frontier tutor move (*Emerald*)

PRIMA OFFICIAL GAME GUIDE

383 Groudon™

GROUND

GENERAL INFO
SPECIES: Continent Pokémon
HEIGHT: 11'06"
WEIGHT: 2,095 lbs.
ABILITY: Drought
The sun shines when Groudon enters battle.

STATS

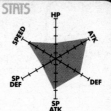

EVOLUTIONS

DOES NOT EVOLVE

LOCATION(s):

RUBY	Rarity: **Only One**	Cave of Origin (After awakening it)
SAPPHIRE	Rarity: **None**	Trade from *Ruby/Emerald*
FIRERED	Rarity: **None**	Trade from *Ruby/Emerald*
LEAFGREEN	Rarity: **None**	Trade from *Ruby/Emerald*
COLOSSEUM	Rarity: **None**	Trade from *Ruby/Emerald*
EMERALD	Rarity: **Only One**	Marine Cave
XD	Rarity: **None**	Trade from *Ruby/Emerald*

MOVES

Level	Attack	Type	Power	ACC	PP	Level	Attack	Type	Power	ACC	PP
—	Mud Shot	Ground	55	95	15	35	Earthquake	Ground	100	100	10
5	Scary Face	Normal	—	90	10	45	Fire Blast	Fire	120	85	5
15	Ancientpower	Rock	60	100	5	50	Rest	Psychic	—	—	10
20	Slash	Normal	70	100	20	60	Fissure	Ground	—	30	5
30	Bulk Up	Fighting	—	—	20	65	Solarbeam	Grass	120	100	10
						75	Eruption	Fire	150	100	5

TM/HM

TM/HM#	Name	Type	Power	ACC	PP	TM/HM#	Name	Type	Power	ACC	PP
TM02	Dragon Claw	Dragon	80	100	15	TM28	Dig	Ground	60	100	10
TM05	Roar	Normal	—	100	20	TM31	Brick Break	Fighting	75	100	15
TM06	Toxic	Poison	—	85	10	TM32	Double Team	Normal	—	—	15
TM08	Bulk Up	Fighting	—	—	20	TM34	Shock Wave	Electric	60	—	20
TM10	Hidden Power	Normal	—	100	15	TM35	Flamethrower	Fire	95	100	15
TM11	Sunny Day	Fire	—	—	5	TM37	Sandstorm	Rock	—	—	10
TM15	Hyper Beam	Normal	150	90	5	TM38	Fire Blast	Fire	120	85	5
TM17	Protect	Normal	—	—	10	TM39	Rock Tomb	Rock	50	80	10
TM20	Safeguard	Normal	—	—	25	TM40	Aerial Ace	Flying	60	—	20
TM21	Frustration	Normal	—	100	20	TM42	Facade	Normal	70	100	20
TM22	Solarbeam	Grass	120	100	10	TM43	Secret Power	Normal	70	100	20
TM23	Iron Tail	Steel	100	75	15	TM44	Rest	Psychic	—	—	10
TM24	Thunderbolt	Electric	95	100	15	TM50	Overheat	Fire	140	90	5
TM25	Thunder	Electric	120	70	10	HM01	Cut	Normal	50	95	30
TM26	Earthquake	Ground	100	100	10	HM04	Strength	Normal	80	100	15
TM27	Return	Normal	—	100	20	HM06	Rock Smash	Fighting	20	100	15

MOVE TUTOR
FireRed/LeafGreen and Emerald Only

Body Slam*	Mimic	Thunder Wave*	
Double-Edge	Substitute	Rock Slide*	
Mega Punch*	Counter*	Swords Dance*	
Mega Kick*	Seismic Toss*		

Emerald Only

Defense Curl*	Mud-Slap*	Swagger
Dynamicpunch*	Psych Up*	Swift*
Endure*	Rollout	Thunderpunch*
Fury Cutter*	Sleep Talk	
Fire Punch*	Snore*	

*Battle Frontier tutor move (*Emerald*)

384 Rayquaza™

DRAGON   FLYING

GENERAL INFO

SPECIES: Sky High Pokémon
HEIGHT: 23'00"
WEIGHT: 455 lbs.
ABILITY: Air Lock
Makes weather effects disappear.

STATS

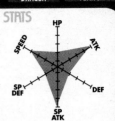

EVOLUTIONS

DOES NOT EVOLVE

LOCATION(s):

RUBY	Rarity: **Only One**	Sky Pillar (After beating Elite Four)
SAPPHIRE	Rarity: **Only One**	Sky Pillar (After beating Elite Four)
FIRERED	Rarity: **None**	Trade from *Ruby/Sapphire/Emerald*
LEAFGREEN	Rarity: **None**	Trade from *Ruby/Sapphire/Emerald*
COLOSSEUM	Rarity: **None**	Trade from *Ruby/Sapphire/Emerald*
EMERALD	Rarity: **Only One**	Sky Pillar (After beating Elite Four)
XD	Rarity: **None**	Trade from *Ruby/Sapphire/Emerald*

MOVES

Level	Attack	Type	Power	ACC	PP	Level	Attack	Type	Power	ACC	PP
—	Twister	Dragon	40	100	20	35	Crunch	Dark	80	100	15
5	Scary Face	Normal	—	90	10	45	Fly	Flying	70	95	15
15	Ancientpower	Rock	60	100	5	50	Rest	Psychic	—	—	10
20	Dragon Claw	Dragon	80	100	15	60	Extremespeed	Normal	80	100	5
30	Dragon Dance	Dragon	—	—	20	65	Outrage	Dragon	90	100	15
						75	Hyper Beam	Normal	150	90	5

TM/HM

TM/HM#	Name	Type	Power	ACC	PP	TM/HM#	Name	Type	Power	ACC	PP
TM02	Dragon Claw	Dragon	80	100	15	TM27	Return	Normal	—	100	20
TM03	Water Pulse	Water	60	100	20	TM31	Brick Break	Fighting	75	100	15
TM05	Roar	Normal	—	100	20	TM32	Double Team	Normal	—	—	15
TM06	Toxic	Poison	—	85	10	TM34	Shock Wave	Electric	60	—	20
TM08	Bulk Up	Fighting	—	—	20	TM35	Flamethrower	Fire	95	100	15
TM10	Hidden Power	Normal	—	100	15	TM37	Sandstorm	Rock	—	—	10
TM11	Sunny Day	Fire	—	—	5	TM38	Fire Blast	Fire	120	85	5
TM13	Ice Beam	Ice	95	100	10	TM40	Aerial Ace	Flying	60	—	20
TM14	Blizzard	Ice	120	70	5	TM42	Facade	Normal	70	100	20
TM15	Hyper Beam	Normal	150	90	5	TM43	Secret Power	Normal	70	100	20
TM17	Protect	Normal	—	—	10	TM44	Rest	Psychic	—	—	10
TM18	Rain Dance	Water	—	—	5	TM50	Overheat	Fire	140	90	5
TM21	Frustration	Normal	—	100	20	HM02	Fly	Flying	70	95	15
TM22	Solarbeam	Grass	120	100	10	HM03	Surf	Water	95	100	15
TM23	Iron Tail	Steel	100	75	15	HM04	Strength	Normal	80	100	15
TM24	Thunderbolt	Electric	95	100	15	HM06	Rock Smash	Fighting	20	100	15
TM25	Thunder	Electric	120	70	10	HM07	Waterfall	Water	80	100	15
TM26	Earthquake	Ground	100	100	10	HM08	Dive	Water	60	100	10

MOVE TUTOR

FireRed/LeafGreen and Emerald Only

Body Slam*	Mimic	Thunder Wave*
Double-Edge	Substitute	Rock Slide*

*Battle Frontier tutor move (*Emerald*)

Emerald Only

Endure*	Mud-Slap*	Snore*
Fury Cutter*	Psych Up*	Swagger
Icy Wind*	Sleep Talk	Swift*

385 Jirachi™

STEEL | PSYCHIC

GENERAL INFO

SPECIES: Wish Pokémon
HEIGHT: 1'00"
WEIGHT: 2 lbs.
ABILITY: Serene Grace

Moves that have extra effects will occur
more frequently when Jirachi attacks.

STATS

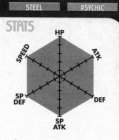

EVOLUTIONS

DOES NOT EVOLVE

LOCATION[s]:

RUBY	**Rarity: None**	Receive from *Colosseum* Bonus Disk
SAPPHIRE	**Rarity: None**	Receive from *Colosseum* Bonus Disk
FIRERED	**Rarity: None**	Only available from *Colosseum* Bonus Disk
LEAFGREEN	**Rarity: None**	Only available from *Colosseum* Bonus Disk
COLOSSEUM	**Rarity: None**	Only available from *Colosseum* Bonus Disk
EMERALD	**Rarity: None**	Only available from *Colosseum* Bonus Disk
XD	**Rarity: None**	Only available from *Colosseum* Bonus Disk

MOVES

Level	Attack	Type	Power	ACC	PP	Level	Attack	Type	Power	ACC	PP
—	Wish	Normal	—	100	10	25	Refresh	Normal	—	100	20
—	Confusion	Psychic	50	100	25	30	Rest	Psychic	—	—	10
5	Rest	Psychic	—	—	10	35	Double-Edge	Normal	120	100	15
10	Swift	Normal	60	—	20	40	Future Sight	Psychic	80	90	15
15	Helping Hand	Normal	—	100	20	45	Cosmic Power	Normal	—	—	20
20	Psychic	Psychic	90	100	10	50	Doom Desire	Steel	120	85	5

TM/HM

TM/HM#	Name	Type	Power	ACC	PP	TM/HM#	Name	Type	Power	ACC	PP
TM03	Water Pulse	Water	60	95	20	TM29	Psychic	Psychic	90	100	10
TM04	Calm Mind	Psychic	—	—	20	TM30	Shadow Ball	Ghost	80	100	15
TM06	Toxic	Poison	—	85	10	TM32	Double Team	Normal	—	—	15
TM10	Hidden Power	Normal	—	100	15	TM33	Reflect	Normal	—	—	20
TM11	Sunny Day	Fire	—	—	5	TM34	Shock Wave	Electric	60	—	20
TM15	Hyper Beam	Normal	150	90	5	TM37	Sandstorm	Ground	—	—	10
TM16	Light Screen	Psychic	—	—	30	TM40	Aerial Ace	Flying	60	—	20
TM17	Protect	Normal	—	—	10	TM42	Facade	Normal	70	100	20
TM18	Rain Dance	Water	—	—	5	TM43	Secret Power	Normal	70	100	20
TM20	Safeguard	Normal	—	—	25	TM44	Rest	Psychic	—	—	10
TM21	Frustration	Normal	—	100	20	TM45	Attract	Normal	—	100	15
TM24	Thunderbolt	Electric	95	100	15	TM48	Skill Swap	Psychic	—	100	10
TM25	Thunder	Electric	120	70	10	HM05	Flash	Normal	—	70	20
TM27	Return	Normal	—	100	20						

MOVE TUTOR

FireRed/LeafGreen and Emerald Only

Body Slam*	Substitute	Dream Eater*
Double-Edge	Thunder Wave*	Metronome
Mimic		

Emerald Only

Defense Curl*	Icy Wind*	Swagger
Dynamicpunch*	Mud-Slap*	Swift*
Endure*	Psych Up*	Thunderpunch*
Fire Punch*	Sleep Talk	
Ice Punch*	Snore*	

*Battle Frontier tutor move (*Emerald*)

386 Deoxys™ (Attack Forme)

PSYCHIC

GENERAL INFO

SPECIES: DNA Pokémon
HEIGHT: 5'05"
WEIGHT: 134 lbs.
ABILITY: Pressure

STATS

(Stat hexagon: HP, ATK, DEF, SP ATK, SP DEF, SPEED)

EVOLUTIONS

DOES NOT EVOLVE

LOCATION[s]:

RUBY	Rarity: **None**	Deoxys does not take this form in this game
SAPPHIRE	Rarity: **None**	Deoxys does not take this form in this game
FIRERED	Rarity: **Only One**	Birth Island (Only accessible with the Aurora Ticket gained via special download at live events)
LEAFGREEN	Rarity: **None**	Deoxys does not take this form in this game
COLOSSEUM	Rarity: **None**	Deoxys does not take this form in this game
EMERALD	Rarity: **None**	Deoxys does not take this form in this game
XD	Rarity: **None**	Deoxys does not take this form in this game

MOVES

Level	Attack	Type	Power	ACC	PP	Level	Attack	Type	Power	ACC	PP
—	Leer	Normal	—	100	30	25	Psychic	Psychic	90	100	10
—	Wrap	Normal	15	85	20	30	Super Power	Fighting	120	100	5
5	Night Shade	Ghost	—	100	15	35	Cosmic Power	Psychic	—	—	20
10	Teleport	Psychic	—	—	20	40	Zap Cannon	Electric	—	50	5
15	Taunt	Dark	—	100	20	45	Psycho Boost	Psychic	140	90	5
20	Pursuit	Dark	40	100	20	50	Hyper Beam	Normal	150	90	5

TM/HM

TM/HM#	Name	Type	Power	ACC	PP	TM/HM#	Name	Type	Power	ACC	PP
TM01	Focus Punch	Fighting	150	100	20	TM29	Psychic	Psychic	90	100	10
TM03	Water Pulse	Water	60	100	20	TM30	Shadow Ball	Ghost	80	100	15
TM04	Calm Mind	Psychic	—	—	20	TM31	Brick Break	Fighting	75	100	15
TM06	Toxic	Poison	—	85	10	TM32	Double Team	Normal	—	—	15
TM10	Hidden Power	Normal	—	100	15	TM33	Reflect	Psychic	—	—	20
TM11	Sunny Day	Fire	—	—	5	TM34	Shock Wave	Electric	60	—	20
TM12	Taunt	Dark	—	100	20	TM39	Rock Tomb	Rock	50	80	10
TM13	Ice Beam	Ice	95	100	10	TM40	Aerial Ace	Flying	60	—	20
TM15	Hyper Beam	Normal	150	90	5	TM41	Torment	Dark	—	100	15
TM16	Light Screen	Psychic	—	—	30	TM42	Facade	Normal	70	100	20
TM17	Protect	Normal	—	—	10	TM43	Secret Power	Normal	70	100	20
TM18	Rain Dance	Water	—	—	5	TM44	Rest	Psychic	—	—	10
TM20	Safeguard	Normal	—	—	25	TM48	Skill Swap	Psychic	—	—	10
TM21	Frustration	Normal	—	100	20	TM49	Snatch	Dark	—	100	10
TM22	Solarbeam	Grass	120	100	10	HM01	Cut	Normal	50	95	30
TM24	Thunderbolt	Electric	95	100	15	HM04	Strength	Normal	80	100	15
TM25	Thunder	Electric	120	70	10	HM05	Flash	Normal	—	70	20
TM27	Return	Normal	—	100	20	HM06	Rock Smash	Fighting	20	100	15

MOVE TUTOR

FireRed/LeafGreen and Emerald Only

Body Slam*	Mimic	Thunder Wave*	Counter	Mega Punch*	Seismic Toss*
Double-Edge	Substitute	Dream Eater*	Rock Slide*	Mega Kick*	

*Battle Frontier tutor move (*Emerald*)

386 Deoxys™ (Defense Forme)

PSYCHIC

GENERAL INFO

SPECIES: DNA Pokémon
HEIGHT: 5'05"
WEIGHT: 134 lbs.
ABILITY: Pressure

STATS

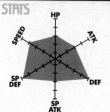

EVOLUTIONS

DOES NOT EVOLVE

LOCATION[s]:

RUBY	Rarity: **None**	Deoxys does not take this form in this game
SAPPHIRE	Rarity: **None**	Deoxys does not take this form in this game
FIRERED	Rarity: **None**	Deoxys does not take this form in this game
LEAFGREEN	Rarity: **Only One**	Birth Island (Only accessible with the Aurora Ticket gained via special download at live events)
COLOSSEUM	Rarity: **None**	Deoxys does not take this form in this game
EMERALD	Rarity: **None**	Deoxys does not take this form in this game
XD	Rarity: **None**	Deoxys does not take this form in this game

MOVES

Level	Attack	Type	Power	ACC	PP	Level	Attack	Type	Power	ACC	PP
—	Leer	Normal	—	100	30	30	Snatch	Dark	—	100	10
—	Wrap	Normal	15	85	20	35	Iron Defense	Steel	—	—	15
5	Night Shade	Ghost	—	100	15	35	Amnesia	Psychic	—	—	20
10	Teleport	Psychic	—	—	20	40	Recover	Normal	—	—	20
15	Knock Off	Dark	20	100	20	45	Psycho Boost	Psychic	140	90	5
20	Spikes	Ground	—	—	20	50	Counter	Fighting	140	100	20
25	Psychic	Psychic	90	100	10	50	Mirror Coat	Psychic	—	100	20

TM/HM

TM/HM#	Name	Type	Power	ACC	PP	TM/HM#	Name	Type	Power	ACC	PP
TM01	Focus Punch	Fighting	150	100	20	TM29	Psychic	Psychic	90	100	10
TM03	Water Pulse	Water	60	100	20	TM30	Shadow Ball	Ghost	80	100	15
TM04	Calm Mind	Psychic	—	—	20	TM31	Brick Break	Fighting	75	100	15
TM06	Toxic	Poison	—	85	10	TM32	Double Team	Normal	—	—	15
TM10	Hidden Power	Normal	—	100	15	TM33	Reflect	Psychic	—	—	20
TM11	Sunny Day	Fire	—	—	5	TM34	Shock Wave	Electric	60	—	20
TM12	Taunt	Dark	—	100	20	TM39	Rock Tomb	Rock	50	80	10
TM13	Ice Beam	Ice	95	100	10	TM40	Aerial Ace	Flying	60	—	20
TM15	Hyper Beam	Normal	150	90	5	TM41	Torment	Dark	—	100	15
TM16	Light Screen	Psychic	—	—	30	TM42	Facade	Normal	70	100	20
TM17	Protect	Normal	—	—	10	TM43	Secret Power	Normal	70	100	20
TM18	Rain Dance	Water	—	—	5	TM44	Rest	Psychic	—	—	10
TM20	Safeguard	Normal	—	—	25	TM48	Skill Swap	Psychic	—	100	10
TM21	Frustration	Normal	—	100	20	TM49	Snatch	Dark	—	100	10
TM22	Solarbeam	Grass	120	100	10	HM01	Cut	Normal	50	95	30
TM24	Thunderbolt	Electric	95	100	15	HM04	Strength	Normal	80	100	15
TM25	Thunder	Electric	120	70	10	HM05	Flash	Normal	—	70	20
TM27	Return	Normal	—	100	20	HM06	Rock Smash	Fighting	20	100	15

MOVE TUTOR

FireRed/LeafGreen and Emerald Only

Body Slam*	Mimic	Thunder Wave*	Counter	Mega Punch*	Seismic Toss*
Double-Edge	Substitute	Dream Eater*	Rock Slide*	Mega Kick*	

*Battle Frontier tutor move (*Emerald*)

386 Deoxys™ (Normal Forme)

PSYCHIC

GENERAL INFO
SPECIES: DNA Pokémon
HEIGHT: 5'05"
WEIGHT: 134 lbs.
ABILITY: Pressure

STATS

HP · SPEED · ATK · DEF · SP DEF · SP ATK

EVOLUTIONS

DOES NOT EVOLVE

LOCATION[s]:

RUBY	Rarity: None	Must trade from *Pokémon FireRed* or *Pokémon LeafGreen*, and then Deoxys takes Normal Form.
SAPPHIRE	Rarity: None	Must trade from *Pokémon FireRed* or *Pokémon LeafGreen*, and then Deoxys takes Normal Form.
FIRERED	Rarity: None	Birth Island (Only accessible with the Aurora Ticket gained via special download at live events)
LEAFGREEN	Rarity: None	Deoxys does not take this form in this game
COLOSSEUM	Rarity: None	Must trade from *Pokémon FireRed* or *Pokémon LeafGreen*, and then Deoxys takes Normal Form.
EMERALD	Rarity: None	Deoxys does not take this form in this game
XD	Rarity: None	Deoxys does not take this form in this game

MOVES

Level	Attack	Type	Power	ACC	PP	Level	Attack	Type	Power	ACC	PP
—	Leer	Normal	—	100	30	25	Psychic	Psychic	90	100	10
—	Wrap	Normal	15	85	20	30	Snatch	Dark	—	100	10
5	Night Shade	Ghost	—	100	15	35	Cosmic Power	Psychic	—	—	20
10	Teleport	Psychic	—	—	20	40	Recover	Normal	—	—	20
15	Knock Off	Dark	20	100	20	45	Psycho Boost	Psychic	140	90	5
20	Pursuit	Dark	40	100	20	50	Hyper Beam	Normal	150	90	5

TM/HM

TM/HM#	Name	Type	Power	ACC	PP	TM/HM#	Name	Type	Power	ACC	PP
TM01	Focus Punch	Fighting	150	100	20	TM29	Psychic	Psychic	90	100	10
TM03	Water Pulse	Water	60	100	20	TM30	Shadow Ball	Ghost	80	100	15
TM04	Calm Mind	Psychic	—	—	20	TM31	Brick Break	Fighting	75	100	15
TM06	Toxic	Poison	—	85	10	TM32	Double Team	Normal	—	—	15
TM10	Hidden Power	Normal	—	100	15	TM33	Reflect	Psychic	—	—	20
TM11	Sunny Day	Fire	—	—	5	TM34	Shock Wave	Electric	60	—	20
TM12	Taunt	Dark	—	100	20	TM39	Rock Tomb	Rock	50	80	10
TM13	Ice Beam	Ice	95	100	10	TM40	Aerial Ace	Flying	60	—	20
TM15	Hyper Beam	Normal	150	90	5	TM41	Torment	Dark	—	100	15
TM16	Light Screen	Psychic	—	—	30	TM42	Facade	Normal	70	100	20
TM17	Protect	Normal	—	—	10	TM43	Secret Power	Normal	70	100	20
TM18	Rain Dance	Water	—	—	5	TM44	Rest	Psychic	—	—	10
TM20	Safeguard	Normal	—	—	25	TM48	Skill Swap	Psychic	—	100	10
TM21	Frustration	Normal	—	100	20	TM49	Snatch	Dark	—	100	10
TM22	Solarbeam	Grass	120	100	10	HM01	Cut	Normal	50	95	30
TM24	Thunderbolt	Electric	95	100	15	HM04	Strength	Normal	80	100	15
TM25	Thunder	Electric	120	70	10	HM05	Flash	Normal	—	70	20
TM27	Return	Normal	—	100	20	HM06	Rock Smash	Fighting	20	100	15

MOVE TUTOR
FireRed/LeafGreen and Emerald Only

Rock Slide*	Double-Edge	Thunder Wave*	Substitute	Mega Punch*	Dream Eater*
Counter	Seismic Toss*	Body Slam*	Mega Kick*	Mimic	

*Battle Frontier tutor move (*Emerald*)

386 Deoxys™ (Speed Forme)

PSYCHIC

GENERAL INFO
SPECIES: DNA Pokémon
HEIGHT: 5'05"
WEIGHT: 134 lbs.
ABILITY: Pressure

STATS

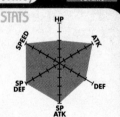

EVOLUTIONS

DOES NOT EVOLVE

LOCATION(s):

RUBY	Rarity: **None**	Deoxys does not take this form in this game
SAPPHIRE	Rarity: **None**	Deoxys does not take this form in this game
FIRERED	Rarity: **None**	Deoxys does not take this form in this game
LEAFGREEN	Rarity: **None**	Deoxys does not take this form in this game
COLOSSEUM	Rarity: **None**	Deoxys does not take this form in this game
EMERALD	Rarity: **Only One**	Birth Island (Only accessible with the Aurora Ticket gained via special download at live events)
XD	Rarity:	Deoxys does not take this form in this game

MOVES

Level	Attack	Type	Power	ACC	PP	Level	Attack	Type	Power	ACC	PP
5	Night Shade	Ghost	—	100	15	30	Swift	Normal	60	—	20
10	Double Team	Normal	—	—	15	35	Agility	Psychic	—	—	30
15	Knock Off	Dark	20	100	20	40	Recover	Normal	—	—	20
20	Pursuit	Dark	40	100	20	45	Psycho Boost	Psychic	140	90	5
25	Psychic	Psychic	90	100	10	50	Extremespeed	Normal	80	100	5

TM/HM

TM/HM#	Name	Type	Power	ACC	PP	TM/HM#	Name	Type	Power	ACC	PP
HM01	Cut	Normal	50	95	30	TM21	Frustration	Normal	—	100	20
HM04	Strength	Normal	80	100	15	TM22	Solarbeam	Grass	120	100	10
HM05	Flash	Normal	—	70	20	TM24	Thunderbolt	Electric	95	100	15
HM06	Rock Smash	Fighting	20	100	15	TM25	Thunder	Electric	120	70	10
TM01	Focus Punch	Fighting	150	100	20	TM27	Return	Normal	—	100	20
TM03	Water Pulse	Water	60	100	20	TM29	Psychic	Psychic	90	100	10
TM04	Calm Mind	Psychic	—	—	20	TM30	Shadow Ball	Ghost	60	—	20
TM06	Toxic	Poison	—	85	10	TM31	Brick Break	Fighting	75	100	15
TM10	Hidden Power	Normal	—	100	15	TM32	Double Team	Normal	—	—	15
TM11	Sunny Day	Fire	—	—	5	TM39	Rock Tomb	Rock	50	80	10
TM12	Taunt	Dark	—	100	20	TM40	Aerial Ace	Flying	60	—	20
TM13	Ice Beam	Ice	95	100	10	TM41	Torment	Dark	—	100	15
TM15	Hyper Beam	Normal	150	90	5	TM42	Façade	Normal	70	100	20
TM16	Light Screen	Psychic	—	—	30	TM43	Secret Power	Normal	70	100	20
TM17	Protect	Normal	—	—	10	TM44	Rest	Psychic	—	—	10
TM18	Rain Dance	Water	—	—	5	TM48	Skill Swap	Psychic	—	100	10
TM20	Safeguard	Normal	—	—	25	TM49	Snatch	Dark	—	100	10

MOVE TUTOR
FireRed/LeafGreen and Emerald Only

Body Slam*	Mimic	Seismic Toss*
Counter*	Mega Kick*	Substitute
Double-Edge	Mega Punch*	Thunder Wave*
Dream Eater*	Rock Slide*	

Emerald Only

Dynamicpunch	Icy Wind*	Swagger
Endure*	Mud-Slap*	Swift*
Fire Punch*	Sleep Talk*	Thunderpunch*
Ice Punch*	Snore*	

*Battle Frontier tutor move (*Emerald*)